A Citizen's Guide to Utah State Government

Office of Legislative Research and General Counsel
State Capitol Complex
W210 House Building
Salt Lake City, Utah 84114-5210
(801) 538-1032

Legislative Printing
Salt Lake City

FOREWORD

This book explains in a simple, easy-to-read manner how state government works, what powers and responsibilities the state judicial, executive, and legislative branches have, and how state government interacts with the federal and local governments. Written by the Office of Legislative Research and General Counsel, the policy and legal staff of the Utah State Legislature; this book targets two main audiences: Utah's legislators and Utah's citizens.

UTAH LEGISLATORS

This book will be a helpful tool to legislators in providing background information on state government and state demographics. The Utah Legislature is a part time body of 104 legislators. Most legislators have outside employment as business people, attorneys, dentists, farmers, ranchers, school teachers, or in other occupations or professions. Legislators are often parents and have other civic responsibilities. The bottom line is that legislators are very busy people who must still legislate for the state. In addition, there is a high rate of turnover in the Utah Legislature. Every two years (as a result of elections), anywhere from one-fourth to one-third of the Utah Legislature is new. This book will help legislators, especially new ones, by providing a one volume reference book on the workings of state government.

UTAH'S CITIZENS

This book helps Utah's citizens understand how their state government works. For example, a high school student has a research report due in a civics class. She has decided to write about how public education is funded in the state. This book has an entire chapter dealing with public education and another chapter that explains the state's tax structure. Much of what she is looking for can be found in this one book. A citizen is concerned about land-use planning in his community, another wants to know how judges get and keep their positions, yet another wants to understand the sales taxes his small store must collect. Various chapters in the book cover all of these issues in clear, straightforward language.

A reader of this book has at his or her reach a basic outline of state government. In addition, the book provides important historical, economic, demographic, and population data that show the major trends that have made Utah what it is today and what it will likely be in the future. This book is designed to answer fundamental questions about state government for both the state's legislators and the general public.

Michael E. Christensen, Ph.D.
Director
Office of Legislative Research and General Counsel

Copyright © 2005 Office of Legislative Research and General Counsel

ISBN 0-9778482-0-5

ACKNOWLEDGMENTS

Chapter 1: An Historical, Demographic, and Economic Overview of Utah
  written by Michael Christensen and Phil Dean

Chapter 2: Utah Law
  written by Jerry Howe and Robert Rees

Chapter 3: Utah Administrative Rules
  written by Art Hunsaker and Susan Creager Allred

Chapter 4: Citizen Participation and Elections
  written by John Fellows, Nina Norton, John Cannon, and Eric Weeks

Chapter 5: The Executive Branch
  written by Arek Butler, John Cannon, Ben Christensen, Dee Larsen, Rich North, and John Fellows

Chapter 6: The Legislative Branch
  written by Gay Taylor, John Fellows, John Cannon, and Rich North

Chapter 7: The Judicial Branch
  written by Jerry Howe, Esther Chelsea-McCarty, and Rich North

Chapter 8: Fiscal Management
  written by Bryant Howe and Rebecca Rockwell

Chapter 9: Agriculture and Food
  written by Jeanenne Larson and Emily Brown

Chapter 10: Business and Labor
  written by Patricia Owen and Mark Steinagel

Chapter 11: Community and Economic Development and Workforce Services
  written by James Wilson and Art Hunsaker

Chapter 12: Public Education
  written by Connie Steffen and Dee Larsen

Chapter 13: Higher Education
  written by Connie Steffen, Dee Larsen, and Spencer Burton

Chapter 14: Environmental Quality
  written by Brian Allred and Spencer Burton

Chapter 15: Health
    written by Mark Andrews and Cathy Dupont

Chapter 16: Human Services
    written by Mark Andrews and Cathy Dupont

Chapter 17: Natural Resources
    written by Jeanenne Larson and Emily Brown

Chapter 18: Public Safety, Criminal Law, and Corrections
    written by Susan Creager Allred, Stewart Smith, and Jami Momberger

Chapter 19: Regulation of Public Utilities
    written by Rich North

Chapter 20: Transportation
    written by Shannon Halverson and Ben Christensen

Chapter 21: Relationship of State and Federal Governments
    written by Gay Taylor, John Cannon, Brian Allred, Brett Hopper, and Bryant Howe

Chapter 22: Local Government
    written by Robert Rees and Joseph Wade

Chapter 23: Utah and the Future
    written by Michael Christensen

Editors:
    Michael E. Christensen, Editor in Chief
    Mary Catherine Perry
    M. Gay Taylor
    John Q. Cannon
    Cassandra N. Bauman, Copy Editor

Utah Legislature
OFFICE OF LEGISLATIVE RESEARCH AND GENERAL COUNSEL

Michael E. Christensen, Director
M. Gay Taylor, General Counsel
Bryant R. Howe, Assistant Director
John L. Fellows, Deputy General Counsel
John Q. Cannon, Managing Policy Analyst
Mark J Allred, Information Systems Manager
Beverlee LeCheminant, Administrative Assistant

Allison Morgan, Policy Analyst
Angela D. Oakes, Associate General Counsel
Arek Butler, Research Assistant
Arthur L. Hunsaker, Policy Analyst
Benjamin N. Christensen, Policy Analyst
Brooke Anderson, Legislative IT Staff
Brooke Ollerton, Legislative Secretary
Cassandra Bauman, Legislative Support Technician
Catherine J. Dupont, Associate General Counsel
Chris Calcut, Legislative IT Staff
Chris Peterson, Supervising Document Technician
Christopher R. Parker, Associate General Counsel
Clay Hatch, Legislative Information Liaison
Constance C. Steffen, Policy Analyst
Courtlan Erickson, Law Clerk
Dee S Larsen, Associate General Counsel
Emily Brown, Associate General Counsel
Eric N. Weeks, Associate General Counsel
Esther Chelsea-McCarty, Associate General Counsel
Glen Johnson, Legislative IT Staff
Glenda S. Whitney, Legislative Secretary
J Brian Allred, Policy Analyst
James L. Wilson, Associate General Counsel
Jeanenne Larson, Associate General Counsel
Jerry D. Howe, Policy Analyst
Joseph T. Wade, Policy Analyst

Joy L. Miller, Legislative Secretary Supervisor
Karen R. Brown, Legislative Data Management
Leif Elder, Research Assistant
Lorraine Ripley, Paralegal
Marilee Miller, Law Clerk
Mark D. Andrews, Policy Analyst
Mark B. Steinagel, Policy Analyst
Maureen Wilson, Legislative Data Management
Nancy Ellison, Document Technician
Nancy McPherson, Receptionist
Nina Norton, Paralegal
Patricia Owen, Associate General Counsel
Peggy R. O'Connor, Document Technician
Phalin L. Flowers, Legislative Secretary
Phillip V. Dean, Policy Analyst
Rebecca L. Rockwell, Associate General Counsel
Richard C. North, Policy Analyst
Robert H. Rees, Associate General Counsel
Shannon Halverson, Associate General Counsel
Shelley Day, Legislative Information Liaison
Stewart E. Smith, Policy Analyst
Susan C. Allred, Associate General Counsel
Thomas R. Vaughn, Associate General Counsel
Tony F. Graf, Legislative IT Staff
Tracey Fredman, Legislative Secretary
Wendy L. Bangerter, Legislative Secretary

Article XIX. Public Buildings and State Institutions 34
Article XX. Public Lands 34
Article XXI. Salaries 34
Article XXII. Miscellaneous 34
Article XXIII. Amendment and Revision 34
Article XXIV. Schedule 35

Chapter 3: Utah Administrative Rules 37
Background 37
Division of Administrative Rules 38
Administrative Rules Review Committee 40
Legislative Repeal of Rules 40
Agency Actions that Must be in Rule 40
Executive Branch Review of Rules 41

Chapter 4: Citizen Participation and Elections 43
Qualifications to Vote 43
Means of Voting 43
Voting Process at Polling Place 44
Getting Elected 44
Political Parties 46
Registered Political Parties 47
Benefits and Obligations of Registered Political Parties 47
Election Process: Nominating Candidates and Electing Public Officials in Utah 47
    Declarations of Candidacy 47
    Unaffiliated Candidates and Write-in Candidates 47
    Partisan Candidates 48
    Partisan Elections 48
    Nonpartisan Elections 48
Initiative and Referendum 49
Citizen Involvement in Government 54
    State Government Internet Web Sites 54
    State Government Address and Telephone Numbers 54
    Citizen Participation in the Election Process 54
    Voter Information Pamphlet 55
        Candidate Information 55
        Ballot Measures Information 55
        Judicial Information 56
        Voter Assistance Information 56
    Candidate and Political Party Web Sites 56
Access to Government Meetings and Documents 56
    Open and Public Meetings 56
    Public Notice of Meetings 56
    Access to Minutes and Audio Recordings 57
    Government Records Access and Management Act 57
    How to Request a Government Document 57
Lobbying and Lobbyist Regulation 58

TABLE OF CONTENTS

Chapter 1: An Historical, Demographic, and Economic Overview of Utah 1
    Geography 1
    Climate, Streams, and Vegetation 2
    The Early Peoples of Utah 3
        Desert Archaic and Fremont Cultures 3
        Anasazi Culture 3
        Shoshonean Culture 4
    Trappers and Explorers 6
    Mormon Settlement of Utah 7
    From Territory to Statehood 8
    Industry and Employment Trends 9
        Economic History 9
        Employment Trends 10
    Population and Demographic Trends 13
        Utah's Employment Picture in the Twenty-first Century 17
    Wealth and Poverty 19
        Gross State Product 19
        Income Measures 19
        Poverty Rates 20
        Cost of Living 21

Chapter 2: Utah Law 23
    State and Federal Constitutions 23
        Purposes of Constitutions 23
        Powers of the National and State Governments 24
    Utah Constitution Historical Background 25
    Article I. Declaration of Rights 26
    Article II. State Boundaries 27
    Article III. Ordinance 27
    Article IV. Elections and Right of Suffrage 27
    Article V. Distribution of Powers 28
    Article VI. Legislative Department 28
    Article VII. Executive Department 29
    Article VIII. Judicial Department 30
    Article IX. Legislative Apportionment 31
    Article X. Education 31
    Article XI. Local Governments 32
    Article XII. Corporations 3
    Article XIII. Revenue and Taxation 3
    Article XIV. Public Debt 3
    Article XV. Militia ....
    Article XVI. Labor ....
    Article XVII. Water Rights ....
    Article XVIII. Forestry ....

  Registration and Licensing 58
  Denial of License 58
  Disclosure of Expenditures 58
  Lobbyist Ethics 58
  Enforcement of Ethical Rules Governing Lobbyists 59
 Political History 59
  Party Control of the Legislature 59
  Party Control of the Governor's Office 61

Chapter 5: The Executive Branch 63
 Governor 63
  Election Process 63
  Powers and Duties 64
  Executive Power 64
   Chief Executive 64
   Appointive Powers 65
   Removal 66
   Boards and Commissions 67
   Budget 67
   Governor's Office of Planning and Budget 68
   Executive Orders 68
   Emergency Power 68
  Governor's Legislative Power 69
   Policy Innovator 69
   Veto Power 69
   Power to Convene Special Sessions 70
  Governor's Judicial Power 70
   Judicial Appointment 70
   Pardons 70
   Extradition 70
  Military Power 71
   Commander in Chief 71
  Comparison of Gubernatorial Powers 71
  Vacancy in the Office of Governor 73
   Vacancy 73
   Emergency Interim Governor 73
   Impeachment 74
  Office Organization 74
 Lieutenant Governor 75
  Governor's Adviser 75
  Acting Secretary of State 75
  Chief Election Officer 75
 Attorney General 76
  Legal Adviser of State Officers 77
   Opinions 77
   Litigation Control 77
  Criminal Prosecutor 77

        Chief Prosecutor 77
           Investigator 78
    Public Advocacy 78
    Office Organization 78
State Auditor 79
    Fiscal Audits 79
    Other Powers 79
    Agency Organization 80
State Treasurer 80
    Accounting for Public Funds 80
    Investing Public Funds 80
Department of Administrative Services 81
    Executive Director 81
    Divisions of the Department 81
Division of Human Resource Management 84
    Career Service System 84
    Decentralization 85
Retirement 85
    Retirement Systems 85
    Retirement Contribution Rates 86
    Retirement Benefits 86
    Independent Entities 88
    Independent State Agencies 88
    Independent Corporations 88
    Nonprofit Quasi-public Corporations 89
Department of Technology Services 89
    Executive Branch Web Site Visits 90
    Legislative Branch Web Site Visits 90
    Judicial Branch Web Site Visits 90

Chapter 6: The Legislative Branch 93
    Legislative Sessions 93
    Annual General Sessions 93
    Veto Override Sessions 94
        Reconsideration Before Adjournment 94
        Reconsideration After Adjournment Sine Die 94
    Special Sessions 94
    Impeachment Proceedings 94
    Extraordinary Sessions of the Senate 95
Role of Committees 95
    Legislative Management Committee 95
    Executive Appropriations Committee 96
    Appropriations Subcommittees 96
Interim Committees and Special Legislative Committees 97
    Temporary Committees, Boards, Panels, and Task Forces 98
    Standing Committees 98
Lawmaking Process 99

Rules of Procedure	99
Three Readings Required in Each House	99
Open and Public Meetings	100
Quorum Is Required in Each House	100
Bills to Contain Only One Subject	100
Each House Shall Keep a Journal of its Proceedings	100
Effective Dates of Bills	100
Effective Dates of Resolutions	101
Procedures Outlined in Legislative Rules	102
How a Bill Becomes a Law	102
The House of Representatives	102
The Senate	103
Bills Presented to Governor for Approval or Veto	104
Other Resolutions (House/Senate/Joint/Concurrent)	104
Who Can Be a Legislator	105
Constitutional Qualifications	105
Length of Terms	105
Salary and Compensation	105
Ineligibility of Legislator for Civil Office of Profit	105
Each House is the Judge of the Election and Qualifications of its Members	106
Legislator Ethics	106
Legislative Ethics Committees	106
Legislative Privilege	107
The Appropriations Process	107
The Governor's Budget	107
Appropriation Subcommittees	107
Executive Appropriations Committee	108
Governor's Approval of the Appropriations Act	108
Balance Budget Is Required	108
Sources of Funding	108
General Fund	108
Uniform School Fund	108
Transportation Fund	109
Constitutional Powers and Restrictions on Powers	109
Limitations on Legislative Powers	109
Prohibition Against Private or Special Legislation	109
The Legislature May Not Authorize Lotteries	109
Special Privileges Forbidden	110
The Lending of Public Credit	110
State Prohibited from Taxing for Political Subdivision	110
Unlawful Delegation of Legislative Authority	110
Reapportionment and Redistricting	111
U.S. Constitution Census Requirement for Reapportionment	111
Utah Constitution Requirement for Redistricting	111
Utah Legislative Process for Redistricting	111
Congressional and Case Law Standards	111
Equal Protection	112

  Nondilution of Racial Minority Influence 112
  Political Gerrymandering 112
 Legislative Staff Offices 112
  Office of Legislative Research and General Counsel 113
  Office of Legislative Fiscal Analyst 113
  Office of Legislative Auditor General 114
  Legislative Printing Office/Bill Room 114
 Use of Information Technology 114

Chapter 7: The Judicial Branch 117
 Constitutional Powers 117
  Judicial Council as Overseer 117
  Rulemaking 118
  Regulation of Practice of Law 118
 Utah Courts 118
  Supreme Court 119
  Court of Appeals 119
  District Courts 119
  Juvenile Courts 121
  Justice Courts 121
  Court Administrators 121
 Administration 122
  Judicial Council 122
  Court Administrator 123
  Administrative Office of the Courts 124
 Judicial Selection, Retention, Discipline, and Removal 124
  Federal Model 124
  Federal Courts 125
  State Model 125
   Selection 125
   Judicial Nominating Commissions 126
   Gubernatorial Appointment 127
   Senate Confirmation 127
   Retention Elections 127
   Discipline and Removal 128
 The Judicial Process 128
  Civil Actions 128
  Criminal Actions 129
 Grand Jury 129
  Indigent Representation 130
 Use of Information Technology 130

Chapter 8: Fiscal Management 131
 Tax Structure for State and Local Governments 131
 Changes in Major State and Local Revenues 132
 Property Tax 133
  Introduction and Historical Highlights 133

    What is Taxable? 133
    Privilege Tax 134
    Tax Equivalent Payments 134
    Who Pays the Tax? 135
    When and How is the Tax Collected? 135
    Equalization 137
    Valuation Date/Tax Payment Due Date 137
    Truth in Taxation 138
    Appeals 138
    Where Does the Tax Revenue Go? 138
    Why Does This Tax Matter? 139
Sales and Use Tax 140
    Introduction and Historical Highlights 140
    What is Taxable? 140
    Who Pays the Tax? 141
    When and How is the Tax Collected? 141
    Where Does the Tax Revenue Go? 141
    Why Does This Tax Matter? 142
Income Tax 142
    Individual Income Tax 142
    Corporate Franchise and Income Tax 143
    Gross Receipts Taxes 143
    What is Taxable? 143
    Who Pays the Tax? 143
    When and How are the Taxes Collected? 146
    Where Does the Tax Revenue Go? 147
    Why Does This Tax Matter? 147
Other Taxes 147
State Tax Commission 148
    Structure 148
    Powers and Duties 148
Tax Comparisons 149
    Utah's Dependency Ratio 149
    National Comparisons: State and Local Revenue Only 149
    Comparisons with Selected Western States 151
Funding of Government Services 153
    General Fund 153
    Uniform School Fund 154
    Combined General Fund and Uniform School Fund 155
    Transportation Fund 155
    Sources of Revenue for Local Governments in Utah 156
State Budget 158

Chapter 9: Agriculture and Food 163
Division of Administrative Services 164
Division of Conservation and Resource Management 164
    Agricultural Loans 164

Environmental Quality	165
Soil Conservation Commission	165
Division of Marketing and Development	165
Division of Animal Industry	166
Animal Health	166
Animal Identification and Elk Farming	166
Meat Inspection	167
Aquaculture	167
Diagnostic Laboratory	167
Division of Chemistry Laboratory	167
Division of Plant Industry	168
State and Federal Pesticide Program	168
Fertilizer and Pesticide Registration and Nursery, Fruit and Vegetable Program	168
Seed Inspection, Feed and Hay Certification, and Noxious Weed Program	168
Insect Control and Plant Quarantine	169
Grain and Hay Inspection Program	169
Division of Regulatory Services	169
Food Compliance	170
Meat, Egg & Poultry Compliance	170
Dairy Compliance	170
Weights and Measures	170
Labeling and Product Compliance	170
Programs	171
Animal and Wildlife Damage and Prevention	171
Agricultural Mediation Service	171
Horse Racing Regulation	171
Chapter 10: Business and Labor	**173**
Alcoholic Beverage Control	173
Utah as a Control State	174
Role of the Commission	175
Role of the Department	175
Department of Commerce	176
Role of the Department	176
Role of the Divisions	177
Administration	177
Division of Consumer Protection	177
Division of Corporations and Commercial Code	178
Division of Occupational and Professional Licensing	178
Division of Public Utilities	180
Committee of Consumer Services	180
Division of Real Estate	181
Division of Securities	181
Department of Financial Institutions	182
State Regulation under the Dual System	183
Depository Financial Institutions in General	184
Role of the Department	184

Insurance Department 185
Labor Commission 187
    Right to Work State 187
    Role of the Labor Commission 188

Chapter 11: Community and Economic Development and Workforce Services 191
    Increasing Interest in Economic Development 191
        National Efforts 191
        International Development 191
    Department of Community and Economic Development 192
        Role of the Department 192
    Department of Community and Economic Development Reorganized 193
    Role of the Divisions within the Governor's Office of Economic Development 194
        Division of Business Development 194
        Division of Tourism 195
    Role of the Divisions within the Department of Community and Culture 195
        Division of Housing and Community Development 196
        Division of Fine Arts 196
        Division of State History 197
        State Library Division 197
        Utah Division of Indian Affairs 198
    Other State Community and Economic Development Entities 198
        Utah Technology Commission 198
        Utah Capital Investment Corporation 199
        Utah State Fair Corporation 199
        Heber Valley Historic Railroad Authority 199
        Utah Science Center Authority 199
        Homeless Coordinating Committee 199
        Utah Housing Corporation 199
    Department of Workforce Services 199
        Background 199
        Federal Welfare and Job Training Reform 200
        Role of the Department of Workforce Services 200
            Employment Development Division 200
            Unemployment Insurance Division 201
            Division of Adjudication 201
            Workforce Development and Information Division 202
            State Council on Workforce Services 202
            Regional Councils 202

Chapter 12: Public Education 205
    Utah's Unique Demographics 205
    Governance of Public Education: The Legislature's Role 207
    Governance of Public Education: State Board of Education 207
        State Board of Education Membership and Election Process 207
        State Board of Education Powers and Duties 208
        State Superintendent and State Office of Education 209

Public Education System	210
School Districts	210
Local School Boards	211
District Officers	211
Charter Schools	211
Utah Schools for the Deaf and the Blind	212
Financing Public Education in Utah	212
Enabling Act and Utah Constitution	212
Guiding Principles	213
State, School District, and Federal Participation in School Funding	213
Educational Reform	215
Utah Performance Assessment System for Students (U-PASS)	215
No Child Left Behind	215
Competency-based Education	216
Student Performance	216

Chapter 13: Higher Education 219

Organizational Overview	219
Board of Regents	220
Commissioner of Higher Education	220
Institutions	220
Research/Teaching Universities	221
Metropolitan/Regional Universities	221
State Colleges	221
Community Colleges	222
Technical Colleges	222
Institutional Leadership	222
Boards of Trustees for Colleges and Universities	222
College and University Presidents	223
Utah College of Applied Technology Administration	223
Financing Higher Education	224
Revenue Sources	224
Funding Process	224
Outcomes	225
Current Issues	225
Affordability	225
Efficiency	226

Chapter 14: Environmental Quality 229

History	229
Department of Environment Quality	229
Purpose of the Department	230
Powers of the Department	230
Executive Director	230
Divisions within the Department of Environmental Quality	231
Establishment of Divisions	231
Division of Air Quality	231

Division of Drinking Water 231
Division of Environmental Response and Remediation 232
Division of Solid and Hazardous Waste 232
Division of Radiation Control 233
Division of Water Quality 234

Chapter 15: Health 235
Utah's Health Status 235
United Health Foundation Ranking 235
Morgan Quitno Ranking 235
Areas for Concern 235
Motor Vehicle Deaths and Injuries 235
Obesity 235
Suicide 236
Access to Health Care 236
Effects of No Medical Coverage 236
Coverage Rates 236
Reasons for No Coverage 236
Persons Most Likely Not to Have Coverage 236
Coverage Types, Enrollment, and Regulation 237
Government Sponsored Plans 237
Employer Sponsored Self-Funded Plans 237
Commercial Health Insurance Plans 238
Enrollment and State Regulatory Authority 238
Public Health 239
Public Health at Statehood 239
Public Health Today 239
Department of Health 240
Division of Community and Family Health Services 240
Division of Epidemiology and Laboratory Services 241
Bureau of Environmental Chemistry 241
Bureau of Forensic Toxicology 241
Bureau of Epidemiology 241
Bureau of Communicable Disease Control 241
Bureau of Laboratory Improvement 242
Bureau of Microbiology 242
Division of Health Care Financing 242
Medicaid 242
Center for Health Data 244
Division of Health Systems Improvement 244
Bureau of Emergency Medical Services 245
Office of Child Care Licensing 245
Bureau of Health Facility Licensing, Certification and Resident Assessment 245
Office of Primary Care and Rural Health 245
Office of the Medical Examiner 245
Office of Emergency Preparedness and Bioterrorism 245
Funding 245

  Summary 246
 Local Health Departments 246

Chapter 16: Human Services 247
 Role of Government in Human Services 247
 Department of Human Services 247
  History 247
  Current Structure 247
   Division of Aging and Adult Services 248
   Division of Child and Family Services 249
   Division of Services for People with Disabilities 249
   Division of Substance Abuse and Mental Health 250
   Division of Juvenile Justice Services 250
   Office of the Public Guardian 250
   Office of Licensing 250
   Office of Recovery Services 251
  Funding 251
  Summary 251

Chapter 17: Natural Resources 253
 Department of Natural Resources 253
 Division of Forestry, Fire and State Lands 254
  Forestry, Fire and State Lands Advisory Council 254
  State Forester 254
  Wildfires 254
  Lone Peak Conservation Center 254
  Utah Forest Practices Act, Forest Stewardship Program, and Forestry Landowner
    Assistance Program 255
  Mineral Leases and Deposits 255
  Range Management 255
  Great Salt Lake 255
 Division of Oil, Gas and Mining 255
  Board of Oil, Gas and Mining 256
  Minerals Mining Program 256
  Coal Mining Program 256
  Oil and Gas Program 256
  Reclamation Program 256
 Division of Parks and Recreation 257
  Board of Utah State Parks and Recreation 257
  Overview of State Parks System 257
  Other Statutory Responsibilities 257
  Boating Safety Program 257
  Off-highway Vehicle Program 258
  Riverway and Trail Projects 258
 Division of Water Resources 258
  Interstate Streams 259
  State Water Planning 259

Conservation and Education 259
Weather Modification 260
Board of Water Resources and Water Development 260
Division of Water Rights 260
Appropriations 260
Adjudication and Distribution 261
Wells, Dams, and Studies 261
Division of Wildlife Resources 261
Wildlife Board 261
Organization 261
Hunting and Fishing 262
Habitat Section 262
Aquatics Section 262
Wildlife Section 262
Law Enforcement 262
Conservation Outreach 262
Major Challenges 263
Utah Geological Survey 263
The Utah Geological Survey Board 263
Energy and Minerals Program 263
Geological Hazards Program 263
Geological Mapping Program 264
Groundwater and Paleontology Program 264
Geologic Information and Outreach 264
Recovery Programs 264
Property Rights Ombudsman 264

Chapter 18: Public Safety, Criminal Law, and Corrections 267
Crime Rates: In Utah, the Mountain States, and the Nation 267
Criminal Offenses 268
Sentencing by the Court 268
Utah Sentencing Commission 271
Board of Pardons and Parole 271
Department of Corrections 272
Division of Institutional Operations 273
Bureau of Clinical Services 273
Adult Probation and Parole 273
Utah Correctional Industries 273
Administrative Services Division 273
Funding 273
Incarceration Rates 274
Juvenile Justice Services 275
Department of Public Safety 276
Division of Operations 276
Utah Highway Patrol 276
Communications Bureau 277
Bureau of Forensic Services 277

Table of Contents • xix

      Highway Safety Office 277
      State Bureau of Investigation 277
   Division of Homeland Security 277
      Emergency Services 277
      State Fire Marshal 278
      Criminal Intelligence Center 278
      Administrative Services 278
      Employee Development Center 278
   Division of Regulatory Services 278
      Driver License Division 278
      Bureau of Criminal Identification 278
   Division of Administrative Services 278
   Peace Officers Standards and Training Academy 279

Chapter 19: Regulation of Public Utilities 281
   Public Service Commission 281
   Division of Public Utilities 282
   Committee of Consumer Services 282
   Electrical Deregulation 282
   Electric Energy Rates 283
   Natural Gas Price Comparison 283

Chapter 20: Transportation 285
   Department of Transportation 285
      Role of the Department 285
      Transportation Commission 286
      Role of the Divisions 286
   Transportation Planning 287
      Project Selection 288
   Highways 288
      Highway Jurisdiction 288
         State Highways 288
         County Highways 288
         Municipal Highways 289
      Highway Funding 289
         Transportation Fund 289
         Centennial Highway Fund 291
         Transportation Investment Fund of 2005 292
         Corridor Preservation Funds 292
         B and C Roads Account 293
         Federal Funding 293
         Funding for Long Range Planning 293
         Funding for the Statewide Transportation Improvement Program 294
   Highway Operations 294
      Highway Maintenance 294
      Intelligent Transportation Systems 295
      Transportation Demand Management 295

      Access Management 295
      Motor Carrier Services 295
   Current Challenges 296
      Funding 296
      Legacy Parkway 298
   Public Transportation 298
   Light Rail and Commuter Rail Transit 302
   Aeronautics 304

Chapter 21: Relationship of State and Federal Governments 307
   Federal Supremacy 307
      Concurrent Power 307
      State Laws 308
      Exclusive Federal Authority 308
      When Federal Law Is Not Exclusive 308
      Implied Preemption vs. Expressed Preemption 309
      Congressional Intent to Preempt 309
   State Preemption Over Local Governments 309
   Federal Funds Received by State Agencies 310
   Influence of Federal Land Ownership in Utah 310
      Land Managed by Federal Agencies in Utah 311
      Wilderness 311
      Payments in Lieu of Taxes 311
      Impact of Federal Land Ownership 312

Chapter 22: Local Government 313
   General Background 313
      Differences Between State & Local and Federal & State Relationships 313
      General Purpose Local Government vs. Limited Purpose Local Government 313
   Counties 314
      History 314
      Current Status 314
      Utah Constitutional Provisions 317
         Counties Recognized as Legal Subdivisions 317
         Moving a County Seat 317
         Changing County Lines 317
         Optional Forms of County Government 317
         Public Debt Limits 317
      Changing County Boundaries 317
         Dividing a County 318
         Consolidating Counties 318
         Major Boundary Change 318
         Minor Boundary Adjustment 318
      Classification 318
      Forms of County Government 320
         County Commission Form 320
         Expanded County Commission Form 320

  County Executive-Council Form 320
  Council-Manager Form 320
 Uniform Fiscal Procedures 320
 Land Use Regulation and Townships 321
Municipalities (Cities and Towns) 321
 History 321
 Current Status 321
 Utah Constitution Provisions 327
  Charter Cities 327
  Municipalities Forbidden from Disposing of Water Rights 327
  Public Debt Limits 327
 Incorporation, Dissolution, and Boundary Changes 327
  Incorporation 327
  Annexation 328
  Boundary Adjustments 329
  Withdrawal/Disconnection 329
  Consolidation of Municipalities 329
  Dissolution of Municipalities 329
 Classification 329
 Forms of Municipal Government 331
 Uniform Fiscal Procedures 332
 Land Use Regulation 332
Limited Purpose Local Governments 332
 Special Districts 333
 Local Districts and Rewrite of Special District Statutes 333
 Independent and Dependent Districts 334
 Special Service Districts 334
 Redevelopment Agencies 335
 Interlocal Cooperation Entities and Interlocal Cooperation Agreements 336
 Associations of Governments 337

Chapter 23: Utah and the Future 343
 Long-term Projections 343
  Population 343
  Demographics 345
  Urbanization 347
  Employment 348
 Summary 349

List of Figures and Tables

Chapter 1: An Historical, Demographic, and Economic Overview
    Figure 1-1 Total Population of Utah 13
    Figure 1-2 County Population in Utah 14
    Figure 1-3 Total Fertility Rates 15
    Table 1-1 Utah Nonagricultural Employment Distribution by Industry 17
    Figure 1-4 Utah Nonagricultural Employment 18
    Figure 1-5 Seasonally Adjusted Unemployment Rates 18
    Figure 1-6 Utah Gross State Product 19
    Figure 1-7 Median Household Income as a Percentage of U.S. 20
    Figure 1-8 Percentage of Persons in Poverty 21

Chapter 3: Utah Administrative Rules
    Figure 3-1 Utah Administrative Rulemaking Process 39

Chapter 4: Citizen Participation and Elections
    Table 4-1 Federal Government 44
    Table 4-2 State Government 45
    Table 4-3 Local School Districts 45
    Table 4-4 County Government 46
    Table 4-5 Municipal Government 46
    Table 4-6 Initiative – Enacting or Amending State Law 49
    Table 4-7 Initiative – Enacting or Amending a County or Municipal Ordinance 51
    Table 4-8 Referendum – Vetoing a New State Law 52
    Table 4-9 Referendum – Vetoing a County or Municipal Ordinance 53
    Table 4-10 Number of Seats and Political Affiliation of the Utah Legislature 59
    Figure 4-1 Party Strength in the Utah State Senate 60
    Figure 4-2 Party Strength in the Utah House of Representatives 61
    Table 4-11 Governors of Utah 61

Chapter 5: The Executive Branch
    Figure 5-1 Executive Branch 65
    Table 5-1 Method of Appointment in Event of Vacancy 66
    Table 5-2 Governors' Institutional Powers 72
    Figure 5-2 Governor's Office 74
    Figure 5-3 Attorney General's Office 78
    Table 5-3 Divisions within the Department of Administrative Services 82
    Figure 5-4 Department of Administrative Services 84
    Table 5-4 Noncontributory Retirement Contribution Rates 86
    Table 5-5 Utah Retirement Defined Benefit Summary – 2005 System Comparison 87
    Figure 5-5 Web Site Access 91

Chapter 6: The Legislative Branch
    Figure 6-1 Legislative Branch 95
    Figure 6-2 Appropriations Committee and Subcommittees 97

Figure 6-3 Interim and Special Legislative Committees 98
Figure 6-4 Standing Committees 99

Chapter 7: The Judicial Branch
Figure 7-1 Judicial Branch 118
Figure 7-2 Court Districts in Utah 120
Table 7-1 Number of District Court Judges and Commissioners 121
Table 7-2 Judicial Qualifications 122
Figure 7-3 Federal Courts 125
Table 7-3 Selection of Judges 126
Table 7-4 Case Filings by District 129

Chapter 8: Fiscal Management
Figure 8-1 Utah's Three Major Taxes: Individual Income, Property, and State and Local Sales and Use 132
Figure 8-2 State and Local Sales and Use, Individual Income, and Property Taxes Revenues in Utah 132
Figure 8-3 Property Taxes: Where Does the Money Come From? 135
Figure 8-4 Percent of All Property Tax Base That is Locally Assessed and Centrally Assessed 136
Figure 8-5 How Taxing Entities Can Overlap to Create Tax Districts 137
Figure 8-6 Property Taxes: Where Does the Money Go? 139
Figure 8-7 Distribution of Property Tax Revenue 139
Figure 8-8 Utah Gross Taxable Sales by Major Component 141
Figure 8-9 Sales and Use Tax: Where Does the Money Go? 142
Figure 8-10 Percentage of Utah Individual Income Tax Revenue Paid by Federal Adjusted Gross Income 144
Figure 8-11 Percentage of Utah Individual Income Tax Returns by Adjusted Gross Income 144
Figure 8-12 Percentage of Corporate Franchise and Income Tax Returns by Corporation's Utah Net Taxable Income 145
Figure 8-13 Percentage of Corporate Franchise and Income Tax Revenue by Corporation's Utah Net Taxable Income 146
Figure 8-14 Individual Income and Corporate Franchise and Income Taxes: Where Does the Money Go? 147
Figure 8-15 State Tax Commission 148
Figure 8-16 Number of School-age Children Per 100 Working Adults 149
Figure 8-17 State and Local Tax Revenue Per Person 150
Figure 8-18 State and Local Tax Revenue as a Percentage of Total Personal Income (comparison) 150
Figure 8-19 State and Local Tax Revenue as a Percentage of Total Personal Income 151
Figure 8-20 Initial Direct Business Tax Burden as a Percentage of Gross State Product .. 152
Figure 8-21 Effective Initial Household and Business Tax Burdens 153
Figure 8-22 The General Fund: Where Does the Tax Money Come From? 154
Figure 8-23 The Uniform School Fund: Where Does the Tax Money Come From? 154
Figure 8-24 Combined General Fund and Uniform School Fund: Where Does the Tax Money Come From? 155

Figure 8-25 Transportation Fund: Where Does the Money Come From? 156
Figure 8-26 Sources of Revenue for Utah Counties 156
Figure 8-27 Sources of Revenue for Municipalities (Government Funds Only) 157
Figure 8-28 Sources of Revenue for Utah Special Service Districts with Budgets Larger than $50,000 157
Figure 8-29 Utah State Government Budget: Where Does the Money Go? 158
Figure 8-30 Utah State Government Appropriations History 159
Figure 8-31 Revenue from Major State Tax Sources 159
Figure 8-32 Revenue from Major State Tax Sources as a Percentage of Total Utah Personal Income 160
Figure 8-33 Revenue from Major State Tax Sources per Person 161

Chapter 9: Agriculture and Food
Figure 9-1 Department of Agriculture and Food 164

Chapter 10: Business and Labor
Figure 10-1 Alcoholic Beverage Control States 174
Figure 10-2 Department of Alcoholic Beverage Control 176
Figure 10-3 Department of Commerce 177
Figure 10-4 Complaints Received by the Division of Consumer Protection 178
Figure 10-5 Total Licenses by Profession 179
Figure 10-6 Number of Regulated Utilities in Utah 180
Table 10-1 Real Estate Licensing in Utah 181
Figure 10-7 Stockbrokers Licensed in Utah 182
Figure 10-8 Department of Financial Institutions 183
Figure 10-9 Utah State-Chartered Credit Unions Converting to Federal Charters 183
Figure 10-10 Insurance Department 186
Figure 10-11 States with Right-to-Work Laws 188
Figure 10-12 Labor Commission 189

Chapter 11: Community and Economic Development and Workforce Services
Figure 11-1 Governor's Office of Economic Development 193
Figure 11-2 Department of Community and Culture 194
Figure 11-3 Department of Workforce Services 203

Chapter 12: Public Education
Figure 12-1 Total Fertility Rates 205
Figure 12-2 Selected Age Groups as a Percentage of Total Population 206
Figure 12-3 Utah Public Education Spending per Pupil 206
Figure 12-4 Actual and Projected School-age and Working-age Populations 207
Figure 12-5 Utah State Office of Education 209
Table 12-1 Public School Enrollment 210
Figure 12-6 Sources of School District and Charter School Revenue 213
Table 12-2 Percentage of Total School District Revenue from Local Sources 214
Figure 12-7 Iowa Test of Basic Skills 216
Table 12-3 National Assessment of Educational Progress Average Scale Scores 217
Table 12-4 American College Test 217

Table 12-5 Advanced Placement Exam 217
Table 12-6 Student Proficiency on Criterion-referenced Tests 218

Chapter 13: Higher Education
Figure 13-1 Utah System of Higher Education 220
Table 13-1 Institutions of Higher Learning by Type 221
Figure 13-2 Utah System of Higher Education Revenue Sources 224
Figure 13-3 Utah System of Higher Education Enrollment 226

Chapter 14: Environmental Quality
Figure 14-1 Department of Environmental Quality 230

Chapter 15: Health
Figure 15-1 Utahns' Sources of Health Care Coverage 238
Figure 15-2 State Regulation of Utah Health Care Coverage 239
Figure 15-3 Department of Health 240
Figure 15-4 Medicaid Spending Growth 243
Figure 15-5 Medicaid Enrollment Growth 243

Chapter 16: Human Services
Figure 16-1 Department of Human Services 248

Chapter 17: Natural Resources
Figure 17-1 Department of Natural Resources 253

Chapter 18: Public Safety, Criminal Law, and Corrections
Figure 18-1 Index Crime Rate 268
Figure 18-2 Violent Crimes 268
Figure 18-3 Property Crime Rate 269
Figure 18-4 Comparison of Incarceration Rates (U.S. vs. Western States vs. Utah) 269
Table 18-1 Utah's Penalty Structure 270
Figure 18-5 Department of Corrections 272
Figure 18-6 Utah's Average Daily Inmate Population 274
Figure 18-7 Department of Public Safety 276

Chapter 19: Regulation of Public Utilities
Figure 19-1 Electrical Energy Price Comparison 283
Figure 19-2 Natural Gas Price Comparison 284

Chapter 20: Transportation
Figure 20-1 Department of Transportation 286
Figure 20-2 Transportation Fund Revenue 289
Figure 20-3 Transportation Fund Distribution 290
Figure 20-4 Utah Fuel Tax Rates 290
Figure 20-5 Centennial Highway Fund: Major Categories 292
Table 20-1 Utah Highway Capacity Needs 294
Figure 20-6 Revenue Growth: Sales and Use Tax vs. Fuel Tax 296

Figure 20-7 Utah Fuel Tax Burden 297
Figure 20-8 Average Annual Fuel Tax Paid Per Vehicle 297
Table 20-2 Utah Transit Authority: Formation and Key Funding Authorization History .. 299
Table 20-3 Utah Transit Authority: Light Rail and Commuter Rail History 303
Table 20-4 Aviation Fuel Tax Funds Distribution 305

Chapter 21: Relationship of State and Federal Governments
Figure 21-1 Federal Funds Received by Agency 310
Table 21-1 Land Managed by Federal Agencies in Utah 311
Figure 21-2 Payments in Lieu of Taxes Paid to Utah 312

Chapter 22: Local Government
Figure 22-1 Counties in Utah 315
Table 22-1 Classification of Counties and County Populations 316
Figure 22-2 Number of Counties by Class 319
Figure 22-3 Percentage of State's Population by Class of County 319
Figure 22-4 County Population as a Share of State Population 319
Table 22-2 Population of Utah Municipalities and Counties 322
Figure 22-5 Location of Municipalities in Utah 326
Table 22-3 Classification of Municipalities 330
Figure 22-6 Statewide Population Per Class of Municipality 330
Figure 22-7 Municipalities Per Class 331
Table 22-4 Optional Forms of Municipal Government 331
Figure 22-8 Associations of Governments in Utah 328
Table 22-5 Activities of Utah's Seven Associations of Governments 340

Chapter 23: Utah and the Future
Table 23-1 Utah Population Projections by County 344
Figure 23-1 Growth of School-age Population 345
Figure 23-2 Growth of Retirement-age Population 346
Figure 23-3 Utah Proportion of Population Projections by Age Group 347
Figure 23-4 Actual and Projected Nonagricultural Payroll Employment Growth 348
Table 23-2 Projected Industry Growth 348

Chapter 1

An Historical, Demographic, and Economic Overview of Utah

In order to understand Utah government, it is helpful to have at least a basic understanding of Utah's geography, history, and its current economic and demographic make-up. This chapter is designed to provide the reader with that basic overview.

GEOGRAPHY

Utah is the thirteenth largest state in the nation, encompassing 84,916 square miles or 54.3 million acres. However, among the eleven contiguous western states Utah ranks only

> **In this chapter:**
>
> Geography (p. 1)
> Climate, Streams, and Vegetation (p. 2)
> The Early Peoples of Utah (p. 3)
> Trappers and Explorers (p. 6)
> Mormon Settlement of Utah (p. 7)
> From Territory to Statehood (p. 8)
> Industry and Employment Trends (p. 9)
> Population and Demographic Trends (p. 13)
> Wealth and Poverty (p. 19)

ninth in size, being larger than only Idaho and Washington. Utah is divided into three major physiographic provinces: the Colorado Plateau, the Great Basin, and the Rocky Mountains. Each of these provinces largely influences what those regions have become and what Utah is today.

The Colorado Plateau is the largest of the three major provinces. It is a high mountain plateau of layered sedimentary rock that covers almost all of the eastern half of Utah and is bordered on the north and west by the Rocky Mountains. The Colorado Plateau is home to some of the world's most spectacular scenery. The area contains five national parks, six national monuments, a national recreation area, and several state parks. From dinosaur bones and many other fossils to deep canyons carved by ancient rivers, this area is one of the wonders of the world. Millions of visitors come to Utah each year to see this area's natural wonders. The plateau also contains significant deposits of hydrocarbons—coal, oil, oil shale, tar sands, gilsonite, and natural gas. In addition, there are large quantities of uranium, potash, and vanadium. Mountain grassland provides summer grazing for cattle and sheep.[1] The streams that flow out of the mountains provide essential water for crops and people.

The Rocky Mountains Province consists of two dissimilar mountain ranges: the Wasatch and Uinta ranges. The Wasatch Range, like most mountain ranges in the nation, runs north and south. The Wasatch Range begins in southern Idaho and runs to Nephi, Utah. The Uintas run, rather unusually, east and west for about 150 miles, from the Wasatch Range east to the Colorado border. Both mountain ranges are important to the state for many reasons but mostly for the snow that falls upon them each winter. This snow melts in the spring and makes the numerous streams that run down its canyons. These streams in turn fill the lakes and man-made reservoirs that are used for water storage, for agriculture, and for municipal and industrial purposes. Without water from these mountain streams, modern life in Utah would be impossible. These mountains also provide exceptional summer and winter recreational activities. Summer camping, fishing, and hiking are very popular. In the winter, the many ski resorts attract skiers from all over the world.

The Great Basin is the third region of the state. It is the second largest in area and by far the most heavily populated. The Great Basin covers most of the western half of Utah and goes well into Nevada. It is the remnant of the much larger Lake Bonneville, a large body of water that covered much of Utah, Nevada, and the southern part of Idaho centuries ago. The lowest area of the Great Basin is the Great Salt Lake, the main remnant of the once enormous lake. The elevation of the Great Salt Lake varies depending on annual rainfall. At its lowest level in 1963, the lake stood at 4,191.30 feet above sea level—a very low level, but not surprising given the region was in its sixth year of drought. In the mid-1980s, the lake was at the opposite end measuring 4,211.86 feet above sea level, after several years of above average rainfall.[2] Since the Great Salt Lake has no outlet, it is one of the saltiest lakes in the world. It is a shallow lake with depths seldom over thirty feet. It provides limited recreation: mainly sail boating and sunbathing. There are some industries that benefit from the salty lake. Brine shrimp and shrimp eggs are harvested for hatcheries and for use in home aquariums. A few companies gather the salt from the lake through large evaporation ponds and market it.

A smaller remnant of Lake Bonneville is Utah Lake which is located about forty miles south of the Great Salt Lake. In contrast to its northern and much larger sister, Utah Lake is a fresh water lake where boating and fishing are popular. It is even more shallow than the Great Salt Lake with depths seldom over eight feet.

CLIMATE, STREAMS, AND VEGETATION

Utah ranks only behind Nevada as the driest state in the nation. Despite this desert sounding statistic, the state actually has three climatic regions: humid, sub-humid or semi-arid, and arid. It will come as no surprise that the humid region is located in the mountain ranges of the state. There rainfall ranges between thirty and fifty inches a year. Much of this moisture comes in the form of snow during the winter and early spring months. By contrast, the arid regions of the state receive eight inches or less of rainfall each year. The mountain valleys and benches receive between twelve and sixteen inches of rainfall each year.[3]

The rivers and streams according to one author, "are small in volume, short in length and variable in seasonal flow."[4] Even Utah's two major rivers—the Colorado and the Green—fit this description when compared to the great rivers of the United States. That does not mean the mountain streams of the state are not important. It is these streams that fill the lakes and man-made reservoirs of the state during the spring sufficiently to provide water for agriculture as well as municipal and industrial uses.

The Rocky Mountains divide the state not only into the Great Basin and the Colorado Plateau, but they also divide the state into two drainage systems. All rivers east of the Rocky Mountains flow into either the Green or Colorado rivers. All streams west of the Rocky Mountains flow into the Great Basin and ultimately what is not used ends up in the Great Salt Lake, Utah Lake, or Sevier Lake, which is the smallest of the remnants of Lake Bonneville.

Because of the variety in elevation and climate, plant life is richly varied. In the highest mountains Alpine Fir and Engelmann Spruce are typical, as are mountain grasses and beautiful mountain flowers. Just below them in elevation grow Douglas Fir, Blue Spruce, and Quaking Aspen. In the lower mountains Pine, Shrubby Maple, Scrub Oak, Sumac, Serviceberry, and Big Tooth

Maple are common. In the foothills Chokecherry, Pinon, and Juniper are found. In the grasslands are numerous grasses and sagebrush and in the deserts Mesquite and Creosote bushes and Joshua trees. Along the water courses Willows, Cottonwoods, Red Birches, and Mountain Alders are commonplace. In the valleys that today house most Utahns, very few trees grew at the time Utah was colonized. As a result, numerous species of trees have been imported and now line many commercial streets and most residential ones. The same can be said for flowers, shrubbery, and grasses.[5]

The tremendous variety in Utah geography and climate allows for a wide variety in wildlife as well. The larger animals of the state include mule deer, elk, moose, and some buffalo. The state's predators include bears, cougars, wolves, coyotes, badgers, and wolverines. Small herbivores such as squirrels, chipmunks, prairie dogs, beavers, and such reptiles as snakes, lizards, and horned toads are prevalent.[6]

THE EARLY PEOPLES OF UTAH
Desert Archaic and Fremont Cultures

The earliest peoples of Utah, as archeologists have so far determined, lived in the Great Basin as early as 11,000 B.C. Named the Desert Archaic Culture by scholars, they were a primitive people who lived in caves and brush and wood huts. They took advantage of the seeds, roots, and small game that lived in the area by the lakes. They lived in extended family units in groups of thirty or so. They seemed to have either moved, died, or been absorbed by other peoples by about A.D. 400.

The Fremont Culture emerged in the place of the Desert Culture. Though retaining the hunting-gathering lifestyle of their predecessors, the Fremont people also began growing crops of beans, corn, and squash. The Fremont tribes that lived near the lakes and streams of northern Utah also relied on fishing and the many native plants that grew along the waters' edges. They engaged in extensive trading with the tribes around them and thereby improved their economic status. The Fremont people covered a very large area of central and northern Utah but also eastern Nevada, southern Idaho, southwestern Wyoming, and western Colorado.

Their housing was superior to the huts and caves of their predecessors, living in well-built partially below-ground pit houses. They also built surface storage facilities and made fine basketry, pottery, and leather moccasins. Their distinctive basketry was made by "weaving coils of brush, bulrush, or other pliable native material around a single rod of juniper, willow, or other stiffer but bendable woods."[7] Their grey-fired pottery was distinctive in that it had granular rock or sand mixed in with the clay that prevented cracking and ensured even drying. Some of their rock art has been preserved and is visible in various places in Utah. Between the tenth and thirteenth centuries, the Fremont peoples began to diminish mainly due to a reduction in regional rainfall.

Anasazi Culture

In the southern part of Utah along the Colorado Plateau, the Anasazi Culture developed at about 385 B.C. The Anasazi culture can be divided into three periods, Basket Maker I, II, and III, with each period signifying the development of a more sophisticated society. The Basket Maker I people began planting corn and living in fixed dwellings. This culture existed until approximately the beginning of the first century A.D. Basket Maker II people developed flood plain irrigation for the growing of their crops of beans, squash, and corn. They also used native plants such as cactus fruit, beeweed grasses, sunflowers, pine nuts, serviceberry, and sedges to name a few. Wild animals like rabbit, mountain sheep, and mule deer added to the variety of their diet. Basket Maker III people developed about A.D. 750 and advanced their agriculture even further, relying on their farming for over 50 percent of their food and only 20 percent on wild plants.[8]

As their agricultural skills developed the Basket Maker cultures became more and more sedentary living in fixed shelters called pit houses. These were below ground level dwellings (generally four to five feet deep) of some sophistication. The walls were lined with sandstone slabs, the floors covered with packed clay or sandstone. These dwellings included benches, grinding stations, fire pits, and tunnels connecting ante rooms and storage areas. Significant trade between the Anasazi and other regional tribes became quite extensive. The Anasazi ceramicware were traded for copper, turquoise, shells, obsidian, and other ornaments.

Beginning around A.D. 750, the Anasazi culture developed into what archeologists call the Pueblo culture. Like the Anasazi culture, the Pueblo culture advanced through three phases. The biggest difference between the two cultures is that Pueblo began building its dwellings above ground and made of sandstone or river cobbles held together by mud. Probably more important was that the above-ground structures were connected rather than the separate pit-houses of the Anasazi.

As the climate changed and became warmer and drier, the Pueblo people were forced to move to higher elevations to access the greater rainfall, but not so high that the shorter growing season of the higher levels threatened their crops. The climate change forced the Pueblo people to live in more concentrated communities in order to maximize division of labor. Some of these elaborate structures can still be seen in several places in southern Utah. The Pueblo culture made extensive use of the local woods. "From local juniper, saltbrush, mountain mahogany, cottonwood, oak squawbrush, willow . . . they made construction members in their houses, agricultural digging sticks, throwing sticks, cradleboards, arrow shafts, and bows."[9] The Pueblos also made beautiful ceramic pottery by coiling ropes of clay to the desired height. Their use of stone allowed them to develop hammers, pestles, polishing and grinding stones, awls, arrows, and axes. They also drew some of the best rock art of the area. Newspaper Rock in Canyonlands National Park is one example of such artwork as are the petroglyphs in Dry Fork Canyon and White Canyon in Natural Bridges National Monument.

Despite these advancements over the Basket Makers, life for the Pueblos was harsh, dangerous, and generally short. Infectious disease from the lack of sanitation, the dangers of childbirth, and parasite infestation all limited life expectancy. The best studies have concluded that "80 percent of females died between ages 16 and 26, many probably in childbirth; and 40 percent of the males died before the age of 26. Few people lived past 50 years of age."[10]

By the twelfth and thirteenth centuries, the Pueblo culture faced such severe uncertainty in rainfall that many began abandoning Utah. Those that remained fought over the scarce water resources. To protect themselves higher cliff dwellings were constructed that can be seen today in many parts of the Southwest. The fate of the Pueblo culture is not clearly known, though most scholars believe they joined the tribal cultures of New Mexico and Arizona.

Shoshonean Culture

By A.D. 1100, a new Indian culture moved into Utah. These Numic or more commonly called Shoshonean peoples, namely the Northern and Western Shoshoni, the Northern Ute, and Southern Paiute came from what is now southern California. Whether these Shoshonean people conquered the Pueblo culture and Fremont peoples, forced them out, or just assisted them in leaving is unknown. What is known is that the Shoshonean proved much more adaptable to the dry climate of the region than either the Fremont or Anasazi. One reason is they brought different tools that allowed them to harvest more efficiently the seeds of the native plants. The Fremont used "horn sickles and coiled, flat winnowing-parching trays. The Shoshonean people brought with them paddle-shaped seed beaters and deep, triangular-twined winnowing trays . . . " which allowed them to gather much more food in less time.[11] The Shoshoneans did not plant crops to the degree that either the Fremont or Anasazi did, but still cultivated squash, beans, sunflowers, and corn.

The Shoshonean peoples eventually covered most of Utah. The Northern Shoshoni were located in northern Utah, southern Idaho, and Wyoming. The territory of the Utes was the largest. It covered most of the state with the exception of the most southern and northern portions and well into Colorado. The Gosiute, also known today as Goshute, settled in northwestern Utah and northeastern Nevada. The Southern Paiute inhabited southwestern Utah, southern Nevada, and northern Arizona. The Gosiutes probably dwelt in some of the driest and dreariest territory of the American West. "They roamed the desert in family bands, gathering seeds and insects, trapping small game, hunting antelope and deer, wearing skin blankets in winter and little of anything in summer and improvising wikiups of brush for shelter. They were few in number and peaceable in disposition."[12] The Southern Paiutes lived on lands only slightly less foreboding. And their lifestyle was similar with the exception of some irrigation agriculture of small gardens.

The Utes were divided into several bands covering different parts of Utah. The Uinta Utes lived in what is today the Uintah Basin; the Timpanogot Utes lived around Utah Lake; the San Pitch Utes lived south of the Timpanogots in Juab and Sevier counties; the Pah Vant Utes lived in the counties of Millard and Sevier; and the Sheberetch and Weeminuche Utes lived in the southern most portions of eastern Utah, just above the Navajos. Most of the Ute bands adopted the horse into their culture as it was introduced by the Spaniards. This allowed them to hunt for food and trade with other tribes over a much larger area than other Utah tribes. This nomadic hunter-gather lifestyle was supplemented by some planting of crops by the Pahvants and Weeminuche who planted corn, beans, and squash. The Timpanogot Utes became excellent fishermen, using various means to catch fish from Utah Lake such as lures, lines, weirs, and nets as well as spears and arrows. All Ute bands hunted for large game including mountain sheep, deer, antelope, bear, buffalo, and elk. Small game such as rabbits, sage grouse, and squirrels added to their diet. The Utes also enjoyed many insects such as crickets and grasshoppers and thought of them as delicacies. They caught these insects in organized drives, then dried or roasted them.[13]

Most of the Shoshoni people lived in conically shaped tents that were easily disassembled since many moved their dwellings with the seasons. Some were covered with animal skins as is often portrayed in movies, but most "used willows, grass, or brush."[14] Clothing was "unpretentious" and simple. Breechcloths for men made of animal skins; for women a short leather skirt or sage-bark dresses. They did weave blankets and robes and made leather moccasins for the colder seasons.[15]

Utes, Paiutes, and Shoshonis formed governments around bands and family groups, not on a tribal wide structure. The system worked more through consensus rather than dictatorship. The native American population of Utah prior to the coming of the white man is difficult to estimate but the best scholars guess that at the time of Columbus, about 19,300 people lived in the Central Mountain Region which would include Utah.

About 1620, the last of the native American tribes entered Utah. The Navajos began entering southeastern Utah, though the biggest portion of their tribal territory existed in Arizona and New Mexico. They were an adaptable people which allowed them to incorporate customs of the peoples that they conquered, lived next to, or with. They are known for their beautiful blankets, pottery, and adobe and rock architecture that was built up against the mountainsides.

In summary of the earliest peoples of Utah, it can be said that the general lifestyle was hunter-gatherer significantly supplemented in some areas by the cultivation of crops. As the climate changed over the years of their existence so did their ways. Some adapted, some moved on, and some just seem to have disappeared. Overall they were few in number and spread into tribal groups over various regions of the state. Where they lived impacted their lifestyle as would be expected. By today's standards they lived very simplistic lives that were harsh and short. Nevertheless the fact that they lived here for over thirteen thousand years before the coming of the Europeans and then the Mormons proved that they were tough and adaptable at least to a significant degree.

TRAPPERS AND EXPLORERS

It was not until after the Lewis and Clark expedition in 1804-06 that a long established fur trade expanded into the trans-Mississippi west. This expansion deeply affected Utah for these itinerant and courageous fur trappers explored Utah and lived much of the time in its mountains and valleys. The trappers came into the West to obtain beaver pelts which had come into great demand as a result of a fashion change: the growing popularity of beaver hats. The many rivers and streams of the West were full of beavers, thus attracting trappers employed by companies from Great Britain, the United States, and Mexico. Fur trappers set traps for the beavers and caught, killed, and skinned them. When loaded to the hilt with the pelts, the trappers traveled to their respective company headquarters, turned in the pelts, got new supplies, and headed back to the mountains to repeat the cycle all over again. By the mid-1820s, the cycle changed and the company came to the mountains in order to improve efficiency of operation. These annual get-togethers became known as rendezvous. This new method kept the trappers in the mountains for more time each year. For three straight years, 1826-28, Utah became the place for these famous rendezvous. Cache Valley hosted the event in 1826 and for the next two, the southern end of Bear Lake held the rendezvous. They were great and wondrous events—trappers, company suppliers, and executives came as did Indians, artisans, and other merchants to trade and sell wares. Games, contests of skill and, of course, tall tales were all part of the week-long experience.

By the 1840s, the fur trapping business was in steep decline. A change in styles and an enormous reduction in the number of beavers (thus making trapping more difficult and expensive) made profitability near impossible. But before the industry died, Utah had been explored like never before and this knowledge was reported to Americans in word, books, and maps. Utah names come from this era and these colorful adventurers. The cities of Ogden and Provo are named after two prominent trappers Peter Skeen Ogden and Etienne Provost. Cache County is named for the caches of fur and other items stored there by trappers.

In addition to the fur trappers who provided substantial knowledge about the west to Americans, government explorers were also crucial to the greater understanding of the West. U.S. government sponsored explorations of Utah played a significant role in its settlement and economic development. Most of the men who conducted the explorations were part of the Army Corps of Topographical Engineers. Their excellent maps and well-written descriptions of the areas including the plants and animals and peoples were read by many in the eastern states. Of all the government explorers, none is more well-known than John C. Fremont. This colorful American and one-time presidential candidate conducted three explorations of the West that included routes through Utah in 1843-44, 1845-46, and 1853-54. During these trips, Fremont confirmed earlier reports of the fur trappers that none of the lakes of Utah drained into the Pacific Ocean and named the region the Great Basin. He also named Antelope Island in the Great Salt Lake because of the large numbers of these animals on the island. He made clear that the Jordan River connected Utah Lake to the Great Salt Lake.

Captain Howard Stansbury made significant scientific contributions to the knowledge of Utah. His explorations of Utah (1849-50) resulted in the first land-based round trip of the Great Salt Lake. When his team left the Salt Lake Valley they had completed for the first time a "complete scientific investigation . . . of this portion of the Great Basin."[16] On his way back to Washington, Stansbury also discovered a new route across Wyoming that would later be used by the Overland Stage, Pony Express, and the Union Pacific Railroad.

John W. Gunnison, a lieutenant in the Army assigned to the Corp of Engineers, accompanied Stansbury on his exploration of Utah and played a significant role in the mapping of Utah Lake and the Jordan River. When the Stansbury journey was over he helped his commander prepare the report for the federal government with maps that proved so helpful to travelers and settlers. Gunnison is also famous for his book on the Mormons that covered their history and theology. The book has been recognized as "probably the most objective work to that date on the subject and had wide appeal as was evidenced by its eight domestic and two foreign editions published prior to 1890."[17]

The publications of John Wesley Powell have made him a household name among people interested in the West. Powell, who lost an arm in the Civil War while serving in the Union army, is most famous for his trips down the Green and Colorado Rivers and for his scholarly publications: *Explorations of the Colorado River* (1875), *Geology of the Uinta Mountains* (1876), and *Report on the Lands of the Arid Regions of the United States With a More Detailed Account of the Land of Utah* (1878). He is probably most famous for his preaching of the "gospel of rational use of natural resources."[18] He believed the West to be fundamentally different than the East to a significant degree because of the paucity of rainfall. As a result, efficient use of water through irrigation and a different distribution of land were essential to survival in the West.

MORMON SETTLEMENT OF UTAH

One historian has written that, until 1847, "Utah was a wilderness, inhabited by small bands of Indians and traversed periodically by Spanish missionaries, and traders, American and British fur trappers, government explorers, and California bound pioneers."[19] The settlement of the Mormons in Utah changed this area dramatically and permanently. The Mormons, or members of The Church of Jesus Christ of Latter-day Saints (LDS Church), came to Utah as a result of persecution in several other areas of the East beginning in New York and Ohio. From there, the Mormons moved to Missouri and then to Illinois. Though initially welcomed by residents of the areas where they settled, animosity soon developed and each time the Mormons were forced to leave. In Illinois, they built a new city they called Nauvoo on the eastern banks of the Mississippi River. In 1844, the church's founder Joseph Smith was killed by a mob and the survival of the entire community seemed seriously threatened.

Brigham Young, who took the reins of the LDS Church after the death of Smith, made the decision to move west because he and the other church leaders could see that they could not peaceably survive in Nauvoo. In early 1846, the Mormons began leaving Nauvoo by crossing the Mississippi River into Iowa, an only partially settled prairie territory. During 1846, the Mormons traversed across Iowa. Poorly organized, and in serious want of supplies, many experienced serious suffering. The advance party built way stations at Garden Grove, about halfway across Iowa and Mt. Pisgah another twenty-five miles west. At the Missouri River, the western border of Iowa, the Mormons created two communities. Kanesville on the eastern bank of the Missouri River and Council Bluffs on the western bank both became important Mormon settlements. The challenge of moving such a large group of people across Iowa without proper preparation proved so difficult that the plan to send an advance party to the Great Basin had to be delayed to 1847.

On April 4, 1847, the advance party of about 150 people led by Brigham Young left Council Bluffs and headed west. Rather than following the Oregon Trail, which ran along the south side of the Platte River, the Mormons traveled on the north side of the river to avoid competition for forage and wood. The trip across Nebraska to Fort Laramie, Wyoming went well. Shortly after Fort Laramie they crossed the Platte River and traveled along the Oregon Trail through South Pass and on to Fort Bridger. Toward the end of June the Mormons met several fur trappers who provided them more information on the Great Basin. Moses "Black" Harris and Thomas "Peg-leg" Smith both recommended Cache Valley rather than the Great Basin as a settlement place. Jim Bridger whom the Mormons met a few days later, spoke more favorably about the Great Basin.

On July 22, 1847, a portion of the advance party entered the Salt Lake Valley. They chose a campsite around present day 500 East between 1700 South and 2100 South, and planted crops. By that evening they had picked what they believed to be the best place to plant crops—near present-day 400 South and between Main and State Streets. By the evening of the next day, crops had been planted and City Creek Canyon had been diverted for irrigation. It was not until July 24 that Brigham Young and the remainder of the advance party arrived in the valley. By the time winter set in, some 1,500 settlers had arrived. The community was organized and assigned all essential tasks for survival. "One group staked out, plowed, harrowed, and irrigated thirty-five acres, planting potatoes, corn, buckwheat, beans, turnips, and other garden produce. Another group laid out a city in 135 ten-acre blocks. . . . Others were assigned to build cabins and a fort. . . . Another committee, . . . located timber in a nearby canyon . . . Others were assigned to hunt, try their luck fishing and to extract salt from the Great Salt Lake."[20]

Not content with settling just the valley of the Great Salt Lake, Brigham Young sent scouting parties and then settlers throughout the West and beyond. One historian writes, "The Mormon settlement of Utah was a remarkable accomplishment by a group of strong leaders and thousands of dedicated, obedient followers who were intent on establishing the Kingdom of God on earth. Their combined efforts produced the most impressive colonizing program in the history of the American West."[21] Within the first decade of their arrival, Mormons had settled over one hundred towns from the Salt Lake Valley south to San Bernardino in southern California. When the leader of this great settlement plan—Brigham Young—died in 1877, "more than 300 settlements had been established in the present states of Utah, Idaho, Wyoming, Arizona, Nevada, California, and Hawaii."[22]

Much of Utah's population growth over the first few decades resulted from continued immigration to the area from the LDS Church's aggressive missionary program. The mission of the LDS Church was to gather "scattered Israel" to Zion in preparation of the second coming of Jesus Christ. To accomplish this "gathering" missionaries were sent to the Eastern states, Great Britain, Europe, and other places as well. The 1850 census showed that Utah had a population of 11,380, a remarkable feat for just three years. By 1860, Utah had almost quadrupled its population to 40,273. By 1870 it had more than doubled to 86,786; of that amount 30,702 or 35.4 percent were foreign born.

FROM TERRITORY TO STATEHOOD

When the Mormons first settled in the Great Basin in 1847, the territory was part of the nation of Mexico. That changed quickly as a result of the Mexican War of 1846-48. In the Treaty of Guadalupe-Hidalgo, 1848, the United States acquired over a million square miles of land including Texas, California, New Mexico, and Utah. The next year, the Mormons applied for statehood. The state of Deseret was huge—ranging from the Colorado Rockies on the east to the Sierra Nevada Mountains on the west and south to San Bernardino, California. But such a vast state was too much for Congress to swallow especially since the population requirement of 60,000 residents had not yet been attained. Shortly thereafter, Utah's political status took the more traditional route to statehood, that of a territory first. The Compromise of 1850 gave territorial status to both New Mexico and Utah, and statehood to California. President Millard Fillmore appointed Brigham Young as the territory's first governor and Young took the oath of office on February 5, 1851.

Over the next forty-six years Utah applied for statehood five other times (1861, 1872, 1882, 1887). All met with failure because Congress believed that Utah had not sufficiently separated church and state and because Congress generally opposed the practice in Utah of plural marriage. By the late 1880s, the LDS Church realized that things must change if statehood were ever going to become a reality. The President of the LDS Church, Wilford W. Woodruff, announced an official declaration which stated that the LDS Church would no longer perform plural marriages or teach polygamy. The last obstacle to statehood remained—separation of church and state. This was done by the dissolution of the two functioning political parties—Liberal and Peoples—and the adoption of the two national parties—Republican and Democrat. With this accomplished, the state applied once more for statehood and Congress finally obliged. Utah became the forty-fifth state in the union on January 4, 1896.

INDUSTRY AND EMPLOYMENT TRENDS

Since the Mormon settlement of Utah beginning in 1847, Utah's economic structure has grown from a substantially isolated agrarian economy to a diversified economy involved in the increasingly connected global marketplace.

Economic History

Prior to the arrival of the Mormon pioneers, minimal economic activity existed in the mostly unknown area now known as Utah. Various explorers, trappers, and traders had spent time in the area and a few pioneer wagon trains, including the ill-fated Donner party, had previously passed through the area, which was sparsely populated by various Indian tribes.

In 1847, upon seeing the isolated Salt Lake Valley, Brigham Young famously declared, "This is the [right] place," then quickly set out to settle the valley and the region. Despite the difficult climate and growing conditions, Mormon pioneers successfully established many agrarian colonies throughout the West, based on an ideal of community self-sufficiency. As of 1860, slightly more than half of the population worked in agriculture, while most of the other half labored in mining coal and iron and processing products from farms and mines to be used locally.

This largely agrarian economy, however, would not last for long. The California Gold Rush of 1849 sparked significant interest in westward expansion. Many people passed through Utah on their way to the Pacific coast, resulting in contact and trade between the Mormon settlements and the travelers. In addition, two highly important economic developments occurred within the next two decades—completion of the transcontinental telegraph in Salt Lake City in 1861 and completion of the transcontinental railroad at Promontory Point in 1869. These important ties with the rest of the expanding United States facilitated significant increases in general commerce, mining, and banking; industries which were initially discouraged by Mormon leaders because these activities would likely bring about the end of the isolation and self-sufficiency that the Mormon pioneers initially sought.

Utah's precious metal mining industry began in 1863 with the first formal mining claims in Bingham Canyon. Mining quickly developed into an important industry for the territory. During the latter part of the 1800s and the early 1900s, mining and other non-agricultural industries became more and more important in the territorial and state economy, sometimes with the encouragement of, and sometimes against the will of, Mormon leaders. Although not as important as in earlier decades, agriculture still played a key role in the overall economy.

While Utah was not a wealthy state prior to the 1930s, the Great Depression nonetheless had a significant impact on the young state. Per capita income dropped 50 percent in 1932 and even by 1940 had only climbed to about 82 percent of the pre-Depression level. During the 1930s, Utah's average unemployment rate was 26 percent. With the establishment of various New Deal programs, Utah received substantial federal aid that went for such construction projects as Pineview, Hyrum, Deer Creek, and Moon Lake dams.[23]

Ultimately, however, it took World War II to lift the state and the nation from the Depression. For the first time in the twentieth century, the state reached full employment during the war years. In addition to providing more jobs, World War II and the subsequent Cold War brought substantial changes to the composition of the Utah economy. Among these changes was a sizable increase in the manufacturing and government (especially national defense) industries and a continual decrease in the importance of agriculture in the state's economy. Building upon this economic foundation, the service, technology, and tourism-related industries have become increasingly important to the state's economy at the end of the twentieth century and into the twenty-first century.[24]

Employment Trends

The industries of any economy are usually divided into three main groups: agriculture, goods-producing, and service-producing. The goods-producing industries are (1) mining, (2) manufacturing, and (3) construction. There are five service-producing industries: (1) services; (2) trade; (3) finance, insurance, and real estate; (4) government; and (5) transportation, communication, and utilities. Such categories are important in understanding employment trends and changes in the economy; but it is important to understand that these categories are somewhat arbitrary and therefore not completely precise. Despite these inherent weaknesses in the categories, there is value in using them to view changes in employment over the decades.

In Utah during the early pioneer period, agriculture was the dominant industry. The census of both 1850 and 1860, showed that over 50 percent of the labor force was employed in agriculture. A decline in agricultural employment subsequently occurred and has continued to the present. Today, agriculture employs about one percent of the total Utah labor force. This trend is a national one. As science and new inventions improved agricultural productivity, fewer farmers were needed to supply the demand for food and other agricultural products. The result was that farmers left for the cities to find new employment opportunities.

During the early years of territorial Utah, goods-producing industries, especially manufacturing and construction, were also major employers. In the 1850 census almost half of all nonagricultural workers were employed in the goods-producing industries. The largest was manufacturing, employing just over 30 percent of all nonagricultural jobs. Construction employed about 16 percent. Mining, the other goods-producing industry, had not had much of a chance to get started in Utah and employed less than 2 percent.

The service-producing sector was small in 1850, employing about 12 percent of the nonagricultural workers. Two sub-categories of the service-producing sector, professional services and education services, only employed seventy-five people and twenty-four people respectively. Trade employment was second to services, employing almost 5 percent of the nonagricultural work force. Financial services and government work were virtually nonexistent during the early pioneer times. These two sectors combined employed only about 1 percent of the nonagricultural work force.

As the population of Utah grew and the territory became more established, employment trends changed substantially. More services became available to Utah citizens. By 1890 (the census just before statehood) Utah showed significant growth in the service-producing sector. Service-employment had more than doubled since the 1850 census. Domestic and personal services, which had employed only two people in 1850, now employed more than six thousand and represented 9 percent of the total work force. Professional services, which had employed fifty-one people in 1850, now employed over eighteen hundred people. Domestic, personal, and educational services now employed 13 percent of all workers. Trade had also grown; in 1890 this industry had increased its share of the workforce to 7 percent.

The transportation and communications industries were very small in early Utah. The United States mail service was established with a post office in 1850. The firm of Russell, Majors, and Waddell held the mail contracts for many of the early years. The transportation industry was dominated by overland freighting, most of which was done by individual entrepreneurs. A few large firms such as Halladay and Warner, as well as Livingston and Kinkead, operated until the coming of the railroad. Both the telegraph and railroad came to Utah in the 1860s, tying the state into the national economy and national affairs.

By 1890, Utah employment trends were showing signs of a more modern era. Railroads employed almost 2,100 people. Financial services had grown from five workers in 1850 to over 1,900, and employed three percent of the nonagricultural work force. Government too had grown by 1890; though it still was the smallest sector, it employed 1,231 people: 785 in the military and 446 in civilian work.

The Great Depression had a dramatic impact on employment trends throughout the United States. One of its main impacts was the establishment of the welfare state and the corresponding growth of government services and regulation. By 1940, things had changed dramatically. Government in Utah now employed around 7,000 people, about 2,900 of them federal employees. With America not yet involved in World War II, only 121 Utahns were in the military.

The 1940 census, taken just prior to America's entrance into World War II, showed the continued shift to the services industries. Services employed 56 percent of the work force. Reflecting the modern era, major growth was seen in transportation, communications, and public utilities. These industries had grown from 8 percent of the work force to almost 11 percent. The fastest-growing industry in this sector was utilities. Twenty years earlier, only 235 people were employed in the electric and gas utilities, but in 1940 more than 2,200 people worked in this burgeoning industry. The two major employers were Utah Power and Light Company and Mountain Fuel Supply Company. Wholesale and retail trade also continued its rapid growth. In 1920, about 15,000 people were employed in this field; by 1940, that number had grown to almost 29,000. Professional, domestic, and personal services had grown from 20,000 employees in 1920 to 27,000 in 1940. As a result, this industry grew from 13.7 percent of the work force to 18.2 percent.

In the 1950s, the transportation, communications, and utilities industries peaked as a percentage figure of state employment—they were over 11 percent. Twenty-one thousand people worked in these industries, half of them for railroads. It was also the railroads' apex. By 1970, railroad employment was half of what it had been in 1950. New competitors like trucking and airlines took much of the transportation business away from the iron horse. With the increased use of the telephone and radio and the beginning of television, the communications sector grew rapidly. Government also continued to grow during the 1950s, especially the federal government. In 1950, government employment amounted to over 9 percent of the state's nonagricultural work force, with the federal government alone accounting for 7 percent.

Between 1960 and 1970, the service-producing industries grew from about 71 percent of the nonagricultural work force to almost 77 percent. Forty-three percent of the total growth came from government. During this time, government grew by 37,800 jobs or 61 percent. The biggest factor in this growth in government services was the field of education. In 1960, education employees comprised 32 percent of government employment; by 1970 they amounted to 37 percent. The reason for this growth was the need to educate the nation's baby-boom children—those born between 1946 and 1964. Two service industries also reflected the changing societal demands brought about by new technologies and a more affluent society: medical and health care services grew by almost 7,000 jobs (107 percent), and personal business services grew by about the same number of jobs, with a 57 percent increase.

During the 1970s, the trend to increased service employment was somewhat hidden because of an almost decade-long economic boom in Utah. The worldwide OPEC oil crisis created a great demand for Utah's natural resources. Mining and manufacturing grew rapidly. Construction employment also grew because of this growing economy and because of the construction of the Intermountain Power Project in Delta. Goods-producing employment in the 1970s actually increased as a percent of total employment—from 23.3 percent in 1970 to 24.9 percent in 1980. This was in direct contrast to what was happening nationally. In the nation, goods-producing employment during the period fell from 33.3 percent to 28.4 percent.

Between 1980 and 1990, Utah's economy not only resumed its long-term trend toward greater service-oriented employment, but actually increased the rate of the shift. This is especially true of the following service-producing industries: services (especially business and health services), trade, finance, insurance, and real estate. The acceleration of the shift was due primarily to a downturn in the goods-producing sector. The energy boom of the 1970s became an energy bust in the 1980s. Prices for coal, oil, copper, and uranium all dropped dramatically, affecting employment in all these operations. With a decline in mining and construction employment, and only modest gains in manufacturing, the employment growth in the service-producing industries was dramatized.

Service-producing employment created 97 percent of all new jobs in the state during the 1980s. Services created over 80,000 new jobs alone. The fastest-growing services again were medical and health services (18,600 jobs) and business services (13,000 jobs). Medical services employment growth was exemplified by the growth of the University of Utah Medical Center, which became one of the larger employers in the Salt Lake Valley. Its prestige made Salt Lake City a regional medical center, which was a major boon to Utah's overall economy. Medical services and inventions such as the artificial heart were spin-offs of this huge facility. Utah also became a major center for computer-related business services. WordPerfect Corporation, for example, located in Utah County, became the largest word processing software program manufacturer in the world. The second-fastest-growing service sector was trade, which grew by 29 percent with the creation of almost 44,000 new jobs. Retail trade especially—with food stores up 8,000 jobs, eating and drinking establishments up 12,000, and general retail up 9,000—dominated trade growth.

One service-producing sector—government—bucked this trend of dramatic employment growth during the 1980s. Government continued to grow in actual numbers, but at a slower rate than the other service sectors. The result of this slower growth was that private-sector employment as a percentage of total employment grew dramatically. In 1970, government (federal, state, local) was the single biggest employer in Utah, employing 28 percent of all nonagricultural workers. In other words, the private sector at the time employed 72 percent of all workers. With the tremendous growth of the service-producing sector and the very modest growth of government, employment in the private sector rose from 72 percent in 1970 to a post-World War II high of 79.2 percent in 1990.[25]

In summary, agriculture dominated the early Utah economy. However, as the state developed, the goods-producing industries—mining, manufacturing, and construction—became major employers. In the twentieth century, especially in the post-World War II period, Utah shifted to a service-based economy. In the *2004 Economic Report to the Governor*, Utah economists pointed out that in 2001, the service-producing industries accounted for 76.2 percent of the state's Gross State Product. Specifically, services accounted for 20.6 percent, finance, insurance, and real estate 20.1 percent, government 14.7 percent, transportation, communications, and utilities 7.9 percent, and trade 6.0 percent. By comparison the goods-producing industries represented just 22.6 percent of the economy. Of that, manufacturing represented 14.9 percent, construction 5.8 percent, and mining 1.9 percent. Agriculture represented only 1.2 percent of the Utah economy.[26]

POPULATION AND DEMOGRAPHIC TRENDS

In 1850, the U. S. Census counted 11,380 people living in Utah. Of that number, 18 percent were foreign born as a compared to a national average of 10 percent. Ten years later, the census counted 40,273 Utah residents, an almost fourfold increase. Of that number, an astounding 32 percent were foreign born. Nationally, the percent of foreign born had increased also, but only to 13 percent. In 1870, Utah's population had grown to 86,786 more than doubling the population of 1860. The foreign born population had now increased to 35.4 percent compared to 14 percent nationally. This was the highest point for the foreign born population in the state. After 1870, foreign born residents gradually declined as a percent of the state's population. The reason for such high percentages of foreign born people in the early part of the state's history is the LDS Church's call to converts from all over the world to come to "Zion" and help build the Kingdom of God. The result was a dramatic migration of Mormon converts, mostly from Europe to Utah. Later, the LDS Church changed its directive and urged its members to stay where they were and build the LDS Church in their native countries.

By 1900, the state's population had increased to 276,749, but with only 24 percent of the population foreign born. By 1920, Utah's foreign born population was virtually the same as the nation (13 percent).[27] Figure 1-1 shows Utah population growth through 2004 and a 2010 projection.

Figure 1-1

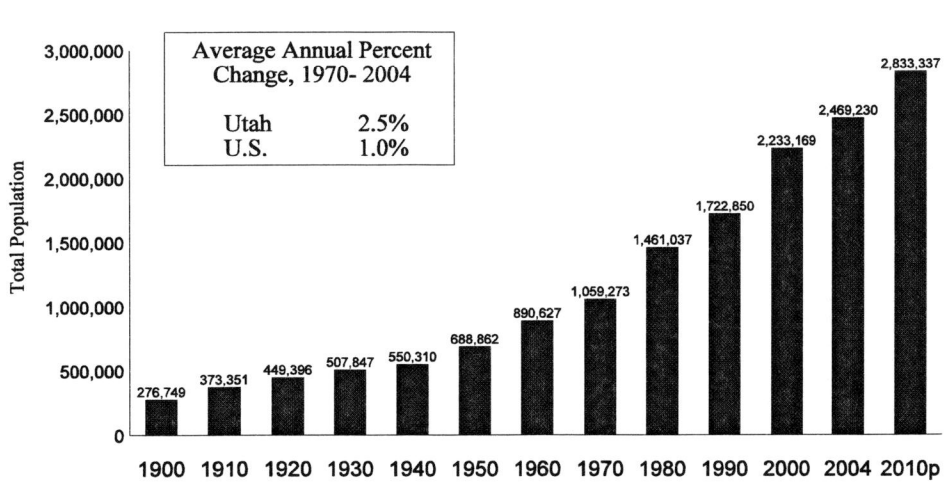

Total Population of Utah
1900 to 2004 and Projected 2010

In the 1950s, Utah experienced a trend sweeping the nation, one which had been going on prior to World War II but which jumped by leaps and bounds after the war—suburbanization. This movement of people from the cities to the suburbs transformed America and Utah. For much of the nation's history the trend had been from farm to city. Now the second phase of American urban history took hold. During this decade, Utah's population grew from 688,862 to 890,627, an increase of 194,537 or 29.3 percent. Of that increase, 96.4 percent occurred in just four counties: Salt Lake, Utah, Davis and Weber. Salt Lake County alone grew by 108,140 or 53.6 percent of the state's total population increase. Weber County, the state's next largest county grew from 83,319 to 110,744, an increase of 32.9 percent. Utah County, the state's third largest county, grew from 81,912 to 106,991, an increase of 30.6 percent. Davis County, however, grew fastest. It more than doubled its population from 30,867 to 64,760. Both Utah and Davis counties would show continued rapid growth over the next several decades.

The reasons for the population growth in these counties were several. Most important is the increase in economic opportunities. The shift from an agricultural economy to an industrial economy caused the shift from farm to city. The shift from an industrial economy to a service-information economy helped spur the shift from city to suburb. But other factors were important as well. People left the cities to get away from crime, congestion, and pollution. In the suburbs those that left—the middle to upper economic classes—found they could have greater control over their communities, schools, and local governments. As the people moved, so did the businesses and retail establishments. Urban sprawl had become an American movement which Utah mirrored.

The growth of the four big urban counties continued over the next several decades. In 1950, Salt Lake, Weber, Davis, and Utah counties accounted for 68.4 percent of the state's entire population. By 1980, that percent had grown to 77.2 percent. In 2004, these same four counties accounted for 76.0 percent of the state's population. The reason for the slight decline is the significant growth of a few other counties. The most phenomenal growth rate of any county in the state over the last thirty years is that of Washington County. With its desert climate of mild winters, warm falls and springs, and very hot summers, "Dixie" as it is nicknamed, exploded in population. Between 1970 and 1980 it almost doubled its population, growing from 13,669 to 26,065. By 1990 it had almost doubled again to 48,560 and by 2000 to 90,354 and the 2004 estimate is a population of 117,316—a phenomenal sevenfold increase in just thirty-three years. Cache County at the opposite end of the state also showed impressive growth. It grew from a population of 42,331 in 1970 to 100,182 in 2004. When the four large urban counties of Salt Lake, Davis, Utah, and Weber are combined with Cache and Washington counties they account for 87 percent of the states entire population. The other twenty-three counties account for only 20 percent. Figure 1-2 shows current urbanization.[28]

Figure 1-2

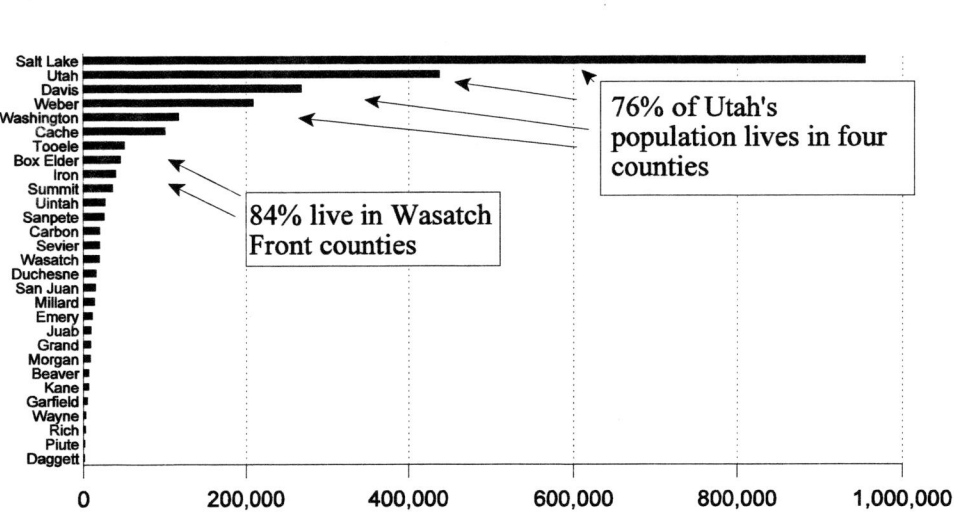

The enormous growth of the big four counties has spawned growth in neighboring counties, most notably Tooele and Summit counties. With a population of 21,545 in 1970, Tooele has more than doubled to 50,075 in 2004. The main reason for Tooele's growth is its proximity to the expansion of southwestern Salt Lake County. Summit County has also shown explosive growth, increasing from a population of 5,879 in 1970 to 35,090 in 2004—almost a six-fold increase. Summit County's attraction is more than its shared border with Salt Lake County. The county is in the Wasatch mountains and features great skiing and other winter recreational activities, cool summers, and the attraction of an old mining town turned tourist mecca and home to the wealthy—Park City.

Utah has always been a state that has grown faster than the nation. In 1900, just after Utah became a state, Utah's population accounted for 0.36 percent of the nation's population. By 1950, it amounted to 0.45 percent and in 2003, 0.82 percent.

Like any other state or nation for that matter, Utah population growth is dependent on two factors: natural increase and net migration. Natural increase is the difference between births and deaths and net migration is the difference between those that move into the state and those that move out. Combined, these two figures determine Utah's population growth.

Of these two figures, natural increase is the most important in Utah's population increase. The reason for this is twofold. First, Utah has a high fertility rate, well above the national average. As shown in figure 1-3, Utah has always had a fertility rate above the national average though it has declined over the decades.[29] Second, Utah's net in-migration is normally modest. Only when the state has a strong economy does Utah experience net migration. For example, from 1969 to 2003, Utah's population grew by 1,356,358. Of that increase, 996,438 or 73.5 percent is the result of natural increase; only 389,331, or 28.7 percent is net-migration. However, over shorter periods these percentages can change significantly. For example, in the years 1991-2001, Utah's economy was so strong that it attracted 233,153 in-migrants compared to a natural increase of 328,591. In other words, during this eleven-year period, net-migration accounted for 41.1 percent of the state's population increase and natural increase fell to 57.9 percent. Interestingly, in both 1992 and 1993, net-migration was more than natural increase—the only time that has happened in the post World War II period.

Figure 1-3

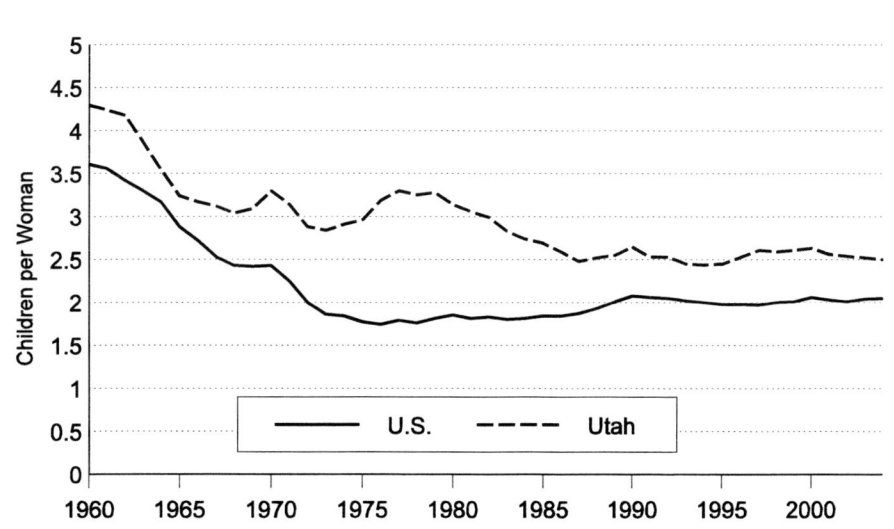

The population projections for the state show a population of 2.83 million residents by 2010, 3.49 million by 2020, and 4.58 million by 2030. Of these increases, approximately 80 percent will come from the state's natural increase and only 20 percent from net-migration. This growth rate will continue to be faster than the nation but because of the state's small population base, will result in the state going from 0.9 percent of the nation's population in 2010 to 1.0 percent in 2020, and 1.1 percent in 2030.

Utah's high fertility rate not only impacts the state's population growth, it also impacts other statistics: median age, dependancy ratios, and per capita income. Utah's 2000 median age as calculated by the U.S. Bureau of the Census is 27.1, the youngest in the nation and 8.2 years below the nation's median age of 35.3. Not only does Utah have the youngest median age, it is a full 5.2 years younger than Texas at 32.3, which has the second youngest median age. By comparison, West Virginia is the oldest state with a median age of 38.9.[30]

Because there are so many children as a result of the state's high birth rate, Utah also stands out in another national statistic–per capita income. In 2003 the per capita income of the U.S. stood at $31,100. Utah ranked forty-seventh with a per capita income of only $25,230 or 78.9 percent of the national average. In fact, Utah has ranked well below the national average for decades because of the state's high birth rate. Since 1970, Utah per capita income has ranged between 85 percent and 75 percent of the nation's. Though this indicates that Utah is a very poor state, other measurements of wealth indicate otherwise. When states are measured according to household income, Utah looks much better with a household income that is 112.7 percent of the national average for the three-year average of 2000-02.[31] Another measurement of households in Utah is poverty. Utah has very low poverty rates. For the same period 2000-02 period, Utah's poverty rate stood at 9.3 percent—well below the national average of 11.7 percent.

In summary, three points are important in understanding Utah population and demographic trends. First, the state has grown faster than the nation as a whole in every decade but one since it became a territory in 1850. Nevertheless, this faster growth has been insignificant relative to the explosive growth of such states as California, Texas, and Florida which have accounted for much of the nation's entire population growth in the last fifty years. Utah has also not grown as fast as Arizona, Colorado, and recently Nevada. Second, most of the state's growth rate is the result of natural increase, driven by a birth rate that has been consistently higher than the national average. Third, this high birth rate makes Utah the youngest state in the nation with a median age several years lower than the national average. It is also the reason that the state's per capita income is one of the lowest in the nation though other measurements, like household income, tend to show another picture.

Utah's Employment Picture in the Twenty-first Century

Today, Utah's economy is rather broadly based, with important connections to the national and world economy. Agricultural employment has consistently declined as a percentage of total employment, from slightly more than 50 percent in 1850 to approximately 1 percent in 2003. Nonagricultural employment is diversified across various industries (see table 1-1). As the manufacturing, defense, technology, service, and tourism industries have become increasingly important to the state's economy over time, Utah's economy has also become more and more tied to economic and political events occurring throughout the nation and the world. Although this means the state will be affected by overall economic trends nationwide, the diversity of the economy helps shield the state somewhat from the impact of economic downturns in a particular sector.

Table 1-1

Utah Nonagricultural Employment Distribution by Industry, 2003	
Trade, transportation, utilities	20.1%
Government	18.2%
Professional/business services	12.3%
Health services/private education	10.6%
Manufacturing	10.6%
Leisure and hospitality	9.4%
Construction	6.3%
Financial activity	5.9%
Other services	3.1%
Information	2.9%
Natural resources	0.6%

One recent example of Utah's connection with the broader economy is the effect of the recent economic recession on Utah employment. As shown in figure 1-4, between 1951 and 2001, Utah only experienced three years of job loss in total nonagricultural employment, with the last year of net job loss occurring in 1964. However, in 2002 and 2003, feeling the effects of the national recession, Utah experienced two successive years of job loss. As of September 2005, Utah's unemployment rate was 4.6 percent, corresponding to 57,600 unemployed Utahns. By comparison, 5.1 percent were unemployed nationally. Furthermore, Utah's job market has rebounded. From September 2004 to September 2005, Utah's employment had grown to 3.6 percent, while the nation grew by 1.7 percent.[32] Figure 1-5 shows these trends.

Figure 1-4

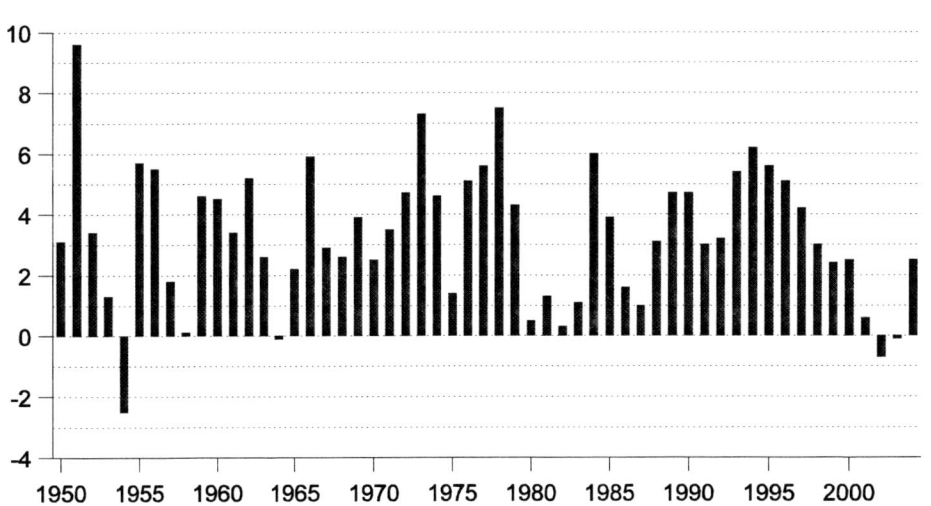

Figure 1-5

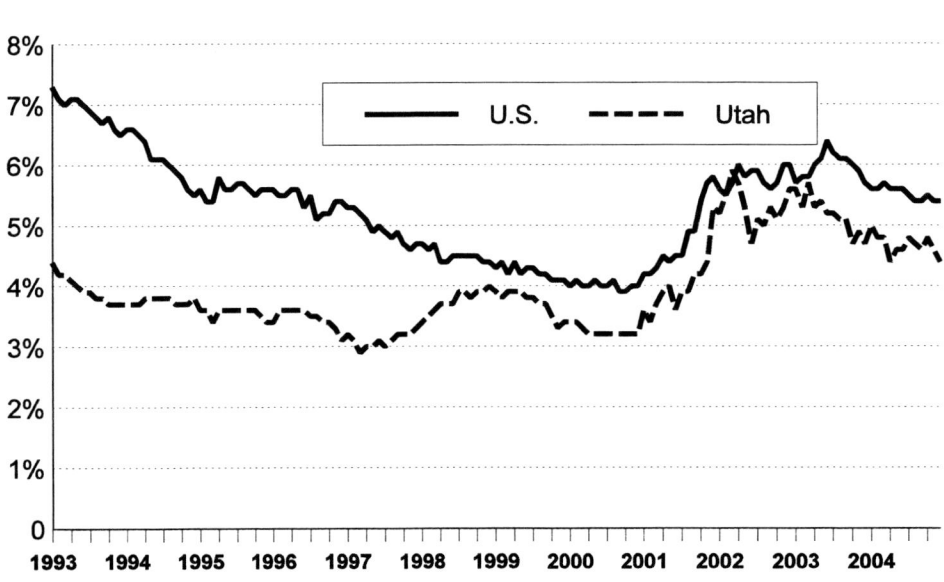

WEALTH AND POVERTY

Below are various measures used to evaluate the wealth and poverty of a state and its residents and how Utah ranks according to these measures.

Gross State Product

Gross State Product (GSP), the state equivalent of the more widely known national Gross Domestic Product measure, represents the value of goods and services produced within a state. Over the fifteen-year period from 1987 to 2001, Utah's nominal GSP has grown from approximately $25 billion to approximately $70 billion. While some of this nominal growth is due to inflation, Utah's real GSP has grown significantly during this time period as the state's economy has substantially expanded. When adjusted for inflation, GSP has doubled from $32 billion in 1987 to $64 billion in 2001. The recent recession significantly slowed Utah's GSP growth rate, as real GSP only grew by 0.6 percent in 2001, by far the slowest growth rate since 1987.[33]

Figure 1-6 shows the changes in the make-up of Utah's GSP between 1987 and 2001. As can be seen, there has been a significant shift from the goods-producing industries (e.g., mining, manufacturing, and construction) to the service-producing industries (mainly services and the combined categories of finance, insurance, and real estate (FIRE)). The service industry has grown from about 10 percent of the Utah economy to about 22 percent. Almost copying that trend, FIRE has grown from about 16 percent to 21 percent. Meanwhile two of the three goods-producing industries have declined as a percent of the Utah economy. Only construction has seen growth. Mining has fallen from about 7 percent to 3 percent and manufacturing has declined from about 18 percent to 15 percent.

Figure 1-6

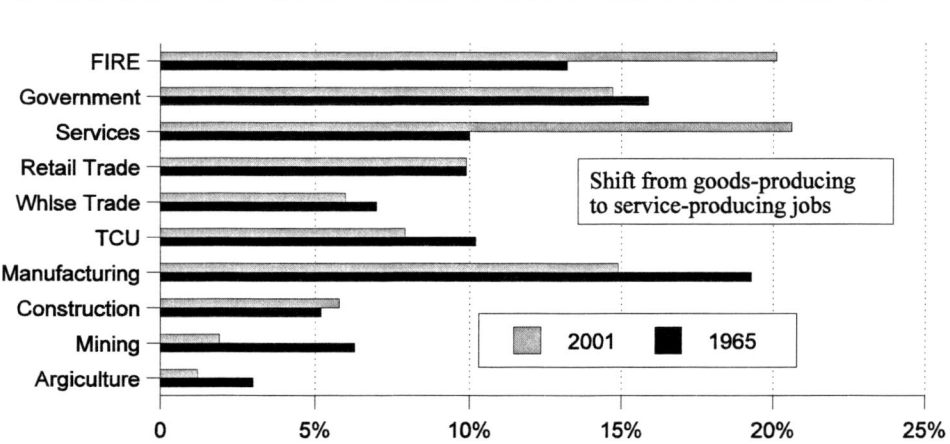

FIRE: Finance, Insurance, Real Estate: TCU: Transportation, Communication, and Utilities

Income Measures

It is difficult to clearly compare Utahns' income with the income of other states' residents because of Utah's high birth rate. One common method of comparing income levels is per capita personal income. As already discussed, Utah's per capita personal income in 2003 was $25,230, which corresponds to 79 percent of the national average and ranks forty-seventh in the nation. However, the per capita figure is skewed by the disproportionately high household size in Utah as compared to the rest of the nation, due to a higher birth rate resulting in a relatively greater percentage of non-income-producing children. As a result, Utah has fewer adult workers per capita than other states, resulting in a lower income per capita. Another method of income comparison is average annual pay of workers covered by unemployment insurance. Using this measure, Utah has average annual pay of $30,580, which corresponds to 83 percent of the national average and ranks thirty-sixth in the nation. When using median household income, another method of comparing income levels, Utah fares much better. Utah's median household income is $48,537, which corresponds to 113 percent of the national average and ranks twelfth in the nation, as shown in figure 1-7.[34]

Figure 1-7

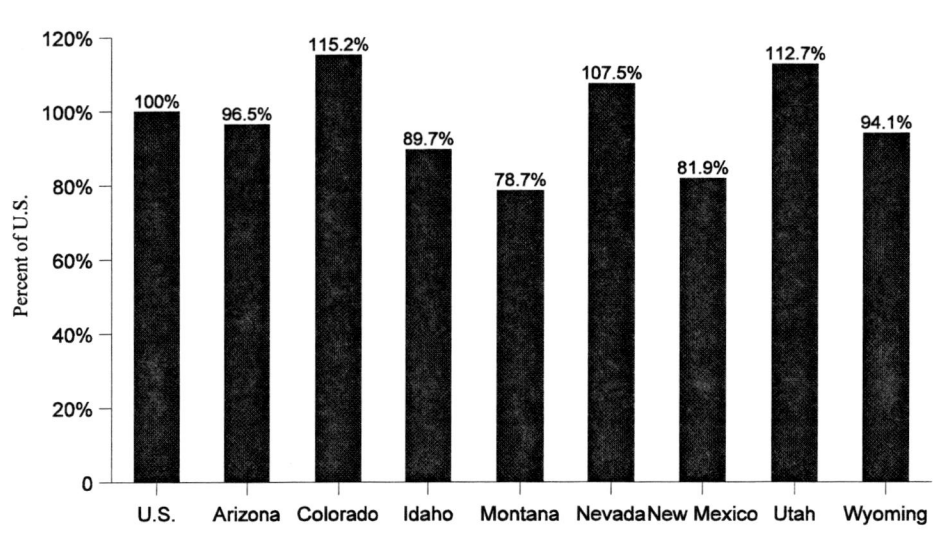

Poverty Rates

With a poverty rate of 9.3 percent, Utah has a poverty rate below the national average of 11.7 percent. This makes Utah's poverty rate the fourteenth lowest in the nation, as shown in figure 1-8.[35]

Figure 1-8

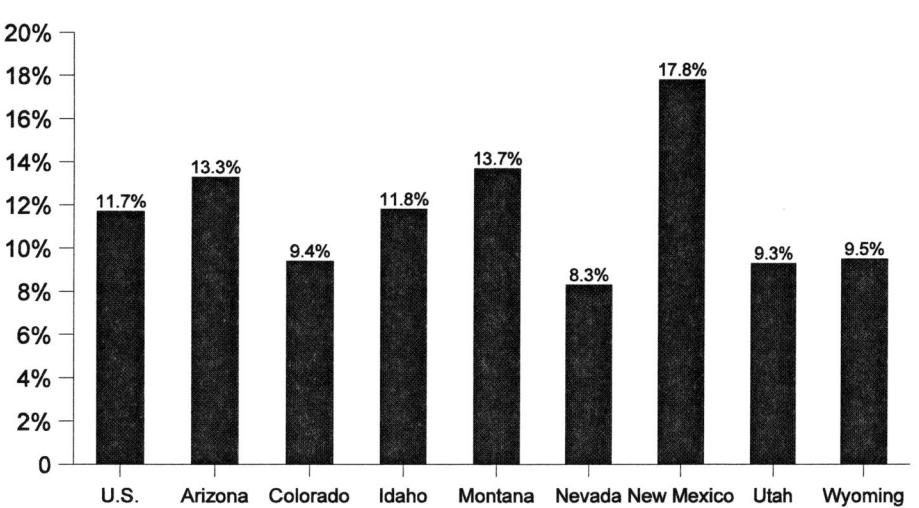

Percentage of Persons in Poverty
Utah and Mountain States, Three-Year Average, 2000-2002

Cost of Living

Cost of living can have a major impact on a person's standard of living. For example, a person living in San Francisco, California at an annual salary of $40,000 would have a much different standard of living than a person living in Cedar City, Utah with the same salary. Similarly, a cost of living lower than the national average would offset some effects of below-average per capita income. The American Chamber of Commerce Researchers Association compiles a point-in-time cost of living index for approximately 270 urban areas, based on information related to housing, groceries, utilities, transportation, health care, and miscellaneous goods and services voluntarily reported by local chambers of commerce. According to this index, the cost of living in most Utah urban areas is somewhat below the national average (represented by a composite score of 100). Cedar City (88.7), St. George (91.6), Logan (93.0), and Provo-Orem (95.3) all rank below the national average, while Salt Lake City measured slightly above the national average (102.7).[36]

Chapter 2

Utah Law

STATE AND FEDERAL CONSTITUTIONS

"There are only two things that all governments have in common. One is a capacity to raise revenues, usually in the form of taxation, to support government activities. The other is coercion—the ability to compel inhabitants to abide by the government's rules."[1] Like governments in the rest of the world, the United States raises revenue and makes laws. But how the United States generates its revenues and makes and enforces its laws is fundamentally different from other governments.

One explanation of why the United States differs from most other governments originates with its unique governmental structure, known as federalism, in which two sovereign governments rule over the same place and people. The manner in which these governments rule is known as a constitutional democracy. And as its name implies, this system relies heavily on constitutions.

Purposes of Constitutions

Most basically, constitutions may be defined as the fundamental law that organizes how a government will operate.[2] Under this definition, any document that defines the operation of government is a constitution, even if that document exists in Hitler's Germany or Stalin's Russia. It is not uncommon for governments to have constitutions. However, the form and structure of the United States Constitution and the relationship between it and the individual state constitutions is so rare, some scholars have called it "a new model of government in which a written document defining the states' lawful powers is a higher authority than the actions of any political leader or institution."[3]

> **In this chapter:**
>
> State and Federal Constitutions (p. 23)
> Utah Constitution Historical Background (p. 25)
> Article I. Declaration of Rights (p. 26)
> Article II. State Boundaries (p. 27)
> Article III. Ordinance (p. 27)
> Article IV. Elections and Right of Suffrage (p. 27)
> Article V. Distribution of Powers (p. 28)
> Article VI. Legislative Department (p. 28)
> Article VII. Executive Department (p. 29)
> Article VIII. Judicial Department (p. 30)
> Article IX. Legislative Apportionment (p. 31)
> Article X. Education (p. 31)
> Article XI. Local Governments (p. 32)
> Article XII. Corporations (p. 32)
> Article XIII. Revenue and Taxation (p. 32)
> Article XIV. Public Debt (p. 33)
> Article XV. Militia (p. 33)
> Article XVI. Labor (p. 33)
> Article XVII. Water Rights (p. 34)
> Article XVIII. Forestry (p. 34)
> Article XIX. Public Buildings and State Institutions (p. 34)
> Article XX. Public Lands (p. 34)
> Article XXI. Salaries (p. 34)
> Article XXII. Miscellaneous (p. 34)
> Article XXIII. Amendment and Revision (p. 34)
> Article XXIV. Schedule (p. 35)

The challenge facing all governments is one of having enough strength to accomplish its legitimate objectives, such as providing for a national defense, creating and enforcing laws, and taxing its citizens, but not being so strong that it can undermine the rights of its citizens. As James Madison explained to Thomas Jefferson, "It is a melancholy reflection that liberty should be equally exposed to danger whether the government have too much power or too little power."[4] The genius of the American constitutional framework is that the national and state constitutions limit and even prohibit some governmental actions while providing governments with enough authority for it to accomplish its legitimate objectives. Balancing these objectives is the primary purpose of both the state and federal constitutions in the American governmental system.

In addition to defining how a government will operate, American constitutions also define the powers and duties, terms of office, and qualifications of its leaders, and provide for the structure of governmental institutions, including the procedures that are to be followed when these leaders and institutions exercise legitimate governmental authority. The framers of the American constitutions recognized and addressed the problem of power that was later warned against by the British historian Lord Acton: "Power tends to corrupt and absolute power corrupts absolutely."[5] By dividing the legitimate use of governmental powers into three separate departments (legislative, executive, and judicial) and by granting certain constitutional rights to citizens that governments are legally obligated to respect, the state and federal constitutions established a framework in which no individual or government institution could exercise absolute power. Separating the powers of government was designed to reduce corruption, which would in turn preserve individual liberty.

Powers of the National and State Governments

Because the state and federal constitutions share some common principles, it is a common misconception to view the state governments "as smaller versions of the national government in the United States."[6] The United States Constitution can be understood as a delegation of power from the people to the national government, whereas state governments are assumed to have inherent powers that may be exercised unless those powers are either limited or prohibited.

Provisions of the United States Constitution therefore contain grants of power, including the power to engage in foreign affairs, establish an army, provide a currency, and declare war. In some circumstances the powers granted by the federal constitution are limited, including the prohibition placed on the government of prosecuting an individual for an act that was legal at the time the act was committed (i.e., *ex post facto* laws) or providing for writs of *habeas corpus*, which prevent the government from holding a prisoner indefinitely without charge. Powers not granted under the federal constitution are effectively denied to the federal government.

The authority of the states is different. States are assumed to possess inherent powers unless the powers have been delegated to the national government or prohibited by a state's own constitution. As a consequence, a state may not exercise powers exclusively granted to the federal government or limited by its own state constitution. Limitations on state authority common in state constitutions include limitations on debt, balanced budgets, and requirements to respect certain individual rights. In Utah, for example, the state must establish and maintain a public school system that is open to all the children of the state and is prohibited from imprisoning someone for delinquent debts.

On many issues the constitutions clearly define whether the federal or state government is responsible for the exercise of certain powers. The federal government, as previously noted, is exclusively authorized to create a currency, regulate interstate commerce, establish a national defense, and provide foreign affairs, whereas the state is exclusively authorized to create counties, cities, and towns; regulate intrastate commerce; and organize voter registration. On other issues, including public health, transportation, law enforcement, and taxation, the state and federal government share powers. It is often within the sphere of sharing powers where conflicts arise between the state and federal government. Chapter 21, *Relationship of State and Federal Governments*, provides a more complete discussion of this topic.

UTAH CONSTITUTION HISTORICAL BACKGROUND

Like other state constitutions, the Utah Constitution establishes the basic framework of state government and articulates basic principles that government must follow. While Utah's constitution shares some similarities with the constitutions of other states, Utah's history leading to the adoption of the constitution is unique and provides an important historical backdrop to the Utah Constitution.

When members of the LDS Church first settled the valley of the Great Salt Lake in 1847, they looked to their church authorities for leadership.[7] Between 1847 and 1849, the ecclesiastical government also served as the civil government of the settlement, known as Deseret.[8]

In the winter and spring of 1849, the settlers created a provisional government by adopting a constitution to govern their "State of Deseret."[9] In many respects, the 1849 constitution of the State of Deseret was similar to the Illinois Constitution of 1818, the state from which most early Mormon settlers had fled and whose constitution they had lived under in Nauvoo, Illinois.[10]

In July 1849, the Deseret General Assembly passed a memorial requesting the State of Deseret's admission to the Union and elected a delegate to present the 1849 constitution to Congress. Congress rejected the memorial and instead, on September 9, 1850, passed an act establishing the Territory of Utah.[11]

In 1856, the people of the Territory of Utah made another attempt at statehood. The constitutional convention used the 1849 convention of Deseret as a model.[12] Because of congressional hostility toward the LDS Church, largely over the issue of polygamy, the delegates from the Utah territory did not even present the 1856 constitution or the petition for statehood to Congress.[13]

Additional constitutional conventions were held and constitutions drafted in 1862, 1872, 1882, and 1887. The 1872 constitutional convention was noteworthy because people who were not members of the LDS Church participated as delegates for the first time. The 1882 constitution was the first to name the state "Utah" instead of "Deseret."[14] On each of these occasions, the petition for statehood was unsuccessful, primarily because of a mistrust of the proposed state's ability to establish a government separate from the ecclesiastical government of the LDS Church and the LDS Church's practice of polygamy.

Following an 1890 announcement from the President of the LDS Church that church members would "refrain from contracting any marriage forbidden by the law of the land,"[15] the territorial legislature in 1892 criminalized polygamy, bigamy, and cohabitation.[16] In 1894, Governor West declared that the Territory of Utah was ready for statehood and that the conditions established by Congress had been met.

In 1894, for the first time in all of Utah Territory's attempts at statehood, Congress officially authorized the Territory of Utah to hold a constitutional convention and directed the President to admit Utah to the Union when all of Congress' conditions were met. Congress passed Utah's Enabling Act on July 16, 1894, authorizing the people of the Territory of Utah to "form a constitution and State government, and to be admitted into the Union on an equal footing with the original States."[17] The Enabling Act provided for the election of delegates to a constitutional convention to convene in March 1895.

The 1895 Utah Constitutional Convention resulted in the adoption of Utah's constitution that became effective at statehood. The convention derived provisions from earlier proposed Utah constitutions and other states' constitutions, primarily Nevada, Washington, Illinois, and New

York.[18] On a 31,305 to 7,607 vote, the majority of voters approved the constitution for ratification and adoption in an election held November 1895. President Grover Cleveland proclaimed the admission of the State of Utah into the Union on January 4, 1896, and the 1896 constitution took effect. The articles of the Utah Constitution are discussed below.

ARTICLE I. DECLARATION OF RIGHTS

Article I consists of twenty-nine sections setting forth basic rights of Utah citizens, fundamental principles of Utah law, and limitations on state government. Of the twenty-nine sections, twenty-one have not been changed since the original 1896 constitution. Section 28, relating to the rights of crime victims, was added in 1995, and Section 29, defining marriage and prohibiting recognition of other domestic unions, was added in 2005.

The basic rights set forth in Article I include the rights to do the following:
- Enjoy and defend life and liberty
- Possess and protect property
- Worship and assemble peaceably
- Keep and bear arms
- Bail
- Trial by jury in capital cases
- Appear and defend in person and by counsel in criminal prosecutions, be confronted by witnesses, and have a speedy trial
- A remedy by due course of law for an injury done to the person, property, or reputation

Article I includes the following fundamental principles:
- All political power is inherent in the people, who have the right to alter or reform their government
- The State of Utah is an inseparable part of the Federal Union, and the U.S. Constitution is the supreme law of the land
- A preliminary examination in a criminal case is limited to determining whether probable cause exists
- Offenses shall be prosecuted by information rather than indictment
- The military shall be in subordination to the civil power
- All laws of a general nature shall have uniform operation
- The enumeration of rights in the constitution is not to be construed to deny others retained by the people
- Victims of crimes have the rights to be treated with fairness, respect, and dignity, to be informed of and present and heard at important proceedings, and to have the sentencing judge consider reliable information about the character of the person convicted
- Marriage consists only of the legal union between a man and a woman, and no other domestic union may be recognized as a marriage or given substantially the same legal effect

Limitations on government contained in Article I include restrictions against:
- Infringing the rights of conscience, making a law respecting an establishment of religion or prohibiting the free exercise of religion, requiring a religious test as a qualification of public office or voting, or appropriating public money for religious purposes
- Suspending the privilege of habeas corpus
- Depriving a person of life, liberty, or property without due process of law

- Requiring excessive bail, imposing excessive fines, inflicting cruel and unusual punishment, or treating arrested persons with unnecessary rigor
- Abridging freedom of speech or of the press
- Imprisoning a person for debt
- Taking or damaging private property without just compensation[19]

ARTICLE II. STATE BOUNDARIES

Article II contains a precise legal description of the state's boundaries using longitude and latitude as markers. When the "State of Deseret" first sought statehood in 1849, the area "included the lower third of what is now California, a major part of Arizona, part of New Mexico, parts of Oregon, Idaho, and Wyoming, the western third of Colorado, and all of Nevada."[20] The current Utah boundaries are significantly smaller than originally requested in 1849.

Since adopted in 1896, the boundaries of Utah have not changed. Although discussions of receding the border city of Wendover, Utah to Nevada have taken place, it does not appear likely that the state boundary will be changed any time soon.[21]

ARTICLE III. ORDINANCE

Article III contains four provisions required by Utah's Enabling Act, a law passed by Congress in 1894 to authorize the Territory of Utah to become a state. As required in the Enabling Act and by Article III itself, these four provisions are irrevocable without the consent of the United States and the people of the state. Except for a minor amendment to the second provision in 1947, Article III remains in its original form as enacted in 1896.

The first provision guarantees perfect toleration of religious sentiment, but forever prohibits polygamous or plural marriages. Under the second provision, the people of the state forever disclaim all right to the unappropriated public lands of the United States and lands owned by Native Americans or Native American tribes lying within the boundaries of the state. The second provision also prohibits lands in Utah that are owned by persons residing outside the state from being taxed at a higher rate than lands owned by residents of the state. In the third provision, the state assumes all debts and liabilities of the Territory of Utah. The fourth provision requires the legislature to make laws for the establishment and maintenance of a public school system and requires that the system be open to all children of the state and free from sectarian control.[22]

ARTICLE IV. ELECTIONS AND RIGHT OF SUFFRAGE

Article IV establishes the qualifications to vote in Utah elections, determines that general elections are to be held on the day after the first Monday in November during even-numbered years, and allows the legislature to provide by statute for special elections. With the adoption of this article in 1896, Utah became one of only a few states that extended the voting franchise to women. This right was not granted to women under the United States Constitution until 1920.

To vote in a Utah election, a person must be a citizen of the United States, at least eighteen years of age, and a resident of Utah for not less than thirty days prior to the election. The state is prohibited from requiring a person to own property in order to vote or hold office, but it is authorized to use voting machines, provided that all elections are done by secret ballot.

A person convicted of a felony, treason, or a crime against the elective franchise such as voting fraud, or who is mentally incompetent, may neither vote nor hold elective office until these rights have been restored as provided by statute.

Moreover, no Utah voters, except those who commit treason, a felony, or breach of the peace, may be arrested on election days, and no voter may be required to perform militia duties on election days except in time of war or public danger.

Finally, all officers appointed or elected under authority of the Utah Constitution are required to subscribe to the following oath: "I do solemnly swear (or affirm) that I will support, obey, and defend the Constitution of the United States and the Constitution of this State, and that I will discharge the duties of my office with fidelity."[23]

ARTICLE V. DISTRIBUTION OF POWERS

Although one of the shortest articles in the constitution, Article V is nevertheless one of the most important. It distributes the powers of the state government among three branches: legislative, executive, and judicial. It prohibits any person charged with the exercise of powers belonging to one of the departments from exercising any function that is exclusive to either of the others, unless the constitution expressly directs or permits.[24]

ARTICLE VI. LEGISLATIVE DEPARTMENT

Article VI sets forth qualifications of legislators. It also describes the powers and duties of the legislative department.

The article requires each legislator to be a citizen of the United States, at least twenty-five years old, a qualified voter in the district from which elected, a resident of the state for three years immediately prior to the filing deadline, and a resident of the district from which elected for six consecutive months. A legislator becomes ineligible to continue in office after ceasing to be a resident of the district from which elected.

Members of the House of Representatives serve two-year terms; members of the State Senate serve four-year terms. Legislators are protected from liability for actions they take in their legislative capacity and are immune from arrest fifteen days prior to sessions, during sessions, and while returning from sessions, except in the case of treason.

This article vests the legislative power of the state in the State Senate, the Utah House of Representatives, and the legal voters of the state through an initiative and referendum process. The power of the people to initiate or refer legislation to the legislature is subject to time, manner, and condition requirements, which are to be established by the legislature in statute.

General sessions under the original constitution were held biennially and lasted sixty days. In 1969, the constitution was amended to provide for a sixty-day general session during odd-numbered years and a twenty-day budget session in even-numbered years. Over time, budget sessions increasingly resembled general sessions, and in 1985 the constitution was amended to provide for annual general sessions of forty-five days. In 1993, the beginning date of annual general sessions was moved from the second Monday in January to the third Monday. On extraordinary occasions, the governor may by proclamation convene the legislature into session, commonly referred to as a special session, for up to thirty days in order to transact legislative business.[25] The governor is required to give forty-eight hours advance public notice of a special session. Legislative sessions are to be open to the public whenever legislative business is transacted, whether in general or special sessions. Each house is also required to keep a journal of its proceedings that includes the votes of its members.

For a bill to become law, it must contain a single subject that is clearly expressed in its title, be read three separate times in each house, and receive at least a majority vote in each house. Upon final passage in each house, bills may not take effect until sixty days after the adjournment of the session unless, by a two-thirds vote of all its members, the legislature directs otherwise.

With respect to internal administration, the presiding officer in each house is required to certify the accuracy of bills and resolutions and ensure that a quorum is present. Each house is authorized to compel the attendance of its absent members, to be the judge of the election and qualification of its own members, to punish them for disorderly conduct, to expel them for cause with a two-thirds vote, and to adopt other rules it considers necessary for its proceedings.

As a check against abuses of executive and judicial power, the legislature is authorized to remove the governor and other state and judicial officers from office for high crimes, misdemeanors, or malfeasance in office. This removal process is known as impeachment. Under the provisions of this article, the House of Representatives is vested with the sole power of impeachment, but only upon a two-thirds vote of all of its members. Upon the house's affirmative vote for impeachment, the senate shall hold a trial, and, if convicted by a two-thirds vote of all senators, the state or judicial officer shall be removed from office and prevented from holding an office of public trust, profit, or honor in the state.[26]

ARTICLE VII. EXECUTIVE DEPARTMENT

This article identifies the officers making up the executive department of government and sets forth their qualifications and authority. The provisions relating to the governor's duties are more extensive than those relating to the duties of the other officers.

While Article VII states that the executive power of the state is vested in a governor, it also provides for other executive branch officers. The other officers are lieutenant governor, auditor, treasurer, and attorney general. Each officer is elected to a four-year term, is required to reside within the state during his or her term of office, and is required to perform duties that are prescribed by the constitution and by statute. Since 1981, this article has required the governor and lieutenant governor to be elected as a team. The office of superintendent of public instruction, established in the 1896 constitution, was eliminated as a constitutional office in 1951. The superintendent of public instruction is now appointed by the State Board of Education.

To be eligible for the office of governor or lieutenant governor, a person must be at least thirty years old at the time of election. For the offices of attorney general, auditor, and treasurer, a person must be at least twenty-five years old at the time of election. Each person must also be a registered voter and a resident of the state for five years preceding the election. In addition, to be eligible for the office of attorney general a person must be a member in good standing of the Utah State Bar.

Article VII authorizes the governor to convene the legislature into session "on extraordinary occasions" to transact legislative business specified by the governor. This session convened by the governor is commonly referred to as a special session. The governor is required to give forty-eight hours advance public notice of any business to be conducted during a special session. If the legislature disagrees about the time when a special session should adjourn, the governor is authorized to adjourn the legislature.

Article VII gives the governor veto authority over bills passed by the legislature and also authority to disapprove any item of appropriation contained in a bill.

The governor has significant appointive powers under Article VII. If there is a vacancy in the offices of lieutenant governor, auditor, treasurer, or attorney general, the governor appoints a person to fill the vacancy. The governor is also authorized to appoint, with the consent of the senate, all state court judges, members of the Board of Pardons, and state and district officers whose offices are established by the constitution or created by law but whose appointment is not specifically provided for.

Article VII provides for the lieutenant governor to take over the powers and duties of the office of governor if the governor dies, is impeached or removed from office, resigns, or due to a disability is unable to discharge the duties of the office, until the disability ceases or until the next general election when the vacancy is filled by election. If the lieutenant governor is fulfilling the powers and duties of the office of governor during a time that the office is vacant, and the lieutenant governor resigns, dies, is removed, or becomes incapable of performing the duties of office, the president of the senate is required to act as governor. If the president of the senate resigns, dies, is removed, or becomes incapable of performing the duties of office, the speaker of the house acts as governor. Although Article VII does not specifically state that a lieutenant governor actually becomes governor when there is a vacancy in the office of governor, the lieutenant governor was sworn in as governor in 2003 following the only time in Utah's history that a governor has resigned from office. Article VII also provides a procedure for determining the disability of a governor or person acting as governor.

Article VII establishes a Board of Pardons and Parole that may grant parole, remit fines, commute punishments, and grant pardons after convictions, except in cases of treason or impeachment. The article also authorizes the governor to grant temporary respites or reprieves in all cases of convictions for offenses against the state except treason or conviction on impeachment.[27]

ARTICLE VIII. JUDICIAL DEPARTMENT

This article describes the powers and duties of the respective courts within the judiciary, provides for the internal administration of the judiciary, establishes the qualifications to be a justice or judge, and creates a procedure for the selection and retention of justices and judges.

The judicial powers of the state are vested in the Utah Supreme Court, in a district court, and such other courts as the legislature by statute shall establish. State statutes provide for a supreme court, a court of appeals, district courts, juvenile courts, and justice courts. All of these courts, except justice courts, are known as courts of an official record since an official record of the court proceedings is kept and the judges and justices of these courts must be admitted to practice law in Utah.

The Judicial Council, with the chief justice as its presiding officer, is the policy body of the judiciary and as such is responsible to adopt all other rules for the administration of the courts. These rules comprise the Utah Code of Judicial Administration.

The Utah Supreme Court, in addition to its adjudicative duties involving original and appellate jurisdiction, is responsible to adopt the rules of evidence, procedure, and appellate procedure, which are to be used in the courts of the state. The legislature may amend the rules of evidence and procedure on a two-thirds vote of all members elected to both houses.

The Utah Supreme Court is also responsible to adopt the rules to authorize retired judges and judges pro tempore to perform any judicial duties. Additionally, the Utah Supreme Court is responsible to govern the practice of law, including admissions and discipline.

To be eligible as a justice of the Utah Supreme Court, a person must be a United States citizen, at least thirty years old, a resident of the state for five years preceding selection, and admitted to practice law in Utah. To be eligible as a district, juvenile, or appellate court judge, a person must be a United States citizen, at least twenty-five years old, a resident of the state for three years preceding selection, and admitted to practice law in the state. The qualifications for justice court judges are provided in statute, but the state may not require a justice court judge to be admitted to practice law.

Supreme court justices, and district, juvenile, and appellate court judges may not practice law, hold elective non-judicial public office, or hold office in a political party. Moreover, judges must reside in the geographic district in which they are selected. No change in either the number of judges or in the geographic districts may have the effect of removing a judge from office. The legislature may establish mandatory retirement of justices and judges, but it may not diminish their salaries during a term of office.

The governor fills judicial vacancies by appointment from a list of qualified applicants certified by a Judicial Nominating Commission. Once appointed by the governor, the judicial candidate is subject to confirmation by a majority of all those elected to the Utah Senate. At the first general election held more than three years from the initial appointment, every justice and judge must face an unopposed judicial retention election. Upon receiving an affirmative vote, justices of the Supreme Court serve a ten-year term, while juvenile, district, and appellate court judges serve a six-year term. At the conclusion of a term of office, a justice or judge may seek an additional term by filing to stand for retention election.

To provide for judicial accountability, the Judicial Conduct Commission is established to investigate and hold confidential hearings regarding complaints against any justice or judge. This commission may order the reprimand, censure, suspension, removal, or involuntary retirement of any justice or judge for: an action which constitutes willful misconduct in office; final conviction of a crime punishable as a felony; willful and persistent failure to perform judicial duties; disability that seriously interferes with the performance of judicial duties; or conduct that is prejudicial to the administration of justice or which brings the judicial office into disrepute.[28] The Utah Supreme Court shall, prior to the implementation of any order of discipline, review the proceedings of the Judicial Conduct Commission, and, as it finds just and proper, either implement, reject, or modify the order of discipline.[29]

ARTICLE IX. LEGISLATIVE APPORTIONMENT

Under this article, the legislature is required to divide the state into congressional, legislative, and other districts at the first session following each decennial census taken by the federal government. The article also sets the number of state senators at no more than twenty-nine, and provides that the number of state representatives must be at least twice but no more than three times the number of state senators. Currently there are twenty-nine state senators and seventy-five representatives.[30]

ARTICLE X. EDUCATION

This article provides for the establishment and maintenance of the state's education system, which consists of public education and higher education. Public education includes all public elementary and secondary schools, otherwise known as K-12, and others as designated by the legislature. Public education is to be free and open to all the children of the state, except that the legislature may authorize the imposition of fees in the secondary schools. The general control and supervision of public education is vested in the State Board of Education, which shall be directed by a state superintendent of public instruction.

Higher education includes all public universities and colleges and others as designated by the legislature. The legislature is required to provide for the general control and supervision of higher education, although the constitutional provision does not specify the name of the supervising entity or its organizational structure. One provision recognizes that the two state universities existing at the time of statehood, Utah State University and the University of Utah, would be governed by the territorial laws in effect in 1896 with respect to those universities' rights, franchises, and endowments.

Both the public education and the higher education systems are to be free from sectarian control. No public funds may be appropriated to a school or educational institution controlled by a religious institution, and no partisan or religious qualification or test may be required as a condition of employment, admission, or attendance at any of the state's education systems.

In addition to the legislature's plenary powers of taxation, this article provides two funding mechanisms for the education systems of the state: the State School Fund and the Uniform School Fund. The State School Fund's primary source of revenue is the original federal land grant to support public and secondary schools. The primary source of revenue of the Uniform School Fund is the state tax on income.[31]

ARTICLE XI. LOCAL GOVERNMENTS

Article XI recognizes counties as legal subdivisions of the state and provides that they shall continue until changed as provided by statute. In order for a county seat to be moved, Article XI requires a two-thirds countywide vote in favor and prohibits a proposition to move the county seat from being submitted more than once in four years. The article also requires any county boundary change, other than a minor adjustment, to be approved by a majority of voters of each county whose boundary is affected. The article requires the legislature to provide for optional forms of county government and requires voter approval for the adoption of an optional form of government.

Article XI prohibits the legislature from creating cities or towns by special laws and requires the legislature to provide for the incorporation, organization, and dissolution of cities and towns and for their classification in proportion to population. The article limits the legislature's ability to authorize the construction of a railroad, telegraph, telephone, or electric light plant within a city or town without the permission of the city or town. Following a 1933 amendment, the article also provides a process for a city's adoption of a charter and specifies certain powers conferred on charter cities. Tooele is currently the state's only charter city. Article XI also prohibits cities and towns from disposing of any of their water rights.

The article permits the legislature to authorize the creation of special service districts to provide statutorily specified services to identifiable areas of a county, city, or town. A county, city, or town that has established a special service district is authorized to levy taxes upon the land within the district, and the special service district is authorized to issue bonds to pay for providing the service. The authority to levy taxes or issue bonds is conditioned upon voter approval.

Article XI also states that the legislature may provide for the establishment of other political subdivisions of the state or other governmental entities to provide services and facilities as provided by statute. These other entities may exercise only those powers and perform only those functions that are specified in statute.[32]

ARTICLE XII. CORPORATIONS

At statehood, the corporations article contained twenty sections. It was written in an era when states felt compelled to curb the growing power of trusts and monopolies.[33] One section that was repealed in 1982 prevented a person who held a business license issued by a municipality from holding an office within that municipality, such as mayor or city council member.[34] Of the remaining nineteen sections, thirteen were repealed in 1992, five were amended, and only one was left unchanged.

The remaining sections of the article establish a free market system to promote the dispersion of economic and political power, prohibit monopolies, prevent the malicious interference with a person obtaining employment, require common carriers to provide services without discrimination, and permit corporations to be formed under general laws, but prevents the formation of corporations by special laws.[35]

ARTICLE XIII. REVENUE AND TAXATION

Article XIII is the most amended article of the Utah Constitution. It was completely rewritten and reenacted in 2003. It sets forth the revenue and taxation policy of the state.

This article requires all tangible property in the state to be taxed at a uniform and equal rate, unless it is subject to a specific exemption. Property that is exempt from property tax under Article XIII includes property owned by the state and other governmental entities; property owned by a nonprofit entity used exclusively for religious, charitable, or educational purposes; places of burial; farm equipment and machinery; and certain water rights. In addition to the property specifically identified in Article XIII as exempt, the article also authorizes the legislature to provide an exemption for property including inventory held for sale in the ordinary course of business; property used to generate electrical power for irrigation purposes; up to 45 percent of the value of residential property; household furnishings; and property owned by a disabled veteran. The legislature is also authorized to provide for a remission or abatement of the taxes of the poor.

Although Article XIII does not contain the same detailed provisions on other types of taxes as it contains on the property tax, the article does state that nothing in the constitution may be construed to prevent the legislature from providing for other taxes. The article also requires the legislature to impose taxes each year sufficient to pay the ordinary expenses of the state, or, in other words, to balance the state's budget. The article earmarks all revenue from the income tax for public and higher education, and earmarks all income from fees, taxes, and other charges related to the operation of motor vehicles for roads, driver education, and traffic law enforcement.

Article XIII establishes the Utah State Tax Commission and provides for its membership and authority. The commission consists of four persons, no more than two of whom may belong to the same political party. The commission is charged generally with the administration and supervision of the state's tax laws. The article also establishes a board of equalization in each county to adjust and equalize the valuation and assessment of the real and personal property within the county.[36]

ARTICLE XIV. PUBLIC DEBT

This article on public debt serves on one hand to authorize the state and its local governments to incur debts and on the other to strictly limit the debts they can incur. In addition to limiting debts to a percentage of the value of taxable property, the provisions in this article also require that debt proceeds may only be expended for the purposes for which the debt was incurred.

The debts of the state are limited to 1.5 percent of the value of the taxable property of the state, except in cases of war or insurrection when the state is authorized to exceed the limit. The state is also prohibited from assuming the debts of any county, city, town, or school district.

A county, city, town, school district, or other political subdivision may not incur debt that is to be repaid from property tax revenues unless the debt is approved by voters. Even voter approved debt may not exceed certain limits. A county may not incur debt in excess of 2 percent of the value of taxable property in the county. A city, town, school district, or other municipal corporation may not incur debt in excess of 4 percent of the value of taxable property within the entity's boundaries. However, a first or second class city may incur additional debt of up to 4 percent, and any other city and town may incur additional debt of up to 8 percent, if the additional debt is for supplying the city or town with water, artificial lights, or sewers.[37]

ARTICLE XV. MILITIA

Article XV states that the militia shall consist of all able-bodied male inhabitants of the state between eighteen and forty-five years of age. The article also requires the legislature to provide for the militia's organization, equipment, and discipline.[38]

ARTICLE XVI. LABOR

Serving as a protection of the workforce, this article, among other things, protects the rights of labor, prohibits the employment of children in underground mines and the involuntary contracting of convict labor, and requires the legislature to pass laws providing for the health and safety of employees in factories, smelters, and mines. It prohibits the legislature from limiting the amount of damages recoverable in injuries that result in death, and authorizes the legislature to provide for a minimum wage for women and children. The article also establishes that eight hours shall constitute a day's work on projects done or aided by the state, a county, or a municipal government.[39]

ARTICLE XVII. WATER RIGHTS

This article has remained unchanged from the 1896 constitution and states simply that all water rights existing at the time of the adoption of the constitution are recognized and confirmed.[40]

ARTICLE XVIII. FORESTRY

This article requires the legislature to enact laws to preserve forests on state lands, including forests that may be transferred to the state from the federal government.[41]

ARTICLE XIX. PUBLIC BUILDINGS AND STATE INSTITUTIONS

This article was repealed January 1, 1989.[42]

ARTICLE XX. PUBLIC LANDS

Section 1 of this article specifies that lands acquired by the state through grant, gift, or otherwise are to be held in trust for the people, to be disposed of as may be provided by law, for the respective purposes for which they have been granted, donated, or otherwise acquired.

Section 2 specifies that land granted to the state by Congress at statehood to support public schools, universities, and other facilities and institutions, together with lands that have been added to them by purchase, exchange, or other means, are school and institutional trust lands. These school and institutional trust lands are distinct from the public lands under Section 1 which are held in trust for other beneficiaries and purposes.[43]

ARTICLE XXI. SALARIES

This article was repealed January 1, 1993.[44]

ARTICLE XXII. MISCELLANEOUS

This article contains some miscellaneous items which, among other things, establish Salt Lake City as the seat of state government, provide for a homestead exemption, make it a felony for a public officer to use public money for an unauthorized purpose, and create a permanent state trust fund which shall receive appropriations from the 1998 tobacco settlement agreement.[45]

ARTICLE XXIII. AMENDMENT AND REVISION

Article XXIII provides two ways to change the constitution. One method is by an amendment passed by two-thirds of both houses of the legislature and approved by a majority of the voters voting on the proposal at the next general election. The amendment process involving the legislature and the approval of the voters has been used frequently. The other method is by the legislature, by a two-thirds vote and approved by the voters, calling for a constitutional convention. If a convention is called, the convention is required to consist of not less than the number of members as are in both houses of the legislature.[46] Since the 1895 constitutional convention to formulate the original 1896 constitution, there has never been a constitutional convention held in Utah. The legislature proposed a constitutional convention in the 1960s to rewrite and modernize the almost seventy-year old constitution, but the proposal was rejected by the voters.

ARTICLE XXIV. SCHEDULE

Without legal significance today, this article was critical at the time of statehood in making the transition from a territory to a state. By assuring a smooth transition, it was important to provide that the territorial laws would continue, that contracts, judgments, and prosecutions would not be interrupted or invalidated, and that prisoners could still be confined under lawful commitment. While these provisions have long since served their purposes, they are of some historical significance.[47]

Chapter 3

Utah Administrative Rules

Administrative rules demonstrate that "the devil is in the details." Rules are written by state agencies to flesh out the details the legislature, when passing laws, chooses to direct the agency to provide by rule. This power to make rules is delegated by the legislature to the executive branch, but the legislature exercises oversight of the rulemaking process to ensure that the rules reflect legislative intent. Rules have the effect of law—the public is required to obey them—and they often affect a citizen's daily life more directly than laws passed by the legislature.

> **In this chapter:**
>
> Background (p. 37)
> Division of Administrative Rules (p. 38)
> Administrative Rules Review Committee (p. 40)
> Legislative Repeal of Rules (p. 40)
> Agency Actions That Must Be in Rule (p. 40)
> Executive Branch Review of Rules (p. 41)

BACKGROUND

Lawmaking is a function of the legislative branch. In the 120 years prior to the New Deal of 1933, legislatures were the only branch of government that passed laws. Executive branch agencies executed those laws without any power to clarify or provide procedural details regarding statutes passed by the legislature.

Beginning at the federal level during the New Deal, and rapidly expanding into state government, legislatures began delegating some of their power to make laws to executive branch agencies.[1] At first, the power granted was very narrow; legislatures specified in statute the kinds of rules that an agency could make, the subject matter of those rules, and the limits of the agencies' power to make rules. And when legislatures attempted to grant broader power to agencies to make rules without limiting the scope of the rules, early court decisions invalidated those grants of power on the grounds that the legislature had unconstitutionally delegated its power to make laws to the executive branch.

Courts eventually allowed legislatures to grant to agencies broad rulemaking powers without requiring the legislatures to set limits or standards on the exercise of that power. But in recent years that trend has lost momentum and the courts have limited and defined circumstances in which state agencies can make rules. For example, in *State of Utah v. Gallion*, the Utah Supreme Court reaffirmed that "there are certain *essential legislative functions* which cannot be transferred to others."[2] In that case, the essential function was the authority to determine what constitutes a crime and what the punishment would be for its violation. The court clearly stated the legislature "may not delegate that power either expressly or by implication."[3]

Of critical importance is the public's right to respond to proposed rules. The Utah Administrative Rulemaking Act, passed by the legislature in 1983, ensured that the public's right to be involved in the rulemaking process would be preserved.

DIVISION OF ADMINISTRATIVE RULES

The rulemaking act requires agencies to submit proposed rules to the division for publication on the division's Web site.[4] The rulemaking act also requires a public comment period during which agencies accept written comment on proposed rules and hold public hearings if requested by concerned groups or individuals, or as required by law. The division is also required to periodically publish all current state agency rules regardless of how long they have been in place.[5]

Figure 3-1 details the administrative rulemaking process that each state agency must follow when making a rule.

The impact of the Division of Administrative Rules' efforts to ensure proper notice and publication of rules and the opportunity for public comment on them is significant. Rules that in years past were often published only within the agency with no public scrutiny, or were created on a case by case basis to address a public inquiry, have now been published widely and the public awareness has increased fairness and equitable treatment.

The quality of rules submitted by state agencies has improved steadily and significantly. Factors contributing to this improvement include:
- Increased public input and concern over the content of administrative rules
- Division training on rulewriting for state agencies
- An increased number of state agencies involving the public and concerned groups in administrative rule development prior to rule publication
- Effective review and feedback on agency rulemaking by staff in the Governor's Office of Planning and Budget
- Oversight by the Administrative Rules Review Committee

Citizens who feel harmed by a rule may go beyond the public comment process by approaching the agency directly and requesting an administrative hearing.[6] After exhausting all options through communicating directly with the state agency, citizens may request a judicial review of the rule by filing a complaint with the county clerk in the district court where the citizen lives or in Salt Lake County District Court. They may also contact a member of the legislature's Administrative Rules Review Committee and request a hearing on the rule.

A citizen may submit to a state agency a proposed draft for an administrative rule, whether it be an alternative to a current rule or a proposal for rulemaking that the state agency has yet to implement.[7] Interested persons may visit the Division of Administrative Rules' Web site, www.rules.utah.gov, to find more information on state agency rulemaking.

Figure 3-1

UTAH ADMINISTRATIVE RULEMAKING PROCESS

A Summary of the Path a Proposed Rule* Takes. For the requirements of the process, see *Utah Code*, Title 63, Chapter 46a; and *Utah Admin. Code*, Title R15.

AUTH-ORIZATION	PREPROPOSAL	PROPOSAL	COMMENT PERIOD	ADOPTION	ENFORCEMENT

An agency must be authorized to regulate. The Utah Constitution, state statute, federal law, or court order may authorize rulemaking.	• The agency identifies a need for a new rule or a change to an existing rule. The need for a rule may come from different sources, including comments received from the public, new legislation, an adjudication establishing a principle of law, a petition for rulemaking, etc.
	• The agency is encouraged to develop each rule in partnership with interested parties.
	• The agency prepares a proposed rule.
	• The agency drafts the rule text and marks the text to show additions with underlining and deletions with strike-out surrounded by brackets.
	• The agency completes a rule analysis as outlined in UTAH CODE ANN. Subsection 63-46a-4(5).
	• The agency is encouraged to create and maintain an "administrative record" to document its decision-making process.
	• The agency's department head (typically a member of the Governor's Cabinet, or a person at an equivalent level) comments on fiscal impacts the rule may have on businesses.
	• The agency may prefile the rule with the Governor's Office of Planning and Budget.
	• A person may request that his name be placed on a mailing list for advanced notice of rulemaking. This request is directed to the agency responsible for writing the rules.
		• The agency files the proposed rule with the Division of Administrative Rules.
		• The Division of Administrative Rules provides a copy of the rule to the Governor's Office of Planning and Budget for executive branch review.
		• The agency notifies interested persons: (1) who have requested notice; (2) who the agency is required by law to notify; and (3) who, in the judgement of the agency, should be notified. Minimum notice is a copy of the rule analysis.
		• The Division reviews the rule analysis for completeness and compliance with the Utah Administrative Rulemaking Act and related rules.
			• A person may submit public comment regarding a proposed rule directly to the agency during the comment period (the name of a contact person and that person's phone number, fax number, E-mail address, and mailing address are included in the rule analysis).
			• The agency accepts public comment during the period it designates on the rule analysis (no fewer than 30 days and no more than 119 days after publication of the rule).
			• The agency considers the public comment it has received.
			• The Administrative Rules Review Committee may ask the agency to appear before the committee.
			• A person may request that the agency hold a public hearing about a specific proposed rule.
			• The agency:
			  • may hold a hearing at its option; OR
			  • must hold a hearing when requested by: (1) another state agency; (2) ten interested persons; or (3) an interested association having not fewer that ten members (The request for a hearing must be made within 15 days of publication of the rule in the BULLETIN, must be held before the rule is made effective, and must be no fewer than seven nor more that 30 days after the agency received the request.); OR
			  • must hold a hearing when required by other law.
				The agency notifies the Division of Administrative Rules of the rule's effective date (no fewer than 31 days and no more than 120 days after publication of the rule in the BULLETIN). If the Division of Administrative Rules does not receive a Notice of Effective Date on or before the 120th day, the rule lapses. To enact the rule, the agency must start the rule-making process over again.	• The agency enforces the rule.
					• The Administrative Rules Review Committee may ask the agency to appear before the committee.
					• A person may petition the agency to change or repeal an existing rule, or enact a new rule.

The Division publishes the rule in the UTAH STATE BULLETIN and summarizes the rule in the UTAH STATE DIGEST; which are available at http://www.rules.utah.gov

The Division codifies and publishes the effective rule in the UTAH ADMINISTRATIVE CODE available at http://www.rules.utah.gov

Comment received, new legislation, adjudication establishing a principle of law, etc., may require the agency to amend or repeal an existing rule or promulgate a new rule (begin again at "preproposal").

NOTE: "Agency" means "each state board, authority, commission, institution, department, division, officer, or other state government entity . . . which is authorized or required by law to make rules, adjudicate, grant or withhold licenses, grant or withhold relief from legal obligations, or perform other similar actions or duties delegated by law." "Agency" does not include the legislative or judicial branches, or state political subdivisions. (UTAH CODE ANN., Section 63-46a-2(2)).
* A proposed rule is the most common type of rule filing. The requirements for other types of filings (120-Day (Emergency) Rules, Five-Year Reviews and Extensions, etc.) vary.

Utah Division of Administrative Rules ◆ 4120 State Office Building ◆ Salt Lake City, UT 84114-1201 ◆ Phone: 801-538-3764 ◆ Fax: 801-538-1773 ◆ rulesonline@utah.gov   6/2003

ADMINISTRATIVE RULES REVIEW COMMITTEE

Legislatures have searched for additional ways to make the administrative rulemaking process more open and responsive to the public. Utah's legislature has created the Administrative Rules Review Committee to serve such a purpose.

The legislature's Administrative Rules Review Committee is a ten-member group of legislators established in 1983 to exercise continuous oversight of rulemaking by state agencies.

The committee serves three main purposes: first, it ensures that state agencies draft rules within statutory boundaries and preserve legislative intent; second, it provides a forum where the rulemaking concerns of citizens, legislators, and other interested groups can be addressed; and third, it provides a means for feedback to the legislature on the programs and activities of state agencies.

The committee not only reviews proposed rules, but reviews actions taken by an agency that are not in rule but, due to their impact on the public, perhaps should be in rule. The committee also reviews instances in which an agency is not following the requirements of its own rules.

LEGISLATIVE REPEAL OF RULES

The committee may also recommend to the legislature that a rule be repealed. This is done through an annual legislative bill that reauthorizes for a one-year period all the rules of the executive branch agencies except for those rules listed specifically in the legislation.[8] This structure was approved by the legislature and allowed to go into law by the governor in 1989 after considerable debate between the legislative and executive branches.

The committee annually identifies rules that fail to meet its review criteria, including statutory authorization, compliance with legislative intent, fiscal impact, or negative effects on the public or local governments. In most instances, agency representatives make rule changes suggested by the committee. If agency representatives choose not to change a rule to address the committee's concerns, the committee typically recommends to the legislature that the rule be repealed in the next general session.[9]

From 1989 to 1993, the committee also reviewed all existing state administrative rules. Hundreds of rules were repealed, rewritten, or streamlined as a result of this review.

AGENCY ACTIONS THAT MUST BE IN RULE

In 2001, the Administrative Rules Review Committee noted that some agency actions that directly affected the public were not being submitted as rules. In 2002, at the recommendation of the committee, the legislature's annual reauthorization of state agency rules also repealed the policies of several state institutions of higher education that restricted the statutorily granted rights of concealed firearm permit holders at campus facilities.[10] At press time, the larger issue of state law and a state institution of higher education's rights regarding firearms has been appealed to the Utah Supreme Court.

In 2002, the committee pursued the issues raised by the repeal of those policies. After lengthy study and debate, the legislature passed legislation in the 2003 General Session which stated, in a clarification of existing statutory language, that if an agency's written statement authorizing it to take action fits within the definition of a rule, particularly as the action affects the public, it is a rule, whether or not the agency complies with the notice, publication, and comment requirements of the Utah Administrative Rulemaking Act. However, the agency cannot enforce the rule unless it complies with the notice, publication, and comment requirements.[11] In other words, an agency can neither enforce its actions nor escape a public or legislative review of its actions simply by not submitting a written description of those actions as an administrative rule.

EXECUTIVE BRANCH REVIEW OF RULES

By executive order,[12] the Governor's Office of Planning and Budget (GOPB) provides a review of administrative rules for the benefit of executive branch agencies. GOPB staff has provided this policy review since March 1988. Agency directors work with the GOPB staff to implement the findings in the review.

An essential part of the review is asking questions of the agency to help it identify what it hopes to accomplish with a rule so that when the agency implements it, potential legal and enforcement concerns have been addressed. The following are some typical questions, as provided on the GOPB's Web site, www.governor.state.ut.us/gopb:

- What purposes are served by departments or agencies in making a rule?
- What are the impacts on citizens and the business community?
- What are the legal or liability questions raised by the rule?
- Are there conflicts or overlaps in policy with other government entities?
- What is the cost impact on the state budget of a rule?

Agencies have the discretion to classify proposed rule changes as "nonsubstantive"—meaning a change so minor that, in the agency's view, it does not merit publication, written public comment, or public hearing. Therefore, it is the GOPB staff's responsibility to verify the appropriateness of the nonsubstantive designation.

GOPB staff also coordinates with the Division of Administrative Rules and the Administrative Rules Review Committee to resolve concerns with administrative rules as they arise.

Chapter 4

Citizen Participation and Elections

Citizen participation is fundamental to representative democracy. Voting is perhaps the most common and most central way that a citizen may be involved in democracy. Political party processes, initiatives, and referenda also allow citizens a way to be involved in their government. Statutes allowing access to government records and requiring the public's business to be done in public also enhance citizens' participation. This chapter will discuss some of these ways that citizens may access and be involved in government.

In this chapter:

Qualifications to Vote (p. 43)
Means of Voting (p. 43)
Voting Process at Polling Place (p. 44)
Getting Elected (p. 44)
Political Parties (p. 46)
Registered Political Parties (p. 47)
Benefits and Obligations of Registered Political Parties (p. 47)
Election Process: Nominating Candidates and Electing Public Officials in Utah (p. 47)
Initiative and Referendum (p. 49)
Citizen Involvement in Government (p. 54)
Access to Government Meetings and Documents (p. 56)
Lobbying and Lobbyist Regulation (p. 58)
Political History (p. 59)

QUALIFICATIONS TO VOTE

The Utah Constitution and Utah statutes provide that an individual is entitled to vote if that individual is a citizen of the United States, at least eighteen years of age, a resident of Utah for thirty days prior to an election, and registered to vote. These requirements allow an individual to vote in regular general elections, statewide or local special elections, municipal general elections, municipal primary elections, and in special district and bond elections.[1] Primary elections are a special case; if a registered political party chooses to close the primary election, a voter may vote in the Western States Presidential Primary election or regular primary election only if the voter meets the political party affiliation requirements designated by the registered political party.[2]

Utah statute designates a specific voter registration form to be filled out, but provides alternative means for registration other than with the county clerk's office. Registration can be done by mail, satellite registrar, upon application for or renewal of a driver's license, at a discretionary voter registration agency, or at a public assistance agency.[3]

MEANS OF VOTING

In general, voters are able to vote at their neighborhood voting precinct on election day. However, if sixty days before an election, less than five hundred persons are registered to vote in a voting precinct, the county legislative body may require persons to vote by absentee ballot.[4] The county clerk is required to (1) mail an absentee ballot to all registered voters in that precinct with information that there is no polling place for the election, (2) give instructions and deadlines for returning the absentee ballot, (3) warn that failure to comply with absentee ballot instructions may result in voting ineligibility for that election, and (4) compare and verify the signature on each absentee ballot with the voter's signature that is maintained on file.[5]

Any registered voter who wishes to vote by absentee ballot can do so by applying for an absentee ballot with the appropriate election officer by the Friday before election day or, if the voter is overseas, no later than twenty days before election day.[6] A person voting by absentee ballot at the office of the election officer shall apply for and cast a ballot no later than the day before the election.[7] Special absentee ballots are available for Utah military members or others living abroad, which allow them to vote in county, state, and national elections during their absence from the state or the country.[8]

VOTING PROCESS AT POLLING PLACE

At the polling place, a registered voter gives his or her name to one of the election judges, which is usually sufficient to receive a ballot. However, on some occasions the voter may need to show proof of identification or proof of residence.[9] If the voter establishes identity and residence to the satisfaction of the election judge, and the voter's name is found on the official register, the judge gives the voter a ballot to vote. If the election judge questions or challenges the voter's identity or residence, or the voter's name is not found on the official register, the voter will receive a provisional ballot to vote.[10] A provisional ballot will later be counted if a state or local election official can verify that the individual is registered.[11]

A disabled, illiterate, or blind voter may be assisted at the polling place by a person of the voter's choice, but the assistant may not be the voter's employer, an agent of the employer, an officer or agent of the voter's union, or a candidate for office.[12]

GETTING ELECTED

Tables 4-1 through 4-5 outline election dates and terms of offices for various levels of government offices in which elected candidates may serve. Regular general elections are partisan elections except for the State School Board; local school boards; Utah Supreme Court justices; Utah Court of Appeals, district court, and juvenile court judges; county justice court judges; and constables.

Table 4-1

Federal Government

Candidates run for various federal and state elective offices in regular general election years. A "regular general election" is held each even-numbered year. However, depending on the term of office or other considerations (e.g., vacancies), each office will not be up for election in every even-numbered year.

ELECTIVE OFFICE	TERM OF OFFICE	ELECTION DATE
President/Vice President	4-year term	Regular General Election held in even-numbered years
U.S. Senate	6-year term	
U.S. House of Representatives	2-year term	

Table 4-2

State Government

State offices are four-year terms except for state representatives (two-year terms) and state supreme court justices, who are subject to unopposed retention elections. Terms of state senators and state school board members are staggered so that some are elected every two years.

ELECTIVE OFFICE	TERM OF OFFICE	ELECTION DATE
Governor/Lieutenant Governor	4-year term	Regular General Election held in even-numbered years
Attorney General	4-year term	
State Auditor	4-year term	
State Treasurer	4-year term	
State Senator	4-year term[13]	
State Representative	2-year term	
Utah Supreme Court Justice	Unopposed retention election 3 years after gubernatorial appointment, then every 10 years	
Utah Court of Appeals Judge	Unopposed retention election 3 years after gubernatorial appointment, then every 6 years	
District Court Judge		
Juvenile Court Judge		
State School Board	4-year staggered terms, non-partisan	

Table 4-3

Local School Districts

ELECTIVE OFFICE	TERM OF OFFICE	ELECTION DATE
Local School Boards	4-year staggered terms	Regular General Election held in even-numbered years

Table 4-4

County Government

County offices are four-year terms unless provided otherwise in an optional plan for county government. County commission and county council member terms are staggered so that some are elected every two years.

ELECTIVE OFFICE	TERM OF OFFICE	ELECTION DATE
County Mayor (if applicable)	4-year term	Regular General Election held in even-numbered years
County Commission or County Council members	4-year term	
County Assessor	4-year term	
County Attorney, District Attorney, or both	4-year term	
County Auditor	4-year term	
County Clerk	4-year term	
County Recorder	4-year term	
County Sheriff	4-year term	
County Surveyor	4-year term	
County Treasurer	4-year term	
County Constable	4-year term	
County Justice Court Judge	4-year term, unopposed retention election	
Township Planning Commission	4-year staggered terms[14]	

Table 4-5

Municipal Government

Local government elective offices are filled in municipal general election years. A "municipal general election" is held each odd-numbered year. However, depending upon the term of office or other considerations (e.g., vacancies) each office will not be up for election in every odd-numbered year. Municipal general elections are generally nonpartisan.

ELECTIVE OFFICE	TERM OF OFFICE	ELECTION DATE
Elected Offices in Cities and Towns		Municipal General Election held in odd-numbered years
Mayor	4-year term	
City Council or City Commission or Town Council	4-year staggered terms	
Elected Offices in Special Districts	4-year term	Municipal General Election held in odd-numbered years
Special District Board		

POLITICAL PARTIES[15]

Political parties are not part of state or local government. U.S. Supreme Court decisions have held that they are independent political associations. Statutes or state or local government procedures mandating particular internal party processes or leadership have been struck down by the Court as violating the First Amendment's protection of the fundamental right to freely associate—to participate in a political party.[16] Consequently, Utah's constitution and statutes impose only limited requirements on the rights of political parties, including the right to register as a political party with the state and the right to participate in and partially dictate who may vote in the party's primary election.

REGISTERED POLITICAL PARTIES

An organization of voters that wishes to be identified as a "registered political party" files an application with the lieutenant governor on or before March 1 of a regular general election year. Political parties that have previously received a total vote for any of its candidates equivalent to 2 percent or more of the total votes cast for all representatives in Congress need only file the petition with the lieutenant governor. Other organizations of voters must file a petition signed by at least two thousand registered voters asking that the political party be recognized as a registered political party.[17] In May 2004, the six registered political parties in Utah were the Republican Party, Democratic Party, Green Party, Libertarian Party, Personal Choice Party, and Constitution Party. Because the Green Party and the Constitution Party failed to receive enough votes in the 2004 election to automatically qualify as a registered political party, only the Republican Party, Democratic Party, Libertarian Party, and Personal Choice Party were registered political parties as of April 2005. The Green Party and Constitution Party, however, were circulating petitions to again qualify as registered political parties for the 2006 election.

BENEFITS AND OBLIGATIONS OF REGISTERED POLITICAL PARTIES

Registered political parties have benefits in that they are able to reserve a political party name, use the state's election apparatus to select party nominees through a primary election, and may have the party's candidates listed on the primary and general election ballots under the party's name. However, with those benefits comes the registered political party's obligation to (1) file a copy of the party's constitution and bylaws with the state; (2) ensure that the constitution and bylaws meet certain requirements; (3) designate a "party liaison" to communicate with the state on the party's behalf; and (4) comply with certain deadlines, such as providing the names of the party's candidates to the lieutenant governor and county clerks.[18]

ELECTION PROCESS: NOMINATING CANDIDATES AND ELECTING PUBLIC OFFICIALS IN UTAH

Declarations of Candidacy

For regular general elections (even-numbered years), Utah statute requires each candidate–except write-in candidates—to file a declaration of candidacy between March 7 and March 17 before the next regular general election, and to pay the required filing fee.[19] There is an exception to this requirement for lieutenant governor candidates—who must file within five days of nomination, candidates for president and vice president of the United States—who must be certified by the registered political party by September 3, and write-in candidates—who must file a declaration of candidacy no later than fourteen days before the election.[20] For municipal general elections (odd-numbered years), each candidate must file a declaration of candidacy or nominating petition between July 15 and August 15 of any odd-numbered year and pay the filing fee if required by municipal ordinance.[21]

Unaffiliated Candidates and Write-in Candidates

Candidates who are "unaffiliated" with a party must file a certificate of nomination that complies with statutory requirements. An unaffiliated candidate must submit to the country clerk for certification a statutorily-required certificate of nomination petition form[22] and an attached signature sheet containing at least one thousand registered voters' signatures[23] for a state office, and three hundred signatures or at least 5 percent of the registered voters residing within a political subdivision for a local office.

Unaffiliated candidates who comply with statutory requirements are entitled to all the rights and subject to all the penalties that apply to candidates selected by a registered political party. A candidate who has filed a declaration of candidacy may not file a certificate of nomination as an unaffiliated candidate in the same year.

Write-in candidates for any office must file a declaration of candidacy no later than fourteen days before the regular general election or municipal general election in which the person intends to become a write-in candidate.[24] The candidate must make a declaration before the appropriate filing officer that the candidate meets the requirements of the office. Write-in candidacy is not available for the office of county attorney or district attorney.[25]

Partisan Candidates

The process for nominating a political party's candidates is established by the political party's constitution and bylaws. The process commonly used by Republican and Democratic parties is to begin with party caucuses held in each voting precinct the last Monday or Tuesday of March.

County party conventions are usually held in April. County candidates and state candidates whose districts are located entirely within the county are selected in one of two ways. The candidates may be selected as the party's nominee if they receive a certain percentage of the vote designated in the party's bylaws. Sixty percent is a common figure, but the percentage may vary from election to election if the party's bylaws are changed. If no candidate receives the requisite percent of the delegate vote, the two candidates receiving the most votes face each other in a primary election held the fourth Tuesday in June. The winner of the primary election becomes the party's nominee for the regular general election.

State party conventions are held in early May. State and federal candidates, and county candidates whose districts include more than one county, are selected in one of the two ways described for county party conventions.

Partisan Elections

Primary elections are held the fourth Tuesday in June. A political party may elect to "close" the primary election, meaning that only registered party members may vote, or partially close the primary election, meaning that only certain classes of voters may vote. For example, a party may allow only registered party members and voters unaffiliated with any other political party to vote in its primary election.

Candidates nominated by the political parties, unaffiliated candidates, and write-in candidates face each other in the regular general election held the first Tuesday after the first Monday in November.

Instead of actually electing the president and vice president of the United States, Utah voters elect a slate of presidential electors chosen by the political party according to procedures specified in the party's bylaws. Each political party's presidential electors are pledged to vote for their party's candidates when the electoral college meets on the first Wednesday in January after the presidential election. Those presidential electors elected by the voters gather at the lieutenant governor's office on that date and cast their votes for president and vice president as part of the electoral college.[26]

Nonpartisan Elections

Nonpartisan elections are contested elections where candidates do not identify themselves as affiliated with a particular political party. To nominate municipal candidates when more than two candidates file for the same office, a nonpartisan primary election is held on the first Tuesday after the first Monday in October.[27] Third, fourth, and fifth class cities and towns may avoid a primary election by passing an ordinance that requires that candidates for municipal office in those municipalities be nominated at a political party convention or committee.[28] The political party may be either a political party that was a registered political party with the state at the last regular general election, or may become qualified as a municipal political party by filing a petition signed by municipal voters with the city recorder or town clerk. Third, fourth, and fifth class cities and towns may also require that candidates for municipal office file nomination petitions signed by the percent of registered voters in the municipality established in a municipal ordinance.[29]

Municipal and special district officers are elected in the municipal general election which is held the first Tuesday after the first Monday in November in odd-numbered years.

INITIATIVE AND REFERENDUM

The legislative power of the state is vested in the people as well as in the legislature. The people's legislative power is exercised through the citizen initiative and referendum process. Utah's initiative process allows citizens to draft state, county, or municipal laws and place them on the ballot for a popular vote if the procedural and subject matter requirements are met. Through the Utah referendum process, citizens are also constitutionally allowed to veto a new state law, except those passed by a two-thirds vote,[30] or a new county or municipal ordinance enacted by the respective legislative bodies before the ordinance goes into effect.

The Utah Supreme Court has held that the initiative and referendum power of the people to enact laws is "sacrosanct" and a fundamental right, "coequal" to the lawmaking power of the legislature: "The power of the legislature and the power of the people to legislate through initiative and referenda are coequal, coextensive, and concurrent and share 'equal dignity.'"[31] The court has emphasized that the voter's right does not commence at the ballot box, but begins upon the signing of a petition.[32] Courts generally afford a presumption of validity to statutes enacted by the initiative process because they are reluctant to contradict the popular will. Tables 4-6 through 4-9 outline initiative and referendum processes.

Table 4-6 summarizes the initiative process for state laws.

Table 4-6

INITIATIVE – ENACTING OR AMENDING STATE LAW
Title 20A, Chapter 7, Part 2

Initiative processes in Utah may be direct or indirect. In the direct process, citizens draft laws and place them on the ballot for a popular vote if the procedural and subject matter limitations are met. In the indirect process, proposals may first be submitted to the legislature, which has the opportunity to act on the proposed legislation before it is placed on the ballot.[33] Utah's statutory scheme provides for a preliminary filing of an application with the appropriate elections officer, preliminary fiscal analysis by the Governor's Office of Planning and Budget, circulation of an initiative petition for signatures of registered voters, submission of the signed petition to the appropriate elections officer for a determination of "sufficiency," and certification to the ballot for a popular vote.

APPLICATION FOR THE DIRECT OR INDIRECT INITIATIVE PROCESS

To place an initiative enacting or amending state law on the general election ballot, an individual must file an application on-line, in person, by fax, or by mail with the lieutenant governor in the State Elections Office.[34]

- The lieutenant governor will accept or reject the application.[35]
- If the application is accepted, the Governor's Office of Planning and Budget or local budget officer, will prepare an initial fiscal impact estimate based on the laws proposed by the initiative.[36]
- Sponsors must hold at least seven public hearings in designated regions throughout the state before circulating a statewide initiative petition.[37] Public hearings are not required for local initiatives.
- "Qualification" of the initiative petition for the regular general election ballot—or obtaining the statutorily required number of legal signatures[38]—must be completed within one year after the application is filed.[39]

DIRECT INITIATIVE PROCESS

To place an initiative petition on the general election ballot:
- A sponsor must obtain legal signatures equal to 10% of all votes cast for governor statewide in the last gubernatorial election and 10% of votes cast for governor in at least twenty-six Utah State Senate districts.[40]
- Signed and verified initiative packets must be submitted to the county clerk for certification of signatures by June 1 to appear on the general election ballot.[41]
- If "at any time not less than four months" before the general election, the lieutenant governor declares the initiative petition sufficient, the proposed law shall appear on the ballot at the next regular general election.[42]
- An initiative that has qualified for the ballot is delivered by July 6 to the Office of Legislative Research and General Counsel to receive an impartial ballot title.[43] The petition and ballot title are returned to the Lieutenant Governor's Office by July 20.[44] The verified title must be certified to the county clerks by September 1 to be printed on the official ballot.

Return and Canvass:[45]
- After the state board of canvassers completes its canvass, the lieutenant governor certifies to the governor the number of votes for and against the proposed law.
- If the initiative passes, the governor issues a proclamation that the initiative petition approved by the voters has the full force and effect of law.
- If two laws, or their parts, approved at the same election are entirely in conflict, the measure receiving the greatest number of affirmative votes becomes law, regardless of the difference in the majorities the measures received.

Effective Dates and Amendments:[46]
- A law proposed by initiative petition that is submitted to and approved by the people does not take effect until at least five days after the date of the official proclamation of the governor. If the initiative petition specifies an effective date, the law takes effect on that date. If the initiative petition does not specify an effective date, the law takes effect five days after the official proclamation of the governor.
- The governor may not veto a law adopted by the people.
- The legislature may amend or repeal any initiative approved by the people at any legislative session.
- A law proposed by initiative petition and adopted by the people is subject to referendum the same as other laws.
- No later than sixty days after the date of an election where an initiative has passed, the Governor's Office of Planning and Budget will prepare a final fiscal impact statement on the cost associated with the new law. If the final fiscal impact statement exceeds the initial fiscal impact estimate by 25% or more, the Legislature may amend or repeal the law or it may pass a joint or concurrent resolution informing the people that they may act to repeal the law.[47]

INDIRECT INITIATIVE PROCESS

To submit an initiative petition to the legislature:
After completing the application process, a sponsor must obtain legal signatures equal to 5% of all votes cast for governor statewide in the last gubernatorial election; and 5% of votes cast for governor in at least twenty-six Utah State Senate districts.[48]

Verification:
- Signed and verified initiative packets must be submitted to the county clerk for verification of signatures by November 15 to be submitted to the legislature at the next general session.[49]
- If the lieutenant governor declares the initiative petition sufficient not less than ten days before the beginning of the annual general session, the lieutenant governor delivers a copy of the petition to the president of the State Senate, speaker of the House of Representatives, and to the Office of Legislative Research and General Counsel.[50]
- An initiative petition that has qualified to be submitted to the legislature is submitted to (1) the Office of Legislative Research and General Counsel for a legislative review note and technical corrections; and (2) the Office of Legislative Fiscal Analyst for a fiscal note.

Consideration by the legislature:
- The legislature may direct its staff to make grammatical and other technical corrections, prepare a fiscal note, and prepare a legislative review note.
- The legislature must enact or reject the proposed initiative without change or amendment.

Effective Dates:
- A proposed law submitted to the legislature takes effect: sixty days after the final adjournment of the legislature that passed it; or on the effective date included in the proposed law if passed by a two-thirds vote of the members of each house.
- A law proposed by initiative petition—and enacted by the legislature—is subject to referendum the same as other laws.[51]

Table 4-7 summarizes the initiative process for county and city ordinances.

Table 4-7

INITIATIVE – ENACTING OR AMENDING A COUNTY OR MUNICIPAL ORDINANCE
Title 20A, Chapter 7, Parts 4 and 5

Utah's local initiative process allows the people to enact or amend county or municipal ordinances by submitting a proposed ordinance or amendment to the local legislative body, who will (1) adopt the proposed law, (2) reject the proposed law and submit the proposed law or amendment to the voters, or (3) adopt a competing law that is submitted to the voters at the same time as the initiative proposal.

APPLICATION FOR THE LOCAL INITIATIVE PROCESS

To circulate an initiative petition, a person must file an application with the local county or municipal clerk and follow the application process shown in table 4-6.

To submit an initiative petition to a local legislative body or to a vote of the people, a sponsor must obtain legal signatures equal to a designated percentage of the votes cast in the county, city, or town for all candidates for governor at the last gubernatorial election. The percentages required are:

Percent Required	Total votes cast for gubernatorial candidates
10%	greater than 25,000
12½%	10,000 but less than 25,000
15%	2,500 but less than 10,000
20%	500 but less than 2,500
25%	250 but less than 500
30%	less than 250[52]

Certification of signatures by county clerk:
- Signed and verified initiative packets must be returned to the county clerk within 120 days of the regular general election (county initiatives) or the municipal general election (municipal initiatives).[53]
- Within ninety days of the election, the county clerk shall check the name of each person verifying signature packets, and within sixty days of the election, shall certify whether or not each signer is a registered voter, and deliver all initiative packets to the local clerk.[54]

Action by the local legislative body:
- If the required number of legal signatures is obtained, the local clerk delivers the proposed law to the local legislative body at its next meeting, who must adopt or reject the proposed law within thirty days.[55] During the thirty days, the legislative body may adopt a competing local law that is submitted to the voters at the same time as the initiative proposal.
- If a county or municipal legislative body rejects a proposed county or municipal ordinance or amendment, the respective county clerk or the municipal recorder or clerk will submit the proposed ordinance or amendment to the voters at the next regular general election for a county proposal, or the next municipal general election for a municipal proposal.[56]

Evaluation by the local clerk – Initiative to be submitted to the voters:
- The local clerk shall declare the petition "sufficient" or "insufficient" depending upon whether or not it received the required percentage of legal signatures.
- A "sufficient" initiative petition is delivered to the county or municipal attorney to receive a citizen's (county or city) initiative number and an impartial ballot title. Within fifteen days, the local attorney must return the initiative petition and impartial ballot title to the local clerk to be printed on the official ballot.[57]

Return and Canvass:[58]
- After the local board of canvassers completes its canvass, the local clerk certifies to the local legislative body the number of votes for and against the proposed ordinance.
- The local legislative body issues a proclamation that the initiative petition approved by the voters has the full force and effect of law.
- If two laws, or their parts, approved at the same election are entirely in conflict, the measure receiving the greatest number of affirmative votes will be law, regardless of the difference in the majorities the measures received.

Effective Dates:
- Any proposed law submitted to and approved by the voters takes effect on the date specified in the initiative petition. If the initiative petition does not specify a date, an approved law takes effect five days after the date of the official proclamation of the vote by the county legislative body.[59]
- The local legislative body may amend or repeal any laws approved by the people at any meeting after the law has taken effect.[60]
- No later than sixty days after the date of an election where an initiative has passed, the local budget officer will prepare a final fiscal impact statement on the cost associated with the new law. If the final fiscal impact statement exceeds the initial fiscal impact estimate by 25% or more, the local legislative body may amend or repeal the law or may pass a resolution informing the people that they may act to repeal the law.[61]

Table 4-8 summarizes referendum procedures to challenge state laws.

Table 4-8

REFERENDUM – VETOING A NEW STATE LAW
Title 20A, Chapter 7, Part 3

Utah's constitution allows the people to veto a new state law enacted by the legislature except when the law passed the legislature by a two-thirds vote.

APPLICATION FOR THE STATE REFERENDUM PROCESS

An individual must file an application with the lieutenant governor in the State Elections Office within five calendar days after the end of the legislative session at which the law was passed.[62]

To have a law passed by the legislature submitted to a vote of the people:
- A sponsor must obtain legal signatures equal to 10% of all votes cast for governor statewide in the last gubernatorial election; and 10% of votes cast for governor in at least fifteen counties.[63]
- Sponsors must collect signatures, and deliver the signed and verified referendum packets to the county clerk no later than forty days after the legislative session.[64]

Certification by county clerks and transfer to the lieutenant governor:
- Within fifty-five days after the legislative session, the county clerk must check the name of each person who verified the signature packets, certify that each petition signer is a registered voter, and deliver the signature packets to the lieutenant governor.[65]

Evaluation by the lieutenant governor and transfer to county clerks:
- The lieutenant governor shall declare the referendum petition "sufficient" or "insufficient" no later than sixty days after the end of the legislative session,[66] and direct that the referendum petition be submitted to the voters at the next general election or at a statewide special election called by the governor.[67]
- A referendum petition that has been declared sufficient is delivered to the Office of Legislative Research and General Counsel to receive an impartial ballot title, and must be returned to the lieutenant governor within fifteen days.[68]
- The lieutenant governor certifies the verified title to the county clerks to be printed on the official ballot.

Return and Canvass:
- After the state board of canvassers completes its canvass, the lieutenant governor certifies the results to the governor. Based upon the result, the governor declares whether or not the law was successfully vetoed by the people.[69]

Effective Dates:[70]
- Any proposed law submitted to the people by referendum petition that is approved by the voters does not take effect until at least five days after the date of the official proclamation of the governor.
- The governor may not veto a successful referendum.

Table 4-9 summarizes referendum procedures to challenge county and city ordinances.

Table 4-9

REFERENDUM – VETOING A COUNTY OR MUNICIPAL ORDINANCE
Title 20A, Chapter 7, Part 6

Utah's constitution allows the people to repeal an ordinance enacted by the local legislative body.

APPLICATION FOR THE LOCAL REFERENDUM PROCESS

An individual must file an application with the local clerk within forty-five days after the passage of the local law.[71]

To have a law passed by the local legislative body submitted to the vote of the people, a sponsor must obtain legal signatures equal to a designated percentage of the votes cast in the county, city, or town for all candidates for governor at the last gubernatorial election. The percentages required are:

Percent Required	Total votes cast for gubernatorial candidates
10%	greater than 25,000
12½%	10,000 but less than 25,000
15%	2,500 but less than 10,000
20%	500 but less than 2,500
25%	250 but less than 500
30%	less than 250[72]

Land use laws have different signature requirements.[73]

Certification by county clerks and transfer to local clerks:
- Signed and verified referendum packets must be returned to the county clerk within 120 days of any regular general election (county referenda) or municipal general election (local referenda).[74]
- Within ninety days of the general election, the county clerk shall verify each name. Within sixty days of the general election, the county clerk shall certify that each signer is a registered voter and deliver all referendum packets to the local clerk.[75]

Evaluation by local clerks:
- The local clerk shall declare the petition "sufficient" or "insufficient" depending upon whether or not it received the required percentage of legal signatures.[76]
- A "sufficient" referendum petition is delivered to the local attorney to receive a citizen's (county or city) referendum number and an impartial ballot title. Within fifteen days, the local attorney must return the referendum petition and impartial ballot title to the local clerk to be printed on the official ballot.[77]

Return and Canvass:
- After the local board of canvassers completes its canvass, the local clerk certifies to the local legislative body the number of votes for and against the law proposed by referendum petition.
- The local legislative body issues a proclamation that the laws proposed by referendum petition that were approved by the voters to be in full force and effect as the law of the local jurisdiction.
- If two laws or their parts approved at the same election are entirely in conflict, the measure receiving the greatest number of affirmative votes will be law, regardless of the difference in the majorities the measures received.[78]

Effective Dates:
- The local law remains in effect until repealed by the voters by referendum.
- If the referendum passes, the local law that was challenged by the referendum is repealed as of the date of the election.[79]
- The local legislative body may amend any laws approved by the people at any meeting after the law has taken effect.[80]

CITIZEN INVOLVEMENT IN GOVERNMENT

Citizen involvement in government and public policy formation is part of Utah's culture and tradition. Driven by the expectation that government should be accountable to the electorate, a menu of communication resources allowing citizens to connect with their government is in place. Developing communication technology, coupled with traditional methods, produce an environment that allows citizens the opportunity to interact productively with state government.

State Government Internet Web Sites

The executive, legislative, and judicial branches of government have Internet Web sites[81] to which any person can link at home, at a public library, or whereever there is a computer that allows Internet access.

At these Web sites, citizens can transact government business; search the Utah Code; monitor legislative activity; research legal, legislative, and administrative actions; and communicate with elected officials and agency employees via electronic mail.

"Utah dot gov" (www.utah.gov) is the general portal to all executive branch agencies as well as to the legislative and judicial branches of state government on the Internet.

State Government Address and Telephone Numbers

State government offices are located throughout the state for the purpose of administrating state programs and for ease of communication with citizens. Location of these offices can be obtained on the Internet or in the telephone directory.

The blue-edged pages in the front of the white pages of the telephone directory provide telephone numbers to government offices. Telephone numbers are also provided on the government agency Web sites.

Citizen Participation in the Election Process

Political parties select candidates to stand for election for public office in Utah. They sponsor and organize neighborhood meetings and county and state conventions—all for the purpose of nominating individuals whose names will appear on primary and general election ballots.

Primary elections are held throughout the state on the fourth Tuesday of June of each even-numbered year for the purpose of nominating candidates for the general election ballot. Municipal primary elections are held the Tuesday following the first Monday in October before the regular municipal election for the purpose of nominating candidates for office in municipalities and special districts.[82]

A general election is held on the first Tuesday after the first Monday in November of each even-numbered year. Voters, at the general election, choose persons to serve the terms established by law for the following federal and state offices: president and vice president of the United States, senators and representatives to the U.S. Congress, governor, lieutenant governor, attorney general, state treasurer, state auditor, state senators and state representatives, county officers, state school board members, local school board members, and any elected judicial officers.[83]

Also considered on the general election ballot are proposals to amend the Utah Constitution and citizen initiatives or referenda that have qualified for the ballot.[84]

Municipal general elections—where municipal and some special district officers are elected—are held on the first Tuesday after the first Monday in November of each odd-numbered year.[85] Proposed local initiatives and referenda that have qualified for the ballot as provided by law are also considered at these elections.[86]

Special elections may be called by the governor, the legislature, and the local legislative body of a local political subdivision for any purpose authorized by law.[87] Dates for special elections are prescribed by state law.

The lieutenant governor, as the chief elections officer in the state, administers state and federal election laws including coordinating with local, state, and federal officials.[88] County clerks in Utah's twenty-nine counties administer and supervise election procedures in their respective counties.[89]

The lieutenant governor's Web site—http://www.utah.gov/ltgovernor—provides access to pertinent information regarding state and local election law. Qualifications for office and filing requirements and deadlines are also available at this Web site.

Voter Information Pamphlet[90]

A voter information pamphlet is published by the lieutenant governor before regular general even-numbered year elections. It is distributed to newspapers of general circulation in the state at least fifteen days before the date of the election. County clerks also receive copies of the pamphlet and distribute it without charge upon request. The pamphlet is also placed at polling places. This pamphlet is "designed to inform the voters of the content, effect, operation, fiscal impact, and the supporting and opposing arguments of any measure submitted to the voters by the legislature or by initiative or referendum petition."[91]

Candidate Information

The voter information pamphlet also contains a list of all candidates for constitutional offices, a list of candidates for each legislative district, and a one hundred-word statement of qualifications for each candidate for the office of governor, lieutenant governor, attorney general, state auditor, or state treasurer.

Ballot Measures Information

Ballot measures, such as state initiatives, state referenda, and proposed state constitutional amendments, are in the voter information pamphlet. This information includes the number and ballot title of the measure, and the final vote cast by the legislature on the measure if it is a measure submitted by the legislature or by referendum. An impartial analysis of each measure is prepared by the Office of Legislative Research and General Counsel. Written arguments in favor, written arguments in opposition, and rebuttals to the arguments against the measure are provided. The names and titles of the authors of the arguments and rebuttals follow each argument and rebuttal.

To assist voters in understanding proposed state constitutional amendments, the proposed changes are printed in their entirety, with new language underlined and deleted language placed within brackets.

Judicial Information

The judicial portion of the voter information pamphlet is prepared by the Judicial Council and includes a description of the judicial selection process, the judicial performance evaluation process, and the judicial retention election process. A list of the criteria and minimum standards of judicial performance is also included.

The names of judges, the counties in which they are subject to retention election, a short biography containing each judge's professional qualifications, and a recent photograph help voters identify judicial candidates for retention election.

A statement declaring whether or not the judge met retention standards along with an explanation of any deficiency the judge may have had in meeting the standard is presented. Judicial Council certification and informal or formal Utah Supreme Court reprimands with supporting reasons are also made public in this section of the voter information pamphlet.

Voter Assistance Information

Ballot marking procedures used by each county, voter registration information, obtaining absentee ballots, and a list of all county clerks with offices and telephone numbers complete the substance of the voter information pamphlet.

Candidate and Political Party Web Sites

Upon filing for political office, many candidates identify personal Internet Web sites. These sites are used to communicate the candidate's public policy positions, give background biographical data for the candidate, encourage and facilitate contributions to their campaign, solicit and recruit volunteer help, and convey other information considered helpful and useful to winning elections. Political parties also maintain Web sites for many of the same reasons.

ACCESS TO GOVERNMENT MEETINGS AND DOCUMENTS

Open and Public Meetings

The public's business is transacted in public. The legislature emphasized that policy in the state's Open and Public Meetings Act[92] as follows: "[T]he Legislature finds and declares that the state, its agencies and political subdivisions, exist to aid in the conduct of the people's business. It is the intent of the law that their actions be taken openly and that their deliberations be conducted openly."[93]

Exceptions to this policy of openness are very narrow. A public body may close a meeting only by strictly complying with statutory guidelines set forth in the act.[94] An affirmative vote of two-thirds of the members of the public body present at an open meeting is required to close a meeting.[95] The minutes of the meeting must reflect the reason for holding the closed meeting and the vote cast by each member by name either for or against closure.[96] Action taken in the closed meeting is restricted and cannot include approval of any ordinance, resolution, rule, regulation, contract, or appointment.[97]

Recognized reasons for closing a meeting are limited to the following: (1) discussion of the character, professional competence, or physical or mental health of an individual; (2) strategy sessions to discuss collective bargaining, pending or reasonably imminent litigation, or purchase, exchange, sale, or lease of real property; (3) discussion regarding deployment of security personnel, devices, or systems; and (4) investigative proceedings regarding allegations of criminal misconduct.[98]

Public Notice of Meetings[99]

Public meetings must be advertised. Regular meetings that are scheduled in advance over the course of a year shall give notice at least once each year of its annual meeting schedule and include the time, date, and place of the meetings. In addition, public notice must be given at least twenty-four hours before the meeting is convened. This public notice must contain not only the time, place, and date of the meeting but also the meeting agenda.

Public notification is satisfied by posting a written notice at the principal office of the public body or at the building where the meeting is to be held and providing notice to at least one newspaper of general circulation within the geographic jurisdiction of the public body or to a local media correspondent. In addition to the legal notice required, public notices for state-scheduled open meetings are routinely available on the Internet.

Access to Minutes and Audio Recordings

Minutes or digital recordings of open meetings are required and are accessible to the public. Records of closed meetings must also be made and kept. Those records are protected under Title 63, Chapter 2, Government Records Access and Management Act. Disclosure of records of a closed meeting can be made pursuant to a court order.

Listening to live audio or viewing live video of senate and house floor debate during the annual general session is now possible over the Internet. Live audio of interim committee meetings is also available. The legislature's homepage, www.le.utah.gov, is the electronic portal through which the debate and meetings are broadcast.

Government Records Access and Management Act

Access to government documents is an important component of open government. Recognizing two basic tenets, the public's right of access to information concerning the conduct of the public's business and the right of privacy in relation to personal data gathered by governmental entities, the legislature has facilitated public access to public documents.

The Government Records Access and Management Act,[100] enacted by the legislature in 1991, allows government documents to be classified as public, private, controlled, or protected and establishes the criteria for those classifications. The act establishes processes for the orderly examination and copying of government documents. The act establishes deadlines with which governmental entities must respond to information requests either by providing the requested documents or by stating the reasoning for denying access to the requested information. Appeals processes for information denials and fees for recouping costs incurred by agencies who provide access to records are also detailed in the act.

By making government documents and records available to the public, the legislature fulfills its intent to (1) promote the public's right of easy and reasonable access to unrestricted public records; (2) specify those conditions under which the public interest in allowing restrictions on access to records may outweigh the public's interest in access; (3) prevent abuse of confidentiality by governmental entities by permitting confidential treatment of records only as provided in the act; (4) provide guidelines for both disclosure and restrictions on access to government records, which are based on the equitable weighing of the pertinent interests and which are consistent with nationwide standards of information practices; (5) favor public access when, in the application of this act, countervailing interests are of equal weight; and (6) establish fair and reasonable records management practices.[101]

How to Request a Government Document

Utah's Government Records Access and Management Act establishes each person's right to inspect any public record free of charge during normal working hours and the right to take a copy of the record by paying a minimal fee.[102]

A person making a request for a record shall furnish the governmental entity with a written request containing the person's name, mailing address, daytime telephone number, if available, and a description of the records requested that identifies the record with reasonable specificity.[103]

LOBBYING AND LOBBYIST REGULATION

Lobbyists are individuals who are employed by, or who contract with an individual or entity to influence the legislative branch, executive branch, or both. They have a significant presence in public policy formation and their impact in the law-making process has resulted in legislation requiring disclosure and regulation of their activities.

Registration and Licensing

A person desiring to lobby the legislature must first register with and obtain a license from the lieutenant governor if the person is "employed by a principal or contracts for economic consideration, other than reimbursement for reasonable travel expenses, with a principal to lobby a public official."[104]

The lobbyist-applicant files the application and pays a $25 fee. The license entitles the lobbyist to lobby on behalf of one or more principals and expires on December 31 of each even-numbered year.

Denial of License

The lieutenant governor can suspend a lobbyist license for up to five years for any lobbyist who is convicted of bribery or offering a bribe, fraudulently altering the draft of any bill or resolution, fraudulently altering an enrolled copy of any bill or resolution, or preventing the legislature or public servants from meeting or organizing. The lieutenant governor can also suspend for up to one year a lobbyist license for any lobbyist who is: guilty of threatening any harm to a public servant, party official, or voter with the purpose of influencing that public servant's, party official's, or voter's action, decision, opinion, recommendation, nomination, vote, or other exercise of discretion; or guilty of disturbing the legislature or an official meeting.[105]

Disclosure of Expenditures[106]

Certain lobbyist expenditures for gifts to and entertainment of public officials are part of the public record and are found on the lieutenant governor's Web site.

An annual lobbyist financial report must be filed with the lieutenant governor's office by January 10 of each year. The report discloses expenditures exceeding a $50 daily limit made to benefit public officials or members of their immediate families.

Depending on the value of the expenditures made to benefit a public official, public officials may be listed by name in the disclosure report. The report will also disclose bills and resolutions by short titles that are the subject of the lobbyist's interest.

Lobbyist Ethics

Legislative rules establish a code of ethics for lobbyists.[107] Lobbyists are required to adhere to the highest standards of ethical conduct. Those standards include a requirement prohibiting lobbyists from attempting to influence any legislator, elected or appointed state official, state employee, or legislative employee through deceit or by threat of violence or economic or political reprisal, if the lobbyist's intent is to alter or affect decisions, votes, opinions, or other actions.[108]

A lobbyist may not knowingly provide false information, omit information, or conceal information in any manner on the lobbyist registration and disclosure reports. Lobbyists are prohibited from participating in committee assignments or legislative leadership races. Misusing legislative office supplies and equipment violates the code of ethics. Engaging in sexual harassment, offering employment to any legislator, and using or disclosing any records classified as private, protected, or controlled also violates the code of ethics.[109]

Enforcement of Ethical Rules Governing Lobbyists[110]

Legislators may file complaints, using procedures established in house and senate rules, alleging that a lobbyist has violated the lobbyist code of ethics. Legislative rules allow for any complaint of an ethics violation by a lobbyist be resolved by a legislative adjudication process outlined in house and senate rules. The rules also outline penalties that may be imposed for violation of the lobbyist code of ethics.

POLITICAL HISTORY

Party Control of the Legislature

During Utah's history as a state, fifty-six legislatures have been seated. Republicans have controlled the Utah House of Representatives thirty-nine of these legislatures and the Democrats have controlled the House the remaining seventeen. Senate Republicans have controlled the Utah State Senate for thirty-seven legislatures and the Democrats for nineteen.

Table 4-10[111]

Number of Seats and Political Affiliation of the Utah Legislature
1896 to 2005

Year	House				Senate				Total Both Houses
	Republican	Democrat	Other	Total	Republican	Democrat	Other	Total	
1896	31	14	0	45	12	6	0	18	63
1897	2	40	3	45	0	17	1	18	63
1899	15	26	4	45	2	14	2	18	63
1901	28	17	0	45	8	10	0	18	63
1903	38	7	0	45	12	6	0	18	63
1905	41	4	0	45	15	3	0	18	63
1907	37	8	0	45	18	0	0	18	63
1909	43	2	0	45	18	0	0	18	63
1911	37	8	0	45	16	2	0	18	63
1913	30	15	0	45	17	1	0	18	63
1915	23	19	4	46	12	5	1	18	64
1917	1	44	1	46	4	14	0	18	64
1919	10	37	0	47	0	18	0	18	65
1921	46	1	0	47	11	7	0	18	65
1923	45	10	0	55	19	1	0	20	75
1925	46	9	0	55	19	1	0	20	75
1927	49	6	0	55	19	1	0	20	75
1929	29	26	0	55	11	9	0	20	75
1931	41	14	0	55	11	9	0	20	75
1933	9	51	0	60	10	13	0	23	83
1935	4	56	0	60	4	19	0	23	83
1937	4	56	0	60	1	22	0	23	83
1939	15	45	0	60	2	21	0	23	83
1941	16	44	0	60	4	19	0	23	83
1943	21	39	0	60	6	17	0	23	83
1945	15	45	0	60	5	18	0	23	83
1947	39	21	0	60	11	12	0	23	83
1949	19	41	0	60	11	12	0	23	83
1951	30	30	0	60	8	15	0	23	83

Year	House				Senate				Total Both Houses
	Republican	Democrat	Other	Total	Republican	Democrat	Other	Total	
1953	39	21	0	60	15	8	0	23	83
1955	33	27	0	60	16	7	0	23	83
1957	40	23	1	64	15	10	0	25	89
1959	22	42	0	64	12	13	0	25	89
1961	28	36	0	64	11	14	0	25	89
1963	34	30	0	64	13	12	0	25	89
1965	30	39	0	69	12	15	0	27	96
1967	59	10	0	69	23	5	0	28	97
1969	48	21	0	69	20	8	0	28	97
1971	29	40	0	69	16	12	0	28	97
1973	44	31	0	75	16	13	0	29	104
1975	35	40	0	75	14	15	0	29	104
1977	40	35	0	75	12	17	0	29	104
1979	51	24	0	75	19	10	0	29	104
1981	58	17	0	75	22	7	0	29	104
1983	58	17	0	75	24	5	0	29	104
1985	61	14	0	75	23	6	0	29	104
1987	48	27	0	75	21	8	0	29	104
1989	48	27	0	75	22	7	0	29	104
1991	44	31	0	75	19	10	0	29	104
1993	49	26	0	75	18	11	0	29	104
1995	55	20	0	75	19	10	0	29	104
1997	55	20	0	75	20	9	0	29	104
1999	54	21	0	75	18	11	0	29	104
2001	51	24	0	75	20	9	0	29	104
2003	56	19	0	75	22	7	0	29	104
2005	56	19	0	75	21	8	0	29	104

Figure 4-1

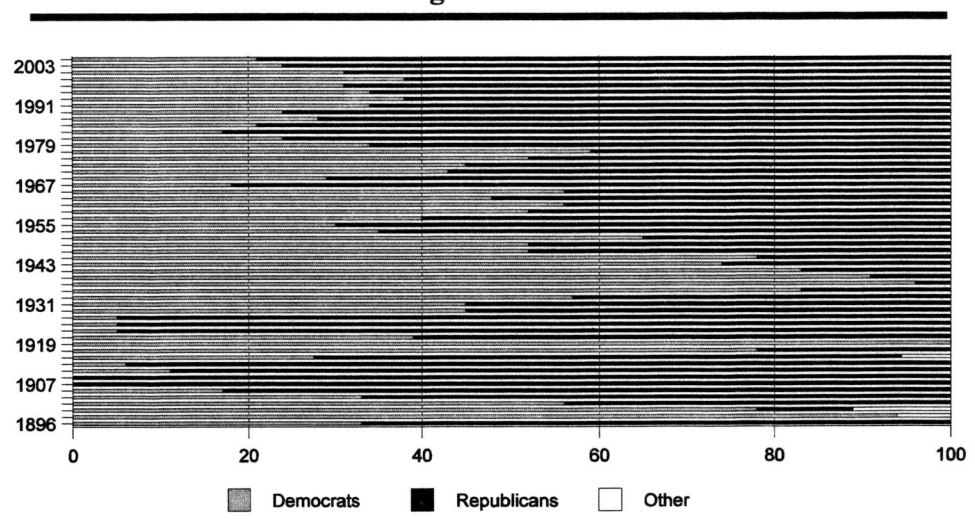

Figure 4-2

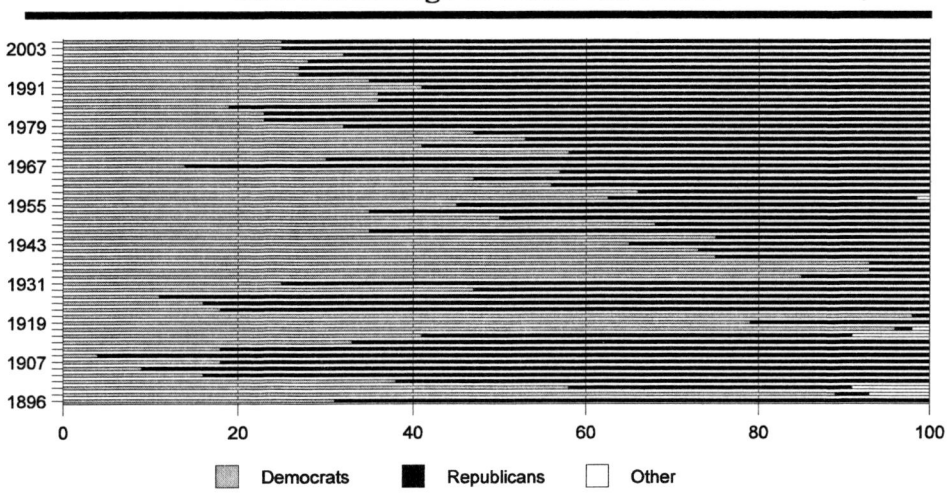

Party Control of the Governor's Office

Since statehood in 1896, sixteen governors have served Utah—eleven Republicans and five Democrats.

Table 4-11[112]

Governors of Utah 1896 to 2005		
Name	**Term of Office**	**Political Party Affiliation**
Heber Manning Wells	1896-1904	Republican
John Christopher Cutler	1905-1908	Republican
William Spry	1909-1916	Republican
Simon Bamberger	1917-1920	Democrat
Charles Rendell Mabey	1921-1924	Republican
George Henery Dern	1925-1932	Democrat
Henry Hooper Blood	1933-1940	Democrat
Herbert Brown Maw	1941-1948	Republican
Joseph Bracken Lee	1949-1956	Republican
George Dewey Clyde	1957-1964	Republican
Calvin Lewellyn Rampton	1965-1976	Democrat
Scott Milne Matheson	1977-1984	Democrat
Norman Howard Bangerter	1985-1992	Republican
Michael Okerlund Leavitt	1993-2003	Republican
Olene Smith Walker	2003-2004	Republican
Jon M. Huntsman, Jr.	2005-20xx	Republican

Chapter 5

The Executive Branch

At the federal level and in all fifty states, our governments are divided into three branches: legislative, executive, and judicial. The chief executive of the national government is the president and the chief executives of the fifty state governments are the governors. It is their responsibility, as head of their states, to see that the laws of their respective states are executed and to run the day-to-day operations of the executive branch under which almost all state agencies operate.

> **In this chapter:**
>
> Governor (p. 63)
> Lieutenant Governor (p. 75)
> Attorney General (p. 76)
> State Auditor (p. 79)
> State Treasurer (p. 80)
> Department of Administrative Services (p. 81)
> Division of Human Resource Management (p. 84)
> Retirement (p. 85)
> Department of Technology Services (p. 89)

Executive power in Utah was first officially granted by the 1850 Organic Act of the United States Congress. This act established the Territory of Utah, organized a territorial government, and gave executive power to a territorial governor. The territorial governor was not a locally elected individual. Instead, the governor was appointed by the president of the United States and held complete veto power over any legislation with no recourse by the territorial legislature. The executive authority continued in this powerful, non-elected arrangement until 1896 when Utah was granted statehood. At that time, the newly-written constitution of the State of Utah vested the executive power of government in an executive department consisting of a popularly elected governor, secretary of state, state auditor, state treasurer, attorney general, and superintendent of public instruction. The superintendent of public instruction and the secretary of state were removed from the constitution in 1950 and 1980 respectively.

Since 1984, the first election after the office of lieutenant governor was created in the Utah Constitution, the office of the lieutenant governor has essentially replaced the secretary of state. However, the executive branch is more than its executive officers; the executive function encompasses most operations of government. The average citizen usually comes in contact with this wide-ranging executive function at the "street level"—the social worker, highway engineer, highway patrol officer, park ranger, and numerous other state employees. This chapter will discuss the authority and duties of these executive officers, vital support organizations, and some important state and independent agencies.

GOVERNOR

Election Process

To be eligible for the office of governor, an individual must be a qualified voter, at least thirty years of age, and a resident of Utah for at least five years before the election. An individual cannot be an officer of the United States government while serving as governor (this prohibition applies to all state officers). The term of office for the governor is four years with no limit as to the number of terms an individual may serve. The governor is elected jointly with the lieutenant governor, and their names appear together on the election ballot. A vote for one is a vote for the other. This constitutional provision is important: if the governor and the lieutenant governor are elected separately (or if some other entity, such as the legislature appoints the lieutenant governor) there is the possibility of serious contention and acrimony at the head of the government. For example, by allowing the governor to choose the lieutenant governor, the state avoids the situation of a lieutenant governor who, as "acting governor," attempts to contravene the existing governor's agenda while the governor is out of the state on official business.

During the election, the candidate who receives the highest number of votes in the election wins the election. If there is a tie in the election for governor, the legislature votes on who shall take office.[1] According to state law, after the election, the Kearns Mansion in Salt Lake City is the official residence of the governor.[2] As with other state officers, the governor receives a salary in an amount established in statute.

Powers and Duties

The Utah Constitution vests all executive power of the state "in the [g]overnor who shall see that the laws are faithfully executed" and shall "transact all executive business."[3] The office of governor is quite powerful and is essential in the operation of government. Indeed, as the head of state government, the governor is constitutionally directed to exercise some authority within all the governmental powers including executive power, legislative power, judicial power, and military power.

Executive Power
Chief Executive

The term "chief executive" connotes ultimate administrative and managerial responsibility. According to former Governor Scott M. Matheson, the "management and operation of state government [is] the most significant and traditional gubernatorial role."[4] The governor oversees and directs all executive agencies and institutions in the state and supervises "the official conduct of all executive and ministerial officers."[5] The governor ensures that all executive offices are filled and communicates with department and agency leaders to provide policy direction. To help the governor maintain administrative control, state law allows the governor to require an officer, commission, or board to make special written reports at any time. As the chief executive, the governor is the sole official organ of communication between the government of the state and the government of any other state and of the United States. As boundaries slowly disappear in today's information age of high speed communication and economic mobility, the governor is not simply concerned with interests internal to the state, but must also look outward to develop relationships with regional, national, and even international entities.

Figure 5-1

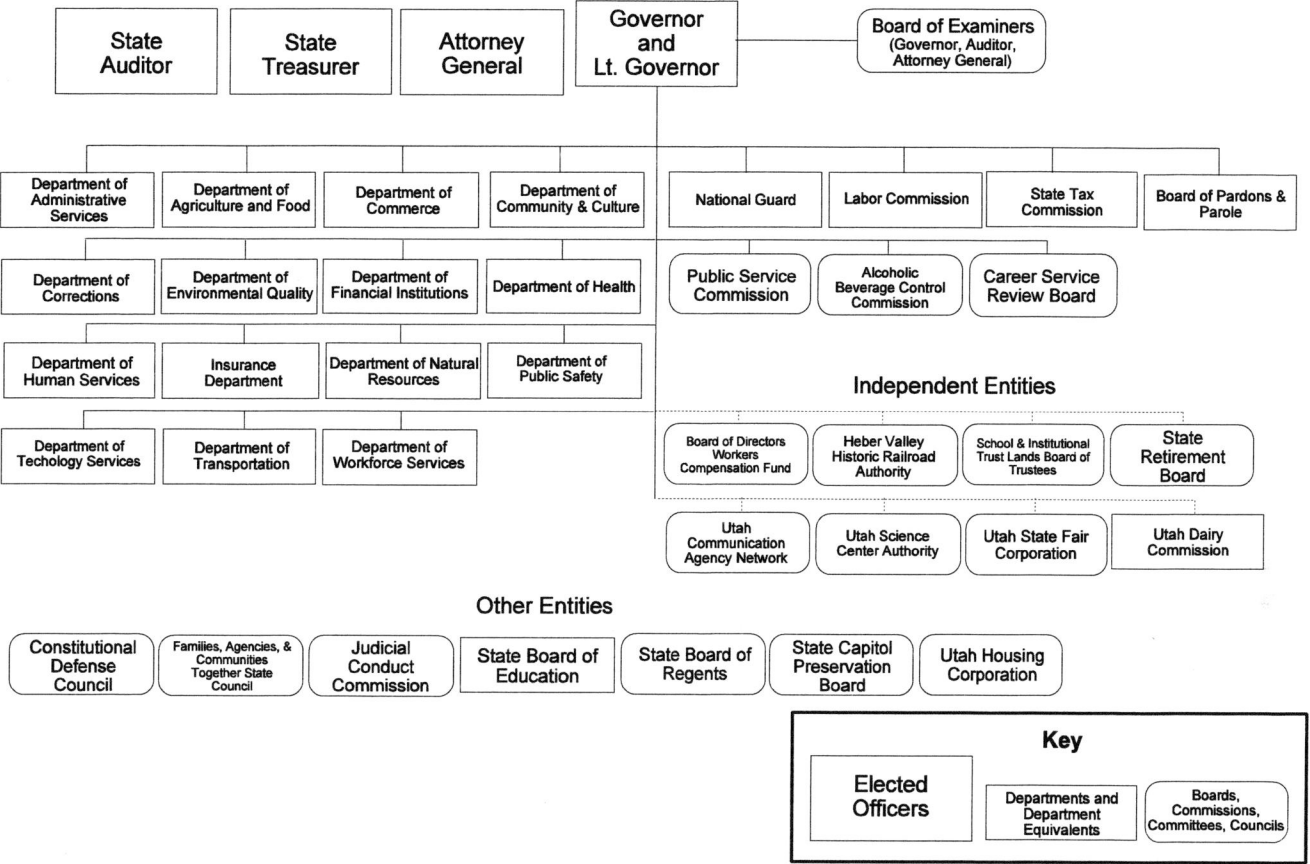

Appointive Powers

The Utah Constitution grants the governor the power to "nominate, and by and with consent of the Senate, appoint all State and district officers whose offices are established by [the] Constitution, or which may be created by law."[6] This power is crucial to the governor's ability to control the administration of government. Government operations are too large for the governor to supervise and manage single-handedly. Appointive powers allow the governor to place trusted individuals into key subordinate positions that assist the governor in executing state law and pursuing policy programs. This appointive power more fully allows the governor to be held accountable for governmental shortcomings than a system providing the governor with little control in choosing subordinate executive leadership.

The governor's appointive power essentially takes two forms. The first is the power to appoint executive department and agency heads that operate in a subordinate capacity to the governor. The Commissioner of Agriculture and the executive director of the Department of Commerce are examples of this type of office. These appointees usually serve "at the pleasure of the governor" and the governor wields significant political influence over them. The second aspect of the governor's appointment power is the filling of vacancies in positions of important government leadership. The governor is responsible to fill the vacancies in the following type of positions:

- Elected executive officers
- State judges
- Elected state senators and representatives
- Elected federal legislators

- Numerous executive boards and commissions

When filling vacancies of executive officers and board members, the governor immediately appoints a temporary replacement, who serves "until the next meeting of the Senate."[7] Once the senate meets, the governor then nominates a permanent replacement for the office. The governor has the authority to convene the senate in an extraordinary session for "transaction of executive business"[8] and has historically used this authority to get the required consent for an appointment.

As noted above, many of the governor's appointments—whether nominating individuals for executive agency positions or filling midterm vacancies—require the approval of the State Senate. Whenever a vacancy occurs in any position that requires senate approval, the governor must submit the name of a nominee to the senate for consent within three months of the vacancy in the office (unless specifically stipulated by state law).[9] If the senate does not approve the nominee, the office is considered vacant and the nominating process begins again. A majority vote is required to gain senate approval.

There are diverse procedures regulating all of the governor's various appointment responsibilities. Each method of appointment has a different effect on the governor's political influence and power concerning that position. Table 5-1 shows the conditions placed on the offices the governor is responsible for filling in the event of a vacancy.

Table 5-1

Method of Appointment in Event of Vacancy				
Type	Origin of Name(s) for Nomination	List Size	Senate Approval	Important Details
Lieutenant Governor	Governor	N/A	No	Holds office until the next general election when the governor is elected
Executive Officers[10]	State Central Committee	3	No	Must be from the same political party as prior officeholder
Agency Directors	Governor	N/A	Yes	Most serve "at the pleasure" of the governor
Judges	Judicial Nominating Commission	at least 3	Yes	The governor must appoint someone within 30 days after receiving the list of nominees
State Legislators	Political party	1	No	Must be from the same political party as prior officeholder
U.S. Representative	N/A	N/A	N/A	Governor must call a special election
U.S. Senator	State Central Committee	3	No	Same political party as the prior officeholder
Boards and Commissions	Governor, agency directors, legislative leadership, etc.		Sometimes	There are hundreds of these positions, most of which have specific term limits

Removal

While it is true that appointment power provides the governor with some degree of influence and control concerning subordinate executive leadership, that influence is not all-reaching. Even though the governor can easily remove an executive department appointee who serves "at the pleasure of the governor," removal of many other officers and board members is more protected. Although state law stipulates that at "any time during a recess of the legislature, the governor may remove any gubernatorial appointee for official misconduct, habitual or willful neglect of duty or other good and sufficient cause,"[11] it is often a difficult task to determine what is "sufficient cause."

Boards and Commissions

Utah has approximately 400 executive boards and committees including policy, advisory, and licensing boards and many nominating committees. Currently, the governor has the authority to appoint or confirm members to about 275 of these executive boards.[12] In addition to appointing many of the members to these boards, the governor must, according to state law, serve as a member of many boards and commissions, including:
- Board of Examiners
- Constitutional Defense Council
- Education Commission of the States
- Interstate Oil Compact Commission
- State Armory Board
- State Bonding Commission
- State Building Ownership Authority
- State Capitol Preservation Board

However, the governor may, and usually does, assign the lieutenant governor to serve in his place as a member on some of these boards.[13]

The governor issues an annual report of all executive boards and commissions and maintains a database containing information about all executive boards, commissions, committees, councils, task forces, advisory groups, working groups, or study groups.[14] To be included in the database, a board or commission must have a limited and defined membership, operate for more than six months, and be created by an executive branch official. This database is accessible to the public on the Internet.[15]

Budget

The budget is the most important public policy tool of the governor. It can also be a powerful political tool. Like most organizations, government requires money to operate and provide services. Thus, allocation of state funds to the various departments and agencies becomes not only a powerful executive function, but also an important policy instrument. Even though it is the legislature that determines the state budget and appropriates state funds, the governor is still able to emphasize policy directives by recommending statutory changes and proposing various increases or decreases in agency budgets. In simple terms, the budget process follows these general rules:
- The governor recommends a proposed budget—an estimate of the expected revenues to be received for a particular fiscal year—and a recommendation about how those revenues should be spent
- The governor submits the proposed budget to the legislature for its review
- The legislature passes a budget
- The governor implements and administers the budget passed by the legislature

The governor's proposed budget is a projection of revenues and a program of expenditures for the next fiscal year. By law, the budget must list all assets, liabilities, reserves, appropriations, surpluses, deficits, anticipated deficits, debts, and funds of the state.[16] This list includes an itemized estimate of appropriations for the legislature and its supporting offices, all executive departments, the judicial department, all debts, and all salaries mandated by law. For comparison purposes, it also charts the previous year's revenues and expenditures.

The director of the Governor's Office of Planning and Budget is also the "Federal Assistance Management Officer" and as such studies the administration and effect of federal assistance programs in the state. The director advises the governor (and the legislature through the Office of

Legislative Fiscal Analyst and the Executive Appropriations Committee) of recommended alternative methods and procedures for the administration of these federal assistance programs.

When proposing the budget, the governor is not free to apportion money in whatever way he chooses. By law, "on-going appropriations" cannot be altered by the governor. Likewise, the governor does not have the authority to redirect earmarked funds such as income tax revenues, which are constitutionally required to fund public and higher education.

By law, the governor has three days to submit the budget for the next fiscal year to the legislature once it has convened in annual general session. The budget is submitted to the presiding officer of each house of the legislature. The legislature considers the governor's proposed budget and then appropriates the monies in what becomes the official budget.

Governor's Office of Planning and Budget

It is impossible for the governor to single-handedly prepare such an enormous and complicated document as the proposed state budget. The governor is assisted in preparing the budget by the Governor's Office of Planning and Budget (GOPB). GOPB combines the state budget office and the state planning coordinator under one office headed by a director who is appointed by the governor. The state planning coordinator is also appointed by the governor and acts as the governor's adviser on state, regional, metropolitan, and local governmental planning matters relating to public improvements and land use. Overall, GOPB provides coordination and leadership for policy issues and initiatives of the governor. As part of the budgetary process, GOPB receives itemized estimates of revenues and expenditures from every state department, agency, institution, board, commission, and bureau that applies for state funds and appropriations. With the governor's direction, GOPB then prepares an itemized budget document which balances state expenditures and revenues and recommends an appropriation amount for each state department, agency, institution, board, commission, and bureau.

Executive Orders

The governor has the power to issue executive orders. There are three basic types of governor's executive orders:

1. Formal, ceremonious, and political orders, usually issued as a proclamation—often used to proclaim a day of honor or to publicly commemorate an event
2. Communication with subordinate officials regarding requests or directions for the execution of the duties of the executive branch
3. Orders that have the force of law—usually requires some constitutional or statutory provision that authorizes the executive order

Emergency Power

The governor is given special executive authority during times of emergency or disaster. In these situations, the governor is responsible for the continuity of government operations and essential services. For example, under the provisions of the Disaster Response and Recovery Act,[17] in a state of emergency the governor may:

- Use all available resources of state government to cope with the emergency
- Suspend the sale, dispensing, or transportation of alcoholic beverages, explosives, and combustibles
- Clear private or public land of anything threatening public safety
- Temporarily suspend or modify laws or regulations to be able to provide housing for disaster victims
- Suspend provisions of any order or rule of any state agency if doing so helps respond to the emergency

- Promulgate orders and rules that have the full force of law
- Purchase or lease public or private land in compliance with existing eminent domain law

The governor may also declare an "energy emergency."[18] This type of emergency may exist if there is a severe disruption or shortage in the supply of energy resources that threatens the availability of essential state services or endangers the public health and safety. In these wide-ranging circumstances, the governor may restrict, curtail, adjust, or allocate energy resources in the state in an attempt to alleviate the emergency situation.

Governor's Legislative Power
Policy Innovator

The governor is often seen as a policy innovator. While the governor does not legislate in the classic sense of the term, the governor acts as an issue catalyst. He picks the issues and sets the state policy agenda. As a single voice, it is easy for the governor to powerfully define issues and set standards. Constitutionally, the governor is to recommend to the legislature any "measures as may be deemed expedient."[19] One important way the governor accomplishes this mandate is during the annual "State of the State" address. During the address, the governor highlights policy programs and legislative desires—the things that the governor hopes that the legislature will act on. However, the governor is not limited to a single address; frequently, the governor uses public appearances, press conferences, media interviews, and private correspondence to promote his policy initiative.

The governor's influence on legislation is not limited to the state level. State governors are sometimes referred to as "federal systems officers."[20] This term connotes the governor's influence on federal policy concerning not only individual states but all states in general. When necessary, the governor travels to Washington, D.C. in an effort to influence federal spending and policy concerning all states. Additionally, the governor often works through the National Governors Association to help shape and implement national policy and to solve state problems. Over the last couple of decades the National Governors Association has become a significant force in influencing national policy.

Veto Power

The governor does have one very powerful direct legislative power, the veto. Each bill passed by the legislature must be presented to the governor. Once a bill has been received from the legislature, the governor must do one of four things:
1. Sign the bill
2. Do nothing (which allows the bill to take effect without written approval by the governor)
3. Veto the bill and return it to the legislature
4. If it is an appropriations bill, veto part(s) of the bill and sign the remaining parts into law[21]

If the governor signs the bill, it becomes state law. If the governor is presented with a bill during the legislative session, and the governor does nothing, within ten days (not counting Sunday or the day the bill is received) the bill becomes law without a signature. If the legislature has adjourned, the governor has twenty days to act before it becomes law without a signature. If the governor dislikes the bill, the governor may reject and return it with the written objections to it. This is called a veto. The governor must veto the bill within the time frames mentioned above or the bill becomes a law.[22] However, any law that is enacted by the voters through the initiative process cannot be vetoed by the governor.

If a bill is vetoed and returned with the governor's objections, the legislature may reconsider the bill. After reconsideration, the legislature may vote to override the governor's veto. To override the governor's veto, the legislature must obtain at least a two-thirds vote of all members elected to the legislature in both the Utah State Senate and the Utah House of Representatives. If the governor returns the bill after the legislature has adjourned, the legislature may reconvene to override the gubernatorial veto.[23]

The governor was given "line-item" veto powers by a constitutional amendment in 1980. If a bill is an appropriations bill, the governor can veto specific items from the bill without vetoing the entire bill.

The veto is often considered the governor's most significant legislative power. The veto involves the governor in the legislative process in both direct and indirect ways. Often, it is the unspoken threat of veto that helps shape legislative language and content. The governor's veto can also provide the governor with administrative powers by limiting executive agencies from gaining support in a "legislative end run around the governor's adverse budget decision."[24] Indeed, the veto can alter the governor's relationship with the legislature for the worse. It may increase the formal confrontations between the two branches of government, which in turn lead to legislative procedures that neutralize or lessen the impact of the gubernatorial veto. The veto can also lead to increased litigation between the two branches.

Power to Convene Special Sessions

Another legislative power of the governor is the authority to convene a special session of the legislature. During the special session, the legislature is only authorized to discuss the item (or items) relevant to the purpose for which the session was called.[25] The governor must give at least forty-eight hours of advance public notice of the purpose of the special session.

Governor's Judicial Power

Judicial Appointment

The governor has a limited but important role in the Utah judicial system: the responsibility to nominate and appoint judges and justices in the state courts. The governor must nominate an individual from a list generated by the appropriate Judicial Nominating Commission. This nomination must then be approved by a majority vote of all members of the senate before the nominee is appointed to the position.[26] The governor also appoints members to both the Trial and Appellate Nominating Commissions, which are the judicial nominating commissions that generate the lists of individuals for judge or justice from which the governor can choose.

Pardons

The governor has only a limited power of executive clemency. Unlike some chief executives in other states, the governor of Utah cannot pardon a conviction. Instead, the governor may grant a respite or reprieve of a conviction until the next session of the Board of Pardons. The Board of Pardons then has the power to continue the governor's respite or reprieve, commute the punishment, or pardon an offense. The governor's power of respite and reprieve does not extend to convictions of treason or impeachment. In case of treason, the governor may suspend the sentence until the case is reported to the legislature at the next annual general session, where the legislature then decides to pardon, commute, or execute the sentence.[27] The governor also appoints all the members of the Board of Pardons with the consent of the senate.[28]

Extradition

Extradition is the surrender of an alleged criminal from one state to another state that has criminal jurisdiction to prosecute the individual. State law,[29] federal law,[30] and the federal constitution[31] all obligate the governor to extradite any person who has fled justice from another state and is found in Utah. In this situation, the governor may call upon the attorney general for help in investigating extradition demands of another state.[32] If the governor refuses to extradite the fugitive to another state for whatever reason, that state may seek to enforce extradition through an order of mandamus in federal court.[33] Of course, the reverse is also true: the governor may demand the return of any fugitive to Utah from another state and seek compliance through the judiciary if the demand is refused.[34]

Military Power
Commander in Chief

The governor commands the state's militia except when it is called into service by the United States government.[35] The governor may order into active service the National Guard, the unorganized militia, or portions of either as necessary.[36] The unorganized militia, with certain exceptions, consists of able-bodied citizens who are not members of the National Guard.[37] Reasons the governor may order the National Guard or militia into active duty may include disaster, emergency, or to "execute the laws, to suppress insurrection, or to repel invasion."[38] Historically, the governor has used the National Guard to assist local authorities in times of natural disaster. The governor is empowered to issue all orders and regulations concerning the organization, discipline, training, equipment, and maintenance of the state militia as necessary to conform to federal law. As the commander in chief, the governor appoints and commissions all officers of the state militia.[39]

Comparison of Gubernatorial Powers

Over the past fifty years, political scientists have maintained data on the institutional powers of the governors of the fifty states. Institutional powers are the powers given the governor by the state constitution or state statutes. These powers are "the structure into which the governor moves on being elected to office."[40] Table 5-2, created by Thad Beyle, charts the following six important institutional powers held by governors:

1. *Separately Elected Executive Branch Officials (SEP).* The more executive branch officials that are separately elected, the less institutional power of the governor.
2. *Tenure Potential (TP).* The longer the term of office and the greater number of terms the governor can serve, the greater the potential power.
3. *Appointment Power (AP).* The greater number of positions the governor may appoint and the fewer constraints on those appointments, the greater potential power.
4. *Budget Powers (BP).* The more responsibility the governor has over the budget with the least amount of oversight, the greater the gubernatorial power.
5. *Veto Powers (VP).* The stronger the veto powers, the greater the gubernatorial power.
6. *Party Control (PC).* If the governor's party controls the legislature, there should be more cooperation and gubernatorial power.

Each category is assigned a numeric score from one to five. The higher the score, the greater the governor's power in that category. A complete explanation of the scoring method is provided in the endnotes.[41] It is interesting to note that the Utah governor has, along with Illinois and New York, the highest-rated governor's institutional power score (GIP). The GIP is calculated by taking the total of all the institutional powers scores and dividing it by six. Of course, this index is not an exact predictor of a governor's power (or personal and professional ability). Nevertheless, it is an indicator of the structural powers of the governor's office. Comparatively speaking, Utah's governor has extensive institutional power granted by the constitution and statute.

Table 5-2

Governors' Institutional Powers
2002

State	SEP	TP	AP	BP	VP	PC	Total	GIP
Alabama	1	4	2	3	4	2	16	2.7
Alaska	5	4	3	3	5	4	24	4
Arizona	2	4	2.5	3	5	1	17.5	2.9
Arkansas	2.5	4	2.5	3	4	2	18	3
California	1	4	3.5	3	5	4	20.5	3.4
Colorado	4	4	3	3	5	4	23	3.8
Connecticut	4	5	3.5	3	5	2	22.5	3.8
Delaware	2.5	4	3.5	3	5	3	21	3.5
Florida	3	4	1.5	3	5	4	20.5	3.4
Georgia	1	4	1	3	5	3	17	2.8
Hawaii	5	4	3	3	5	2	22	3.7
Idaho	2	4	2	3	5	5	21	3.5
Illinois	4	5	3.5	3	5	4	24.5	4.1
Indiana	3	4	3.5	3	2	3	18.5	3.1
Iowa	3	5	3.5	3	5	2	21.5	3.6
Kansas	3	4	3.5	3	5	2	20.5	3.4
Kentucky	3	4	3.5	3	4	3	20.5	3.4
Louisiana	1	4	3.5	3	5	2	18.5	3.1
Maine	5	4	4.5	3	2	4	22.5	3.8
Maryland	4	4	3	5	5	2	23	3.8
Massachusetts	4	4	3.5	3	5	1	20.5	3.4
Michigan	4	4	3.5	3	5	2	21.5	3.6
Minnesota	4	5	4	3	5	3	24	4
Mississippi	1.5	4	3	3	5	4	20.5	3.4
Missouri	2.5	4	2.5	3	5	2	19	3.2
Montana	3	4	2.5	3	5	4	21.5	3.6
Nebraska	3	4	3	4	5	3	22	3.7
Nevada	2.5	4	3.5	3	2	3	18	3
New Hampshire	5	2	3	3	2	4	19	3.2
New Jersey	5	4	3.5	3	5	3	23.5	3.9
New Mexico	3	4	3	3	5	4	22	3.7
New York	4	5	3.5	4	5	3	24.5	4.1
North Carolina	1	4	3.5	3	2	3	16.5	2.8
North Dakota	3	5	3.5	3	5	4	23.5	3.9
Ohio	4	4	3.5	3	5	4	23.5	3.9

State	SEP	TP	AP	BP	VP	PC	Total	GIP
Oklahoma	1	4	1.5	3	5	4	18.5	3.1
Oregon	1.5	4	3	3	5	3	19.5	3.3
Pennsylvania	4	4	4	3	5	2	22	3.7
Rhode Island	2.5	4	4	3	2	1	16.5	2.8
South Carolina	1	4	2.5	2	5	4	18.5	3.1
South Dakota	3	4	3.5	3	5	4	22.5	3.8
Tennessee	4.5	4	4	3	4	4	23.5	3.9
Texas	1	5	1.5	2	5	4	18.5	3.1
Utah	**4**	**4.5**	**3**	**3**	**5**	**5**	**24.5**	**4.1**
Vermont	2.5	2	5	3	2	2	16.5	2.8
Virginia	2.5	3	3.5	3	5	2	19	3.2
Washington	1	4	3	3	5	3	19	3.2
West Virginia	2	4	4	5	5	4	24	4
Wisconsin	3	5	3.5	3	5	2	21.5	3.6
Wyoming	2	4	3.5	3	5	2	19.5	3.3

SOURCES: For SEP, CSG 2002, 161-168; TP CSG 2002, 145-146; AP, CSG 2002, 34-37; BP, CSG 2000, 20-21 and NCSL 1998; VP, GSG 2002, 104-105 and 150-151; NCSL 2003.

Vacancy in the Office of Governor

Vacancy

The Utah Constitution provides for an orderly transfer of executive power if a vacancy occurs in the office of governor. If the governor is impeached, resigns, or is otherwise incapacitated, the duties of governor fall to the following officers in this order: (1) lieutenant governor, (2) president of the Utah State Senate, and (3) speaker of the Utah House of Representatives.[42]

In 2003, despite an orderly transfer of executive power, there was some debate about whether the lieutenant governor actually becomes the governor or becomes an *acting* governor. The constitution states the "powers and duties of the Governor shall devolve upon the Lieutenant Governor."[43] Some experts understand this language to mean the lieutenant governor stays the lieutenant governor but has the powers and duties of the governor—an acting governor. Others argue that the phrase "shall devolve" means "succession" and the lieutenant governor becomes the governor—with the important authority to appoint a new lieutenant governor. Concerning this matter, the Utah attorney general in 2003 issued an opinion stating the phrase "shall devolve" means the lieutenant governor succeeds to the office of governor and becomes governor, following the example of the president and vice president of the United States.[44] Nevertheless, the issue has not been settled in a Utah court. Concerning the president of the senate and the speaker of the house, it is much clearer in the law that one becomes an *acting* governor.

Emergency Interim Governor

Utah state law provides for a possible major emergency or disaster in which neither the governor nor any of the replacement officers listed above are available to exercise the powers and duties of the office of governor. In this situation the executive powers fall to the following officers in this order: (1) attorney general, (2) state auditor, and (3) state treasurer.[45]

In this emergency situation, the interim governor exercises the powers and duties of the office of governor "until the governor, lieutenant governor, president of the senate, or speaker of the house becomes available or a new governor is elected and qualified."[46] Again, in this situation, it is clear that the replacement becomes the *acting* governor, not *the* governor.

Impeachment

The governor is subject to impeachment for high crimes, misdemeanors, or malfeasance in office.[47] Impeachment is a criminal proceeding instituted against a public official by the legislature. Impeachment is a two step process: the impeachment hearing and the trial hearing. The impeachment hearing is conducted by the Utah House of Representatives which has the "sole power of impeachment,"[48] or the sole power to bring charges against the governor (or other state or judicial officer). For the governor to be impeached, a two-thirds vote of all elected members of the Utah House of Representatives is required.

If the impeachment vote is successful, the senate then tries the impeachment. The chief justice of the supreme court presides at the trial if the governor is being tried. A two-thirds vote of all elected members of the senate are needed to convict the governor (or other state or judicial officer). If the governor is convicted, the judgment may be that the governor is suspended or removed from office and disqualified to hold any office in state government. Whether the governor is convicted or not, the governor may still be criminally prosecuted or brought before a civil court.

Office Organization

The organization of the governor's office may change from administration to administration; however, some parts of the office organization, like the Governor's Office of Planning and Budget and the Commission of Criminal and Juvenile Justice, are mandated by statute. Of course, with every new administration, some or all of the staff may change.

See figure 5-2 for the organization of the governor's office as of August 2005.

Figure 5-2

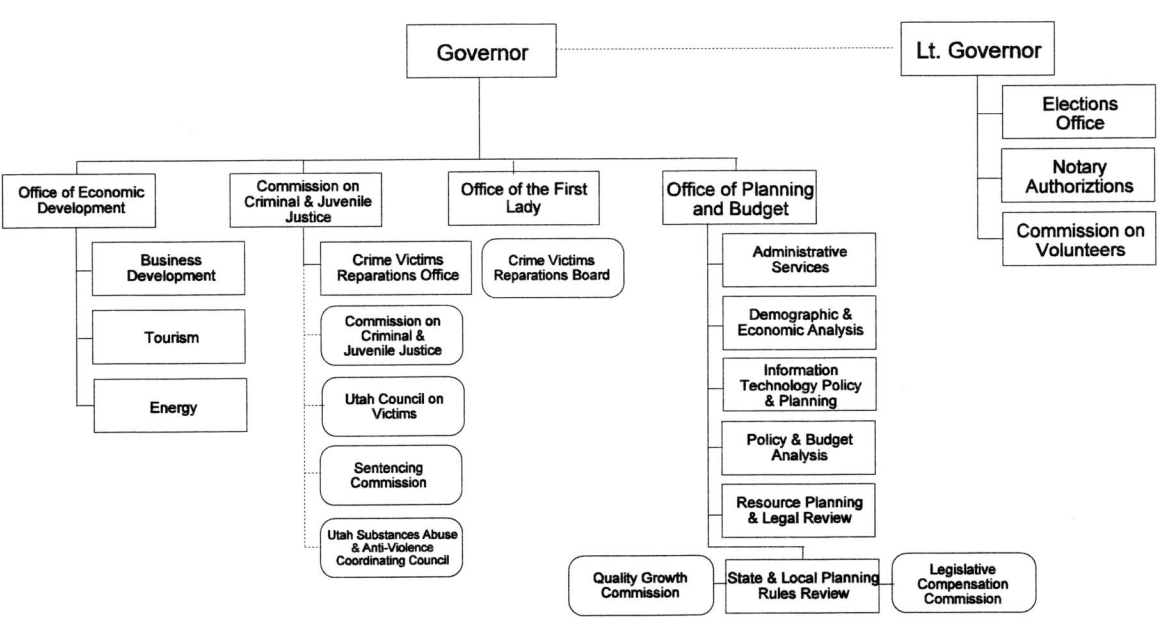

LIEUTENANT GOVERNOR

The lieutenant governor is "the second highest official of the state"[49] and is responsible for the maintenance of the government should the office of the governor be vacated for any reason. As noted earlier, the office of lieutenant governor is a relatively recent position. This office was first created by statute in 1975. At this time, the lieutenant governor took over all statutory duties of the secretary of state with the secretary of state retaining all constitutional duties. At that time, the acting secretary of state became, *ex officio*, the first lieutenant governor. In 1980, by constitutional amendment, the office of secretary of state was repealed and the office of lieutenant governor become a constitutionally-mandated executive office.[50] In 1984 (in accordance with the legislation passed in 1980), the governor and lieutenant governor were placed on the ballot together for the first time. In Utah, the lieutenant governor has "significant responsibilities and duties"[51] that include governor's adviser, acting secretary of state, and chief election officer.

Governor's Adviser

The office of lieutenant governor allows for continuity of political ideology as well as government operations. Electing both the governor and the lieutenant governor at the same time was intended to eliminate any extreme shift in political ideology if the office of governor is vacated. The political closeness of these two offices also allows the lieutenant governor to act as a personal adviser to the governor on policy and administrative matters as well as be assigned to serve on any board or commission in lieu of the governor. The governor may assign or delegate most duties to the lieutenant governor.

State law gives the governor wide latitude in assignments given to the lieutenant governor. For example, the lieutenant governor may be assigned to act as the head of any executive department with the consent of the senate (and without any additional monetary compensation). Moreover, the governor may assign the lieutenant governor to act as the chair of any cabinet group that advises the governor or coordinates intergovernmental or interdepartmental policies or programs. The lieutenant governor can act as liaison between the governor and the state legislature to coordinate and facilitate the governor's programs and budget requests. The lieutenant governor may also act as liaison between the governor and other officials of local, state, federal, international governments, or any other political entities to coordinate, facilitate, and protect the interests of the state.

Acting Secretary of State

The lieutenant governor still performs most of the duties that were once fulfilled by the secretary of state. By law, any reference in the Utah Code to the secretary of state is considered a reference to the lieutenant governor. Moreover, when required by local, state, federal, or international law, the lieutenant governor is designated the secretary of state and performs the duties and functions required by those laws.[52]

The function of the lieutenant governor, when acting as the secretary of state, includes such things as attesting or certifying documents and recording and storing laws and other official documents. In these capacities, the lieutenant governor oversees the state authentication and notarizations offices and maintains the official state registry of all official acts, documents, and instruments that require the governor's official signature. As custodian of records, the lieutenant governor must furnish a certified copy of any record to any person who requests it and pays the fee. Additionally, by constitutional directive, the lieutenant governor keeps custody of the Great Seal of Utah.[53]

Chief Election Officer

One of the most important duties of the lieutenant governor is to serve as Utah's "chief election officer."[54] In this capacity, the lieutenant governor ensures the integrity of the state's elections by exercising direct supervisory authority over federal, state, and county elections, including public initiatives and referendums. This supervisory authority also extends to any recounts of these elections if necessary.

As chief election officer, the lieutenant governor has considerable authority and responsibility for elections. Past lieutenant governors have created a State Elections Office, to assist the lieutenant governor in carrying out these responsibilities. The lieutenant governor's election duties also include:
- Assisting county clerks in unifying the election ballot
- Preparing election information for the public and making it available to the news media
- Receiving and answering any election questions from the government or the public
- Maintaining an election file on opinions received from the attorney general
- Maintaining election returns and statistics
- Certifying to the governor the names of those persons who have received the highest number of votes for any state office
- Performing certain other duties required by federal laws, such as overseeing the National Motor Voter Registration Act and the Help America Vote Act

Despite playing a powerful role in the election process, the lieutenant governor cannot assume any of the regular responsibilities assigned to the county clerks, city recorders, town clerks, or other local election officials.

ATTORNEY GENERAL

The position of attorney general has a long history dating back to medieval England when the king appointed a special attorney to represent the legal interests of the crown. Over the years, the authority of this office gradually expanded until the attorney general of England "emerged as foremost legal adviser to all departments of government and the principal representative of the government's interest in litigation."[55] In this form, the office of attorney general carried over from the British system to the American colonies and eventually to the new American state and federal governments.

In January 1850, the Utah provisional government (in anticipation to becoming a territory) passed an ordinance that created the office of Utah attorney general. This office was to be elected by the legislature for a term of four years. In 1851, the first territorial legislature firmly established the position of attorney general in Utah. However, some of the fledgling territorial ordinances concerning the legal power of Utah's probate court "created a jurisdictional conflict with the federal government" and in 1874 the U.S. Congress passed the Poland Act repealing the office of Utah Attorney General.[56] Consequently, Utah did not have an attorney general until twenty-two years later, when it was granted statehood in 1896.

With the new state constitution, the position of attorney general was reinstated in the Utah government, but this time as a popularly-elected executive officer. According to the constitution, to be eligible for the office of attorney general an individual must be at least twenty-five years of age, a resident of Utah for at least five years, admitted to practice before the Utah Supreme Court, and be a member in good standing of the Utah State Bar.[57] The attorney general is elected every four years in the general election at the same time as the governor and the lieutenant governor and serves a four-year term.[58] There is no limit to the number of terms that the attorney general may serve. As an executive officer, the attorney general is subject to impeachment.

The office of attorney general is charged with much responsibility and wide-ranging authority. In fact, the attorney general occupies "the middle of a well-traveled intersection of law, politics, and public policy, delicately, sometimes even perilously, poised between the tensions of scholarship and activism; professional responsibility and public duty; political conflict and the search for legal certainty."[59] The important roles fulfilled by the Utah attorney general include legal adviser, criminal prosecutor, and public advocate.[60]

Legal Adviser of State Officers

The attorney general is the chief law officer of the state and acts as "the legal adviser of the state officers."[61] As chief legal adviser, the attorney general conducts legal business such as:
- Prosecuting for and defending the state in courts of justice
- Acting as legal adviser of state officers
- Preparing legal documents and instruments
- Giving legal opinions regarding questions of law

In addition, unless specifically permitted by law, the attorney general has the "sole right to hire legal counsel"[62] for state executive agencies.

There are some limitations to the attorney general's authority as adviser to state officers. The governor may appoint legal counsel to advise the governor as a result of a constitutional amendment passed in 1992.[63] Certain agencies or organizations that the legislature (or constitution) has created to be independent of executive control are not within the advisory jurisdiction of the attorney general. Generally, these independent agencies administer no public moneys, and are not under the direct supervision or control of an executive department agency or officer. In addition, if a regular state executive officer such as the state treasurer serves on a non-executive agency or board, such as the Utah State Retirement Board, this state officer is not bound to the attorney general's legal direction while acting in this independent capacity.[64] The legislature and the judicial department each have constitutional authority to appoint their own legal counsel to provide all legal services.[65]

Opinions

The attorney general is instructed by statute to "give the attorney general's opinion in writing and without fee"[66] to the legislature, any state officer, board, commission, county attorney, or district attorney. This mandate to advise state officers is one of the attorney general's original functions and continues to be one of the most important. Opinions can take many forms including formal opinions and informal opinions.

Informal opinions include any direct correspondence between the client agency and the attorney general's office including letters, memoranda, and oral advice. If the client desires the opinion to be memorialized, the opinion will usually be put into letter format. Most of these informal opinions, whether they are verbal or written, are not public information due to the strict attorney-client privilege that must be maintained by the Office of the Attorney General.

Formal opinions are infrequent and are written only on issues that are of major (usually state-wide) importance and controversy. These opinions are generally published and accessible online.[67] These formal opinions provide valuable guidance to state executive officials and agencies, but are not binding upon courts although courts generally give attorney general opinions "substantial weight and due consideration."[68] When it comes to the actual writing of an opinion, the State Agency Counsel Division prepares the majority of the attorney general's opinions.

Litigation Control

Utah statutes grant the attorney general the power to determine the state's legal policy by initiating legal action on behalf of the state.[69]

Criminal Prosecutor
Chief Prosecutor

The attorney general is the chief prosecutor in Utah.[70] The attorney general exercises supervision over the district and county attorneys and has the final control of litigation and appeals. Utah courts have determined that, in the absence of express legislative restriction, the attorney general has the authority to prosecute any criminal activity.[71] This gives the attorney general extremely wide-ranging powers of prosecution concerning perceived criminal activity throughout the state. Usually, the Criminal Division of the attorney general's office assists county attorneys in homicide cases and other complex matters and takes the lead in prosecution of multi-county cases and conflict-of-interest cases. Through the Criminal Division, the attorney general employs specialized prosecutors who cover a wide range of criminal prosecutions including insurance fraud, narcotics enforcement, medicaid fraud, welfare fraud, and criminal fraud.

Investigator

An important part of prosecution is investigation. The Office of the Attorney General has broad investigation authority. The Investigation Division investigates multi-county and multi-victim cases involving white-collar crime, organized crime, government corruption, computer crime, criminal real estate fraud, and child abuse. This division also assists in major street crime investigations, such as homicide, when requested by local authorities.

Public Advocacy

In the past, the duty of the attorney general was to represent the king, or the sovereign. In today's representative democracy, the courts have affirmed that the attorney general's duty remains to the sovereign—the state's citizens—rather than to the "machinery of government."[72] Public advocacy is a broad term; it can range from "child support enforcement, consumer protection, antitrust action, rate and utility regulation and advocacy to the provision of services to crime victims."[73] The Utah courts have determined that the attorney general has the duty to intervene in legal proceedings on behalf of the public interest because the attorney general is in a much more informed and advantageous position to bring a suit than the individual citizen.[74]

Office Organization

Figure 5-3

Attorney General's Office

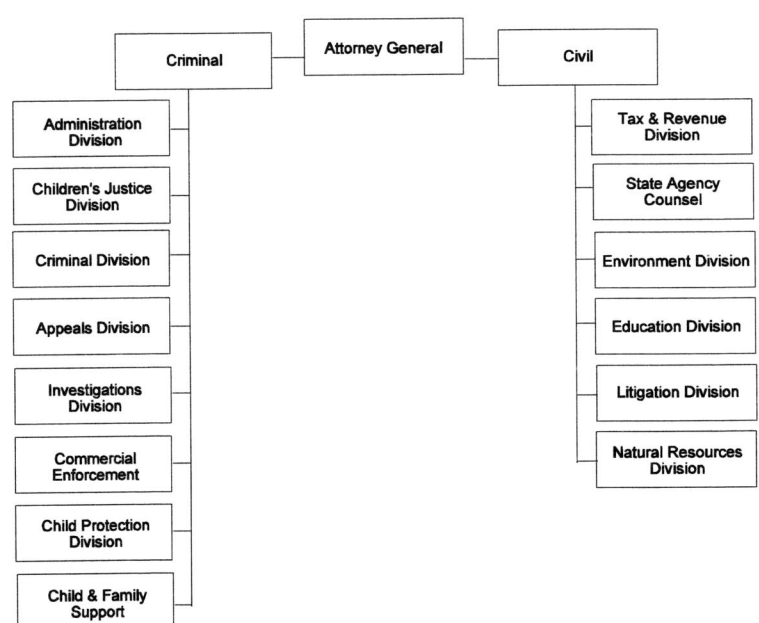

STATE AUDITOR

The Utah Constitution provides for a state auditor who is a popularly-elected executive officer. To be eligible for this office, an individual must be at least twenty-five years of age and a qualified voter who has been a resident citizen of Utah for at least five years prior to election.[75] The state auditor audits the state's accounts and agencies and is independent of other executive or administrative officers of the state.[76] This independence is important because the state auditor strives to objectively ensure that public funds are spent appropriately and lawfully in accordance with federal, state, and local law.[77]

The state auditor's operations are process-oriented. The state auditor primarily conducts fiscal post audits, ensures there is no fraud or abuse of public funds, determines the reliability of financial statements and adequacy of internal controls and the degree of compliance with legal and contractual requirements, reviews revenues and expenditures and encumbrances, and ensures compliance to legal and contractual requirements and procedure.

Recently, the legislature amended the state auditor's duties to allow the office to conduct performance and special-purpose audits.[78]

Fiscal Audits

The state auditor closely reviews revenues received or accrued, expenditures paid or accrued, the amount of unexpended or unencumbered balances of the appropriations to the agencies, departments, divisions, commissions, and institutions, and the cash balances of the funds in the custody of the state treasurer. Through the process of the audit, the state auditor ensures that the government entity maintains honesty and integrity in fiscal affairs, accuracy and reliability of financial statements, effectiveness and adequacy of financial controls, and compliance with state and federal law.

Other Powers

The state auditor is granted broad authority in Utah statute concerning both internal and external operations. For example, the state auditor is not limited in the selection of personnel or in the determination of the reasonable and necessary expenses of his office.[79] Equally, the office has the jurisdiction to audit all the state's permanent and special funds, state agencies and departments, independent agencies, and public corporations.[80] State law gives the auditor "access to all offices of public entities during business hours for the inspection of their records, regardless of any general limitation on access to records provided in an entity's individual statute."[81] The state auditor may also stop the payment of the salary of any state official or state employee who refuses to comply with the instructions of the state auditor, controlling board, or department head concerning financial procedures. Additionally, the state auditor can withhold state-allocated funds or the disbursement of property taxes from any state taxing or fee-assessing unit to ensure that those organizations comply with state budgeting and financial reporting laws and procedures.[82]

Under the Government Records Access and Management Act, the auditor has the authority to control and protect public access to records for a variety of reasons. These types of records include those that would incriminate a public employee, disclose the identity of a government whistle blower, and records that would disclose an outline of any audit survey plans or audit program. The auditor has the authority to disclose records of this type at the auditor's discretion.[83]

There are, of course, constraints placed on the state auditor's authority. The office must conform to the generally accepted government auditing standards and procedures. Also, the state auditor cannot audit work that the auditor performed before becoming state auditor. When this conflict arises, the legislature is required to designate how the work is to be audited.

Agency Organization
There are three divisions within the state auditor's office:
- *Financial Audit Division*. This division is responsible for fiscal audits of all state departments, agencies, colleges, universities, state funds, and federal grants.
- *Local Government Division*. This division provides consulting, assistance, training, and budget forms to local government units to help ensure uniform accounting, budgeting, and financial reporting. It also reviews the independent audits of all local government units.
- *Special Projects Division*. This division performs any special requests audits and reviews such as internal control reviews, legal compliance audits, and fraud investigations.

STATE TREASURER

The final executive department office created by constitutional authority is the state treasurer. The state treasurer is "the custodian of public moneys."[84] Public moneys include any funds that are owned, held, or administered by a state entity regardless of the source of the funds, as well as funds of independent state agencies and public corporations. Two important duties of the state treasurer as the state's "custodian" of public funds are to account for public funds and invest public funds.

Accounting for Public Funds

The treasurer receives and disburses all monies in public funds.[85] This involves an enormous amount of money and a great responsibility, totaling billions of dollars each year. The treasurer receives these monies from the various state agencies, allocates those monies into their proper funds, and then pays all warrants drawn on those funds by the Division of Finance. It is also the treasurer's responsibility to protect the public funds by procuring insurance against loss.

The state treasurer is held accountable for the integrity of the state funds.[86] At the request of either house of the legislature, or of any legislative committee, the treasurer must give information in writing as to the condition of the treasury, or about any subject relating to the duties of the office. The treasurer must "keep the books open at all times" for the inspection by the governor, the state auditor, or any member of the legislature.[87] On the other hand, because the treasurer is responsible for the condition of the state funds, the treasurer is authorized to inspect the books, papers, and accounts of any state entity.

If the state treasurer is suspected of negligence in keeping the books or in taking care of the public monies, the governor must take possession of all books and state property in the possession of the treasurer and temporarily suspend the state treasurer from office. The state auditor then conducts an investigation and reports to the governor. If the state auditor finds that the state treasurer has acted negligently or fraudulently, the governor must replace the state treasurer and turn all information over to the legislature for the impeachment process. The appointed treasurer holds the office until a new treasurer is elected or the old one is reinstated.[88]

Investing Public Funds

The state treasurer manages the hundreds of millions of dollars of investments and debt accrued by the state. As investment manager, the treasurer must direct the investment of public funds into various securities and markets that effectively increase and safeguard state assets. In this capacity, the conduct of the treasurer is governed by the State Money Management Act and the State Money Management Council.[89] The State Money Management Act gives directions and authority to the state treasurer and the State Money Management Council in the disposition of investments concerning Utah funds. The State Money Management Act does not govern funds of the Workers' Compensation Fund, Utah State Retirement Board, Utah Housing Corporation, or the endowment funds of higher education institutions.[90]

One major fund the state treasurer manages is the Utah Public Treasurers Investment Fund (UPTIF). This fund allows Utah local governments, city and county treasurers, state boards, commissions, institutions, departments, divisions, agencies, school districts, and other public bodies to manage idle monies more effectively. The UPTIF acts as a "pool" that these state and local entities can temporarily place idle funds into and then draw back as needed. Allowing these public organizations access to this managed fund provides higher rates than smaller organizations could broker on their own. Larger denomination securities are exempt from certain investment service charges normally assessed by banks and brokers further reducing costs. The UPTIF allows organizations immediate access to funds, saving the burden of predicting exactly how long funds will be available for investment.[91]

In fulfilling investment responsibilities, the treasurer may hire a state financial adviser on a fee-for-service basis. In addition to assisting the state treasurer, this financial adviser may advise other executive officials, such as the director of the Division of Finance, as well as members of the legislative branch on the issuance of bonds and public debt. The treasurer also serves on many boards and commissions including the State Bonding Commission and the Utah Capital Investment Board.

DEPARTMENT OF ADMINISTRATIVE SERVICES

With over twenty thousand state employees spread across nineteen departments and numerous agencies and commissions, the task of coordinating administrative services of the executive branch of government is undeniably immense. The Department of Administrative Services (DAS) provides central management and coordination of regular business and office needs as well as specialized agency and public administrative concerns.[92] These services allow the government to operate on a day-to-day basis and are as commonplace as procurement, financial accounting, and vehicle maintenance, or as extraordinary as debt collection or the writing of administrative rules which carry the force of law.

The department was created in 1981. Before its creation, separate agencies like the Department of Finance managed many of the regular administrative services now carried out by DAS. In 1981, the legislature combined the Department of Finance with other departments such as the Department of Systems Planning and Computing in an attempt to streamline and unify the government's administrative services—an important principle behind the formation of DAS. DAS is charged with serving the public interest by "providing services in a cost-effective and efficient manner" and "eliminating unnecessary duplication."[93] Above all, DAS is charged to "protect the public interest by ensuring the integrity of the fiscal accounting procedures and polices that govern the operation of agencies and institutions."[94]

Executive Director

The Department of Administrative Services is lead by an executive director who is appointed by the governor and confirmed by the senate. The executive director serves at the "pleasure of the governor"[95] and is responsible to the governor, and the public, for the discharge of the executive director's duties. The executive director provides leadership and coordination for the seven divisions which fulfill the diverse administrative needs of Utah government.

Divisions of the Department

In the 2005 General Session, DAS underwent some restructuring by the legislature. The Department of Human Resource Management was moved to the DAS as a division, whereas the Division of Information Technology Services was changed to the Department of Technology Services with the director holding a cabinet level position. Table 5-3 details the major divisions and offices within DAS as well as the important policy and coordinating boards that oversee and assist these divisions or offices.[96]

Table 5-3

Divisions within the Department of Administrative Services

Administrative Rules	• Regulates the rulemaking process and ensures state agency compliance with the Utah Administrative Rulemaking Act (Title 63, Chapter 46a) • Maintains the official compilation of the Utah Administrative Code **Policy Board:** No policy-making board. The legislature's Administrative Rules Review Committee does review existing rules and has a close relationship with the DAS but the committee does not give the division operational directions.
Archives	• Assists Utah government agencies in the efficient management of their records, preserves records of enduring value, and provides quality access to public information[97] • Acts as a consultant for state agencies and local governments concerning questions of records management • Creates schedules to facilitate the transfer of records that have long-term value from government agencies to the archives • Provides training, microfilm processing, and off-site records storage for state agencies **Policy Board:** The State Records Committee must approve the retention schedule and the Utah State Historic Records Advisory Board gives some direction on historical record management.
(Office of) Child Welfare Parental Defense	• Develops contracts with attorneys to serve as parental defense attorneys in child welfare cases falling under Title 78, Chapter 3a, Parts 3 and 4 of the Utah Code (cases involving protective child custody and the termination of parental rights) • Provides assistance and advice to contracted parental defense attorneys • Develops educational and training programs for contracted parental defense attorneys • Provides information and advice to assist contracted parental defense attorneys to comply with their professional, contractual, and ethical duties
(Office of) Debt Collection	• Manages the collection of state receivables by contracting with private collection agencies[98] • Develops policies and procedures for accounting, reporting, collecting and writing off monies owed to the state • Prepares quarterly and annual reports of the state's receivables • Oversees receivable programs of state agencies to ensure they follow state policies • Does not receive state funding but is funded with fees and interest from overdue receivable accounts **Policy Board:** No policy-making board.
Facilities & Construction Management	• Purchases, constructs, and maintains most state facilities and buildings[99] • Selects private sector architects and engineers for projects • Awards construction bids to the most competitive contractors • Provides services to state agencies such as roofing, paving, and grounds maintenance **Policy Board:** State Building Board

Divisions within the Department of Administrative Services

Finance	• Maintains accounting and payroll systems • Maintains a data warehouse of financial information for decision-making • Produces the state's financial reports • Operates the state's travel agency • Controls the hundreds of unrestricted and restricted funds, including trust funds • Reviews and monitors agency compliance of all state contracts • Processes payments of state vendors and contractors • Accounts for all state revenues collected by all agencies • Prepares the statewide cost allocation plan **Policy Board:** None
Fleet Operations	• Acts as the state's motor pool • Handles all administrative and operational duties of purchasing, leasing, maintaining, and coordinating the state's vehicle fleet • Manages yearly vehicle registration, licensing, emissions and safety inspection • Operates as an internal service fund agency by financing its operations by leasing vehicles to state agencies or entities • Operates twelve "mini-motor pools" through the state and leases vehicles on either a long or short-term basis. • Provides emergency roadside assistance for state employees using state vehicles • Manages the surplus property program **Policy Board:** Motor Vehicle Review Committee
Human Resource Management	*See Division of Human Resource Management discussion on the following page.*
Purchasing & General Services	• Acts as the agent between most state entities and the private sector vendors who provide goods and services • Assists state agencies in obtaining needed goods and services • Administers the procurement process and negotiates and awards contracts • Acts as the government mail and copy service • Division director serves as the state's Chief Procurement Officer **Policy Board:** State Procurement Policy Board
Risk Management	• Acts as the state's insurer • Responsible for the administration of all policies, contracts, terms, rates, adjustments, claims, and awards regarding state agencies • Insures property, vehicles, equipment, personnel, and other items • Provides training and administrative support to help decrease costly accidents involving the state's personnel, property, and equipment • Assists the Attorney General's Office in evaluating, defending, and setting claims against the state • Division director serves as the State Risk Manager **Policy Board:** No policy-making board

The Executive Branch

Figure 5-4

Department of Administrative Services

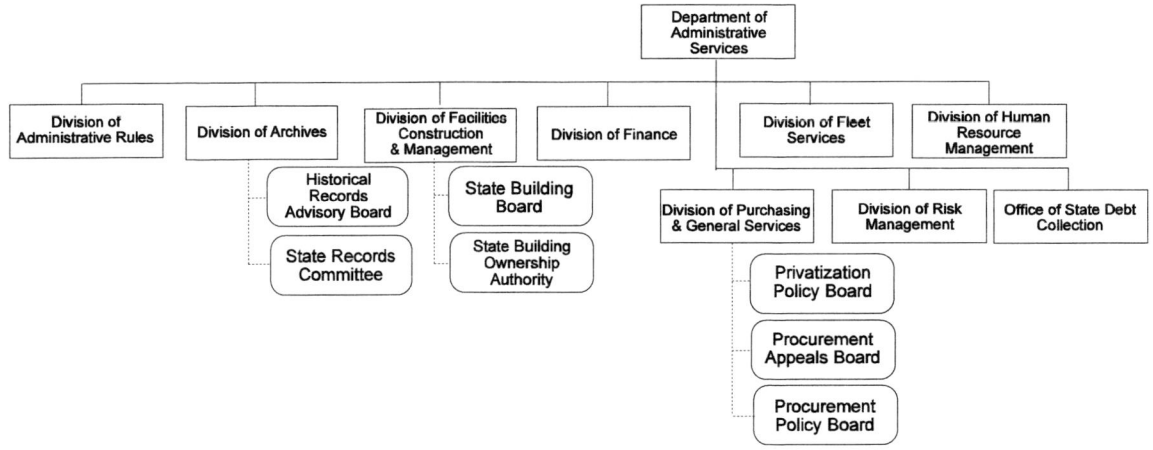

DIVISION OF HUMAN RESOURCE MANAGEMENT

Historically, effectively managing human resources is one of government's biggest challenges. Unlike the private sector, where profit is the bottom line, government goals are to provide order, secure the rights of its citizens, provide essential services, educate the young, and build state infrastructure. Yet, over the years, concerns have arisen over efficiency and waste within the public sector. For example, in early American history most government positions were filled using the spoils system. This was a system of appointment based on political favor that often led to corruption, waste, and incompetence.[100] In the late 1800s, the federal government led the way in civil service reform by enacting the Pendleton Act of 1883. The Pendleton Act "altered the institutional arrangement of federal personnel management" and created what become known as the *merit system*.[101] The merit system is a system of hiring, retention, and promotion based on ability and performance. These federal civil service reforms resulted in reforms at the state and local level.

Career Service System

The Department of Human Resource Management will change from a cabinet-level department to a division of the Department of Administrative Services on July 1, 2006.[102] The division will be headed by a director appointed by the governor and answering to the executive director of the Department of Administrative Services. The department's purpose is to provide an effective system of personnel management to increase the government's capacity in the hiring, training, and retaining of quality employees and to operate and maintain the state's Career Service System. The Career Service System (Utah's version of the merit system) seeks to implement the following principles:[103]

- Recruit, select, and advance employees on the basis of ability, knowledge, and skills
- Ensure open consideration of qualified applicants
- Provide for equitable and competitive compensation system
- Train employees to assure high-quality performance
- Retain employees on the basis of performance
- Terminate an employee whose inadequate performance cannot be corrected
- Ensure fair treatment of applicants and employees without regard to race, color, religion, sex, national origin, political affiliation, age, or disability
- Provide information to employees regarding their political rights and the prohibited practices

- Provide a formal procedure for processing the appeals and grievances of employees without discrimination, coercion, restraint, or reprisal

Decentralization

Utah state law currently allows the Department of Human Resource Management (DHRM) to "contract with any [state government] agency to allow the agency to perform specified personnel functions on its own behalf."[104] Most large agencies follow this contract procedure. Commencing July 1, 2006, persons performing personnel functions for an agency under contract with DHRM will become DHRM employees and will work within agencies to perform personnel functions as a DHRM field office.[105] The availability of on-site human resource functions gives state agencies more flexibility to manage their own personnel according to each unique situation. In fact, the functions of state government are incredibly diverse and each state agency may have distinct human resource needs depending on its own mission and structure. Therefore, the Utah Human Resource Management System allows contracted state agencies to write their own policies and handle certain human resources functions including:
- Writing initial job descriptions
- Offering recommendations for position classifications and grade allocations
- Selecting qualified applicants for appointment and promotion to vacant positions
- Conducting performance appraisals
- Disciplining employees
- Maintaining individual personnel records

However, DHRM cannot contract out the design and administration of the state pay plan, state classification system, or schedule of assignments. Each agency also agrees to allow DHRM to:
- Study all position classifications within each agency
- Conduct periodic desk audits
- Define all agency human resource functions
- Monitor the state agencies personnel practices
- Maintain a centralized personnel record system[106]

The contracts between DHRM and agencies ensure that agencies set up and maintain working environments that conform with both state and federal law. For example, all employers must operate under many federal laws such as the Americans with Disabilities Act (ADA), the Fair Labor Standards Act (FLSA), and the Family and Medical Leave Act (FMLA). These laws seek to protect all employees, not just civil servants, by ensuring they receive fair pay, leave, and due process protections.

RETIREMENT

Retirement Systems

In accordance with Title 49, Utah State Retirement and Insurance Benefit Act, retirement systems have been established to cover employees of the state, government funded educational institutions, counties, municipalities, and other political subdivisions. The Utah State Retirement Systems consists of six different systems that include a total membership of retired and active (currently employed) members of 158,597 as of December 31, 2004. The systems and the percent of total membership of each system are as follows:
- Non-contributory, 83.6 percent
- Contributory, 7.2 percent
- Public safety, 7.2 percent
- Firefighters, 1.6 percent
- Governors and legislators, 0.3 percent
- Judges, 0.1 percent

Each system is different because:
- Each system is separate and self-contained
- Each system has different benefits (although many benefits are similar)
- Benefit costs may be different from one system to another because of actuarial differences
- Some systems have unique funding sources (i.e., fire fighters have a fire insurance premium tax and judges have court fines used to fund their systems)
- Each system was developed independently over time

Funding for the retirement systems has been (nine-year average 1995-2004) as follows:
- Investment income, 68.8 percent
- Employer contributions, 24.9 percent
- Transfers from systems, 3.6 percent
- Member contributions, 2.2 percent
- Court fees and fire insurance premium tax, 0.6 percent

Retirement Contribution Rates

Based on actuarial projections, a contribution rate is calculated each year and approved by the Utah State Retirement Board. The contribution rate is the percent of eligible employee salary that the employer is required to pay into the retirement fund each year. This contribution is required to keep retirement systems funded on an actuarially sound basis. The contribution rates are paid in addition to the salary paid to public employees. The historical contribution rate in the Public Employees Noncontributory System (expressed as percentage of salary) is shown in table 5-4. For fiscal year 2005, the Utah State Retirement Board has recommended a contribution rate increase to 13.38 percent of salary. This 1.68 percent of salary increase represents approximately $50 million.

Table 5-4

| Noncontributory Retirement Contribution Rates ||
Fiscal Year	Percent of Salary
1998	14.16%
1999	14.16%
2000	14.16%
2001	13.68%
2002	10.40%
2003	10.40%
2004	11.70%
2005	13.38%
2006	13.38%
Average	**12.82%**

Source: Data provided by the Utah State Retirement System.

Retirement Benefits

A member who retires from employment with a participating employer in a state retirement system is eligible for different defined benefits based on:
- The retirement system the member is in
- Eligibility for retirement, which is based on age and number of years of service
- Service benefit formula, which is based on the percent of final average salary applied to each year of service
- Final average salary, which is based on the average of the member's highest salary for two to five years depending on which retirement system the member is part of
- Cost of living adjustment provided each year based on inflation

Table 5-5 is a comparison of the defined benefits provided by the different Utah retirement systems.

Table 5-5

Utah Retirement Defined Benefit Summary – 2005 System Comparison

	Public Employees' Noncontributory	Public Employees' Contributory	Public Safety Noncontributory and Contributory	Firefighters'	Judges' Noncontributory and Contributory	Governor's and Legislative Service
Participants	State/Public Education Classified School Higher Education Political Subdivisions Other governmental entities	Same as Non-Contributory	Peace Officers, Correctional Officers, and approved Special Function Officers	Full-time Firefighters regularly assigned to a fire department	Judges of the Supreme, Appellate, District, Circuit, and Juvenile Courts	Governors and Legislators
Total Members Active / Retired	132,643 85,046 / 23,774	11,341 3,393 / 6,518	11,412 7,173 / 3,047	2,601 1,591 / 933	197 106 / 84	403 95 / 221
Eligibility for Retirement	any age 30 years age 60 20 years (AR) age 62 10 years (AR) age 65 4 years any age 25 years (FAR or employee/employer purchase of up to 5 years immediately prior to retirement)	any age 30 years age 60 20 years (AR) age 62 10 years (AR) age 65 4 years optional employee/employer purchase of up to 5 years immediately prior to retirement	any age 20 years age 60 10 years age 65 4 years	Same as Public Safety	any age 25 years age 55 20 years (FAR) age 62 10 years age 70 6 years	**Legislators** age 62 10 years (AR) age 65 4 years **Governors** age 62 10 years (AR) age 65 4 years
Service Benefit Formula	2% x FAS (all years)	2% after 7/1/75 x FAS 1.25% for years prior to 7/1/75 x FAS	2.5% x FAS x 1st 20 years 2% x FAS x years above 20	Same as Public Safety	5% x FAS x 1st 10 years 2.25% x FAS x 2nd 10 years 1% of FAS x remaining years	**Legislators** - $10/month per year of service increased semiannually up to 2% based on CPI $25.20/month, as of 07/05 **Governors** - $500/month per term increased semiannually up to 2% based on CPI $1,140/month as of 07/05
	No maximum benefit	No maximum benefit	70% maximum benefit of FAS reached at 30 years		75% maximum benefit of FAS reached at 22.5 years	
Final Average Salary Definition	Average of highest 3 years	Average of highest 5 years	Average of highest 3 years	Same as Public Safety	Average of highest 2 years	N/A
Cost of Living Adjustment	Up to 4% annually (CPI) (Simple) after 1 year	Same as Non-Contributory	Up to 2.5% annually (CPI) (Simple) after 1 year	Up to 4% annually (CPI) (Simple) after 1 year	Up to 4% annually (CPI) (Compounded) after 1 year	Up to 4% annually (CPI) (Simple) after 1 year
Employer Defined Contribution Benefit % of Salary	State/School: 1.5% 401(k) Local government: Optional	State/School: None Local government: Optional	State: None Local government: Optional	State: None Local government: Optional	None	N/A

AR = Actuarial Reduction (3% per year under age 65)
FAR = Full Actuarial Reduction
FAS = Final Average Salary

Source: Utah Retirement Systems Comprehensive Annual Financial Report for year ended December 31, 2003 and Title 49, Utah State Retirement and Insurance Benefit Act, *Utah Code Annotated 1953*

Independent Entities

Independent entities are entities created or permitted by the state that have a public purpose relating to the state or its citizens.[107] They are governed by a board or commission appointed as specified in enabling legislation. An independent entity can exist as an independent state agency or an independent corporation.

Independent State Agencies

There are six independent state agencies in Utah: Heber Valley Historic Railroad Authority, School and Institutional Trust Lands Administration, Utah Communications Agency Network, Utah Dairy Commission, Utah Science Center Authority, and Utah State Retirement Office.

The Heber Valley Historic Railroad Authority was created to operate and maintain a scenic and historic railroad in and around the Heber Valley.[108]

The School and Institutional Trust Lands Administration was created to manage lands that Congress granted to the state for the support of common schools and other beneficiary institutions, under the Utah Enabling Act.[109]

The Utah Communications Agency Network is a board and executive committee created to administer the creation, administration, and maintenance of the Utah Communications Agency Network to provide public safety communications services and facilities on a regional or statewide basis for the benefit and use of public agencies and state and federal agencies.[110]

The Utah Dairy Commission was created to conduct a campaign of research, nutritional education, and publicity, showing the value of milk, cream, and dairy products; encourage local, national, and international use of Utah dairy products and by-products, through advertising or otherwise; investigate and participate in studies of problems peculiar to producers in Utah; and promote, protect, and stabilize the state dairy industry.[111]

The Utah Science Center Authority was created to foster the development of science, technology, engineering, arts, tourism, cultural, and educational facilities in order to further the welfare of the citizens of the state and its economic growth.[112] The Utah Science Center has operated since 1995 through the Discovery on Wheels outreach program reportedly serving thousands of students each year. The Leonardo at Library Square is the home of the Utah Science Center and sponsors forums, programs, alliances, and connections to encourage science and technology exploration and hands-on experimentation.

The Utah State Retirement Office was created to establish and administer retirement systems and the Utah Governors' and Legislators' Retirement Plan for members which provide a uniform system of membership, retirement requirements, benefits for members, funding on an actuarially sound basis, contributions, economy and efficiency in public service, and a central administrative office and a board to administer the various systems, plans, and programs established by the legislature or the Utah State Retirement Board.[113]

Independent Corporations

The Utah Housing Corporation is an independent body politic and corporate, constituting a public corporation to assist financing the construction, development, rehabilitation, or purchase of residential housing for low and moderate income persons through low interest loans and other means.[114]

The Utah State Fair Corporation is an independent public nonprofit corporation created to have general management, supervision, and control over all activities relating to the state fair and have charge of all state expositions except as otherwise provided by statute.[115]

Nonprofit Quasi-public Corporations

The Utah Capitol Investment Corporation is an independent quasi-public nonprofit corporation created to mobilize venture equity capital for investment in a manner that will result in a significant potential to create jobs and to diversify and stabilize the economy of the state.[116]

The Workers' Compensation Fund is a nonprofit, quasi-public corporation created to insure Utah employers against liability for compensation based on job-related accidental injuries and occupational diseases; and assure payment of this compensation to Utah employees who are entitled to it.[117]

During the 2001 General Session, the legislature passed H.B. 28 "Independent Entities Act," which provides additional regulations for independent entities and corporations. The bill outlines a process for a legislative committee to review independent entities and determine whether they should be repealed, made a state agency, privatized, made an independent state agency, or made an independent corporation. H.B. 28 took effect July 1, 2002 and created the Legislative Independent Entities Committee, which replaced the Quasi-governmental Entities Committee and took over its duties as well as additional responsibilities. During the 2003 General Session, the legislature changed the name of the committee to the Retirement and Independent Entities Committee from its former names, the Quasi-Governmental Entities Committee and the Independent Entities Committee. This committee is a statutorily created interim committee of the legislature. The Committee is composed of five senators and nine representatives. By legislative rule, senate members constitute the Senate Retirement and Independent Entities Standing Committee and house members constitute the House Retirement and Independent Entities Standing Committee.[118] Members of the committee are also the members of the Retirement and Independent Entities Appropriations Subcommittee of the Joint Appropriations Committee.[119] The committee is required to comply with the rules of legislative interim committees.

The committee has responsibility to:
- Determine which entities should be treated as independent entities
- Determine the extent to which consistency in the statutes for each independent entity should be provided
- Determine from which provisions of the Utah Code, if any, each independent entity should be exempt
- Determine whether or not the state should receive services from or provide services to each independent entity
- Request and hear reports from each independent entity
- Review the annual audits of each independent entity
- Follow statutory guidelines in reviewing a proposal to create a new independent entity
- Recommend the appropriate method of changing the organizational status of any entity
- Study entities created by interlocal agreement to determine if they should be subject to the Independent Entities Act
- Report annually to the Legislative Management Committee

DEPARTMENT OF TECHNOLOGY SERVICES

Utah state government's use of computers began in the early 1960s and evolved through several different organizational models before the legislature created the Division of Information Technology Services in 1990.[120] Originally housed within the Department of Administrative Services, the Division of Information Technology Services provided the centralized delivery of enterprise type (mainframe) computing and telecommunication services to state agencies and the public where economies of scale and standardization dictated their use. Other services provided by the division include microwave and satellite communications.

From 1960 to 1990, computer use migrated from the centralized delivery of services via mainframe and dumb terminals, to personal computers and local area networks within agencies. By the mid-1990s, with the advent of the Internet, personal computers dominated the delivery of computing services statewide. Mainframe computing was still part of the process for enterprise type services, such as wide area networks and email, but agencies primarily relied upon personal computers as their work tool of choice.

Distributed computing (personal computers) via local or wide area networks and the Internet is now the preferred model for delivering agency services to the public. Those services include all types of licensing by the state such as business, drivers and motor vehicles, and hunting and fishing. All state agencies are required by the legislature to provide on-line, public access to information and services.[121]

The transformation of technology use in state government has necessitated administrative changes in the Division of Information Technology Services as well. In the mid-1990s the legislature authorized the governor to appoint a chief information officer. The chief information officer's primary duties were to help develop and coordinate the implementation of state information technology policy. The chief information officer also served as a member of the legislature's Utah Technology Commission,[122] a government-wide policy recommending entity.

In 2005, the legislature, having studied the rapid change in technology and its delivery for the previous two years, authorized a major reorganization of state technology assets and personnel.[123] Key aspects of that change include the creation of a Department of Technology Services with the chief information officer as the executive director, reassignment of all state technology personnel, and all technology funding to be coordinated and authorized by the new department. The transition to the new department will take place over 2005 and 2006 with a final effective date of July 1, 2006.[124]

While distributed computing has become the primary work tool for state agencies, the Department of Technology Services continues (by statutory mandate) to provide centralized, mainframe services which, in addition to traditional services such as networks, also provides critical broadband access to the Internet, security, and host to the state's primary Web site, www.utah.gov.

Executive Branch Web Site Visits

As shown by figure 5.5, Web site visits for the executive branch increased by 22 percent from 2002 to 2003. There was a 10 percent increase in visits from 2003 to 2004. The fall quarter (Oct. - Dec.) of each year represents the most active visit period for executive branch Web site visits.[125]

Legislative Branch Web Site Visits

Web site visits for the legislative branch increased by 58 percent from 2002 to 2003. The upward trend has continued with a 23 percent increase in visits from 2003 to 2004. The legislature receives most visits during the annual general session from January to March each year.[126]

Judicial Branch Web Site Visits

Web site visits for the judicial branch increased by 28 percent from 2002 to 2003, and from 2003 to 2004 visits increased 46 percent. The months from May through October over the 2002-04 period represent the most active time period for visits.[127]

Figure 5-5

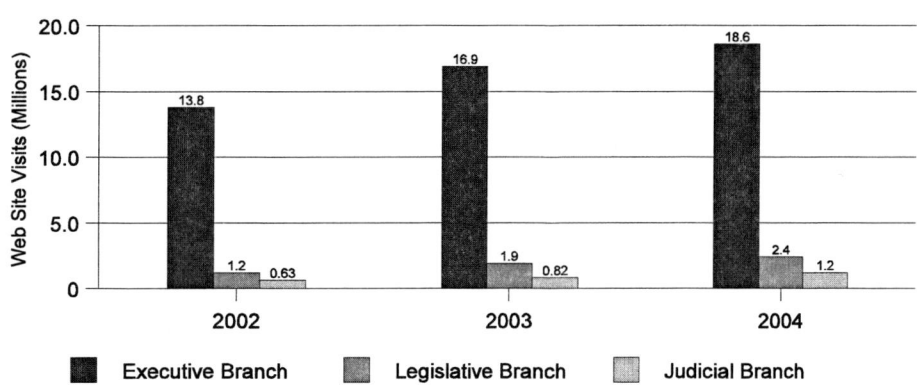

The Executive Branch • 91

Chapter 6

The Legislative Branch

The Utah Legislature is a part-time legislature, whose members come from all walks of life, including lawyers, doctors, real estate developers, educators, farmers, ranchers, manufacturers, miners, homemakers, and retirees. There are 75 members of the House of Representatives and 29 members of the State Senate, making a total of 104 legislators who comprise the Utah Legislature.[1]

> **In this chapter:**
>
> Legislative Sessions (p. 93)
> Role of Committees (p. 95)
> Lawmaking Process (p. 99)
> How a Bill Becomes a Law (p. 102)
> Who Can Be a Legislator (p. 105)
> The Appropriations Process (p. 107)
> Constitutional Powers and Restrictions on Powers (p. 109)
> Limitations on Legislative Power (p. 109)
> Reapportionment and Redistricting (p. 111)
> Legislative Staff Offices (p. 112)
> Use of Information Technology (p. 114)

LEGISLATIVE SESSIONS

The Utah Legislature holds various types of legislative sessions:
- Annual general sessions
- Veto override sessions
- Special sessions
- Impeachment sessions
- Senate extraordinary sessions for confirmation of gubernatorial appointments

Each type of session has its own purpose, time limitations, and requirements for convening which must be followed in order that the actions taken during the session are valid.

The speaker of the House of Representatives and the president of the State Senate are the presiding officers of their respective houses and are formally elected by their membership at the opening of the annual general session. However, in practice they are selected by the majority party caucuses. They are responsible for the flow of work during all sessions of the legislature, and their duties are stated in house and senate rules.[2]

Annual General Sessions

The legislature meets in annual general session beginning on the third Monday in January.[3] The annual general session runs forty-five days. Saturdays, Sundays, and holidays are included as part of this forty-five calendar day session.[4] Legislators generally meet Monday through Friday of each week including the holidays that occur during this time.

All sessions of the legislature are open to the public and are broadcast over the Internet as well.[5] Legislative sessions focus on topics of high interest to the public and to legislators. Legislators address those and other topics by introducing legislation to enact new laws, amend existing laws, or repeal existing laws. The legislation enacted by the legislature and signed or not vetoed by the governor becomes state law. It represents the public policy of the state of Utah. Legislation is introduced, debated, and addressed each year during the annual general session; however, legislators also may address emergency and other legislation in special sessions called by the governor.

Veto Override Sessions

The Utah Constitution permits the legislature to override a gubernatorial veto by a two-thirds vote of both houses of the legislature.[6] A veto override session may be held during a general or special session of the legislature, or a veto override session may be convened by the legislature after it has adjourned *sine die*.

Reconsideration Before Adjournment

A bill vetoed by the governor while the legislature is still in session, is returned to its original house with the governor's objections. If upon reconsideration the bill again passes both houses by a two-thirds vote, the bill becomes law.[7]

Reconsideration After Adjournment Sine Die

The legislature may call itself into session to reconsider a bill vetoed by the governor after adjournment *sine die* of the session at which the bill was passed, in a session "not to exceed five calendar days."[8] The presiding officers must poll the members of their respective houses, and if two-thirds of the members approve, the legislature shall be convened in a veto override session within sixty days after the session at which the legislation was passed.[9]

No amendments or substitutions may be made to the legislation under consideration: the legislation retains the number and entire substance that it had when it passed in the previous legislative session. The only vote taken is whether or not to override the governor's veto.[10] A two-thirds vote in each house is required to override a governor's veto.

Special Sessions

The governor has exclusive power to convene the legislature into special session for no more than thirty days, except in cases of impeachment.[11] The legislature may consider only the legislative business specified in the governor's call, and may act only upon items germane to or within the apparent scope of subject specified in the governor's call.

If, while the legislature is in special session, the governor determines that there is other legislative business that the legislature needs to consider, the governor may add those items to the special session agenda if the governor provides forty-eight hours advance public notice of the items. The forty-eight hour advanced public notice is not required if an emergency has been declared, or if the legislature has approved the consideration of the item by a two-thirds vote of each house.[12]

Impeachment Proceedings

The thirty-day limitation on special sessions does not apply when the legislature is conducting impeachment proceedings. Impeachment procedures are established by constitutional mandate in Article 6, Sections 17 through 21, by statute, and in legislative rules.[13]

The removal of the governor or other state or judicial officer must be based on "high crimes, misdemeanors, or malfeasance in office"[14] and involves both the House of Representatives and the State Senate. The role played by each of these bodies is distinct. First, the House of Representatives commences the "impeachment" by drafting and approving a Resolution of Impeachment and detailing the offenses warranting impeachment in what is called the Articles of Impeachment.[15]

After the house has voted for impeachment, the senate sits as a court of impeachment in order to render a judgment. The senate tries the accused official and votes to either acquit or convict on each offense detailed in the Articles of Impeachment.[16] A constitutional two-thirds majority is required to convict the official.

Extraordinary Sessions of the Senate

The senate meets in extraordinary session to act only on "executive business"—the review, confirmation or rejection of individual executive and judicial appointments by the governor.[17] Senate confirmation, also known as "advice and consent," is required for certain executive or judicial appointments by constitution and by statute. The senate's power to accept or reject proposed appointments is a key check and balance undergirding Utah's separation of powers.

ROLE OF COMMITTEES

Generally, all members of the legislature hold membership on two standing committees and one joint appropriation subcommittee during the forty-five-day general session of the legislature. Legislators also are members of two interim committees that meet during the period of time between general sessions. All of these committees work under the direction of chairs, who are appointed by the president of the State Senate and the speaker of the House of Representatives.[18]

Figure 6-1

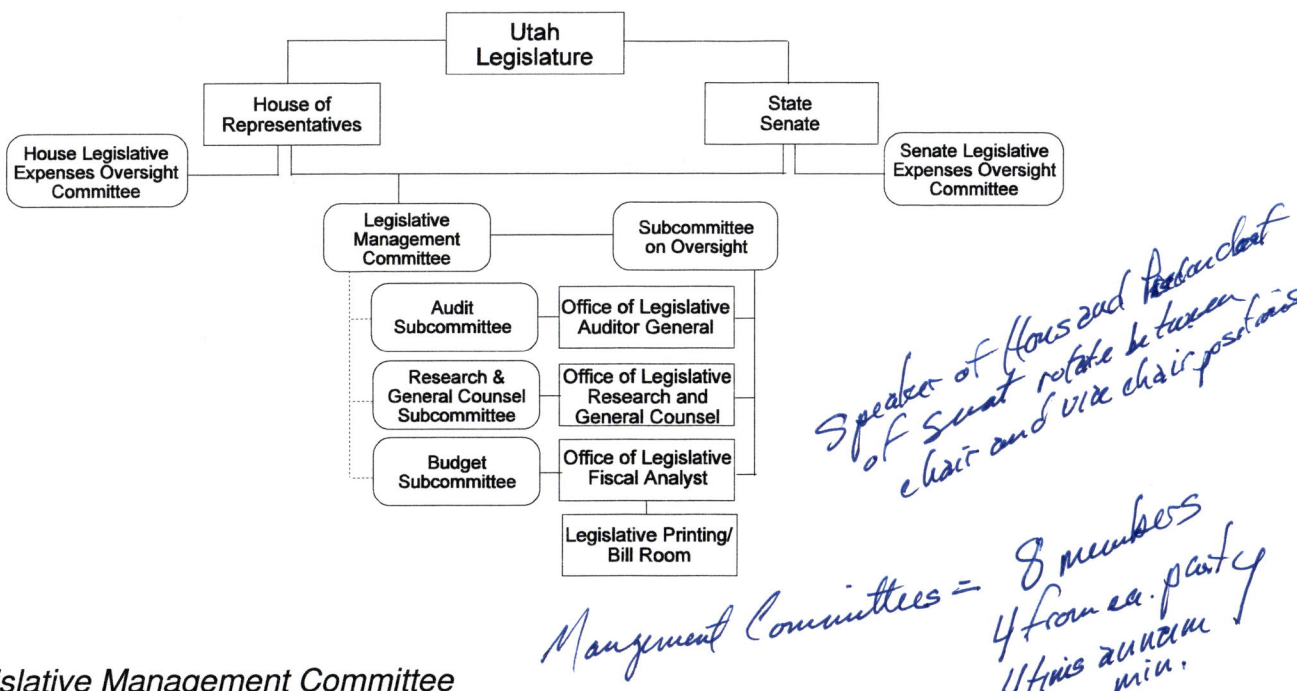

Legislative Management Committee

Utah statute has established as permanent legislative committees a House Management Committee and a Senate Management Committee. Each committee consists of eight members from each house, four members from each political party elected to leadership[19] of each house, and additional members chosen at the beginning of each annual general session as needed to complete the full membership.

The two management committees meeting jointly comprise the Legislative Management Committee. The speaker of the house and the president of the senate annually rotate between the chair and vice chair positions. The committee meets as often as necessary, but not less than four times a year.

Responsibilities of the Legislative Management Committee include:

- Assigning studies to appropriate interim committees
- Considering requests from interim committees to conduct additional studies and approving the study requests, unless there are inadequate funds to perform a study or the study is being conducted by another committee
- Establishing a budget for each interim committee
- Setting times and places for committee meetings
- Employing staff directors
- Developing and adopting personnel policies for the legislative staff
- Determining travel policies
- Acting on special study budget requests
- Assisting new legislative leadership

Executive Appropriations Committee[20]

The Executive Appropriations Committee is composed of the house and senate appropriations chairs, legislative leadership of both parties in the senate and the house, and other members as outlined in joint legislative rules. The committee works with appropriation subcommittees to prepare the state's budget. The Executive Appropriations Committee prepares and approves the final version of the appropriations acts, the School Finance Act, and any bonding authorizations. Those bills are then separately reviewed and must be approved by the House of Representatives, State Senate, and the governor.

Appropriations Subcommittees

There are ten[21] appropriations subcommittees appointed from the members of the house and senate by the speaker of the house and the president of the senate. The subcommittees hold public meetings to review and decide on the allocation of available funds to the affected state entities. Each subcommittee considers a specific portion of the budget and makes recommendations to the Executive Appropriations Committee. The Executive Appropriations Committee may alter the budget recommendations as necessary in order to balance the budget and make a final appropriations bill.[22] Each of the appropriations subcommittees are staffed by one or more legislative fiscal analysts.[23] Figure 6-2 shows the relationship of the Executive Appropriations Committee to its subcommittees.

Figure 6-2

Appropriations Committee and Subcommittees

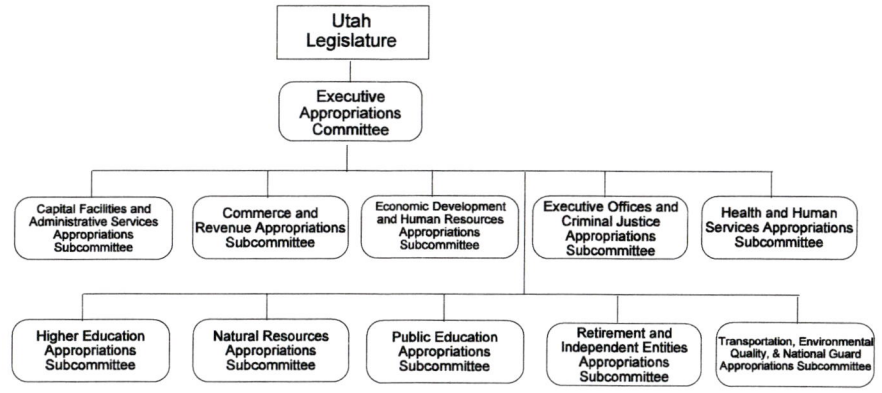

Interim Committees and Special Legislative Committees

Legislators from the State Senate and the House of Representatives are appointed and jointly serve as members of various "interim committees." Generally, these committees meet jointly on the third Wednesday of every month between sessions from April through November.

The purpose of ongoing interim committees is to (1) study key issues facing the state, including requesting and reviewing professional staff reports, (2) receive public comment between legislative sessions concerning matters being considered by the legislature, (3) recommend for the upcoming session legislation that implements the committees' findings, and (4) make recommendations for study proposals and other relative matters of concern to the legislature. Study assignments are approved by the legislature in a resolution and are chosen as interim topics by the Legislative Management Committee, or by a committee's own initiative with approval of the Legislative Management Committee.

A report of the work done by the ongoing interim committees is prepared by the Office of Legislative Research and General Counsel and is issued before each legislative session. Copies of reports and recommendations of the interim committees are mailed to each legislator, to each elective state officer, to the state library, and are available on the legislature's Web site—http://www.le.utah.gov. Figure 6-3 shows ongoing interim committees and represent the various subject areas studied by the legislature.

Figure 6-3

Interim and Special Legislative Committees

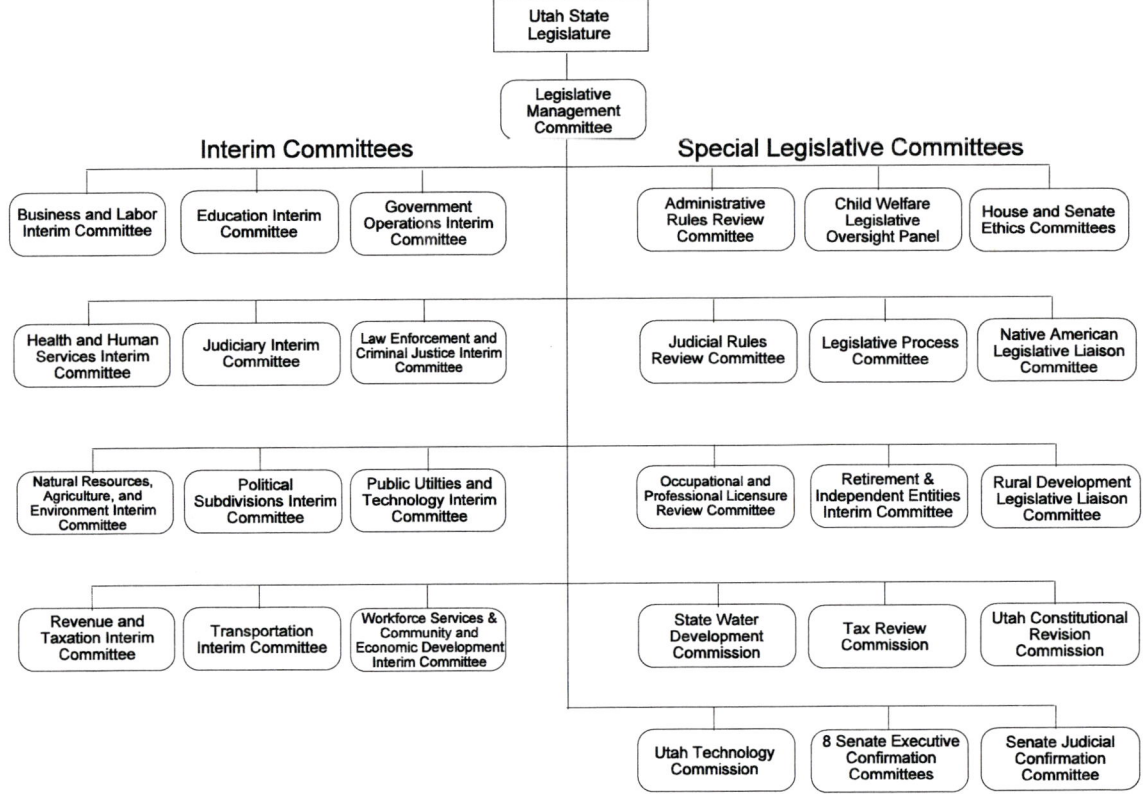

Temporary Committees, Boards, Panels, and Task Forces

The leadership of each house decides how many task forces and commissions it will permit each year depending upon priority of current legislative concerns and moneys available to fund task force and commission studies. These committees, boards, panels, and task forces in which "legislative participation is required by law,"[24] are sometimes loosely referred to as an "interim committee." However their pattern is usually prescribed in a specific law. They are set up to function for predetermined periods of time in order to study current issues of legislative concern.

Standing Committees

Standing committee meetings are held by the house and senate during the annual general session and offer citizens the opportunity to listen to and comment on bills and resolutions being considered by the legislature. Following the first reading in a house, a bill usually is referred to the respective house Rules Committee. The Rules Committee recommends to the presiding officer the standing committee to which the bill should be referred. Upon receipt of the rules committee report, the speaker or president refers the measure to the appropriate standing committee. The standing committee then reviews the bill and may receive testimony in a public meeting. The standing committee may amend, hold, table, substitute, or make a favorable recommendation on the bill.[25]

Following the standing committee hearing, the bill is returned to the full house with a committee report. The committee may report the bill out favorably, favorably with amendments, favorably as a substitute, or report that the bill has been tabled. Figure 6-4 lists the various standing committees for the house and senate.

Figure 6-4

Standing Committees

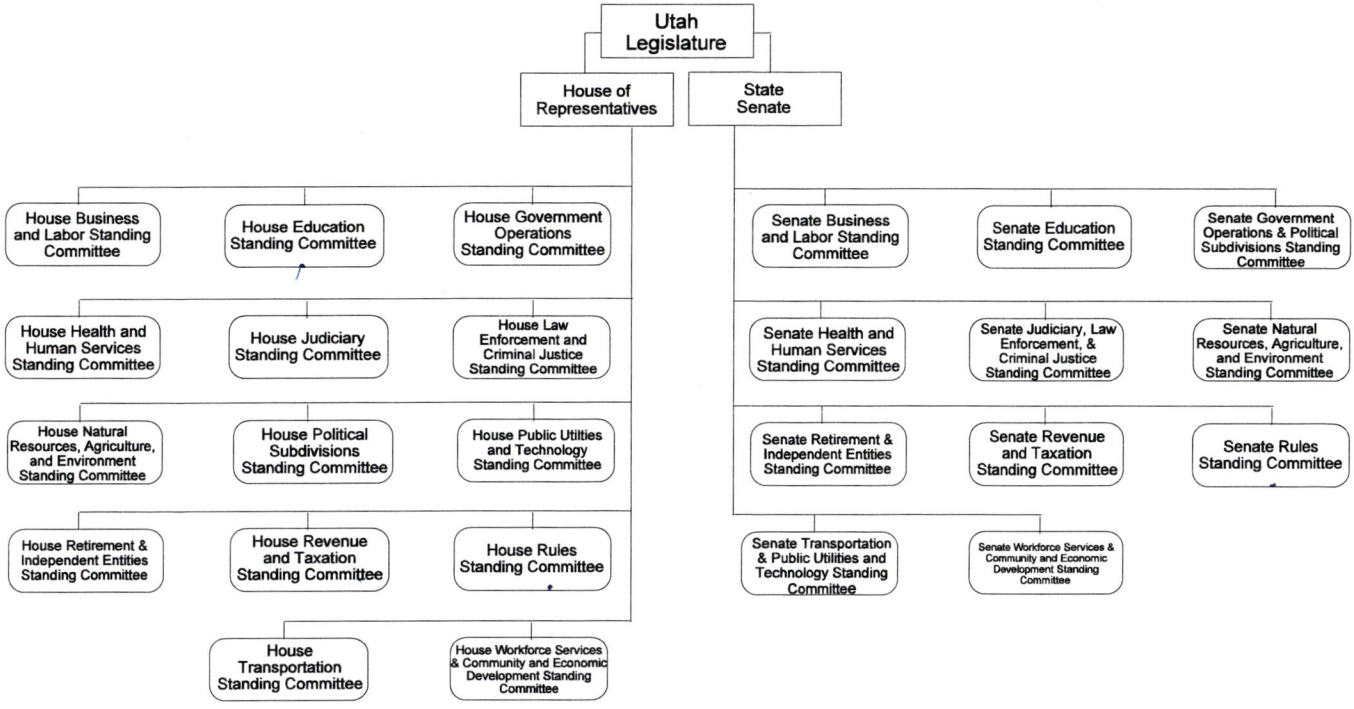

LAWMAKING PROCESS

Although the legislature has flexibility in enacting rules of procedure to govern its own legislative process, there are constitutional provisions that create specific requirements and limitations for the passage of a bill. In those limited situations where the Utah Constitution mandates procedure, the validity of a bill can hinge upon whether or not the legislature followed the proper procedure during the bill's enactment. If the constitution does not mandate a procedure, courts will give deference to the legislative process in passing a bill and will not invalidate a bill for failure to follow an internal rule of legislative procedure.

Rules of Procedure

The Utah Constitution gives the house and senate power to make rules to govern their own procedures.[26] This broad mandate is limited by a few Utah constitutional provisions that mandate the way the legislature must do business. For example, the Utah Constitution requires that (1) each bill must have three readings in each house,[27] (2) the sessions of the legislature shall be public,[28] (3) a quorum of members shall be in attendance to transact business,[29] (4) with limited exceptions, bills shall contain only one subject,[30] (5) each house shall keep a journal of its proceedings,[31] and (6) legislation becomes effective on a certain date unless otherwise specified.[32]

Three Readings Required in Each House

Each bill must be read three times in both the house and the senate except when the house in which the bill is pending, suspends the requirement by the two-thirds vote.[33] This requirement dates back to English times when reprinting a bill was an issue. This practice provided that legislators would be informed as to what the bill proposed to do. Today, this requirement is suspended in part, as allowed by the Utah Constitution, to instead require three readings of the short title of the bill, not three readings of the entire bill.

Open and Public Meetings

"All sessions of the Legislature, except those of the senate while sitting in executive session, shall be public. . . ."[34] The legislature enacted the Open and Public Meetings Act[35] to clarify the requirement that state, agency, and political subdivision meetings must be open to the public, with only limited exceptions. The act requires posting public notice at least twenty-four hours in advance of any meeting. Minutes or a tape recording must be made of the meeting. Now all legislative meetings are available on CD-rom and are on the legislature's Web site and the senate and house floor debates and interim committee meetings are broadcast live through the legislature's Web site.

Quorum Is Required in Each House

A majority of the members of each house must be present to transact legislative business.[36] The legislature has the authority to compel the attendance of those absent so that such business may be transacted.

Bills to Contain Only One Subject

Utah's Constitution prohibits bills from containing more than one subject, except for appropriation bills and bills for the codification or revision of laws.[37] The purpose of the single subject provision is to prevent the legislature from combining into one bill separate measures that legally have no proper relationship with one another.[38]

The provision also requires that the bill's subject be clearly expressed in its title. The general purpose of the title is to protect the public by ensuring that individual members of the legislature and the public at large are "fairly appraised" of the subject matter contained in the legislation. Being "fairly appraised" would constitute having "notice of the general subject matter" and the "interests likely to be affected."[39] The title should be so worded that it is broad enough to include the subject of the legislation, but specific enough to restrict or limit the act to matters that are legitimately included within the single subject.

Each House Shall Keep a Journal of its Proceedings

The House of Representatives and the State Senate are each required to keep a journal of its proceedings.[40] The journal contains general proceedings and votes taken on each measure. The Office of Legislative Research and General Counsel consults the journal during the enrollment of bills to verify that passage of each bill followed all constitutionally required procedures. Courts may refer to legislative house journals when the valid enactment or constitutionality of a law has been challenged. The legal community in general and interested citizens may consult the journals when reviewing the legislative history of a bill in an attempt to learn the legislative intent behind a particular enactment or amendment.

Effective Dates of Bills

In general, if no effective date is specified in a bill, the bill becomes effective sixty days after the session in which it was passed adjourns.[41] However, the legislature's power to enact laws includes the power to specify in the bill a future day, or a "delayed effective date," at which the bill will take effect.[42] A delayed effective date requires only a majority approval in each house.

Early Effective Dates. A bill may also become effective earlier than the sixty days after the session in which it passed if the earlier effective date is specified in the bill, and the bill receives the approval of two-thirds vote of all the members elected to each house. If the early effective date bill receives a majority vote in each house, but less than a two-thirds vote in either house, the bill will pass, but the early effective date is not given effect. The bill takes effect sixty days after the session at which it passed.

An early effective date bill that receives a two-thirds vote of each house may take effect upon signature of the governor.[43] If the governor allows an early effective date bill to go into effect by *not signing* the bill, the bill will take effect the day after the Article 7, Section 8 time limit for the governor to sign, which is ten days after presentment during the session, or twenty days after the session if presentment is after the session. When an early effective date bill is vetoed by the governor, the bill becomes effective only if the veto is overridden by the legislature. The date of the veto override vote becomes the effective date of the bill.

Retroactive Effective Dates. There are limited circumstances in which a bill may be given retrospective operation[44] to a date that precedes the passage of the bill.[45] This most often occurs in tax laws where retrospective operation is used to provide consistency in a tax obligation during an entire tax year. Utah statutory law provides that no statute is retroactive "unless expressly so declared."[46] Unlike early effective dates, a retrospective operation provision does not require a constitutional two-thirds vote of each house.[47]

A later statute or amendment will not be applied in a retroactive manner to deprive a person of substantive rights or impose greater liability upon the person. The Utah Supreme Court has recognized exceptions that include: amendments for clarifying statutes;[48] or procedural or remedial statutes that do not enlarge, eliminate, or destroy vested rights.[49] The key issues are whether an amendment is procedural or substantive, and whether vested rights are affected.

The legislature's power to enact retrospective laws is limited particularly in the criminal area. Both the federal and state constitutions specifically prohibit states from enacting any ex post facto law.[50] An ex post facto law is defined as "a law that impermissibly applies retroactively, especially in a way that negatively affect a person's rights, as by criminalizing an action that was legal when it was committed."[51] The purpose of this constitutional provision is to ensure that individuals have fair warning of legislative acts and to restrain the legislature from enacting laws creating arbitrary and potentially vindictive prosecution.[52]

Effective Dates of Resolutions

Bills and resolutions are distinctly different; bills require effective dates, while most resolutions do not. Resolutions become effective on the day that the resolution receives final approval from:
- The House of Representatives or the State Senate if it is a single house resolution
- The State Senate if it is a House Joint Resolution or the House of Representatives if it is a Senate Joint Resolution
- The governor if it is a concurrent resolution having passed the State Senate and the House of Representatives[53]

A resolution form is used instead of a bill to (1) express sentiment or opinion, (2) carry out the inner administration of the legislative body, and (3) propose a constitutional amendment in a joint resolution.[54] Except for joint resolutions proposing constitutional amendments, or amending the rules of procedure or evidence adopted by the supreme court, most resolutions are not considered to be law because they do not have the binding effect of a statute, and are immediately effective upon passage by the last required entity.

Joint resolutions amending, enacting, or repealing constitutional provisions are considered to be laws that do require specific effective dates, and they must receive a two-thirds vote of the members of each house. After a joint resolution amending the Utah Constitution is passed by the legislature, it is submitted to the people for approval and final passage at the next general election. The changes to the Utah Constitution contained in the resolution become effective only upon the approval of the voters and on the date specified in the resolution.[55]

Procedures Outlined in Legislative Rules

Other procedures are required by legislative rules. If legislation passes the legislature without following all of these rules, it will still be valid legislation. Examples of procedures required in legislative rules include:

- Giving priority to calendaring bills that have been heard by a legislative committee that meets between sessions of the legislature, most commonly referred to as interim committees[56]
- Providing a hearing by both a house and senate standing committee in order to pass[57]
- Considering bills in the order they appear on the calendar[58]
- Reprinting house amendments on lilac colored paper and senate amendments on goldenrod colored paper[59]
- Determining the procedures followed by conference committees[60]

HOW A BILL BECOMES A LAW

In Utah, the official lawmaking process proceeds through five major phases: introduction, committee action, floor action, enrollment, and governor's action. The first three phases take place in each house. Then the bill is returned to the original house for enrollment by the Office of Legislative Research and General Counsel. If the bill is vetoed by the governor, the legislature may override the veto with a constitutional two-thirds vote in both houses.

How a bill becomes a law is best illustrated by walking a bill through the legislative process in both houses, beginning in the house and proceeding to the senate. This procedure would work in reverse for a bill beginning in the senate and proceeding to the house.

The House of Representatives

1. *First Reading*. The house bill is introduced by title and read for the first time, then referred to the Rules Committee where the bill is examined for proper form and fiscal impact.
2. *Rules Committee*. The Rules Committee reports back to the house, orders that the bill be printed with the fiscal note for distribution, and recommends to the speaker of the house the standing committee to which the speaker should assign the bill.
3. *Committee Hearing*. The assigned standing committee, in public session, holds a meeting to review the bill. The committee may amend, hold, table, substitute, or make a favorable recommendation on the bill.
4. *Second Reading (committee action)*. The committee report is read to the house and adopted by motion. Adoption[61] of the standing committee report in the house is considered the second reading of three constitutionally required readings. The bill is then placed at the bottom of the third reading calendar and cannot be considered until the following day, except under suspension of the rules.
5. *Third Reading*. The bill is read to the house by title a third time and then explained by the sponsoring representative who answers questions that may be asked. Other representatives may speak and propose amendments to the bill.
6. *Consent Calendar*. The consent calendar is used in both houses to facilitate action on bills that carry the unanimous recommendation of the standing committee to which they were assigned. A standing committee, with a unanimous favorable vote by a quorum of the committee and upon request of the sponsor, may recommend that a bill be placed on the consent calendar. A bill certified as a consent calendar bill by a committee chair will be placed on the consent calendar following its second reading and remains on the calendar unless objected to by six members in the house. A bill remaining on the consent calendar for three days is considered for final passage without debate.[62]

7. *Vote.* On the third reading, the constitutional vote requirements apply as well as legislative rules which require legislators to vote, regardless of any conflict of interest. A motion for "previous question," which requires a two-thirds vote in the house, closes debate and stops further amendment to the bill.[63] In order for the bill to pass, the bill must receive at minimum the constitutional simple majority of the house's total membership (thirty-eight votes is a majority of the seventy-five votes possible).[64]
8. *Transmittal.* If the bill passes the house, the bill is certified with a communication informing the senate that the bill has passed the house, and is transmitted to the senate for a similar procedure.

The Senate

1. *First Reading.* The bill is read by title a first time and referred to the Rules Committee where the bill is assigned to a standing committee.
2. *Committee Hearing.* The committee may amend, hold, table, substitute, or make a favorable recommendation on the bill. In the senate, a motion for "previous question" to end debate in committee requires a majority vote. A motion for "previous question" is not allowed on the senate floor.
3. *Standing Committee Report.* The standing committee report is read to the senate, and the bill is placed at the bottom of the Second Reading Calendar. The senate's adoption of the standing committee report is not considered the second reading of the bill.
4. *Second Reading.* The bill is read a second time and debated. It is voted on and must pass in order to advance to third reading. The bill is then placed at the bottom of the third reading calendar and cannot be considered until the following day, except under suspension of the rules.
5. *Third Reading.* The bill is read a third time and debated. To pass, the bill must receive at a minimum, the constitutional majority of the total members of the senate (fifteen votes is a majority of the twenty-nine votes possible).[65]
6. *Final Vote.* On the third reading, the constitutional vote requirements apply as well as legislative rules which require legislators to vote, regardless of any conflict of interest.[66]
7. *Consent Calendar.* Similar procedure as in the House of Representatives except only three members of the senate are enough to remove a bill from the consent calendar.[67]
8. *Concurrence or Conference Committee.* Any amendments made *in the second house* must be approved by the first house. If there is a disagreement between the houses on any modifications, a conference committee is formed by three senators appointed by the president of the senate and three representatives appointed by the speaker of the house. The conference committee attempts to work out a compromise on the bill. The conference committee report and the bill must then be approved by each house for a bill to pass. If the conference committee report and actions are rejected by either house, a new conference committee can be established. If a compromise cannot be reached, the bill dies.[68]
9. *Signature of Presiding Officers and Enrollment.* After the bill has passed both houses, it is signed by both presiding officers. The Utah Constitution requires the presiding officers of each house to sign all bills and joint resolutions within five days after adjournment of the legislature.[69] This action is considered ministerial by the presiding officers who cannot veto the bill.[70] The bill is then examined by the Office of Legislative Research and General Counsel in a process called enrollment.[71] Enrollment is a final examination to find any technical errors and to verify all data (e.g., readings, vote totals, and amendments). The office prepares the bill in final form with all amendments included and returns it to the house of origin. This enrolled bill is an exact, accurate, and official copy of the enacted bill.

10. *Signature of the Governor.* The final bill is printed and sent to the governor for the governor's signature. If the governor fails to sign the bill, the bill automatically becomes law without the governor's signature. The governor has the power to veto the bill and send objections to the presiding officers of the House of Representative and the State Senate.[72]
11. A bill enacted at a legislative session is effective sixty days following adjournment, unless another date is specified within the bill.[73]

Bills Presented to Governor for Approval or Veto

After the Office of Legislative Research and General Counsel has enrolled the bill, the house of origin sends the bill to the governor for approval. If the governor signs the bill, it becomes law sixty days following adjournment, unless a different effective date is specified in the bill.

If the legislature is in session and the governor fails to sign a bill within ten days after receiving it (Sunday and legal holidays excepted), the bill automatically becomes law without the governor's signature sixty days following the legislative session.

The governor has the power to veto specific appropriation items by a line item veto. However, the governor is still under obligation to identify the specific items vetoed, along with the reasons for disapproval.

After the legislature adjourns, the governor has twenty days to make a decision about each bill. The governor may veto any bill and send objections to the presiding officer of the house where the bill originated within the twenty-day period. If the governor fails to take any action within the twenty days, the measure becomes law without the governor's signature.[74]

If the governor vetoes a bill before the end of the session, the legislature may reconsider the bill and override the veto with a constitutional two-thirds vote of both houses. If the governor vetoes a bill or an appropriation item after the legislature had adjourned *sine die*, the speaker and the president poll their members on the matter of a veto override session. If two-thirds of the members of each house are in favor of reconvening, the legislature will reconvene for a maximum of five days solely for the purpose of reconsidering action on the vetoed items. The legislature's action on vetoed legislation is a simple yes or no vote. No further amendments may be considered. A vetoed bill becomes law or an item of appropriation takes effect on its original effective date if, upon reconsideration, it receives a two-thirds vote in each house.[75]

Other Resolutions (House/Senate/Joint/Concurrent)

Except for joint resolutions amending the Utah Constitution or amending Utah Supreme Court Rules of Evidence or Procedures, resolutions generally have no force of law. They are considered an expression of the legislature and are printed in the session laws but are not "codified" (placed in the Utah Code). The type of resolution a sponsor chooses often depends upon whether one house, both houses, or both houses and the governor support a particular concept or proposal. Resolutions may be one of the three following types:

Simple Resolution. A simple resolution is a resolution passed by a single house. It is used to initiate action involving only that house, such as establishing a committee or altering the house's rules.

Joint Resolution. A joint resolution is passed by both houses. It is used for matters involving both houses such as appointing joint committees or issuing joint communiques. Proposals to amend the Utah Constitution or supreme court rules of procedures or evidence must be by joint resolution and receive the concurrence of both houses.

Concurrent Resolution. A concurrent resolution is passed by both houses and signed by the governor. It is used to express the position of the state on a specific matter.

If a legislator decides to use a concurrent resolution, the legislator generally secures the governor's support before filing the resolution. Once introduced, a resolution may not change from one type (concurrent, joint, or single house) to another. A new resolution must be introduced. Also, a concurrent or joint resolution that is only passed by a single house by the end of a legislative session does not become a simple resolution; it fails.

WHO CAN BE A LEGISLATOR

Constitutional Qualifications

The Utah Constitution establishes who is eligible and ineligible to serve as a state senator or representative. A person is eligible to be a legislator if the person is a U.S. citizen, at least twenty-five years of age, a qualified voter from his or her respective district, a three-year resident of Utah immediately prior to filing, and a six-month resident of the district immediately prior to filing.[76] In addition, "[n]o person elected to the office of senator or representative shall continue to serve in that office after ceasing to be a resident of the district from which elected."[77] Utah law requires all legislative candidates to file campaign finance statements.[78] Failure to file a summary report results in disqualification of the legislative candidate.[79]

The Utah Constitution also restricts any person, with some specific exceptions, who holds a public office of profit or trust under authority of the United States or the state from serving in the legislature.[80]

Length of Terms

The length of terms for state senators and representatives is also established by constitution. Members of the House of Representatives are chosen every two years in November of even-numbered years.[81] Terms of senators are four years; however, the constitution requires the staggering of senators' terms such that nearly half of the senate is elected every two years at the same time and places as state representatives.[82]

Salary and Compensation

The Utah Constitution provides for salary and compensation for legislators during legislative sessions and for attendance at interim committee meetings. The constitution also prohibits the legislature from increasing the salaries of its members. The governor, however, is authorized to appoint a citizens' salary commission to make recommendations to the legislature in even-numbered years for salary changes, which the legislature may "accept, reject or lower, . . . but may not, in any event increase."[83] Any salary changes take place January 1 of each odd-numbered year.

The legislature is required to provide in statute a means to reimburse expenses that legislators incur while carrying out their responsibilities during legislative sessions.[84] Legislators may receive additional per diem compensation and mileage for attendance at meetings of interim committees equal to rates established for regular legislative sessions.[85]

Ineligibility of Legislator for Civil Office of Profit

The Utah Constitution provides that "[n]o member of the Legislature, during the term for which he was elected, shall be appointed or elected to any civil office of profit under this State, which shall have been created, or the emoluments of which shall have been increased, during the term for which he was elected."[86] The purpose of this section is to guard against legislative dishonesty and give assurance to the public that a legislator is not having his judgment on bills improperly swayed, or personally profiting "by virtue of any enactments of the legislature of which he is a member."[87]

Nonetheless, the Utah Supreme Court also stated that there are cases in which this provision should not be applied rigidly or literally. In a 1964 case,[88] the court considered whether an *across-the-board* salary increase by the legislature to all state officers would disqualify a member of the legislature who had passed the salary increase during the legislator's term from running for a state office during that same term for which the legislator was elected. The court determined that an across-the-board salary increase was an incident where there was no possibility of legislative impropriety of conduct, and could, in effect deprive the public of an otherwise qualified candidate.[89]

Each House is the Judge of the Election and Qualifications of its Members

Each house of the legislature is required to judge the election and qualification of its members.[90] The power to determine the election and eligibility of its members preserves the integrity and independence of the legislature and prevents the encroachment on the legislature's powers by the executive and judicial branches.

Though no challenge has been made to date to the proper election of a legislator, clearly the constitution vests the power of judgment of process in the house to which the legislator is elected. Likewise, if a challenge is made to a legislator's qualifications, this constitutional provision gives each house the exclusive authority to judge whether or not a legislator meets the relevant Utah constitutional provisions that establish the qualifications for legislative service:

- Article 6, Section 5 establishes age, residency, and citizenship requirements for legislative service
- Article 6, Section 6 prohibits any person holding a public office of profit or trust under authority of this state from being a member of the legislature
- Article 5, Section 1 prohibits a person who exercises the powers of one branch of state government from exercising the functions of another branch of state government

"Qualifications" has been construed broadly by the courts such that the legislature's right to judge a member's qualifications also includes the right to decide when a member has become disqualified, which decision is not subject to court review.[91] However, the Utah Supreme Court has suggested that intervention by the courts might be appropriate should the house or senate consider qualifications or disqualifications other than those mandated by the constitution.[92]

Legislator Ethics

Because Utah has a part-time legislature, many legislators also work outside the legislature in part-time or full-time positions. To reconcile the functions of privately employed legislators who have their own private interests with maintenance of high ethical standards, Utah statute and legislative rules provides guidelines for judging conflicts of interest.[93] Legislators are required to vote on all measures regardless of any conflict of interest. Legislators must orally declare any conflict of interest directly to the house, senate, or legislative committee before voting on any legislative matter, and the declaration is noted in the respective journal[94] of the house or senate or in the minutes of a committee meeting. A legislator also must file a public document disclosing the general legislative areas in which a legislator may have a conflict of interest with the respective secretary of the State Senate or the chief clerk of the House of Representatives.[95]

Legislative Ethics Committees

The legislature has established a committee on ethics in each house that is responsible for enforcing the rules of ethical conduct.[96] If a member is found guilty of unethical conduct, the Ethics Committee recommends appropriate action to the member's respective house. Acceptance of a recommendation for expulsion requires a two-thirds vote of all members in the respective house.[97] All other recommendations require a majority vote.

The senate and house ethics committees attempt to oversee legislative behavior and prevent or report conduct in various areas, including action that destroys the independence of judgment of a legislator, exercise of undue influence upon any governmental agency or entity, or any act that would be an abuse of official position or a violation of trust.

Legislative Privilege

The Speech or Debate Clause of the Utah Constitution[98] provides civil and criminal immunity to legislative branch members engaged in actions they take within the legitimate legislative sphere.[99] This immunity frees legislators to represent the interests of their constituents and effectively discharge their public duty without fear of being called into court by aggrieved members of the public. The intent of the provision is not to protect legislators against prosecutions for their own personal benefit, but to allow the legislative process to continue, uninterrupted, for the benefit and welfare of the people.

Most case law with respect to legislative immunity revolves around what constitutes the legitimate legislative sphere, or what are protected legislative functions. Courts have identified certain areas deserving protection that include (1) speeches on the floor of the legislature, (2) voting on the floor or in committee, (3) circulation of information to other legislators, (4) participation in committee proceedings and reports, (5) issuance of subpoenas pursuant to committee investigations, (6) field investigations, (7) arrangements for seating the press in the gallery, and (8) decisions about what kind of lobbying to allow on the floor of the chamber.[100]

Courts have also identified areas in which legislators are not generally entitled to protection that include (1) personnel actions dealing with food service employees,[101] (2) accepting bribes,[102] and (3) morning prayers.[103]

THE APPROPRIATIONS PROCESS[104]

The Governor's Budget[105]

Each year the governor prepares a budget (an estimate of expenditures and the expected revenues for a fiscal year) for which the legislature has a responsibility to review and approve funding for all of state government. An extensive amount of work is carried out by many individuals before the governor's budget is presented to the legislature in January of each year. Between the previous July and September, state agencies prepare budget requests on forms issued in June by the Governor's Office of Planning and Budget (GOPB). Upon receipt of the agency budget requests, GOPB in September and October, review the requests and prepare a summary for the governor.

During October and November, GOPB holds hearings on the agencies' budget requests and prepares the governor's estimates of proposed expenditures and expected revenues for the upcoming fiscal year, or the "Governor's Budget," which is issued in December. The governor's budget includes an estimate for the legislative department certified by the speaker of the house and the president of the senate, without revision. It also includes an estimate for the judicial department certified by the state court administrator without any revisions, although it may have separate recommendations.

Meanwhile, between September and December, the Office of Legislative Fiscal Analyst makes revenue estimates in conjunction with the Governor's Office of Planning and Budget, assists the legislature by analyzing the governor's budget, and makes recommendations to the legislature about budget amounts.[106]

Appropriation Subcommittees

During the annual general session of the legislature, the legislature reviews the governor's budget and its accompanying message, reviews the fiscal analyst's recommendations, and refers the agency budgets to joint appropriations subcommittees. The ten appropriations subcommittees hold hearings with the agencies during the general session of the legislature, make decisions on the individual line items, and report back their recommendations to the Executive Appropriations Committee.

Executive Appropriations Committee

During the last several weeks of the session, the Executive Appropriations Committee holds hearings with the chairs of the appropriations subcommittees and the agencies. The responsibilities of the Executive Appropriations Committee is to approve the actions of the subcommittees, recommend further action, and if necessary, make alterations to balance the budget. The Executive Appropriations Committee gives final directions to the Office of Legislative Fiscal Analyst to prepare the appropriations acts for action by the entire legislature.[107]

Ultimately, the legislature debates and passes an appropriations act which funds state government operations from July 1-June 30 of the following year. In addition, one or more supplemental appropriations acts are also passed, which include additional funding for state government operations and fund any bills that have passed that have an additional impact on the budget.

Governor's Approval of the Appropriations Act

As with all other bills, the governor reviews the appropriations bills and signs, vetoes, or lets the bills pass into law without signature. However, the Utah Constitution provides the governor with the power to veto any single item of appropriation while approving other portions of the bill. This power extends only to items of appropriation.[108] As a general rule, conditions placed on an appropriation may not be vetoed. The one subject rule precludes the inclusion of substantive legislation in an appropriations bill.[109]

After the budget has been adopted, it becomes the responsibility of the governor and the executive branch to implement the budget in conformance with the terms set forth by the legislature.[110] Excess funds in accounts at the end of the fiscal year are closed out (lapsed) except for certain funds which are made nonlapsing either in the appropriations act or in other Utah statutes.

Balance Budget Is Required

Utah's constitution requires a balanced budget.[111] It provides that "[f]or any fiscal year, the legislature may not make an appropriation or authorize an expenditure if the State's expenditure exceeds the total tax provided for by statute and applicable to the particular appropriation or expenditure."[112]

Sources of Funding[113]

Budgeted revenues are estimates of anticipated receipts as determined by the Legislative Fiscal Analyst and approved by the Executive Appropriations Committee. This committee, in conjunction with the Office of the Legislative Fiscal Analyst, prepares allocations of state funds for each of the joint appropriations subcommittees. Other sources of funding may be available for subcommittee use, such as federal funds, dedicated credits revenue, trust accounts and restricted revenue. Key revenue categories are noted briefly below.

General Fund

The primary revenue source is the sales tax, although there are several other taxes and fees that contribute to the General Fund (e.g., insurance, inheritance, severance, beer, and cigarette taxes). General funds can be spent at the discretion of the legislature, as the Utah Constitution allows.

Uniform School Fund

The Uniform School Fund is largely comprised of revenues generated by one tax, the individual income tax. The corporate income and franchise taxes are also an important revenue source for this fund. The Utah Constitution mandates that interest and dividends from the Uniform School Fund may only be used to fund the state's public education system.[114]

Transportation Fund

Revenue for the Transportation Fund is primarily from fees and taxes on motor fuel. This revenue is constitutionally restricted to pay costs of administration, construction, maintenance, and repair of state and local roads, driver education, and enforcement of motor vehicle laws.[115]

CONSTITUTIONAL POWERS AND RESTRICTIONS ON POWERS

In general, all powers not specifically delegated to the federal government in the U.S. Constitution are reserved to the states. The Tenth Amendment specifically clarifies this delegation of powers stating: "The powers not delegated to the United States by the Constitution, nor prohibited by it to the States, are reserved to the States respectively, or to the people."

The Utah Constitution gives the legislative power of the state to the Utah Legislature through the State Senate and the House of Representatives, and to the legal voters of the state through the initiative and referendum process.[116] The Utah Supreme Court has held that the extent of the legislature's power is inherently broad. As a general rule, absent any express or implied constitutional restraint, the legislature may act on any subject within the sphere of government, and enact all laws necessary to carry out the purposes of government.[117]

LIMITATIONS ON LEGISLATIVE POWERS

Although the legislature's lawmaking power is inherently broad, there are a number of constitutional provisions that limit this power. These provisions include prohibitions against laws that (1) constitute private or special legislation, (2) authorize lotteries, (3) create special commissions with special privileges, (4) lend the state's credit, (5) impose taxes for political subdivisions, or (6) delegate overly broad rulemaking authority to administrative agencies that would constitute an unlawful delegation of legislative authority.

Prohibition Against Private or Special Legislation

The legislature enacts most legislation through general laws. A "general law" is one that applies to and operates uniformly upon all members of a legislatively created class of persons, places, or things. A law that requires licensing and registration of all motor vehicles that use public roadways is an example of a general law. Utah Constitution Article 6, Section 26 states that "[n]o private or special law shall be enacted where a general law can be applicable."

A special law classifies its objects unreasonably.[118] Special legislation differs from general legislation only in that the law does not apply uniformly to a particular class, but excludes some members thereof. A special law *may* be constitutional if (1) the classification is reasonable, (2) general legislation is unable to cover the same issues that the special legislation covers, and (3) the special legislation accomplishes a public purpose. An example of a special law held unconstitutional by the Utah Supreme Court was a law that required mercantile and commercial houses in cities with a population of ten thousand or more to close at 6 p.m., while drugstores and houses dealing in perishable goods were exempt from the closing requirement.[119]

The Legislature May Not Authorize Lotteries

The Utah Constitution prohibits the legislature from enacting laws that would legalize gambling: "The Legislature shall not authorize any game of chance, lottery or gift enterprise under any pretense or for any purpose."[120] The Utah Supreme Court has made several rulings on what does or does not constitute a lottery. "Double cash bingo" did not constitute a lottery because a bingo card was free; thus, there was no valuable consideration required to be paid for the chance to win.[121] On the other hand, a player's "time, attention, thought, energy, and money" spent in transportation to the store to buy a game card for a chance to win was considered to be "consideration" with respect to game cards issued by oil companies.[122] Punch board was held not to be a game of chance in violation of this provision, but a game of skill. The Utah Supreme Court has determined that one player is likely to be more skillful than another and the player's skill does not alter the nature of the game.[123]

Special Privileges Forbidden

The State is the source of all local government powers, and grants cities the "authority to exercise all powers relating to municipal affairs."[124] However, another constitutional provision forbids the legislature from creating special commissions[125] or boards that may usurp the functions of local governments. The Utah Constitution prohibits the legislature from delegating any powers to special commissions or authorities that interfere with or perform municipal functions.[126]

The Lending of Public Credit

The Utah Constitution prohibits the state from "lending its credit" to a private enterprise. This means that the state, a county, city, town, school district or other political subdivision is prohibited from acting as a surety or guarantor for the debts of a private entity.[127] A government entity is free, however, to make loans and grants to private entities as long as there is an underlying public purpose.

In the November 2004 General Election, Utah voters adopted a constitutional amendment that changed this constitutional provision to allow for the state or a public institution of post-secondary education to acquire an equity interest in a private business entity as consideration for the sale, license, or other transfer of intellectual property that it had developed. The amended provision also provides that the state or institution may hold or dispose of the equity interest.

State Prohibited from Taxing for Political Subdivision

The Utah Constitution places restrictions on the legislature's ability to interfere with a local government authority's power to levy local taxes. It provides that the "[l]egislature may not impose a tax for the purpose of a political subdivision of the State, but may by statute authorize political subdivisions of the State to assess and collect taxes for their own purposes."[128]

The Utah Supreme Court in *Mountain States Tel. & Tel. Co. v. Garfield County*, considered whether the legislature had interfered with the right of the county under local self-government to assess and levy taxes for its own purposes. The court upheld a statute that required a statewide uniform levy upon real property to fund local tax assessment, collection, and distribution costs by determining that the tax had a larger statewide purpose.[129] The tax financed the assessment, collection, and distribution of ad valorem property taxes in each county, ensuring that local county taxing authorities had sufficient funds to perform their duties.

State action will be considered to be a violation of the constitution if the legislature imposes a tax for only a local purpose. However, if there is a state public purpose as well as a county purpose for a tax, then the legislature's tax may be permissible.[130]

Unlawful Delegation of Legislative Authority

The Utah Constitution's separation of powers provision divides the powers of government between the legislative, executive, and judicial departments.[131] This provision prohibits any person charged with powers belonging to one of these departments from exercising any functions belonging to either of the other departments, unless expressly directed or permitted by the Utah Constitution.

Article 6 of the Utah Constitution defines the powers vested in the Utah Legislature. The executive branch does not have expressed or implied rulemaking authority. That authority stems only from the legislative branch through statutory grants of authority.

The Utah Supreme Court has ruled that the legislature does not violate the separation of powers provision by delegating rulemaking authority to an administrative agency.[132] However, the Utah Supreme Court has interpreted the Utah Constitution as limiting the ability of the legislature to delegate rulemaking authority to an administrative agency in two ways. First, the legislature must not delegate an essential legislative function to an administrative agency; and second, the legislature must provide sufficient policies and standards to guide the administrative agency in its rulemaking authority.[133]

REAPPORTIONMENT AND REDISTRICTING

U.S. Constitution Census Requirement for Reapportionment

The United States Constitution specifically requires that a population census be taken every ten years for the primary purpose of reapportioning congressional seats in the U.S. House of Representatives.[134] Reapportionment must be carried out for the entire country at one time, and the census is taken as of April 1 in the year ending in zero, with the population data available to the states by April or May in the year ending in the number one.[135]

Without prescribing an apportionment procedure, the U.S. Constitution specifies that the number of congressional seats is to be equally apportioned to each state according to its population.[136] U.S. statute provides that the total number of congressional seats must equal 435. Each state must have at least one representative in the U.S. House of Representatives and the remaining 385 seats are distributed in accordance with the highest ratio of population.[137] Each state is then responsible for its own "redistricting" process—the process of dividing the state into single member congressional districts that are nearly equal in population.

Utah Constitution Requirement for Redistricting

The Utah Constitution provides the Utah Legislature with exclusive authority to redistrict congressional, legislative, and other state district boundaries.[138] After the chief clerk of the U.S. House of Representatives certifies to the governor the number of congressional seats to which Utah is entitled, "redistricting" takes place in order to define the geographic boundaries for each district. Utah Constitution, Article IX, Section 1 requires that the redistricting process be completed by the general session following the receipt of the census data. Utah Constitution, Article IX, Section 2 provides that the senate may not exceed "twenty-nine in number, and the number of representatives shall never be less than twice nor greater than three times the number of senators."

Utah Legislative Process for Redistricting

The legislative process for redistricting is not outlined in Utah statute. Traditionally, the speaker of the house and the president of the senate appoint a joint committee on redistricting. The committee determines the redistricting process, which usually includes public hearings throughout the state. The committee also adopts specific guidelines for determining geographic boundaries in order to comply with constitutional, statutory, and case law standards. The legislature works with nonpartisan staff in the Office of Legislative Research and General Counsel to draw district lines in accordance with committee adopted guidelines.

Congressional and Case Law Standards

In drawing congressional and legislative district lines, the legislature is constrained by various legal requirements established by the United States and Utah constitutions, state and federal laws, and case law. The legal requirements limit, but do not totally restrict, the legislature's discretion in redistricting decisions. The intent of the requirements is to ensure that basic concepts of fairness are incorporated into the naturally political redistricting arena. Examples of guidelines a redistricting committee may adopt to draw district lines in compliance with constitutional, statutory, and case law requirements are (1) establishing total population deviations for congressional and legislative plans; (2) drawing lines to maintain communities of interest, respecting political subdivision boundaries where possible, drawing districts as contiguous and compact as practicable, and not drawing districts to intentionally protect or defeat any incumbent; (3) providing for single member districts; and (4) drawing lines to enhance the influence of minority groups in the electoral process.[139]

Equal Protection

Under the United States Supreme Court's and the Utah Supreme Court's interpretations of the United States and Utah constitutions, there is consensus that all districts must be equal in population. However, the courts have imposed different standards for congressional, legislative, and other state districts. For congressional districts, the standard is "as equal in population as practicable"[140] and is very restrictive. For legislative and other state districts, that standard is "substantially equal in population."[141] In 2001, Utah's Redistricting Committee adopted an overall deviation standard of 2 percent (plus or minus 1 percent) for congressional districts and 8 percent (plus or minus 4 percent) for legislative and state school districts. Final deviations of adopted redistricting plans were within these ranges.

Nondilution of Racial Minority Influence

The Voting Rights Act of 1965 put an end to literacy tests and poll taxes. Section 2 of the Voting Rights Act attempts to secure the right to vote for racial and language minorities[142] by prohibiting states and political subdivisions from imposing or applying voting qualifications, prerequisites to voting, or other standards, practices, or procedures that result in the denial or abridgment of the right to vote on account of race or color.[143] Section 2 of the Voting Rights Act has been used to attack redistricting plans on the ground that they discriminated against minority groups and abridged minorities' right to vote by diluting the voting strength of their population in the state. In 1986, the U.S. Supreme Court struck down North Carolina's redistricting plan, holding that any redistricting plan that serves to minimize or cancel out the voting strength of a protected minority group or which is motivated by an intent to discriminate against the group is unconstitutional.[144]

Although considerations of the race of persons within a district should be a factor in drawing district lines, it may not be the sole factor. In the 1990s, in the *Shaw v. Reno* cases, which originated in North Carolina,[145] the U.S. Supreme Court held that states that drew plans solely in reliance on race in an effort to comply with the Voting Rights Act, also violated the equal protection clause. Although race can and sometimes must be a factor in drawing plans, it cannot be the exclusive factor.[146]

Political Gerrymandering[147]

Although for years the U.S. Supreme Court had ruled that they had no jurisdiction to decide cases where a minority political party alleged discrimination in the creation of Congressional or legislative districts, the Court reversed that position in 1986. In *Davis v. Bandemer*,[148] the Court reviewed an Indiana redistricting plan and ruled that partisan gerrymandering is an issue that courts may at least review. Although the court agreed to review the question in that case, they concluded that a violation of the Equal Protection Clause had not been proven.[149]

When the U.S. Supreme Court again considered political gerrymandering of the Pennsylvania congressional redistricting plan in *Veith v. Jubelirer*,[150] it did not provide much additional guidance in the political gerrymandering arena. After that case, it is still impossible to tell whether or not a court would even consider a lawsuit alleging a political gerrymandering violation of the Equal Protection Clause.

LEGISLATIVE STAFF OFFICES

The Office of Legislative Research and General Counsel, the Office of Legislative Fiscal Analyst, the Office of Legislative Auditor General, and the Legislative Printing Office are nonpartisan staff offices that serve the legislature. The responsibilities of each of these offices are carried out under the supervision of the Legislative Management Committee and its oversight subcommittees. The Legislative Management Committee employs, upon recommendation of the appropriate subcommittee and approval of both houses by a majority vote, the legislative auditor, legislative fiscal analyst, the director of the Office of Legislative Research and General Counsel, and the legislative general counsel. These individuals are appointed for six-year terms; and each one is subject to removal for cause upon a majority vote of both houses or by a two-thirds vote of the Legislative Management Committee.[151]

Office of Legislative Research and General Counsel

The Office of Legislative Research and General Counsel provides research and legal services to the legislature.[152] These services include legal review and policy analysis of current law and proposed legislation and all legal support services for the legislature, including representing the legislature, its members, and its staff offices in litigation. Utah Constitution Article VI, Section 32(2) provides that "[t]he Legislature may appoint legal counsel which shall provide and control all legal services for the Legislature unless otherwise provided by statute."[153] The Office of Legislative Research and General Counsel is that legal counsel to the legislature. The office promotes an understanding of critical legislative issues, serves as a liaison with other government agencies and the public, and is responsible for giving advice and counsel regarding proposed changes in the law and for drafting legislation.

The office reviews all proposed legislation before introduction in a session and prepares requested amendments and substitute bills or resolutions after the legislation has been introduced. The office is also required to review each bill for constitutionality and to attach a legislative review note and any interim committee note to the last page of the printed bill. Before bills passed by the legislature are submitted to the governor, the office reviews each bill to determine if it meets the constitutional standards for final passage and through the enrolling process, makes technical corrections. The office prepares the chapterization of the bills that are adopted in each session and provides the Legislative Printing Office with the update and enrolled copies of all legislation for creation of the Laws of Utah. Following each session, document technicians update the statutory database of the Utah Code[154] for statutory searches and bill drafting purposes.[155] This database of legislation is available online at http://www.le.utah.gov.

The office also provides legal, research, and administrative support for standing and interim committees, task forces, and legislative commissions. Attorneys and policy analysts produce research reports, prepare briefing papers, and make presentations before legislative committees. They work with committee and task force chairs to produce agendas, publish minutes, and prepare handouts and mailings (both electronic and hard copy).

A legislative information section maintains resource center that is available to legislators, their committees, legislative staff, and the public.

Office of Legislative Fiscal Analyst

The fiscal analyst is given duties and responsibilities relating to fiscal oversight in both statute and legislative rule.[156] Thirty days prior to each legislative session, the Office of Legislative Fiscal Analyst is to receive from the governor proposed budget recommendations. The fiscal analyst is required to review this executive budget before the legislature convenes and to make recommendations and comments to the legislature on each item or program. The fiscal analyst not only recommends specific levels of funding, but also (1) highlights instances in which the administration may be failing to carry out the expressed intent of the legislature, (2) calls attention to each proposed new service contained in the governor's budget, and (3) points out items that have been previously denied by the legislature.[157]

The fiscal analyst and staff are responsible for providing a fiscal note on all legislation that identifies the legislation's fiscal implications, either estimated cost or cost savings. The fiscal notes represent an independent appraisal, but are in no way binding upon the legislature. Additionally, the office prepares detailed revenue estimates for all state operating funds.

The office staffs the Executive Appropriations Committee and the joint appropriations subcommittees and has responsibility for drafting the appropriation acts and the School Finance Act. Following the legislative session, the fiscal analyst prepares and issues the "Appropriations Report" which contains a summary of all appropriations, denials, reductions and increases, revenue measures, new programs, and expressed legislative intent.

Office of Legislative Auditor General

The major function of the Office of Legislative Auditor General is to conduct performance audits of state departments, institutions, school districts, special districts, and state colleges and universities.[158] Performance audits may show the efficiency of operating costs of an agency or program, indicate places where an agency or program is not effective in its design to serve the public, or reveal noncompliance or discrepancies in interpreting the legislature's intent for creating the agency or program.

Written audit requests may be submitted to the legislative auditor general by legislators, legislative committees, legislative subcommittees, or legislative task forces. Other audit assignments are developed as a result of committee study assignments, allegations from the public, and concerns identified as a result of previous audits. All audit assignments are reviewed and approved by the Audit Subcommittee of the Legislative Management Committee.

A summary report of all audit findings goes to each legislator, a complete report is sent to members of the appropriate committees, and copies of reports are available to the general public.[159]

Legislative Printing Office/Bill Room

The Legislative Printing Office/Bill Room operates under the direction of the legislative fiscal analyst to provide printing, typesetting, and graphic services to the legislature, its staff offices, and other state agencies. During the legislative session, the Bill Room's responsibilities include preparation of the daily house and senate journals, house and senate bills, amendments, agendas, minutes, status sheets, and miscellaneous printing.[160] In the interim, the Legislative Printing Office publishes the final house and senate journals, *Laws of Utah*,[161] reports, manuals, audits, and other state agency publications.

USE OF INFORMATION TECHNOLOGY

The legislature's use of information technology began in the early 1980s and focused on bill processing, tracking, status, calendars, and voting records. Other early uses of information technology included policy research, budget processing, and communications. Mainframe computer technology provided the backbone for the legislature's information technology systems at that time.

By the mid-1990s, as information technology evolved from mainframes to personal computers, the legislature adopted the new technologies to further increase productivity. With the adoption of personal computing and network technologies, the legislature begin offering new services that included Web sites providing information about legislators, committees, research, bills, and access to the Utah Code. Trends in research on the use of the legislature's Web site is also discussed in Chapter 5, *The Executive Branch*.

Figure 5-5 indicates trends in research on the use of the legislature's Web site.

The legislature also began employing email technology to provide another means of communication with the public and governmental entities. Other new services are audio streaming and wireless technology. The legislature's Web site also provides video streaming of the annual general session which is live and recorded and live audio broadcast of legislative committee meetings and general sessions. Both the State Senate and the House of Representatives as well as all three legislative staff offices are fully computerized and networked.

While implementing information technology changes within the legislative branch of government, the legislature also created the Information Technology Commission to review and recommend statewide information technology policies.[162] The commission's membership represents all three branches of government, along with public education, higher education, the Public Service Commission, and private individuals involved with information technology. Charged with developing statewide information technology policy, the commission has served as the primary legislative entity for that purpose.

In 2003, the Information Technology Commission was expanded to include all types of technology with an emphasis on information, aerospace, and biotechnology.[163] In recognition of the new legislative assignments, the name was changed to the Utah Technology Commission to more accurately reflect the additional duties. At the same time, the legislature also created the Utah Technology Industry Council, which is a private-sector body charged with making business recommendations to the commission in statutorily authorized joint meetings. Together, the commission and council are designed to develop state-wide technology policies for both the public and private sectors.

The legislature considers technology to be a key to improving citizen access to government, a growth industry for Utah's business community, and a communication tool for connecting and improving the lives of everyone living in Utah.

Chapter 7

The Judicial Branch

The judiciary is usually considered the third branch of government—the other two being the executive and legislative. The framers of the federal constitution considered this branch the weakest of the three. Despite this initial perspective on the judiciary, this branch has proven to be a powerful and enormously influential part of the national scene. The same can be said for the fifty state court systems. Two experts on state governments wrote this about our state court systems, "[t]hey determine the division of powers between state and local governments, outline relations within families and among contractors, define individual rights and liberties, and levy criminal sanctions. Their rulings affect people who never go to court. Decisions on school segregation, medical malpractice, usury limits, and product liability affect all of us."[1]

> **In this chapter:**
>
> Constitutional Powers (p. 117)
> Utah Courts (p. 118)
> Administration (p. 122)
> Judicial Selection, Retention, Discipline, and Removal (p. 124)
> The Judicial Process (p. 128)
> Grand Jury (p. 129)
> Use of Information Technology (p. 130)

CONSTITUTIONAL POWERS

"The judicial power of the state shall be vested in a Supreme Court, in a trial court of general jurisdiction known as the district court, and in such other courts as the Legislature by statute may establish."[2] With that broad language, the framers of the Judicial Article to Utah's Constitution in 1984 laid the groundwork for the current Utah judicial system for which the Utah Supreme Court, the district court, and the legislature share responsibility.

In carrying out their responsibilities, the legislature and the Judicial Council, working under the framework of the Utah Constitution which establishes the Utah Supreme Court and district courts, have created a court system, overseen by the Administrative Office of the Courts, that addresses the needs of the citizens of the state as expeditiously as possible.

Judicial Council as Overseer

The Judicial Council, chaired by the chief justice of the Utah Supreme Court, has the major responsibility for oversight of the courts.[3] Through the Administrative Office of the Courts, the Judicial Council directs the day-to-day activities of the various departments within the judicial system. The Judicial Council's administrative responsibilities include rulemaking and, in conjunction with the Utah Supreme Court, hiring of the state court administrator.

Figure 7-1

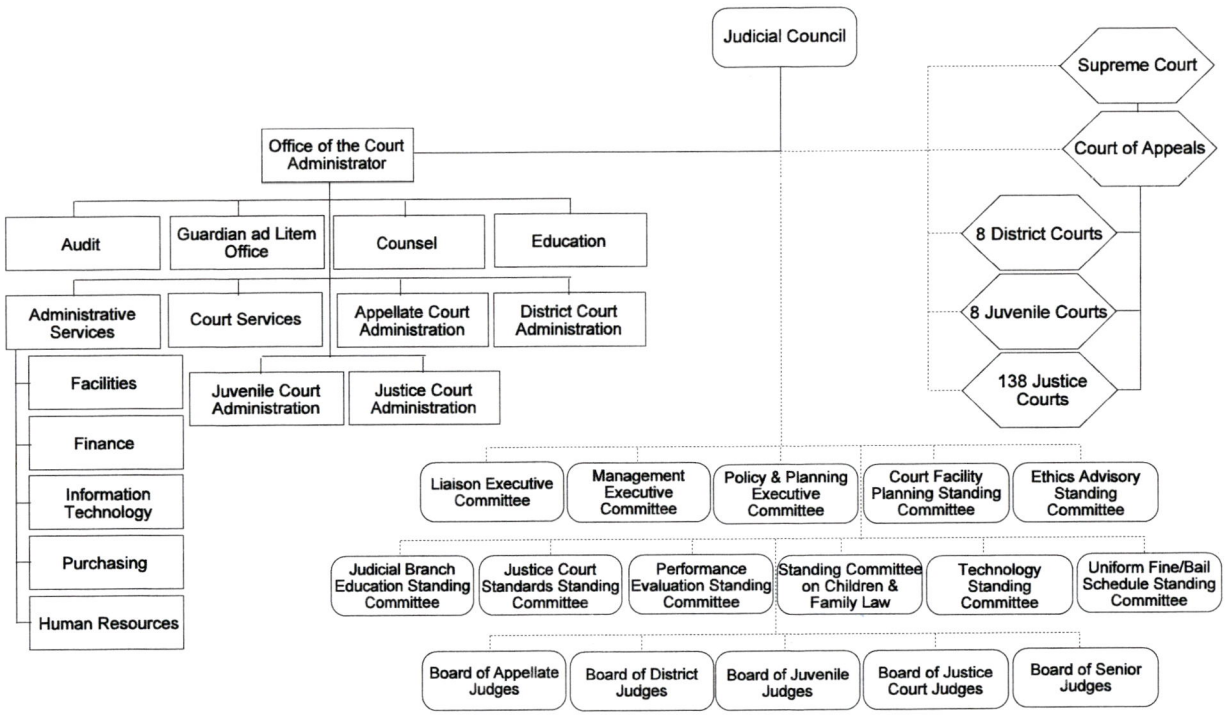

Rulemaking

Rules are the main governing tool for the courts in Utah. They determine practice, procedure, administration, qualifications for certain positions, and establish programs. The Utah Supreme Court is charged with adopting "rules of procedure and evidence to be used in the courts of the state."[4] The Judicial Council is responsible for promulgating the Rules of Judicial Administration, which are internal administrative rules that regulate the day-to-day routines of the Administrative Office of the Courts as well as attorney and judicial conduct.[5] It should be noted that the Utah Constitution gives the legislature the authority to amend rules of procedure and evidence adopted by the Utah Supreme Court.[6] The legislature may not, however, amend judicial administration rules as they are the rules that govern the internal workings of the courts.

Regulation of Practice of Law

The Utah Supreme Court is also constitutionally tasked with the regulation of the practice of law.[7] This includes admission standards for attorneys practicing law in Utah, the administration of the state bar exam, admission of those candidates who successfully pass the exam, and discipline of those whose conduct as practicing attorneys do not meet the standards set out in the Rules of Professional Conduct. While much of this aspect of the court's responsibilities is delegated to the Utah State Bar, the Utah Supreme Court is the final arbiter of Rules of Professional Conduct and reviews all recommendations for attorney discipline.

UTAH COURTS

The Utah Supreme Court and district courts are created by the constitution; all other courts in Utah are created by the legislature. These are the Utah Court of Appeals;[8] juvenile courts;[9] and justice courts,[10] which include small claims courts. Circuit courts, which the legislature created in 1977, were repealed in 1996 and their functions merged into the district courts.

Supreme Court

As the highest court in the state, the Utah Supreme Court is the final arbiter of legal disputes. The court of last resort for interpretations of state law, the Utah Supreme Court is made up of five justices. The chief justice is elected by the membership to serve a term of four years. An associate chief justice is elected in the same manner for a term of two years.

The Utah Supreme Court has original jurisdiction to decide matters of state law referred to it by a court of the United States, and to issue extraordinary writs or enforce any of its orders, judgments, or decrees.[11] Its appellate jurisdiction includes interlocutory appeals, cases certified to it from the Utah Court of Appeals, the discipline of members of the Utah State Bar, first degree and capital felony convictions in district court, final orders of certain formal adjudicative proceedings, and regarding the discipline of judges, a review of any Judicial Conduct Commission order of discipline.

Court of Appeals

There are seven judges on the Utah Court of Appeals. Sitting in rotating panels of three, appellate judges hear all cases appealed from the judgment of a trial court except those reserved to the Utah Supreme Court, and final adjudicative orders of state agencies.[12] A presiding judge is elected by the membership and serves for a two-year term. The responsibilities of the presiding judge include the rotation and scheduling of panels and acting as a liaison between the Utah Court of Appeals and the Utah Supreme Court.[13]

District Courts

As the trial court of general jurisdiction within the state, the district court is the workhorse of the judiciary. Except for adjudicatory matters appealed directly to the Utah Court of Appeals and actions filed directly with the Utah Supreme Court by law, "[t]he district court has original jurisdiction in all matters civil and criminal."[14] This includes civil lawsuits, divorce, child custody, probate, and criminal actions prosecuted by the state.

The judicial system is divided into eight geographic districts, with each district comprised of at least three counties (see figure 7-2). In total there are seventy district court judges in the state.

Figure 7-2

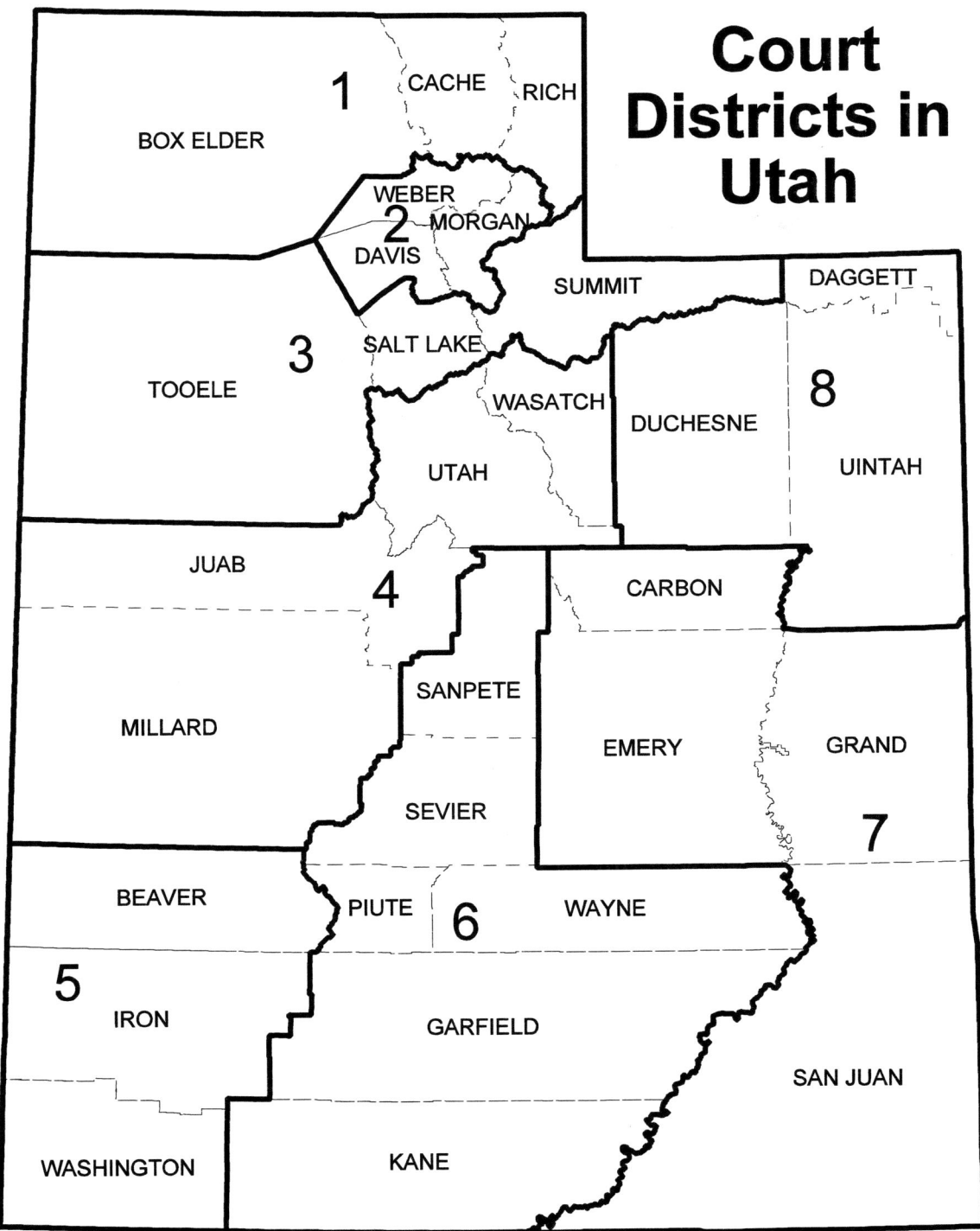

In addition to judges, the district courts also employ court commissioners.[15] These quasi-judicial officers of the court hear specific types of cases and make recommendations to judges as to final resolution. Court commissioners are regulated by the Judicial Council. There are currently eight court commissioners serving in three district courts throughout the state (see table 7-1).

Table 7-1

Number of District Court Judges and Commissioners

District	Counties	# of Judges		# of Commissioners
		District	Juvenile	
1	Box Elder, Cache, Rich	4	2	0
2	Weber, Davis, Morgan	14	5	3
3	Salt Lake, Summit, Tooele	28	9	4 district, 1 juvenile
4	Utah, Wasatch, Juab, Millard	12	4	1
5	Beaver, Iron, Washington	5	2	0
6	Garfield, Kane, Piute, Sanpete, Sevier, Wayne	2	1	0
7	Carbon, Emery, Grand, San Juan	3	2	0
8	Daggett, Duchesne, Uintah	2	1	0

Juvenile Courts

Divided into the same eight geographic districts as the district court system and holding equal status with the district court,[16] the juvenile court generally has exclusive original jurisdiction over persons under eighteen years of age who violate any federal, state, or municipal law, and any child who is abused, neglected, or dependent. One exception is child custody in connection with a divorce when there is no allegation of abuse. Juvenile courts also have concurrent jurisdiction with the district and justice courts over adults contributing to the delinquency and neglect of a minor.

Traffic offenses committed by minors are handled by the juvenile court only if the minor is under sixteen years of age. If the minor is over sixteen years of age, the juvenile court only handles specific enumerated offenses that include automobile homicide, driving under the influence, and reckless driving.[17]

The twenty-six juvenile court judges across the state are selected by the same process as district court judges. There is also one juvenile court commissioner in the Third Judicial District.

Justice Courts

Dealing with Class B and C misdemeanors and infractions committed within their jurisdiction is the mainstay of justice courts. They are also responsible for local ordinance violations, and small claims actions. Established by municipalities and counties, these courts' jurisdiction is limited to their local government's boundaries.

The judges for these courts, county and municipal, are hired and treated differently than state court judges. County judges are initially appointed by a county commission and must stand for a retention election every four years. Municipal judges are appointed by city officials for four-year terms. Retention is by reappointment. Judges may be both county and municipal judges and, while a person applying for a judicial position in all other courts is required to be licensed to practice law in Utah, no such requirement exists for justice court judges.

Court Administrators

Each level of courts employs an administrator. The state court administrator is appointed by the Utah Supreme Court and serves at the pleasure of both the Utah Supreme Court and the Judicial Council.[18] The state court administrator is responsible for the overall management of the court system within the state. Administrators for the appellate, district, juvenile, and justice courts are appointed by the state administrator in consultation with the chief justice of the Utah Supreme Court and the specific court's board of judges.

Table 7-2

Judicial Qualifications*

Court	Age	Utah Residency	Bar Membership
Supreme Court	30	5 years	Yes
Court of Appeals	25	3 years	Yes
District Court	25	3 years	Yes
Juvenile Court	25	3 years	Yes
Justice Court	25	3 years	No

*All judges must be citizens of the United States.

ADMINISTRATION
Judicial Council

Article VIII of the Utah Constitution creates a judicial council as the policy-making body of the Utah judiciary which is charged with the responsibility to adopt rules for the administration of the courts.[19] The council must be comprised of at least one representative from each court, and each court must elect one or more of its members to serve on the council.[20] In addition to the chief justice, the Utah Supreme Court is to elect one of its members to the council. One member is elected from the court of appeals, five members are elected by the board of district court judges, two members are elected by the juvenile court, three members are elected by the justice court judges, and one commissioner is elected by the Board of Commissioners of the Utah State Bar.

The chief justice of the Utah Supreme Court serves as the presiding officer of the council, as the chief administrative officer for the courts, and is responsible to ensure uniform adherence to the law and the rules adopted by the council and for the administration of the courts. Moreover, the presiding officer is to preside at council meetings, supervise and implement the policies of the council, and among other things, to serve as the chief spokesperson for the judiciary.[21]

In meeting its constitutional responsibilities, the Judicial Council created the Utah Code of Judicial Administration. The Code of Judicial Administration contains chapters on:
- Administration of the Judiciary
- Appellate Court Operations
- District Court Operations
- Judicial Council Organization
- Judicial Council Procedure
- Justice Court Operations
- Juvenile Court Operations
- Local Supplemental Rules
- Operation of the Courts[22]

As an independent constitutional entity responsible for the administration of the courts, the Judicial Council adopts rules regarding its roles and responsibilities, organization, and membership.[23] Within the chapter governing the organization of the Judicial Council, for example, a rule-making procedure has been adopted which governs the format of court rules, establishes an opportunity for a forty-five day public comment period, and allows rules to be adopted without public comment when doing so is considered by majority vote of the council to be in the best interest of the Judiciary.[24]

These rules also permit the Judicial Council to create executive committees which consist of a Management Committee, Policy and Planning Committee, and a Liaison Committee. Each of these committees is comprised of members of the Judicial Council and each committee's role and responsibilities are defined by rule.[25] The Liaison Committee, for example, is charged with the responsibility to review legislation affecting the authority, jurisdiction, organization, or administration of the judiciary. It may, under certain circumstances, take a position opposing, or endorsing legislation.[26]

In addition to the Judicial Council and its executive committees, the rules grant the Judicial Council authority to establish the following standing committees: Technology Committee, Uniform Fine and Bail Schedule Committee, Performance Evaluation Committee, Ethics Advisory Committee, Justice Court Standards Committee, Judicial Branch Education Committee, Court Facility Planning Committee, and Children and Family Law Committee. The duties, responsibilities, and membership of these standing committees are also provided by rule.[27]

The rules also authorize the council to create ad hoc committees or task forces that may consider issues outside the scope of the standing committees and make recommendations to the council. Finally, the rules authorize the council to establish appellate, district, juvenile, justice, and senior court judge boards in an attempt to increase the level of participation and communication with the council and the courts.[28]

The Judicial Council has adopted rules governing public notice of its meetings and having its meetings open to the public.[29] The council is required, for example, to publish an annual meeting schedule and post a public notice and agenda at least twenty-four hours prior to each meeting. Due to unforeseen circumstances of an urgent nature, however, the Judicial Council, by rule, may hold a meeting without posting a public notice, but only after it has attempted to contact all the members of the council, a quorum is present for a meeting, and a majority of those present vote to hold the meeting.

Except under certain circumstances, such as when the character or mental health of an individual, the sale of real estate, or similar matters are discussed, the Judicial Council is required to open its meetings to the public. These rules do not apply, however, to the Judicial Council's management committee, policy and planning committee, liaison committee, or any of the council's standing or ad hoc committees, including the board meetings of the appellate, district, juvenile, justice, and senior court judges.[30] It should also be noted that a legislator or a representative of the Office of Legislative Research and General Counsel may attend any meeting of the Judicial Council at which a rule of the council is under consideration, and may comment on the rule.[31]

Court Administrator

The chief administrative officer of the courts is the chief justice. By statute, the Utah Supreme Court is to appoint a professional administrator of the Judicial Council, who shall have the title of the administrator of the courts.[32] Once appointed by the Utah Supreme Court, the administrator of the courts is to serve under the general supervision of the chief justice, within the policies established by the Judicial Council, and at the pleasure of both the Utah Supreme Court and the Judicial Council. The administrator of the courts is responsible, among other duties, to organize and administer all the non-judicial activities of the courts, to assign and supervise all the work of all the non-judicial officers of the courts, and to assist the chief justice in implementing the rules established by the Judicial Council.[33]

In addition to preparing a budget for the entire court system, administering all of the procurement activities for the operation of the courts, and developing uniform procedures for the management of court business, the administrator of the courts is also responsible, under the supervision of the chief justice, for establishing positions and salaries for assistant court administrators, including the positions of appellate court administrator, district court administrator, juvenile court administrator, and justices' court administrator. Administrators for a specified court are appointed by the administrator of the court, with the approval of the chief justice, and with the concurrence of the respective board of judges as established by the Judicial Council.[34]

Administrative Office of the Courts

The administrator of the courts and any assistants appointed by the administrator are known collectively as the Administrative Office of the Courts.[35] The Administrative Office of the Courts is primarily responsible to provide administrative support to the Utah court system. Beginning with three employees in 1973, the Administrative Office of the Courts now employs approximately one hundred people with an annual budget in 2003 of just over $9 million.[36]

Since the creation of the Administrative Office of the Courts, and under the direction of the Judicial Council, Utah courts operate under standardized policies and procedures. Non-judicial activities and employees of the courts are organized and administered in a consistent manner. All levels of Utah courts have an administrator while the state court administrator serves the Utah Supreme Court and the Judicial Council.

In addition to exercising its statutory powers, duties, and responsibilities,[37] the Administrative Office of the Courts is also responsible for a number of legislatively enacted directives that include (1) Alternative Dispute Resolution Program, which was established to promote the efficient operation of the courts by encouraging alternative dispute resolution to secure the just, speedy, and inexpensive determination of civil actions; (2) Data Processing Department, which has developed and implemented a court records database that is accessible to the entire judicial system; (3) the position of a Capital Law Clerk, who advises judges who conduct trials involving capital offenses; and (4) administrative services to the Guardian ad Litem program, which is responsible to assure that minors receive qualified legal services in abuse, neglect, and dependency proceedings.

JUDICIAL SELECTION, RETENTION, DISCIPLINE, AND REMOVAL

Federal Model

The federal judiciary is comprised of the U.S. Supreme Court (the highest court in the land), courts of appeals, and district courts, the latter of which hold trials. The federal judiciary is independent from both the legislative and executive branches of the federal government. Each of the branches are equal to the others in the sense that each was designed to perform an independent and indispensable function in the government. While the highest officers in the legislative and executive branches are elected to office, judges in the federal judiciary are not elected. Federal judges are appointed by the president of United States and are subject to confirmation by the United States Senate.

When the federal judiciary was established, Article III of the U.S. Constitution provided that federal judges would "hold their office during times of good behavior." The constitution does not define "good behavior" and as a consequence federal judges have been substantially insulated from political pressures and popular public opinion. It is in this way that the federal judiciary is able to exercise its powers and duties independently. Since only a very few federal judges have been removed from office through impeachment and conviction, the practical effect is that once appointed and confirmed, federal judges usually serve in office until they retire or die.

The federal judiciary is also different from the executive and legislative branches in that judges, unlike the president, senators, and representatives, do not have age, residency, and citizenship requirements.

Federal Courts

The federal judiciary consists primarily of the same three levels of courts found in Utah: supreme court, court of appeals, and district court. The nation is divided into districts (trial courts) and circuits (for the Court of Appeals). Utah is its own district, but is part of the Tenth Circuit Court of Appeals. In general, federal courts handle matters that reach beyond the boundaries of a state, such as federal taxes, bankruptcy, immigration, interstate commerce, patent and copyright issues, and specific federal offenses in criminal matters. Figure 7-3 shows the geographic boundaries of the eleven federal circuit courts.

Figure 7-3

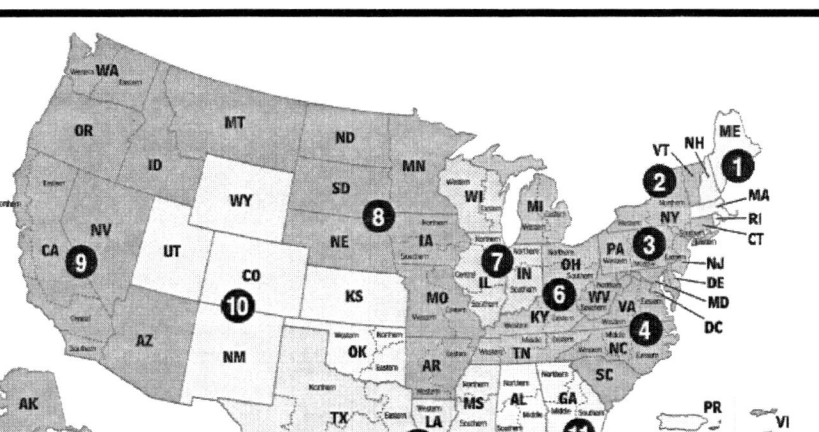

Federal Circuit Courts

State Model
Selection

Each state is authorized to establish its own court system. Although each state decides for itself the structure of its courts, every state has an equivalent to a state supreme court, the highest court in the state; most have a court of appeals; and all have some form of trial court. Many states also have specialized courts that adjudicate matters of a single subject. Family courts, specialized tax courts, and juvenile courts are examples of limited jurisdiction courts.

In addition to deciding the structure of its court system, states also decide the method of judicial selection. All state judicial selection methods are either by election or appointment. Table 7-3 shows how each state selects its judges. Unlike federal judges who are appointed for life, nearly all state court judges require reappointment or reelection to serve additional terms of office.

Most states select their judges in either partisan or nonpartisan elections. Utah, prior to 1984, permitted election of its judges. However, in 1985, the judicial selection process was changed; not because Utah's electorate made poor selection choices, but rather because of the unavoidable consequences contested elections had on the judicial system. When Utah was debating its judicial selection methods, one astute observer noted that "there is no harm in turning a politician into a judge, he may become a good judge. The curse of the elective system is that it turns every judge into a politician. Judges selected through contested elections are obliged to engage in political activities in ways that prejudice their judicial independence."[38] Among other issues, it was simply seen as inappropriate to require judges to seek campaign contributions from community leaders and lawyers who may appear in court as litigators, petitioners, and respondents.[39]

Utah now fills judicial vacancies through an appointment process known today as merit selection. This process includes a judicial nominating commission, gubernatorial appointment, and senate confirmation; subsequent terms of office are filled by an uncontested retention election. This merit-based system avoids the conflicts of interest inherent in an elective system and is a model supported by both the American Judicature Society and the American Bar Association.

Table 7-3

Selection of Judges[40]

Partisan Election	Nonpartisan Election	Election by Legislature	Merit Plan
Alabama	Arizona	Connecticut	Alaska
Arkansas	California	Rhode Island	California
Georgia	Florida	South Carolina	Colorado
Indiana	Idaho	Vermont	Indiana
Illinois	Kentucky	Virginia	Iowa
Kansas	Michigan		Kansas
Louisiana	Minnesota		Missouri
Mississippi	Montana	**Appointment by Governor**	Nebraska
Mew Mexico	North Dakota	Delaware	Oklahoma
New York	Ohio	Hawaii	Tennessee
North Carolina	Oregon	Maryland	Utah
Pennsylvania	Oklahoma	Massachusetts	Wyoming
Tennessee	South Dakota	New Hampshire	
Texas	Washington	New Jersey	
West Virginia	Wisconsin		

Judicial Nominating Commissions

Whenever a vacancy occurs in a juvenile, district, or appellate court, the governor shall fill the vacancy by appointment from a list of at least three nominees certified to the governor by the judicial nominating commission having authority over the vacancy.[41] Each nominating commission has authority over a certain geographic region which is known as a judicial district. The appellate court nominating commission has authority for vacancies occurring on both the supreme court and the court of appeals. The trial court nominating commissions have authority for vacancies for both the district and juvenile courts.

The composition and procedures of the nominating commissions are provided in statute. The Appellate Court Nominating Commission is responsible for the nomination of justices of the supreme court and judges of the court of appeals.[42] The Trial Court Nominating Commissions are responsible for the nomination of district and juvenile court judges.[43]

The composition and procedures of both the Appellate Court Nominating Commission and Trial Court Nominating Commission are identical in that each is comprised of seven voting members, no more than four of whom may be from the same political party, and two of whom must be selected from a list of six names provided by the Utah State Bar. The chair of every commission is selected by the governor and no legislator may serve as a member of any nominating commission. The chief justice of the Utah Supreme Court is an *ex officio* member of every nominating commission, and is charged with the duty to ensure that each commission follows the rules adopted by the Judicial Council.[44] No later than forty-five days after convening, each nominating commission is required to certify a list of qualified nominees to the governor. The Appellate Court Nominating Commission is required to certify at least five but no more than seven nominees to the governor, and the Trial Court Nominating Commission is required to certify at least three but no more than five nominees to the governor.

Gubernatorial Appointment

Once a judicial nominating commission has nominated a judicial candidate, the governor receives the names of the nominees, along with each nominee's application materials and any public comments received by the Judicial Nominating Commission about the nominee. The governor is then required to appoint one of the nominees within thirty days.[45] In the event the governor fails to make an appointment within the required thirty-day period, the chief justice of the Utah Supreme Court shall make the appointment from the same list of nominees provided to the governor within twenty days.[46] Although the governor's selection procedures are not codified in statute or rule, the governor traditionally conducts a series of interviews with each judicial nominee.

Senate Confirmation

Before the person appointed by the governor to fill a judicial vacancy may take office, the Utah State Senate is required to confirm the appointee by majority vote within sixty days of the appointment. If the senate either fails to confirm the appointment within the required time period, or if the senate confirmation vote does not pass by a majority vote, the office shall be considered vacant and the entire selection process shall begin over with the judicial nominating commission.[47]

In summary, the nominating commissions ensure that the pool of candidates from which the governor must select are chosen based on legal qualifications and experience, and not political consideration. This method of judicial selection provides a process by which the interests of all three branches of state government are recognized.

Retention Elections

For additional terms of office, judges in Utah are not required to face the appointing authority, the legislature, or a contested election for each additional term in office, as is the case in more than forty other states.[48] Instead, every justice and judge of the juvenile, district, appellate, and supreme court is required to face the electorate in an unopposed retention election.[49]

At the first general election held more than three years after a justice or judge is initially appointed and confirmed by the senate, the justice or judge shall be subject to an unopposed retention election. After initial voter approval, justices of the Utah Supreme Court shall be subject to retention elections every tenth year; and judges of the juvenile, district, and court of appeals shall be subject to retention elections every sixth year. If at any retention election, a justice or judge does not receive a majority of affirmative votes to retain, the justice or judge is removed from office and may not be nominated by a judicial nominating commission to fill a judicial vacancy until the term for which the judge failed to be retained has expired.

Each justice or judge that stands for a judicial retention election is required to be evaluated by the Judicial Council. To assist the Judicial Council in making a determination as to whether or not a judge has met the minimum standards for certification, the council has established certification standards. Although no judge has failed to be certified by the Judicial Council for not meeting the minimum standards, two judges have nevertheless been removed in a retention election.

Discipline and Removal

The Judicial Conduct Commission investigates and conducts confidential hearings regarding complaints against any justice or judge. This commission is authorized to order the reprimand, censure, suspension, removal, or involuntary retirement of any justice or judge for action which constitutes willful misconduct in office; final conviction of a crime punishable as a felony under state or federal law; willful and persistent failure to perform judicial duties; disability that seriously interferes with the performance of judicial duties; or conduct prejudicial to the administration of justice which brings the judicial office into disrepute, which includes a violation of the Code of Judicial Conduct.[50]

Upon a recommendation for discipline, the Utah Supreme Court reviews the proceedings of the Judicial Conduct Commission as to both law and fact, and the court may permit the introduction of additional evidence. After its review, the court, as it finds just and proper, is required to issue an order either implementing, modifying, or rejecting the recommendation for discipline issued by the Judicial Conduct Commission.[51]

Provisions for impeachment are found in the federal constitution and in forty-nine of the fifty state constitutions. In Utah, Article VI of the Utah Constitution provides for impeachment as a procedure for removing state and judicial officers for misconduct in office, typically described as high crimes, misdemeanors, and malfeasance in office.[52] Impeachment is a legislative procedure for removal of certain state and judicial officers under limited circumstances that does not involve either the executive or judicial branch, except in the impeachment of the governor, in which case the chief justice serves as the presiding officer in the senate during the trial.[53]

Impeachment consists of two procedures: the first is the sole responsibility of the House of Representatives which begins with articles of impeachment that describe the alleged misconduct and culminates with a vote of whether or not to impeach.[54] Upon a majority vote by the House of Representatives to impeach, the second procedure entails a trial by the State Senate using the articles of impeachment passed by the House of Representatives.[55] If convicted in the trial by the State Senate, the subject of the impeachment is removed from office and is disqualified from holding any office of honor, trust, or profit in Utah. Regardless of the charges contained in the articles of impeachment, the trial in the State Senate is limited to whether or not the subject of the impeachment shall be removed from office. Whether the subject of the impeachment trial is convicted or acquitted, that person may be nevertheless liable to prosecution, trial, and punishment in a court of law.[56]

A governor, state officer, or judicial officer in Utah has never been impeached by the House of Representatives or tried by the State Senate. However, the House of Representatives did file articles of impeachment against one judge, but the judge resigned after the Judicial Conduct Commission recommended an order of discipline to the Utah Supreme Court and before the House of Representative voted on the articles of impeachment.[57]

THE JUDICIAL PROCESS

There are two basic types of actions within the court system: civil and criminal.

Civil Actions

Most citizens come into contact with the civil aspect of the judicial system. Civil litigation and dispute resolution cover problems that arise between two or more private persons. Civil litigation may involve personal injury in an accident, contract disputes, probate of a will, administration of a trust, property disputes between landowners, divorce and other actions that most often do not involve federal, state, or local governments.

Criminal Actions

The criminal system is a prosecutorial system in which federal, state, or local authorities address the contravention of specific laws and mete out penalties accordingly. Criminal actions are titled "State" or "United States" versus the criminal defendant. This indicates that the government is a party with a stake in the outcome. Through the passage of statutes and ordinances, governing bodies control which actions may be so titled. Table 7-4 shows the number of case filings, both civil and criminal, from July 1, 2003 to June 30, 2004.

Table 7-4

	Case Filings by District			
	Fiscal Year 2004*			
District	Civil**	Criminal	Juvenile	Total
1	6,851	1,552	3,619	12,022
2	60,778	11,641	10,126	82,545
3	69,128	13,505	19,588	102,221
4	53,342	10,102	7,128	70,572
5	4,940	2,573	3,637	11,150
6	1,516	753	1,385	3,654
7	2,262	1,120	1,680	5,062
8	2,287	1,191	1,426	4,904
Totals	201,104	42,437	48,589	292,130

*Source: Utah Caseload Statistics, http://www.utcourts.gov/stats/
**Figure includes all district court case filings except criminal, and traffic and misdemeanor filings in justice courts.

GRAND JURY

The traditional notion of a grand jury is that of a citizen panel sifting through mounds of evidence and calling witnesses in order to decide whether the government has enough evidence to prosecute "public enemy number one." Because of the expense and perceived seriousness of calling a grand jury, this is often the case. However, a grand jury can be formed to investigate any crime. In Utah, the formation of a grand jury is a two-step process.

A panel of five district court judges from throughout the state is appointed by the chief justice of the Utah Supreme Court. The panel is required to hold hearings in each judicial district at least once every three years.[58] At the hearings, the panel receives information from prosecutors and testimony from witnesses under oath concerning criminal activity within the state. If the panel feels that there is sufficient reason to call a grand jury, it will make findings in writing and may order a grand jury summoned. Alternatively, the panel may refer any information it receives to the county, district, or city attorney, or attorney general for investigation and prosecution.

The qualifications and selection method for grand jurors are the same as for regular jurors, but once sitting, the similarities end. The grand jury is an independent, investigative body. It may call and interrogate witnesses, request the production of documents or other evidence, and require that the prosecutor draft reduced charges. In addition, even though its proceedings are conducted in secret, a complete record is made and kept. Once an indictment is made, it is sealed until a judge orders it public.[59]

Because of the expense, grand juries are used sparingly in Utah. The federal government requires a grand jury indictment for all criminal prosecutions, but the Utah system of county, district, and city attorneys makes that type of system unnecessary. Only two grand juries have been empaneled within the state in the last ten years.

Indigent Representation

"In all criminal prosecutions, the accused shall . . . have the Assistance of Counsel for his defence."[60] The U.S. Supreme Court, in *Gideon v Wainwright*, 372 U.S. 335, elaborated on the Sixth Amendment by declaring that if a person cannot afford to hire an attorney the state must provide an attorney for that person. This is only true, however, in criminal prosecutions where a person's life or liberty might be affected. For those infractions and misdemeanors where there is no possibility of incarceration, there is no right to a state-appointed attorney. This was recently reaffirmed by the U.S. Supreme Court in *Alabama v. Shelton*, 535 U.S. 654, where the Court affirmed the vacation of the defendant's suspended sentence because the conviction was obtained without the defendant being accorded the assistance of counsel.

Title 77, Chapter 32, Indigent Defense Act, describes the requirements and qualifications for indigent defense in Utah. Divided into seven distinct parts, the act addresses how the state determines which defendants qualify for indigent defense services, standards to be met by state and local governments as well as attorneys in the representation of indigents, compensation for attorneys appointed by the court to represent indigent defendants, and representation of prisoners. The act creates two trust funds for the funding of indigent defense in felony and capital cases.

USE OF INFORMATION TECHNOLOGY

The legislature authorized the creation of the Administrative Office of the Courts in the 1973 Court Administrator Act. The administrative office is statutorily charged with providing centralized services to the courts including information services and technology.

Actual court data processing on a state level began in 1967 with the Juvenile Court's use of computers to keypunch data intake forms. By 1981, a State Judicial Information System (SJIS) became operational and was designed to collect statistics statewide on court activities. Other supporting information technology systems developed during the 1980s include the Trial Court Information System and the Courts Information System. The SJIS was upgraded in 1991 following recommendations of the Utah Commission on Justice in the Twenty-first Century.[61]

In the early 1990s, a standing committee on court technology was created to develop a long-term master plan for information technology use by the courts. Planning for the new information systems included providing for technology for the district, juvenile, and justice courts as well as the jury system.

Following the move to a new state court building in 1998, the Administrative Office of the Courts has continued to upgrade technology facilities and services for both public and private use. Those upgrades include broadband access to the Internet and the development of Web sites. Other examples of network-based improvements include the ability to file and retrieve court documents on line, and access to court staff and records. The public, the legal community, and others have made widespread use of the court's Internet access as demonstrated in figure 5-5.

Chapter 8

Fiscal Management

Oliver Wendell Holmes wrote, "Taxes are what we pay for civilized society."[1] Taxes are frequently levied without reference to any particular government service or expenditure. So while most taxpayers are willing to pay their share, they want to know that they are being treated fairly and that their tax dollars are being spent frugally and correctly.

This chapter provides a brief description of the taxes imposed by the state and by local governments in Utah, the purpose being to explain how the Utah tax system works. The chapter focuses on the three major tax categories of the Utah system—property tax, sales and use tax, and income tax.

In this chapter:

Tax Structure for State and Local Governments (p. 131)
Changes in Major State and Local Revenues (p. 132)
Property Tax (p. 133)
Sales and Use Tax (p. 140)
Income Tax (p. 142)
Other Taxes (p. 147)
State Tax Commission (p. 148)
Tax Comparisons (p. 149)
Funding of Government Services (p. 153)
State Budget (p. 158)

For each of these major taxes, this chapter explains how the tax developed, what is taxable, who pays the tax, when and how it is collected, where the revenue goes, and why the tax is important. A brief description of other taxes levied in Utah, information about the State Tax Commission, and a comparison of Utah's tax system with other states is also included. Finally, this chapter outlines into which funds tax revenues are received and the general purposes for which they are spent.

TAX STRUCTURE FOR STATE AND LOCAL GOVERNMENTS

A balanced tax system is often compared to a stool with three legs. Each leg represents a different tax and all three legs are equal in that each tax raises roughly the same amount of revenue. Just as a three-legged stool gives more strength and stability than a one- or two-legged stool, tax experts believe a balanced tax system provides strength and stability to a state's revenue and gives the state the best chance of meeting many important goals. Among those goals is to provide adequate revenue, a fair and proportional distribution of the cost of providing public goods and services, moderate and stable levels of taxation, and an equilibrium between the growth of tax revenues and a taxpayer's income.

Only states that have a unique opportunity to export their taxes to nonresidents are in a position to ignore this revenue diversification principle. Nevada, with its gaming industry, and Wyoming, with its large natural resource base, are examples of states without a diverse tax base. Incidentally, neither of these states impose an individual income tax.

The three taxes represented by the legs are sales and use taxes, property taxes, and taxes based on income. As shown in figure 8-1, these three types of taxes raised more than $5.4 billion in revenue in fiscal year 2004 (the fiscal year goes from July 1, 2003 to June 30, 2004). The largest amount of revenue comes from sales and use taxes at 38 percent, followed by the individual income tax, and property taxes. These three tax types generate the major sources of revenue for state and local governments in Utah and the same is true for most other states as well.

Figure 8-1[2]

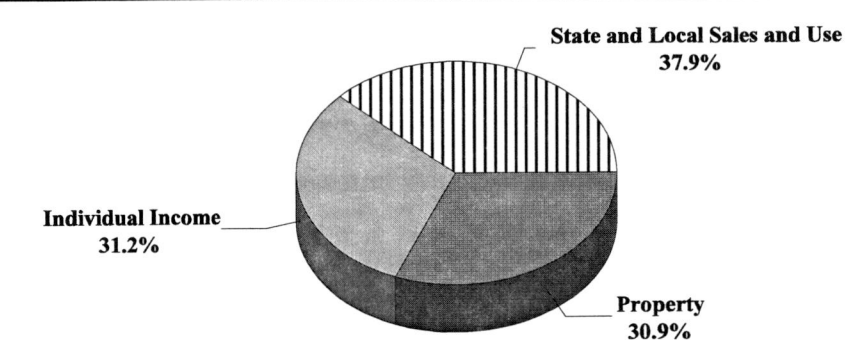

Utah's Three Major Taxes: Individual Income, Property, and State and Local Sales and Use
Fiscal Year 2004

Total Revenue: $5,451,257,497

CHANGES IN MAJOR STATE AND LOCAL REVENUES

During the period from 1982 to the present, as portrayed in figure 8-2, revenues from state and local sales and use taxes and individual income taxes grew significantly. Property tax revenues grew more slowly because the legislature cut property tax rates imposed by school districts and exempted a larger portion of the value of primary residences from the property tax. Imposition of "truth in taxation" laws have also correlated with slower growth in property tax revenues. Probably one of the most remarkable aspects of the revenue growth during the 1990s was the strong growth of the individual income tax, due primarily to the state's fast-growing economy.

Figure 8-2[3]

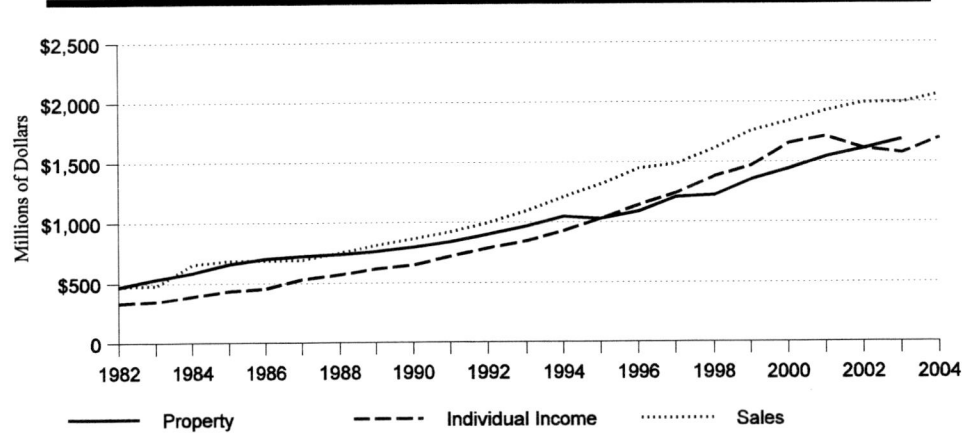

State and Local Sales and Use, Individual Income, and Property Taxes Revenues in Utah
Fiscal Year 1982 to 2004

PROPERTY TAX
Introduction and Historical Highlights

The first general tax imposed on the value of all real and tangible personal property ("ad valorem tax") within the boundaries of Utah dates back to 1878, prior to Utah's statehood in 1896.[4] Historically, the property tax was the principal revenue source for funding state and local governments. For example, in 1890, revenues generated by the property tax represented 97 percent of total state and local government revenues.[5] Over time, state and local government reliance on the property tax has declined significantly, to 23 percent of all state and local taxes for fiscal year 2002.[6] However, because the property tax is less sensitive to changes in the business cycle, the property tax remains a stable source of revenue for funding public education and local governments.[7]

Utah's property tax is rooted in the Utah Constitution, and was provided for when the Utah Constitution was adopted in 1896.[8] Since the adoption of the Utah Constitution, numerous constitutional amendments have authorized exemptions and special treatment of property by the legislature.[9] The exemptions and special treatments of property under the Utah Constitution are described below. Significantly, in 2002, voters approved a constitutional amendment to substantially reorganize, clarify, and simplify Article XIII, Revenue and Taxation, of the Utah Constitution. This change became effective January 1, 2003.[10]

Throughout the history of the property tax in Utah, there have been several recurring issues that have challenged state and local governments, the courts, tax administrators, and taxpayers.[11] These issues include the establishment and equalization of property values within and among counties and among types of property, limiting growth in property taxes, ensuring public disclosure when property taxes are increased, and providing property tax relief.[12]

What is Taxable?

Utah Constitution Article XIII, Section 2 states "all tangible property in the State that is not exempt under the laws of the United States or under this Constitution shall be assessed at a uniform and equal rate in proportion to its fair market value, to be ascertained as provided by law; and taxed at a uniform and equal rate."[13]

The Utah Constitution provides for some significant exemptions to the property tax.[14] These exemptions may generally be separated into two categories: property for which the Utah Constitution requires an exemption, and property that the legislature may by statute exempt from property tax. The Utah Constitution also authorizes the legislature to provide for special treatment for certain property.[15]

The Utah Constitution requires an exemption from property tax for the following property:
- Property owned by the state
- Property owned by a public library
- Property owned by a school district
- Property owned by a political subdivision of the state, other than a school district, and located within the political subdivision
- Property owned by a political subdivision of the state, other than a school district, and located outside the political subdivision unless the legislature by statute authorizes the property tax on that property
- Property owned by a nonprofit entity used exclusively for religious, charitable, or educational purposes
- Places of burial not held or used for private or corporate benefit
- Farm equipment and farm machinery
- Water rights, reservoirs, pumping plants, ditches, canals, pipes, flumes, power plants, and transmission lines to the extent owned and used by an individual or corporation to irrigate

land that is within the state and owned by the individual or corporation, or by an individual member of the corporation[16]

Utah Constitution Article XIII, Section 2 provides that the legislature may, by statute, exempt the following from property tax:

- Tangible personal property constituting inventory present in the state on January 1 and held for sale in the ordinary course of business
- Tangible personal property present in the state on January 1 and held for sale or processing and shipped to a final destination outside the state within twelve months
- Property to the extent used to generate and deliver electrical power for pumping water to irrigate lands in the state if the exemption accrues to the benefit of the users of pumped water as provided by statute
- Up to 45 percent of the fair market value of residential property, as defined by statute
- Household furnishings, furniture, and equipment used exclusively by the owner of that property in maintaining the owner's home
- Property owned by a disabled person who, during military training or a military conflict, was disabled in the line of duty in the military service of the United States or the state
- Property owned by the unmarried surviving spouse or the minor orphan of a disabled person described above or a person who during military training or a military conflict, was killed in action or died in the line of duty in the military service of the United States or the state[17]

Utah Constitution Article XIII, Sections 2 and 3 identify several types of property that are allowed to receive special treatment by the legislature by statute. These types of property and a summary of the special treatment the property may receive are as follows:

- The legislature may provide by statute that land used for agricultural purposes be assessed based on its value for agricultural use
- The legislature may by statute determine the manner and extent of taxing livestock
- The legislature may by statute determine the manner and extent of taxing or exempting intangible property, except that any property tax on intangible property may not exceed 0.005 of its fair market value and if any intangible property is taxed under the property tax, the income from that property may not also be taxed
- The legislature may exempt from property tax by statute certain tangible personal property required by law to be registered with the state before it is used on a public highway or waterway, on public land, or in the air if the legislature provides for the payment of uniform statewide fees or uniform statewide rates of assessment or taxation on that property in lieu of the property tax
- The legislature may by statute provide for the remission or abatement of the taxes of the poor[18]

Privilege Tax

In general, property that is exempt from the property tax, which is used to conduct a business for profit, is subject to the privilege tax.[19] For example, a business conducted for profit that has operations on federal land is exempt from the property tax, but would be subject to the privilege tax. This tax is assessed, collected, and distributed in the same manner as the property tax.[20]

Tax Equivalent Payments

"Tax equivalent property" means property on which any tax equivalent payment is made.[21] A "tax equivalent payment" means a payment required or authorized by statute to be made in lieu of property taxes on tax exempt property when required by a contract authorized by statute.[22]

Who Pays the Tax?

Figure 8-3 shows the various types of property that are included in the property tax base. Primary residential property is the largest percentage of the base at 44.8 percent, followed by commercial and industrial property, then by other types of real property.

Figure 8-3[23]

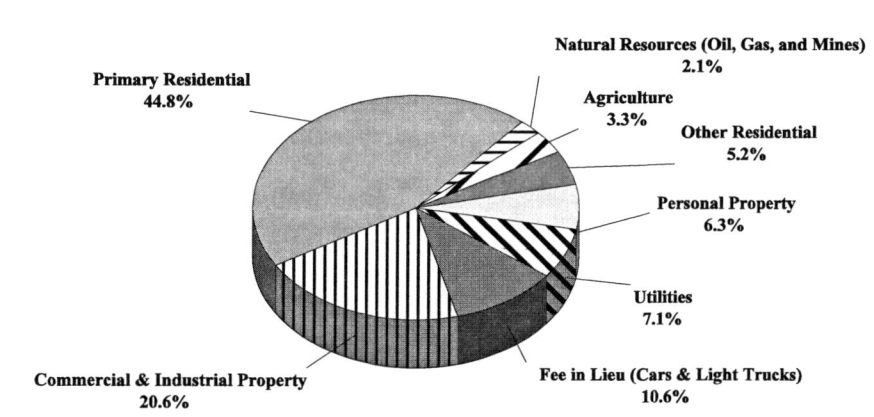

Property Taxes: Where Does the Money Come From?
2003 Tax Year

Total Property Taxes Charged: $1,686,338,334

While all taxable property is required to be valued at fair market value, the amount of property taxes that a taxpayer pays depends on the number of taxing entities that impose taxes on the property and the rate at which those entities impose a property tax. Rates may vary widely across the state depending on factors such as the number of taxing entities and the level of rates.

When and How is the Tax Collected?

The property tax is levied by numerous taxing entities including all 29 counties, all 40 school districts, over 230 cities and towns, and approximately 300 special districts. Currently, the state does not impose a property tax for general state purposes. The location of the property determines the rate of tax that will be imposed. The lowest rates will generally be found in rural areas where relatively few governmental services are provided and the highest rates in cities with higher levels of governmental services.

It is also important to note that the state's general obligation debt is dependent on property tax.[24] Constitutionally, property values establish the state's debt limits and property taxes are the principal source of revenue to repay general obligation bonds issued by local governments.[25]

County assessors have the obligation to place a market value on all residential, commercial, and industrial properties within their county except for properties required by statute to be assessed by the State Tax Commission as discussed below. The State Tax Commission also conducts regular studies to ensure that assessed values are equal to market value.[26]

The Utah Constitution and state statutes require that certain types of property be assessed by the State Tax Commission.[27] These are called centrally assessed properties. Some examples of centrally assessed properties include the real and personal property of airlines, railroads, and public utilities; geothermal fluids and geothermal resources; mines; mining machinery; property or surface improvements upon or appurtenant to mines or mining claims; other property which operates as a unit across county lines if the values must be apportioned among more than one county or state; and in some cases mines and mining claims.[28] The primary rationale behind central assessment of these types of property is the complexity and often multi-jurisdictional nature of the property.

Figure 8-4 shows the relationship between the percentage of property taxes that are locally or centrally assessed from 1987 through 2003. It shows that the percentage of the property tax base that is locally assessed has been increasing and the percentage of the property tax base that is centrally assessed has been decreasing. This shift has been caused by the greater growth and development of residential and commercial properties when compared to centrally assessed companies, such as mines and transportation companies which have not grown significantly.

Figure 8-4[29]

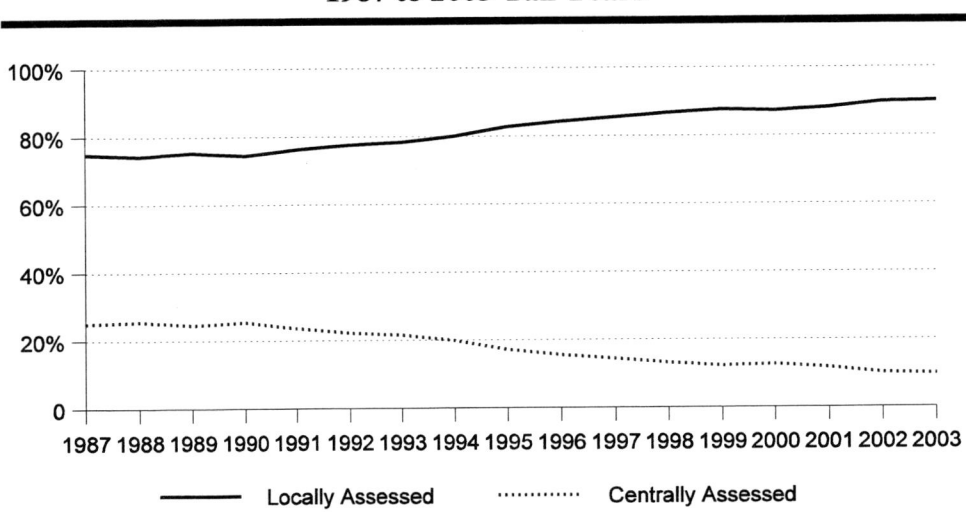

Various taxing entities often overlap one another. The location of a property determines which entities may levy a property tax against that particular property. Figure 8-5 shows how overlapping taxing entities combine to determine the property tax to which a given property is subject. In this example, eight different taxing districts are created as shown in the figure. Taxing district 6, which receives services from all four taxing districts, has the highest tax rate.

Figure 8-5

How Taxing Entities Can Overlap to Create Tax Districts

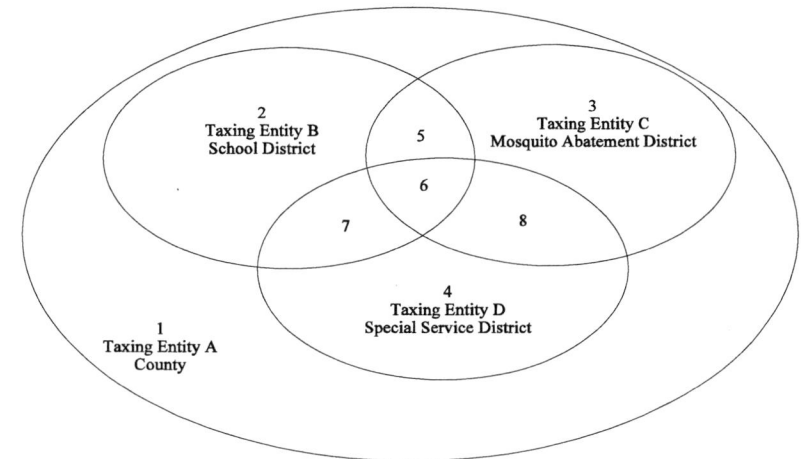

Equalization

The purpose of equalization is to ensure that all property is assessed based upon its fair market value using the same standards throughout the state. The State Tax Commission monitors both intra-county and inter-county equity. Intra-county equity refers to the equality or uniformity of assessments within a county. Inter-county equity refers to the equality or uniformity of assessments among the state's twenty-nine counties.

Property tax assessments are generally required to be equitable throughout the state.[30] In order to keep assessment values current and equitable, county assessors are required to update property values on an annual basis by doing a systematic review of market data and conducting a detailed review of the characteristics of each property every five years.[31] Additionally, the State Tax Commission is required to conduct an annual assessment/sales ratio study and to order adjustments or corrective action by any individual county based on the study results.[32]

The county legislative body of each county acts as the county board of equalization.[33] This board is responsible to ensure that property taxes are equitable within the county. The county board of equalization is responsible for:
- Adding property to the assessment roll
- Making corrections to the assessment roll that may raise or lower property values
- Raising or lowering the value of a class or group of properties
- Adjusting assessments based on taxpayer appeals
- Granting certain exemptions[34]

Valuation Date/Tax Payment Due Date

In general, real and tangible personal property are assessed on the basis of fair market value as of January 1 each year.[35] All of the dates for assessments, hearings, and appeals are set out in a property tax calender which is produced by the State Tax Commission's Property Tax Division. Payment of all taxes on real property is due by November 30 of each year.[36] Taxes on personal property are due at various times during the year, depending on factors such as the type of property or the county in which the property is located.

Truth in Taxation

To fully inform taxpayers, Utah law requires taxing entities that propose to increase their property tax revenues in any given fiscal year to go through a public notice and hearing process known as "truth in taxation."[37] Utah's "truth in taxation" laws, which were first enacted in 1985 as part of the Tax Increase Disclosure Act,[38] are revenue-driven, not rate-driven. This means that the requirements to publish notice and hold a "truth in taxation" hearing are based upon the budgeted property tax revenues of a taxing entity, not the rate charged.

In general, Utah law requires notice to be published and "truth in taxation" hearings to be held when a taxing entity elects to budget more revenue than was budgeted for the previous year.[39] However, the taxing entities are permitted to keep property tax revenues generated by "new growth," which includes value added to the tax rolls such as value added as a result of a new subdivision or a new business.[40]

For example, if a taxing entity's budgeted revenues would increase because property values rise 10 percent as the result of inflation or revaluation, but the taxing entity does not lower its property tax rate proportionately, it must advertise and hold a "truth in taxation" hearing. The hearing is required because increases in value due to inflation or revaluation are not considered to be new growth.

State law requires two forms of public notice when a taxing entity proposes a tax increase. First, the county auditor must send a notice to every property owner within the taxing entity.[41] The notice discloses the property's current year and previous year market values, the potential tax impact of the proposed revenue increase, instructions for appealing the property market value, and the date, time, and place of any public hearings where proposed increases will be discussed.[42] In addition, a taxing entity must advertise any proposed increase in a newspaper as provided by statute.[43]

Appeals

If a property owner disagrees with the value set by the county assessor on either real or personal property, an appeal may be filed with the county board of equalization.[44] The law assumes that the assessor has established an accurate, equitable value. Therefore, the burden of proof is on the property owner to provide facts to support a claim of improper valuation.[45] Appeals relating to centrally assessed property are made to the State Tax Commission.[46] Decisions of a county board of equalization may be appealed to the State Tax Commission and courts.[47] A State Tax Commission decision may be appealed to a court.[48]

Where Does the Tax Revenue Go?

Taxing entities that are authorized to levy property taxes include counties, municipalities, school districts, and various special districts as provided by statute. Figure 8-6 shows the proportion of property tax revenues that went to the various taxing entities, with school districts receiving the largest portion. Figure 8-7 shows how these proportions have changed during selected years. Figure 8-7 shows that between 1980 and 1997, the portion of property tax revenue going to school districts decreased from 59 percent to 50 percent. This was because in the mid-1990s the legislature reduced the property tax levy for the minimum basic school program.

Figure 8-6[49]

Property Taxes: Where Does the Money Go?
2003 Tax Year

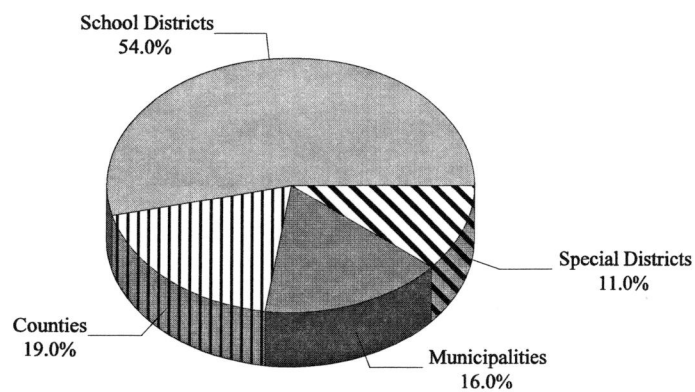

Figure 8-7[50]

Distribution of Property Tax Revenue
1980, 1997, and 2003 Tax Years

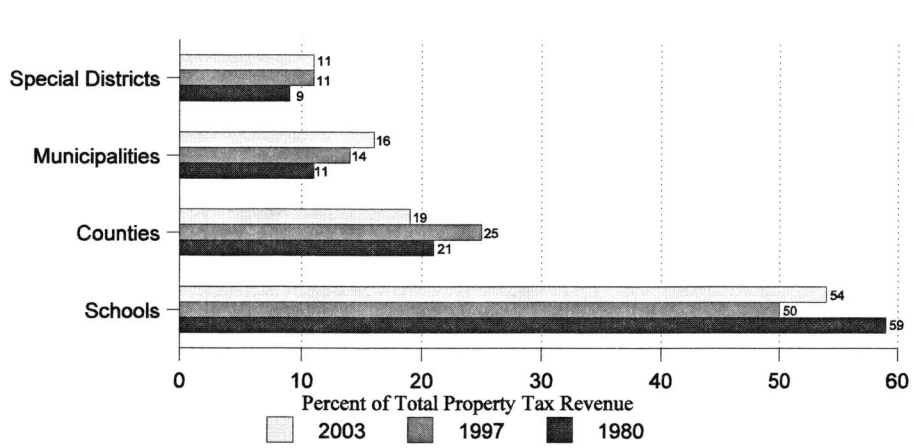

Why Does This Tax Matter?

The property tax is important in the financing of public education and local government. As discussed above, the property tax is also a stable revenue source. For local school boards it is the only major source of revenue that may be adjusted to meet local needs and to provide for school buildings. It is also a major source of revenue for counties, municipalities, and most special districts.

The property tax also limits the amount of debt government can incur and constitutionally acts as a guarantee that the debt will be paid.[51] This guarantee is an important element in the high credit rating the state and its political subdivisions currently receive.

Fiscal Management • 139

SALES AND USE TAX
Introduction and Historical Highlights

Sales taxes were first introduced as a revenue source in 1933 when property tax collections dropped dramatically because of the Great Depression.[52] The use tax was added in 1937 to complement the sales tax.[53] A person is subject to a use tax, which is administered in the same manner as a sales tax, if for a transaction involving tangible personal property the seller did not collect the tax and the purchaser stores, uses, or consumes the tangible personal property within the state.[54] Since the enactment of the state sales and use taxes, the transactions that are subject to state sales and use taxes, as well as the tax rates and exemptions that apply to state sales and use taxes, have been amended many times. In addition, since 1933, portions of the revenues generated by state sales and use taxes have been designated by statute for particular uses, or "earmarked," in increasing frequency.[55]

The first local option sales and use tax was enacted in 1959.[56] At the time this local option tax was enacted, the tax was distributed to local governments on the basis of point of sale, which is where the sale occurred.[57] In 1982, the Utah Constitution was amended to allow revenue sharing among political subdivisions, and in 1983 the local option sales and use tax was amended to establish a distribution formula that, over a period of years, shifted from 100 percent point of sale to 50 percent point of sale communities that were growing rapidly but did not have a large commercial base.[58] This local option sales and use tax still retains point of sale and population distribution components.[59]

Since the enactment of the first local option sales and use tax in 1959, numerous local option sales and use taxes have been enacted.[60] Currently, there are at least eighteen statutory authorizations to impose a local option sales and use tax under Utah's Sales and Use Tax Act.[61] These sales and use taxes vary in their distribution, and a number of these taxes are earmarked for particular purposes.[62]

Another significant source of legislative changes in the structure of state and local sales and use taxes is the state's involvement with the Streamlined Sales Tax Project (SST), which is a multistate effort to simplify and modernize sales and use tax laws. One of the objectives of SST is to facilitate the collection of sales and use taxes by sellers that do not have a physical presence in a state ("non-nexus sellers"). Although the U.S. Supreme Court has concluded that a seller without sufficient presence in a state may not be required to collect sales and use taxes on behalf of that state, the Court has recognized Congress' power to change federal law to require such collections.[63] Until Congress acts, states hope to encourage the voluntary collection of sales and use taxes by non-nexus sellers by making complex sales and use tax laws more uniform and easing compliance burdens.

In 1999, the legislature enacted legislation to authorize the State Tax Commission to enter into negotiations with other states to develop uniform sales and use tax procedures and study ways to simplify the administration of the sales and use tax.[64] Between 2000 and 2005, legislation was enacted to appoint delegates to the Streamlined Sales Tax Implementing States, develop uniform sales and use tax procedures, and simplify and modernize administration of the sales and use tax.[65] To date, a significant portion of Utah sales and use tax law complies with the requirements established to participate in SST. Other laws that are necessary to be in substantial compliance with the requirements for participation in SST are scheduled to take effect on July 1, 2006.[66]

What is Taxable?

The sales and use tax is imposed on the sale of goods and some services.[67] Some types of sales are excluded from the system entirely,[68] such as sales of legal, accounting, physician, or other similar services. In addition, many types of sales or certain classes of taxpayers are statutorily exempt from paying sales and use taxes.[69] Government, religious, and charitable organizations are generally afforded sales and use tax exemptions.[70] Other exemptions are provided in the interest of efficiency, to carry out social policy, or to facilitate economic development. The Utah Tax Review

Commission[71] is responsible to review each of these exemptions every eight years to see if the exemptions are still appropriate and useful.[72]

Who Pays the Tax?

As shown in figure 8-8, retail trade (purchases by individuals) accounts for 57.7 percent of the sales and use tax base, while business purchases account for another 25.8 percent. Certain taxable services account for another 12.8 percent.

Figure 8-8[73]

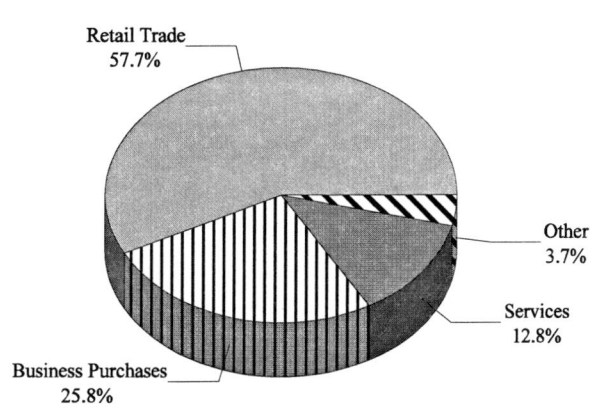

Utah Gross Taxable Sales by Major Component
2004 Calendar Year

Retail Trade 57.7%
Other 3.7%
Services 12.8%
Business Purchases 25.8%

When and How is the Tax Collected?

As noted above, sales and use taxes are imposed on a purchaser for retail sales, leases, or rentals of tangible personal property or certain services, such as public accommodations and services provided by hotels.[74] Sales and use taxes may be collected and remitted by the seller or paid by the purchaser.[75] Individuals are required to report transactions subject to a use tax on the individual income tax return and remit any unpaid use taxes with that return.[76]

State sales and use taxes and most local option sales and use taxes are remitted to the State Tax Commission.[77] For local option sales and use taxes remitted to the State Tax Commission, the State Tax Commission distributes the taxes to local governments as provided by statute after deducting a portion of the tax for administrative expenses.[78]

Before a seller may legally sell goods and services in Utah, the seller must obtain a license to do so.[79] Some sellers required to remit sales and use taxes to the State Tax Commission on a monthly basis may retain 1.31 percent of state sales and use taxes and certain local option sales and use taxes and 1 percent of other local option sales and use taxes as specified in statute.[80] This authority for sellers to retain a percentage of sales and use taxes is commonly referred to as the "vendor discount."

Where Does the Tax Revenue Go?

Figure 8-9 shows how revenue from state and local sales and use taxes is distributed. In fiscal year 2004, these state and local sales and use taxes raised nearly $2.1 billion in revenue. Nearly 73 percent of this revenue went to state government where it was deposited into the General Fund either as free revenue or restricted revenue. Restricted revenues are revenues earmarked for certain uses including highways and water development.

Just over 21 percent of all sales and use tax revenues are generated by local option sales and use taxes. Most of these revenues are used by local governments for general government purposes. However, some revenues are earmarked for specific purposes.

Figure 8-9[81]

Sales and Use Tax: Where Does the Money Go?
Fiscal Year 2004

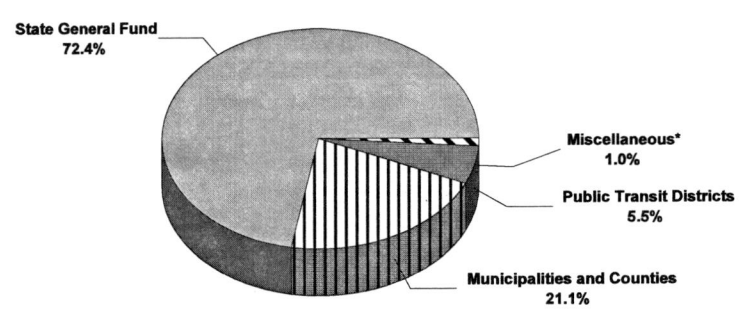

Total State and Local Sales and Use Tax Revenue: $2,065,729,163

Why Does This Tax Matter?

The sales and use tax has become the most significant source of revenue to state government and its operations and to the state's higher education system. It is also a significant source of revenue to the Utah Transit Authority and other public transit districts, to municipalities, and to county governments. Apart from public education, revenue from sales and use tax funds the bulk of state government goods and services. Public safety and law enforcement, health and human services, and universities and colleges are all dependent on sales and use tax revenue. Arts, cultural, recreational, zoological, and other organizations have also benefitted from sales and use tax revenues.

Increasingly, state and local government entities and private organizations want sales and use taxes to be earmarked by statute for a particular purpose.[82] However, earmarking allows some groups to avoid having to justify their budgets and compete with other groups for revenue. Also, some argue that earmarking limits the ability of policymakers to have a wide range of options in the budgeting process.

INCOME TAX

Individual Income Tax

Utah's individual income tax was enacted in 1931, when economic conditions during the Great Depression resulted in a need for revenues.[83] At that time, most state and local government functions were funded by the property tax, and high delinquency rates during the Great Depression placed tremendous pressure on the property tax.[84] The income tax provided a way to impose taxes on individuals who had a means to pay the taxes.[85]

Throughout Utah's history, the individual income tax has been subject to numerous changes.[86] For example, in 1957, the first withholding tax was enacted that applied only to nonresident employees.[87] The withholding tax was expanded to include both resident and nonresident employees in 1959.[88] One of the most significant changes to the income tax rate structure occurred in 1973. Prior to 1973, one tax rate structure applied to all taxpayers.[89] In 1973, as part of a major overhaul of the individual income tax, separate tax rate structures were enacted for single individuals, married individuals filing joint tax returns, and married individuals filing separate returns.[90] In addition, in 1973, the individual income tax became more closely linked to the federal individual income tax system.[91]

Corporate Franchise and Income Tax

Utah's corporate franchise tax was enacted in 1931, the same year as the enactment of the individual income tax.[92] In 1959, the corporate income tax was enacted as a counterpart to the corporate franchise tax as a means of taxing corporations engaged in interstate commerce that were not previously subject to the corporate franchise tax but had income derived from Utah sources.[93]

The state corporate franchise and income tax structure has been subject to many changes, including changes in tax rates, the minimum tax, deductions, exemptions, and the application of the tax to corporations with foreign interests.[94] Significant changes were made to the corporate franchise and income taxes in the early 1990s, when the taxes were modernized, simplified, and brought into closer conformance with federal income tax provisions.[95]

Gross Receipts Taxes[96]

The gross receipts tax imposed on nonprofit corporations, other than religious and charitable institutions, that would otherwise not be required to pay corporate franchise and income taxes (e.g., Intermountain Power Project), was enacted by the legislature in 1980.[97] Electrical corporations that received a property tax reduction authorized in 1995 by the legislature (e.g., Pacificorp), were subjected to a gross receipts tax in that same year.[98]

What is Taxable?

In general, taxable income of both individuals and corporations is based on the definition of income used for federal income tax purposes.[99] In the case of individual income taxes, state taxable income is calculated by determining federal taxable income.[100] Federal taxable income includes all sources of revenue to the taxpayer including wages, interest, dividends, rental income, and capital gains.[101] After federal taxable income is calculated, certain additions and subtractions are made as required by statute to arrive at state taxable income.[102]

Each corporation pays an annual tax of 5 percent of its income derived from or attributable to sources within the state, with a $100 minimum tax. The portion attributable to Utah is determined by the amount of property, sales, and payroll the corporation has in Utah. Each of these three factors may be given equal weight, or, beginning in taxable year 2006, a corporation may elect to have the sales factor receive a double weighting.[103] If a corporation makes such an election, the election may not be revoked for five taxable years.[104] Those corporations paying a gross receipts tax pay the tax on all consideration received for a good or service produced or rendered in Utah after the first $10 million.[105]

Who Pays the Tax?

In fiscal year 2004, individuals paid nearly $1.7 billion in income taxes and corporations paid $155.36 million in corporate franchise and income taxes. A tax on gross receipts was also paid as noted above.

Figure 8-10 displays the percentage of individual income tax revenue paid for various income classes. While higher income taxpayers make up a small portion of all Utah taxpayers, they pay a large portion of Utah's individual income taxes. Taxpayers with federal adjusted gross incomes of more than $100,000 paid more than 38 percent of Utah's individual income taxes.

Figure 8-10[106]

**Percentage of Utah Individual Income Tax Revenue
Paid by Federal Adjusted Gross Income**
2002 Tax Year

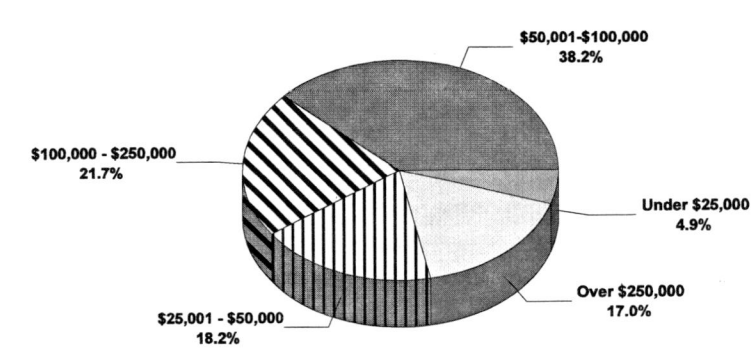

Total: $1,468,090,707

In figure 8-11, the percentage of total individual income tax returns by adjusted gross income is shown. Almost 72 percent of Utah individual income tax returns show an adjusted gross income of $50,000 or less. Just 6.5 percent of all returns show an adjusted gross income of $100,000 or more. Looking at figure 8-10 and figure 8-11 together, the data show that 38 percent of Utah individul income tax revenues are collected from 6.5 percent of returns.

Figure 8-11[107]

**Percentage of Total Utah Individual Income Tax
Returns by Adjusted Gross Income**
2002 Tax Year

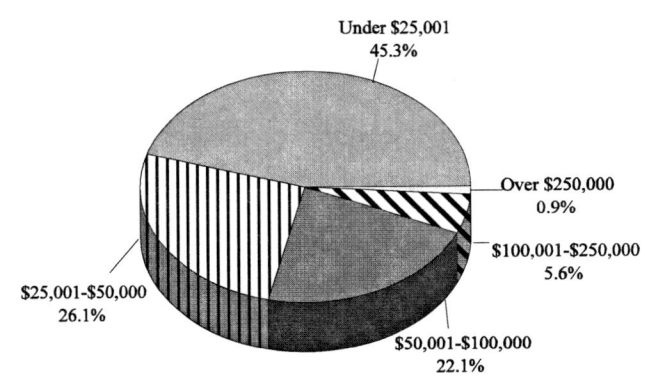

Total Number of Returns: 893,274

Corporate franchise and income taxes are mostly paid by certain types of businesses. A large percentage of corporate franchise and income tax returns are filed by corporations in the manufacturing, transportation, communications, and public utilities sectors.

More than 60 percent of all Utah corporations that file a corporate franchise and income tax return show no taxable income. Figure 8-12 displays the percentage of corporate franchise and income returns by the amount of the corporation's Utah net taxable income. Corporations with no reported Utah net taxable income make up about 63.74 percent of all returns. Those corporations with "positive income" make up 10.4 percent of all returns. The category of "positive income" includes corporations that reported a positive Utah net taxable income, but that paid the minimum tax because the corporation's tax liability was $100 or lower. Just under 2.5 percent of all corporations filing a corporate franchise and income tax return reported a Utah net taxable income of more than $500,000. However, figure 8-13 shows that this 2.46 percent of corporations paid 88 percent of all corporate franchise and income taxes.

Figure 8-12[108]

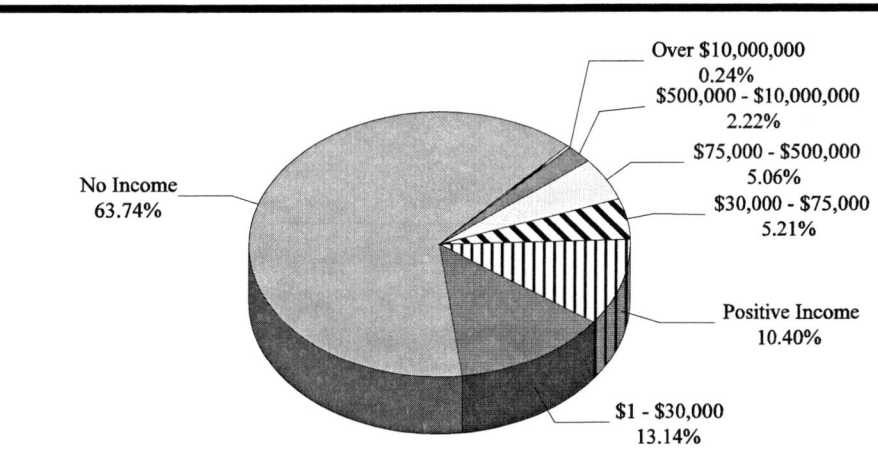

Percentage of Corporate Franchise and Income Tax Returns by Corporation's Utah Net Taxable Income
2002 Tax Year

Total Number of Returns: 21,997

Figure 8-13[109]

Percentage of Corporate Franchise and Income Tax Revenue by Corporation's Utah Net Taxable Income
2002 Tax Year

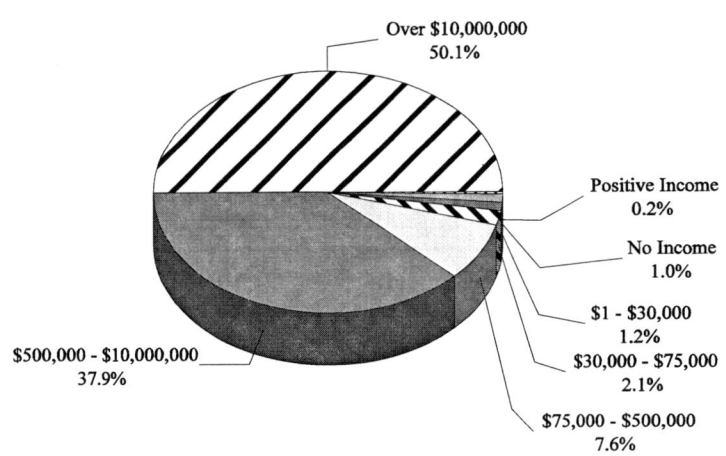

Total: $133,965,164

When and How are the Taxes Collected?

Most state individual income taxes are collected through employer withholding. In general, an employer doing business in Utah or having any income from Utah sources must withhold an amount from an employee's wages that will, as closely as possible, pay the employee's state individual income taxes.[110] In some cases, an employer may also be required to withhold individual income taxes from certain unemployment compensation benefits and annuities.[111]

Certain exemptions from withholding are authorized by statute, including an exemption for employers doing business in Utah for sixty days or less during a calendar year and an exemption for an employee not incurring individual income tax liability.[112] Withholding amounts are established in accordance with tables established by the State Tax Commission.[113]

Unlike state individual income taxes, state corporate franchise and income tax laws require that a corporation meeting certain requirements must prepay a percentage of the corporation's taxes. A corporation is generally required to make quarterly estimated tax payments if the corporation is subject to state corporate franchise or income taxes and has a tax liability of $3,000 or more in the current taxable year or $3,000 or more in the previous taxable year.[114]

Estimated tax payments are generally made in four equal payments on the fifteenth day of the fourth, sixth, ninth, and twelfth months of the corporation's taxable year. A corporation is required to pay a total amount of estimated tax payments of at least 90 percent of the corporation's current year tax liability or 100 percent of the corporation's prior year tax liability.[115] The corporation may choose which of the two above amounts of tax liability to pay.[116]

A corporation required to file a state corporate franchise or income tax return must file the return with the State Tax Commission and pay any tax due on or before the fifteenth day of the fourth month following the close of the corporation's taxable year.[117] A corporation's taxable year for state corporate franchise and income tax purposes must be the same as the corporation's taxable year for federal income tax purposes.[118]

The state gross receipts taxes are not subject to withholding, and returns are filed twice each year on or before the last day of July and January.[119] Otherwise, the gross receipts taxes are subject to the same procedures as the corporate franchise and income taxes.[120]

Where Does the Tax Revenue Go?

Utah Constitution Article XIII, Section 5, Subsection (5) provides that "[a]ll revenue from . . . a tax on income shall be used to support the systems of public education and higher education. . . ."[121] Currently, all revenues generated by the individual income tax, the corporate franchise and income taxes, and the gross receipts taxes are used to support public education and higher education.

Figure 8-14 shows the disposition of individual income tax and corporate franchise and income tax revenues. Over 90 percent of these revenues are used to operate the state's public education system. The rest is used to help finance the higher education system.

Figure 8-14[122]

Individual Income and Corporate Franchise and Income Taxes: Where Does the Money Go?
Fiscal Year 2005 Appropriated

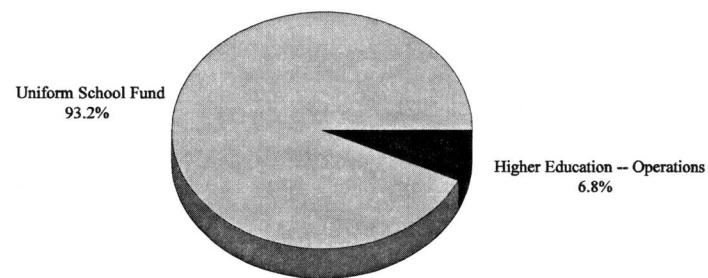

Why Does This Tax Matter?

Taxes on income are a critical source of funding for the public and higher education systems in Utah.[123] Through the minimum school program funded for the most part by income taxes, each child enrolled in a public school in Utah is assured that a definite amount of money will be spent to educate that child.

OTHER TAXES

Throughout Utah's history, a number of miscellaneous taxes have been enacted to supplement state and local revenues. Examples of these miscellaneous taxes are:
- Insurance premium tax, enacted in 1896[124]
- Inheritance tax, enacted in 1901[125]
- Mining severance tax, enacted in 1917[126]
- Motor fuel tax, enacted in 1923[127]
- Cigarette tax, enacted in 1923[128]
- Beer tax, enacted in 1933[129]
- Special fuel tax, enacted in 1941[130]
- Wine and liquor tax, enacted in 1943[131]
- Aviation fuel tax, enacted in 1951[132]
- Oil and gas severance tax, enacted in 1955[133]

- Privilege tax, enacted in 1959[134]
- Tobacco products tax, enacted in 1963[135]
- Municipal energy sales and use tax, enacted in 1996[136]
- Brine shrimp royalty, enacted in 1997[137]
- Radioactive waste facility tax, enacted in 2001[138]
- Municipal telecommunications license tax, enacted in 2003[139]
- Hazardous waste facility and nonhazardous solid waste facility tax, enacted in 2003[140]
- Multi-channel video or audio service tax, enacted in 2004[141]
- Sexually explicit business and escort service tax, enacted in 2004[142]

STATE TAX COMMISSION

Structure

In 1930, the Utah Constitution was amended to create the State Tax Commission.[143] The State Tax Commission consists of four commissioners appointed by the governor with the consent of the senate.[144] Not more than two commissioners may belong to the same political party and commissioners serve four-year terms.[145] The commissioners are required to appoint an executive director, an administrative secretary, an internal audit unit, and an appeals staff.[146] The executive director oversees the day-to-day operations of the State Tax Commission in accordance with a statutorily-required plan that is developed by the commissioners.[147] The executive director is authorized to employ additional staff necessary to perform the duties and responsibilities of the State Tax Commission.[148] Figure 8-15 illustrates the structure of the State Tax Commission.

Figure 8-15

State Tax Commission

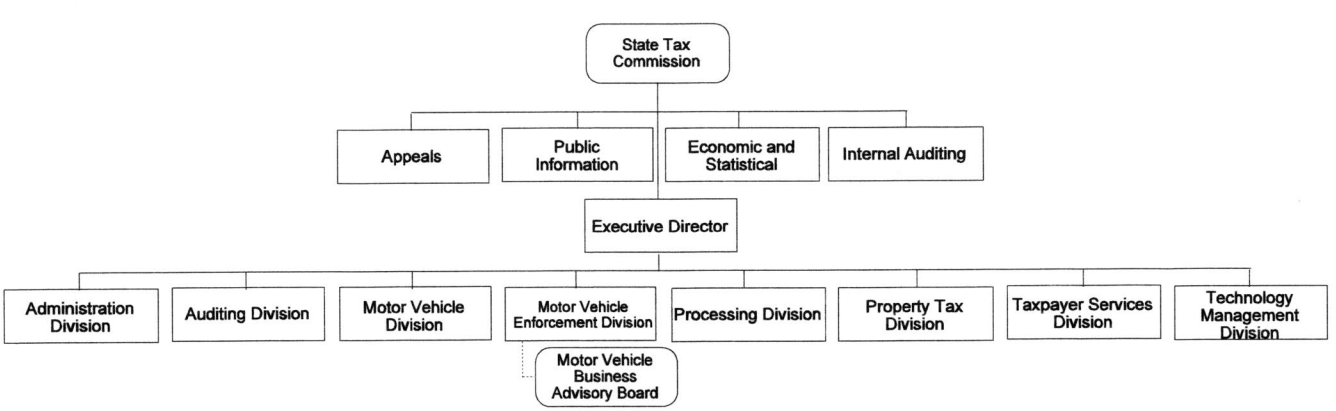

Powers and Duties

The Utah Constitution prescribes that the State Tax Commission shall:
- Administer and supervise the state's tax laws
- Assess mines and public utilities and have other powers of original assessment as provided by the legislature by statute
- Adjust and equalize the valuation and assessment of property among the counties
- As the legislature provides by statute, review proposed bond issues, revise local tax levies, and equalize the assessment and valuation of property within the counties
- Have other powers as may be provided by statute[149]

TAX COMPARISONS

This section explains how Utah compares with other states in state tax revenue per person and in relation to personal income. It also compares Utah with selected other western states in how the overall tax obligation falls on households and businesses.

Utah's Dependency Ratio

An explanation of the taxes paid by Utahns can be summed up as follows: Utah taxpayers pay more of their personal income in state and local taxes than do residents of most other states. The reason for this is simple: the state has more children to educate in its public schools per taxpayer than any other state in the nation. Figure 8-16 shows Utah's school-age "dependency ratio."

Figure 8-16[150]

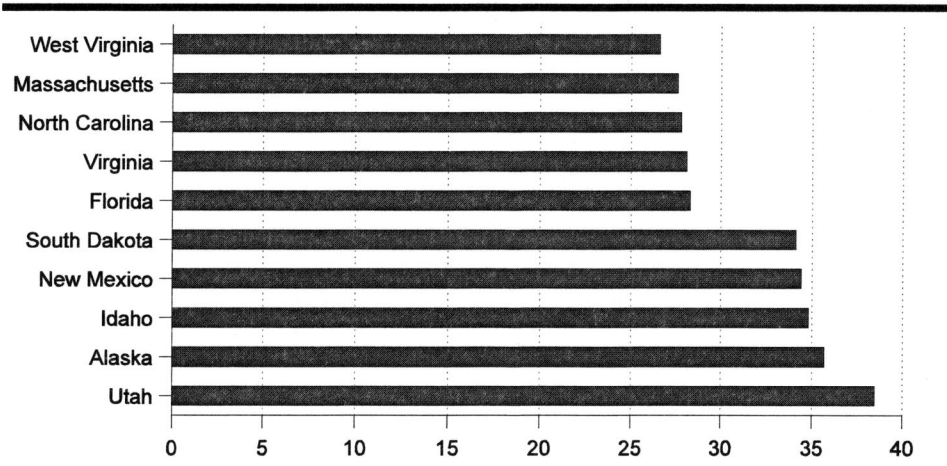

The dependency ratio is the number of school-aged children per number of working adults. Utah has about thirty-eight school-age children per one hundred working adults compared to a national average of thirty school-age children per one hundred working adults.[151] This means that Utah's dependency ratio is about one-fourth higher than the national average.

National Comparisons: State and Local Revenue Only

There are two ways that are traditionally used to compare tax burdens among the states. The first way to compare tax burdens is to simply look at tax revenue per person, regardless of whether a person actually pays any taxes. The second way to compare tax burdens is to compare the amount of taxes paid in relation to personal income. Personal income is the measure of all the income that all persons in the state receive, no matter what the source. Only taxes paid to the state and local governments are used in these comparisons.

Figure 8-17 shows how Utah is ranked in state and local tax revenue per person. As shown in this figure, states with the highest amounts of state tax revenue per person include New Jersey, New York, and Connecticut. In this comparison, Utah is ranked thirty-ninth overall. States with low state tax revenue per person include Alabama, Tennessee, and Mississippi. Utah ranks rather low by this comparison because of the state's relatively large number of children, who have little or no earnings.

Figure 8-17[152]

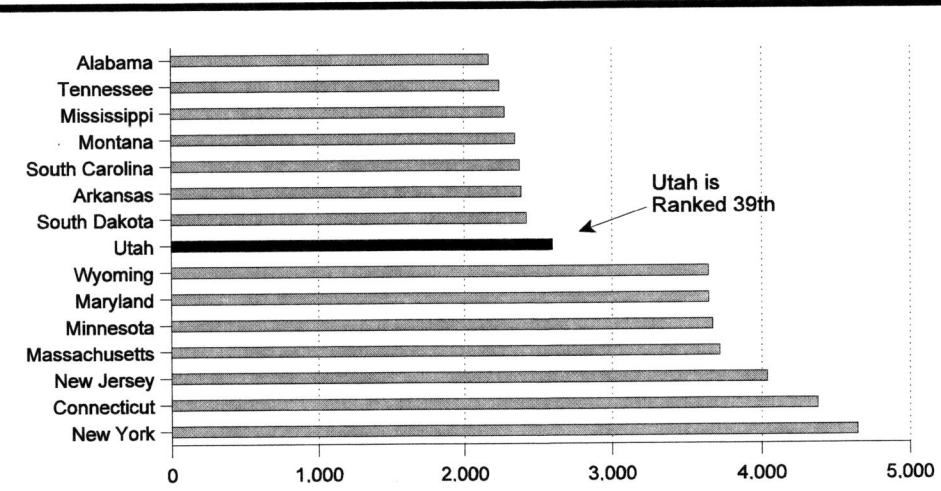

Figure 8-18 shows state and local tax revenue as a percentage of total personal income. In this comparison, Utah is ranked thirteenth overall. Utah ranks higher by this measurement because of the need for funding a large public school system.

Figure 8-18[153]

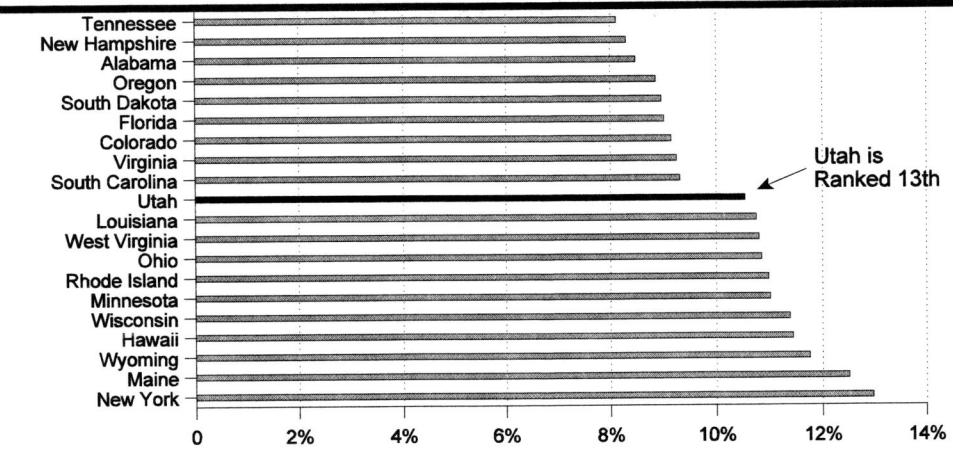

Figure 8-19 displays total state and local tax revenue as a percentage of total personal income from fiscal years 1991 to 2002. Since peaking at 12.26 percent in 1995, state and local taxes as a percentage of total personal income has declined to 10.55 percent in 2002.

Figure 8-19[154]

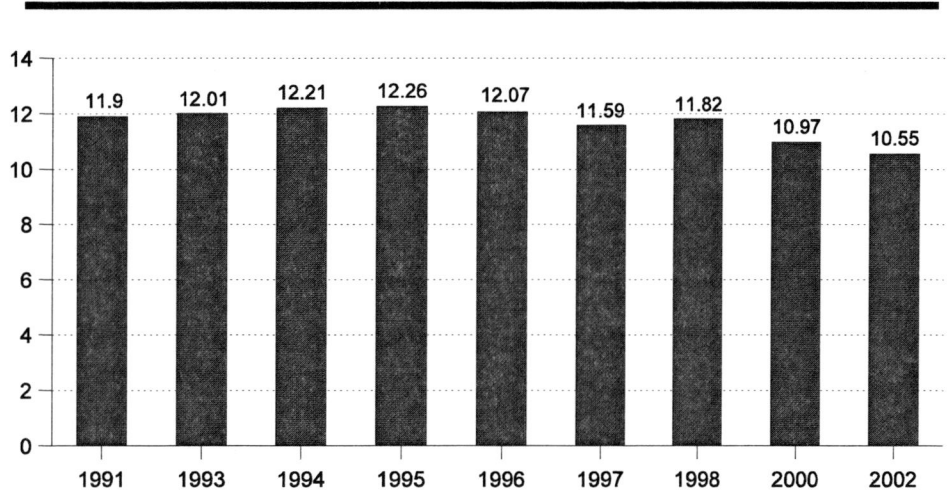

State and Local Tax Revenue as a Percentage of Total Personal Income
Utah, Fiscal Years 1991 to 2002

Comparisons with Selected Western States

The information in this section is taken from studies conducted by the Economic and Statistical Unit of the State Tax Commission.[155] Taxes included in the figures in this section include income taxes, inheritance taxes, property taxes, general sales and use taxes, tourism taxes, severance taxes, unemployment insurance taxes, and other selective taxes. For purposes of the figures in this section, "selective taxes" includes cigarette taxes, beer taxes, gasoline taxes, motor vehicle registration fees, public utility fees, and car rental taxes.

When comparing tax burdens among states, it is useful to choose states with similar tax structures and economic conditions. Utah is unique in that it is bordered by Nevada and Wyoming, which do not impose taxes on either personal or corporate income. As stated above, Nevada receives significant revenue from taxes on gaming, and Wyoming imposes taxes on its abundant natural resources. Montana has no state sales tax, but imposes a severance tax on coal. These taxes on gaming and natural resources can largely be exported to taxpayers in other states, thereby lowering the overall tax burden for the residents of the states that impose those taxes on gaming and natural resources.

Figure 8-20 shows the initial direct tax burden imposed on businesses as a percentage of gross state product. The term "initial direct tax burden" is used to distinguish between the legal and economic incidence of taxes. Figure 8-20 show the legal incidence of taxes, or in other words, the taxes that a business is legally required to pay. However, because taxes are ultimately paid by people, and not businesses, the tax burden must be shifted. This shift describes the economic incidence of taxes. Depending on a variety of factors, the tax burden is either shifted forward or shifted back. When the tax burden is shifted forward, the goods and services that the business sells cost more than they would without the tax. When the tax burden is shifted back, the business' employees are paid less than they would without the tax. The tax burden can also be shifted back to investors in the form of lower returns on investment. It is also important to note that two different measurements are used to compute household and business tax burdens: for households, total personal income is used; for businesses, gross state product is used. Washington businesses bear the highest business tax burden of the states compared. Washington imposes a tax on gross business income, and Washington businesses also pay a portion of the state's relatively high sales tax. As shown in figure 8-20, Utah ranks third highest of the selected western states when comparing business tax burdens.

Figure 8-20[156]

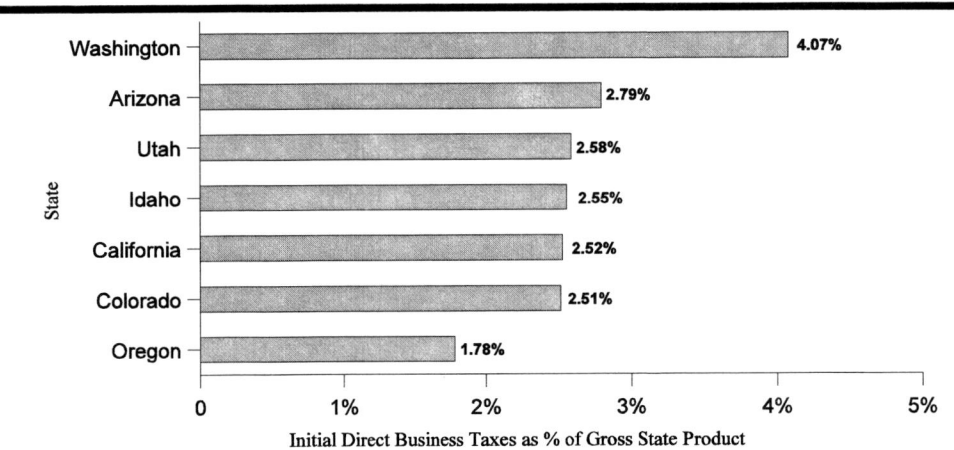

Initial Direct Business Tax Burden as a Percentage of Gross State Product
Utah and Selected Western States, Fiscal Years 2002 to 2003

Figure 8-21 displays the change in effective initial tax burdens for Utah households and businesses since 1985. This figure shows state and local taxes as a percentage of personal income for households and gross state product for businesses. The initial taxes paid by households has grown from 7.6 percent of total personal income in 1985 to 8.5 percent in 1998 then dropped to 7.61 percent in 2003. Increasing home values and income from capital gains account for some of the increase during the 1990s. It is important to note that during this same time frame, the legislature lowered property, individual income, and state sales and use tax rates, but raised tax rates on cigarettes and motor fuel and increased motor vehicle registration fees.[157] The decline in the initial tax burden on households between 2000 and 2003 was partially due to declines in individual income tax revenues.

There are several possible reasons for the decline in the effective initial business tax burden from 4 percent of gross state product in 1985 to 2.6 percent of gross state product in 2003. The percentages displayed in figure 8-21 are not absolute dollar amounts, but rather the proportion of taxes paid by business and gross state product. One possible explanation is that taxes paid by business did not grow as quickly as did gross state product. Another possible explanation is that during this same period of time the legislature expanded the sales and use tax exemption for machinery used in the manufacturing process. A final possible explanation is that corporate franchise and income tax revenue fell from $196 million in fiscal year 1997-98 to $187 million in fiscal year 1999-2000[158] and fell again to $152 million in fiscal year 2002-03.[159]

Figure 8-21[160]

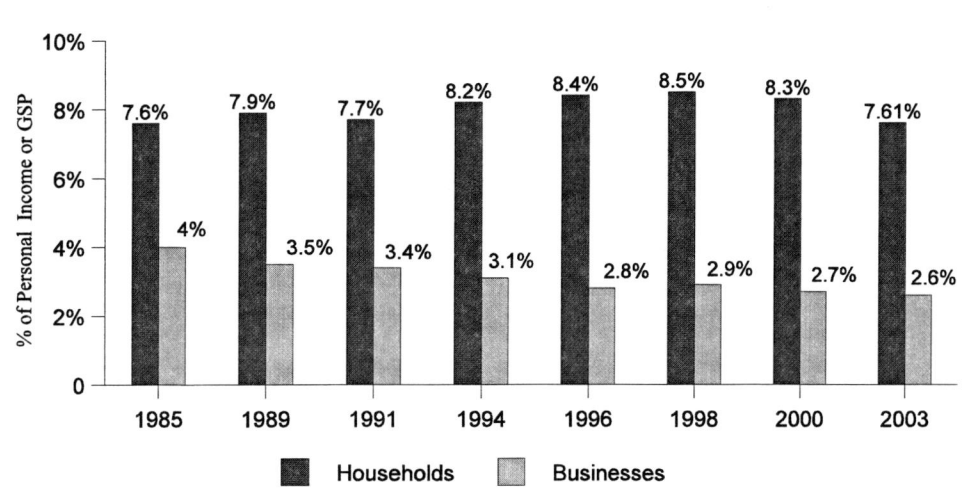

Effective Initial Household and Business Tax Burdens
Utah, Selected Years, 1985 to 2003

FUNDING OF GOVERNMENT SERVICES

Once taxes are collected they must be placed in funds and appropriated to pay for various goods and services that government provides. The legislature appropriates most state tax monies from three funds: the General Fund, the Uniform School Fund, and the Transportation Fund. Each fund has dedicated revenue sources. This section briefly describes the relative importance of these three major funds to the state and to the various local government entities.

General Fund

From the General Fund, the legislature appropriates monies for general state government use and for higher education. Some General Fund revenue is also used to fund the state's public school system. Figure 8-22 shows what tax revenues make up the General Fund. The largest single source of revenue comes from the 4.75 percent state sales and use tax. Two small sources of General Fund revenue, interest and liquor profits, are not included in this figure because they are not tax revenues.

Figure 8-22[161]

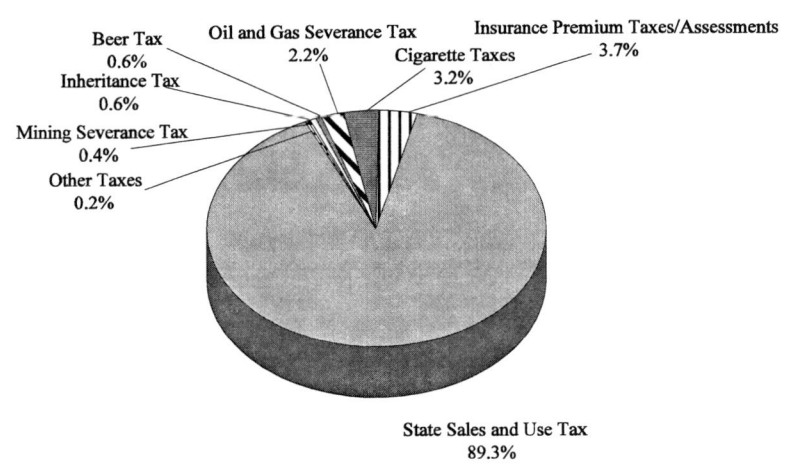

The General Fund: Where Does the Tax Money Come From?
Fiscal Year 2004

Total General Fund Tax Net Revenue: $1,676,877,984

Uniform School Fund

Under the Utah Constitution, monies in the Uniform School Fund may only be used to fund the state's public education system.[162] As shown in figure 8-23 the Uniform School Fund is largely comprised of revenues generated by one tax, the individual income tax. The corporate franchise and income taxes are also an important revenue source for this fund.

Figure 8-23[163]

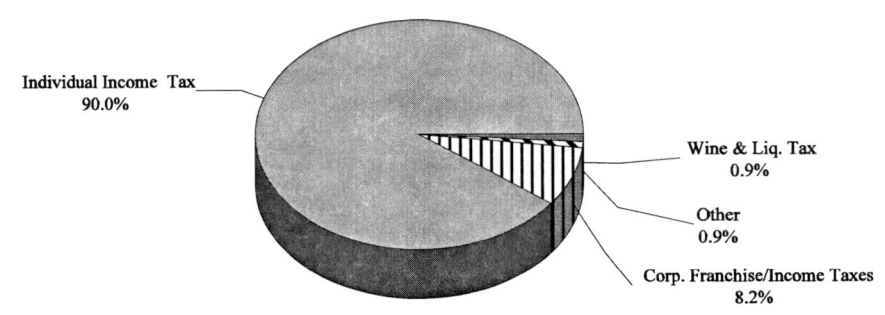

The Uniform School Fund: Where Does the Tax Money Come From?
Fiscal Year 2004

Total Uniform School Fund Tax Net Revenue: $1,888,914,385

Combined General Fund and Uniform School Fund

Figure 8-24 displays the sources of the tax revenue for the combined Uniform School Fund and General Fund for fiscal year 2004. Two tax sources, the individual income tax and the state sales and use tax, make up more than 89 percent of the total of these two funds. Corporate franchise and income taxes make up 4.4 percent of these two funds.

Figure 8-24[164]

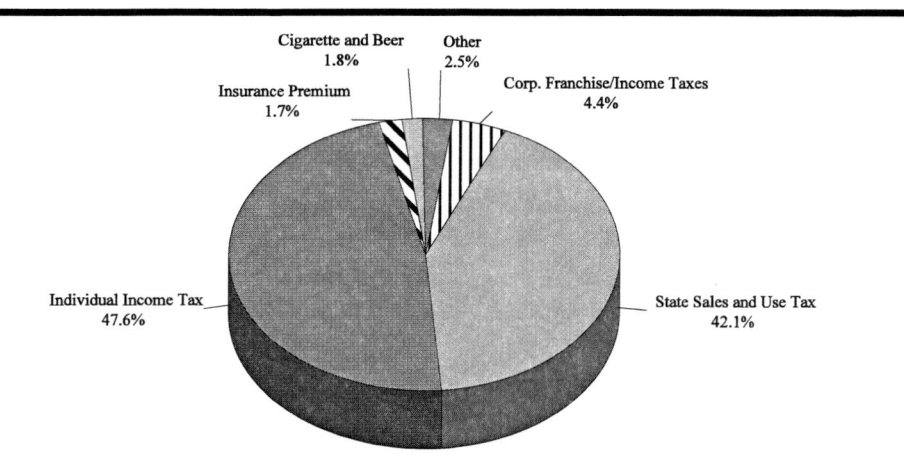

Combined General Fund and Uniform School Fund: Where Does the Tax Money Come From?
Fiscal Year 2004

Total General Fund and Uniform School Fund Tax Net Revenue: $3,565,792,369

Transportation Fund

The Transportation Fund is the third major fund in Utah. The Utah Constitution requires that proceeds from taxes, fees, and other charges related to the operation of motor vehicles on public highways and proceeds from an excise tax on liquid motor fuel used to propel those motor vehicles be used for certain transportation-related purposes.[165] As shown in figure 8-25, more than 73 percent of the revenues deposited into the Transportation Fund come from the state's taxes on motor fuel and special fuel. Motor vehicle registration fees also contribute to this fund. Federal transportation monies do not go into the Transportation Fund, but are provided to Utah as a block grant, so these monies are not included in figure 8-25.

Figure 8-25[166]

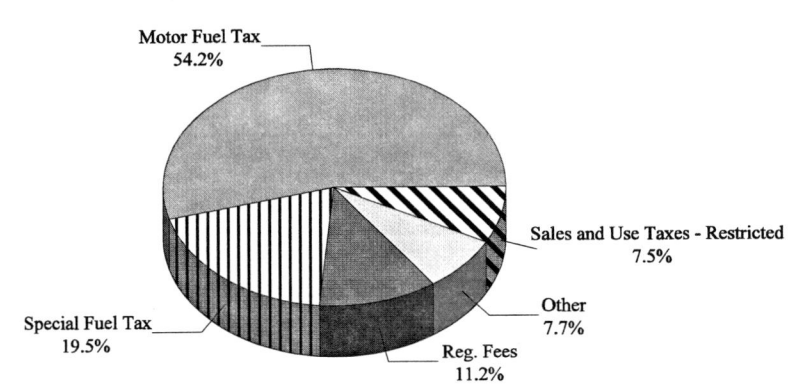

Transportation Fund: Where Does the Money Come From?
Fiscal Year 2004

Total Transportation Fund Net Revenue: $442,825,512

Sources of Revenue for Local Governments in Utah

Units of local government in Utah include counties, cities, towns, school districts, and special districts. These governmental entities rely on a wide range of taxes and fees to fund the various services they provide.

Figure 8-26 displays the revenue sources for the general fund budgets for Utah's 29 counties. Property taxes provide nearly one-third of the revenues for these budgets. Sales and use taxes, charges, and miscellaneous revenues are also major sources of revenue for counties. County general fund budgets provide general county-wide services.[167] Counties have separate budgets for services such as capital projects and municipal-type services.

Figure 8-26[168]

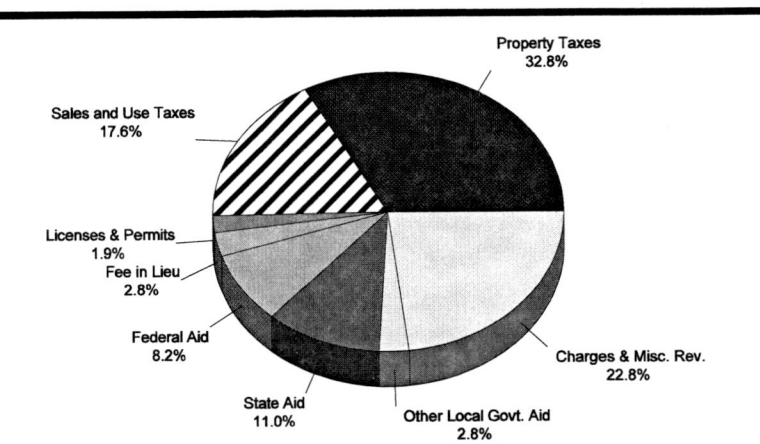

Sources of Revenue for Utah Counties
Fiscal Year 2003

Cities and towns rely on a mix of revenues to fund general operation budgets, with a heavy reliance on property taxes and sales and use taxes. Sales and use taxes have been a growing source of revenue for municipalities in the last few years. Figure 8-27 displays the sources of revenue for municipalities.

Figure 8-27[169]

Sources of Revenue for Municipalities
(Government Funds Only)
Fiscal Year 2003

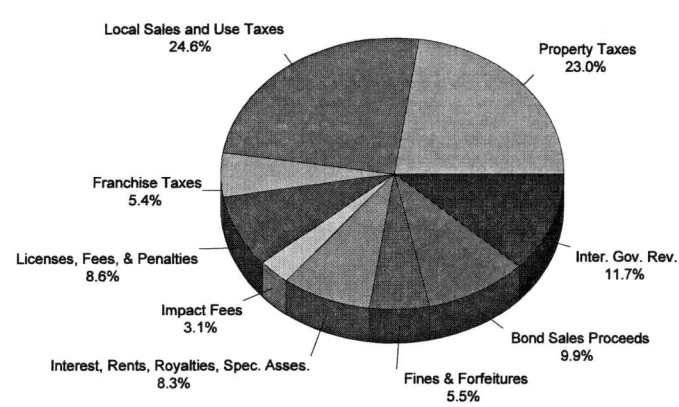

Special districts in Utah provide a wide variety of services including water and sewer services, recreation services, and mosquito abatement services. Many of these services are provided through fees and charges for services. Consequently, fees and charges are a major source of revenue for special districts, as shown in figure 8-28.

Figure 8-28[170]

Sources of Revenue for Utah Special Service Districts
with Budgets Larger than $50,000
Fiscal Year 2002

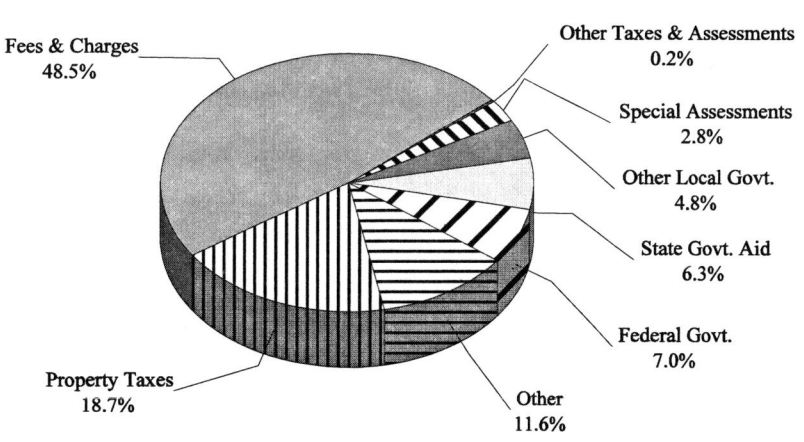

Total Revenue: $535,805,296

Fiscal Management • 157

STATE BUDGET

One of the most important actions during each legislative session is the development and adoption of a budget for state government, the state's system of higher education, and the state's public school system. These budgets rely on a variety of revenue sources including state taxes, fees imposed by state agencies, and grants from the federal government.

There are several ways to view the state's budget, including: all funds, General Fund only, Uniform School Fund only, and combined General Fund and Uniform School Fund. Figure 8-29 displays how all funds in the budget, including all state and federal funds, were allocated for the fiscal year beginning on July 1, 2004 and ending on June 30, 2005. Two-thirds of the state budget is used in just two areas: education and health and human services. While these proportions may change slightly from year to year, the top budget priorities of the state usually remain the same.

Figure 8-29[171]

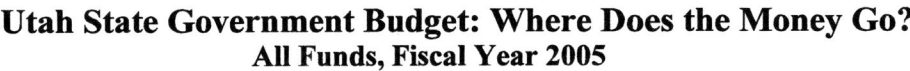

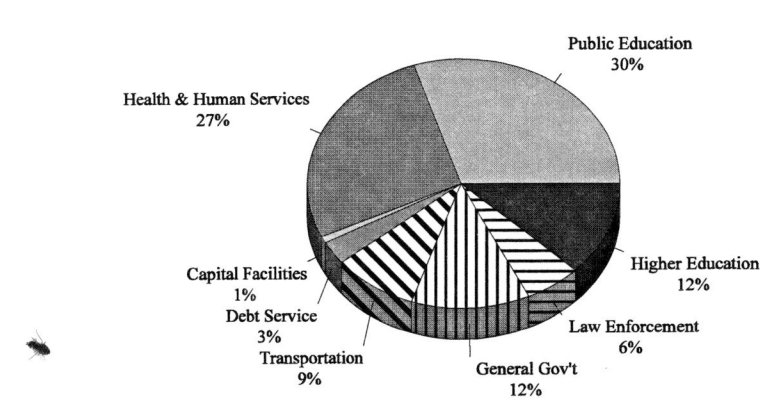

Spending by state government usually grows each year. In fact, as shown in figure 8-30, state government spending, including all sources of funding, has grown from just over $5 billion in fiscal year 1996 to over $8.2 billion in fiscal year 2005. Only in fiscal year 2003 was total spending less than the prior fiscal year. Spending was lower in fiscal year 2003 primarily as a result of reductions in motor fuel tax, individual income tax, and corporate franchise and income tax revenues.

Figure 8-30[172]

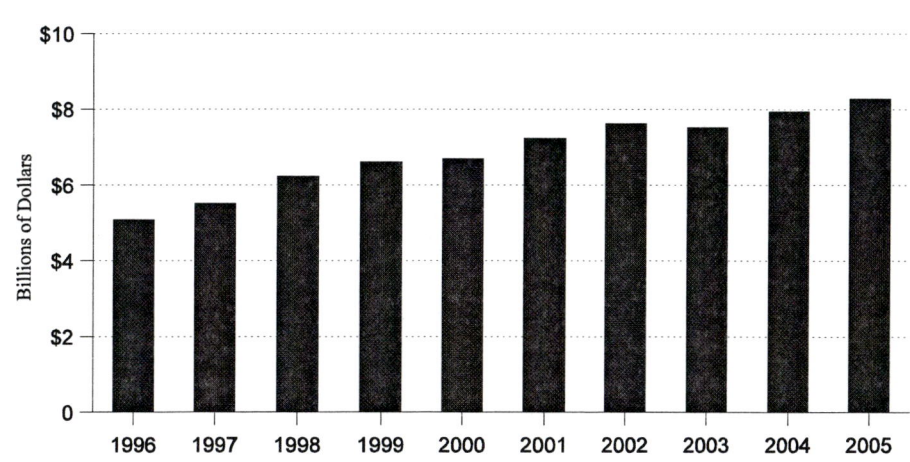

Utah State Government Appropriations History
All Sources of Funding, Fiscal Years 1996 to 2005

Because there are so many variables in the state budget each fiscal year, it is sometimes helpful to break out of the budget the revenues that come only from major state tax sources. These tax sources include the state sales and use tax, individual income tax, corporate franchise and income taxes, estate tax, cigarette tax, beer tax, insurance premium tax, and severance tax. As shown in figure 8-31, these revenues have also generally grown during the last twenty fiscal years, except for the decline after fiscal year 2001.

Figure 8-31[173]

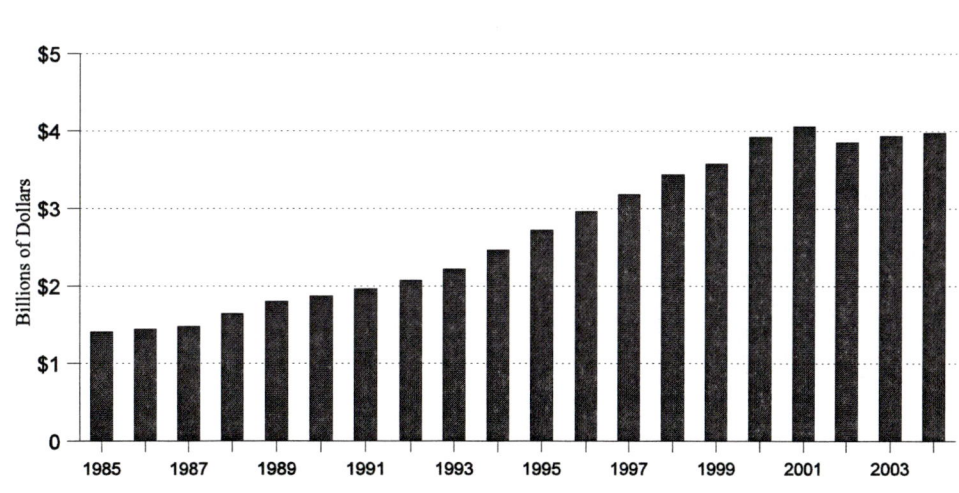

Revenue from Major State Tax Sources
Utah, Fiscal Years 1985 to 2004

Another way to consider changes to state tax revenues is to compare them to changes in total personal income and population. Figure 8-32 displays revenue from major state tax sources as a

Fiscal Management • 159

percentage of total Utah personal income. This shows how much of Utahns' personal income goes to pay major state taxes. Since 1985, this percentage has been fairly constant at between 7 percent and 7.4 percent. However, the downturn in the state's economy in 2002 and 2003, with the corresponding reduction in state tax revenue, resulted in about 6.7 percent of personal income going to major state taxes in 2004.

Figure 8-32[174]

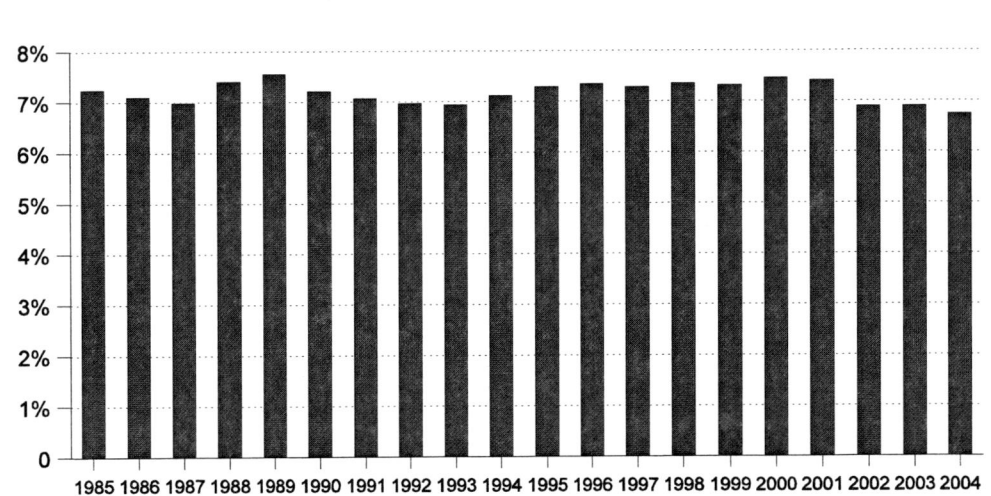

Revenue from Major State Tax Sources as a Percentage of Total Utah Personal Income
Utah, Fiscal Years 1985 to 2004

Figure 8-33 compares changes in total major state tax sources to population and inflation. Nominal (not adjusted for inflation) per person tax revenue grew from about $858 per person in 1985 to $1,766 per person in 2001, then dropped in the subsequent years. Real (adjusted for inflation) per person tax revenue also grew from $858 per person in 1985 to $1,073 per person in 2001 and then dropped to $943 per person in 2004.

Figure 8-33[175]

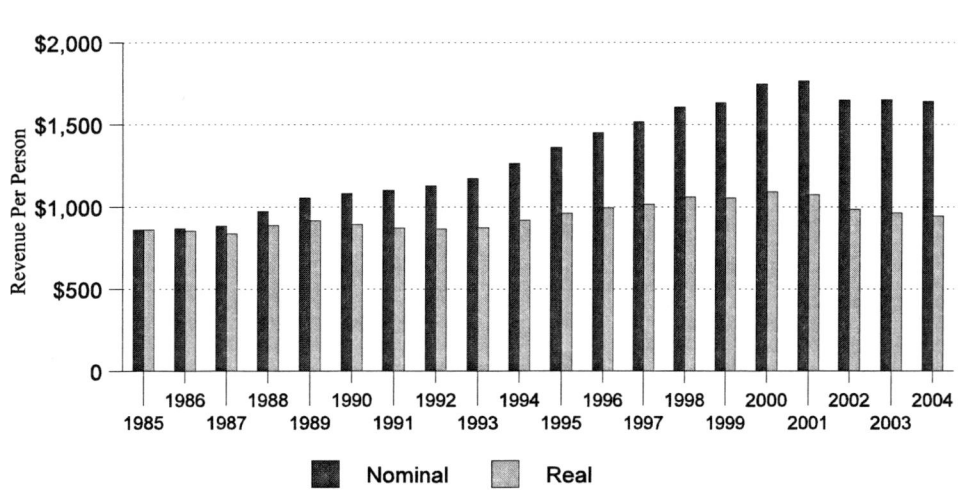

Revenue from Major State Tax Sources Per Person
Utah, Fiscal Years 1985 to 2004

There are several possible explanations as to why real per person major state tax revenues grew by over $200 per person until 2001 and then dropped by over $100 since that time. First, the legislature made a policy decision in the 1990s that it would reduce property taxes substantially, while making smaller tax reductions in state sales and use and individual income taxes. The legislature also increased motor fuel and special fuel taxes in 1997. The legislature reduced property taxes through lowering property taxes imposed by school districts. Because these property taxes are not considered a source of state revenue, they are not included in these figures. Second, the 1990s were a period of strong economic growth in the state with increases in sales and use tax revenues and individual income tax revenues. Nearly every year from 1991 to 2000, state individual income tax revenues grew more than 8 percent annually and state corporate franchise and income taxes also experienced large increases in some years during this period. While part of this was to due to strong wage growth, another factor was the significant increases in income from capital gains and dividends, driven by a booming stock market. When stock market gains began to disappear in 2001, the income tax revenues also decreased.

Chapter 9

Agriculture and Food

The Department of Agriculture and Food is directed by statute to protect and promote Utah agriculture and food by enforcing state laws and administering agricultural services and consumer programs.[1] The department helps protect public health and safety as well as agricultural markets.[2]

The department also enacts rules to ensure an adequate and available supply of agricultural products for consumers.[3] With the recent emphasis on homeland security, the department is also addressing the threat of agri-terrorism and the introduction of foreign animal diseases.[4]

> **In this chapter:**
>
> Division of Administrative Services (p. 164)
> Division of Conservation and Resource Management (p. 164)
> Division of Marketing and Development (p. 165)
> Division of Animal Industry (p. 166)
> Division of Chemistry Laboratory (p. 167)
> Division of Plant Industry (p. 168)
> Division of Regulatory Services (p. 169)
> Programs (p. 171)

The thirteen-member Agricultural Advisory Board advises the department regarding the planning, implementation, and administration of the department's programs.[5] It is composed of members representing the Farm Bureau Federation, the Farmers Union, the Cattlemen's Association, the Wool Growers' Association, the Dairymen's Association, the Veterinary Medical Association, the Livestock Auction Marketing Association, the Association of Conservation Districts, the horse industry, the food processing industry, the manufacturers of food supplements, the Utah Producers Association, and a consumer affairs group.[6]

The department is comprised of seven divisions, as illustrated below:
1. Division of Administrative Services
2. Division of Conservation and Resource Management
3. Division of Marketing and Development
4. Division of Animal Industry
5. Division of Chemistry Laboratory
6. Division of Plant Industry
7. Division of Regulatory Services

These seven divisions help the commissioner of agriculture and food to efficiently administer the department's business.[7] The department is also responsible for administering several programs, including the agricultural wildlife damage prevention program, an agricultural mediation service, and the horse racing commission.

Figure 9-1

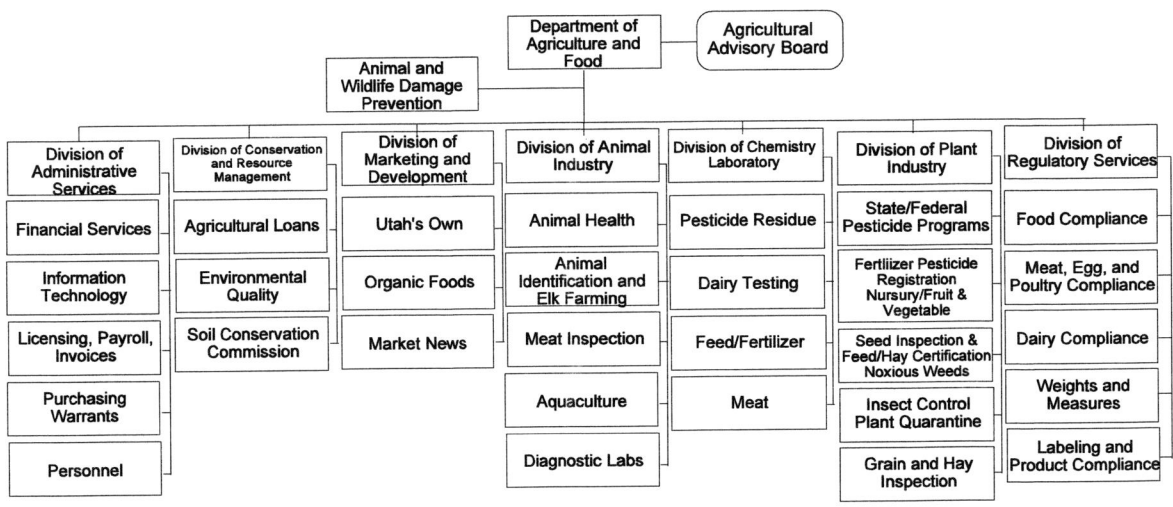

Department of Agriculture and Food

DIVISION OF ADMINISTRATIVE SERVICES

This division provides administrative services to all other divisions in the department and is responsible for all budget, accounting, purchasing, personnel, payroll, policies and procedures, and the day-to-day operations of the department.[8] In addition, the division's information technology section is responsible for the online registration and licensing systems for department business.[9]

DIVISION OF CONSERVATION AND RESOURCE MANAGEMENT

The Division of Conservation and Resource Management administers a variety of programs to help agricultural producers, who hold the majority of private lands and water rights in the state, to protect and enhance Utah's natural resources.[10] The division administers two low-interest revolving loan funds aimed at developing resources and financing new enterprises.[11] The division also provides information and technical assistance for conservation or resource improvements, and monitors and tests agricultural groundwater.[12]

Agricultural Loans

The division administers loan programs to help the agricultural community improve productivity and efficiency and to produce environmental benefits for the people of Utah. These loan programs include the Agriculture Resource Development Loan program, which is a revolving loan fund,[13] and the Rural Rehabilitation Loan program.[14] At present, the division has portfolios with more than one thousand loans, with total assets of more than $35 million.[15]

The Agricultural Resource and Development Loan program has the largest portfolio consisting of approximately 900 loans, with more than $27 million outstanding.[16] The loan program is managed by the division for the Soil Conservation Commission in cooperation with the soil conservation districts throughout the state.[17] The loans finance improvements by landowners to increase the efficiency of agricultural operations, achieve range improvements, foster water and soil conservation, provide disaster assistance, and improve environmental quality.[18]

Based on a 1975 agreement between the U.S. Farm Home Administration and the state, the department, through the division, is responsible for the administration of the Rural Rehabilitation program.[19] This program is funded by both state and federal monies and totals $7.9 million, and consists of approximately seventy-five loans.[20] This program provides low-interest loans for farmers and ranchers who cannot qualify for conventional financing.[21] These loans help financially troubled producers stay in business, assist beginning farmers in obtaining farm or ranch property, and provide financing for a transfer of agricultural properties from one generation to another.[22]

The division also monitors compliance of conservation easements held by the department.[23] These conservation easements on agricultural properties provide an economic incentive for land owners to voluntarily preserve their properties for agricultural purposes, in an effort to preserve open space and habitat.[24]

Environmental Quality

Agricultural production has significant water, soil, and air quality implications for the state. Utah's incentive based agricultural nonpoint source pollution control program is funded largely by federal grants through the Clean Water Act.[25] Under this program, grants are given to operations, after evaluation by an assessment team, to pay for projects to improve manure management or control surface water runoff. In addition, stream stabilization and range and riparian rehabilitation help improve water quality.[26]

The division also administers the agricultural groundwater and rangeland monitoring programs.[27] The division conducts a free, nonregulatory groundwater testing program for privately owned water-supply systems, including wells and springs. Water is tested for bacteria, pesticides, nitrates, and inorganic minerals. The division outlines problems and offers suggestions regarding where well users might seek assistance.[28] As part of the Colorado River Basin Salinity Control Program designed to reduce the salt loading of the river, the division has instituted a salinity credit program. In addition to encouraging improved irrigation practices that will reduce the amount of salt discharged into the Colorado River system, the division also allows producers to purchase salt credits to offset salinity discharges.[29] Finally, through the Rangeland Monitoring Program, the division collects data and estimates range conditions which helps producers have advance warning to obtain alternate feed sources.[30]

Soil Conservation Commission

Soil and water resources require careful management to ensure responsible use and protection from wind and water erosion, sediment, and pollutants. The legislature created the twelve-member Soil Conservation Commission within the department to develop and coordinate the implementation of soil and water conservation initiatives.[31] The commission directs watershed and flood control projects, and gives financial and administrative support to the thirty-eight soil conservation districts in the state.[32]

DIVISION OF MARKETING AND DEVELOPMENT

The Division of Marketing and Development assists with the economic development of the state's agricultural sector by supporting the development of new products and promoting Utah agriculture in local, national, and international markets.[33] The sections and programs within the division include "Utah's Own," Organic Foods, and Market News.[34]

The division was established to help private producers increase local, national, and international market opportunities and add value to locally produced commodities.[35] Asia is a major destination for Utah food exports and agricultural commodities. Top commodity exports include meat, skins, hides, and dairy products. The Utah's Own Program promotes Utah products and has developed a logo in an effort to encourage consumers to use Utah products.[36]

With growing organic production, the Organic Foods program certified 39 operations in 2004 that met the United States Department of Agriculture (USDA) National Organic Program certification standards.[37] Certification offers a third party verification that standards have been met for the production and handling of organic foods. These producers are allowed to use the USDA or UDAF logo on the packaging representing "Certified Organic" products. The division also participates in a USDA cost share program that pays a percentage of certification costs for organic producers.[38] Finally, the Market News section of the division provides accurate and unbiased commodity price information which allows agricultural procedures to make critical business decisions.[39]

DIVISION OF ANIMAL INDUSTRY

The Division of Animal Industry is divided into programs: Animal Health, Animal Identification and Elk Farming, Meat Inspection, Aquaculture, and Diagnostic Laboratory.[40] The division has also developed a mobile emergency response unit which responds to animal disease emergencies, and the division offers training and consultation in biosecurity measures to various groups.[41]

Animal Health

The Animal Health program directs the monitoring of numerous animal disease programs and is particularly focused on the prevention and control of diseases that can be transmitted to humans. The division supports and promotes health assurance programs such as the Utah Cattle Health Assurance program, the Beef Quality Assurance program, the Utah Egg Quality Assurance program, and the National Poultry Improvement Plan.[42]

State law allows inspectors to investigate and quarantine certain animals with infectious diseases that may jeopardize the health of other animals within the state.[43] This program also implements the immunization, testing, and sanitary requirements necessary to prevent the spread of disease.[44] The commissioner of agriculture and food, with approval of the governor, may also destroy any infected livestock capable of spreading disease to other animals.[45]

Animal Identification and Elk Farming

The Animal Identification program is responsible for brand inspection, the administration of the livestock market laws, and elk farming and hunting parks. The Utah Livestock Brand and Anti-Theft Act of 1979 was enacted to protect the Utah livestock industry from the accidental straying or intentional theft of livestock.[46] The department appoints, with the Livestock Brand Board's approval, a state supervisor for livestock brand inspection.[47] Inspections are done on all livestock at the state's weekly auctions, and field inspections are done on all livestock before changing ownership, leaving the state, or going to slaughter.[48] The Livestock Brand Board oversees these procedures and policies, and is comprised of four cattle ranchers, one dairyman, one livestock market operator, and one horse breeder.[49] The Animal Identification program also maintains a central Brand and Mark Registry that lists each brand or mark recorded.[50] The statute requires livestock brands and earmarks to be renewed every five years to keep the brands current.[51]

The Livestock Market Committee advises the division as it administers and enforces the provisions of the Livestock Markets chapter and approves applications for licensing.[52] All operators and weighmen at livestock markets must be licensed by the department and must provide a certified copy of a surety bond filed with the United States Department of Agriculture as required by the U.S. Packers and Stockyards Act.[53]

Since the passage of the Domesticated Elk Act of 1997, many elk farms and hunting parks have been established.[54] This act provides for the regulation of domesticated elk, the inspection of domesticated elk facilities, and specifies requirements relating to the control of disease in domesticated elk facilities.[55] An advisory council gives advice and make recommendations on policies and rules, and has representatives from the Department of Natural Resources, the Department of Agriculture, the livestock industry, the domesticated elk industry, the Division of Wildlife Resources, and wildlife organizations.[56]

Meat Inspection

The Utah Meat and Poultry Products Inspection and Licensing statute directs the division to regulate and inspect meat processing facilities to encourage production in clean, well built, and sanitary facilities.[57] This law also provides guidelines so that the meat and poultry products inspection programs in the state are at least equal to those imposed under the Federal Meat Inspection Act and the Federal Poultry Products Inspection Act.[58]

All slaughterhouses in Utah must be licensed by the department.[59] The law prescribes certain sanitary standards, requires experts in sanitation or other competent investigators to investigate unsanitary conditions, and allows inspectors to refuse to provide inspection service if the sanitary conditions allow adulteration of any livestock or poultry product.[60]

Aquaculture

The purpose of the Aquaculture Act of 1994 is to encourage the practice of aquaculture, or the controlled cultivation of aquatic animals, while protecting the public fishery resource.[61] Several commercial aquaculture facilities and fee fishing facilities have registered with the state and are operating under the Fish Health program.[62]

The Fish Health Policy Board establishes policies designed to prevent the outbreak of disease in aquatic animals and develops aquaculture disease control plans.[63] The board also determines procedures and requirements for health approval certification and creates policies and procedures for an emergency response team to investigate serious threats of disease in aquatic animals.[64]

Diagnostic Laboratory

The Diagnostic Laboratory is a cooperative laboratory between the Utah Department of Agriculture and Food, the USDA, and Utah State University. The department funded the physical facilities, the USDA funds part of the testing for certain diseases, and Utah State University staffs and operates the laboratory. The laboratory monitors and tests farm animals, wildlife, and pets for a variety of diseases.

DIVISION OF CHEMISTRY LABORATORY

The Division of Chemistry Laboratory, directed by the state chemist, conducts chemical, physical, and microbiological analyses for the other divisions within the department.[65] The division, through its three main laboratories, tests various items to ensure label accuracy and to detect undesirable materials.[66]

The Pesticide Laboratory tests herbicides, insecticides, and fungicides to determine whether the listing of active ingredients and their concentrations comply with state labeling laws.[67] It also test plants, fruits, vegetables, soil, water, and milk products for pesticide residues.[68] The Dairy Laboratory tests dairy products and administers an industry laboratory certification program.[69] The Feed and Fertilizer Laboratory tests samples of commercial feed and fertilizer to ensure compliance with state labeling laws.[70] Finally, the Meat Laboratory analyzes meat samples obtained during inspections of plant and processing facilities to determine conformity to federal and state standards.[71]

DIVISION OF PLANT INDUSTRY

The Division of Plant Industry works, through its programs, to ensure that plants, grains, and seeds are properly labeled and disease and pest free.[72] The division is also responsible for ensuring that pesticides and other farm chemicals are applied safely.

State and Federal Pesticide Program

The Utah Pesticide Control Act[73] requires applicators of pesticides to be licenced and certified with the division.[74] The act also authorizes the division to adopt a list of "restricted use pesticides" for the state or designated areas within the state.[75] To determine compliance with the act, the division may periodically sample pesticides, observe and investigate the use and application of pesticides, and inspect equipment used to apply pesticides.[76]

The Pesticide Committee, created by the act, is comprised of nine persons, including members from the Utah State University Extension Service, the Department of Agriculture and Food, the Department of Health, the Division of Wildlife Resources, the Department of Environmental Quality, the Pest Control Association, the Farmers Union, the Farm Bureau Federation, and the agricultural chemical industry.[77] The Pesticide Committee makes recommendations to the commissioner of agriculture and food regarding rulemaking relating to the sale, distribution, use, and disposal of pesticides.[78]

The department is also the lead state agency for pesticide use enforcement under the Federal Insecticide, Fungicide, and Rodenticide Act.[79] The division administers provisions of this federal law by developing programs in cooperation with the Environmental Protection Agency.[80]

Fertilizer and Pesticide Registration and Nursery, Fruit and Vegetable Program

The Utah Fertilizer Act[81] requires that each brand and grade of commercial fertilizer or soil amendment be registered before being distributed, and that the labels be accurate and conform to departmental standards.[82] To enforce the Utah Fertilizer Act, the division periodically inspects commercial fertilizers and soil amendments.[83]

The Utah Pesticide Control Act[84] requires pesticide products to be registered with the division before the sale of pesticides.[85] The act also establishes labeling requirements for pesticides distributed in the state.[86]

Under the Utah Nursery Act,[87] a person must obtain a license from the division to run a nursery. In addition, each type of nursery stock must be sized and graded in accordance with regulations.[88] The division inspects each nursery once a year to determine whether its stock is free of pests and disease and issues a certificate to that effect.[89] Nursery stock found to be infested cannot be offered for sale and may be destroyed or otherwise treated as determined by the division.[90]

The Fruit and Vegetable Grading program is a voluntary program paid for by the packers of fresh fruit or vegetables. Inspectors from the division are licensed to inspect the fresh fruits and vegetables to verify that the produce meets USDA standards. The shipping point sheds, where growers transport their produce for packing and shipping, are also investigated to ensure that health and safety standards are met.

Seed Inspection, Feed and Hay Certification, and Noxious Weed Program

The Utah Seed Act[91] establishes labeling requirements for seeds sold or transported for use in the state.[92] It also requires seed sellers to test the percentage of germination, list the date the seed is offered for sale, and ensure it is free of noxious weed seed.[93] The division also has facilities for testing the purity and germination of seeds, and prescribes by rule uniform methods for sampling and testing seeds.[94] The Agricultural Experiment Station at Utah State University is the state agency responsible for the production, approval, and testing of foundation seeds.[95]

The Utah Commercial Feed Act[96] requires commercial feed distributors to register with the division.[97] In addition, most containers of commercial feed must meet certain labeling requirements.[98] To enforce the Commercial Feed Act, the division periodically inspects commercial feed distributed within the state for ingredients to determine whether a commercial feed is misbranded, adulterated, or otherwise deficient.[99] The division inspects straw and hay bales for weeds through out the state. The division's weed-free certification for hay is important because the certification is required for all hay used on public lands.[100]

In administering the Utah Noxious Weed Control Act[101], the state weed specialist coordinates and monitors weed control programs on a statewide basis.[102] A five-member State Weed Committee advises the division regarding the state noxious weed program.[103] Each county may appoint a county weed control board who is responsible for the formulation and implementation of a county-wide coordinated noxious weed control program designed to prevent and control noxious weeds within its county.[104] The division may require the board to justify in writing any failure to carry out its duties.[105]

Insect Control and Plant Quarantine

The state entomologist inspects insects and plants and may institute quarantines administered by the division.[106] The state entomologist issues phytosanitary certificates that allow Utahns to ship plants and plant products to other states and foreign countries.[107] The state entomologist also administers the Utah Bee Inspection Act and the Insect Infestation Emergency Control Act.[108]

The Utah Bee Inspection Act of 1979 requires registration to raise bees in the state, a license to operate a wax-salvage plant, and a certificate of inspection to import bees.[109] The division and all county bee inspectors have access to all apiaries for enforcement purposes.[110]

Several insects that are problematic to farmers and ranchers in the state include the Apple Maggot, the Cherry Fruit Fly, the African Honey Bee, the Cereal Leaf Beetle, the Gypsy Moth, grasshoppers, and Mormon Crickets. Insect infestation results in extensive crop damage each year.[111] Under the Insect Infestation Emergency Control Act, the legislature created the Decision and Action Committee which is responsible for establishing a system of priorities during an insect infestation emergency and determining whether an area requires the establishment of an insect control district.[112]

The commissioner of agriculture and food, with the consent of the governor, may declare that an insect infestation emergency situation exists which jeopardizes property and resources, and designate the area or areas affected.[113] The commissioner of agriculture and food is authorized to direct and implement all emergency measures that the committee considers necessary to alleviate the emergency condition.[114]

Grain and Hay Inspection Program

The Grain Inspection Service is responsible for ensuring that the grain in Utah is disease and insect free.[115] The service is funded by fees charged for grading grain, one of the many agricultural products that the department grades.[116] The grain grading lab tests submitted samples and samples gathered at the grain inspection facility in Ogden.[117]

DIVISION OF REGULATORY SERVICES

The Division of Regulatory Services has regulatory oversight of Utah agricultural products and services.[118] The division is divided into five programs: Food Compliance, Meat, Egg, and Poultry Compliance, Dairy Compliance, Weights and Measures, and Labeling and Production Compliance.[119]

Food Compliance

The Division of Regulatory Services is charged with the enforcement of the Wholesome Food Act, which prohibits the manufacture or sale of adulterated or misbranded food and the dissemination of any false advertisement.[120] Under the Utah Wholesome Food Act, food that is suspected of being misbranded or adulterated is prevented from moving in commerce by voluntary destructions, hold orders, or releases.[121] Additional regulatory action may include the issuance of warning notices, cease and desist orders, citations, and taking administrative action.[122] Agents of the division are authorized to embargo any adulterated or misbranded food, and can apply to the district court to enter a decree authorizing the food's destruction.[123]

The division may also establish regulations aimed at protecting the public from unsafe substances in foods.[124] The division also registers food establishments, such as bakeries, grocery stories, and water facilities.[125]

Meat, Egg & Poultry Compliance

Through the planned and random compliance reviews, the Meat Compliance program strives to control and limit the sale of adulterated or misbranded meats.[126] The department, through the division, establishes grades and standards of the quality, size, and weight for the sale of eggs and poultry products as well as regulates the sale of eggs generally.[127] Grading is a standardized means of describing the marketability of the product and eggs and poultry can be classified by quality characteristics.[128]

Dairy Compliance

Under the Utah Dairy Act, the division has authority to inspect any premises where dairy products are produced, manufactured, processed, stored, or held for distribution to determine whether such premises are in compliance with state law.[129] The division also has the authority to collect samples of dairy products and to condemn or embargo any dairy product that is adulterated, misbranded, or not produced or processed in accordance with the law.[130]

The division is also responsible for the issuance of licenses and permits to produce milk, operate a dairy plant, manufacture dairy products, haul milk in bulk, and for the wholesale distribution of dairy products.[131]

Weights and Measures

The Regulatory Services Division has authority to establish weights and measures standards for all commodities.[132] The division also has authority to inspect and test weights and measures offered for sale to determine if they are correct.[133] The division may seize weights and measures that are inaccurate and are not corrected within a reasonable time.[134] All weights and measures in the state are referenced to the "state standards" that are housed in the department and the state metrology lab, which are in turn referenced to the national standards. The primary function of the weights and measures program is to ensure that equity prevails in the marketplace for both the buyer and the seller.[135]

Labeling and Product Compliance

The purpose of the Labeling and Product Compliance program is to help protect consumers against fraud and product misrepresentation, to help provide Utahns with hygienically clean products, and to provide allergy awareness when purchasing these articles.[136] Utah law requires manufacturers, supply dealers, wholesalers, and repairers of these products and their components to obtain an annual license before offering items for sale within the state.[137] Product labels are required to indicate whether the product is made with new or used filling materials and to disclose those materials by generic name and percentage.[138] This enables consumers to make price/value/performance-based buying decisions.[139] It also encourages fair competition among manufacturers by establishing uniformity in labeling and component disclosure.[140]

PROGRAMS

The department also administers other programs in addition to the program administered by the seven divisions.

Animal and Wildlife Damage and Prevention

The Utah Wildlife Services program is a cooperative effort between the Utah Department of Agriculture and Food and the U.S. Department of Agriculture to protect livestock through predator management.[141] The Wildlife Services program also works with the Utah Division of Wildlife Resources to protect declining wildlife populations.[142] The program monitors its impact to ensure there are no negative environmental consequences of its activities.[143]

Authorized by the Agricultural Wildlife Damage Act, the Agricultural and Wildlife Damage Prevention Board creates state policy designed to prevent damage to wildlife and agricultural crops. The board oversees the Wildlife Service programs designed to prevent damage to livestock, poultry, and agricultural crops through the selective control of predators and other birds and animals that damage crops.[144] The board is composed of the commissioner of agriculture and food and the director of the Division of Wildlife Resources, who serve as the board's chair and vice chair, together with seven other members: one sheep producer representing wool growers; one cattle producer representing range cattle producers; one person from the United States Department of Agriculture; one agricultural landowner representing agricultural landowners; one person representing wildlife interests; one person from the United States Forest Service; and one person from the United States Bureau of Land Management.[145]

Agricultural Mediation Service

The department administers a certified agriculture mediation program through a grant from the federal government.[146] The program offers mediation services to Utah agricultural producers who may be adversely affected by decisions made by USDA.[147]

Horse Racing Regulation

The Utah Horse Regulation Act creates a regulatory program for monitoring the horse racing industry in Utah.[148] The Utah Horse Racing Commission licenses, regulates, inspects, and supervises all persons and places involved in horse racing.[149] Upon appropriation by the legislature, money from the Horse Racing Account consisting of license fees, revenue from fines, and interest, can be used for the administration of the act, including payment of the costs of public liability insurance, stewards, veterinarians, and drug testing.[150]

Chapter 10

Business and Labor

Government regulation of business and labor in Utah takes many forms, from regulating proprietary schools and banks to requiring licensing for certain occupations; and from operating a state-run alcoholic beverage control system, to overseeing employment relationships. Government regulation of businesses and business transactions generally has as a goal protecting the public from unduly harmful business practices while allowing the free market to produce the best products at the best prices.[1] As with most challenging policy issues, policymakers have struck a balance between an unregulated, "buyer beware" economy and an over regulated, government-run economy. This chapter discusses Utah's current regulatory policy as carried out through five state departments that each regulate different areas of commerce:

> **In this chapter:**
>
> Alcoholic Beverage Control (p. 173)
> Department of Commerce (p. 176)
> Department of Financial Institutions (p. 182)
> Insurance Department (p. 185)
> Labor Commission (p. 187)

1. Department of Alcoholic Beverage Control
2. Department of Commerce
3. Department of Financial Institutions
4. Insurance Department
5. Labor Commission

ALCOHOLIC BEVERAGE CONTROL

Under the Twenty-first Amendment to the United States Constitution, each state is granted powers to regulate alcoholic beverages.[2] States have exercised that authority in a variety of ways, generally through licensing or through the control of the retail, wholesale, or both retail and wholesale distribution of alcoholic beverages.[3] States that control the sale and distribution of alcoholic beverages are often referred to as "control states." As of May 2005, Utah is one of eighteen control states.[4] Figure 10-1 shows as shaded those states that are control states.

Figure 10-1

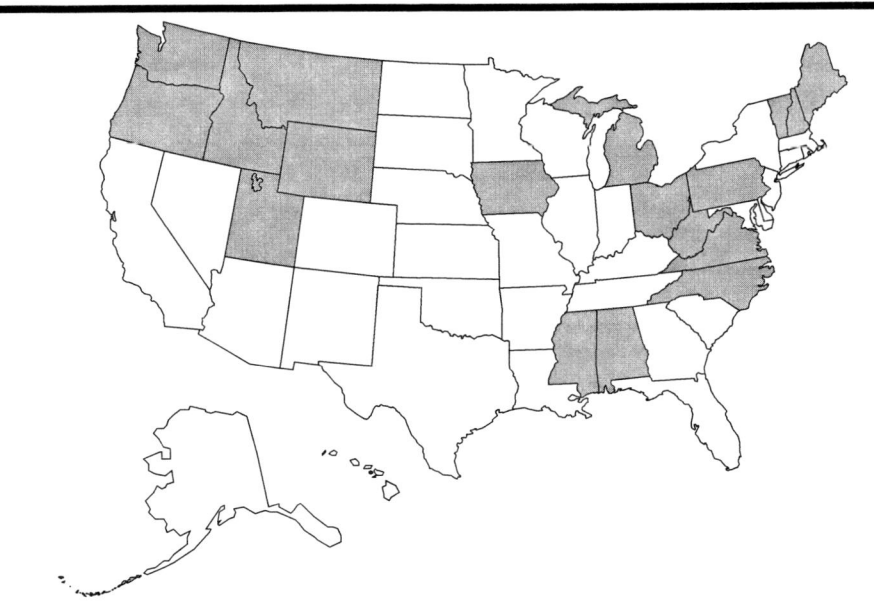

Alcoholic Beverage Control States
2004

Utah as a Control State

Prior to prohibition there existed a variety of statutes regulating alcoholic beverages. After the repeal of federal prohibition in 1933, Utah became a control state when in 1935 the Utah Legislature passed comprehensive legislation under which state stores or packaging agencies were the sole outlets for purchasing liquor.[5] Utah's status as a control state has not changed; however, through the years the legislature has modified Utah's alcoholic beverage statutes.

Utah's Alcoholic Beverage Control Act governs the sale, service, storage, manufacture, distribution, and consumption of alcoholic products.[6] Under that act, alcoholic products are generally categorized as either liquor (distilled spirits, wine and wine-based products, and beer that contains more than 3.2 percent alcohol by weight) or beer (all beer and beer-based products that contain 3.2 percent or less of alcohol by weight).[7] Whether an alcoholic beverage is liquor or beer affects how it is regulated. For example, while beer that contains 3.2 percent or less of alcohol by weight may be sold by grocery stores or convenience stores, packaged liquor is distributed at prices set by the state through state-owned liquor stores or privately-operated package agencies that contract with the state. Retail sale of alcoholic beverages for on-premise consumption is further regulated through the issuance of retail licenses for restaurants, limited service restaurants, on-premise banquet facilities, airport lounges, private clubs, and on-premise beer retailers.[8] Special uses or temporary events where alcoholic beverages are distributed are generally regulated through the use of permits. Licenses are issued to local industry representatives; manufacturers, such as a wineries, distilleries, or breweries; and distributors, such as liquor warehouses or beer wholesalers. Utah also requires certification of out-of-state breweries.[9] Utah's alcoholic beverage control system not only controls the distribution of alcoholic beverages, it has become a major source of revenue.[10]

The Alcoholic Beverage Control Act creates uniformity throughout the state in many areas involving the regulation of alcoholic beverages. The act addresses regulatory control by local authorities. The act governs except where local authorities are expressly granted regulatory control by the act. The act also provides that "[n]othing in [the act] precludes local authorities from regulating the sale, storage, service, or consumption of alcoholic beverages if that regulation does not conflict with the provisions of [the act]."[11]

Role of the Commission

The Alcoholic Beverage Control Commission consists of five part-time commissioners appointed by the governor with the consent of the senate with no more than three commissioners from the same political party.[12] A commissioner is generally appointed to a four-year term, but may be removed by the governor for cause after a public hearing, the procedural requirements of which are outlined by statute.[13] The commission is to meet at least monthly and is the general policymaking body on the subject of alcoholic product control.[14] The commission is directed to conduct, license, and regulate the sale of alcoholic beverages in a manner and at prices that:

- Reasonably satisfy the public demand and protect the public interest, including the rights of citizens who do not wish to be involved with alcoholic products
- Will promote the reduction of the harmful effects of over consumption of alcoholic beverages by adults and consumption of alcoholic beverages by minors[15]

Among its several duties, the Alcoholic Beverage Control Commission, through rule, sets policy establishing criteria and procedures for:

- Granting, denying, suspending, or revoking permits, licenses, and package agencies
- Controlling liquor merchandise inventory
- Determining the location of state stores, package agencies, and outlets[16]

Another example of a commission power or duty is to fix prices at which liquors are sold that are the same for state stores, package agencies, and outlets.[17] Subject to statutory requirements, the commission also decides the number and location of state stores, package agencies, and outlets.[18]

Role of the Department

The public business of alcoholic beverage control is governed by the Alcoholic Beverage Control Commission but operated by the Department of Alcoholic Beverage Control.[19] The administrative head of the department is a director of alcoholic beverage control appointed by the commission with the approval of the governor.[20] The director may be removed from office for cause by a majority vote of the commission after a public hearing before the full commission, the procedural requirements of which are outlined in statute.[21]

The Alcoholic Beverage Control Commission and the Department of Alcoholic Beverage Control work hand-in-hand. For example, the commission requires the director of the department to follow sound management principles and to report periodically to the commission. In turn, the commission is to receive, consider, and act in a timely manner upon all reports, recommendations, and matters submitted by the director, and do all things necessary to support the department in properly performing the department's duties and responsibilities.[22]

The department conducts the day-to-day operations of the state's liquor stores and package agencies and administers the state liquor laws. It is state policy that alcoholic beverage control be operated as a public business using sound management principles and practices.[23] The business function is to service the public demand for alcoholic beverages; however, the commission and department may not promote or encourage the sale or consumption of alcoholic beverages.[24]

Figure 10-2

Department of Alcoholic Beverage Control

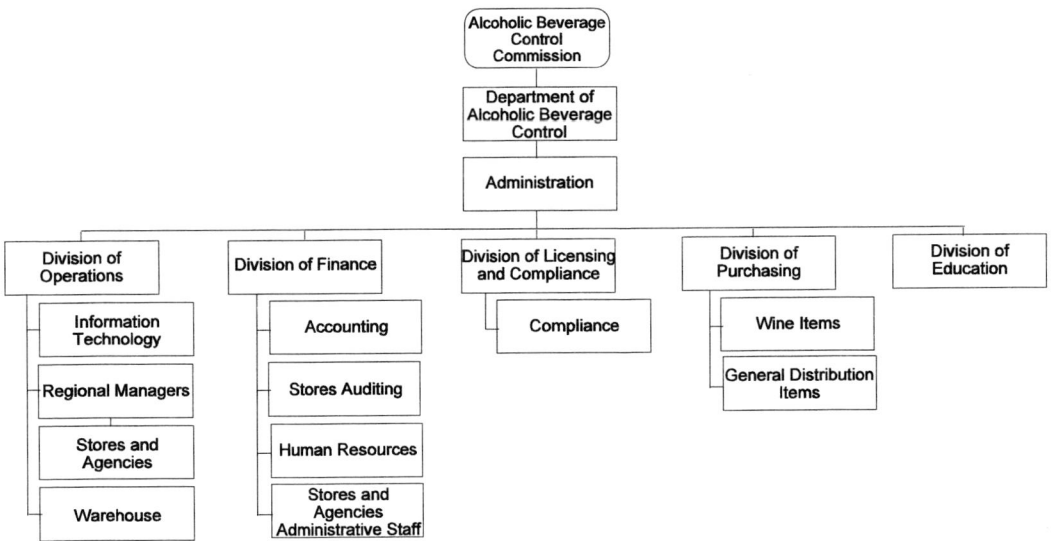

DEPARTMENT OF COMMERCE
Role of the Department

Utah's businesses and occupations have a pronounced physical and economic impact on the health, safety, and welfare of the citizens of the state. While the overall impact is generally beneficial to the public, the potential for harm and injury frequently warrants intervention by state government.[25] The Department of Commerce was created in order to achieve an environment where businesses may thrive and where the public is protected. The department's mission statement, "to protect the public interest by ensuring fair commercial and professional practices"[26] summarizes its regulatory activities. It licenses occupations and professions, investigates complaints against licensees and businesses, investigates fraud and other harmful business practices against consumers, and performs other functions that ensure fair commercial and professional practices.

The department was established in 1941.[27] Until 1989, the department was known as the Department of Business Regulation.[28] From its creation until 1983, it was led by a three-member commission that had oversight authority over the insurance department, banking department, and department of registration.[29] The commissioners were members of the public service commission, state securities commission, and the trade commission. However, the department's role has changed as the economy has shifted from agriculture and manufacturing to services and information. An executive director, chosen by the governor with the consent of the senate, now leads the Department of Commerce. The department accomplishes its mission through activities achieved in the following:

- Administration
- Division of Consumer Protection
- Division of Corporations and Commercial Code
- Division of Occupational and Professional Licensing
- Division of Public Utilities
- Division of Real Estate
- Division of Securities

Figure 10-3

Department of Commerce

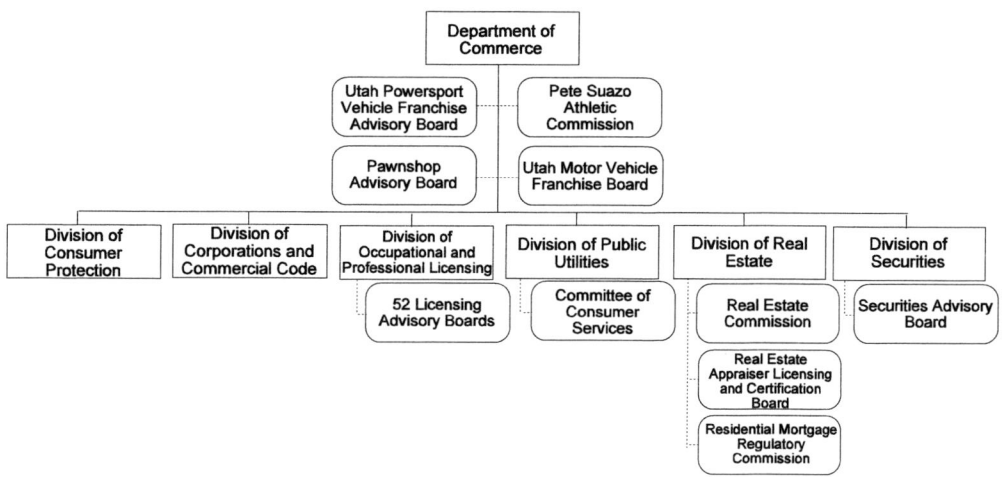

Role of the Divisions
Administration

Administration oversees and coordinates the activities of the divisions. In it is housed the executive director and the rest of the department's executive staff. Administration is responsible for information technology support, budgeting, bill-paying, payroll, and other operational aspects of the department as a whole.[30]

Division of Consumer Protection

The legislature created the Division of Consumer Protection in 1983.[31] Prior to 1983, it was called the trade commission. The trade commission's original mission was to protect the public from unfair business practices.[32] The division still has a similar mission, but the division's regulatory responsibilities have increased as the economy has become more complex. Since 1983, the number of Utah Code chapters that the division administers has grown from four to thirteen. The division administers the following acts:
- Unfair Practices Act
- Music Licensing Practices Act
- Utah Consumer Sales Practices Act
- Business Opportunity Disclosure Act
- New Motor Vehicles Warranty Act
- Credit Services Organizations Act
- Charitable Solicitations Act
- Health Spa Services Protection Act
- Telephone and Facsimile Solicitation Act
- Telephone Fraud Prevention Act
- Prize Notices Regulation Act
- Utah Postsecondary Proprietary Schools Act
- Price Controls During Emergencies Act

The division is led by a director who is appointed by the executive director of the Department of Commerce with the approval of the governor.[33] During fiscal year 2004, the division completed and closed investigations on 2,456 complaints from the public regarding unfair business practices (see figure 10-4).[34] Most of the complaints resulted in voluntary compliance from the business, administrative action by the division, or dismissal of the complaint.

Figure 10-4

Complaints Received by the Division of Consumer Protection
July 1, 2003 to June 30, 2004

Complaints Received	3,567
Complaints Assigned to an Investigator	2,552
Administrative & Civil Cases Closed	2,456
Actions on Complaints	
Voluntary Compliance	878
Administrative Action	332
Insufficient Evidence	204
Unfounded	207
Criminal cases referred to Attorney General	10
Other Actions	825

Division of Corporations and Commercial Code

The Division of Corporations and Commercial Code was created in 1984 to "assume certain duties and responsibilities previously delegated to the secretary of state."[35] The division is responsible for administering Utah Code provisions dealing with corporations and other forms of business entities doing business in Utah. The division registers businesses seeking to incorporate in Utah, provides certificates of authority to foreign corporations seeking to transact business in the state, registers trademarks, and performs other regulatory activities that ensure the integrity of the business climate for business entities that transact business in Utah.[36]

The division is led by a director who is appointed by the executive director of the Department of Commerce with the approval of the governor. The director holds office at the pleasure of the governor.

Division of Occupational and Professional Licensing

In 1985, the legislature created the Division of Occupational and Professional Licensing to regulate various occupations and professions that are subject to state licensing in Utah.[37] It is the largest division within the Department of Commerce, and during 2004 the division regulated 151,254[38] individuals and entities (see figure 10-5).

The division is led by a director who is appointed by the executive director of the Department of Commerce with the approval of the governor. The director holds office at the pleasure of the governor. The division works closely with boards that oversee the licensing requirements for each occupation and profession.

Occupational regulation is not new for Utah's government. Even prior to achieving statehood, the Utah Territorial Legislature passed a law to regulate the practice of medicine.[39] For many years, the Division of Regulation governed occupational licensing. Currently, the Division of Occupational and Professional Licensing has responsibilities that include:[40]

- Investigating the activities of any person whose occupation or profession is regulated by the division

- Taking action against persons in violation of the laws and rules administered and enforced by the division
- Seeking injunctions and temporary restraining orders to restrain unauthorized activity
- Issuing, refusing to issue, revoking, suspending, renewing, refusing to renew, or otherwise acting upon any license
- Preparing lists of licensees and making these lists available to the public

Figure 10-5

Total Licensees by Profession
(as of 6/30/04)

Acupuncturists	66
Advanced Practice Registered Nurses (3)	958
Alternative Dispute Resolution Providers (3)	58
Architects	1,892
Athlete Agents	13
Building Inspectors (2)	497
Burglar Alarm Agents	1,347
Burglar Alarm Companies	137
Certified Court Reporters	134
Certified Nurse Midwives (3)	112
Certified Public Accountants	3,730
Certified Public Accountancy Firms	638
Certified Registered Nurse Anesthetists	184
Chiropractic Physicians	720
Construction Trades Instructors (4)	29
Contractors	18,034
Controlled Substance Handler	24
Controlled Substance Purchaser/Distributors	14
Cosmetologist/Barbers and Interns	19,896
Cosmetology/Barber Instructors	980
Cosmetology/Barber Schools	36
Deception Detection Examiners and Interns	26
Dental Hygienists (2)	1,425
Dentists (4)	2,165
Dietitians	506
Electricians (5)	8,696
Electrologists	148
Electrologist Instructors	3
Electrology Schools	1
Engineers--Professional and Structural	7,235
Environmental Health Scientists & In-Train	245
Estheticians (2)	1,245
Esthetician Instructors	51
Esthetics Schools	12
Factory Built Housing Dealers	67
Funeral Service Directors and Apprentices	313
Funeral Service Establishments	94
Genetic Counselors	22
Geologists	923
Health Care Assistants	8,988
Health Facility Administrators	298
Hearing Instrument Specialists and Interns	103
Land Surveyors	669
Landscape Architects	313
Licensed Practical Nurses (2)	3,323
Marriage and Family Therapists and Interns	486
Massage Therapists and Apprentices	4,379
Nail Technicians	2,487
Nail Technician Instructors	46
Nail Technician Schools	6
Naturopathic Physicians (3)	16
Occupational Therapists and Apprentices	586
Optometrists (3)	403
Osteopathic Physicians	244
Pharmacists, Preceptors, Interns, Technicians	5,128
Pharmacies (15)	1,128
Physical Therapists	1,446
Physician Assistants	458
Physician/Surgeons	6,955
Plumbers (4)	4,103
Podiatric Physician	183
Pre-need Funeral Arrangement Providers and Sales Agents	251
Private Probation Officers	58
Professional Counselors and Interns	522
Professional Employer Organizations	67
Psychologists and Psychology Residents	778
Radiology & Practical Technicians	2,173
Recreational Therapists (3)	750
Registered Nurses (2)	18,882
Respiratory Care Practitioners	1,099
Security Companies	61
Security Personnel (2)	5,417
Social Workers (3)	5,214
Speech-Language Pathologists & Audiologists (3)	634
Substance Abuse Counselors	341
Veterinarians and Interns	583
TOTAL LICENSEES	151,254

*Occupations having multiple license classifications are noted in parentheses

The division receives a substantial portion of its funding from licensee fees, which typically range from $30 to $200.[41] Each license issued by the division is on a two-year renewal cycle.

Aside from professional licensing and enforcement of licensing standards, the division also oversees two other programs: the medical malpractice pre-litigation program and the Residence Lien Recovery Fund. The medical malpractice pre-litigation program requires that a person wishing to initiate a medical liability case against a health care provider must first participate in an informal, nonbinding panel hearing with the division before the case can go to trial.[42] The Residence Lien Recovery Fund protects homeowners from liens that are placed on their home by unpaid suppliers or subcontractors when the homeowner has contracted with a licensed contractor and has paid the licensed contractor for the materials or services.[43]

Division of Public Utilities

The public utility industry in Utah is still primarily comprised of monopolies that are regulated by the Public Service Commission in order to protect the public interest. The Division of Public Utilities assists the Public Service Commission in regulating 152 utilities by providing the commission with objective and comprehensive information, evidence, and recommendations governing the regulation of public utilities in Utah (see figure 10-6).[44]

Figure 10-6

Number of Regulated Utilities in Utah
Fiscal Year 2004

Electric	13
Natural Gas	2
Telecom--ILEC*	21
Telecom--CLEC**	75
Water and Sewer	37
Railroads	4
Total	152

*Incumbent Local Exchange Carrier
**Competitive Local Exchange Carrier

The division audits and tracks utility operations, handles and investigates consumer complaints, and monitors utility operations to ensure compliance with statutes and Public Service Commission rules and orders.[45]

The division was created in 1983.[46] The director of the division is appointed by the executive director of the Department of Commerce and serves at the pleasure of the executive director. This division is also discussed in Chapter 19, *Regulation of Public Utilities*.

Committee of Consumer Services

The Committee of Consumer Services was created in 1977 to represent the interests of residential and small commercial utility consumers.[47] The committee is made up of six members from different areas of the state and different economic backgrounds.[48] Committee members are chosen by the governor with the consent of the senate. The committee assesses the impact of utility rate changes and other regulatory actions on residential and small commercial consumers; assists residential consumers and those engaged in small commercial enterprises in appearing before the Public Service Commission; and advocates for positions most advantageous to a majority of residential and small commercial consumers before the Public Service Commission.[49] This committee is also discussed in Chapter 19, *Regulation of Public Utilities*.

Division of Real Estate

Utah's Division of Real Estate, created in 1979,[50] works to improve the quality of the real estate industry in Utah by licensing and educating real estate professionals, educating the public, and enforcing state real estate laws through investigation and administrative actions against violators.[51] The division is led by a director who is appointed by the executive director of the Department of Commerce with the approval of the governor. The director holds office at the pleasure of the governor.[52]

Table 10-1

Real Estate Licensing in Utah[53]					
	2000	2001	2002	2003	2004
Appraisers	1,781	999	1,003	991	1,034
Real Estate Professionals	14,624	14,762	15,260	16,223	17,500
Mortgage Lenders	0	1,227	7,709	11,020	14,746

The division regulates three main professions within the real estate industry: appraisers, real estate professionals (agents and brokers), and mortgage lenders (see table 10-1).[54] The number of persons licensed as appraisers remained steady over the past five years, while the number of licensed real estate professionals slowly increased during the period. In contrast, residential mortgage broker licensing has rapidly increased, because residential mortgage lending regulation within the Department of Commerce is a recent activity. Prior to passage of the Utah Residential Mortgage Practices Act in 2000,[55] residential mortgage lending regulation occurred primarily through regulation of financial institutions. However, in recent years, residential mortgage lending through a mortgage broker, rather than through a home buyer's financial institution, has become more common.[56]

The Real Estate Commission assists the Division of Real Estate in its duties.[57] Its membership includes five members appointed by the governor with the consent of the senate. Four of the members are real estate professionals and one is a member from the general public. The commission has authority to make rules for the administration of the Real Estate Code, conduct hearings related to any real estate licensee or applicant for licensure, establish fees, advise the division, and conduct other activities as outlined in statute.[58]

Division of Securities

The Division of Securities was created in 1983.[59] Prior to the creation of the division, the security industry in Utah was regulated by a security commission made up of the business regulation commission. Currently the division is led by a director, appointed by the executive director of the Department of Commerce with the governor's approval. The director of the division holds office at the pleasure of the governor.[60] A Securities Advisory Board helps the director establish policy matters, budgetary matters, registration requirements, division rules, and reasonable fees.[61]

The division administers and enforces the Utah Uniform Securities Act. The Division administers the act by registering securities; reviewing exemptions; issuing no-action letters and interpretative opinions; licensing securities professionals; and providing investor education opportunities.[62] In 2003, the division regulated over 80,000 licensees, more than 90 percent of which are from the East Coast.[63] As is apparent in figure 10-7, the number of licensed stockbrokers fluctuates.

Figure 10-7

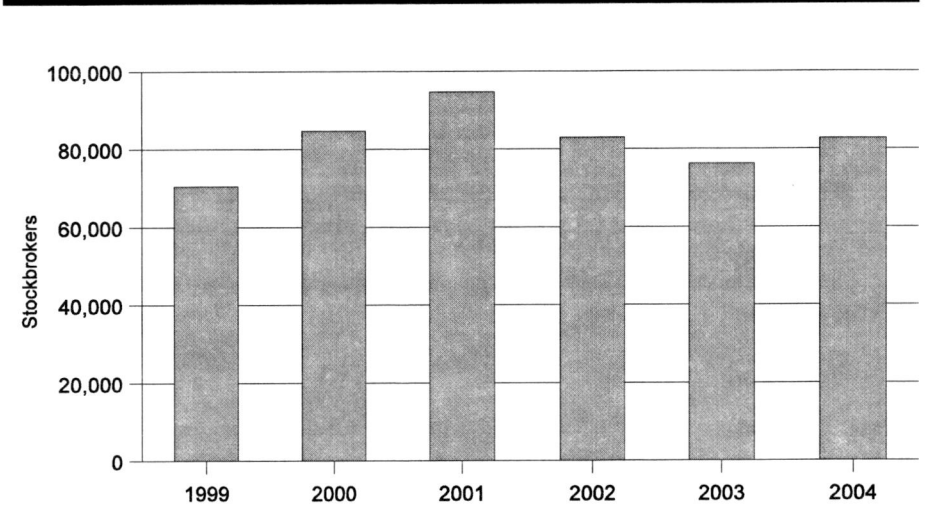

The division is staffed with numerous investigators, auditors, and other professionals who investigate alleged violations of Utah's securities laws. The division also investigates complaints involving persons licensed by the division. Upon discovering a violation, the division may bring a civil or administrative action, or refer the investigation for criminal prosecution.

DEPARTMENT OF FINANCIAL INSTITUTIONS

Beginning with the supervision of state chartered banks in 1896,[64] regulation of Utah's financial institutions has been an important role for state government. The regulation of financial institutions has evolved from the secretary of state regulating banks to the present day Department of Financial Institutions regulating traditional financial institutions and various other entities and persons providing financial services.[65]

Figure 10-8 outlines the structure of the Department of Financial Institutions.

Figure 10-8

Department of Financial Institutions

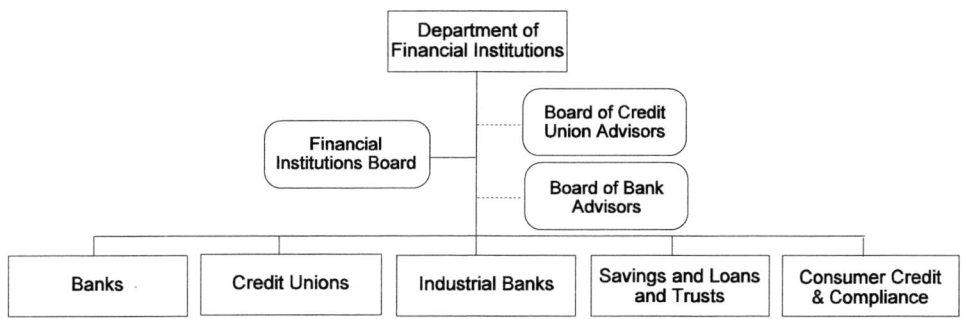

State Regulation under the Dual System

A cornerstone of the United States financial institution industry is the existence of a dual system for chartering of financial institutions. For example, to function as a bank or credit union an institution generally must first be "chartered." Under the dual chartering system, an institution meeting the relevant chartering requirements may choose whether its chartering agency, and hence the primary regulator, is a federal or state agency. For example, a credit union could be chartered under federal law by the National Credit Union Administration which would then be the primary regulator of the credit union's activities. Alternatively, the credit union could be chartered under state law by the commissioner of financial institutions who would then be the primary regulator of the credit union. However, the state-chartered credit union may also be subject to supervision by the National Credit Union Administration as the insurer of deposits of the credit union.

Figure 10-9

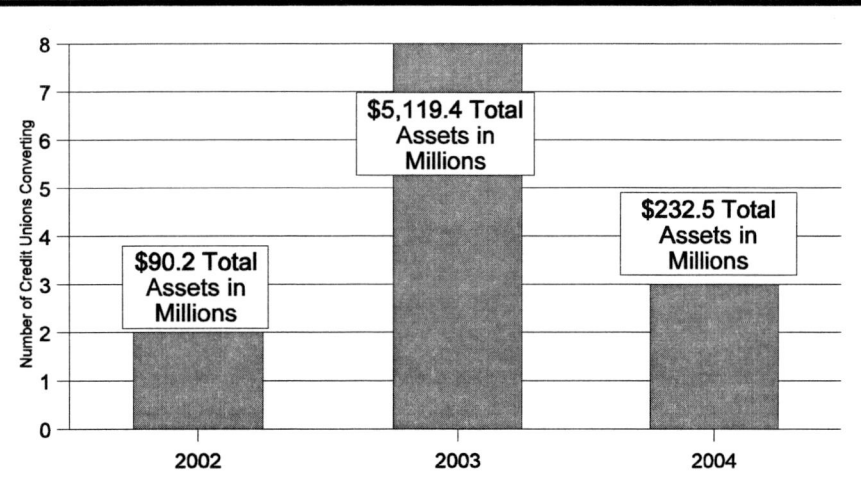

A financial institution may change its charter from state-to-federal or federal-to-state if the institution meets the relevant chartering requirements. For example, in recent years, the state has experienced several conversions of state-chartered credit unions to federally-chartered credit unions.[66] Figure 10-9 shows the number of Utah state-chartered credit unions that converted to a federal charter in 2002, 2003, and 2004.

The dual chartering of financial institutions creates an environment where innovation and responsiveness is encouraged as federal and state agencies seek to meet the needs of the financial institution industry. However, as economies become global, the dual chartering system faces new challenges. The preservation of the dual banking system and the competitive equality of state chartered institutions as compared to federally chartered institutions are express purposes of Title 7, Financial Institutions Act.[67] Examples of other purposes of the Financial Institutions Act include:

- Providing for the supervision, regulation, and examinations of persons furnishing depository, lending, and associated financial services in this state
- Protecting the interests of shareholders, members, depositors, and other customers of financial institutions operating in this state
- Promoting the availability, efficiency, and profitability of financial services in the communities of this state
- Cooperating with federal regulators and regulators from other states in regulating financial institutions, in improving the quality of regulation, and in promoting the interests of this state in interstate matters
- Providing to the commissioner of financial institutions sufficient powers and responsibilities to carry out the purposes of the Financial Institutions Act[68]

Depository Financial Institutions in General

Types of depository financial institutions supervised by the Department of Financial Institutions include state-chartered banks, credit unions, industrial banks, and savings and loan associations.[69] In its simplest terms, the Department of Financial Institutions supervises state-chartered depository institutions to ensure that they operate in a safe and sound manner within a competitive environment. However, there are differences in how financial institutions are treated on both the state and federal levels. For example, a credit union is exempt from paying income tax,[70] but is limited in who can be members of the credit union.[71] Commercial banks generally are subject to income taxes. Whether or not these differences create undue competitive advantages has been debated by the banking and credit union industries within the state for many years. The debate has led to litigation[72] and legislative action modifying the Utah Credit Union Act, Title 7, Chapter 9 of the Utah Code.[73] As several credit unions have moved to a federal charter, the debate has moved to some degree to the federal arena.

Role of the Department

The Department of Financial Institutions is responsible for executing the laws of this state relating to financial institutions; other persons subject to the Financial Institutions Act, Title 7, of the Utah Code; and the businesses financial institutions and other persons conduct.[74] The Department of Financial Institutions also functions as an administrative body under Title 70C, Utah Consumer Credit Code, and Title 70D, Mortgage Financing Regulation, of the Utah Code.

The chief executive officer of the Department of Financial Institutions is the commissioner of financial institutions, who is appointed by the governor with the consent of the senate for a four-year term, and subject to removal by the governor.[75] Along with the commissioner, there is the Board of Financial Institutions, the chief examiner, the supervisor of banks, the supervisor of savings and loan associations, the supervisor of industrial banks, the supervisor of credit unions, and other supervisors, examiners, and personnel as may be required to carry out the duties, powers, and responsibilities of the Department of Financial Institutions.[76]

An example of the powers of the commissioner is the power to supervise the conduct, operation, management, examination, and statements and reports of examinations of financial institutions and other persons subject to the jurisdiction of the department.[77] The commissioner's powers also include, after considering certain factors, the power to authorize a state-chartered depository institution to engage in any activity it could engage in if federally-chartered, and to grant to a state-chartered depository institution all additional rights, powers, privileges, benefits, or immunities it would possess if it were federally-chartered.[78] The commissioner has similar power to authorize a depository institution chartered by this state to engage in any activity that a Utah branch of an out-of-state depository institution of the same class may engage in.[79]

In addition to supervising state-chartered financial institutions, the Department of Financial Institutions regulates selected nondepository institutions to varying degrees such as:[80]
- Trust companies[81]
- Depository institution holding companies[82]
- Money transmitters, wire transferors, and issuers of travelers checks and money orders[83]
- Loan production offices[84]
- Independent escrow agents[85]
- Residential mortgage lenders, brokers, and servicers[86]
- Consumer lending[87]
- Check cashers and deferred deposit loan lenders[88]
- Title lenders[89]

The Department of Financial Institutions also has jurisdiction over second mortgage lenders, mortgage servicers, and depository institutions or affiliates engaged in first mortgage brokering and lending.[90]

INSURANCE DEPARTMENT

Regulation of insurance companies predates the creation of the Insurance Department in 1909 and demonstrates a consistent state policy requiring the regulation of insurance.[91] This pattern of regulating the insurance industry and products continues today with the Insurance Department being the executive branch entity charged with administering Title 31A, Insurance Code. Examples of the several purposes of the Insurance Code is ensuring the solvency of insurers; the fair and equitable treatment of policyholders, claimants, and insurers; and that Utah has an adequate and healthy insurance market, characterized by competitive conditions, the spirit of innovation, and the exercise of initiative.[92]

The chief officer of the Insurance Department is the insurance commissioner, who is appointed by the governor with the consent of the senate.[93] The commissioner may appoint up to three persons to assist the commissioner.[94] The commissioner is required to employ a chief examiner and may employ such other professional, technical, and clerical employees as necessary to carry out the duties of the Insurance Department.[95] Although statute does not divide the Insurance Department into divisions, the department currently is generally organized around multiple divisions. For example, the Department has divisions for the various types of insurance it oversees (e.g., Health Insurance Division, Life Insurance Division, and Property and Casualty Insurance Division which would include the areas of motor vehicle and homeowners insurance).[96] In addition to general administrative or licensing divisions, the Insurance Department maintains a Fraud Division and an Examination Division.[97] The department also includes other components such as boards. Figure 10-10 outlines the structure of the Insurance Department.

Figure 10-10

Insurance Department

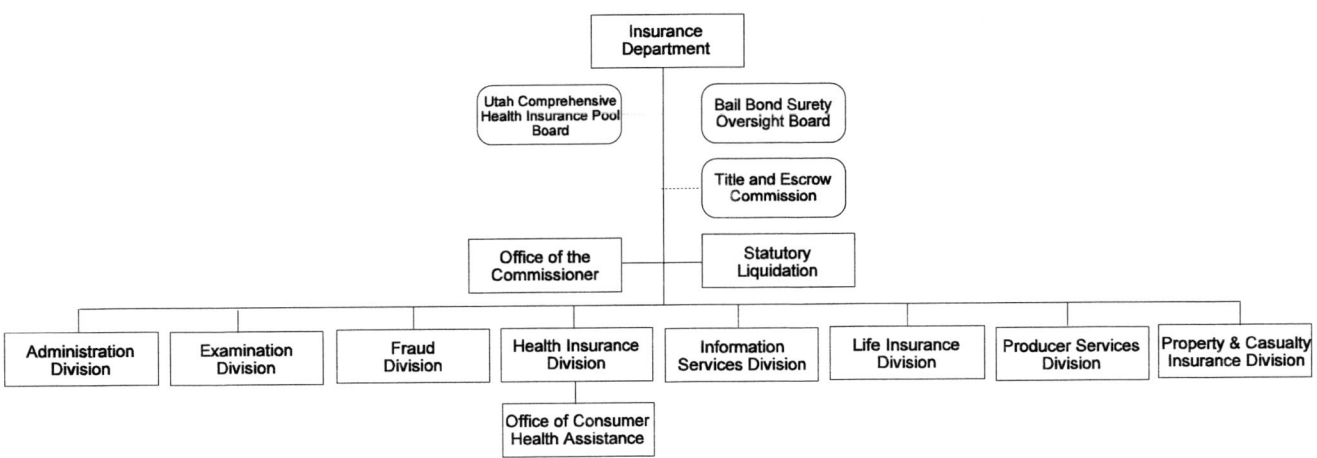

A person must comply with the Insurance Code to engage in an insurance business, act as an insurance producer or consultant, or engage in insurance adjusting in Utah.[98] Insurers are generally granted certificates of authority in order for them to conduct business in the state. In a 2003 report, the Insurance Department reports nearly 1,950 insurers doing business in Utah.[99]

As part of its supervision of insurers operating in the state, the Insurance Department monitors the financial condition of insurance companies incorporated in Utah. The commissioner may petition a court to place an insurer incorporated in Utah into formal rehabilitation or liquidation proceedings if the insurer becomes insolvent. These proceedings are court supervised with the commissioner appointed as the rehabilitator or liquidator.[100] During 2003, the commissioner, as liquidator, administered the liquidation of five insurance companies.[101]

In addition to granting certificates of authority to insurers doing business in the state, a major function of the Insurance Department is to license many participants in the insurance industry. For example, the Insurance Department licenses producers (persons who sell, solicit, or negotiate insurance) in the following lines of authority:

- Life insurance
- Variable contracts
- Accident and health insurance
- Property insurance
- Casualty insurance
- Title insurance
- Workers' compensation insurance
- Personal lines insurance
- Surplus lines[102]

As of August 2004, the state has licensed over forty-six thousand producers.[103] Examples of other license classifications include a customer service representative, consultant, adjuster, third party administrator, managing general agent, reinsurance intermediary, or bail bond surety company.

Premiums or rates charged by insurance companies are also addressed by the Insurance Code. Although rates are typically set on the basis of market forces, with some exceptions, the Insurance Department has a general responsibility to monitor and disapprove rates charged by insurers that are excessive, inadequate, or unfairly discriminatory. Examples of the underlying purposes for this monitoring include protecting policyholders and the public against the adverse effects of excessive, inadequate, or unfairly discriminatory rates; encouraging independent action by and reasonable price competition among insurers so that rates are responsive to competitive market conditions; and providing formal regulatory controls for use if independent action and price competition fail.[104]

Beyond acting as regulator of insurance products, insurers, and other market participants, the Insurance Department plays other roles. For example, the insurance commissioner has duties and powers related to insurance guaranty associations.[105] The Insurance Department provides consumer services such as those provided by the Office of Consumer Health Assistance that, among its several functions, investigates and works to resolve consumer complaints.[106] The Insurance Department, through its Fraud Division, investigates and takes action against insurance fraud violators.[107] The department also participates in a program designed to provide health insurance to those who are uninsurable in the competitive market through a nonprofit entity created in the department called the "Utah Comprehensive Health Insurance Pool." The health insurance pool is under the direction of a twelve-member board of directors[108] and has as its purpose to provide low cost access to health insurance coverage to residents of Utah who are denied adequate health insurance and are considered uninsurable.[109] For further discussion of the health insurance pool, see Chapter 15, *Health*.

LABOR COMMISSION

Government regulation of business includes not only protection of the public interest in business transactions, but also oversight of the relationship between employers and employees. Regulation of the relationship between employers and employees is considered an important role of government because employees spend a major portion of their lives in the workplace and both their socioeconomic stability and demand on government services is tied to their ability to succeed in the workplace.

Right to Work State

Twenty-three states, including Utah, have laws that allow employees to decide for themselves whether or not to join or financially support a union[110] (see shaded states in figure 10-11). These states are typically called "right-to-work" states.

Figure 10-11

States with Right-to-Work Laws
2004

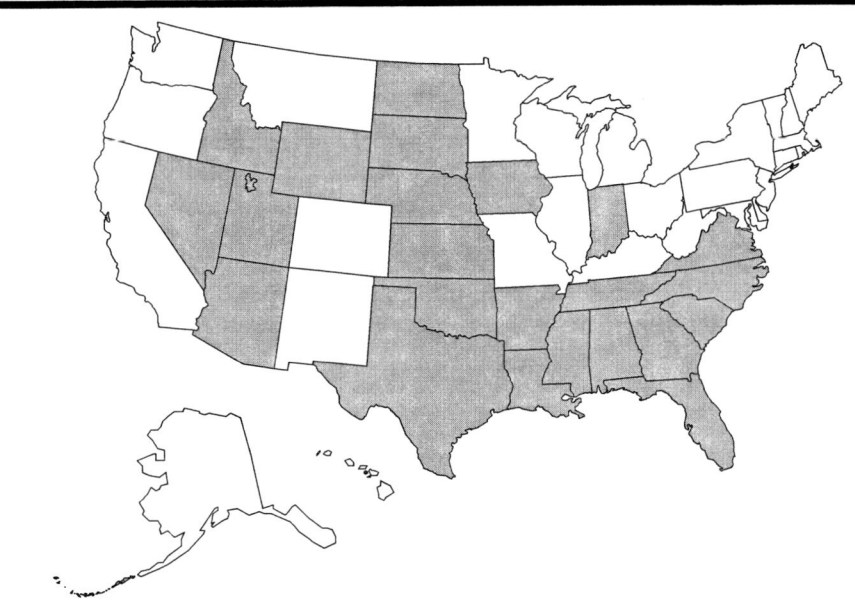

In Utah, unions exist, but employers and unions cannot make "any express or implied agreement, understanding or practice . . . whereby any person not a member of such union, organization or any other type of association shall be denied the right to work for an employer. . . ."[111] Any workplace must be open to all employees, union and non-union alike. Agreements that limit employment in an organization to members of a union are forbidden in Utah law. Utah's prohibition of these types of agreements is an important component in understanding Utah's labor policy.

Role of the Labor Commission

The Labor Commission seeks to provide a safe and fair work environment for Utah employees without unnecessarily interfering with the private interests of employers and employees.[112] The Labor Commission, formerly known as the Industrial Commission, was originally created in 1919 with a three-member, full-time bipartisan body appointed by the governor with the consent of the senate.[113] In 1997 the commission name and structure were changed.[114] Now a single commissioner is chosen by the governor with the consent of the senate. The commissioner serves as the state labor executive and "has all of the policymaking functions, regulatory and enforcement powers, rights, duties, and responsibilities outlined in" Utah's labor laws.[115] Utah's labor laws are administered through five divisions overseen by the commissioner:[116]

- *Adjudication.* The Division of Adjudication adjudicates claims or actions brought under the Utah Labor Code.
- *Administrative Services.* The Division of Administrative Services provides support services to each division in budgeting, accounting, personnel, legal, and information technology services.
- *Antidiscrimination and Labor.* The Division of Antidiscrimination and Labor administers the Utah Antidiscrimination Act, Utah Fair Housing Act, and other sections of the Utah Labor Code when specified by statute.

- *Industrial Accidents.* The Division of Industrial Accidents administers the regulatory requirements of the Utah Labor Code concerning industrial accidents and occupational disease, which requires administering the workers' compensation system in Utah.
- *Safety.* The Division of Safety administers the regulatory requirements of Title 34A, Chapter 7, Safety, and Title 40, Chapter 2, Coal Mines.
- *Utah Occupational Safety and Health.* The Division of Occupational Safety and Health administers the Utah Occupational Safety and Health Act.

Aside from the divisions, other entities within the commission aid the commission in its duties. The Labor Relations Board, comprised of the commissioner and a representative of both employer and employee groups, is a constitutionally created board that administers collective bargaining laws.[117] An Appeals Board reviews decisions or rulings made under some areas of the Utah Labor Code. Advisory boards advise the commission, commission divisions, and the legislature in setting labor policy for the state. Figure 10-12 outlines the structure of the Labor Commission and related entities.

Figure 10-12

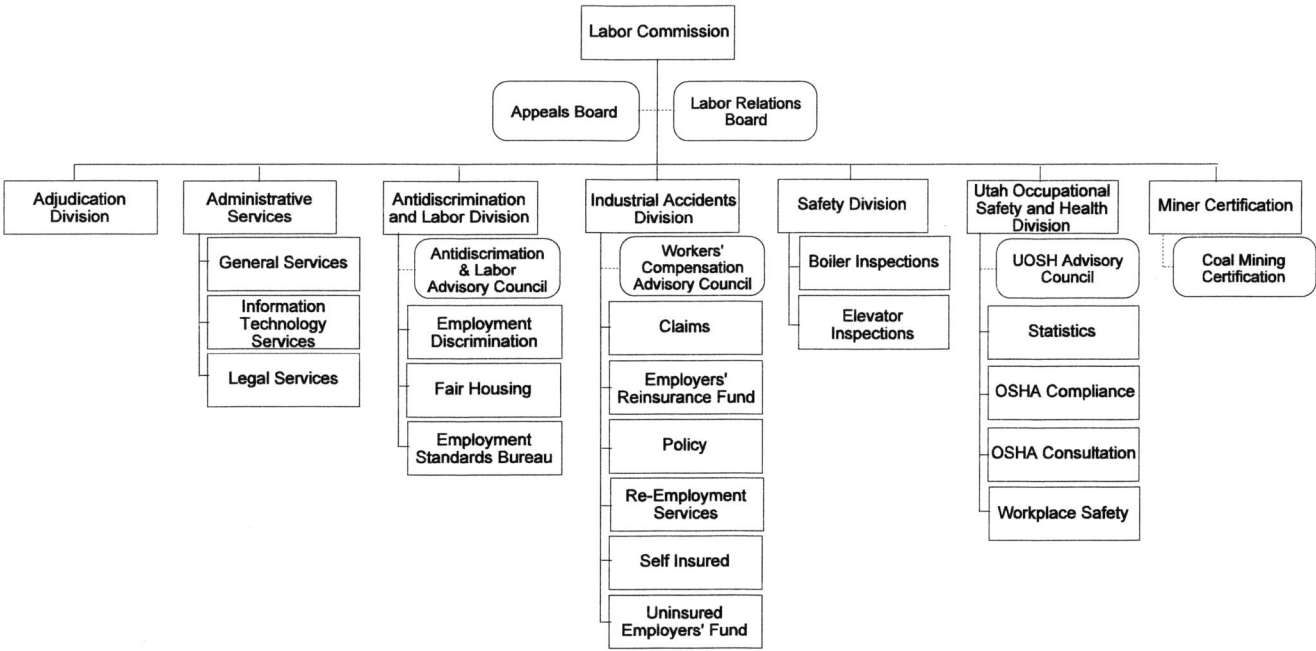

Chapter 11

Community and Economic Development and Workforce Services

INCREASING INTEREST IN ECONOMIC DEVELOPMENT

National Efforts

It has been suggested by well-known economic planners that a succinct two-word description for economic development is "buying jobs."[1] The mission of the National Business Development Program within Utah's Department of Community and Economic Development seems to suggest much more. That mission is to create quality jobs by proactively recruiting new or expanding companies to the state. The National Business Development Program also coordinates state and local economic development resources to recruit companies outside the state that will create jobs in Utah with above average wages and benefits.

> **In this chapter:**
>
> Increasing Interest in Economic Development (p. 191)
> Department of Community and Economic Development (p. 192)
> Department of Community and Economic Development Reorganized (p. 193)
> Role of the Divisions within the Governor's Office of Economic Development (p. 194)
> Role of the Divisions within the Department of Community and Culture (p. 195)
> Other State Community and Economic Development Entities (p. 198)
> Department of Workforce Services (p. 199)

This program has taken the lead in developing marketing strategies and materials for other programs and entities within the Department of Community and Economic Development's Division of Business and Economic Development, assisting them in developing advertising, promotional materials, and brochures. The program's results are measured by the number of companies assisted to relocate or expand in Utah annually and the number of jobs these companies create in the state. As a snapshot in time of the program's success, it assisted forty-six companies that created over eleven thousand jobs to locate in Utah during the years 2000-04.[2] The program was moved to the Governor's Office of Economic Development in 2005 as a result of a major restructuring of the Department of Community and Economic Development.

International Development

There seems to be an assumption embedded in economic development in America that citizens can control their destiny. That is, if an individual or community or state has a vision, and can find the right resources, it can do anything. As the states and their citizenry seek to grow and develop their respective economies, it would appear that they are proceeding on the basis of a presumption that somewhere in the world there is money, natural resources, and markets that if they can find and put together the state and its communities can succeed.

A focal point of this undertaking at the state level in Utah has been the efforts of the International Business Development Office within the Utah Department of Community and Economic Development. Since 1982, the office has assisted Utah companies and communities in identifying and developing receptive markets throughout the world for their products and services. Its mission has been and continues to be the building of Utah's global economy and international presence. Its strategies for accomplishing this mission include:
- Promoting a business-friendly environment in Utah by educating Utahns about the advantages of international business, increasing statewide knowledge of international business opportunities, and preparing Utah companies to do international business
- Promoting the Utah brand by developing an awareness of Utah throughout the world and providing Utah's international visitors with the highest quality Utah experience
- Developing partnerships and alliances by strengthening existing international relationships and establishing new ones beneficial to Utah business
- Increasing international investment capital in Utah by strategically recruiting foreign investors and identifying the advantages of making foreign investments in the state[3]

Many of theses strategies are implemented through diplomatic channels and therefore the office's success becomes somewhat difficult to quantify. However, the office has recently developed performance indicators which base the success of its program on such measures as the number of international business seminars sponsored annually and attendance at the seminars, the number of international trade agreements entered into during the year, and the number of working international partners within the state. The office was moved to the Governor's Office of Economic Development in 2005 as a result of a major restructuring of the Department of Community and Economic Development.

DEPARTMENT OF COMMUNITY AND ECONOMIC DEVELOPMENT
Role of the Department

The legislature created the Department of Community and Economic Development in 1979. This new entity merged the Department of Developmental Services, whose main purpose had been to promote and develop aesthetic and cultural values, tourism, and the attraction of new business to the state, with the Department of Community Affairs, whose primary function had been to assist local governments in resolving problems related to population shifts and making optimal use of federal grants and assistance programs for local governments. Other state activities such as state libraries and Indian affairs were also brought into the new department. The department managed a broad range of community and economic development activities and adopted a threefold mission of promoting job creation, facilitating economic growth, and enhancing the quality of life within the state.

The department's responsibilities consisted of:
- Promoting community and economic development within the state
- Administering and coordinating all state or federal grant programs that are, or become, available for community and economic development
- Performing economic development planning for the state
- Coordinating the program plans of its various divisions

The department consisted of the following seven divisions:
1. Division of Business and Economic Development
2. Division of Housing and Community Development
3. Division of Fine Arts
4. Division of State History

5. Division of Travel Development
6. State Library Division
7. Division of Indian Affairs[4]

DEPARTMENT OF COMMUNITY AND ECONOMIC DEVELOPMENT REORGANIZED

In the 2005 General Session, the Utah Legislature, acting in response to recommendations from newly-elected Governor Huntsman, made major changes to the long-established department described above. It created within the Governor's Office as of July 1, 2005, the Governor's Office of Economic Development and gave it the business development and tourism duties and responsibilities previously held by the Division of Business and Economic Development and the Division of Travel Development within the Department of Community and Economic Development. In addition, the Utah Energy Office, once part of the Department of Natural Resources, was dissolved and its duties assigned to the Governor's Office of Economic Development. Figures 11-1 and 11-2 show the current structure for the administration of community and economic development at the state level resulting from this legislative action.

Figure 11-1

Governor's Office of Economic Development

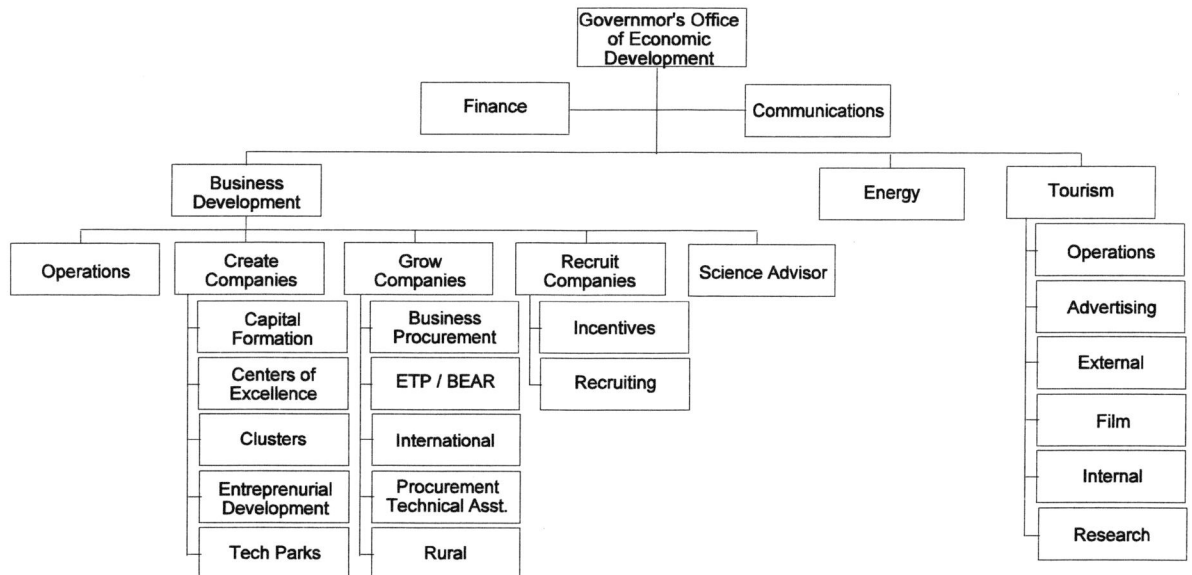

Figure 11-2

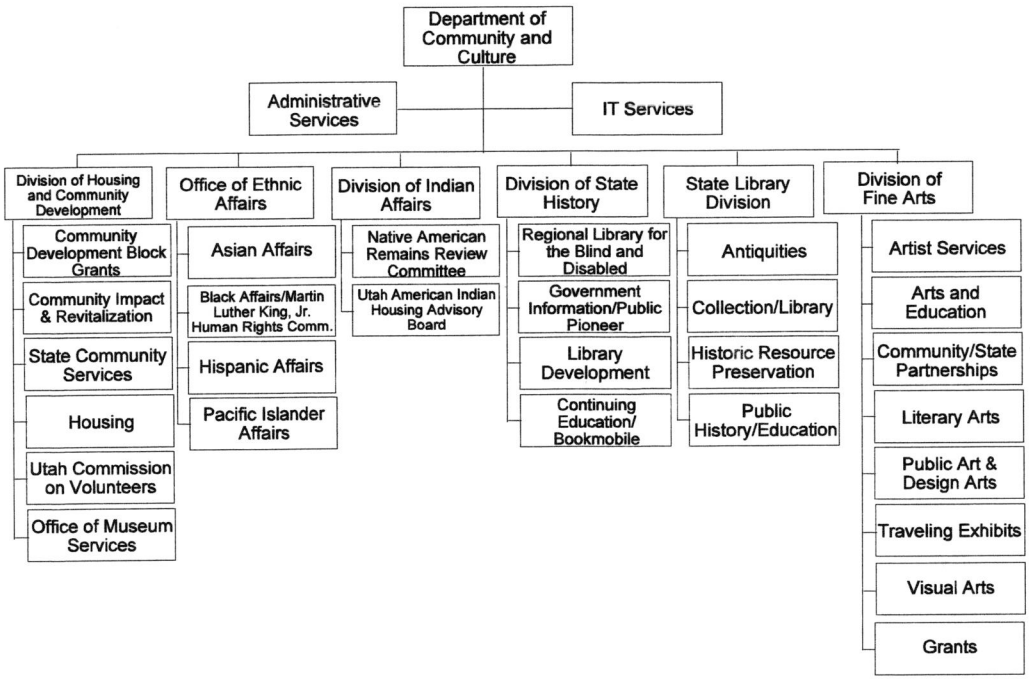

The Governor's Office of Economic Development is directed by statute to be responsible for economic development within the state and to administer and coordinate all state or federal government grant programs which are, or become, available for economic development. The office is under the administration of a director appointed by the governor. The director serves at the pleasure of the governor and is responsible for:
- Administering, directing, controlling, organizing, and managing the office
- Seeking federal grants, loans, or participation in federal programs related to community and economic development[5]

ROLE OF THE DIVISIONS WITHIN THE GOVERNOR'S OFFICE OF ECONOMIC DEVELOPMENT
Division of Business Development

The Division of Business and Economic Development was originally created within the Department of Community and Economic Development to be the industrial promotion authority of the state and to enhance the economic, commercial, financial, agricultural, and civic welfare of Utah. The division is also responsible for creating, developing, attracting, and retaining businesses and industry within the state. The division performs its duties by participating in or sponsoring the development of new technology companies, the retention and expansion of Utah's existing business base, and the recruitment of businesses and direct investment from outside the state.[6]

The division has a fifteen-member board, appointed by the governor. The board establishes broad policies for the division and advises it on matters related to business and economic development within the state. The board also works to obtain favorable rates, fares, charges, and classification for transportation of persons and property by common carriers operating within the state.

The division has a number of programs and offices that have been established to assist it in promoting and developing business and the state's economy. They include business expansion and development, the National Business Development Program, the International Business Development Office, the Utah Film Commission, the State Advisory Council on Science and Technology, Enterprise Zones, Centers of Excellence, the Industrial Assistance Fund, the Community Economic Development Project Fund, the Utah Technology Alliance, the Tourism Marketing Performance Fund, Aerospace and Aviation Development Zones, and the Office of Rural Development.

These programs and offices provide a number of incentives to businesses that are either expanding within or looking to move into the state. As examples, the Utah Enterprise Zone Program, established in 1988, allows certain types of businesses locating to or expanding in a designated geographic zone to claim state tax credits against individual income taxes or corporate franchise and income taxes. The Industrial Assistance Fund, which was created in 1991, encourages the creation of quality jobs in Utah by providing financial assistance to companies for expenses related to the establishment, relocation, or development of industry in Utah. The Centers of Excellence Program provides funding to Utah's public universities to identify marketable technologies and transfer those technologies to Utah companies to generate new high-paying jobs. Other business incentives offered through the division's programs include tax credits, rebates and exemptions, performance grants based on the creation of new jobs, and job-training helps.[7] The division was absorbed into the Governor's Office of Economic Development in 2005 as the Division of Business Development as noted above.

Division of Tourism

Salt Lake City's hosting of the 2002 Winter Olympics brought into focus the importance of tourism to the state's economy. Utah is no longer considered a state of seasonal tourism. This is due in large part to the development and expansion of convention centers along the Wasatch Front that host regional and national conventions and the ever-increasing popularity of winter sports venues in the state touted to have some of the finest deep powder ski slopes in the world. Consequently, Utah has become a year-round Mecca for tourists. It offers those visiting the state a wide range of outdoor activities that have a significant economic impact on transportation, entertainment, food services, lodgings, and retail trade.

The Division of Travel Development as originally created within the Department of Community and Economic Development is the travel development authority of Utah and has been given responsibility for developing a travel promotion program. The division is charged with

- Planning and conducting an information, advertising, and publicity program that markets the tourism attractions of the state
- Developing a plan to increase revenues received from tourism related activities in the state
- Assisting in the coordination of activities and programs with public and private groups that publicize the state's scenic attractions and advantages for tourists

The division has a nine-member advisory board, appointed by the governor with the consent of the senate, to assist it in promoting tourism. The board has authority to solicit and accept contributions from public and private sources to help promote the general interest of the state in tourism.[8] The division was absorbed into the Governor's Office of Economic Development in 2005 as the Tourism Division as noted above.

ROLE OF THE DIVISIONS WITHIN THE DEPARTMENT OF COMMUNITY AND CULTURE

As noted in figure 11-2, the remaining five divisions in the restructured Department of Community and Economic Development are now administered by the newly-named Department of Community and Culture.[9]

Division of Housing and Community Development

The Division of Housing and Community Development was created to assist local governments and citizens of Utah in the planning, development, and maintenance of necessary public infrastructure and services. It is one of the five divisions that remained within the Department of Community and Culture under the 2005 statutory restructuring. More specifically, the division:

- Provides technical assistance to counties, cities, towns, regional planning commissions, community action agencies, and other entities created for the purpose of aiding and encouraging an orderly and productive development of the state and its political subdivisions
- Serves as a clearinghouse for information and data that may be helpful to local governments in discharging their duties and provides information on available federal and state financial and technical assistance
- Assists in funding affordable housing and addressing problems of homelessness
- Supports economic development activities through grants, loans, and direct programs financial assistance
- Assists and supports local governments, community action agencies, and individuals in energy efficiency and anti-poverty activities
- Assists and supports volunteer efforts in Utah[10]

This division is administered by a director appointed by the executive director of the Department of Community and Culture. The division administers a number of programs under its general powers, which include:

- Community development block grants
- Community impact and revitalization
- State community services
- Ethnic affairs
- Housing, to include the Olene Walker Housing Loan Fund
- Home energy assistance targets
- Weatherization
- Museum services
- Utah Commission on Volunteers[11]

Division of Fine Arts

The Division of Fine Arts was originally created by the legislature in 1899 as the Institute of Fine Arts but later became a division of the department. At the present time it is also referred to as the Utah Arts Council, having become a division within the department. Its primary responsibility is to advance the interests of the arts, in all their phases, within Utah. The chief administrative officer of the division is its director who is appointed by the executive director of the department. The director must be experienced in administration and knowledgeable in the arts.

The division has a thirteen-member board, appointed by the governor to four-year terms of office with the consent of the senate. Nine of the board members are to be working artists in the following areas: (1) visual arts, (2) architecture or design, (3) literature, (4) music, (5) sculpture, (6) folklore or folk art, (7) theater, (8) dance, and (9) media arts. The remaining four board members are to be citizens knowledgeable in the arts. The board makes policy for the division and may receive gifts, bequests, and property for the state to enhance and promote the arts. The division also administers a Percent-for-Arts Program and the Utah Arts Endowment Fund, which focus on acquiring works of art used for public buildings and providing moneys to qualifying arts organizations to enable them to create their own arts endowment funds.[12]

Division of State History

The Division of State History is the designated official state authority for state history. It has the following duties and responsibilities:
- To stimulate research, study, and activity in the field of Utah history and related history
- To maintain a specialized history library
- To mark and preserve historical sites, areas, and remains
- To collect, preserve, and administer historical records relating to the history of Utah
- To administer, collect, preserve, document, interpret, develop and exhibit historical artifacts, documentary materials, and other objects relating to the history of Utah for educational and cultural purposes
- To edit and publish historical records
- To cooperate with local, state, and federal agencies and schools and museums in coordinating, collecting, preserving, and exhibiting historical artifacts related to Utah
- To provide grants and technical assistance as necessary and appropriate[13]

The division also has a State Antiquities Section, which is the state authority for the protection and orderly development of archaeological and anthropological resources.

The division is directed by the Board of State History, an eleven-member policy board, whose members are appointed by the governor with the consent of the senate. The board:
- Makes policy to direct the division director in carrying out the director's duties
- Functions as the State Review Board for purposes of the historic preservation program
- Makes recommendations to the director for listings on the State and National Historic Registers
- Functions as the board of the Utah State Historical Society[14]

The division also publishes an historic magazine which is furnished to supporting members of the historical society and others on a subscription basis.

The division director is appointed by the executive director of the department with the concurrence of the Board of State History. The director is required to be qualified by education or training in the field of state history.

State Library Division

The State Library Division functions as the library authority for the state and is responsible for general library services; extension services; the preservation, distribution, and exchange of state publications; legislative reference; and other services considered appropriate for a state library. Its main role is to support libraries throughout Utah so that they can better serve their patrons. The division also provides special library services for state agencies and for individuals in Utah who would not otherwise have access to a public library.

The division has a nine-member State Library Board appointed by the governor. Four of those members are appointed from recommendations made from the State Office of Education, the Board of Control of the State Law Library, the Office of Legislative Research and General Counsel, and the Utah System of Higher Education. Of the five remaining members at least two must be from rural areas of Utah. The division director is appointed by the department's executive director and must have a degree in library science from an institution approved by the American Library Association.

The board and director develop standards for public libraries in Utah and serve as the agency of the state for the administration of any state or federal funds that may be appropriated to further library development within Utah.[15]

Utah Division of Indian Affairs

The Utah Division of Indian Affairs acts as a liaison between state government and Native American tribes in Utah. The purpose of the division is to:
- Develop programs that will allow Indian citizens the opportunity to share in the progress of Utah
- Promote an atmosphere that provides Indian citizens with alternatives so that they may choose for themselves the kind of lives they will live, socially and economically
- Help the tribes and Indian communities find solutions to their community problems
- Promote government-to-government relations between the state and tribal governments

The director of the division must be knowledgeable in the field of Indian affairs, and is appointed by the executive director of the department with the approval of the governor.

The division meets on a regular basis, at least six times each year, with representatives of tribal governments to coordinate the efforts of state and tribal governments in meeting the needs of Native Americans residing in Utah. Tribal representatives to be included in the meetings are selected by their tribal governments as follows:
- An elected official of the Navajo Nation that resides in San Juan County selected by the Navajo Nation government
- An elected official of the Northern Ute tribe selected by the Ute Business Committee
- An elected official of the Paiute Indian tribe selected by the Paiute Indian Tribal Council
- An elected official of the Northwestern Band of Shoshoni Nation that resides in Northern Utah selected by the Northwestern Band of Shoshoni Tribal Council
- An elected official of the Ibapah Band of Goshute Indians that resides in Ibapah selected by the Goshute Indian Tribal Council
- An elected official of the Skull Valley Band of Goshute Indians selected by the Goshute Indian Tribal council
- An elected official of the Ute Mountain Ute Tribe that resides in Utah selected by the Ute Mountain Ute Council
- An elected official of the San Juan Southern Paiute Tribe that resides in Utah selected by the San Juan Southern Paiute tribal government[16]

In addition to the Division of Indian Affairs, the department maintains an Office of Ethic Affairs and separate offices for Asian affairs, Black affairs, Hispanic affairs, and Pacific Island affairs within the Division of Housing and Community Development. These offices act as a liaison between state government and Utah's Asian, Black, and Hispanic communities.

OTHER STATE COMMUNITY AND ECONOMIC DEVELOPMENT ENTITIES

There are also a number of other state entities whose roles and missions are similar to those of the Governor's Office of Economic Development and the Department of Community and Culture. They include the Utah Technology Commission and the Utah Technology Industry Council, the Utah Capital Investment Corporation, the Utah State Fair Corporation, the Heber Valley Historic Railroad Authority, the Utah Science Center Authority, the Homeless Coordinating Committee, and the Utah Housing Corporation.

Utah Technology Commission

The Utah Technology Commission and the Utah Technology Industry Council were created to study the present and future information technology needs of state government; study the technology needs related to the state's economy and quality of life of Utah's citizens; and make recommendations for promoting economic development of the technology industry in Utah. The council was created to recommend policy in these areas to the commission. The commission consists of thirteen members: eight legislators; one representative from the executive branch; one representative from the judicial branch; one representative from public education; one representative from higher education; and the chief information officer on information technology.[17]

Utah Capital Investment Corporation
The Utah Capital Investment Corporation works to enhance, promote, and increase venture capital investment in Utah.[18]

Utah State Fair Corporation
The Utah State Fair Corporation has general management and control over all activities relating to the state fair and is in charge of all state expositions.[19]

Heber Valley Historic Railroad Authority
The Heber Valley Historic Railroad Authority operates and maintains a scenic historic railroad in and around the Heber Valley.[20]

Utah Science Center Authority
The Utah Science Center Authority was established to promote the development of science, high technology, engineering, the arts, tourism, cultural, and educational facilities to further the welfare of citizens of Utah and its economic growth.[21]

Homeless Coordinating Committee
The Homeless Coordinating Committee endeavors to ensure that services provided to the homeless by state agencies, local governments, and private organizations are provided in a cost-effective manner. The committee consists of the state planning coordinator, the state superintendent of public instruction, and the executive directors of the Department of Community and Culture, the Department of Workforce Services, and the Department of Health, or their designees.[22]

Utah Housing Corporation
The Utah Housing Corporation was established to assist in providing housing for low and moderate income persons who could not otherwise have decent, safe, and sanitary housing. The corporation funds its housing programs by issuing tax-exempt state revenue bonds. Because the bonds are tax exempt, it can sell them at relatively low interest rates. Its debts are payable solely from payments received by the corporation from mortgage borrowers and other revenues generated internally by the corporation. The corporation is governed by a nine-member board of trustees: the executive director of the department; the commissioner of the Department of Financial Institutions; the state treasurer or the treasurer's designee; and six public trustees, appointed by the governor, who represent the mortgage lending industry, the home building and real estate industry, and the public at large.[23]

DEPARTMENT OF WORKFORCE SERVICES
Background
Before Utah became one of the nation's leading welfare reform and job training success stories, Utahns seeking assistance were required to make a series of visits to different government facilities spread throughout their community. At each destination they found a separate government agency providing a unique slice of needed services such as food stamps, child care, and job training, with little or no coordination among the agencies.

A 1992 audit of state employment and job training programs by the Office of the Legislative Auditor General described state employment and training programs as "fragmented among 23 separate state and federal programs which are administered by six different state agencies . . . each created by a separate piece of legislation. . . . [The six] agencies in turn are accountable to separate state legislative standing and appropriations committees. Each program also has its own advisory board and regional network of service delivery offices. . . . [These] programs provide similar services to overlapping client populations. . ." and "tend[s] to be driven more by the needs of the institutions than by the needs of its customers."[24]

In response to the audit, and anticipating that welfare reform would soon take the national stage, Utah focused on developing improved welfare, job placement, and job training services. Challenges were identified through a legislative audit and a Governor's Task Force on Workforce Services. A consensus emerged to streamline and consolidate welfare and job training services. By the time federal welfare reform was passed in 1996, the state had passed the first of two pieces of legislation reorganizing Utah's welfare and job training effort. The new approach signaled a shift to a process driven more by the needs of those seeking assistance.

Federal Welfare and Job Training Reform

The Personal Responsibility and Work Opportunity Reconciliation Act of 1996 and the Workforce Investment Act of 1998 overhauled welfare and job training in the United States by:
- Eliminating the Aid to Families with Dependent Children (AFDC) program, an entitlement to public assistance with no requirements to seek employment or improve skills
- Replacing AFDC with the Family Employment Program (FEP), which implements lifetime limits on cash assistance and an individual work plan designed to prepare persons receiving assistance for employment
- Introducing one-stop welfare and employment service centers
- Establishing state and regional workforce services boards to help states and communities organize their welfare and job training assistance to their citizens[25]

FEP establishes a lifetime eligibility limit on cash assistance of sixty months and allows states to select a shorter time limit. FEP's major funding comes from a United States Department of Health and Human Services grant, Temporary Assistance to Needy Families (TANF). Eligibility to receive these benefits depends on a client's efforts to prepare for employment, including the development by the client and the case worker of an employment plan, a sort of written path to finding a job that includes specific job skill development and job seeking activities.[26] The six-year TANF grant ended September 30, 2002, but Congress has since passed year-long extensions of the block grants by resolution.

Role of the Department of Workforce Services

Legislation establishing the Utah Department of Workforce Services was passed in the 1996 and 1997 General Sessions and the department officially began operating July 1, 1997, allowing a year to accomplish the necessary consolidation and transition. The department administers public assistance and job training programs, provides information and organizational support for child care programs throughout the state, administers the Unemployment Compensation Fund, adjudicates appeals of determinations by the fund, and staffs the State Council on Workforce Services.[27]

Employment Development Division

The Employment Development Division (commonly referred to as the Operational Support Division) administers public assistance programs, determines eligibility for those programs within boundaries set by statute, provides child care assistance for children through its Office of Child Care, and works in cooperation with the Utah Housing Corporation, the Division of Housing and Community Development, and local housing authorities to help clients qualify for affordable housing.

Although Utah's thirty-eight "one-stop" employment centers allow clients to receive a full range of public assistance and job training services, being sent to several different people in the same building can still leave the client feeling disconnected and lost in the bureaucratic shuffle. To address the problem, the division assigns a single case worker to each client requesting public assistance. The case worker is a client's single point of contact with the department and the client's connection to the full range of services, including cash assistance, employment counseling, child care, food stamps, and many others. When services beyond the case worker's expertise are needed, it is the case worker who coordinates the delivery of those services with other employees.

The legislature has exercised a federally-provided option and set the lifetime limit for receiving cash assistance at thirty-six months. The average time clients have spent in the program is two years, the same as under the AFDC program. However, the higher client numbers indicate that more individuals are being hired than under the former program.

The Office of Child Care provides information and organizational support to child care programs throughout Utah. Its duties include:
- Providing child care subsidy services for income-eligible children through age twelve and for income-eligible children with disabilities through age eighteen
- Providing information to employers as they determine how to provide child care in the workplace
- Providing information to the public on obtaining quality child care and coordinating services for quality child care training
- Working collaboratively with the State Board of Education, the department, and the Department of Health for the delivery of quality child care and early childhood programs and school age programs throughout Utah
- Researching child care programs and public policy that will improve child care quality and accessibility
- Providing planning and technical assistance for the development and implementation of programs in communities that lack child care, early childhood programs, and school age programs
- Providing organizational support for the formation of nonprofit organizations approved by the Child Care Advisory Committee[28]

Unemployment Insurance Division

The legislature has provided for the compulsory setting aside of unemployment reserves to be used for the benefit of unemployed persons and sets the contribution rates paid. The division receives contributions from employers to the Unemployment Compensation Fund and administers the fund. The division must also ensure that individuals seeking unemployment benefits are legally entitled to the benefits.[29]

Division of Adjudication

If an employer wishes to appeal the Unemployment Insurance Division's decision or determination of Unemployment Compensation Fund contribution liability, the appeal is heard by the Division of Adjudication. An appeal must be initiated within ten days of the employer receiving notice of the determination. At the hearing, both the employer and the division are afforded the opportunity to make arguments in support of their point of view before a salaried, impartial administrative law judge. The judge then makes a determination to either uphold the determination of the division, modify the determination, or reverse it. If the employer appeals the decision of the administrative law judge, The Workforce Appeals Board may hear the case. Appeals beyond the board must be brought before the court of appeals.[30]

Workforce Development and Information Division

The Workforce Development and Information Division provides the state and the United States Department of Labor with Utah's labor statistics, including the unemployment rate, wage data, and job growth statistics. This information is based on data collected from employers each quarter.

The division is also responsible for reporting to the department and to the United States Department of Labor on how the state is doing in meeting the outcomes and requirements of federal workforce law. The division also contracts with the Department of Labor to provide economic data services, including the development of software and analysis of data, for use nationwide.[31]

State Council on Workforce Services

The membership of the State Council on Workforce Services is drawn from the education community, small and large employers, employee organizations, veterans, and the Utah State Office of Rehabilitation. A key statutory responsibility of the council is to annually develop a workforce services plan. The plan must include:
- A projected analysis of the workforce needs of employers and clients statewide
- Policy standards, when required by law or considered necessary by the council, to ensure statewide programs are consistent across regional workforce services areas
- Outcome-based standards for measuring program performance to ensure equitable service
- Oversight of regional compliance with state policies
- Elements of regional workforce services plans that relate to statewide initiatives and programs
- Strategies to ensure program responsiveness, universal access, and unified case management and to eliminate unnecessary barriers to services
- Assistance to employees facing unemployment dislocation and their employers

In addition to developing the workforce services plan, the State Council on Workforce Services:
- Oversees workforce services regions to ensure that their plans are consistent with state policy guidelines and that service delivery follows the regional plan
- Evaluates program performance and client satisfaction and develops plans to improve performance and satisfaction levels
- Uses marketing tools to improve understanding and visibility of workforce services efforts
- Coordinates the planning and delivery of services with public and higher education, vocational rehabilitation, and human services[32]

Regional Councils

Regional councils were established to ensure that the unique workforce needs of each region of the state are addressed. The five geographic regions, together with their planning regions, are:
1. Northern Region and the Bear River and Three County Planning Regions
2. Central Region and Salt Lake and Tooele counties
3. Mountainland Region and Utah, Summit, and Wasatch counties
4. Eastern Region and the Uintah Basin and Four Corners Planning Regions
5. Western Region and two multi-county planning regions

Regional council membership includes individuals representing small and large employers, employee organizations, clients, county governments, public and higher education, veterans, the Utah Office of Rehabilitation, a state economic development board, applied technology, and the Health and Human Services Departments. Regional councils are required to annually develop a regional workforce services plan which must include:
- A projected analysis of the regional workforce needs of employers and clients
- Assurances that state policy standards will be incorporated into the regional workforce services design

- A regional budget outlining administration and client support services expenditures
- The location of employment centers and staff levels to deliver services
- The services to be provided including assessment and support services, job training options, job placement, and employer outreach
- Identification of targeted occupations for which training will be approved
- Regional outcome-based performance standards that ensure equitable client services
- Regional oversight that includes a process to evaluate program effectiveness and develop plans to improve programs
- Internal and external marketing strategies to improve the understanding and visibility of regional workforce services efforts
- Coordination of apprenticeship training
- Strategies to provide assistance to employees facing employment dislocation and their employers

In addition to developing the workforce services plan, regional councils also:
- Determine the locations of employment centers
- Develop training priorities for the region
- Work cooperatively with the State Council to oversee regional operations and ensuring that services are delivered according to the regional plan
- Address concerns within the region related to apprenticeship training coordination[33]

Figure 11-3

Department of Workforce Services

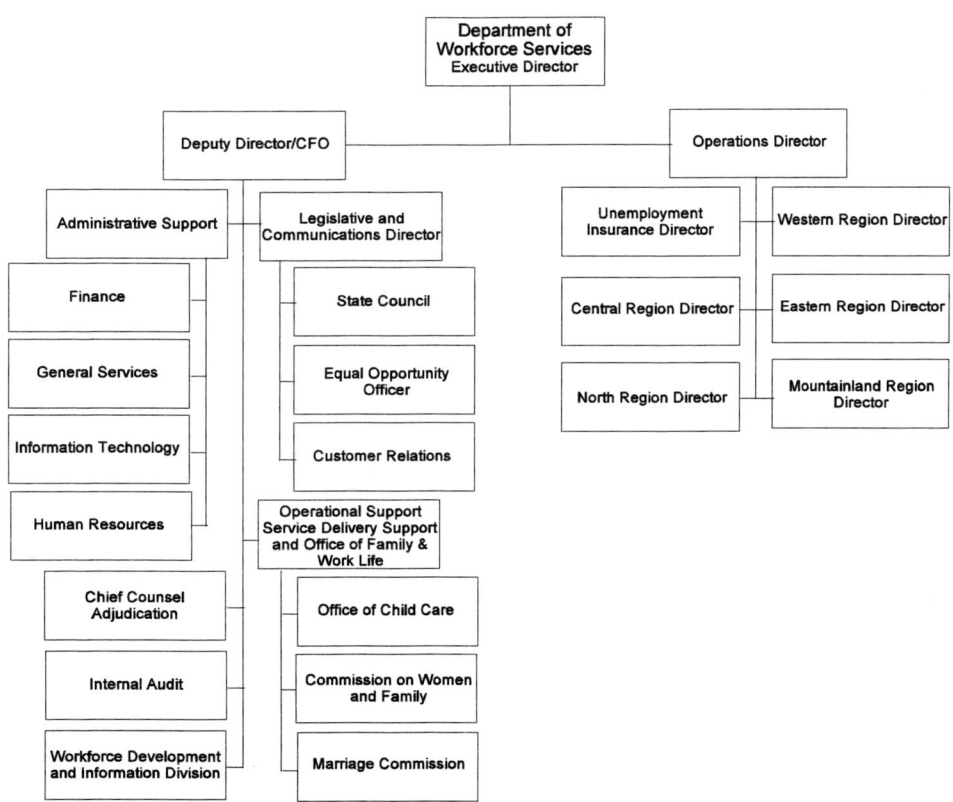

Chapter 12

Public Education

UTAH'S UNIQUE DEMOGRAPHICS

Education is a public undertaking that generates a high degree of attention from citizens and the media and claims the largest portion of tax dollars in the state. Utah faces unique circumstances that challenge the state to establish and maintain a public education system within Utah's available resources. A major factor in Utah's educational challenge has been the state's high birth rate and large number of school-age children. As shown in figure 12-1, although Utah's fertility rate has declined slightly over recent decades, the rate still leads to an unusually high number of school-age children.

> **In this chapter:**
>
> Utah's Unique Demographics (p. 205)
> Governance of Public Education: The Legislature's Role (p. 207)
> Governance of Public Education: State Board of Education (p. 207)
> Public Education System (p. 210)
> Financing Public Education in Utah (p. 212)
> Education Reform (p. 215)
> Student Performance (p. 216)

Figure 12-1[1]

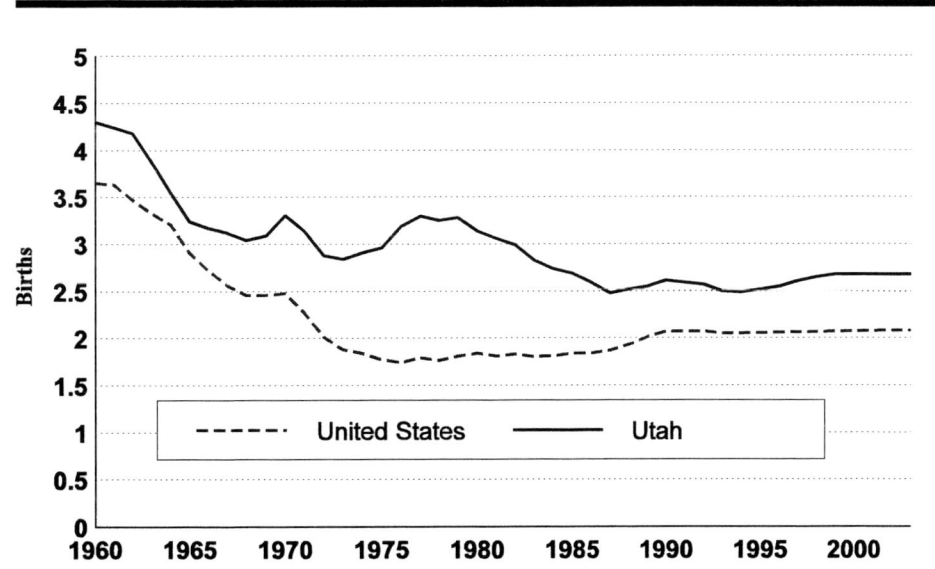

Figure 12-2 shows the population by major age group for Utah compared to the United States. Among the states, Utah has the highest percentage of school age children as a proportion of the total population.[2]

Figure 12-2[3]

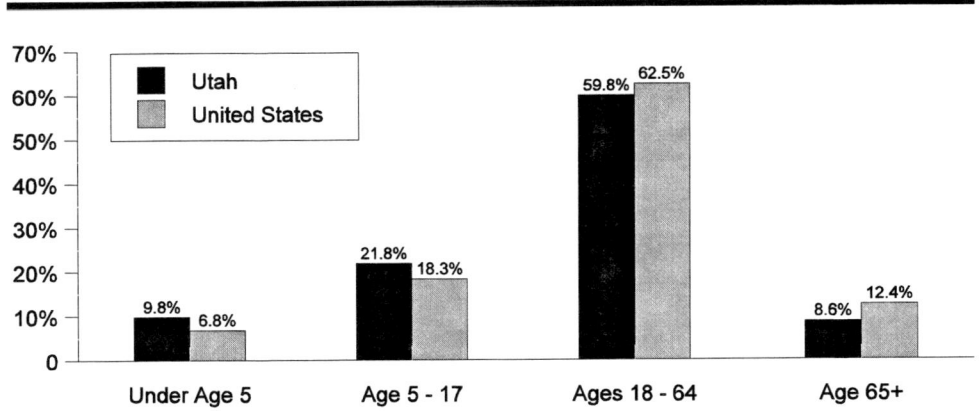

Utah has traditionally made significant effort to support public education and its citizens bear a relatively high tax burden. In 2002, the state ranked fifteenth in state and local taxes paid as a percent of personal income.[4] More recently, the growth in the state's economy in the 1990s was used to provide additional support to public education in Utah. As shown in figure 12-3, Utah's public education spending per pupil increased from $2,959 in 1990 to $5,787 in 2001.

Figure 12-3

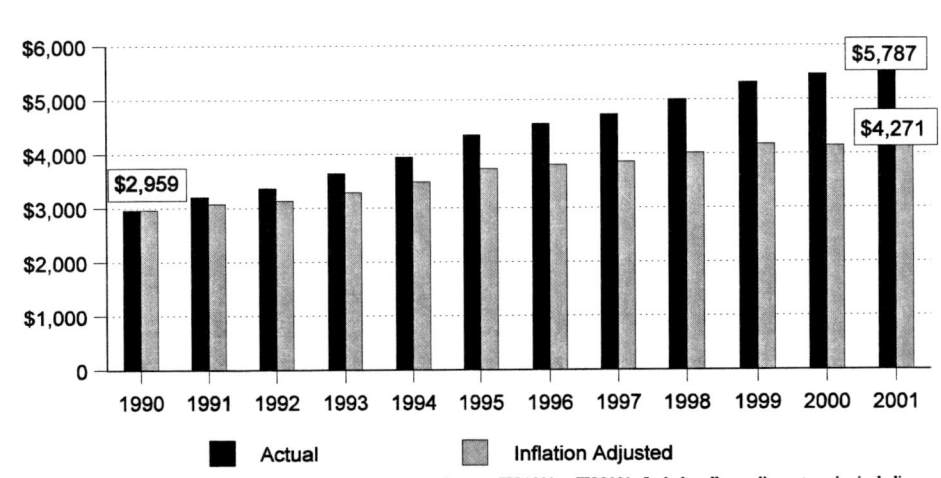

Despite these high tax efforts to support public education, Utah's unique demographics make it difficult to compare favorably with other states. Utah ranks last among the states in elementary and secondary school per pupil expenditures. Utah's per pupil spending in the 2003-2004 school year was less than half the per pupil expenditures of eight states.[5]

The ability of the state to fund the public education system may be even more difficult in the near future. Beginning in 2004, Utah is projected to experience a school-age population boom. By 2020, the school age population is projected to reach 753,950, which is 47 percent greater than it was in 2000.[6] Figure 12-4 shows actual and projected school-age and working-age populations from 1980 to 2030.

Figure 12-4[7]

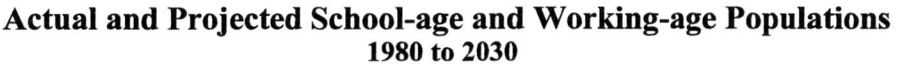

Actual and Projected School-age and Working-age Populations
1980 to 2030

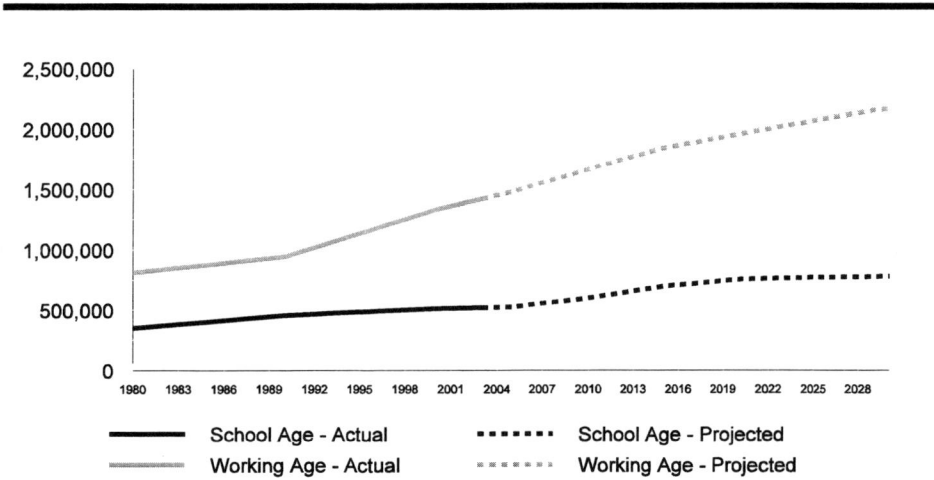

GOVERNANCE OF PUBLIC EDUCATION: THE LEGISLATURE'S ROLE

The Enabling Act requires the state to provide for the establishment and maintenance of a system of public schools open to all children of the state and free from sectarian control.[8] The state responsibility to provide public education is specifically assigned to the legislature in two provisions of the Utah Constitution:
- "The Legislature shall provide for the establishment and maintenance of the state's education systems including a public education system, which shall be open to all children of the state."[9]
- "The public education system shall include all public elementary and secondary schools and such other schools and programs as the Legislature may designate."[10]

The legislature therefore has the responsibility and authority to create laws that provide for the establishment and maintenance of the Utah public education system.

GOVERNANCE OF PUBLIC EDUCATION: STATE BOARD OF EDUCATION
State Board of Education Membership and Election Process

The Utah Constitution establishes a State Board of Education, but allows the membership of the board and its election process to be established by statute. The State Board of Education consists of fifteen nonpartisan members, each elected to a four-year term, to represent one of the fifteen state school board districts that are established by the legislature during the redistricting process that follows each U.S. census.[11]

By November 1 of each year preceding a general election year, the governor appoints a single statewide nominating and recruiting committee consisting of twelve members who represent business, industry, and education interests. The committee is first charged with recruiting candidates to file for membership on the seats of the State Board of Education which are subject to election. The committee is later required to review the candidates who filed for the seats in accordance with the election laws and submit a list of at least three candidates for each state board position to the governor by July 1 of the general election year. The governor then selects two candidates for each district for the State Board of Education from the lists submitted by the state board district nominating and recruiting committee and the names are placed on the nonpartisan section of the ballot.

The four-year terms of the board members are staggered so that either seven or eight of the fifteen seats are open for election every two years in a general election year. In the event of a vacancy on the state board, the position is filled by the governor, with the consent of the senate, for the remainder of the vacated term.

State Board of Education Powers and Duties

The Utah Constitution provides that "general control and supervision of the public education system shall be vested in the State Board of Education."[12] Utah law declares that "general control and supervision" as used in the Utah Constitution means the State Board of Education's control and supervision is directed to the whole system. The board may not govern, manage, or operate school districts, institutions, and programs, unless granted that authority by statute.[13] Accordingly, the State Board of Education does not operate local public schools, which is a responsibility reserved to local school boards in Utah.

The primary functions of the State Board of Education are to direct the whole public education system, establish rules and minimum standards for the public schools, provide leadership and administrative support functions, provide advisory services, administer state and federal accountability testing programs, approve formulas to divide and distribute state education funds to districts and charter schools, and compile education information and make reports on education in Utah. Included among the state board's specific statutory responsibilities where the board establishes rules, sets minimum standards, or administers programs are the following:

- Educator qualifications and certification
- Educator evaluation
- Administrative services
- Access to programs
- Attendance
- Competency levels
- Graduation requirements
- Discipline and control
- School accreditation
- The academic year
- Curriculum and instruction requirements
- School libraries
- Services to the disabled
- State reimbursed bus routes
- Financial, statistical, and student accounting requirements[14]

The board is authorized to adopt rules and policies in accordance with its responsibilities under the constitution and state laws, and may interrupt disbursements of state aid to any district which fails to comply with its rules.[15]

State Superintendent and State Office of Education

The Utah Constitution requires the State Board of Education to "appoint a State Superintendent of Public Instruction who shall be the executive officer of the board."[16] The state superintendent of public instruction advises school district superintendents, school boards, and other school officers upon all matters involving the welfare of the schools.[17] The state superintendent is also responsible to administer all educational programs assigned to the State Board of Education in accordance with the policies and the standards established by the board.

Included among the state superintendent's duties outlined in statute are the following:
- Investigating matters pertaining to public schools
- Holding conferences and meetings on educational topics
- Presenting a report of the public school system
- With the approval of the board, preparing and submitting to the governor a budget to be included in the budget that the governor submits to the legislature[18]

The state superintendent's annual report contains the most comprehensive information available about Utah's public school system, including summaries of education programs and detailed education statistical and financial data. The superintendent's annual report is available online, along with other education information, at www.usoe.k12.us/schoolinfo.htm.

State law also authorizes the State Board of Education to "appoint other employees as necessary for the proper administration and supervision of the public school system."[19] While the State Office of Education is not created or described in statute, its employees assist the State Board of Education and the state superintendent of public instruction in fulfilling their statutory responsibilities. Within the state office, associate superintendents supervise various programs. Figure 12-5 illustrates the management responsibilities of the three associate superintendents and also shows the principal programs that are administered by the State Office of Education.

Figure 12-5

Utah State Office of Education

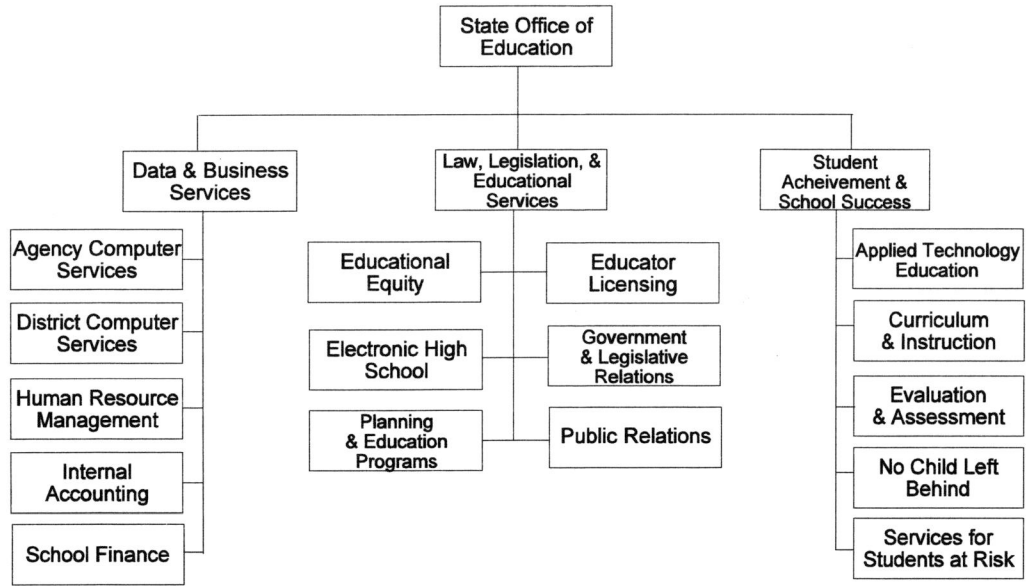

PUBLIC EDUCATION SYSTEM

School Districts

Utah's public education system includes forty school districts, each governed by an elected local school board and a superintendent. The system also includes charter schools. Table 12-1 shows Utah's public school enrollment for its forty school districts and charter schools for the 2003-04 school year.

Table 12-1

Public School Enrollment
October 2003-04

District	Enrollment	District	Enrollment
Alpine	51,118	Nebo	23,900
Beaver	1,472	North Sanpete	2,370
Box Elder	10,529	North Summit	969
Cache	13,315	Ogden	12,963
Carbon	3,622	Park City	4,059
Daggett	132	Piute	307
Davis	60,025	Provo	13,103
Duchesne	3,900	Rich	454
Emery	2,434	Salt Lake	23,966
Garfield	969	San Juan	2,979
Grand	1,474	Sevier	4,316
Granite	69,072	South Sanpete	2,772
Iron	7,443	South Summit	1,312
Jordan	74,761	Tintic	250
Juab	1,939	Tooele	10,508
Kane	1,200	Uintah	5,607
Logan	5,872	Wasatch	4,022
Millard	3,083	Washington	20,317
Morgan	1,955	Wayne	518
Murray	6,482	Weber	28,196
		Charter Schools	3,253
		Total	**486,938**

Source: Utah State Office of Education

210 • *Public Education*

Local School Boards

The board of education of a school district with a student population of less than twenty-four thousand students consists of five members, while the board of a school district with a student population of twenty-four thousand or more students consists of seven members. Each local school board member is elected to a four-year term to represent a geographic area within the school district.

The powers and duties of local school boards are to:
- Establish, locate, and maintain elementary, secondary, and applied technology schools
- Make and enforce rules necessary for the control and management of the district schools
- Spend minimum school program funds for programs and activities for which the State Board of Education has established minimum standards or rules
- Purchase, sell, and make improvements on school sites, buildings, and equipment and construct, erect, and furnish school buildings
- Do all other things necessary for the maintenance, prosperity, and success of the schools and the promotion of education within the district[20]

District Officers

Each local school board is required to "appoint a district superintendent of schools who serves as the board's chief executive officer."[21] The superintendent shall hold an administrative/supervisory license or a letter of authorization from the State Board of Education to serve as superintendent.

Each board shall appoint a business administrator who, subject to the direction of the district superintendent of schools, shall keep an accurate record of board meetings and be the legal custodian of all district records. The business administrator is also responsible for district funds, including keeping accurate records of all revenues received and their sources, using uniform budgeting, accounting, and auditing procedures, and preparing a detailed annual financial statement for the district.[22]

A local school board may also "appoint other necessary officers who serve at the pleasure of the board."[23] This statute gives school districts the authority to hire other administrators and education specialists who assist the superintendent and local school board in administering local school board policy.

Charter Schools

Beginning in 1998, charter schools have been authorized by the legislature as a school choice option within the public education system.[24] A charter school is created with the approval of its governing charter by a local school board or the State Board of Education. A charter school may be a new school or the conversion of an existing public school to charter status. Charter schools provide an opportunity to use diverse instructional approaches within unique academic environments.

In recent years, there has been a growing number of charter schools in operation. During the 2004-05 school year, twenty-two charter schools are scheduled to be in operation, with a combined student enrollment of over thirty-two hundred students.[25] School districts are also granting more charters, with five schools having received charters from their local school boards to be in operation by the fall of 2005.

During the 2004 General Session, the legislature created a new State Charter School Board, which authorizes the establishment of charter schools at the state level, subject to final approval of the State Board of Education. The charter board also has the responsibility to promote charter schools in the state and to assist and provide technical support to charter schools. The charter board is required to annually study charter school statutes and board rules and submit a report with its recommendations to the legislature.

A charter school is a public school. A charter school is required to operate in accordance with its charter and other statutes applicable to public schools, except as specifically exempted in statute.[26] The State Board of Education's rules also apply to charter schools, but a charter school may request a waiver of any rule that inhibits the charter school from accomplishing its charter mission. Specifically, charter schools may not charge tuition, may only charge fees like other public schools, are subject to health and safety laws, and are subject to state and federal accountability testing programs, such as U-PASS and No Child Left Behind. A charter school that violates its charter or other laws may have its charter terminated by its authorizing board.

Utah Schools for the Deaf and the Blind

Individuals from birth through age twenty-one who are hearing impaired, visually impaired, or dual sensory impaired may receive educational services from the Utah Schools for the Deaf and the Blind. The schools' main campus is in Ogden, which includes dormitory facilities for students enrolled in a residential program. Students from the residential program and students bussed to the schools from nearby counties receive specialized instruction in self-contained classrooms. Hearing and visually impaired students in other parts of the state receive instruction through the Utah Schools for the Deaf and Blind in self-contained classrooms located in public schools.

In addition to the self-contained classrooms for students ages three through twenty-one, the schools provide (1) parent-infant programs to develop young children's communication skills; (2) consultant teachers to assist hearing and visually impaired students mainstreamed in regular classrooms; and (3) through the Education Resource Center, media for sensory impaired children and young adults, such as captioned films and books in braille and large print.

The Utah Schools for the Deaf and the Blind are governed by the State Board of Education. An institutional council for the Schools for the Deaf and the Blind advises the State Board of Education on the needs of, and educational programs for, the hearing and visually impaired.[27]

FINANCING PUBLIC EDUCATION IN UTAH

Fundamental elements of Utah's school funding scheme are set forth in Utah's Enabling Act and the Utah Constitution. Guiding principles and the specific mechanics of public school funding are spelled out in the Utah Code.

Enabling Act and Utah Constitution

The Enabling Act contains a means for funding the public school system. Upon admission, four sections of each township, comprising nearly one-ninth of Utah's landmass, were granted to the state for the support of public schools. The proceeds of those lands, known as school trust lands, constitute a permanent fund, only the interest of which may be expended for the support of public schools. In addition to the land grant, 5 percent of the net proceeds from the sale of federal lands within Utah are to be distributed to the state for deposit in a permanent fund for public schools.[28]

In accordance with the Enabling Act, the Utah Constitution directs the legislature to provide for the establishment and maintenance of a public education system, consisting of elementary and secondary schools, that is open to all children of Utah and free of sectarian control. The Utah Constitution also dictates that public elementary and secondary schools shall be free, except the legislature may authorize the imposition of fees in secondary schools.[29]

Certain revenues are dedicated, and accounts created, by the Utah Constitution for the funding of the public school system. A permanent trust fund known as the State School Fund is established.[30] The contents of the State School Fund include (1) revenue from the sale and use of school trust lands, (2) revenues from nonrenewable resources on other state lands, and (3) 5 percent of the net proceeds from the sale of federal lands within the state. The principle of the fund is to be invested by the state and held in perpetuity. Only the interest and dividends earned on fund monies may be expended for the support of public schools.

Another fund created by the Utah Constitution is the Uniform School Fund into which interest and dividends from the State School Fund are deposited along with other monies designated for public schools such as income tax revenue.[31]

The major revenue source dedicated, in part, to the public education system by the Utah Constitution is income tax revenue. Income tax proceeds are earmarked for both the public and higher education systems; however, all but a small fraction of income tax revenue is used to fund public elementary and secondary schools.[32]

Guiding Principles

The logic of the complicated system of formulas for appropriating and distributing monies for public schools can best be understood by reviewing a set of guiding principles stated in the Utah Code. Those principles are:

- All children of Utah are entitled to reasonably equal educational opportunities regardless of their place of residence in the state and of the economic situation of their respective school districts
- Although the establishment of an educational system is primarily a state function, school districts should be required to participate on a partnership basis in the payment of a reasonable portion of the costs of a minimum program
- Each locality should be empowered to provide education facilities and opportunities beyond the minimum program[33]

State, School District, and Federal Participation in School Funding

Under Utah law, the responsibility for paying the costs of public education is shared by the state and school districts. The federal government's intervention in education has increased over the past few decades, so school districts now rely on federal funds for a significant part of their budget. As shown in figure 12-6, of the total revenues received by school districts and charter schools for the 2003-04 school year, the state provided 55.4 percent, district tax levies, tuition, fees, and investments provided 34.7 percent, and the federal government provided 8.7 percent.

Figure 12-6

Sources of School District and Charter School Revenue
2003-2004 School Year

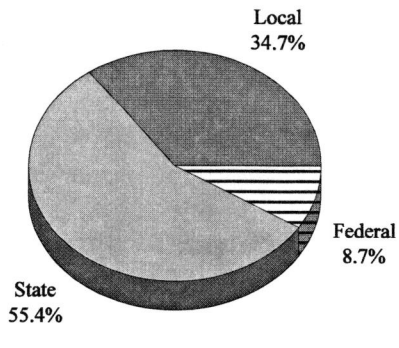

Source: Utah State Office of Education

The large contribution of the state serves to mitigate the varying capabilities of the forty school districts in raising tax revenue for schools. Each school district is required to impose a property tax within the district known as the basic levy. Proceeds of the basic levy are used to pay for the cost of the basic program in the district. The basic program consists of a certain amount of money per student, which is established each year in statute, and additional monies for professional staff, administrative costs, and rural schools. If the proceeds of the basic levy imposed by a school district are not sufficient to pay the costs of the district's basic program, the state pays the balance. Alternatively, if the basic levy generates more money than the cost of the district's basic program, the excess revenue is deposited into the Uniform School Fund. In the past, a few districts were able to raise more than was needed to pay for the basic program and had to transfer the excess to the Uniform School Fund. However, after the basic levy was decreased in 1995, no district has independently fully funded its basic school program.

School districts may raise additional monies for the operation and maintenance of schools by imposing other property tax levies as specified in statute. If a school district elects to impose taxes to expand school funding beyond the basic program, the state will guarantee that certain district levies will generate a minimum amount per student. District levies that are guaranteed by the state to generate a minimum amount per student are (1) a voter-approved leeway of up to 0.0016 per dollar of taxable value; (2) a local school board-approved leeway of up to .0004 per dollar of taxable value; and (3) a local school board-approved leeway for the school district's K-3 Reading Improvement Program of up to .000121 per dollar of taxable value.[34]

The sources of state revenue used for the public education system include (1) income taxes, (2) interest and dividends earned on the State School Fund, (3) a $2.50 fee per vehicle registration designated for driver education, (4) liquor taxes, (5) unclaimed property, and (6) forfeitures.[35]

Nearly all state funds distributed to school districts are designated for the operation and maintenance of schools. The state provides money for capital facilities to school districts that generate relatively low amounts of tax revenue per pupil. In fiscal year 2004-05, $27 million was appropriated under the capital facilities program.[36]

Schools districts are empowered to authorize property tax levies to generate monies for the construction or renovation of schools. Or, if voters within a school district approve a bond, the district may impose a property tax levy for debt service.

Federal dollars received by school districts are designated for particular student populations or federal programs. Significant federal dollars are directed towards (1) education of disabled, disadvantaged, and non-English speaking students; (2) adult and vocational education; and (3) school meals.

The percent of total school district revenue that is derived from local sources, including district tax levies for operations and maintenance and capital facilities, tuition, fees, and investments, by district is shown in Table 12-2.

Table 12-2

Percentage of Total School District Revenue from Local Sources
2003-2004 School Year

District	Percent	District	Percent
Alpine	30.4%	Nebo	28.2%
Beaver	39.2%	North Sanpete	23.4%
Box Elder	28.1%	North Summit	77.0%
Cache	24.6%	Ogden	28.5%
Carbon	40.6%	Park City	86.2%
Daggett	59.4%	Piute	15.5%

District	Percent	District	Percent
Davis	30.6%	Provo	32.7%
Duchesne	23.0%	Rich	38.2%
Emery	45.8%	Salt Lake	47.3%
Garfield	33.7%	San Juan	20.4%
Grand	42.1%	Sevier	24.3%
Granite	32.3%	South Sanpete	19.8%
Iron	38.2%	South Summit	12.1%
Jordan	39.8%	Tintic	11.6%
Juab	33.1%	Tooele	31.7%
Kane	38.4%	Uintah	31.7%
Logan	33.0%	Wasatch	49.4%
Millard	49.5%	Washington	39.6%
Morgan	38.6%	Wayne	21.7%
Murray	43.6%	Weber	28.5%

Source: Utah State Office of Education

EDUCATIONAL REFORM

Rising costs of education and the need for a more highly skilled workforce have spurred efforts nationwide to improve the performance of the public education system. Utah, also, has instituted educational reform measures. Another motivation for reform in Utah is the challenge of having to accommodate a huge increase in student enrollment expected between 2004 and 2020.

Utah Performance Assessment System for Students (U-PASS)

U-PASS, established by legislation enacted in 2000, is designed to determine the effectiveness of school districts and schools in assisting students to master fundamental skills. It incorporates (1) assessments of skills; (2) reporting of results to parents, teachers, and the State Board of Education; and (3) the identification of schools not achieving state-established acceptable levels of student performance in order to assist those schools in raising performance levels.

Assessments administered under U-PASS include (1) norm-referenced achievement tests of all students in grades 3, 5, 8, and 11; (2) criterion-referenced achievement testing of students in all grade levels in language arts, mathematics, and science; (3) writing assessments of students in grades 6 and 9; and (4) a tenth grade basic skills competency test.

No Child Left Behind

The federal No Child Left Behind Act of 2001 imposed an assessment and accountability system on school districts receiving federal education monies. Fortunately, the assessments under U-PASS were sufficiently comprehensive that Utah was able to use its criterion-referenced tests to comply with the assessment requirements of No Child Left Behind.

Although the federal and state assessment programs are complementary, the federal and state methods of evaluating school performance differ. Under No Child Left Behind, schools are evaluated based on the percentage of students in the school who score at or above the proficient level on language arts and mathematics tests. Schools are also held accountable under No Child Left

Behind for the performance of various student subgroups, including ethnic minorities, English language learners, students with disabilities, and disadvantaged students. The U-PASS Accountability Plan, which was implemented beginning in the 2004-05 school year, not only examines the proficiency of a school's student body, but also the progress that individual students make from year to year. The state is seeking sufficient flexibility from the U.S. Department of Education to allow it use the U-PASS Accountability Plan to comply with No Child Left Behind accountability requirements.

Competency-based Education

In 2003 and 2004, the legislature enacted legislation placing an emphasis on competency-based education. This is an educational approach requiring students to master competencies and including a classroom structure and operation that facilitates the acquisition of specified competencies on an individual basis wherein students are allowed to master and demonstrate competencies as fast as they are able.[37] The State Board of Education will be conducting pilot programs implementing competency-based education. The board is also proposing to modify high school graduation requirements to assure that students are able to demonstrate competency in a subject before receiving a passing grade.

STUDENT PERFORMANCE

On tests administered to students nationwide, the average score of Utah students is generally equal to or slightly above the national average. As shown in figure 12-7, Utah students in all grades tested performed above average on the 2004 Iowa Test of Basic Skills.[38]

Figure 12-7

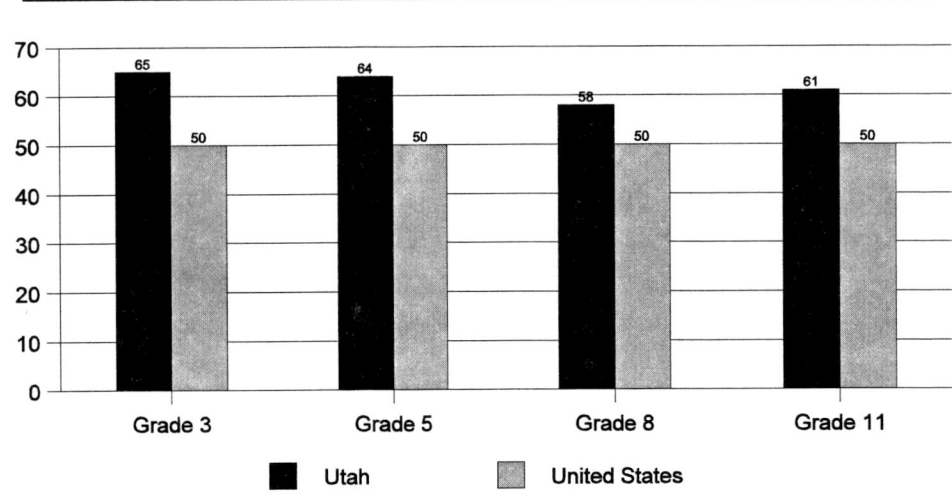

Similarly, on the 2003 NAEP (National Assessment of Educational Progress), which is administered to a sample of students nationwide, the average Utah scores for reading and mathematics were slightly above the average scores nationwide (see table 12-3).[39]

An area where Utah students appear to need improvement is writing. As shown in table 12-3, Utah students in grades 4 and 8 scored below their peers on the 2002 NAEP writing test.[40] To improve students' writing skills, the State Board of Education is modifying curriculum to include writing practice in all subjects.

Table 12-3

NAEP Average Scale Scores		
	Utah	U.S.
Grade 4		
Reading (2003)	219	216
Math (2003)	235	234
Writing (2002)	145	153
Grade 8		
Reading (2003)	264	261
Math (2003)	281	276
Writing (2002)	143	152

At the high school level, Utah students perform as well or slightly better than their peers nationwide as evidenced by scores on the ACT (American College Test)[41] and AP (Advanced Placement) Exam (see tables 12-4 and 12-5).[42]

Table 12-4

ACT 2004		
	Utah	U.S.
Composite Score	21.5	20.9

Table 12-5

AP Exam 2003-2004		
	Utah	U.S.
Percent Passing	68.1	61.4

Whereas Utah students as a whole generally perform at or above the national average, there is considerable variation in student performance among ethnic and income subgroups. Table 12-6 shows student performance on CRTs (criterion-referenced tests), which are administered in all grades statewide to assess mastery of the skills and objectives in Utah's core curriculum. Ethnic minority and low income students, except for Asian students, score significantly below students who are classified as white and not low income.

Table 12-6

Student Proficiency on CRTs
Utah, 2004

	Language Arts Percent Passing	Mathematics Percent Passing
American Indian	50.0%	44.6%
Asian	78.0%	75.6%
Black	58.6%	49.4%
Hispanic	49.9%	47.6%
Pacific Islander	60.3%	55.6%
White	81.0%	74.8%
Low Income	62.9%	59.1%
Not Low Income	83.5%	77.0%

Chapter 13

Higher Education

When pioneer settlers entered Utah in 1847, they began almost immediately to work towards establishing a system of higher education. Only three years later, community leaders incorporated the University of Deseret and began the tradition of Utah higher education that continues today. While Utahns' enthusiasm for education has not wavered, much of the structure of Utah's higher education system has substantially changed. This chapter describes the current system of higher education in Utah. It presents a general overview of the Utah System of Higher Education, including a description of its organizational structure, how it is financed, and the outcomes it has produced. Finally, this chapter considers various issues and challenges that face the Utah System of Higher Education today.

> **In this chapter:**
>
> Organizational Overview (p. 219)
> Financing Higher Education (p. 224)
> Outcomes (p. 225)
> Current Issues (p. 225)

ORGANIZATIONAL OVERVIEW

The Utah Constitution stipulates that "the higher education system shall include all public universities and colleges and such other institutions and programs as the legislature may designate."[1] The constitution further states that "the general control and supervision of the higher education system shall be provided for by statute."[2] Today, statutes regarding higher education comprise all of Title 53B of the Utah Code. These statutes describe the organizational structure of the Utah System of Higher Education and include detailed descriptions of the system's institutions, leadership positions, and the duties and responsibilities pertaining to each leadership position.

An organizational chart of the Utah System of Higher Education is depicted in figure 13-1.

Figure 13-1

Utah System of Higher Education

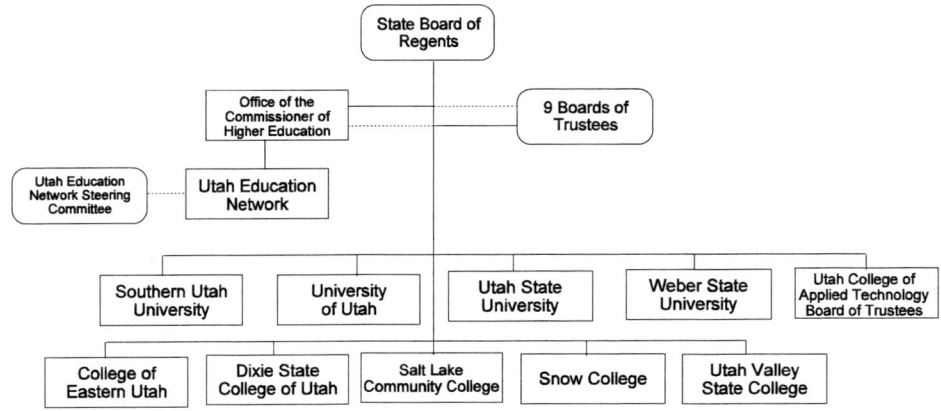

Board of Regents

Utah law vests general control and supervision of higher education with the State Board of Regents. The board is responsible to provide quality higher education for the Utah public, develop and oversee the state's entire system of higher education, and coordinate individual institutions within the system.[3]

The State Board of Regents consists of sixteen voting and two non-voting members. Fifteen of the voting members are appointed by the governor with the consent of the senate. The sixteenth voting member is selected by the governor from a group of individuals nominated by the student body presidents of institutions within the Utah System of Higher Education. The two non-voting board members are appointed by the chair of the State Board of Education.

Commissioner of Higher Education

The State Board of Regents appoints a Commissioner of Higher Education who serves as its chief executive officer. The commissioner serves at the board's pleasure and is responsible for:

- Executing the board's policies and programs
- Compiling and evaluating information regarding the Utah System of Higher Education
- Providing policy recommendations to the board
- Recommending professional and administrative staff for appointment
- Providing state-level leadership in activities affecting higher education institutions[4]

Institutions

The Utah System of Higher Education comprises ten institutions of higher learning, including two research/teaching universities, two metropolitan/regional universities, two state colleges, three community colleges, and a college of applied technology.

Table 13-1

Institutions of Higher Learning by Type

Research/Teaching Universities	University of Utah
	Utah State University
Metropolitan/Regional Universities	Weber State University
	Southern Utah University
State Colleges	Utah Valley State College
	Dixie State College
Community Colleges	Salt Lake Community College
	Snow College
	College of Eastern Utah
Technical College	Utah College of Applied Technology

Research/Teaching Universities

The University of Utah, located in Salt Lake City, is a major urban university. In addition to housing significant programs of sponsored research, the university offers graduate, professional, and undergraduate education in fifteen colleges and professional schools, including top-tier schools of law and medicine. With over 29,500 enrolled students, 2,500 faculty members, and 8,500 staff, the university is the largest institution within the Utah System of Higher Education.[5]

Utah State University, located in Logan, serves as Utah's land-grant institution under state and federal legislation and is a major center for research as well as professional, graduate, and undergraduate education. The seven colleges at Utah State University include over 200 undergraduate majors and 130 graduate degrees. In total, the university enrolls more than 22,500 students and employs over 850 faculty and 1,850 staff.[6]

Metropolitan/Regional Universities

Weber State University, located in Ogden, is the largest regional university in the state system of higher education. With over 18,500 students, 550 faculty, and 800 staff, Weber State University provides instruction in over 200 certificate and degree programs as well as four graduate programs.

Southern Utah University, located in Cedar City, is the only university located in the southern half of Utah. While the majority of the over 5,500 students enrolled at the university are candidates for bachelors degrees, the university also offers certificates, associates degrees, and masters degrees to its students. Students at Southern Utah University are instructed by over 250 faculty members and supported by over 400 staff.

State Colleges

Utah Valley State College, located in Orem, serves over 23,500 students. With more than 800 full-time faculty and 700 staff, the college offers a wide range of education options including certificates, associate degrees, and select bachelor degree programs.

Dixie State College, located in St. George, offers its 7,000 students a choice of four bachelor and six associate degrees as well as certificates in thirty areas of study. Dixie State College employs 200 faculty members and 160 staff.

Community Colleges

Community colleges will soon be the single largest sector in post-secondary education in the United States. Nationwide, enrollment at community colleges has increased by over 325 percent during the last three decades, compared to only 103 percent growth for public four-year colleges. Community colleges have rapidly gained popularity due to an increasing number of high school graduates, escalating college tuition, and stricter admission requirements at many four-year institutions.[7]

Currently, there are three community colleges within the Utah System of Higher Education. Like their counterparts nationwide, Utah's community colleges have experienced significant growth in recent years.

Salt Lake Community College, with its eight campuses located throughout the Salt Lake Valley, offers a choice of 112 programs to over 23,500 students. With more than 850 faculty and 600 staff, Salt Lake Community College is the largest community college within the Utah System of Higher Education.

Snow College, located in Ephraim, offers students a choice of over forty degrees from its five college divisions. Snow College enrolls more than 3,500 students and employs approximately 180 faculty and 170 staff.

The College of Eastern Utah, with its main campus in Price, provides quality education to approximately 2,500 students. With over 400 courses in sixty areas of study, the college offers a wide variety of educational options to its students. Currently, the College of Eastern Utah employs over 80 full-time faculty and more than 100 full-time staff.[8]

Technical Colleges

In 2001, the legislature created the Utah College of Applied Technology (UCAT) by reorganizing nine existing stand-alone applied technology centers as campuses with UCAT. Today, UCAT is considered the tenth institution of higher education within the state system.

The mission of UCAT is to provide Utahns with a short-term practical alternative to traditional forms of higher education and allow them to gain the skills and knowledge to meet the needs of local business and industry. In addition to offering a wide variety of skill certifications, UCAT offers three associate of applied technology degrees that prepare students to enter the workforce or transfer to other Utah institutions of higher learning.

In recent years, enrollment at UCAT has grown remarkably. In 2003, over 28,600 adults and 13,400 secondary students enrolled in programs at UCAT's nine campuses statewide.

Each campus location within UCAT offers post-secondary and extra-secondary applied technology education at market cost to adult students. Students who are still in secondary school may attend class on UCAT campuses, but are not required to pay tuition.[9]

Institutional Leadership
Boards of Trustees for Colleges and Universities

Each college or university is governed by its own board of trustees. In addition to performing the duties and responsibilities delegated to it by the State Board of Regents, the board of trustees is responsible for:

- Facilitating communication between the institution and the community it serves
- Planning and executing fund raising operations
- Selecting recipients for honorary degrees
- Strengthening and maintaining community and alumni support

The board of trustees for an institution other than UCAT consists of ten board members. Eight members are appointed by the governor with the consent of the senate, while two *ex officio* positions are reserved for the president of the institution's alumni association and president of the institution's student association.[10]

College and University Presidents

In addition to having a board of trustees, each institution within the Utah System of Higher Education is led by a president. The State Board of Regents appoints a president to lead each institution after consulting with the institution's board of trustees. The State Board of Regents also determines the length of service and the salary for each institutional president.[11]

Utah law broadly empowers institutional presidents to ensure the efficient administration and operation of their institutions and to take necessary steps to follow the state's master plan for higher education. Institutional presidents are responsible for:
- Appointing administrative officers, deans, faculty members, and support personnel, prescribing their duties, and determining their salaries
- Providing for the constitution, government, and organization of faculty and administration at their institutions
- Overseeing faculty in instruction, examination, admission, and classification of students

The State Board of Regents establishes guidelines for interaction between institutional boards and presidents. These guidelines enumerate certain matters for which institution presidents must consult with the board of trustees before acting.[12]

Utah College of Applied Technology Administration

Board of Trustees. The UCAT board is responsible for prioritizing the budget and building requests of the nine campuses and submitting those prioritized requests to the governor, legislature, and State Building Board. The board also approves the courses and requirements for associate of applied technology degrees. The membership of the UCAT board includes two members of the State Board of Education, two members of the State Board of Regents, and eleven representatives of business and industry.

President. The president of the Utah College of Applied Technology is appointed by the State Board of Regents and serves at the board's discretion. In addition to directing the entire applied technology network of campuses, the UCAT president is responsible for:
- Coordinating activities of the UCAT college campuses
- Developing appropriate associate degrees in applied technology and ensuring their transferability to other institutions
- Establishing minimum standards for UCAT applied technology programs
- Ensuring that secondary students in the public school system have access to UCAT campuses and programs
- Developing and implementing strategies to inform citizens about the availability, cost, and advantages of applied technology education[13]

Campus Board of Directors. Each campus within the Utah College of Applied Technology has a board of directors that is responsible for:
- Preparing and submitting budget requests to the UCAT Board of Trustees
- Conferring with business and industry to determine what skills the market demands, and developing appropriate educational programs
- Establishing human resource and compensation policies
- Developing policies and procedures for admission, instruction and examination[14]

Campus boards of directors have between eleven and fifteen members with representatives from a wide variety of interests including local businesses and education.

Campus Presidents. The president of the Utah College of Applied Technology appoints a campus president for each of the nine UCAT campuses. Each campus president serves at the

discretion of the UCAT president, the UCAT Board of Trustees, and the corresponding campus board of directors. Campus presidents are expected to fulfill the following duties:
- Serve as executive officer for the campus board of directors
- Administer human resource and compensation programs for campus employees
- Execute campus operations under the direction of the board of directors[15]

FINANCING HIGHER EDUCATION
Revenue Sources

The Utah System of Higher Education receives money from a wide variety of sources, including revenue from state appropriations, sales of products and services, research contracts and grants, tuition and fees, and alumni and community donations. Figure 13-2 shows the sources of revenue for the Utah System of Higher Education.

Sales of products and services are the largest source of revenue for the Utah System of Higher Education. The University of Utah Hospital generates the majority of those monies. Other revenue from product sales and services include payments for campus housing and food services.

State appropriations are the second largest revenue source at 21.7 percent, followed by grants and contracts at 18.8 percent. Tuition and fees provide 11.1 percent of total revenues. Remaining revenues include deposits to internal service funds, donations, interest income, and other various sources of money.

State funds for higher education have traditionally come from Utah's General Fund; however, as allowed by a 1996 constitutional amendment, a portion of state funding for higher education now comes from state income tax revenues.[16]

Figure 13-2

Utah System of Higher Education Revenue Sources
Fiscal Years 2002 to 2003

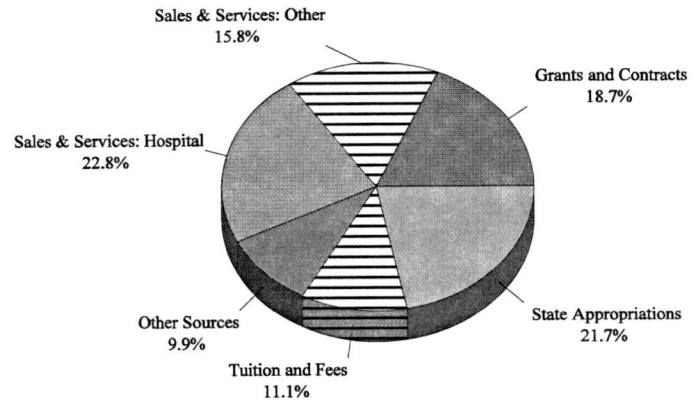

Source: Compiled from data in *Databook 2004-2005*, Utah System of Higher Education

Funding Process

Each year the State Board of Regents sends a recommendation to the legislature for a combined appropriation for the operating budget of all institutions in the Utah System of Higher Education. The board establishes its recommendation for appropriations after carefully considering the proposed operating budgets of each institution within the Utah System. Additionally, the board presents the legislature with an annual recommendation for tuition levels for resident and non-resident students.[17]

After considering the board's recommendations, the legislature appropriates funds for use by institutions of higher education. Each institution is then responsible to use its portion of the appropriated funds for its purchasing, payroll, and other financial affairs under the general supervision of the board.[18]

OUTCOMES

Higher education has produced important benefits for individuals and for the state as a whole. For example, 31 percent of Utahns between ages twenty-five and sixty-five have earned a bachelor's degree; economists estimate that this has increased total personal income in Utah by 9 percent. Other benefits associated with higher education in Utah include above-average voter turnout in elections and high levels of charitable giving.[19] More importantly, the Utah System of Higher Education improves the quality of life for citizens. As a result, Utah has fewer children in poverty and a more educated population than most other states.[20]

In addition to the aforementioned benefits, the Utah System of Higher Education provides many economic benefits to the state. For example, higher education is one of largest employers in Utah with over 26,700 employees statewide.[21]

CURRENT ISSUES

Along with its numerous accomplishments and successes, the Utah System of Higher Education currently faces some unique challenges. These challenges include keeping higher education affordable and encouraging efficiency within the higher education system.

Affordability

Student enrollment in the Utah System of Higher Education has increased dramatically since 1990 (see figure 13-3). As enrollments have increased, institutions within the Utah System of Higher Education have relied more and more on student tuition payments as a source of funding. This increased dependence on tuition funding has resulted in higher tuition costs for students. From 1999-2000 to 2003-04, resident undergraduate tuition in constant dollars has increased from a low of 15 percent at Dixie State College to a high of 47 percent at Utah Valley State College.[22]

Figure 13-3

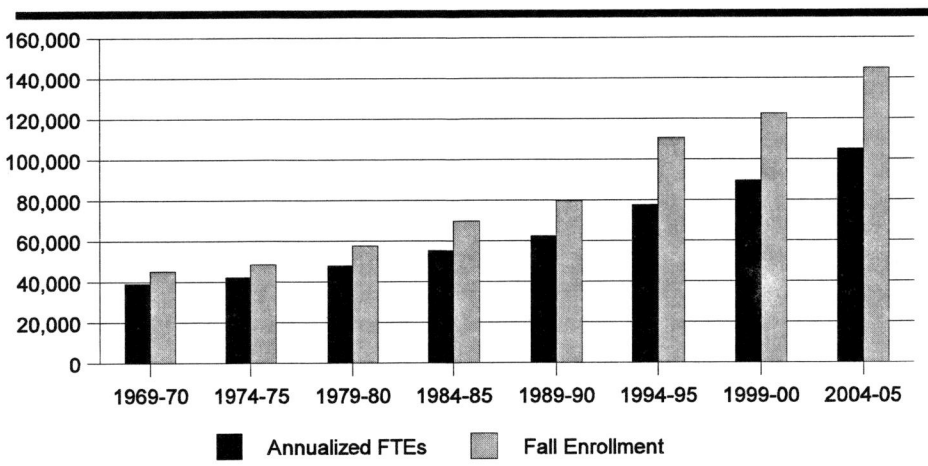

Source: Office of the Commissioner of Higher Education
Note: Annualized FTEs means total hours generated over three semesters (summer, fall, spring) divided by thirty.

As demand for state tax funds for public education, roads, and healthcare continues to increase, there is likely to be continued pressure for tuition increases to fund higher education in the future. Tuition increases, however, are not inevitable. In 2001 the legislature passed a "truth in tuition" bill that requires an institution president to take various steps prior to raising tuition. These steps include holding a public hearing with students and providing students with information on why the tuition increase is needed and how additional revenue will be spent.[23] Thus, students now have a voice in the tuition-hike process.

Despite recent tuition increases, higher education remains relatively affordable in Utah. The average Utah family must spend 17.6 percent of its income to pay for a family member's education at a four-year state college or university. This figure is the lowest of any state and is much lower than the national average of 28.5 percent.[24]

Efficiency

In Utah and throughout the nation, educators and policymakers are under increasing pressure to improve the efficiency of higher education systems. One important measure of efficiency in higher education is the graduation rate of students that enroll as freshmen. Traditionally, the vast majority of students graduated from the same institution in which they initially enrolled. Today, however, an increasing number of students are attending more than one institution during their higher education experience. For example, a nationwide study recently found that 43 percent of students that enroll in a two-year institution transfer at least once during the course of their higher-education experience.[25]

There are many types of inter-institutional transfers. The most common type of transfer involves students who earn credit at a two-year institution and then transfer to a four-year institution with the goal of attaining a bachelor degree. Both students and state education systems benefit from this type of transfer because it allows students to pay less in tuition and allows state systems to enjoy a lower per-pupil cost for education. Lower education costs can increase the availability of higher education to low-income and minority groups and produce a myriad of long-term benefits to society.

Despite the obvious advantages associated with inter-institutional transfers, many state higher education systems are structured in a manner that discourages students from transferring. During the recent past, Utah has taken significant steps to eliminate barriers to inter-institutional transfers and improve the system's efficiency. One such step occurred in 1998 when all Utah institutions implemented a semester system. The universal semester system has facilitated transfers of students' credit hours within the system. Similarly, in 2004 the legislature enacted legislation which directed the Utah System of Higher Education to facilitate transfers by creating common course numbers for General Education and pre-major courses.[26]

In response to this legislative mandate, faculty and academic advisors from each college and university in the Utah System of Higher Education have identified sets of courses similar in content, standards, and rigor, and assigned them a common course number. The quantity of commonly numbered courses within the Utah System increased from thirty-five to over four hundred, and more common numbering of courses is expected in the future. Proponents of the legislation expect that common numbering of courses will eliminate much confusion for transfer students and reduce the amount of remedial work required of them.

While it is difficult to know how beneficial the recent changes in Utah will be, it is clear that Utah is committed to increasing the efficiency and effectiveness of its system of higher education.

Chapter 14

Environmental Quality

HISTORY

From the 1930s to today, state government agencies have been in place to address state environmental issues. Beginning in the 1930s, the Bureau of Environmental Health, a bureau within the Department of Social Services provided environmental oversight. In the 1970s, the legislature replaced the Bureau of Environmental Health with an environmental division comprised of six bureaus. In July of 1991, the legislature created the Department of Environmental Quality (DEQ). DEQ employs over four hundred scientists, engineers, and administrative staff.

> **In this chapter:**
>
> History (p. 229)
> Department of Environmental Quality (p. 229)
> Divisions within the Department of Environmental Quality (p. 231)

DEPARTMENT OF ENVIRONMENT QUALITY

DEQ is administered by an executive director who is appointed by the governor with the consent of the senate.[1] The executive director appoints a division director for each division.[2] Five policymaking boards are created within DEQ.[3] The executive director serves as a member of each board with all remaining members appointed by the governor with the consent of the senate. DEQ policymaking boards include the Air Quality Board (11 members), the Radiation Control Board (13 members), the Drinking Water Board (11 members), the Solid and Hazardous Waste Board (13 members), and the Water Quality Board (11 members).

Figure 14-1

Department of Environmental Quality

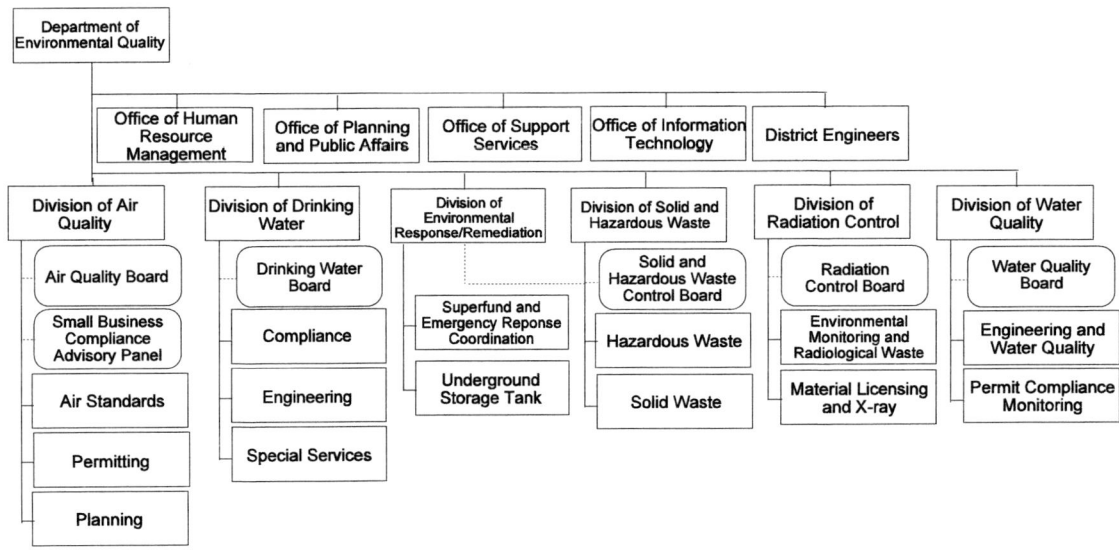

Purpose of the Department

The purpose of DEQ is to provide "coordinated management of state environmental concerns" and to "safeguard public health and quality of life by protecting and improving environmental quality."[4] In accomplishing these purposes, DEQ must consider the benefits to public health and the environment in light of the impacts on economic development, property, wildlife, tourism, business, agriculture, forests, and other interests as well as the costs to the general public.[5]

Powers of the Department

Utah law gives the Department of Environmental Quality various powers and responsibilities and stipulates that DEQ must consult with the Utah Department of Health to assess environmental health risks and to coordinate efficient use of state resources in protecting the public from these risks.[6] Additionally, DEQ has statutory authority to engage in a variety of activities related to environmental quality, including the following:
- Prepare and publish information regarding issues of environmental quality
- Establish and operate programs for protection of public health and the environment from environmental hazards
- Prescribe by rule reasonable environmental quality requirements for local health departments[7]

Executive Director

DEQ is led by an executive director. The legislature establishes the executive director's level of compensation.[8] The executive director's mandatory duties include:
- Administration and supervision of department
- Coordination of policies and programs of department boards, offices and divisions
- Approval of proposed budgets and applications for federal assistance

In addition to the statutory duties listed above, the executive director has the statutory authority to:
- Issue orders to enforce state laws and regulations established by the department
- Establish advisory committees to carry out department purposes

- Make decisions on appointment, removal, and compensation of division directors
- Employ sufficient employees to ensure adequate execution of department purposes[9]

DIVISIONS WITHIN THE DEPARTMENT OF ENVIRONMENTAL QUALITY
Establishment of Divisions

The Utah Environmental Quality Code establishes six divisions within DEQ. Each of the following divisions is charged with administering a specific portion of DEQ's environmental quality responsibilities:[10]

1. Division of Air Quality
2. Division of Drinking Water
3. Division of Environmental Response and Remediation
4. Division of Radiation Control
5. Division of Solid and Hazardous Waste
6. Division of Water Quality

Division of Air Quality

The mission of the Division of Air Quality is to "safeguard human health and quality of life by protecting and enhancing the environment."[11] The division functions under the authority of the Federal Clean Air Act and the Utah Air Conservation Act.[12] The division is divided into three branches, each branch possessing expertise and authority to fulfill specific duties and responsibilities related to air quality.

1. *Permitting Branch.* This branch is responsible for issuing construction permits as well as ongoing operating permits. This branch also houses the Small Business Assistance Program, which is designed to educate small businesses about air pollution and permitting issues.
2. *Planning Branch.* This branch is responsible for identifying, tracking, and analyzing air pollution sources and identifying methods for reduction of air pollution.
3. *Air Standards Branch.* This branch ensures that industries comply with all Utah Air Quality requirements. To help accomplish this task, this branch operates a network of air quality monitors throughout Utah that measure the actual level of pollution in the ambient air. Additionally, this branch monitors mitigation activities associated with lead-base paint and asbestos.[13]

All of the branches of the Division of Air Quality receive input and advice from the Air Quality Board, a group of eleven individuals who represent government, industry, environmental groups, and other interested groups. The Air Quality Board is a non-partisan board that has statutory authority to make rules regarding "control, abatement, and prevention of air pollution from all sources."[14] The board is the also responsible to establish and maintain air quality standards and ensure that Utah entities comply with state and federal air quality regulations.

Division of Drinking Water

The Division of Drinking Water was formed to further the conservation, development, treatment, and protection of Utah's water sources and enforce rules related to public drinking water systems. In addition to administering Utah's public drinking water systems, the division encourages Utah citizens to develop a water conservation ethic to ensure water supplies in the future.[15]

The Division of Drinking Water receives statutory authority from the Utah Safe Drinking Water Act as well as the Federal Safe Drinking Water Act.[16] These acts establish rules for water development, distribution, storage, and treatment. Additionally, Utah law sets up an infrastructure improvement loan program which assists communities in improving water system quality.

The Division of Drinking Water receives input from the state Drinking Water Board and the DEQ executive director.[17] The division divides its responsibilities among three sections.

1. *Compliance Section.* This section encourages water system certification and enforces compliance. Administers over 250 annual sanitary surveys and provides emergency response for drinking-water related problems throughout Utah.
2. *Engineering Section.* This section distributes annually over $10 million in financial assistance to water systems. Oversees water infrastructure construction and inspects water treatment plants.
3. *Special Services Section.* This section encourages source and watershed protection. Coordinates water boards and associations and provides technical assistance to water treatment plants.

Ninety-nine and six-tenths percent of Utah's citizens drink water from a source approved by the Division of Drinking Water.[18] Each year, this division reviews 300 to 400 water plans and conducts over 250 surveys.[19]

Division of Environmental Response and Remediation

The Division of Environmental Response and Remediation is responsible for protecting public health and Utah's environment through environmental response and cleanup of chemically contaminated sites. Other division responsibilities include ensuring that underground storage tanks are used properly and providing chemical usage and emission data to the public and local response agencies.[20]

The Division of Environmental Response and Remediation receives authorization and funding from various federal sources, including the Comprehensive Environmental Response Compensation and Liability Act, the Emergency Planning and Community Right to Know Act, and the Resource Conservation and Recovery Act. The division applies the federal funding and authority it receives to carry out its responsibilities through two regulatory branches – each branch taking responsibility for specific parts of the division's mission.[21] The first branch, known as the Utah Underground Storage Tank Program, seeks to protect human health and the environment from leaking underground storage tanks. The program only regulates underground tanks that contain petroleum products or other hazardous chemicals. In cases that involve such tanks, program staff oversees tank installation, inspection, and removal to ensure compliance with state and federal release-prevention regulations.[22]

The second branch is known as the Utah Superfund and Emergency Response Coordination Program. This branch focuses on real properties that have been contaminated by improper use, storage, or disposal of hazardous wastes. Utah's Superfund program functions in cooperation with the federal Comprehensive Environmental Response, Compensation, and Liability Act of 1980 (CERCLA), also known as the Superfund program. In partnership with the federal Superfund Program, Utah's Superfund program continues to discover and clean up contaminated properties throughout Utah.

In addition to the two regulatory branches, the division provides a program to encourage cleanup and redevelopment of contaminated sites. This program is known as the Brownfield/Voluntary Cleanup Program. The program provides a streamlined, regulatory-friendly environment that promotes voluntary decontamination of problem sites by private firms.

Unlike many of the other divisions within the DEQ, the Division of Environmental Response and Remediation does not have an exclusive policy or advisory board. The Division of Environmental Response and Remediation shares the Solid and Hazardous Waste Control Board with the Division of Solid and Hazardous Waste.

Division of Solid and Hazardous Waste

The Utah Division of Solid and Hazardous Waste (DSHW) exists to protect public health and the environment by ensuring proper management of solid and hazardous wastes within Utah.[23] The

DSHW operates a wide variety of waste-management programs to deal with all levels of waste. These programs range from the regulation of commercial and military hazardous waste to the promotion of oil and tire recycling. The division receives statutory authority from both state and federal laws including, the Federal Resource Conservation and Recovery Act, the Utah Solid and Hazardous Waste Act, the Utah Used Oil Management Act, and the Waste Tire Recycling Act.[24] The DSHW divides its responsibilities into two branches. The first division branch is called the Hazardous Waste Branch; this branch, in turn, is divided into four sections.

1. *Hazardous Waste Management Section.* This section regulates hazardous waste generators in Utah.
2. *Hazardous Waste Facilities Section.* This section regulates Utah's hazardous waste storage and treatment sites.
3. *Chemical Demilitarization Section.* This section ensures safe and proper functioning of Utah's storage and disposal sites for military-generated hazardous waste.
4. *Commercial / Federal Facilities Section.* This section regulates Utah's commercial and federal hazardous waste disposal facilities.

The second branch is the Special Programs Branch which deals with less toxic materials and contains two sections.

1. *Solid Waste Section.* This section administers permitting and compliance programs for non-hazardous solid waste treatment, storage, and disposal facilities statewide.[25]
2. *Planning / Used Oil Section.* This section oversees programs related to recycling and safe disposal of used oil in Utah.

Division of Radiation Control

The mission of the Utah Division of Radiation Control (DRC) is to protect Utah citizens from health hazards posed by various sources of radiation. The DRC receives authority from the Federal Atomic Energy Act and the State Radiation Act. The DRC receives input from the Radiation Control Board.[26] This board guides the development of radiation-control policies and regulations throughout the state. The DRC is divided into eight programs.

1. *X-Ray Program.* Because the use of radiation for medical purposes accounts for the most common type of radiation exposure for average citizens, this program exists to mitigate risks. While it is generally accepted that the benefits of medical radiation exceed the risks, medical radiation can produce significant health risks. The X-Ray Program regulates Utah's more than 2000 medical radiation facilities, educates medical professionals about the risks of radiation, and periodically inspect x-ray machines to ensure that patients do not receive excessive exposure to radiation.[27]
2. *Indoor Radon Program.* The purpose of the division's Indoor Radon Program is to reduce indoor radon concentrations and maintain them below dangerous levels as required by the U.S. Environmental Protection Agency. Much of the radon program is funded by an Environmental Protection Agency grant. The Indoor Radon Program focuses its efforts in five principle areas:
   - Encouraging radon-resistant construction
   - Overseeing real estate disclosure and testing
   - Maintaining local government coalitions
   - Testing public schools
   - Increasing the public's radon awareness[28]
3. *Uranium Mills Program.* Uranium ore has been milled in Utah for decades, and as a result of the milling process, large quantities of pulverized ore have been left behind. This ore, known as "tailings," contains low concentrations of heavy metals and other contaminants that are hazardous to human health. Traditionally, the federal government has assumed

responsibility for regulation of uranium tailings in Utah. However, the DRC has received federal approval to take over regulatory authority for Utah's uranium mills and tailings.[29]

4. *Transportation Program.* In Utah, the transportation of radioactive materials is regulated by three agencies. First, the U.S. Nuclear Regulatory Commission oversees the design, construction, use, and maintenance of shipping containers for hazardous radioactive materials. Second, the U.S. Department of Transportation regulates the conditions of transport for shippers of radioactive material. Third, the Utah Division of Radiation Control inspects waste shipments at Utah's low-level radioactive waste disposal facility.[30]

5. *Low Level Waste Program.* This program ensures safe handling and disposal of low level radioactive waste in Utah. The program regulates Utah's low-level radioactive waste disposal facility.[31]

6. *Radioactive Materials Program.* Through an agreement with the U.S. Nuclear Regulatory Commission, the radioactive materials program licenses and inspects users of certain types of radioactive materials within Utah. There are currently approximately 240 licensees statewide, each of which is subject to periodic unannounced inspections by DRC staff.[32]

7. *Non-Ionizing Radiation Program.* Non-ionizing radiation is every-day radiation that occurs naturally and is produced by many household appliances. Types of natural non-ionizing radiation include ultraviolet and visible light. Other types of non-ionizing radiation are produced by products common in the home or workplace, including power lines, tanning beds, microwave ovens, and cellular phones. While most people only experience low levels of exposure to non-ionizing radiation, high levels of exposure can be harmful to humans. The non-ionizing radiation program of the DRC is responsible for adopting rules to control sources of non-ionizing radiation that constitute a significant health hazards to the Utah public.[33]

8. *Generator Site Access Program.* The Generator Site Access Permit program authorizes waste generators, collectors, and processors to deliver radioactive wastes into Utah for storage and disposal.[34]

Division of Water Quality

The mission of the Utah Division of Water Quality (DWQ) is to "[p]rotect, maintain and enhance the quality of Utah's surface and underground waters for appropriate beneficial uses and to protect the public health through eliminating and preventing water related health hazards which can occur as a result of improper disposal of human, animal, or industrial wastes while giving reasonable consideration to the economic impact."[35] Operational authority for DWQ comes from the Utah Water Quality Act, the Federal Safe Drinking Water Act, and the Federal Clean Water Act.[36] The DWQ receives input from the Utah Water Quality Board.[37] The DWQ's responsibilities are allocated between two branches.

1. *Engineering and Water Quality Branch.* This branch manages water quality through watershed planning, construction assistance, and design evaluation of water-related infrastructure.

2. *Permitting, Compliance, and Monitoring Branch.* This branch protects groundwater through enforcement of permitting regulations. Conducts chemical and biological sampling of groundwater sites to monitor compliance and ensure water quality.

Chapter 15

Health

UTAH'S HEALTH STATUS

Utah is a healthy state! Compared to their fellow Americans, Utahns born today can expect to live longer[1] and suffer much less from many diseases.[2] At least two organizations use a variety of factors to annually rank the overall health status of each state.

> **In this chapter:**
>
> Utah's Health Status (p. 235)
> Access to Health Care (p. 236)
> Public Health (p. 239)
> Department of Health (p. 240)
> Local Health Departments (p. 246)

United Health Foundation Ranking

In *America's Health: State Health Rankings*, United Health Foundation uses six outcome measures and twelve risk factors to produce an overall ranking of state health status.[3] In 2004, Utah ranked second on outcomes and eighth on risk factors for an overall fifth place ranking. Among other things, Utah's high ranking is attributable to low rates of smoking, cancer related mortality, cardiovascular related mortality, violent crime, infectious disease, and children living in poverty.[4]

Morgan Quitno Ranking

In *Health Care State Rankings 2005*, Morgan Quitno Press uses its own seventeen negative risk factors and four positive risk factors to produce an overall health status ranking.[5] In 2005, Utah is ranked as the seventh healthiest state.[6] This is consistent with the state's top ten ranking in nine out of the ten previous years and top five ranking five times during the same period.[7]

Areas for Concern

Notwithstanding Utah's overall favorable comparison to other states, several areas should be of particular concern to Utahns.

Motor Vehicle Deaths and Injuries

Every year in Utah, more than thirty thousand people are injured and more than three hundred die as a result of motor vehicle crashes. Crashes account for over $30 million in inpatient hospitalization charges and are the leading cause of injury death in Utah.[8]

Obesity

Obesity is a leading cause of preventable death in the United States,[9] second only to cigarette smoking.[10] Obesity increases the risk of heart disease, type 2 diabetes, and other chronic diseases. In Utah, the percentage of adults who are obese increased from 39 percent in 1989 to 56 percent in 2003.[11]

Suicide

Every year, over 300 Utahns commit suicide.[12] In 2002, Utah had the tenth highest suicide rate in the nation. Among Utah males, ages fifteen to forty-four, suicide is the leading cause of death.[13]

ACCESS TO HEALTH CARE

Effects of No Medical Coverage

Access to health care—the ability to obtain appropriate medical care—has a direct impact on the status of an individual's and a community's health. Due to the cost of medical care, access is generally determined by a person's ability to obtain coverage of health care costs through private insurance or government programs. Lack of coverage is a concern because compared to people with health care coverage, people without coverage:
- Do not receive as many preventive services
- Are more likely to delay treatment until their conditions are more acute and more costly
- Are more likely to die prematurely

The impacts on health due to lack of coverage may affect normal human development, educational achievement, employment productivity, and peace of mind.[14]

Coverage Rates

In Utah, most people have some type of health care coverage. In 2003, only 5 percent of the population was without coverage for at least twelve months. An additional 10 percent was without coverage for less than twelve months. At any given time in 2003, 9.1 percent of Utahns (214,500 persons) were without coverage.[15] During the same period, the national rate for persons without coverage was 10.1 percent.[16]

Reasons for No Coverage

The 15 percent of Utahns lacking coverage for at least some period of time during the year cite one or more reasons for lack of coverage:
- 66 percent cannot afford it
- 48 percent lost their jobs or changed employers
- 29 percent have employers who do not offer coverage
- 18 percent work temporary or part-time jobs
- 17 percent believe that it is safe to go without coverage[17]

Persons Most Likely Not to Have Coverage

People in the following groups are more likely than others to not have medical coverage:
- People ages twenty-seven to thirty-four with household incomes less than $20,000
- Adults without a high school education
- Adults ages nineteen to twenty-six
- Adults ages nineteen to sixty-four who are divorced, separated, or widowed
- People living outside the Wasatch Front[18]

However, of those actually without coverage:
- 92 percent are high school graduates
- 68 percent live on the Wasatch Front
- 47 percent are full-time employees
- 70 percent live in households with total annual incomes less than $45,000
- 55 percent are less than twenty-seven years of age[19]

Coverage Types, Enrollment, and Regulation

Although 85 percent of the population has insurance or some other type of medical coverage twelve months out of the year and another 10 percent has coverage for at least a portion of the year,[20] the costs and benefits of that coverage vary greatly depending upon the source of coverage. Health care benefits come from three sources: government sponsored plans, employer sponsored self-funded plans, and commercial health insurance plans. Each plan type differs from the others in terms of eligibility, state and federal regulation, and funding source.

Government Sponsored Plans[21]

Medicare. Medicare is available to all persons sixty-five years of age and older and to some persons under sixty-five years of age with a disability. This is purely a federal program created, administered, and funded by the federal government.[22]

Medicaid. Medicaid is available to low income pregnant women, children, people with disabilities, and the elderly. This is a federally authorized and regulated program administered by the states. Due to flexibility granted by Congress, no two states' Medicaid programs are identical. Every dollar spent by Utah on Medicaid is matched by about three federal dollars.

Children's Health Insurance Program (CHIP). CHIP is available to all children living in households at or below 200 percent of the federal poverty level. CHIP is also a federally authorized program with significant implementation leeway granted to the states. Administration of the program is handled by the states. Utah funding of CHIP is matched approximately four to one by federal funds.

Primary Care Network (PCN). PCN is available to low income adults who do not otherwise qualify for Medicaid or Medicare. PCN is a special feature of Utah's Medicaid program and is funded by state and federal monies at the regular Medicaid match rate. Utah hospitals have committed to provide up to $10 million annually in donated services to this program.[23]

Utah Comprehensive Health Insurance Pool (HIPUtah). HIPUtah is available to persons whose health conditions are serious enough to make them "uninsurable" in the portion of the commercial market that sells plans directly to individuals (rather than through employers). This program satisfies a federal insurance requirement, but it was created by, and is entirely administered and funded by, the state.

Government sponsored plans cover Utahns less frequently than other Americans. Medicare covers 13.7 percent of the U.S. population but only 9.2 percent of the Utah population. Similarly, Medicaid covers 12.4 percent of all Americans, but only 7.3 percent of Utahns.[24]

Employer Sponsored Self-Funded Plans[25]

Public Employee Health Program (PEHP). PEHP is available to state and local government employees in Utah. This program is operated by the Utah Retirement Systems and regulated by the federal Employee Retirement Income Security Act (ERISA). Because PEHP is an ERISA plan, Utah lawmakers are limited in their ability to define benefits. However, in practice, PEHP has adopted whatever benefit provisions the legislature has required commercial plans to adopt.

Federal Employee Health Benefit Plan (FEHBP). FEHBP is available to federal employees. This is a federal program, subject to federal, not state, law and regulation.

Nongovernmental plans. These plans are available to employees or members of organizations that assume the risks of insurance by funding their own benefits. These are privately funded plans subject to ERISA. Again, state lawmakers are limited in their ability to affect benefits offered by these plans. Although some of these plans are administered by commercial insurers which are otherwise regulated by the Utah Insurance Department, the department does not regulate these plans.

Commercial Health Insurance Plans[26]

Group plans. These are available to individuals and their families through employers with two or more employees.

Individual plans. These are available to self-employed individuals and others on an individual, rather than a group, basis.

Group and individual plans are subject to state law and are regulated by the Utah Insurance Department.

Figure 15-1

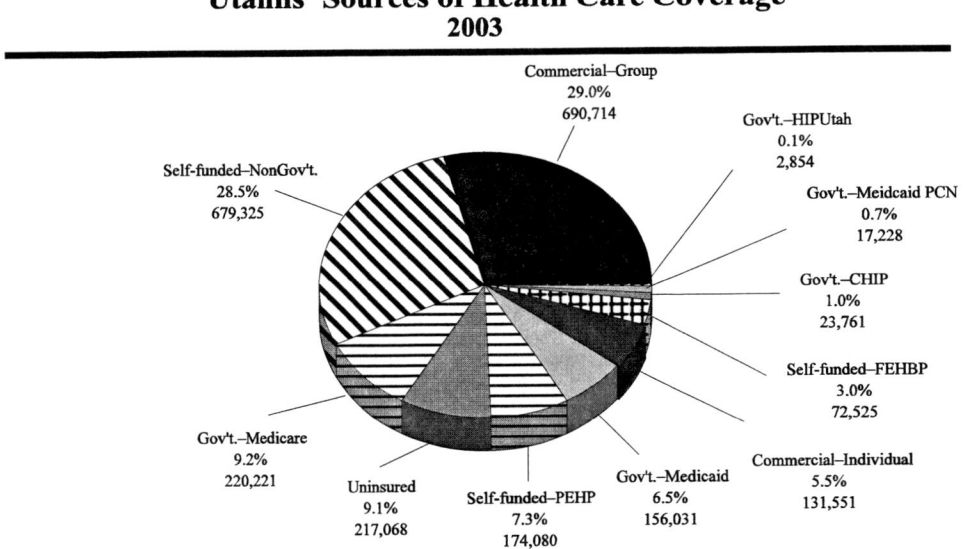

Utahns' Sources of Health Care Coverage 2003

Enrollment and State Regulatory Authority[27]

Figure 15-1 shows that government sponsored plans cover 18 percent of Utah's population (9.2 percent–Medicare, 7.3 percent–Medicaid, and 1.8 percent–other programs). Employer sponsored self-funded plans cover 39 percent of Utah's population (7.3 percent–PEHP, 3.0 percent–FEHBP, and 28.5 percent–nongovernmental plans). Commercial health insurance plans cover 35 percent of the state's population (29.0 percent–group plans, and 5.5 percent–individual plans). Thus, as shown in figure 15-2, state lawmakers and regulators have primary regulatory authority over only 34.5 percent of the medical coverage provided to Utah citizens (by commercial plans). State officials exercise a shared authority with federal regulators over an additional 8.4 percent of coverage (government programs other than Medicare).

Figure 15-2

State Regulation of Utah Health Care Coverage
Number of Covered Persons and Percentage of Population

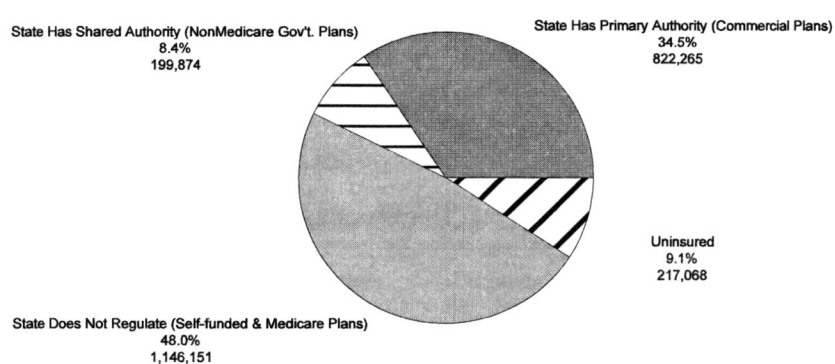

PUBLIC HEALTH

Public Health at Statehood

Public health authorities have always had a rather broad charge with respect to the health of the citizens of Utah. In 1898, only two years after statehood, the legislature created the first State Board of Health. The board was charged with the "general supervision of the interests of the health of the citizens of the state," and given the power "to make such rules and regulations . . . necessary for the preservation of public health." More specifically, the board was directed to investigate the sanitary conditions of "localities" and employments, investigate the causes of diseases, and gather related information for "diffusion among the people."[28]

At this same time the legislature also spelled out the duties of municipal and county health officers to abate or remove the "cause of any special disease or mortality," provide surveillance information to the state board of health on the presence of disease, and report vital statistics to the state, including causes of death.[29]

Public Health Today

While today's state and local health authorities retain the same basic powers and duties as their pre-1900 predecessors, their missions have been expanded, particularly at the state level. For example, today's state health authority, the Utah Department of Health, is charged with a broad array of duties related not only to protecting the public from disease and death, but also to promoting wellness, regulating providers within the health care system, and accomplishing other health related objectives. A sample of these duties includes: publishing information to promote health; reporting on the causes of injury and disability; operating a public health laboratory; regulating health care facilities, child care providers, and ambulance and paramedic services; monitoring the costs of health care; fostering price competition in health care; administering organ donation funds; administering health care delivery programs; and conducting postmortem examinations.[30]

At the local level, the duties of local health departments have also expanded. In addition to other duties, county and multi-county health departments are specifically responsible for the increased public health functions related to food protection, solid waste management, waste water management, and drinking water.[31]

DEPARTMENT OF HEALTH

The following overview of the Utah Department of Health highlights its organization, programs, functions, and funding.

The department consists of seven major organizational units:[32]
1. Division of Community and Family Health Services
2. Division of Epidemiology and Laboratory Services
3. Division of Health Care Financing
4. Center for Health Data
5. Division of Health Systems Improvement
6. Office of the Medical Examiner
7. Office of Emergency Preparedness and Bioterrorism

Figure 15-3 provides an overview of the department's structure, including offices and bureaus within the divisions, and related advisory committees and administrative units.

Figure 15-3

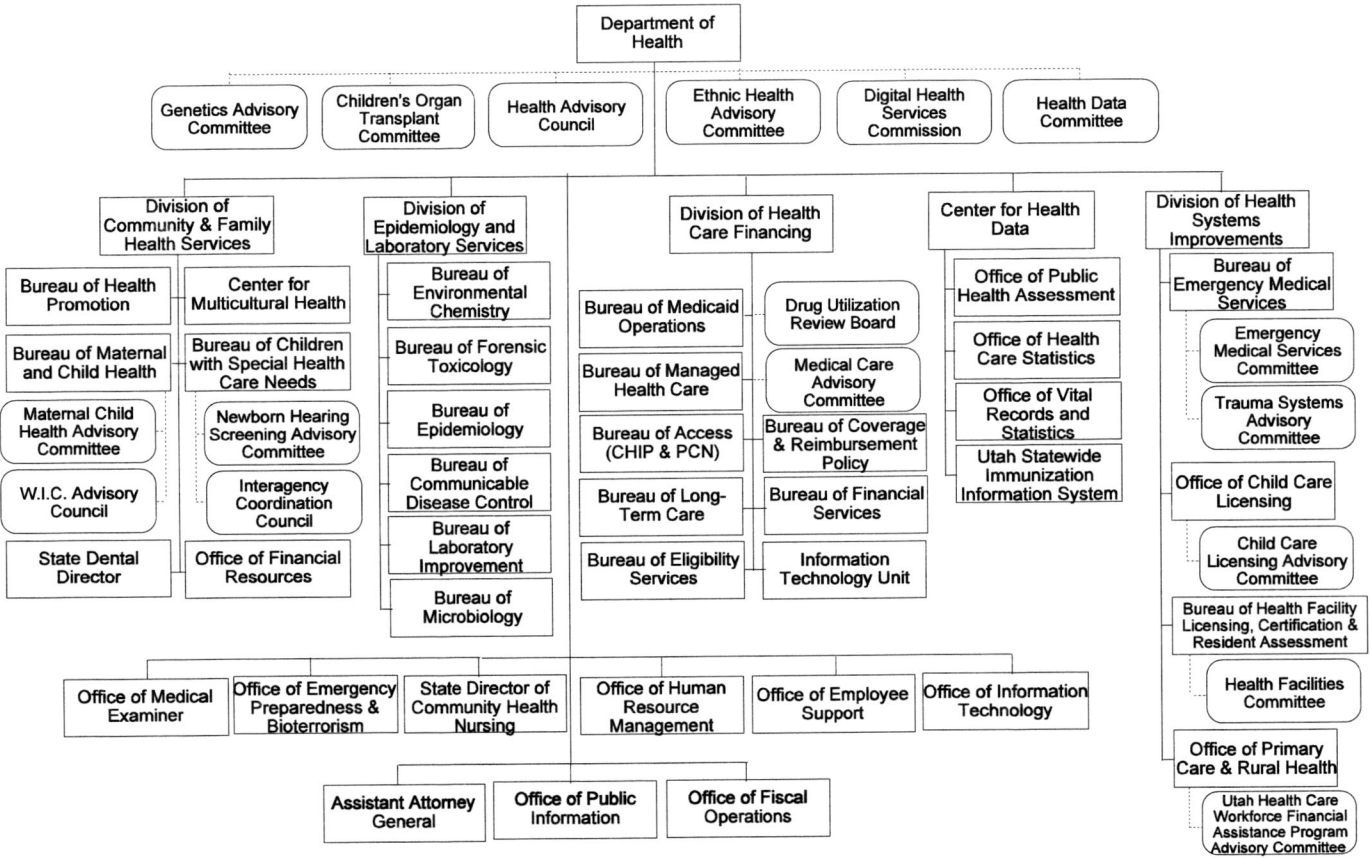

Division of Community and Family Health Services

The Division of Community and Family Health Services consists of six organizational units:
1. Bureau of Health Promotion
2. Bureau of Maternal and Child Health
3. Center for Multicultural Health
4. Bureau of Children with Special Health Care Needs

5. State Dental Director
6. Office of Financial Resources

Working with federal and community partners, including local health departments, this division provides services and programs designed to promote and improve the health of mothers, children, racial and cultural minorities, and other populations with special health care needs. These programs and services address a wide range of diseases and other health issues, including arthritis, asthma, birth defects, cancer, cardiovascular disease, developmental delays in children, diabetes, domestic violence, genomics, immunizations, infant sleep safety, low birth weight, motor vehicle safety, newborn screening, nutrition, oral health, pregnancy, smoking, suicide, overweight, and unintentional injuries. Services are delivered through Baby Your Baby, Baby Watch Early Intervention, Wee Care, WIC (Women Infants and Children), Vaccines for Children, Pregnancy Riskline, Tobacco Quit Line, and many other programs.[33]

Division of Epidemiology and Laboratory Services

The Division of Epidemiology and Laboratory Services is divided into six functional units:
1. Bureau of Environmental Chemistry
2. Bureau of Forensic Toxicology
3. Bureau of Epidemiology
4. Bureau of Communicable Disease Control
5. Bureau of Laboratory Improvement
6. Bureau of Microbiology

Bureau of Environmental Chemistry

The Department of Environmental Quality, the Department of Natural Resources, and public water utilities rely on this bureau to determine compliance with air and water quality standards and to analyze tests of hazardous waste and hazardous spills. The bureau is developing the capacity to detect and quantify chemical terrorism incidents.[34]

Bureau of Forensic Toxicology

State and local law enforcement agencies rely on this division to analyze the results of tests conducted on drivers suspected of driving under the influence of alcohol or other substances. The Office of the Medical Examiner also relies on the bureau to test autopsy specimens.[35]

Bureau of Epidemiology

The Bureau of Epidemiology is responsible for the detection, investigation, and control of communicable and infectious diseases and for surveillance and investigation of health effects associated with environmental hazards.[36] The bureau operates three programs:
1. Disease Outbreak Management Program
2. Environmental Epidemiology Program
3. Surveillance and System Development Program

As part of these programs, the bureau provides assistance and training to local health departments, physicians, hospitals, and schools and is responsible for developing and operating surveillance systems to detect bioterrorism. The bureau also works with local health departments to monitor second-hand smoke and sanitation in public places, including restaurants and swimming pools.[37]

Bureau of Communicable Disease Control

This bureau is responsible for the prevention, control, and treatment of communicable diseases, including HIV, hepatitis C, tuberculosis, and sexually transmitted diseases. The bureau operates an

HIV Prevention Program, an HIV/AIDS Surveillance Program, an HIV/AIDS Drug Assistance Program, an HIV/AIDS Home Health Program, an HIV/AIDS Health Insurance Continuation Program, a Tuberculosis Control Program, a Refugee Health Program, and a Sexually Transmitted Disease Control Program.[38] The bureau also provides technical assistance to local health departments and other public health partners.[39]

Bureau of Laboratory Improvement

This bureau operates under contract with the federal government to inspect and enforce regulations pertaining to all clinical laboratories operating in Utah that perform tests on human samples.[40] The bureau also establishes and enforces standards for laboratories that provide compliance test results to the Department of Environmental Quality.[41]

Bureau of Microbiology

This bureau performs a wide range of infectious disease tests for other units within the Department of Health, local health departments, and private health care providers. The bureau also analyzes newborn screening samples for metabolic, endocrine, and hemotologic disorders.[42]

Division of Health Care Financing

The Division of Health Care Financing operates the state's Medicaid program.[43] Each of the division's eight organizational units are directly related to the program:
1. Bureau of Medicaid Operations
2. Bureau of Managed Health Care
3. Bureau of Access
4. Bureau of Long-term Care
5. Bureau of Eligibility Services
6. Bureau of Coverage and Reimbursement Policy
7. Bureau of Financial Services
8. Information Technology Unit

Medicaid

Medicaid is a state and federal partnership designed to fund health care services for low income pregnant women, children, people with disabilities, and the elderly. In Medicaid, as in private health insurance programs, a relatively small number of enrollees account for a large portion of program costs. Although the elderly and persons with a disability make up only 25 percent of enrollees nationally, they account for 70 percent of Medicaid's costs.[44] A similar pattern exists in Utah.

The exact amount of federal funding of Utah's Medicaid program varies from year to year, but the federal government generally matches about three dollars for every dollar spent by the state. The most recent downturn in the U.S. economy and a new round of medical cost inflation have led to renewed interest nationwide in containing costs and expanding state flexibility for this entitlement program.

As shown in figure 15-4, over the past twenty years total state and federal Medicaid spending in Utah has grown nearly tenfold. From 1985 to 1995 spending increased from $144 million to $552 million, a 14.3 percent average annual rate of growth. From 1995 to 2005, spending increased an additional $841 million, a still large, but somewhat slower, 9.7 percent average annual growth rate.

Figure 15-4[45]

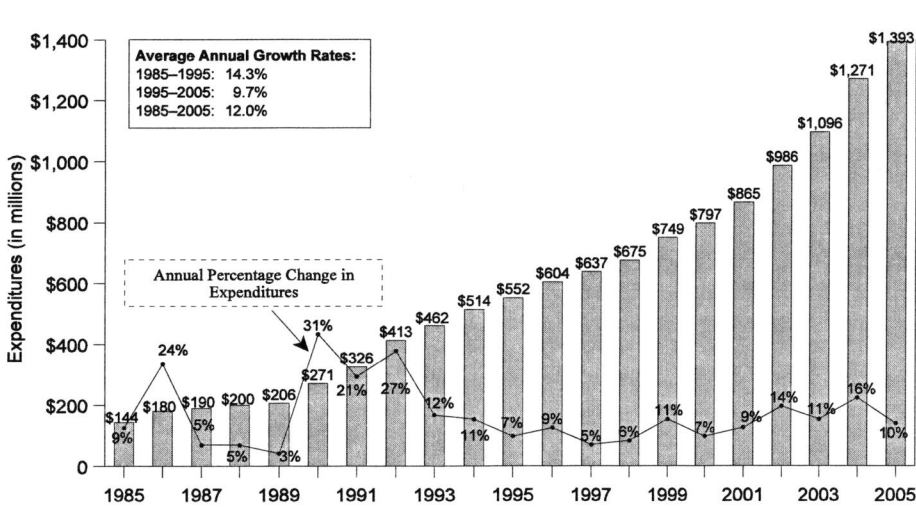

In fiscal year 2005, Utah Medicaid expenditures totaled $1.393 billion.[46] This represented 16 percent of the state's total budget and accounted for 13 percent of General Fund expenditures.[47] Except public education, no other state program received greater funding than Medicaid.[48]

Figure 15-5 shows that from 1995 to 2005, Medicaid enrollment[49] grew from 129,430 to 186,507,[50] an average annual growth rate of 3.7 percent. This rate is significantly lower than the 9.7 percent average annual rate of growth in spending for the same period.

Figure 15-5[51]

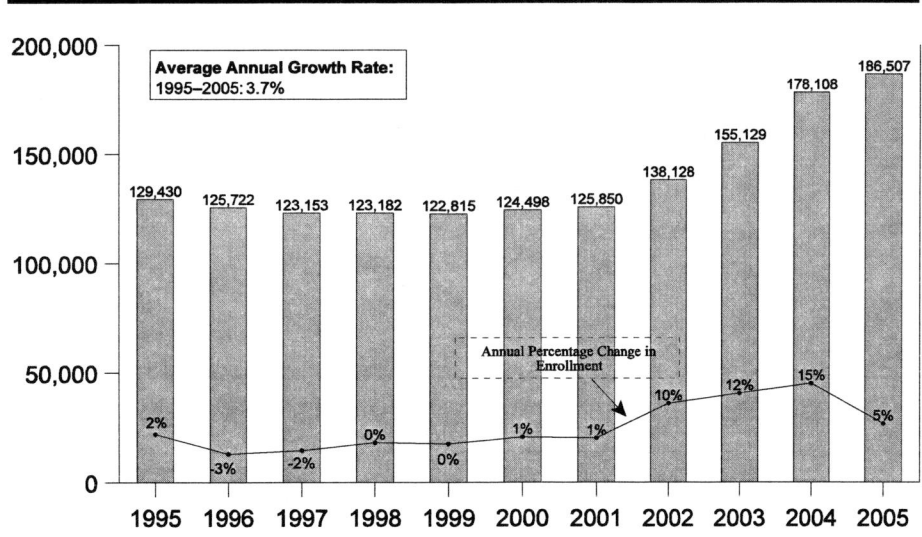

In terms of eligibility and funding, Medicaid is an incredibly complex program (Utah's Medicaid program has at least twenty-nine unique eligibility categories),[52] but its overriding purpose is to encourage and help states expand access to quality health care for individuals who could not otherwise afford that care. Over the years, Utah has expanded that access using various Medicaid and non-Medicaid approaches. Some of the more recent expansions include the Primary Care Network, Covered at Work, and CHIP (Children's Health Insurance Program).

The Primary Care Network is undoubtedly the state's most well known recent attempt to expand access to health care. In 2002, the U.S. Department of Human Services approved the state's request to establish a primary care network expanding limited Medicaid coverage to adults ages nineteen to sixty-four with incomes less than 150 percent of the federal poverty level. Permitting something less than full medical coverage was new to Medicaid and discussed extensively in national gatherings. The Primary Care Network serves about eighteen thousand individuals.[53]

Following implementation of the Primary Care Network, the state also received federal approval to operate Covered at Work, a further expansion of the state's Medicaid program designed to pay $50 per month toward an employee's health insurance premium. This program is designed to make employer-based coverage more affordable and is limited to employees with premiums in excess of five percent of income. Currently, the program serves less than 100 individuals.[54]

An earlier, non-Medicaid approach to expanding access to health care was CHIP (Children's Health Insurance Program). When CHIP was authorized by Congress in 1997, states were given the option to deliver the program as a Medicaid expansion. Utah chose the non-Medicaid route in order to retain greater control over benefit design. CHIP provides health care benefits to children living in homes with incomes at or below 200 percent of the federal poverty level. State funding comes primarily from the Master Settlement Agreement entered into by the state with leading tobacco manufacturers in 1998. Federal funding of the program matches state spending four to one. The program covers about thirty-one thousand children,[55] but is expected to cover an additional twelve thousand children beginning in fiscal year 2006.[56]

Center for Health Data

The Center for Health Data consists of:
- Office of Public Health Assessment
- Office of Health Care Statistics
- Office of Vital Records and Statistics
- Utah Statewide Immunizations Information System (USSIIS)

The Center for Health Data collects, analyzes and publishes a wide array of data related to birth, death, marriage, divorce, morbidity (disease, illness, and injury), hospitalization, patient treatment, abortion, patient safety, managed care performance, consumer satisfaction with managed care providers, and immunizations.

The Center for Health Data works closely with the Health Data Committee, a thirteen-member body with rulemaking authority created by statute within the Department of Health. The committee includes health care providers, insurers, consumers, and public health representatives and is charged to "direct a statewide effort to collect, analyze, and distribute health care data to facilitate the promotion and accessibility of quality and cost-effective health care and also to facilitate interaction among those with concern for health care issues."[57]

Division of Health Systems Improvement

The Division of Health Systems Improvement is responsible for ensuring "basic levels of quality in the [state's] health and child care industries."[58] The division consists of four units:
1. Bureau of Emergency Medical Services
2. Office of Child Care Licensing
3. Bureau of Health Facility Licensing, Certification and Resident Assessment
4. Office of Primary Care and Rural Health

Bureau of Emergency Medical Services

This bureau is responsible for licensing ambulance and paramedic providers, granting permits to ambulances and other emergency response vehicles, coordinating emergency medical services within the state, developing a counseling and support program for personnel exposed to stressful incidents, improving delivery of emergency medical services through grants, establishing and supervising a statewide trauma system that includes health care facilities, and regulating the emergency medical services market by establishing exclusive service areas and maximum rates.[59]

Office of Child Care Licensing

This office licenses and certifies child care provided by families, residential centers, employers, and others.[60]

Bureau of Health Facility Licensing, Certification and Resident Assessment

This bureau licenses, certifies, and ensures regulatory compliance by all health care facilities in the state, including those providing services to Medicare and Medicaid patients. The facilities include hospitals, nursing care facilities, assisted living facilities, home health agencies, and numerous other types of providers.

The bureau conducts pre-admission screenings and continued stay reviews for persons seeking or receiving care in nursing homes or institutions for persons with mental retardation or a mental illness. It also performs background checks for criminal activity or abuse of children, the elderly, or persons with a disability by those associated with licensed facilities.[61]

Office of Primary Care and Rural Health

This office grants monies to public and nonprofit entities to provide primary health care services to medically underserved populations, including "persons of limited English-speaking ability, single heads of households, the elderly, persons with low incomes, and persons with chronic diseases."[62] The office also assists rural communities with needs assessments, grant writing, recruiting, and other tasks related to developing primary health care services.[63]

Office of the Medical Examiner

State law requires the Office of the Medical Examiner to investigate sudden or unexpected deaths, including deaths by violence, drug overdose or poisoning, or disease which may constitute a threat to public health; deaths associated with medical treatment; deaths under suspicious or unusual circumstances; and other specified deaths.[64] The office relies on physicians in local communities to assist with cases outside the Wasatch Front.[65]

Office of Emergency Preparedness and Bioterrorism

This office is responsible for coordinating the activities of various units within the department that detect, communicate, and respond to public health threats resulting from terrorist acts or other emergency situations.[66]

Funding

The Department of Health's $1.8 billion budget is 20 percent of the nearly $9 billion total appropriated to state government in fiscal year 2006.[67] The department's share of General Fund appropriations is somewhat less—16 percent—due to heavy reliance on federal funding for the Medicaid program.[68] Only public education receives a greater portion of total state and federal funding.[69]

Summary

With its $1.8 billion budget and extensive organization, the Utah Department of Health is very different from the first State Board of Health created in 1898. Nevertheless, the department is still carrying out the same basic public health mandate—the prevention of disease, the protection of health, and the collection and dissemination of useful health information. To these core functions have been added numerous other responsibilities intended to promote the health and wellness of Utah's residents.

LOCAL HEALTH DEPARTMENTS

Each county in Utah is required, either individually or in cooperation with one or more other counties, to create a local health department.[70] These departments work cooperatively with the Utah Department of Health to carry out many of the same responsibilities shared by the state. However, local departments are also authorized to develop their own public health standards and enact their own ordinances, as long as they are at least as stringent as those established by the state.[71]

Local health departments carry out much of the monitoring and enforcement activities of public health.[72] By statute, local health departments are specifically responsible for public health functions related to food protection, solid waste management, waste water management, and drinking water.[73]

In fiscal year 2004, the budgets for Utah's twelve local health departments totaled $75 million. Of this amount, $4 million (6 percent) came from state sources, $18 million (24 percent) from federal sources, and $52 million (70 percent) from county or other sources. Rural multi-county health departments rely much more heavily on state and federal funding than urban single-county health departments.[74]

Chapter 16

Human Services

ROLE OF GOVERNMENT IN HUMAN SERVICES

At least since "Great Britain instituted the Elizabethan Poor Relief Act in 1601, government has taken an active interest in the health and welfare of its citizens."[1] For a long period in the United States, this interest was manifest primarily by local communities and states. Although the federal government created the Public Health Service in 1798 and the U.S. Children's Bureau in 1912, the responsibility for most health and welfare functions continued with state and local governments.[2] However, federal involvement in social welfare programs increased tremendously during the New Deal of the 1930s and the "Great Society" of the 1960s.[3] Today, many programs of this type are funded and administered as federal, state, and local government partnerships. The following review of the Utah Department of Human Services highlights government's role in the delivery of a broad array of services designed to improve the social condition of the state's citizens.

> **In this chapter:**
>
> Role of Government in Human Services (p. 247)
> Utah Department of Human Services (p. 247)

UTAH DEPARTMENT OF HUMAN SERVICES

History

The Utah Department of Human Services traces its beginnings to the Department of Health and Welfare created by the Utah Legislature in 1967. Prior to that time, various human services were provided by nine independent agencies.[4]

Over the years the department that has overseen the delivery of human services has undergone numerous organizational and name changes. Several divisions that were once part of the 1967 organization—Health, Welfare, and Corrections—are now separate departments within state government. Specifically, the creation of the Department of Workforce Services was the culmination of efforts over many years to consolidate and simplify the delivery of public assistance, job training, employment, and other welfare services.

Current Structure

Utah's Department of Human Services consists of five divisions and three major offices:[5]
- Division of Aging and Adult Services
- Division of Child and Family Services
- Division of Services for People with Disabilities
- Division of Substance Abuse and Mental Health
- Division of Juvenile Justice Services
- Office of Public Guardian

- Office of Licensing
- Office of Recovery Services

With the exception of the Office of Recovery Services, each of these divisions and offices has a corresponding policy board.[6] Boards possess administrative rulemaking authority to establish policy which each division and office in turn is required to carry out. Appointments of directors of divisions and the Office of the Public Guardian require the concurrence of the corresponding boards.[7] Divisions and offices also have administrative rulemaking authority.[8]

A review of the functions of each division and office highlights the breadth of the department's responsibilities to reach out to and assist persons who are delinquent youths, aged, abused, addicted, disabled, delinquent in support payments, neglected, or mentally ill.[9]

Figure 16-1 provides an overview of the Department of Human Services' structure, including the various administrative offices and bureaus which support the department's primary functions, but are not discussed in this chapter.

Figure 16-1

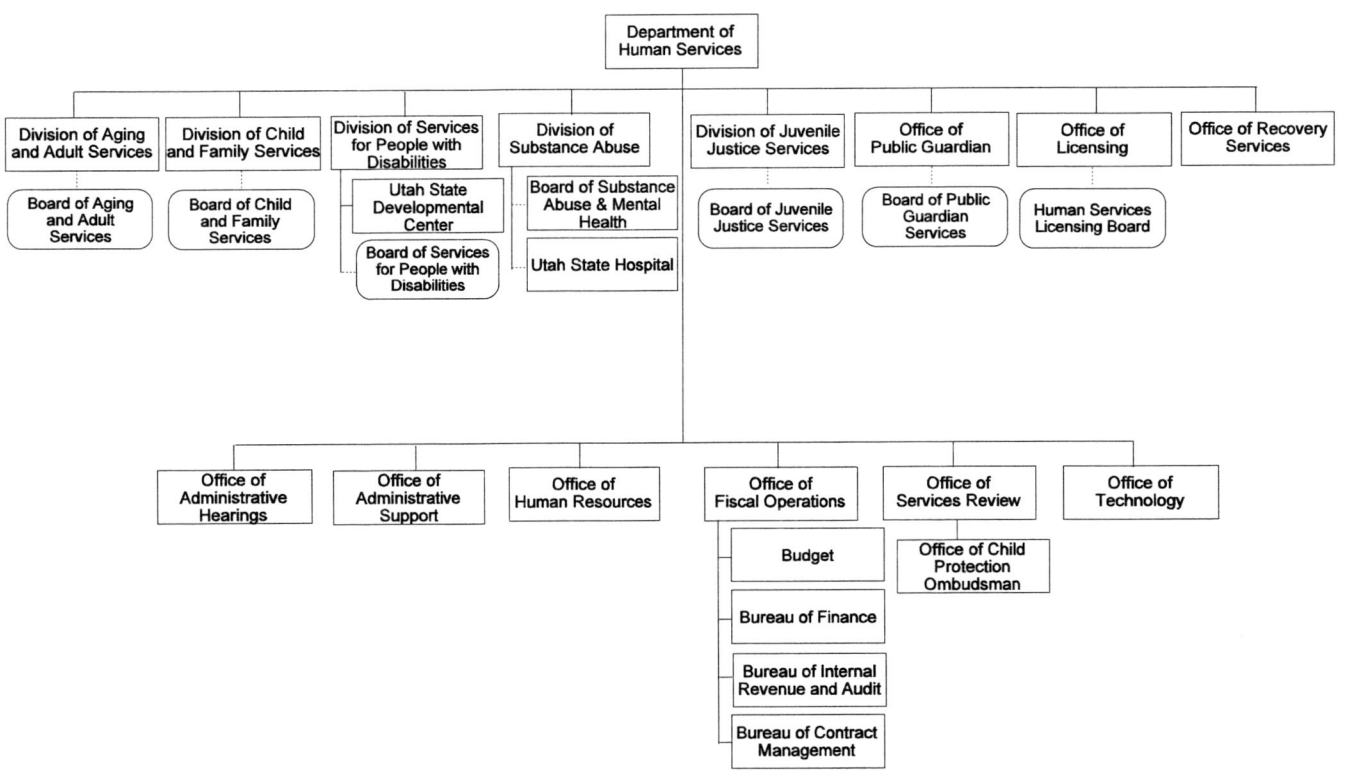

Division of Aging and Adult Services

The Division of Aging and Adult Services "administers, contracts, and monitors services to aging and disabled adults, and investigates abuse, neglect and exploitation of vulnerable adults."[10] These services include nutrition programs (e.g., Meals on Wheels, an in-home program), the Home and Community Based Medicaid Waiver Program for the Elderly, the Senior Community Service Employment Program, the Alternatives Program, the Utah Family Caregiver Support Program, the long-term care ombudsman, and senior centers.[11] The Adult Protective Services unit within the division conducts investigations of abuse, neglect, and exploitation and provides "short-term, limited protective services with the permission of the . . . vulnerable adult or guardian . . . of the vulnerable adult."[12]

Services funded by the division are delivered largely through twelve "area agencies on aging," single or multi-county government agencies designated by the division to "design and implement a comprehensive and coordinated system of services and programs for the aged."[13]

Division of Child and Family Services

The Division of Child and Family Services is charged with protecting the health, safety, and welfare of children who have been abused or neglected. To accomplish this mission, the division investigates allegations of abuse or neglect, provides family preservation services to prevent the separation of children at risk of abuse or neglect from their parents, and provides reunification services to enable children who have been taken into the custody of the state to return to their families when appropriate. The division works closely with foster families, the juvenile court, adoption agencies, and other service providers.[14]

Unlike some other states with county or city child welfare departments, Utah's child welfare system is a centralized, state-administered system consisting of various state-directed agencies. Local governments, however, are important partners in the system, investigating and prosecuting criminal abuse and neglect, and delivering mental health, substance abuse, and other services.

Since 1994 the state's child welfare system has been significantly upgraded in the wake of a legislative audit[15] and a federal lawsuit, *David C. v. Leavitt*,[16] both highlighting serious deficiencies in the system. In response to the legal challenge, the state agreed to oversight by a federal district judge.[17] That oversight is scheduled to end when the state meets the operational objectives set forth in the Performance Milestone Plan adopted by the court in 1999.

The state's compliance with the Performance Milestone Plan is evaluated using three basic tools: one that measures outcomes for children and their families, one that measures the adoption of good practices, and one that measures procedural compliance. According to two of these tools, the state has met the court's performance objectives for the well-being of children and their families and is making substantial improvement implementing good child welfare practices. The third tool, however, indicates the state is not making the same degree of progress in procedural compliance.[18] This tool has recently been the subject of negotiations between the state and the plaintiff and has been modified to more accurately reflect the state's efforts.[19] On several occasions, the federal judge has signaled that the court's oversight might end as early as 2006.

Child welfare agencies in at least fifteen other states are also operating under some type of court directive.[20]

Division of Services for People with Disabilities

The Division of Services for People with Disabilities is responsible for planning, developing, and managing, "an array of services and supports for persons with disabilities and their families throughout the state."[21]

Some of the disabilities that qualify a person for services from the division include mental retardation, cerebral palsy, autism, severe epilepsy, acquired brain injury, and the inability by an adult to use two or more limbs[22] if the disability "results in a substantial functional limitation in three or more areas . . . of major life activity."[23]

Services provided by the division include respite care, assistance with daily activities, assistive technology and adaptive devices, training, supported employment, skill development, and supervised living arrangements.[24] The division also operates the Utah State Developmental Center which provides twenty-four-hour care and intensive services to individuals whose needs cannot be met in a less restrictive setting.[25]

Delivery of services is prioritized based on a standardized needs assessment.[26] Those unable to receive services are placed on a waiting list. Because most of the division clients receive services on a long-term basis, persons waiting for services often must wait until additional funds are appropriated by the legislature.

Division of Substance Abuse and Mental Health

The Division of Substance Abuse and Mental Health has the responsibility to work with thirteen local substance abuse authorities and thirteen local mental health authorities (single or multi-county government agencies) to ensure that a "comprehensive continuum" of mental health and substance abuse services is available throughout the state.[27] The division contracts with the local authorities for services, monitors their performance, and provides technical assistance and training. Local authorities provide services themselves or contract with private providers.[28]

The division operates the Utah State Hospital, a twenty-four-hour inpatient facility that provides mental health services to individuals whose needs cannot be met through local public mental health centers. The hospital also provides evaluations and treatment for persons involved with the criminal justice system.[29]

The division's services are limited by available funding and are allocated to clients on the basis of need.[30]

Division of Juvenile Justice Services

The Division of Juvenile Justice Services provides intervention, supervision, and rehabilitation services to youth offenders and their families.[31] Youth offenders fall into two categories: those who commit status offenses (offenses such as tobacco use or curfew violation that are illegal only due to the youth's age), and those who are delinquent (youth who commit misdemeanor or felony acts).[32]

For status offenders, the division provides assessment, therapy, education, referral to community services, short-term residential placements, and twenty-four-hour crisis counseling. For delinquent youth, the division provides secure detention, home detention, observation and assessment, secure facilities, work camps, day and night reporting centers, non-secure community programs, case management, and parole.[33] More information about the division can be found in Chapter 18, *Public Safety, Criminal Law, and Corrections*.

Office of the Public Guardian

The Office of Public Guardian serves "as a guardian, conservator, or both for [an incapacitated adult][34] upon appointment by a court when no other person is able and willing to do so."[35] Services are limited by available funding and are usually provided only to persons experiencing or at significant risk of abuse, neglect, self-neglect, or exploitation, or who are in life-threatening situations.[36]

The office is authorized to recruit and train volunteers to assist in providing services.[37]

Office of Licensing

"No person, agency, . . . or governmental unit . . . may establish, conduct, or maintain a human services program or facility in this state without a . . . license issued by [the Office of Licensing]."[38] This applies to any "youth program, resource family home, or a facility or program . . . that provides care, secure treatment, inpatient treatment, residential treatment, residential support, adult day care, day treatment, outpatient treatment, domestic violence treatment, child placing services, or social detoxification."[39] These programs and facilities include foster care homes, adoption agencies, and various types of treatment and care programs, including those for persons with a disability, persons with mental illness, and persons abusing drugs or alcohol.[40]

The Office of Licensing evaluates applications for license, conducts criminal and abuse background checks for persons associated with the licensee,[41] grants licenses, conducts compliance surveys, and investigates complaints.[42]

Office of Recovery Services

The Office of Recovery Services collects child support from parents who have been ordered to pay child support. This includes support ordered in divorce or other court proceedings, including cases where a child is in the custody of the Division of Child and Family Services, the Division of Juvenile Justice Services, or the Utah State Hospital and a parent has been ordered under Utah law to pay support. The office also assists in locating parents and establishing paternity.[43]

In addition to enforcing support obligations, the office seeks reimbursement from individuals and third parties, when appropriate, to repay medical expenses paid by the state Medicaid program. This includes recovering expenses from the estate of any person who has received Medicaid benefits while over fifty-five years of age.[44]

In fiscal year 2004, the Office of Recovery Services collected $152.5 million on 74,025 support cases[45] and $18.8 million on 23,044 Medicaid cases for a total collection of $171.3 million on 97,069 cases. The office also helped Medicaid to avoid over $195 million in costs.[46]

Overall, the Office of Recovery Services collected 58.6 percent of the current support due in fiscal year 2003. This collection rate was slightly higher than the national average, 58.1 percent,[47] and twenty-third among the 50 states.[48] Approximately $338 million in unpaid liabilities remains outstanding, nearly all of that representing unpaid child support payments.[49]

Funding

The Department of Human Services' $605 million budget (fiscal year 2006) represents only 7 percent of Utah's nearly $9 billion total budget; however, the $298 million appropriated to the department from the state's General Fund represents 15 percent of total General Fund appropriations. Department programs rely heavily on federal funding, especially Medicaid funding.[50]

Summary

The Utah Department of Human Services, with its five divisions and three offices, plays a wide-ranging, significant role in the constellation of federal, state, local government, and non-government agencies that plan, coordinate, fund, and deliver social welfare services across a broad spectrum of human needs.

Chapter 17

Natural Resources

DEPARTMENT OF NATURAL RESOURCES

Created in 1967 by the legislature, the Department of Natural Resources (DNR) endeavors to sustain and enhance the quality of life for current and future citizens through coordinated and balanced stewardship of Utah's natural resources.[1] DNR now consists of seven divisions:

1. Division of Forestry, Fire and State Lands
2. Division of Oil, Gas and Mining
3. Division of State Parks and Recreation
4. Division of Water Resources
5. Division of Water Rights
6. Division of Wildlife Resources
7. Utah Geological Survey

> **In this chapter:**
>
> Department of Natural Resources (p. 253)
> Division of Forestry, Fire, and State Lands (p. 254)
> Division of Oil, Gas and Mining (p. 255)
> Division of State Parks and Recreation (p. 257)
> Division of Water Resources (p. 258)
> Division of Water Rights (p. 260)
> Division of Wildlife Resources (p. 261)
> Utah Geological Survey (p. 263)
> Recovery Program (p. 264)
> Property Rights Ombudsman (p. 264)

DNR also includes the Natural Resources Policy and Planning Teams, the Recovery Program, the Take Pride in Utah Program, and the Office of the Utah Property Rights Ombudsman.

Figure 17-1

Department of Natural Resources

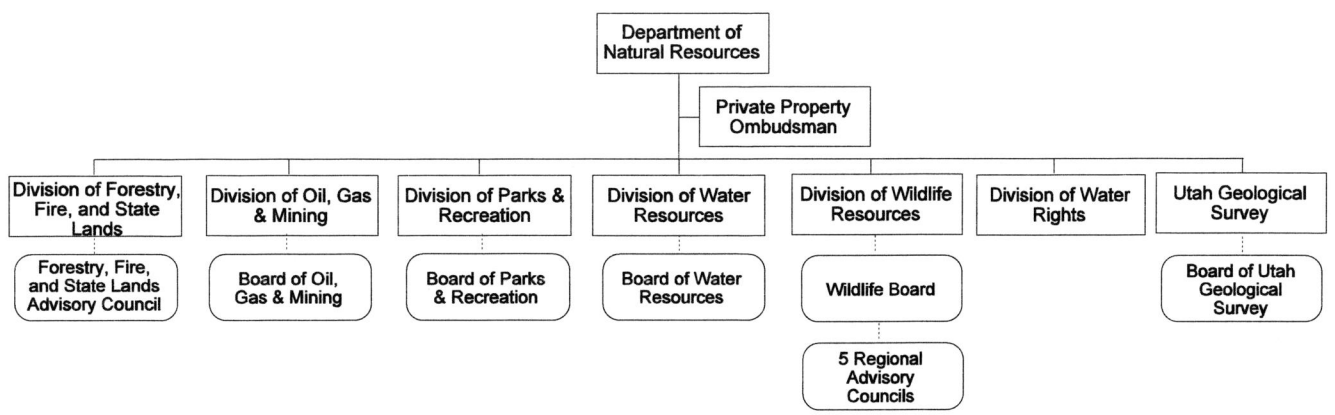

DIVISION OF FORESTRY, FIRE AND STATE LANDS

The Division of Forestry, Fire and State Lands is the executive authority for the management of sovereign lands and the state's mineral estates on nontrust lands. It also manages state forestry and fire control activities.[2] The division administers state lands under land management programs using multiple-use and sustained yield principles and seeks to derive optimum benefit from public trust resources such as mineral leasing on sovereign, lake bed and riverbed lands, and state-owned nontrust lands.

Forestry, Fire and State Lands Advisory Council

Comprised of eight citizens representing specific geographic areas and interests, the Forestry, Fire and State Lands Advisory Council is required to meet at least twice yearly.[3] It advises the division on matters regarding comprehensive land management policies using multiple-use, sustained yield principles.[4] The council studies natural resource issues involving forestry and state lands and recommends appropriate action.

State Forester

The state forester is responsible for making certain that appropriate action is taken to control wildland fires on nonfederal forest, range, and watershed lands. The division is also responsible for protecting nonfederal forest and watershed areas according to conservation principles, and encouraging private landowners in preserving, protecting, and managing forest and other lands throughout Utah.

Wildfires

The focus of the Wildland Fire Protection Program is the protection of lives, property, and natural resources through a cooperative effort with county, local, and federal partners. Emphasis is on the prevention of wildland fire through education and implementation of National Fire Plan projects and Healthy Forest Initiatives. This program also provides wildland fire suppression training and administers fire equipment grants to rural fire departments. If the state forester finds conditions in a given area in Utah to be extremely hazardous, the state forester may close those areas to any forms of use by the public, or limit that use.

State agencies responsible for the administration of state-owned lands allocate funds annually to the division for providing a basic level of fire protection. Counties are responsible for abating any public nuisance caused by uncontrolled fire on privately owned or county owned forest, range, and watershed lands. They may participate in the division's Wildland Fire Protection System. In order to be eligible, the county must adopt a wildland fire ordinance based upon minimum standards established by the division, that requires the county fire department to meet minimum standards for wildland fire training, certification, and wildland fire suppression equipment; and file a budget for fire suppression costs.[5]

To support local fire-fighting efforts, the division administers a cost-sharing program to assist in training and equipping local fire services by providing matching funds to local fire departments. The division also manages the Flame-In-Gos, a highly-trained, elite fire-fighting force composed of prison inmates. They also work on natural resource conservation projects.

Lone Peak Conservation Center

The division operates the Lone Peak Conservation Center where Utah native shrubs are grown to be used in conservation projects. The Lone Peak Conservation Center in Draper provides trained crews and resources for wildland firefighting and natural resource projects. The conservation seedling nursery produces one million native plants each year for conservation needs.

Utah Forest Practices Act, Forest Stewardship Program, and Forestry Landowner Assistance Program

The Utah Forest Practices Act requires persons intending to grow, harvest or process forest products, except landowners on their own land, to register with the division.[6] This notification allows the division to better protect forest, soil, and water resources. The Forest Stewardship Program promotes nonindustrial private forest land management by providing services to landowners through area offices.[7] The Forestry Landowner Assistance Program promotes long-term management of nonindustrial private forest lands.[8] Foresters provide technical assistance and expertise to private landowners through development of forest stewardship plans. Other assistance includes preparing timber sales, windbreak design, water quality and forest health protection. The division also offers financial assistance to help with implementing forest practices identified in management plans.

Mineral Leases and Deposits

Coal and mineral deposits in state-owned lands are reserved to the state, and the division makes all mineral leases, depositing the revenue in the Sovereign Lands Management Account.[9] The legislature then appropriates funds from this account to the division to manage state lands. Purchasers of state-owned land acquire no right, title, or interest in coal or mineral deposits because coal and mineral deposits in state-owned lands may not be sold, but may be leased on a rental and royalty basis. Salts and other minerals in the waters of navigable lakes and streams are reserved to the state and may only be sold by the division on a royalty basis. The division may also issue surface leases of state lands for any period up to ninety-nine years.

Range Management

The division is responsible for the efficient management of all range resources on lands under its administration.[10] The division is responsible for approximately 1,500,000 acres, most of which are submerged. The legislature has directed the division to manage based on sound conservation principles, including improving range conditions. The division issues grazing leases for up to fifteen years on approximately 8,000 acres of state lands based on the fair market value of the lease and determines the number and kind of stock that may be grazed, and regulates the number of days of grazing.

Great Salt Lake

The division is also responsible for preparing and maintaining a comprehensive plan for the Great Salt Lake. It develops strategies to deal with the fluctuating lake level and encourages development of the lake in a manner which will preserve the lake, encourage availability of brines for lake extraction industries, protect wildlife, and protect recreational facilities. The lake and the marshes are important to the waterfowl flyway system, and the division is charged with maintaining and protecting the state, federal, and private marshlands, rookeries, and wildlife refuges while providing public access to the lake for recreation, hunting, and fishing.

DIVISION OF OIL, GAS AND MINING

The Division of Oil, Gas and Mining has stewardship over the state's development of oil, gas, coal, and other mineral resources.[11] When exploration and development activities are complete, the division works to ensure that oil and gas wells are properly abandoned and mining sites are satisfactorily reclaimed. The legislature has declared that it is in the public interest to promote oil and gas production in a manner that will prevent waste and realize the greatest possible economic recovery.

Board of Oil, Gas and Mining

The seven-member Board of Oil, Gas and Mining is a quasi-judicial forum for mineral and energy resource policy and regulatory issues. Members have expertise in oil and gas, mining, royalty matters, environmental protection, and geology.[12] The board provides the first level of administrative appeal to the public on minerals, coal, and oil and gas projects when there are objections. The board is the policy making body for the division. The board and division have exclusive jurisdiction over non-federal lands and cooperative jurisdiction over federal lands in regard to regulation of coal mining, reclamation operations, and oil and gas exploration.

In addition to the duties assigned by the board, the division is responsible for an inspection program that includes production data, pre-drilling checks, and site security reviews and for publishing monthly production reports. It also keeps records of all oil and gas facilities, well logs, directional surveys, and reports on well location, drilling, and production and gas processing plants.

Minerals Regulatory Program

Mining is an important industry in Utah, providing many high-paying jobs. Periodic mine inspections ensure operator compliance with regulations. The Minerals Regulatory Program oversees and regulates large and small mineral mines and exploration projects.[13] Permits are issued to ensure compliance with environmental laws and regulations.

Coal Regulatory Program

The Coal Regulatory Program supports a viable coal mining industry to meet the nation's energy needs, attempts to safeguard the environment, protects public health and safety, and encourages the successful reclamation of mined lands.[14]

Oil and Gas Program

The Oil and Gas Program responds to fluctuations in industry exploration and production activity.[15] This program approves new drilling operations, inspects new and existing oil and gas operations for regulatory compliance, and works to ensure that oil and gas wells are properly plugged and abandoned. As part of this effort, information is collected, processed, and maintained on ownership, production, disposition, and status of oil and gas exploration and production wells and facilities.

A supporting function of the program is permitting and inspecting injection and disposal wells and surface water disposal pits. Water is forced into injection wells to aid recovery of additional oil assets.

The State Tax Commission collects the fee levied for oil and gas produced and deposits it in the Oil and Gas Conservation Account.[16] Account monies are used to pay for administration costs and plugging and reclaiming abandoned oil or gas wells.

Reclamation Program

The Abandoned Mines Reclamation Program attempts to protect public health and safety from hazards at abandoned mines and restores lands damaged by past unregulated mining.[17] An estimated twenty thousand abandoned mines in Utah require on-going efforts to educate the public about the dangers of abandoned mines.[18]

The division works to ensure that the rights of surface landowners are protected from the impacts of mining operations, that surface coal mining operations are conducted so as to protect the environment, and that reclamation occurs as contemporaneously as possible with the mining operation. The division also promotes the reclamation of mined areas left without adequate reclamation.

DIVISION OF PARKS AND RECREATION

The Division of Parks and Recreation is responsible for protecting, preserving, and managing Utah's recreational, cultural, and natural resources.[19] The division manages the resources using a multiple-use principle allowing grazing, fishing, hunting, and mining. It coordinates programs for the development of recreational areas, water conservation, flood control, and wildlife conservation along rivers and streams that are impacted by high density populations or that are prone to flooding.

Board of Utah State Parks and Recreation

The nine-member Board of Parks and Recreation is the policy-making body of the division and represents each of the state's eight judicial districts with one at-large member.[20] The board makes rules governing the use of the state park system to protect state parks and their natural and cultural resources from misuse or damage, including watersheds, plants, wildlife, and park amenities and to provide for public safety and preserve the peace within state parks.

Overview of State Parks System

Created in 1957, the Park Commission was charged with the responsibility of inventorying the state for potential state park areas to join the four parks in existence at the time. The legislature directed the commission to make a survey of Utah's park and recreation potential, with field investigation of areas of scenic, historic, archeological, and geologic interest. The commission completed their survey two years later, identifying 118 potential state park sites. In 1967, the Parks Commission was dissolved, and the Division of Utah State Parks and Recreation was formed within the newly established DNR. Currently, the Utah State Park System is made up of forty-one recreational, heritage, and scenic state parks. Parks are located throughout Utah in mountain valleys, desert canyons and mesa tops, and in proximity to many of Utah's cities and towns.

Heritage parks and museums protect, preserve, research, and interpret the state's unique cultural and natural history resources for the education and enjoyment of all. Museums feature Utah's prehistory from dinosaurs to American Indian culture, and more recent Civil War and Utah pioneer history. Scenic parks reveal the natural resources of our state, while preserving vistas, geologic formations, and fragile ecosystems for future generations to enjoy. Recreation parks provide access to lakes, reservoirs, dunes, campgrounds, day-use areas, trails, and golf courses. Utah's recreation parks provide year-round opportunities, including boating, off-highway vehicle riding, hiking, mountain biking, cross-country skiing, golf, wildlife viewing, and more.

Other Statutory Responsibilities

Utah State Parks has statutory responsibilities to (1) protect state parks, property, and visitors; (2) promote safety for persons and property related to boating and off-highway vehicles; and (3) protect the environment with respect to the use and operation of off-highway vehicles.[21]

To do this the division manages several statewide programs. The division administers the state boating program, off-highway vehicle programs, the Land and Water Conservation Fund, and grant programs for riverways and non-motorized trails.[22] The division has primary authority over boating safety on Utah's lakes, reservoirs, and rivers, and provides a program that offers user education and enforcement of laws and regulations. An all-terrain vehicle and snowmobile program educates users, and promotes safety and protection for people, property and the environment. Utah State Parks oversees statewide motorized and non-motorized trail programs, a recreation grants program, a large law enforcement program, and a state park reservation system.[23]

Boating Safety Program

The division administers the State Boating Act on Utah waters which includes safety, education, and enforcement.[24] This includes the personal watercraft operators education program for youth.

Utah boating law requires personal water craft operators between the ages of twelve to seventeen to receive education and certification.

Off-highway Vehicle Program

The division administers summer and winter off-highway vehicle programs including education, trail maintenance, grant programs, user compliance, accident investigation, and search and rescue.[25] Utah's off-highway vehicle education program instructs children between the ages of eight and sixteen.

Registered off-highway vehicles may be operated on public lands or roads that are signed or designated as open to off-highway vehicle use. Off-highway vehicle riding is not allowed in Utah State Parks, except for Coral Pink Sand Dunes State Park. The U.S. Forest Service, Bureau of Land Management, and other land managing agencies have travel maps indicating areas where off-highway vehicle use is permitted. The Off-highway Vehicle Advisory Council awards matching grants for motorized trail programs using money from the off-highway vehicle restricted account to develop multiple-use trails.

Riverway and Trail Projects

The Riverway Enhancement Advisory Council approves grant money for riverway projects.[26] Cities receive money to beautify trails and develop recreational areas along city rivers. The Utah Recreational Trails Advisory Council recommends matching grants for non-motorized trail projects.[27] These funds are available to any federal, state, or local government entity for the planning, acquisition, and development of recreational trails. This program includes the funds appropriated by the legislature for the Bonneville Shoreline Trail and Centennial Crossing Programs. The State Park's Board awards these grants at its fall meeting based on the recommendations of the Recreational Trails Advisory Council and the Division of Parks and Recreation.

DIVISION OF WATER RESOURCES

The Division of Water Resources has roots extending back to 1909 with the passage of an Act to Provide for a Utah State Conservation Commission to prevent waste of the natural resources in Utah.[28] In 1921, the legislature created the Utah Water Storage Commission to make investigations, looking to a full and proper development and utilization of Utah's water supply.[29] In 1941, the commission was abolished, and its powers and duties were given to the newly created Publicity and Industrial Development Department.[30]

In 1947, the legislature replaced the Publicity Department with the Utah Water and Power Board.[31] At the same time, the legislature implemented a Revolving Construction Fund to provide financial assistance for the construction of water development and conservation projects. This began the legacy of the state's participation in a self-help water development cooperative effort that continues to function today.[32]

With the creation of the DNR in 1967, the legislature dissolved the Water and Power Board and established the Board of Water Resources and the Division of Water Resources to administer the water development funding programs and the state's responsibilities in water resource matters.[33] The board has funded 1,268 water projects. The Water Resources Cities Water Loan Fund, with a $23.4 million principle balance, provides loans to municipalities and water districts to acquire or construct water systems. The Water Resources Construction Fund, with a $30.5 million principle balance, provides loans and grants to develop water conservation and dam projects. The Water Resources Conservation and Development Fund, with a principle balance of $158 million, is a revolving fund established for projects outside the scope of financing by the other funds.

The division acts as the technical advisor for water issues to the board and governor. The division's engineering staff provides technical help to project sponsors, local water suppliers and users, and other state agencies.

Interstate Streams

Geography, history, and national politics have a strong influence on water management in Utah. Drainage basins covering more than half the state are associated with interstate streams. Active participation on selected interstate and state and federal water bodies is essential to protect Utah's interests.

The 1,450 mile-long Colorado River and its tributaries flow through seven states from Colorado to the Gulf of California in Mexico. The rights of these seven states and Mexico to use Colorado River water are governed by a series of compacts. The Upper Basin states, involving Wyoming, Colorado, Utah, and New Mexico, and the Lower Basin states, including California, Nevada, and Arizona, are collectively entitled to an equal portion of Colorado River water in a normal year. In an effort to assure Utah their share of the Colorado River, Congress authorized the Central Utah Project which consisted of a series of diversion and storage dams, aqueducts, and tunnels.

Utah is part of an adaptive management work group of a federal advisory committee that recommends future releases from Glen Canyon Dam and Reservoir on the Colorado River. Those recommendations benefit downstream water users and the river's natural resources. Sufficient progress on the Upper Colorado River endangered fishes recovery program allows Central Utah Projects to continue in the Uintah Basin. The state also works on the Colorado River salinity control program and the annual operating plan for federal facilities on the Colorado River.

The Board of Water Resources, with the approval of the DNR executive director and the governor, designated the director of the Division of Water Resources as Utah's Interstate Streams Commissioner to represent Utah in all interstate conferences and meetings between the state and other compact states to divide interstate waters or to discuss interstate streams issues. The director represents the state on the Upper Colorado River Commission, Bear River Commission, Western States Water Council, Colorado River Basin Salinity Control Forum and Advisory Council, Glen Canyon Adaptive Management Work Group, and is the governor's representative to the Colorado River Management Group.

State Water Planning

The division is responsible to plan for and encourage the use of Utah's water resources to best serve the physical, economic, environmental, and social needs of the people of Utah.[34] The division helps local, state, and federal agencies coordinate water resources planning and development activities. It also maintains the State Water Plan which (1) identifies and quantifies existing and projected municipal, industrial, agricultural and environmental water use; (2) identifies and quantifies water supply sources and develops basin plans for each hydrologic area; and (3) identifies and discusses water-related principles, issues, and proposed recommendations.

Conservation and Education

The water conservation and education programs are focused on activities and programs to help Utahns reduce the per capita municipal and industrial water use of Utah residents.[35] Division efforts in water conservation and education include providing materials and teacher training in public schools; assisting the Governor's Water Conservation Team; working with local water agencies to develop and implement water conservation programs, including education of the general public as to how to use Utah's water wisely; and promoting modification of laws, ordinances, and regulations to promote efficient water use.

Weather Modification

The Division of Water Resources regulates cloud seeding in Utah and cost-shares with local cloud seeding projects. Technological advances are improving the efficiency of the process. In addition, added reservoir storage has increased the ability to store the additional snowpack for use later in the year. Statistical analysis of the cloud seeding program since 1976 has shown an average increase in precipitation of 8 to 20 percent in seeded areas at a cost of about $1 per acre-foot for the additional water.

Board of Water Resources and Water Development

The Board of Water Resources and the Division of Water Resources continue to administer the water development funding programs and the state's responsibilities in water resource matters.[36] The division acts as technical advisor to the board and governor. The board is comprised of eight members, each residing in the river district they represent. The board and staff manage three revolving funds established to build water development projects throughout the state. This self-help water development cooperative effort provides over $20 million annually to water users. The repayments help replenish the funds for future projects. Eligible project sponsors include political subdivisions of the state and incorporated entities such as irrigation companies and private mutual water companies. Typical projects the board funds include wells, pipelines, irrigation distribution systems, water tanks, water treatment plants, dams, and dam safety upgrades. The division's engineering staff can provide technical assistance, as requested, to water users and water suppliers throughout Utah.

DIVISION OF WATER RIGHTS

The Division of Water Rights administers water rights in the state. In 1897 the legislature created the State Engineer's Office.[37] The state engineer is the chief water rights administrative officer. This same year it enacted a new water statute establishing a specific procedure to appropriate water and other related provisions. Originally the office had only limited authority; however, over time the duties and responsibilities have become more clearly defined.

In the early territorial days, rights to the use of public streams of water were acquired by actual diversion and application of water to beneficial use, or by legislative grant. The system underwent a number of changes which shifted the administrative responsibility from the state to the county or local level.

In 1903, the first comprehensive water law was enacted.[38] It placed all water administration in the hands of the state engineer, including a new procedure for initiating water rights by application. To establish a water right, an application must be filed and approved by the state engineer. The state engineer was given general supervision of the waters of the state and of their measurement, apportionment and appropriation, with power to make rules and regulations, subject to review by the courts. In 1967 the State Engineer's Office was made a part of the DNR and the name was changed to the Division of Water Rights.[39]

Appropriations

The state engineer administers several types of water right applications including applications to appropriate water, to change the point of diversion, place or use of water, to file diligence and underground water claims, to resume the use of water, to segregate a water right and to renovate or replace a well.[40] A large percentage of the applications currently being filed are change applications, which are generally transferring irrigation water rights to domestic, municipal, or related uses. The Division of Water Rights maintains a record of all 180,000 water rights of record.

When federal lands are withdrawn or reserved for a specific purpose, unappropriated water will by implication be reserved in an amount sufficient to satisfy the purposes of the withdrawal or reservation. The water use entitlements of most federal reservations have not been determined or quantified, and private individuals who have acquired state-created water rights subsequent to the date of the federal reservations are subject to being divested by the prior federal reserved right.

Adjudication and Distribution

With Utah's limited water supplies and growing demands for water, the state engineer must seek new technology for water distribution and measurement to better manage, regulate and report how the water is used. The state engineer also oversees the distribution of water to water users on forty-five river/groundwater systems that are managed by water commissioners.

The state engineer also plays an integral part in the adjudication of water rights by investigating and updating water rights for each hydrologic area of the state under order by the district court.

Wells, Dams, and Studies

The state engineer has the statutory responsibility to license and regulate water well drillers in the state.[41] The office also inspects approximately four hundred dams annually to ensure safety and public health. A major initiative is underway to rehabilitate the older dams in order to meet current safety standards.[42]

The state engineer also administers natural stream alterations according to the Utah Code and the terms of a general permit from U.S. Army Corps of Engineers.[43] Finally, proper management of water resources requires vital data and information. The division cooperates with other agencies and water users to collect basic data and conduct investigative water resource studies.

DIVISION OF WILDLIFE RESOURCES

The Division of Wildlife Resources is the wildlife authority for Utah charged with protecting, propagating, and managing protected wildlife throughout Utah and is subject to the broad policy-making authority of a seven-member Wildlife Board.[44]

Wildlife Board

Traditionally two separate boards, the Board of Fish and Game and the Board of Big Game Control, established season dates and all rules governing hunting, fishing, and trapping.[45] The legislature consolidated the two boards into a single, seven-member Utah Wildlife Board in the early 1990s.[46] Board members must have experience in wildlife and habitat management or knowledge of recreational wildlife issues.

The division determines facts relevant to the wildlife resources upon which the board establishes the policies best designed to accomplish the preservation and management of wildlife. In establishing policy, the Wildlife Board recognizes that wildlife and its habitat are an essential part of a healthy, productive environment. The board attempts to balance the habitat requirements of wildlife, social and economic activities of society, and the social and economic value of wildlife, including fishing and hunting.

There are also five Regional Advisory Councils, consisting of twelve to fifteen members, from each wildlife region.[47] Members represent agriculture, sportsmen, non-consumptive wildlife interests, locally elected public officials, and federal land agencies. These councils hear recommendations, biological data, and information regarding the effects of wildlife and make recommendations to the Wildlife Board in an advisory capacity.

Organization

The Division of Wildlife Resources consists of a Salt Lake administrative office and five regional offices in Vernal, Ogden, Springville, Price, and Cedar City. For law enforcement purposes, Utah is divided into districts, with conservation officers assigned to each district. For management purposes, the division is divided into six sections with section chiefs and staff headquartered in the Salt Lake City office.

Hunting and Fishing

The division sells hunting and fishing licenses and publishes rules for wildlife-related activities. The division sells over 650,000 hunting and fishing licenses and permits each year. This generates an annual economic impact of $598 million of fishing expenditures and $306 million of hunting related expenditures. Further, wildlife watchers that are not required to purchase hunting and fishing licenses expend another $555.7 million in expenditures for equipment and supplies.[48] These activities make wildlife related expenditures one of the top outdoor related industries in Utah. In recent years, the division has created urban fisheries around the Wasatch Front to provide citizens who could not otherwise easily leave urban areas a chance to participate in fishing activities. It also releases birds to provide more opportunity for upland game hunters.

Habitat Section

The Habitat Section manages fish and wildlife habitat on public land and provides support and expertise to private landowners who wish to create or enhance essential habitat on private land.[49] This involves conservation, enhancement, and rehabilitation of fish and wildlife habitat. The section is also involved in both public and private land use planning and environmental assessments related to the responsible management of growth and development throughout Utah.

Aquatics Section

The Aquatics Section is responsible for the management, conservation, and enhancement of all fishery resources in Utah. The section provides a healthy and diverse sport fishery for citizens. It operates ten state fish hatcheries, stocking up to ten million trout in Utah waters annually. The section also strives to keep fish and aquatic wildlife off the federal threatened and endangered species list by conserving or expanding the range of rare, threatened, and endangered indigenous fish species.

Wildlife Section

The Wildlife Section is responsible for the management and conservation of all terrestrial wildlife in Utah, including big game; small and upland game; waterfowl and migratory birds; mammals such as cougar, otters, and black bears; and raptors, such as eagles and peregrine falcons.[50] The big game program coordinator monitors deer, elk, and other big game species populations and recommends permit numbers and hunt strategies designed to maintain and increase quality hunting opportunities.

Law Enforcement

The Law Enforcement Section works to ensure the protection of Utah's wildlife through the enforcement of all wildlife laws, regulations and proclamations as established by the legislature and the Wildlife Board.[51] The section also manages and administers the statewide Hunter Education Program.[52]

Conservation Outreach

The Conservation Outreach Section provides information and education support for the division.[53] The section is responsible for media outreach efforts such as news releases, video coverage, radio and TV programs, the Wildlife Review magazines, and an interactive website. Project WILD trains and provides required wildlife education curricula to hundreds of K-12 Utah teachers annually. The section also manages and administers the statewide Dedicated Hunter Program.[54]

Major Challenges

Many challenges face the division over the next several years. Urbanization and drought have contributed to habitat loss and degradation that continues to be the single greatest problem facing all wildlife in Utah. The Habitat Initiative, created in 2002, is an effort to rehabilitate up to a million acres of sagebrush-steppe and other essential wildlife habitat over the next twenty years.[55]

UTAH GEOLOGICAL SURVEY

In 1931, the legislature created the Utah Geological and Mineralogical Survey (UGMS). The governor appointed an advisory board, but no funding was appropriated for salaries or operations, and no personnel were assigned to the survey. Geological survey work was carried out by staff of the University of Utah Engineering Experiment Station until 1941, when the UGMS and various other state agencies were placed in the newly created "Utah State Department of Publicity and Industrial Development" (UPID). In 1949, the state disbanded the UPID, and the UGMS was transferred to the State School of Mines and Mineral Industries at the University of Utah.

The legislature then established the Utah Geological Survey in 1967 under the DNR to provide information about Utah's geological environment.[56] Utah has a rich geological spectrum encompassing parts of the Colorado Plateau with flat sedimentary buttes, mesas, and narrow canyons; the Basin and Range with steep, narrow, north-treading mountain ranges separated by wide, flat sediment-filled valleys; and the Middle Rocky Mountains, high mountains with sharp ridge lines and U-shaped valleys carved by streams and glaciers.

The Utah Geological Survey Board

The seven-member Board of the Utah Geological Survey is the policy-making body for the Utah Geological Survey.[57] Board members, appointed by the governor, represent a cross-section of the geological industry in Utah. The present board composition includes representatives from the following sectors: metal mining, oil and gas exploration, coal mining, engineering geology, industrial minerals, academia, and a public-at-large person who represents earth science education. The director of School and Institutional Trust Lands has an *ex officio* position on the board.

The board establishes policies, programs, and priorities based on the needs of the community with regard to the development and use of geologic resources. Organized into five technical programs, the survey investigates energy and mineral resources, identifies geological hazards, maps Utah's geology, evaluates groundwater resources, monitors Utah's archeological and paleontological sites, and evaluates environmental changes. The Utah Geological Survey also operates the Utah Core Research Center containing borehole cuttings and core from over thirty-five hundred holes as a result of oil and gas exploration in Utah.

Energy and Minerals Program

The Energy and Mineral Program inventories mineral and energy resources in Utah to facilitate responsible development.[58]

In addition to managing the Core Research Center, the program maintains databases on Utah's past and present resource development activities, and responds to requests for information about the state's energy and mineral resources from individuals, government agencies, and industry.

Geological Hazards Program

The Geological Hazards Program investigates geological hazards, such as earthquakes, landslides, and radon hazards.[59] Hundreds of small earthquakes are recorded each year in Utah.

While most occur in the Intermountain Seismic Belt running between the Basin and Range to the west and the Middle Rocky Mountains and the Colorado Plateau to the east, the Wasatch Fault presents the greatest earthquake hazard because of its length and proximity to the majority of Utah's residents.

The program responds to requests from government agencies upon request for engineering-geologic investigations and report reviews. The program assists local and state government agencies in planning, zoning, and building regulation by delineating special earthquake risk areas, and reviewing the siting of critical facilities. The program responds to geologic hazard emergencies and compiles geologic hazard maps.

Geological Mapping Program

The Geological Mapping Program maps Utah's geology describing the stratigraphy, structure, geological hazards, bedrock and surficial geology, economic and groundwater resources, and scenic geological resources.[60] The program provides geologic maps to geologists, government agencies, industry, and the public to promote better understanding of Utah's geology, delineate the resource protection of property, and assess geologic hazards. These maps also help describe the potential economic value of property and facilitate wise land-use decisions.

Groundwater and Paleontology Program

The Groundwater and Paleontology Program provides state government and the public with information and detailed studies on Utah's groundwater resources and paleontology resources.[61] Projects include water well siting and cuttings analyses; groundwater contamination analysis; drinking-water source-protection area delineation; geologic framework of aquifers and hydrologic basins; and paleontological locality database, fossil recovery, and analysis. The program publishes records of Utah's fossil resources, provides paleontological and archaeological recovery services to state and local government, and conducts studies of environmental change to aid resource management.

Geologic Information and Outreach

The Geological Information and Outreach Program answers questions and provides information on Utah's geology to the public, educators, industry, and decision makers.[62] It produces non-technical and geologic-overview publications on a variety of topics including geologic guides to various areas of geologic hazards and resources.

The program operates the Natural Resources Map and Bookstore and the DNR library, both of which are Earth Science Information Centers, affiliates of the U.S. Geological Survey, and maintains the Utah Geological Survey and Map and Bookstore Web sites.

RECOVERY PROGRAMS

In 1998, the legislature authorized and funded the Endangered Species Mitigation Fund (ESMF) to allow the DNR to participate in several recovery programs that recover listed species.[63] The ESMF can also be used to restore state sensitive species. In addition to administering the fund the DNR works with counties, water and other resource users, and federal agencies to help public and private groups comply with or resolve issues related to the Endangered Species Act.

PROPERTY RIGHTS OMBUDSMAN

The state employs an ombudsman to assist its citizens in resolving property rights disputes with local government officials and state agencies.[64] The ombudsman analyzes actions with potential takings implications and advises private property owners who have a legitimate potential or actual takings claim against a state or local government entity. The ombudsman may also mediate or conduct arbitration for disputes between private property owners and government entities that involve takings or eminent domain issues.

Chapter 18

Public Safety, Criminal Law, and Corrections

CRIME RATES IN UTAH, THE MOUNTAIN STATES, AND THE NATION

Crime in Utah and in the United States has declined significantly over the past decade. *Crime State Rankings 2005* shows Utah as the seventeenth safest state, as determined by giving equal weight to rates for the offenses of murder, rape, robbery, aggravated assault, burglary, and motor vehicle theft.[1] The sum of these offense rankings places Utah's crime rate well below the national average.[2]

> **In this chapter:**
>
> Crime Rates in Utah, the Mountain States, and the Nation (p. 267)
> Criminal Offenses (p. 270)
> Sentencing by the Court (p. 270)
> Board of Pardons and Parole (p. 271)
> Department of Corrections (p. 272)
> Juvenile Justice Services (p. 275)
> Department of Public Safety (p. 276)

Utah does, however, have a higher than average rate for larceny (commonly known as theft), which accounts for nearly three-quarters of the state's total index crime rate.[3] The index crime rate, a different measuring mechanism, is a measurement that includes larceny and arson, in addition to murder, rape, robbery, aggravated assault, burglary, and motor vehicle theft.[4] As a result, the index crime rate for Utah is higher than the national average (see figure 18-1).[5] As of 2003, Utah had the eighteenth highest index crime rate in the United States.[6] Utah's overall index crime rate in 2003 was 4,474 offenses per 100,000 persons[7] compared to the national average index crime rate of 4,063 offenses per 100,000 persons during the same period of time.[8] These rates are the lowest rates in Utah and in the United States since 1972 (see figure 18-1).[9]

When analyzing crime statistics separately in terms of violent offenses and property offenses, both Utah and national violent crime rates steadily declined over the past several years. Even so, the national violent crime rate is more than double Utah's very low violent crime rate.[10] However, Utah has a disproportionately high rate of property crimes which include burglary, larceny, motor vehicle theft, arson, and damage or destruction of property.

Figure 18-1

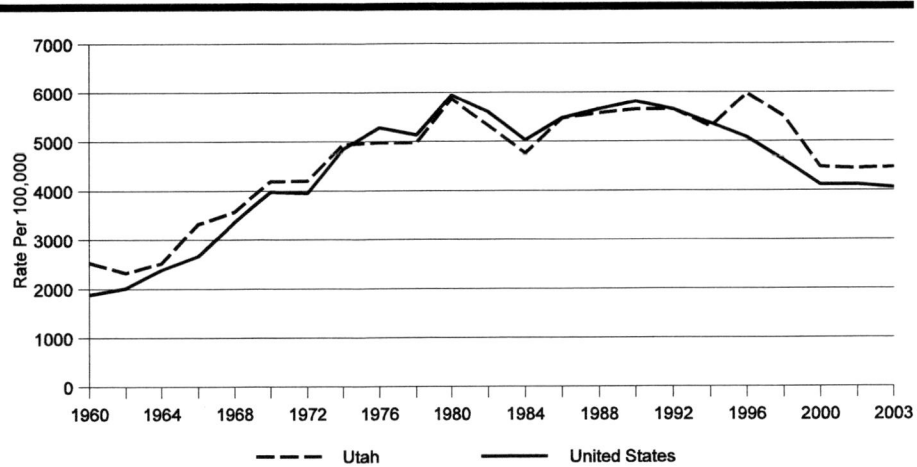

Figure 18-2

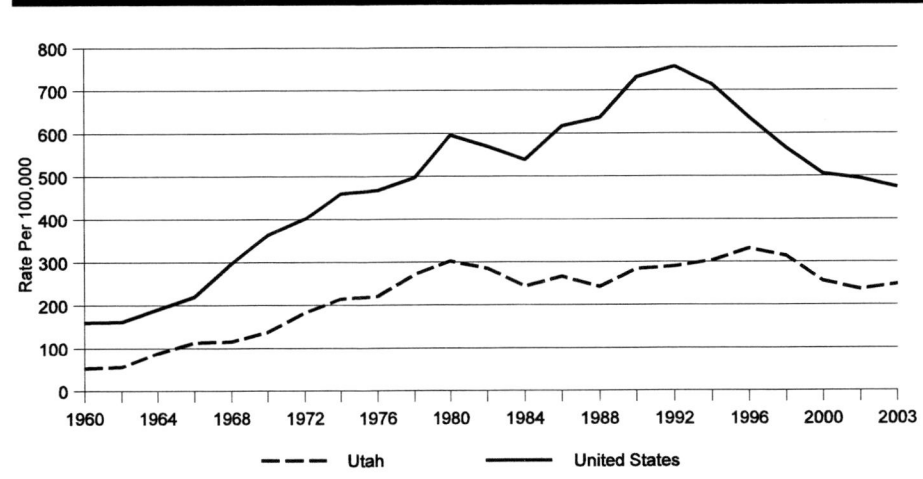

Figure 18-3

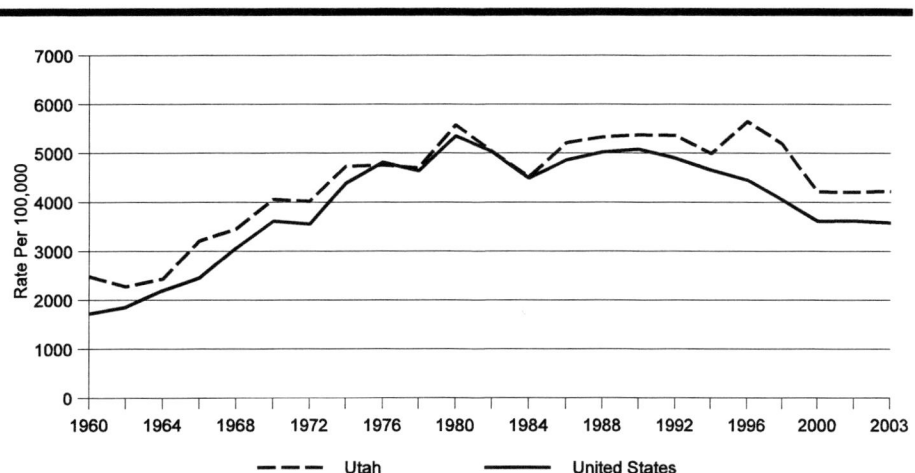

In 2003, Utah ranked fourth in its overall crime rate compared to the other Mountain States.[11] Compared to states of similar population, between 1.7 and 3.0 million people, Utah ranked fifth of nine states[12] in overall crime rate statistics.[13]

While Utah's crime index rate decreased over 27 percent between 1995 and 2003, the incarceration rate (number of people in prison per 100,000 population) has increased 38.7 percent during the same period (see figure 18-4).[14] Utah's incarceration rate as of midyear 2004 was the ninth lowest in the United States, at 239 per 100,000, and also the lowest in the Western States.[15] During this same period, the national average incarceration rate was 486 per 100,000 (see figure 18-4).[16]

Figure 18-4

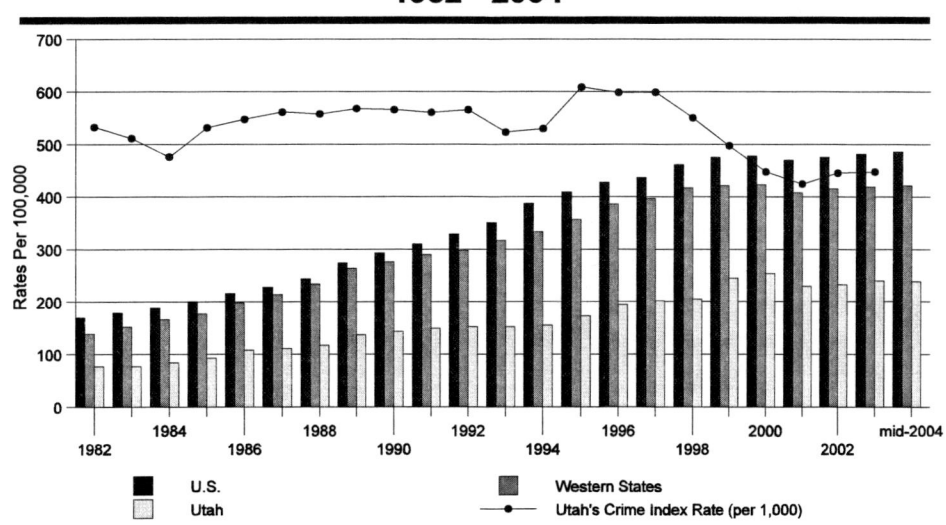

CRIMINAL OFFENSES

Utah's Criminal Code is in Title 76 of the Utah Code.[17] Utah's penalty structure is described in table 18-1.

Table 18-1

Utah's Penalty Structure

Penalty	Fine Not Exceeding	Incarceration
Infraction	$750	No incarceration
Class C misdemeanor	$750	Not to exceed 90 days
Class B misdemeanor	$1,000	Not to exceed 6 months
Class A misdemeanor	$2,500	Not to exceed 1 year
Third degree felony	$5,000	Not to exceed 5 years, but with enhancements for use of a dangerous weapon
Second degree felony	$10,000	Not less than 1 year, and not more than 15 years, but with enhancements for use of a dangerous weapon
First degree felony	$10,000	Not less than 5 years, unless otherwise provided by statute, and up to life
Capital felony	$10,000	Death penalty or life in prison without parole

Corporations, associations, partnerships, government, or governmental instrumentalities are subject to greater fines.[18]

A capital felony in Utah is subject to a sentence of life in prison without parole or the death penalty. In Utah, the death penalty is imposed by lethal injection. Until recently a defendant could elect a firing squad, but this option was repealed in the 2004 General Session, with very limited exceptions for persons on death row at the time the law was passed. Aggravated murder is a capital felony; the elements of the offense are listed in Section 76-5-202 of the Utah Code. Utah does not impose the death penalty for a capital offense if the defendant is determined to be mentally retarded or to have subaverage general intellectual functioning, as defined by statute.[19]

Additional criminal offenses are listed in areas other than Title 76 of the Utah Code when the offense is directly relevant to the specific subject matter of the offense, such as election, environment, and wildlife laws.

SENTENCING BY THE COURT

Utah uses an indeterminate sentencing structure. Under this type of sentencing structure, a judge sentences an offender to prison for a range of time based on the penalty for the offense, rather than a specific amount of time.[20] For example, unless the statute provides otherwise, a person convicted of a first degree felony will be sentenced to a term of between five years and life imprisonment, a second degree felony carries a sentence of between one year and fifteen years, and the sentence for a third degree felony cannot exceed five years. Once incarcerated, the Board of Pardons and Parole then determines how long the offender will actually remain in prison.

The judge also has the option to impose probation in lieu of jail or prison, except when imposing sentence for certain violent offenses and specified offenses against children. In these cases the authority to sentence the offender to probation or to limit the sentence is severely limited.[21]

If the judge is sentencing a defendant for a misdemeanor, the judge establishes the term of any jail time to be served, within the time frame set by statute for the offense. A judge may not sentence an offender to parole. Parole is served after the offender is released from prison and probation is imposed in lieu of jail or prison. If the conditions of either probation or parole are violated, the offender may be sent or returned to jail or prison. An offender usually serves time in a jail if the sentence is one year or less. Prisons serve offenders sentenced to more than one year. However, as discussed later in this chapter, some offenders incarcerated for more than one year may serve time in a jail under the supervision of the Department of Corrections.

Utah Sentencing Commission

The Utah Sentencing Commission is required to develop sentencing guidelines and to make recommendations to the legislature, the governor, and the Judicial Council for the sentencing of juvenile and adult offenders.[22] These guidelines, which are usually updated annually, help to increase equity in criminal sentencing while preserving the discretion of sentencing judges and the role of the Board of Pardons and Parole and the Youth Parole Authority as they make the final decisions on sentencing and releasing offenders. The guidelines provide a frame of reference and a tool. Departure from the guidelines may be made based on aggravating and mitigating factors which, considered with the defendant's history, may be used to increase or reduce the severity of the sentence.

The Utah Sentencing Commission has twenty-seven members and includes legislators, judges, prosecutors, defenders, representatives of law enforcement, rehabilitation treatment professionals, and governmental agencies, including the executive directors of the Board of Pardons and Parole, Department of Corrections, Juvenile Justice Services, and Commission on Criminal and Juvenile Justice.

BOARD OF PARDONS AND PAROLE

The Board of Pardons and Parole[23] is an independent entity within the executive branch.[24] The board has jurisdiction over all offenders committed to the Department of Corrections and makes decisions regarding the length of incarceration, parole supervision, termination of sentence, commutation of sentence, and pardons.[25] The board consists of five full-time members and five *pro tempore* members. The members are appointed by the governor with the consent of the senate, and serve terms of five years. The Commission on Criminal and Juvenile Justice recommends five applicants to the governor, and in selecting these applications shall "consider applicants' knowledge of the criminal justice system, state and federal criminal law, judicial procedure, corrections policies and procedures, and behavioral sciences."[26]

As discussed earlier, Utah uses an indeterminate sentencing structure.[27] The Board of Pardons and Parole then has the obligation of determining when, within this time period, incarcerated individuals should be released.[28]

Within six months of the offender's commitment, the board is required to establish a date for a parole hearing.[29] Before being released, the board is required to interview the offender to consider whether the offender is fit for release.[30] During the hearing, the board receives information from a number of sources to assist with its decision. This information may include reports from mental health experts, victim testimony, information about the offender, and information about the crime committed. In addition, the judge who imposed the sentence may write a statement that sets out the term the judge thinks the offender should serve and the reasons for that decision.[31] The prosecutor is required to produce a full and complete description of the crime; a written record of any plea bargain; a statement of mitigating or aggravating factors; all investigative reports; a victim impact statement which describes the physical, mental, or economic loss suffered by the victim; and any other information the prosecutor believes is relevant to the board's decision.

The board then makes its decision as to when, within the statutorily specified time frame, the offender shall be released, and if the offender is to be granted parole. The board is encouraged to make decisions that are compatible with the sentencing guidelines, except where there are aggravating and mitigating factors. The board's decision is final and cannot be appealed.[32]

The board may grant an offender parole, which means the offender is released from prison prior to serving the maximum term for the offense. Offenders released on parole are subject to the conditions set by the board and are monitored by a parole officer. If the offender violates a term of his parole, the board may revoke the parole status and order the offender to be returned to prison.[33]

DEPARTMENT OF CORRECTIONS

The Utah Department of Corrections (UDC) is supervised by an executive director who is appointed by the governor with the consent of the senate. The director shall be "experienced and knowledgeable in the field of corrections and shall have training in criminology and penology."[34] The department operates correctional facilities, intermediate or "half-way" facilities, and probation and parole services. As funding allows, the department also provides programs for offenders, including work programs and mental health programs. The department's statutory functions, including the correctional industry program, are codified in Title 64, State Institutions, of the Utah Code. The department also provides the community with victim services which are listed at www.udc.state.ut.us/community/victimservices and a searchable online sex offender registry at www.udc.state.ut.us/community/sexoffenders.

Figure 18-5

Department of Corrections

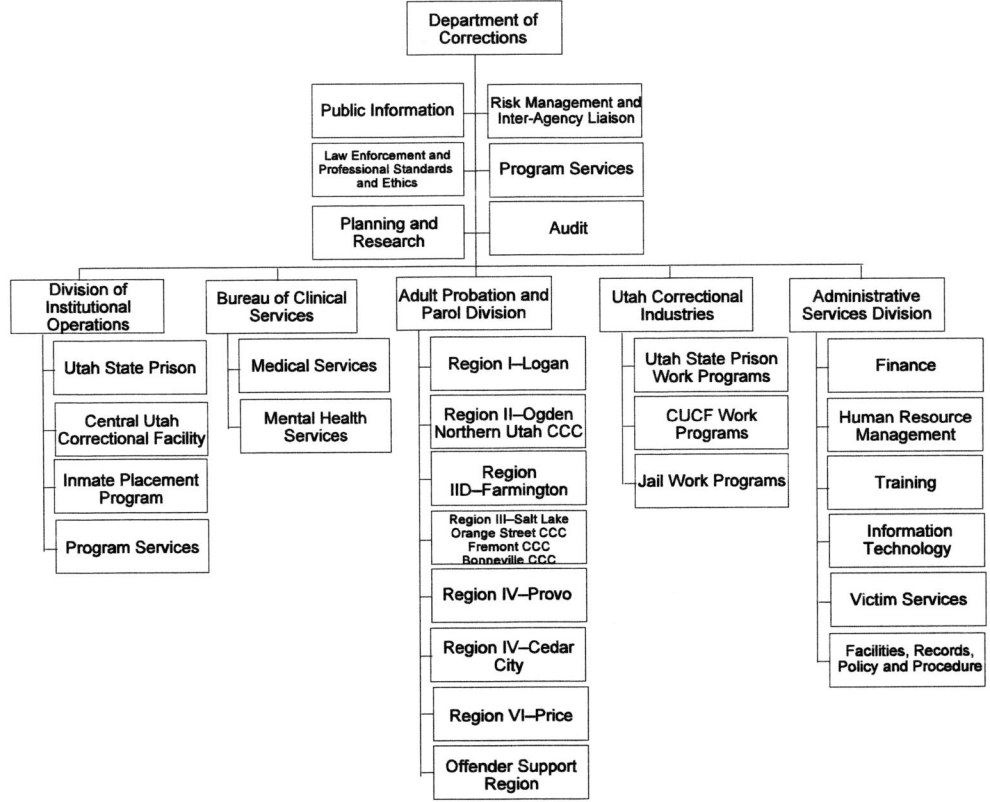

272 • *Public Safety, Criminal Law, and Corrections*

Division of Institutional Operations

The Division of Institutional Operations (DIO) manages the inmate populations in the two state prison facilities and provides oversight of inmates housed in county jail facilities under contract with the state. DIO is also responsible for inmate training, treatment, employment counseling, and education.

Bureau of Clinical Services

The Bureau of Clinical Services provides medical, dental, and mental health care to those incarcerated by the state and ensures these services comply with federal requirements. Treatment is provided by doctors, dentists, nurses, mental health professionals, and aides employed by the department in its facilities or by contract for those housed in contracted facilities.

Adult Probation and Parole

The Adult Probation and Parole Division (AP&P) provides support to the UDC in managing community corrections centers (half-way houses), private treatment contracts, pre-release processes, and in supervising the adult probation and parole population assigned to the department. AP&P also has responsibility for obtaining DNA specimens from offenders, managing the sex offender registry, and providing pre-sentence investigations for the courts.

Utah Correctional Industries

Utah Correctional Industries (UCI) provides work experience and training for inmates to increase their potential for success after being released from prison. The UCI enterprises are self-supporting from the sales of products and services that include: manufacturing of furniture, license plates, and signs; printing; computer refurbishing; data entry and microfilming; community work crews; asbestos abatement; commercial sewing; dairy operations and meat processing; electronics and waste recycling; commissary services; and roofing and construction.

Administrative Services Division

The Administrative Services Division provides management and technical support services to the other divisions in the department to assist them in meeting their statutory missions. The division is responsible for records and facilities management, policies and procedures, information technology, research and planning, audits, human resources, and finance.

Funding

An important trend in corrections is the impact these programs have on state budgets. Corrections is consistently one of the largest single appropriations within Utah's general fund budget. This is not unusual among states.[35] In fiscal year 2006, corrections was third largest of twenty-one categories of general fund appropriations.

Utah funds approximately 90 percent of its corrections budget with general fund monies. The balance consists of dedicated credits, and federal and other funds.[36] The department's appropriated programs and operations budget for fiscal year 2006 was $156,246,600. Utah's total appropriated fiscal year 2006 annual budget for the department was $221,104,200, of which $199,520,700 was general fund money,[37] or about 13 percent of the state's total general fund appropriations.[38] Considering Utah's population and crime rate, the percentage of general funds spent on corrections is consistent with the national average.[39]

Incarceration Rates

One reason corrections continues to demand such a large portion of the state budget is the annual average incarcerated population has continually grown over the past twenty years. The average daily incarceration population for 2004 was 5,875 offenders (see figure 18-6).[40] The average population dropped significantly in July 2001 due to an early release program instigated by the department. While this program had a short-term effect of decreasing the demand for beds in the system, the early release program is not feasible on a long-term basis. The offenders considered for early release were from a finite pool of nonviolent second and third degree felons who were charged with drug and property offenses and who had a parole date already set.[41] As a result of the early release program the number of inmates stabilized for approximately one year. However, the number of inmates continues to rise, and at a faster rate than the state population. In 1983, the incarceration rate was 77 per 100,000 population, but by 2004, the rate was 239 per 100,000 population.[42] In 2004 the United States' rate per 100,000 population was 486, and the western states' rate was 421 (see figure 18-4).

Figure 18-6

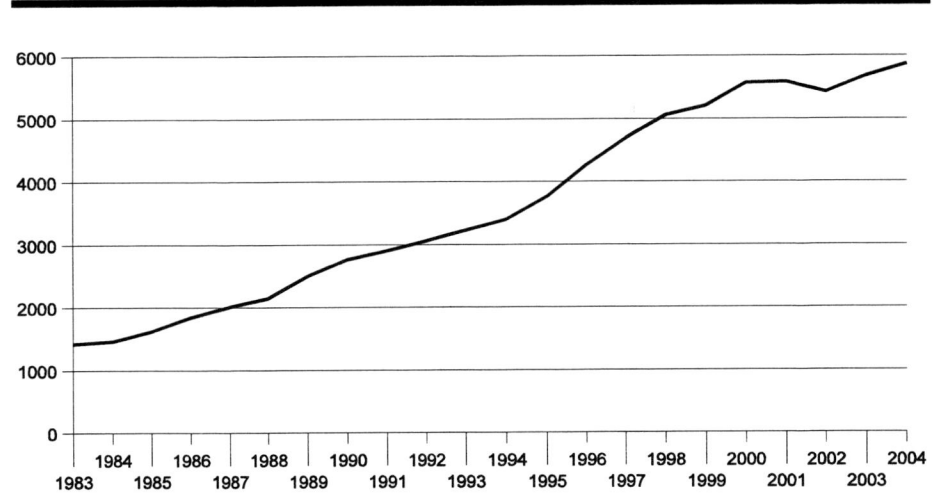

To avoid capital costs and to facilitate the growing number of incarcerated individuals, the department contracts with county jails to house inmates in the county jails rather than in either of the two state prisons. Currently, the department houses approximately 20 percent of the total incarcerated population in county jails through the jail reimbursement program.[43] Twenty of Utah's twenty-six counties with county jails participate in the jail reimbursement program.[44] The department is statutorily required to reimburse counties for 70 percent of the cost to house a felony offender sentenced to jail as a condition of parole.[45] This program benefits the department, the counties, and the inmates. The department saves on infrastructure costs and is able to manage inmates in smaller groups, counties have a labor force for community projects and greater community and economic development through increased jobs, and inmates may be housed closer to family and community ties.[46] If the department expanded the prisons to accommodate this population the cost would exceed $39 million just for construction expenses.[47]

Utah has two prisons. The Utah State Prison is located in Draper, in Salt Lake County, and has capacity for 3,970 inmates. The Utah Correctional Facility is located in Gunnison, which is in Sanpete County, and has a capacity for 1,125 inmates.

JUVENILE JUSTICE SERVICES

The Division of Juvenile Justice Services is located within the Department of Human Services and is responsible for all youth offenders committed to it by juvenile courts for secure confinement or for supervision and treatment in the community.[48] The division administers a continuum of community, secure, and nonsecure programs for these youth offenders.[49]

The division also provides, through its Youth Services, temporary custody, care, risk-needs assessments, evaluations, and control for youth who have not been adjudicated or found by the court to have committed a crime, but who are receiving division services because of behavior issues, family difficulties such as running away, or minor criminal conduct.[50]

The division also operates prevention and early intervention youth services programs. The division must ensure that youth who are receiving services under these programs and who are not in the custody of the division are served separately from youth who are in custody of the division.[51] As part of its programs, the division operates compensatory-service work programs for youth offenders that provide rehabilitation, education, and restitution to victims.

Within the division is the Youth Parole Authority, which is comprised of ten part-time members and five pro tempore members who are residents of Utah. The authority determines appropriate parole dates for youth offenders, based on guidelines established by the Board of Juvenile Justice Services.[52]

A youth offender who has been committed to a secure facility remains in secure confinement until the youth offender reaches the age of twenty-one, is paroled, or is discharged by the division. The committed youth offender is required to appear before the authority within ninety days after commitment for review of treatment plans and establishment of parole release guidelines.[53]

Youth offenders may be paroled upon specified conditions. The parole may be to the offender's own home, to a residential community-based program, to a nonresidential community-based treatment program, or to other appropriate residences. The youth offender remains on parole, regardless of the location, until parole is terminated by the authority. The division supervises youth offenders on parole. The authority may revoke parole upon a finding that the youth offender violated the conditions of parole.[54]

The division also has authority to discharge a youth offender from the division's jurisdiction at any time if it finds that no further purpose is served by secure confinement or community supervision of the youth offender. Any discharge must be in accordance with policies established by the Board of Juvenile Justice Services.[55]

DEPARTMENT OF PUBLIC SAFETY

The Department of Public Safety provides a number of essential services for the citizens of Utah. The director of the department is the commissioner of public safety. The commissioner is appointed by the governor with the consent of the senate and serves for a term of four years.[56] The commissioners's powers and duties include cooperating with appropriate agencies in applying for and distributing highway safety program funds and receiving and distributing federal funding to further the objectives of highway safety.[57]

Figure 18-7 outlines the department's divisions and bureaus.

Figure 18-7

Department of Public Safety

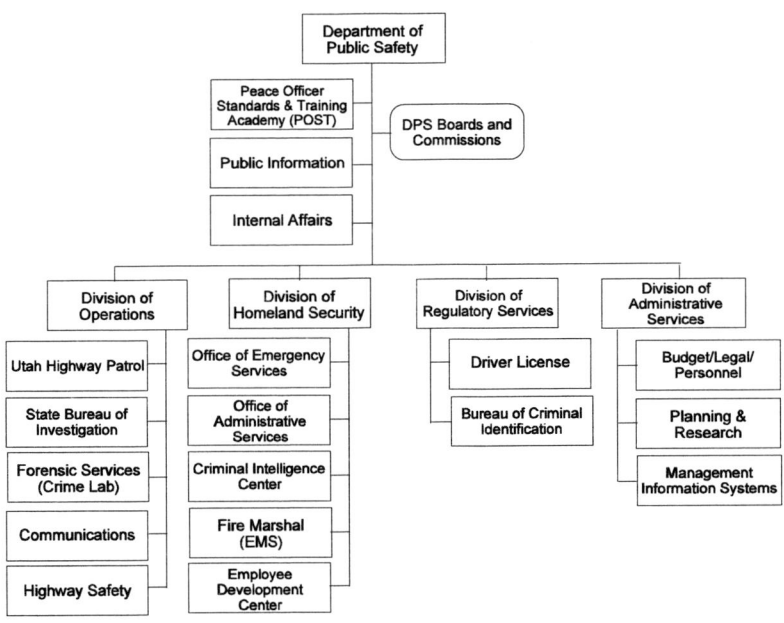

Division of Operations

The Division of Operations oversees the Utah Highway Patrol Division and functions in direct support of the Highway Patrol. The division director is referred to as the "superintendent" and is appointed by the public safety commissioner, with the approval of the governor.[58]

The superintendent's duties include:
- Dividing the state highways into sections for patrolling
- Conducting, with the State Board of Education, a school campaign in highway safety
- Working with community organizations to promote highway safety and reduction of highway accidents

Utah Highway Patrol

The Division of Operations employs "troopers," who are trained peace officers. The troopers carry out the patrolling and policing services provided by the Utah Highway Patrol. Troopers may serve criminal process, and also arrest and prosecute violators of state law.

Statutory duties of the Highway Patrol include:
- Enforcing state laws governing use of the state highways
- Regulating traffic on all highways and roads of the state

- Assisting the governor in an emergency or at other times at the governor's discretion
- Providing security and protection for the governor
- In cooperation with federal, state, and local agencies, enforcing and assisting in the enforcement of all state and federal laws related to the operation of motor carriers in Utah
- Inspecting a vehicle if questions arise regarding the vehicle's safety inspection compliance
- Providing security and protection for the state legislature while in session
- Providing security and protection for the Utah Supreme Court and the Court of Appeals when those courts are in session in Salt Lake City

The Highway Patrol supervises the state vehicle safety inspection program and provides permits to authorized inspection stations. The Highway Patrol also conducts the safety inspections of public and private school buses.

Communications Bureau

The Bureau manages six regional consolidated emergency communications centers. These regional dispatch centers provide emergency communications services and general information to law enforcement, fire and emergency medical responders, and the general public. Five of these centers are enhanced 911 public safety answering points for federal, state, and local government agencies.

Bureau of Forensic Services

This bureau is a full-service crime laboratory system assisting law enforcement agencies and prosecutors in analyzing evidence taken from the crime scenes across Utah. The staff also provides extensive training to law enforcement officers and prosecutors from across the state in crime scene investigation, and evidence collection and preservation.[59]

Highway Safety Office

The Highway Safety Office is the collection point for federal highway safety funds coming into Utah. The office focuses on driver behavioral issues, and provides educational and informational campaigns, such as "Click It or Ticket" for seat belt use, and "You Drink and Drive. You Lose" for impaired driving prevention. The office also promotes safe driving and prevention of highway fatalities by funding extra shifts for law enforcement officers to focus on highway safety enforcement.

State Bureau of Investigation

The State Bureau of Investigation supports several multi-jurisdictional task forces throughout the state working to enforce laws and prevent crimes in the areas of the Internet, gangs, narcotics, alcohol, organized crime, and financial crimes.[60]

Division of Homeland Security

The Division of Homeland Security coordinates emergency management efforts between federal, state, and local governments. These efforts involve preparedness, recovery, response, and mitigation. The division investigates and responds to security threats and intelligence information.[61]

Emergency Services

This office provides functions relating to the planning for and mitigation of potential disasters and emergencies.

State Fire Marshal
This division enforces fire prevention and fire safety rules in public buildings, examines plans for school buildings, promotes fire education, and regulates use of liquified petroleum gas and other combustible materials.

Criminal Intelligence Center
This office collects and disseminates intelligence information.

Administrative Services
This office handles grant management, legal issues, human resources, information technology, facilities, and finance.

Employee Development Center
The center provides ongoing professional development and training for all employees in the department. The center also works with institutions of higher education to centralize and coordinate training for department employees.

Division of Regulatory Services
The Division of Regulatory Services includes:

Driver License Division
The division issues and takes action regarding driving permits and licenses, and maintains records relating to these functions.[62]

Bureau of Criminal Identification
The Bureau of Criminal Identification (BCI) manages the Utah Criminal Justice Information System which is a secure Internet database that provides prosecutors, courts, and law enforcement access to information on suspects, offenders, and prisoners. BCI also links Utah's data into national databases. Other duties of the bureau include:
- Licensing bail bond providers and private investigators
- Conducting handgun purchase background checks as required by the federal Handgun Violence Protection Act
- Issuing concealed firearm permits
- Operating the Automated Fingerprint Identification System which provides fingerprint identification services to law enforcement and certain other agencies in Utah
- Compiling Utah's crime statistics
- Expunging criminal records in accordance with state law
- Providing a Missing Person Clearinghouse that coordinates investigations of missing children, including use of the Amber Alert, providing a toll-free line regarding missing persons, and coordinating and providing assistance in efforts to locate missing persons[63]

Division of Administrative Services
The division provides support services for the department.

Budget, Legal, and Personnel Management contains the functions of budgeting, accounting, legal support, and personnel management.

Planning and Research provides these functions for the department.

Management Information Services provides technical support services for all law enforcement agencies in the state. The division has access to the National Crime Information Center and works with the FBI and the National Law Enforcement and Telecommunication Systems.

Peace Officers Standards and Training Academy

Peace Officers Standards and Training Academy (POST) provides training and certification for peace officers and conducts investigations of allegations of peace officer misconduct.[64] In addition, a twenty-week training course known as the Police Corps Program is hosted by the department and provided by POST. It is federally funded and is intended to address violent crime. The program provides law enforcement training scholarships on a competitive basis to college students who agree to serve as community patrol officers for at least four years after graduation. Police Corps graduates become members of the participating law enforcement agencies in areas of the state having the greatest need for additional police officers.

Chapter 19

Regulation of Public Utilities

Utah's public utility regulatory process includes three statutorily authorized entities: the Public Service Commission, the Division of Public Utilities, and the Committee of Consumer Services in the Department of Commerce.

In this chapter:

Public Service Commission (p. 281)
Division of Public Utilities (p. 282)
Committee of Consumer Services (p. 282)
Electrical Deregulation (p. 282)
Electric Energy Rates (p. 283)
Natural Gas Price Comparison (p. 283)

PUBLIC SERVICE COMMISSION

Utah, like other states, regulates public utilities to address the common issue of monopoly suppliers setting prices without the checks that a competitive marketplace provides. The Public Service Commission (PSC) was created by the legislature in 1917 and given jurisdiction over every public utility in the state.[1] The utility regulatory process was designed to balance the lack of competition and serve two purposes: consumers would receive reliable and fairly priced utility services; and utility investors would receive a fair rate of return. The legislature in the Utah Code, Title 54, Public Utilities Statutes and Public Service Commission Rules, authorized the Public Service Commission to regulate utility rates and services.

The commission operates as an independent state agency with three members nominated by the governor and confirmed by the senate. The commissioners are statutorily charged with exercising legislative, adjudicative, and rulemaking powers in the area of public utility regulation.[2] In practice, the commission conducts its hearings in a quasi-judicial manner by requiring testimony and record-keeping to determine the facts in rate cases and controversies.[3]

For example, a utility company seeking a rate increase would file a request with the commission. The commission would then conduct public hearings where they determine the utility's revenue requirements, the responsibility for revenue requirements among the different consumer classes such as residential and commercial, and the appropriate rate for each consumer class. Following the hearing process, the commission may issue an order setting a new rate.[4]

The rate setting hearings are public and all parties to the process are granted time to provide testimony. Decisions by the commission are subject to review by the district court and the Utah Supreme Court.

In 1975, the legislature amended the commission's jurisdiction by transferring authority for motor carriers safety and security issues to the Utah Department of Transportation.[5]

The PSC regulates three major utility sectors: electrical, gas, and telecommunications. The electrical sector is composed of investor-owned entities, such as Utah Power and Light, which are regulated at both state and federal levels, publicly-owned or municipals, such as Utah Municipal Power Agency, which are not regulated by the state, and cooperatively-owned, such as Utah Rural Electric Association, which are subject to PSC review for rates and other regulation.

The regulation of natural gas centers around its use as a primary fuel source for the generation of electricity, its distribution to residential and commercial customers, and transmission integration. Transmission is primarily regulated at the federal level. The primary provider of natural gas in Utah is Questar Corporation.

The regulation of telecommunication services in Utah includes residential and commercial telephone services provided by the regional Bell operating company, Qwest Communications, and numerous rural exchange providers located across the state. In 1995, the legislature passed H.B. 364, Telecommunications Reform Act, which authorized the de-regulation of telecommunications services.[6]

DIVISION OF PUBLIC UTILITIES

The Division of Public Utilities was created by the legislature in 1983 to address the growing complexity of utility regulation and to provide a state agency independent of the Public Service Commission that could assist in the regulatory process by providing research, analysis, and make utility policy recommendations.[7]

The division director is appointed by and serves at the pleasure of the executive director of the Department of Commerce. The division is authorized to have professional and technical personnel including economists, engineers, accountants, statisticians, lawyers, inspectors, and administrative and support staff.[8] Legal advice is provided through the attorney general.[9] In practice, the division's staff works with the commission in developing information about all aspects of utility operation. That information is used by the commission and the division in a number of venues such as rate hearings, to accurately and fairly regulate utility providers.

COMMITTEE OF CONSUMER SERVICES

The Committee of Consumer Services was created by the legislature in 1977 within the Division of Public Utilities of the Department of Business Regulations.[10] The department's name was changed to the Department of Commerce in 1989 and both the division and the committee continued to be part of that state entity.[11]

In creating the committee, the legislature's stated purpose was to provide a governmental entity to advocate on behalf of residential customers, small commercial businesses, and agricultural enterprises. The committee consists of six members from specified cities along the Wasatch Front and an unincorporated area. Those members shall include the following: a low-income resident; a retired person; a small commercial consumer; a farmer or rancher; and a residential customer. The members are appointed by the governor with consent of the senate for four-year terms.[12] Staffing consists of an appointee by the governor and other professionals, including an attorney assigned from the Utah Attorney General's Office.[13]

The duties of the committee and staff are to assess utility rate changes and regulatory actions, assist residential and small commercial enterprises in appearing before the Public Service Commission, and bring original court actions before the Public Service Commission or any court having appellate jurisdiction over the Public Service Commission.[14] In practice, the committee works with the other state utility regulatory entities and the regulated, private sector utility companies in meeting its legislative charge. The committee also appears before the legislature as requested.

ELECTRICAL DEREGULATION

In 1997, the Utah Legislature created a two-year Electrical Deregulation and Customer Choice Task Force for the purpose of studying and making recommendations regarding the existing regulation of monopoly electrical providers.[15] The task force was charged with determining whether replacement of the existing rate-of-return regulation with market-based, retail competition would provide Utah residents with more choices in selecting their energy providers and at lower costs.

Over the two-year study, the task force considered the deregulation of electric power generation, customer benefits from retail competition in a low-cost energy state, such as Utah, and how other federal/state restructuring efforts might affect deregulation in Utah.

The task force concluded in 1999, after an extensive review of electrical energy regulation and generation, that Utah would be premature in adopting a comprehensive electrical restructuring plan.[16] The task force was reauthorized and continued to meet until December 2004 when it was allowed to "Sunset" and the Public Utilities and Technology Interim Committee was assigned to study the issue.

ELECTRIC ENERGY RATES

One of the critical factors reviewed by states considering the deregulation of electrical energy providers was the customer price over time. Figure 19-1 shows a comparison with the seven other mountain states of electricity prices in nominal dollars per million British Thermal Units[17] (mln/BTU) from 1970 through 2000. It indicates:[18]

- In the 1970s, Utah, at $7.35 per mln/BTU, was more than 10 percent higher than the mountain states average of $6.49, but below the national average of $7.96
- In the 1980s, Utah, at $17.21 per mln/BTU, was more than 10 percent higher than the mountain states average of $15.22, but below the national average of $17.98
- In the 1990s, Utah, at $16.96 per mln/BTU, was below the mountain state average of $17.99 by more than 5 percent and more than 20 percent below the national average of $21.98

Figure 19-1[19]

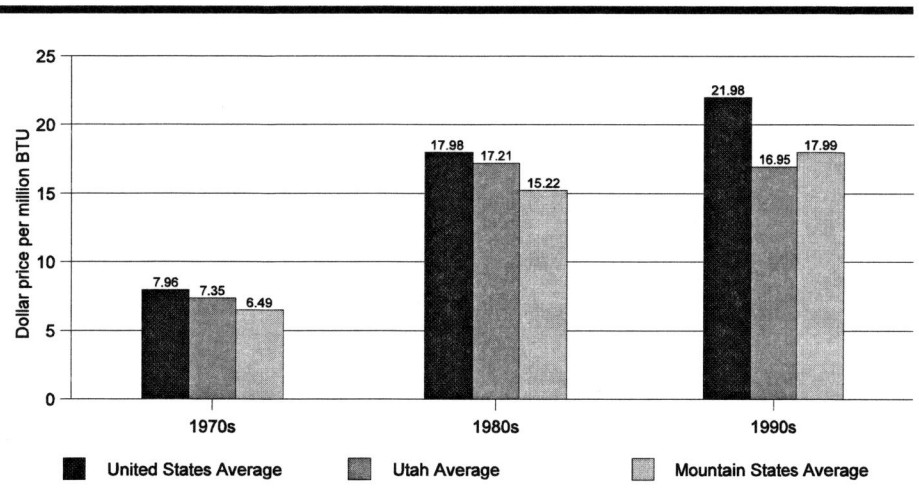

NATURAL GAS PRICE COMPARISON

Natural gas is a market competitor for electricity because it is an alternative fuel source for both residential and commercial customers. As the demand for electricity increased over the 1980s and 1990s, electrical prices also moved upward. This resulted in higher demand for natural gas and natural gas prices rose dramatically over that same time frame.[20]

Average natural gas prices during the 1970s were relatively low and stable across the United States including Utah and the other mountain states. However, beginning in the early 1980s, average natural gas prices soared from $1.77 per thousand cubic feet to $6.29 per thousand cubic feet in 1990, a 255 percent increase.

During that same period of time, Utah average natural gas prices increased 276 percent, from $1.37 to $5.15 per thousand cubic feet and the mountain states average natural gas price rose from a$1.61 to $5.52 per thousand cubic feet, a 243 percent increase. Figure 19-2 details those price comparisons.

Figure 19-2[21]

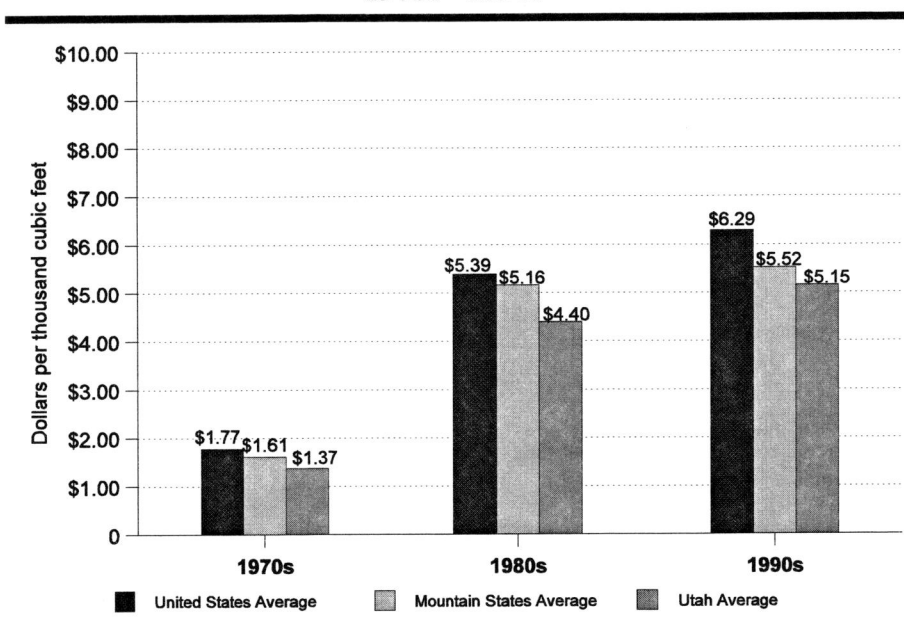

Chapter 20

Transportation

The safe and efficient movement of people and property within Utah is vital to its citizens. The importance of transportation infrastructure to the state's economy and the general well being of its citizens is hard to overstate. Matching resources with transportation needs is a continuing challenge of each successive governor and legislature as well as state, regional, and local officials. The state's transportation needs require continual assessment, advanced planning, thoughtful project development and implementation, and funding. But the obligation does not stop with a completed construction project. Maintenance and operation of transportation infrastructure must be done vigilantly throughout the useful life of each facility.

> **In this chapter:**
>
> Department of Transportation (p. 285)
> Transportation Planning (p. 287)
> Highways (p. 288)
> Highway Operations (p. 294)
> Current Challenges (p. 296)
> Public Transportation (p. 298)
> Light Rail and Commuter Rail Transit (p. 302)
> Aeronautics (p. 304)

DEPARTMENT OF TRANSPORTATION

Role of the Department

The Utah Department of Transportation (UDOT) was established in 1975.[1] Prior to that time, it was known as the State Road Commission. UDOT is responsible for the design, construction, maintenance, security, and safety of transportation systems. UDOT fulfills this responsibility by constructing and maintaining state highways; regulating motor carriers for safety, size, and weight compliance; coordinating with local agencies that provide public transportation services; and regulating aeronautics throughout Utah.

UDOT has identified four strategic goals it uses to further its responsibilities. These goals are (1) take care of what we have, (2) make the system work better, (3) improve safety, and (4) increase capacity.[2] These strategic goals are intended to help ensure that UDOT is providing safe and efficient transportation systems in the most cost effective manner possible.

The executive director, who is appointed by the governor with recommendations from the Transportation Commission and with the consent of the senate, is the chief executive officer of UDOT. As chief executive officer, the executive director is responsible to supervise all state transportation systems and operations of UDOT, to implement rules, priorities, and policies established by the commission, and, when necessary, to bring suits in court in the name of UDOT.[3] The executive director is also responsible to appoint a deputy director. The deputy director must be a registered engineer and is responsible to assist the executive director with program and project development and operation and maintenance of the transportation system.[4]

Transportation Commission

General policy for UDOT is established by a seven-member, part-time Transportation Commission. Each commissioner is appointed by the governor with the consent of the senate for a six-year term. One commissioner is selected from the state at large, while the other six are appointed from specified counties within the state. No more than four of the commissioners may be from the same political party. The commission's duties include determining priorities and funding levels of projects, determining additions and deletions to state highways, holding hearings and otherwise providing for public input on transportation matters, advising the department in state transportation systems policy, and approving settlement agreements of condemnation cases.[5]

Role of the Divisions

UDOT has seven divisions that are identified in Utah statutes:
1. Administrative Services Division
2. Comptroller Division
3. Internal Audit Division
4. Community Relations Division
5. Program Development Division
6. Project Development Division
7. Operations Division

The general administrative duties for UDOT are handled by the Administrative Services Division, the Comptroller Division, the Internal Audit Division and the Community Relations Division. The operations duties are handled by the Program Development Division, the Project Development Division, and Operations Division.[6] The department has also created a Legislative and Government Affairs Division. In addition, UDOT has four regional offices and three district offices which oversee the construction, maintenance, and administration of all states roads within each area (see figure 20-1).

Figure 20-1

Department of Transportation

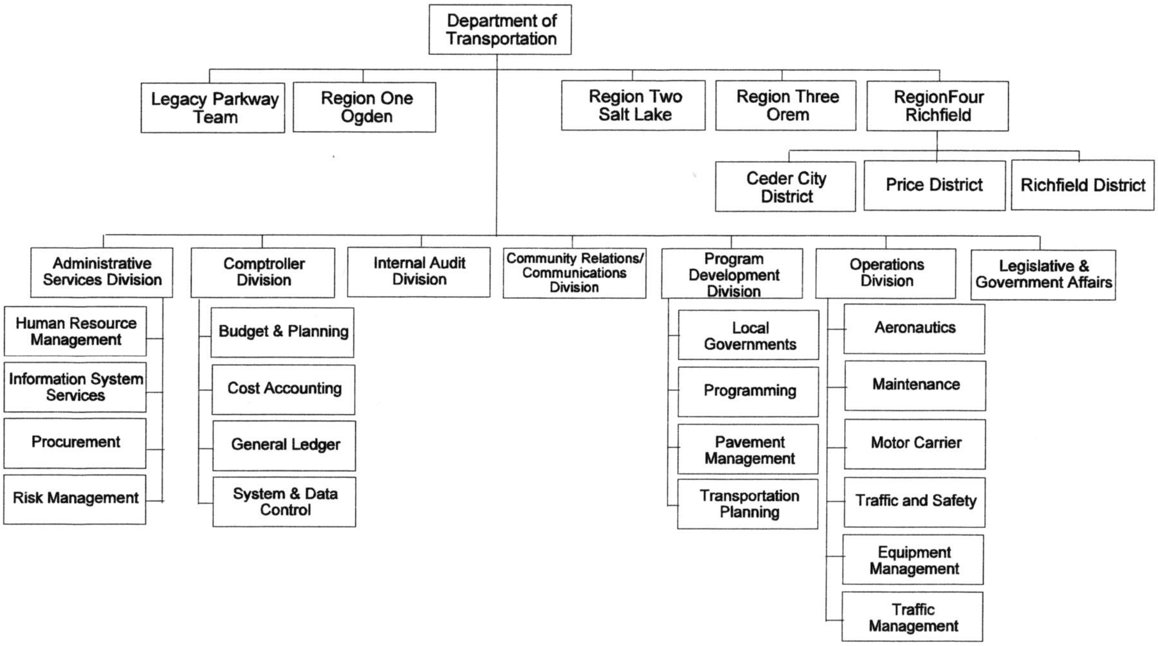

```
                            Department of
                            Transportation
    ┌──────────┬──────────┬─────┴────┬──────────┬──────────┐
 Legacy      Region One  Region Two  Region Three  RegionFour
 Parkway     Ogden       Salt Lake   Orem          Richfield
 Team
                                    ┌──────────┬──────────┐
                                 Ceder City  Price      Richfield
                                 District    District   District
```

Administrative Services Division	Comptroller Division	Internal Audit Division	Community Relations/ Communications Division	Program Development Division	Operations Division	Legislative & Government Affairs
Human Resource Management	Budget & Planning			Local Governments	Aeronautics	
Information System Services	Cost Accounting			Programming	Maintenance	
Procurement	General Ledger			Pavement Management	Motor Carrier	
Risk Management	System & Data Control			Transportation Planning	Traffic and Safety	
					Equipment Management	
					Traffic Management	

TRANSPORTATION PLANNING

Transportation planning is the process of evaluating the demographic characteristics and travel patterns of the regional area to determine alternatives for the transportation system and the most effective use of federal, state, and local funding to meet travel demand in the future.

UDOT is responsible for establishing a Statewide Transportation Improvement Program (STIP), which is a five-year program of highway and transit projects that includes highway projects on the state, city, and county highway systems and projects in National Parks. It is developed through cooperation between UDOT; Metropolitan Planning Organizations; and federal, city, and county governments. The STIP serves two purposes: (1) documenting UDOT's compliance with the requirements of the "Transportation Equity Act of the 21st Century" to be eligible for federal funding, and (2) serving as UDOT's work plan for the development of projects.[7]

UDOT is also required to develop a Long Range Transportation Plan that projects transportation needs over at least a twenty-year period, takes into account estimated population growth, and is financially constrained.[8] In December 2003, UDOT published a thirty-year transportation plan, which is called Utah Transportation 2030.[9] This document identifies projects and strategies that can be implemented with the projected revenues that can reasonably be anticipated. The document also identifies projects that are needed in the future but are not scheduled to be constructed because funding is not available. Prior to its final release, the document was subject to the review, revision, and approval of the Transportation Commission. This document will be updated every three years.[10]

Under federal law, an urbanized area with a population of more than 50,000 is required to establish a Metropolitan Planning Organization (MPO) that is responsible for transportation planning and project programming. All federal funds expended in the MPO planning area must go through this planning process.[11] MPOs are made up of representatives of local government and transportation authorities. Currently in Utah, there are four MPOs: the Wasatch Front Regional Council representing urbanized areas in Salt Lake, Davis, and Weber Counties; Mountainland

Association of Governments representing urbanized areas in Utah County; the Dixie MPO in the St. George urbanized area; and the Cache MPO in the Logan urbanized area. Each MPO must prepare a Long Range Transportation Plan for its area that covers a twenty-year horizon and that is financially constrained based on revenue that it can reasonably expect to be available. In addition, an MPO is responsible to prepare a Transportation Improvement Plan at least once every two years, which is a three-year list of highway and transit projects that will be federally funded.

In 2002, a memorandum of agreement was signed by the Wasatch Front Regional Council, Mountainland Association of Governments, UDOT, and the Utah Transit Authority to establish a Joint Policy Advisory Committee and a Joint Technical Advisory Committee to work cooperatively to address long range highway and transit project priorities, funding mechanisms, and other items of common interest and to provide a seamless transportation process between these organizations. The Joint Policy Advisory Committee is to establish common evaluation criteria for rating and ranking highway projects, establish a common list of prioritized projects needing new sources of funding, and pursue a financial strategy necessary to fund the prioritized list of highway projects.[12]

Project Selection

Currently, the Transportation Commission is responsible to prioritize transportation projects. In 2005, the legislature passed a bill requiring the Transportation Commission to establish a new process for prioritizing new transportation capacity projects. The commission is required to assign each new transportation capacity project a ranking based on a weighted criteria system and make the project ranking publicly available upon request. In addition, if the commission prioritizes a project over a higher ranked project, the commission must hold a hearing and accept public comment on the merits of why the project was prioritized over higher ranked projects.[13]

HIGHWAYS

Highway Jurisdiction

UDOT, counties, and municipalities are the primary agencies involved in providing highways, roads, and streets, collectively referred to as highways. The U.S. Forest Service, National Park Service, and other federal agencies have a collective total of 4,131 miles of highway that are not under the jurisdiction of the state, county, or municipality. Of these federal highways, 79.5 percent are not paved.[14]

State Highways

Under Utah statute, state highways are class A state roads and are under the jurisdiction and control of UDOT. State highways are designated by state route number and a description in state law.[15] UDOT annually submits to the legislature's Transportation Interim Committee a list of highways that the Transportation Commission recommends for addition or deletion from the state highway system. All recommendations must be based on minimum qualifying standards established by the commission. This list, along with any fiscal recommendations, is reviewed by the Transportation Interim Committee before submission to the legislature in a bill form. UDOT is responsible for 5,848 miles of highway, 99.6 percent of which are paved.[16]

County Highways

County highways are class B county roads and are under the jurisdiction and control of the respective counties. County highways are designated county highways or are non-state highways situated outside of incorporated municipal boundaries. County highways may include highways under the control of a federal agency if a construction or maintenance agreement is in effect with the appropriate federal agency. Counties are responsible for 23,786 miles of highway, 23 percent of which are paved.[17]

Municipal Highways

Municipal highways are class C city roads and are under the jurisdiction and control of the respective municipalities. Municipal highways are all highways within the corporate limits of the municipality that are not designated county highways or state highways. Municipal highways may also include highways under the control of a federal agency if a construction or maintenance agreement is in effect with the appropriate federal agency. Municipalities are responsible for 8,845 miles of highway, 92.2 percent of which are paved.[18]

Highway Funding
Transportation Fund

Since 1961, the Utah Constitution has required that the proceeds of any tax or fee related to the operation of a motor vehicle on a highway must be used for highway purposes, excluding costs of collection and administration, driver education, and enforcement of motor vehicle and traffic laws.[19] Highway user-related taxes and fees are deposited in the Transportation Fund. Motor fuel and special fuel taxes make up approximately 84.5 percent of the revenue of the Transportation Fund. Vehicle registration fees make up the next highest percent of the revenue of the Transportation Fund at only 7.4 percent. There is a statutory cap of $11.6 million that may be appropriated from the fund to other agencies for tax collection costs and law enforcement.[20] Of the amount remaining after the $11.6 million is deducted from the Transportation Fund, 25 percent is appropriated into the B and C Road Account which is distributed to counties and municipalities for local roads.[21] The remaining 75 percent is appropriated to UDOT for state highway construction and maintenance (see figures 20-2 and 20-3).

Figure 20-2

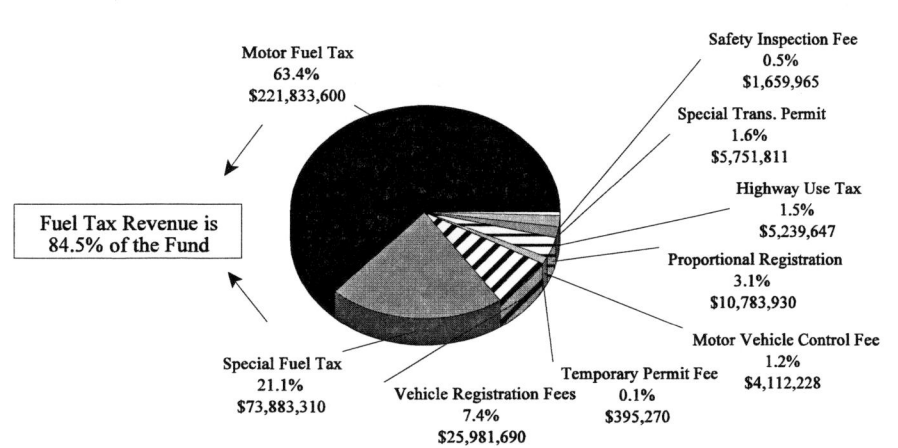

Transportation Fund Revenue
Seven-Year Average, Fiscal Years 1997 to 2003

Total Average Annual Revenue: $349,641,498

Note: Driver license revenues are not included because revenue is dedicated to fund that division.
Source: Annual Statistical Summary, Program Development, Utah Department of Transportation, December 1997-2003

Figure 20-3

Transportation Fund Distribution
Seven-Year Average, Fiscal Years 1997 to 2003

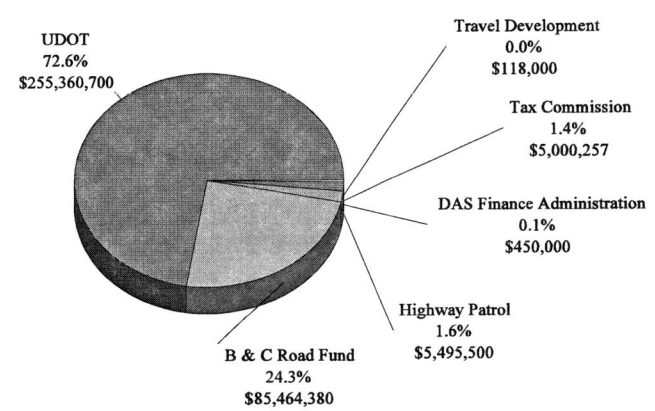

Total Average Annual Distribution: $351,567,390

Note: Driver license revenues are not included because revenue is dedicated to fund that division.
Source: Annual Statistical Summary, Program Development, Utah Department of Transportation, December 1997-2003

Since 1923 when the Utah Legislature enacted a 2.5-cent per gallon tax, the gas tax has been the primary source of funding for state highways in Utah.[22] In 1941, when the gas tax was four cents per gallon, a special fuel tax (diesel fuel tax) at the same rate was enacted by the legislature.[23] Since that time both the motor fuel tax and the special fuel tax have been at the same rate. As of 2004, that rate is at 24.5 cents per gallon (see figure 20-4).

Figure 20-4

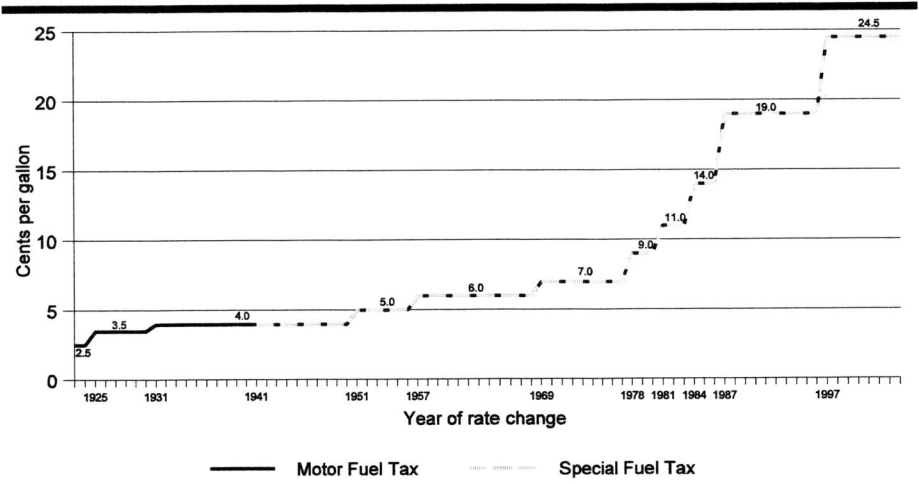

Excludes a 1/4-cent per gallon environmental assurance fee charged since 1997 by participants in the Environmnetal Assirance Program (see Section 19-6-410.5). This fee replaced a 1/2-cent per gallon environmental surcharge for petroleum storage tank cleanup that was enacted in 1990 (see former Section 19-6-410).
Source: Sections 59-13-201 and 59-13-301.

Centennial Highway Fund

The Centennial Highway Fund, created in 1996, consists of appropriations made by the legislature, a portion of the motor fuel tax, special fuel tax, and motor vehicle registration fees, voluntary contributions, and revenues generated by a 1/64 percent sales and use tax rate (see figure 20-5).[24] This fund may only be used for construction, major reconstruction, or major renovation to state and federal highways.[25] The Centennial Highway Fund was created as an eleven-year $2.4 billion program of highway projects. The Centennial Highway Fund was used to fund the $1.56 billion I-15 reconstruction project in Salt Lake County, and it is being used to fund approximately forty other major highway construction and reconstruction projects throughout the state. The initial plan would have provided a $1.9 million deficit at the end of fiscal year 2007. However, current projections show the deficit will be closer to $1.14 billion at the end of fiscal year 2007.[26] Under current revenue and expenditure projections, the Centennial Highway Fund debt will be paid off in fiscal year 2014, seven years later than planned.[27] At least four factors have contributed to this situation:

1. $956 million in increased project costs were added with no additional funding
2. General Fund contributions have not been made as initially planned resulting in
   - Additional bonding
   - A disruption of planned cash flow
   - Planned General Fund contributions being used for other state needs during the state budget shortfalls beginning in fiscal year 2003;
3. The initial project costs estimates were not complete and underestimated the cost of the projects due to the lack of project scope, hasty development of the list, and unclear understanding of project expectations
4. The initial revenue package was overly optimistic (e.g., $200 million in savings from UDOT efficiencies)

Additional bonding was added to the Centennial Highway Fund in response to a lack of current revenue in the plan. The initial Centennial Highway Fund plan for $563 million in bonding included net interest and other bonding costs of $200 million. Instead, $1.679 billion in bonding will be needed with net interest and other bonding costs projected to be $767.7 million.[28] The increased cost associated with increased bonding and paying off seven years later than originally planned will cost an extra $567.7 million.[29] In 2005, the legislature dedicated $59,594,700 of the state sales and use tax revenue to be deposited in the Centennial Highway Fund annually and appropriated an additional $90 million to the Centennial Highway Fund.[30] In previous years, the legislature had annually appropriated $59,594,700 or more from the General Fund to the Centennial Highway Fund since it was created in 1997.

Figure 20-5

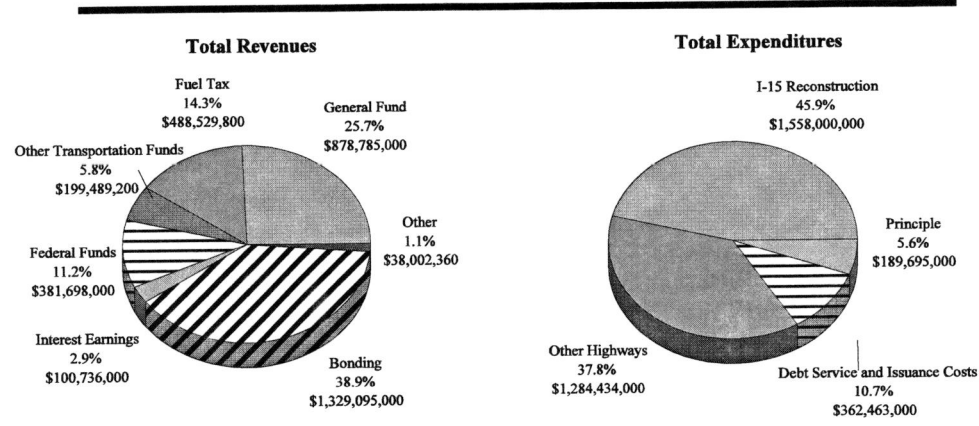

Transportation Investment Fund of 2005

In 2005, the legislature also created the Transportation Investment Fund of 2005. This fund was created to pay the costs of maintenance, construction, reconstruction, or renovation to state and federal highways using the written prioritization process to determine which projects will be completed. Currently, the revenue sources for the fund are appropriations from the legislature and any voluntary contributions. Once the highway general obligation bonds have been paid off and the projects completed that are intended to be paid from revenues deposited in the Centennial Highway Fund, the revenue sources for the Centennial Highway Fund will be deposited in the Transportation Investment Fund of 2005.[31]

Corridor Preservation Funds

Another important aspect of transportation planning and funding is corridor preservation. In 1996, the legislature created the Transportation Corridor Preservation Revolving Loan Fund to provide UDOT with funds to acquire title to property or interests in real property for state, county, or local future planned transportation corridors.[32] Revenue for the fund comes from a 2.5 percent motor vehicle rental tax that is imposed on short term leases or rentals of motor vehicles that do not exceed thirty days and a portion of the revenues generated by the statewide sales and use tax.[33] UDOT has authority to use the money from the fund to purchase property rights up to thirty years in advance for future planned transportation facility construction.[34]

In 2005, the legislature also created the Local Transportation Corridor Preservation Fund and authorized any county legislative body in the state to impose up to a $10 local option transportation corridor preservation fee on motor vehicle registrations and renewals of registration within the county. The county may use the fund monies from the fees generated by motor vehicle registrations in that county to acquire real property or any interests in real property for state, county, and municipal transportation corridors. In addition, a county that is not included in a metropolitan planning organization may use a portion of the revenues generated by a local option transportation corridor preservation fee for countywide transportation planning.[35]

B and C Roads Account

Funding for county and municipal highways is provided through the B and C Roads Account. Early contributions of state-collected highway user revenue to municipalities and counties came from the Motor Vehicle Registration Fund. In 1937, the legislature enacted legislation that authorized and appropriated $800,000 annually to the B and C Roads Account.[36] In 1949, the amount was changed so that all money from the Motor Vehicle Registration Fund went into the B and C Roads Account annually.[37] In 1951, a cap was enacted of $2 million plus 50 percent of the remainder of the Motor Vehicle Registration Fund to go into the B and C Roads Account with the other 50 percent of the remainder going to the Highway Construction and Maintenance Fund to fund state highways.[38]

Ten years later, in 1961, the split of remaining moneys from the Motor Vehicle Registration Fund after the first $2 million was changed to 75 percent to the B and C Roads Account and 25 percent to the Highway Construction and Maintenance Fund.[39] In 1977, the Highway Construction and Maintenance Fund was changed to the Transportation Fund and was used for the deposit of all highway user revenue.[40] In 1981, the formula was changed again to 15 percent of the Transportation Fund going to the B and C Roads Account.[41] One year later in 1982, the split of the Transportation Fund was changed to its current level with 75 percent going to the Department of Transportation for state highways and 25 percent going to the B and C Roads Account for municipal and county highways.[42] In addition to the amounts from the Transportation Fund, a portion of the revenue generated by the statewide sales and use tax is deposited into the B and C roads account.[43] Revenues from the fund are distributed to counties and municipalities using a formula based on road mileage weighted by road type and population.[44]

Federal Funding

Currently under federal law, a gasoline excise tax of 18.4 cents per gallon is imposed.[45] The majority of the revenue from the federal gas tax is deposited into the Highway Trust Fund and is distributed to the states through the Highway Account and Mass Transit Account of the Highway Trust Fund.[46] Federal highway funding to the state has been averaging approximately $238 million per year in apportionment in recent years and approximately $200 million per year in obligation limitation (what can actually be spent). Utah's fiscal year 2004 apportionment totaled $229.6 million.[47] This federal aid is in accordance with the "Transportation Equity Act for the 21st Century" (TEA-21) enacted in 1998 and is vital to the planning, construction, and maintenance of the state highway system.[48] Congress has historically passed a new Federal Transportation Act approximately every six years and provides limitations on how the money can be spent by funding categories. In August of 2005, the "Safe, Accountable, Flexible, and Efficient Transportation Equity Act: A Legacy for Users" (SAFETEA-LU) was enacted, which provides federal funding to the states through the year 2009.[49] UDOT expends considerable effort to effectively program and account for the numerous funding categories. Some of the major categories for federal aid highway funding include: Interstate, Interstate Maintenance, National Highway System, Metropolitan Planning, Congestion Mitigation, Bridge Replacement, and Demonstration Projects. Utah, along with most states, continues to lobby for more flexibility in the use of these federal funds.

Funding for Long Range Planning

UDOT and MPOs are required to develop a fiscally constrained long range plan to address transportation needs.[50] Current planning efforts extend to the year 2030. The plans assume that the equivalent of a five-cent per gallon gas tax increase will be enacted by the legislature every six years beginning in 2005. Under current estimates each penny per gallon increase in the motor fuel and special fuel tax rate yields $13 million annually. A five-cent increase would generate $65 million annually. The anticipated revenues in these plans do not fully fund the transportation needs that have been identified. Total highway needs through the year 2030 exceed $23 billion.[51]

Table 20-1

Utah Highway Capacity Needs 2030	
*WFRC urban area	$10,899,000,000
MAG urban area	**$4,440,000,000**
Cache urban area	$427,000,000
Dixie urban area	$800,000,000
#UDOT, Non-MPO areas	$6,477,000,000
TOTAL CAPACITY NEEDS	$23,043,000,000
***Current available highway revenue through 2030	$10,644,000,000
****Less expected highway expenditures through 2030	$4,105,000,000
Total highway revenues available for capacity	$6,539,000,000
Total Unfunded Highway Capacity Needs (needs less revenues available)	**$16,504,000,000**

*WFRC (Wasatch Front Regional Council)
**MAG (Mountainlands Association of Governments)
#Includes reconstruction and major reconstruction
***Highway revenue sources include available state transportation funds (less UDOT operations and maintenance costs), federal highway funds, 1/4 of 1/4 cent sales tax (Salt Lake County), and Centennial Highway Funds
****Highway expenditures include roadway expenditures, pavement/bridge preservation, routine projects including traffic signals, roadway safety improvements, roadway lighting, and contingencies.
Source: Utah Department of Transportation   November 2004

Funding for the Statewide Transportation Improvement Program

The Statewide Transportation Improvement Program (STIP) is a five-year program of highway and transit projects designed to implement the Long Range Highway Plan.[52] STIP is funded through state and federal transportation dollars and is the primary ongoing program used to address state transportation needs.

HIGHWAY OPERATIONS

UDOT's primary responsibility is the planning, construction, and maintenance of state highways that are safe, reliable, environmentally sensitive, and that serve the needs of the traveling public.[53] UDOT manages over fifty-eight hundred miles of highway. In fulfilling this responsibility, UDOT has identified several focus areas to most effectively further their strategic goals. These areas include highway maintenance, intelligent transportation systems, transportation demand management, and access management. In addition, UDOT regulates motor carriers who rely on the highway infrastructure for the movement of freight within Utah.[54]

Highway Maintenance

UDOT has identified highway maintenance as one of its top priorities to ensure that the existing highway system is adequately maintained. UDOT has adopted a "Good Roads Cost Less" philosophy. To further this philosophy, UDOT divides its maintenance efforts into two categories—preventative maintenance and proactive maintenance. Preventative maintenance includes regularly scheduled treatments of the pavements and bridges which preserve and improve existing highways and significantly reduce future deterioration. UDOT estimates that through its maintenance efforts a good road will cost $0.9 million per mile over thirty years while roads that are not maintained but are then replaced cost $1.5 million per mile over thirty years. Proactive maintenance is the daily maintenance required to keep the system operating, including activities such as snow removal, paint striping, or pot hole patching. UDOT estimates that the total amount of funds needed in 2005 for all maintenance activities will be $144 million, and this amount will increase to $226 million by 2015.[55]

Intelligent Transportation Systems

Intelligent transportation systems is the use of technology to make the transportation system work smarter. UDOT established its CommuterLink program, an intelligent transportation systems network, in 1999. This program is a combination of services and technology combined to increase highway safety, reduce travel delays and crashes, and facilitate traveler information so that transportation system capacity is maximized. The CommuterLink Program includes a CommuterLink website with up-to-date traffic information, roadside assistance and incident management teams, interagency coordination, traffic signal coordination, freeway ramp meters, electronic variable message signs, a voice activated 511 traveler information phone line, closed-circuit television cameras, and congestion sensors used for intersection monitoring and traffic management. Intelligent Transportation Systems has saved over $100 million in annual user costs and has helped reduce traffic delays.[56]

Transportation Demand Management

In addition to constructing and maintaining highways, UDOT is responsible to ensure that highways are working properly and most effectively. UDOT fulfills this responsibility by adopting guidelines and programs that promote a reduction in travel demand through Transportation Demand Management. Its objective is to reduce travel by providing alternatives that meet travel demand. Transportation Demand Management strategies include promoting flexible work hours, vanpools, teleworking, teleconferencing, transit use, and walkable communities. These strategies are part of UDOT's effort to promote a shared solution to the growing demand for travel within Utah.[57]

Access Management

Access management is a method of increasing highway capacity, increasing safety, and enhancing mobility by limiting new driveways, on-street parking, and certain turning movements, and consolidating or restructuring existing driveways if necessary. In 1999, the legislature passed a law to provide incentives for local authorities to implement access management programs by requiring that a local authority implement an access management program to be eligible for transportation corridor preservation funds.[58] In addition, the legislature in 2001 passed a law that requires permits for approach roads and driveways entering state highways to ensure that these approach roads or driveways are consistent with UDOT's plans for access management.[59] The benefits of an access management program include crash reductions and crash severity reductions, traffic congestion reductions, potential reductions in air pollution from vehicle exhausts, highway capacity maximization, and other important economic benefits.[60]

Motor Carrier Services

Trucking is an important industry to Utah's economy. Almost 80 percent of all Utah communities depend solely on the trucking industry to supply needed goods. Approximately 96.4 million tons of freight valued at $42.3 billion is shipped from Utah annually using all transportation modes, and 87.7 million tons of freight valued at $54.4 billion arrives in Utah annually. In addition, these numbers do not include freight passing through Utah or freight being shipped entirely within the state's boundaries. Seventy percent of Utah's freight tonnage is shipped by trucks.[61]

UDOT is responsible to construct and operate ports-of-entry to ensure that motor carriers are complying with state and federal laws.[62] UDOT currently operates ten permanent ports-of-entry and one temporary port-of-entry. UDOT inspects commercial vehicles to ensure compliance with vehicle size, weight, and load restrictions and safety and security requirements and reviews company safety programs. In addition, UDOT conducts educational programs for industry owners, safety managers, drivers, and maintenance personnel so that all are aware of the proper safety policies, procedures, and practices. All commercial motor vehicles are required to stop at ports-of-entry and may purchase required permits at these locations.[63]

CURRENT CHALLENGES
Funding

Increasing demand, inflating costs, and a relatively flat primary funding source contribute to the continuing challenge of funding Utah's highways. Add several recurrent severe budget shortfalls to a reduction in the General Fund commitment to the Centennial Highway Program and the challenge has reached critical levels. On average, fuel tax revenue has grown 7.5 percent per year over the last nineteen years. Over the same time period, on average, sales tax revenue has grown 9.2 percent per year (see figure 20-6).

Figure 20-6

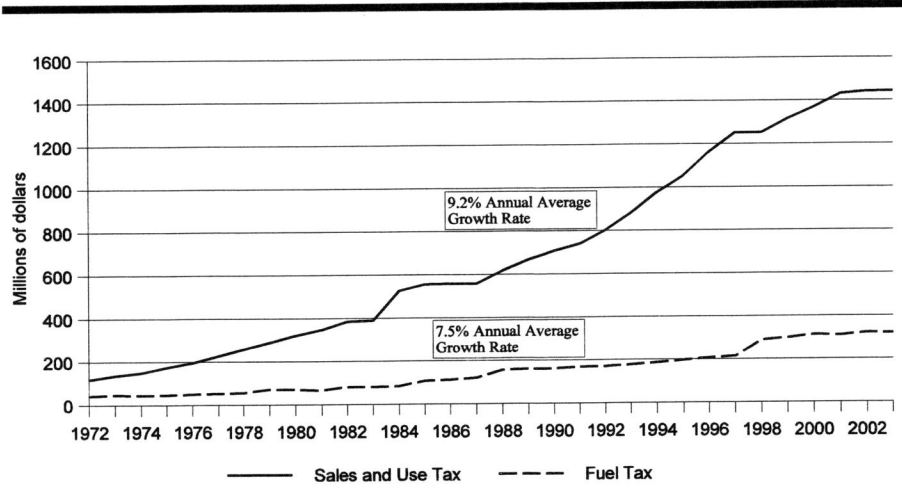

Sales tax revenue grows because of a growing Utah economy and inflation. Fuel tax revenue grows because of increases in fuel tax rates, vehicle miles traveled, motor fuel gallons taxed, and special fuel gallons taxed. Inflation is not a factor in fuel tax revenue growth. Instead, inflation only erodes the purchasing power of fuel tax revenue. More fuel efficient vehicles and increased alternative transportation also reduce fuel tax revenue growth.

Between 1978 and 1987 the fuel tax rate was raised four times, increasing the tax from seven cents to nineteen cents per gallon.[64] Since 1987, the fuel tax rate has been adjusted only once in 1997, when it increased from nineteen cents per gallon to the current rate of 24.5 cents per gallon.[65] The percent of personal income that Utah taxpayers pay in fuel taxes has decreased 39 percent from 0.94 percent in 1972 to 0.57 percent in 2001 (see figure 20-7).[66]

The average annual fuel tax paid per registered vehicle has declined 41 percent from $276 in 1972 to $162 in 2001 based on 2001 dollars (see figure 20-8).[67] The fuel tax burden on Utah taxpayers is the lowest it has been in seventeen of the last eighteen years.

Figure 20-7

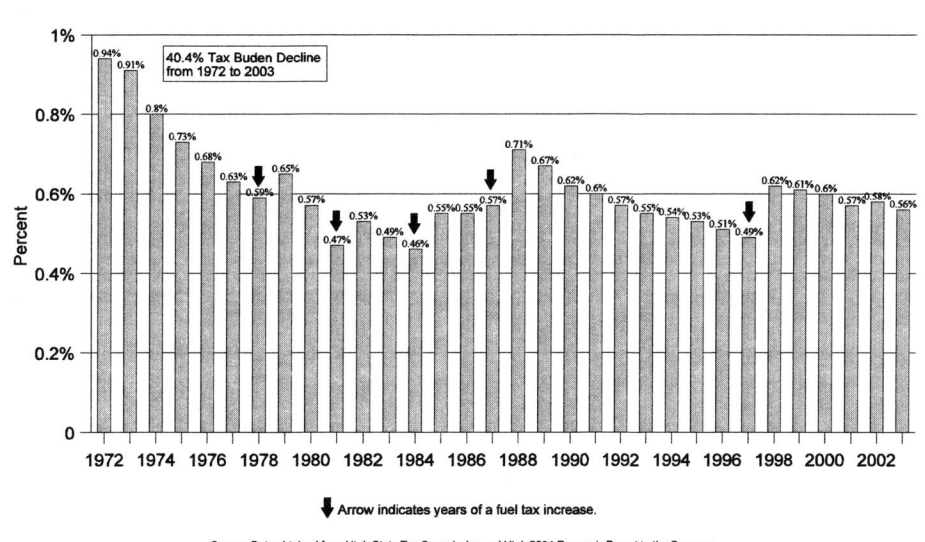

Figure 20-8

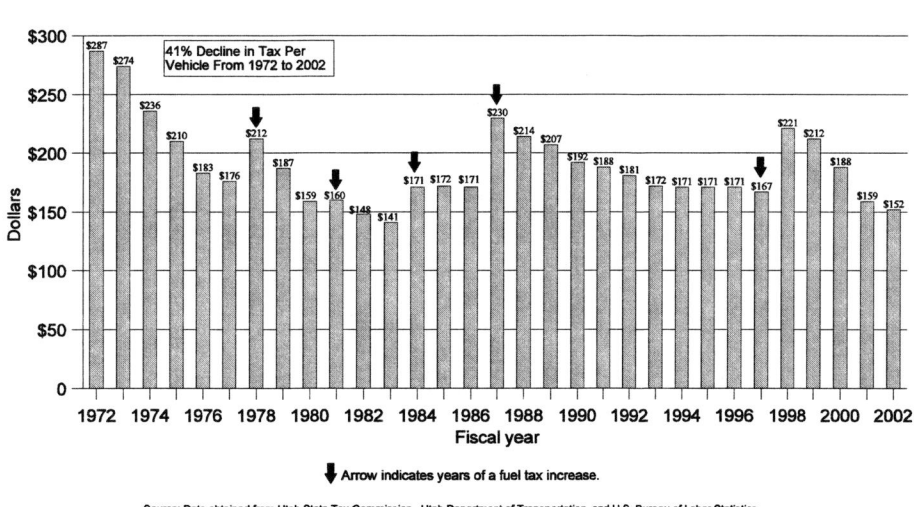

In recent years, Utah's slower economy has reduced General Fund revenues, including those revenues going to the Centennial Highway Fund. Present commitments already made to highway

projects means the legislature must delay highway projects, eliminate highway projects, or find new revenues. If new revenues are considered, options include:
- Periodically increasing fuel tax rates
- Creating an automatic rate adjustment on fuel taxes (tied to inflation)
- Imposing a sales tax on the sale of fuel
- Finding new sources of revenue for highways

Legacy Parkway

In March 1991, a Wasatch Front Regional Council study of the North I-15 Corridor recommended construction of the West Davis Highway (now called Legacy Parkway) from I-215 to Farmington. The final environmental impact statement for this fourteen-mile project was completed in July 2000, and approval was received from the Federal Highway Administration on October 31, 2000 and from the U.S. Army Corps of Engineers on January 9, 2001. On the same day, UDOT gave the design/build contractor, FAK (Fluor-Daniel), a notice to proceed. The project is a fourteen-mile stretch of two-lane highway in each direction designed to provide an alternate roadway for northern Utah commuters between North Salt Lake and Farmington. It includes a pedestrian/equestrian/bike path the entire length of the parkway and a 2,098-acre nature preserve designed to preserve wetlands, buffer development, and ensure a habitat for wildlife. The cost of the project was $451 million and was originally expected to be completed in the fall of 2004.

A majority of the construction on the Legacy Parkway has been halted since November 16, 2001, due to an injunction issued by the U.S. Tenth Circuit Court of Appeals in Denver. On September 16, 2002, the court issued a decision that ordered further environmental analysis by the Federal Highway Administration and the U.S. Army Corps of Engineers.[68] UDOT incurred $17 million in suspension costs due to the court injunction. These agencies are preparing a Supplemental Environmental Impact Statement to respond to the Court. The Supplemental Environmental Impact Statement was available for public review and comment in late 2004, with a public hearing held early in 2005. It is expected that the Supplemental Environmental Impact Statement process will be completed, records of decision presented, and the project advertised for construction early 2006.

During the fall of 2005, the plaintiffs in the original Legacy lawsuit negotiated a settlement with the state. On November 9, 2005, the legislature passed a resolution in a special session approving a settlement agreement which would bar the original plaintiffs from filing a lawsuit on the Supplemental Environmental Impact Statement for Legacy Parkway.[69] Barring future legal complications from other plaintiffs, UDOT hopes to resume construction on Legacy Parkway in the spring of 2006.

The North interchange work on Park Lane (formerly Burke Lane) and Shepard's Lane was completed.

Currently, the Legacy Parkway Project is approximately 33 percent completed, which means:
- 90 percent of the right-of-way has been purchased
- 87 percent of the design has been completed
- 42 percent of the right-of-way has been cleared and stripped
- 34 percent of the right-of-way has received fill dirt

PUBLIC TRANSPORTATION

Public transportation throughout Utah is provided by municipalities and agencies organized as public transit districts. A public transit district is a special district created to provide mass transit services in a certain geographic area—often across municipal and county boundaries. It is a political subdivision created by counties and municipalities under enabling legislation passed by the Utah Legislature in 1969.[70] Currently there are six public transit districts in Utah, which include the Utah Transit Authority covering the Wasatch Front, the Sun Tran Transit District in St. George, the Park

City Transit District, the Snyderville Basin Transit District near Park City, the Cache Valley Transit District, and the Logan Transit District.

A public transit district is governed by a board appointed by the member entities (the counties and municipalities) that created the district. If more than 200,000 people reside within the public transit district boundaries, the board of trustees consists of sixteen trustees, fifteen voting members, and one nonvoting member who is also a member of the Transportation Commission. If 200,000 people or fewer reside within the district boundaries, the board of trustees consists of trustees appointed by the legislative bodies of each municipality, county, or unincorporated area within any county based on one trustee for each full unit of regularly scheduled passenger routes proposed to be served by the district in each municipality or unincorporated area within any county in the following calendar year. A member of the Transportation Commission may also serve as a non-voting member.[71]

A public transit district board of trustees is responsible to determine what facilities should be acquired or constructed and to supervise and regulate every transit facility owned and operated by the district. The board is responsible to appoint a general manager who is in charge of the acquisition, construction, maintenance, and operation of the facilities of the district and of the administration of the business affairs of the district. The general manager, along with other officers of the district appointed by the general manager (including a general counsel, a treasurer, a comptroller, and other officers) manage the business affairs of the district and are responsible to keep the board advised of the needs of the district and to report to the board on the finances and administrative activities of the district.[72]

Public transit districts may be funded from federal, state, and local funds. Currently, counties, cities, or towns are authorized to impose up to 0.50 percent in sales and use tax to fund a public transit district within their areas.[73] In addition, counties are authorized to impose a property tax of up to .0004 per dollar of taxable value for public transit district funding if approved by voters within the county. However to date, a property tax to fund public transit has not been imposed by any county.[74] Additionally, public transit districts may charge a fare for use of the public transit system.

Utah Transit Authority (UTA) is Utah's largest public transit district. It was originally incorporated in 1970 by municipalities and counties by a vote of the people authorizing a 1/4 percent sales tax dedicated to the district.[75] Since its incorporation, UTA has steadily grown to provide public transportation services for the majority of cities along the Wasatch Front. On November 7, 2000, voters in Salt Lake, Davis, and Weber counties approved an additional 1/4 percent sales tax to fund light rail extensions, expand bus service, and establish commuter rail.

Table 20-2

Utah Transit Authority
Formation and Key Funding Authorization History

Date	Who and What	Notes
May 9, 1969	**Legislature** enacts the "Utah Public Transit District Act" which allows the creation and provides for the governance of public transit districts by municipalities and counties and allows public transit districts to issue bonds.	Enacted in the First Special Session, S.B. 4 "Utah Public Transit District Act"; effective date July 9, 1969.[76]
Nov. 4, 1969	Voters in **Salt Lake City, South Salt Lake, Murray, Midvale, Sandy, and Bingham Canyon** voted to create and become members of a public transit district.	
Mar. 3, 1970	The above named jurisdictions incorporated a public transit district to be called the **Utah Transit Authority (UTA)**.	

Date	Who and What	Notes
Nov. 3, 1970	Voters representing the **unincorporated areas of Salt Lake County** approved a proposition to become part of UTA (Oct. 21, 1971 included in Articles of Incorporation).	
Mar. 8, 1973	**Utah Legislature** allows counties to impose a property tax for transit district funding if approved by voters within the county (rate limit is up to .0004 per dollar of taxable value).	S.B. 89 "Funding Public Transit Districts"; effective May 8, 1973 (Note -- this tax has never been imposed)[77]
Mar. 8, 1973 and Feb. 2, 1974	**Utah Legislature** provides temporary share of liquor control profits from the state-operated Liquor Commission to subsidize transit districts.	• H.B. 297 "Liquor Control Fund Distribution"; effective May 8, 1973.[78] • H.B. 32 "Liquor Control Fund Distribution"; effective April 4, 1974.[79] • Other source: "Mass Transit in Salt Lake Valley: 1960 to 1978," Utah Economic and Business Review Vol. 38, #1 January 1978.
Nov. 6, 1973	Voters in **Davis and Weber Counties** approved a proposition to become part of UTA (Mar. 1, 1974 included in Articles of Incorporation).	
Feb. 2, 1974	• **Legislature** authorizes any county within a public transit district to impose a 1/4 of 1% sales tax to fund a <u>no-fare</u> public transit district if approved by the voters within the county. • **Legislature** removes no-fare provision later in 1974.	• H.B. 13 "Local Option Sales Tax -- No-Fare Public Transit Allocation"; effective April 4, 1974.[80] • In the Second Special Session, H.B. 2 "Local Option Sales Tax -- Public Transit Allocation" passed removing the no-fare provision; effective date August 15, 1974.[81]
Nov. 5, 1974	• Voters of **Salt Lake and Weber Counties** adopted the optional 1/4 of 1% sales tax to fund UTA. • Voters of **Davis County** rejected the sales tax. • Voters of **Alta** approved a proposition to become part of UTA and adopted the optional 1/4 of 1% sales tax for its funding (Dec. 23, 1974 included in Articles of Incorporation).	
Nov. 4, 1975	• Voters of **West Jordan, South Jordan, and Riverton** approved a proposition to become part of UTA (Jan. 21, 1976 included in Articles of Incorporation). • **Davis County** voters adopted the optional 1/4 of 1% sales tax to fund UTA.	
Mar. 9, 1977	**Legislature** extends authorization to <u>any municipality</u> or county within a public transit district to impose a 1/4 of 1% sales tax to fund a public transit district if approved by the voters within the <u>municipality</u> or county.	S.B. 348 "Municipal Transit Tax Authorization"; effective date May 10, 1977[82]
Nov. 7, 1978 Feb. 27, 1983 May 2, 1983	• Voters of Provo and Orem approved a proposition to form the Timpanogos Transit Authority (TTA) but rejected the sales tax funding. • TTA board proposed a merger with UTA. • Merger documents signed conditioned on voter approval.	
Aug. 21, 1984	Voters of **Provo and Orem** approved a proposition to become part of UTA and adopted the optional 1/4 of 1% sales tax for its funding (Jan. 1, 1985 included in Articles of Incorporation).	

Date	Who and What	Notes
Nov. 11, 1989	Voters of **Lehi, American Fork, Pleasant Grove, and Lindon** approved a proposition to become part of UTA and adopted the optional 1/4 of 1% sales tax for its funding (Dec. 27, 1989 included in Articles of Incorporation).	
Mar. 12, 1990	**Legislature** authorizes the imposition of a second 1/4 of 1% sales tax to fund a fixed guideway and expanded public transit system with approval of the voters within the county or municipality. In first class counties (Salt Lake County), 25% of the additional 1/4 of 1% sales tax must be used for improvements to I-15.	S.B. 108 "Public Choice on Transit Tax Amendments"; effective date January 1, 1991.[83]
Nov. 6, 1990	Voters of **Springville, Tooele, Grantsville, and unincorporated areas of Erda, Lakepoint, Stansbury Park, and Lincoln** approved a proposition to become part of UTA and adopted the optional 1/4 of 1% sales tax for its funding (Dec. 11, 1990 included in Articles of Incorporation).	
Nov. 2, 1993	Voters of **Alpine, Highland, and Cedar Hills** approved a proposition to become part of UTA and adopted the optional 1/4 of 1% sales tax for its funding (Nov. 30, 1993 included in Articles of Incorporation).	
Nov. 8, 1994	Voters of **Mapleton, Spanish Fork, Salem, Payson, and Provo Canyon** approved a proposition to become part of UTA and adopted the optional 1/4 of 1% sales tax for its funding (Nov. 22, 1994 included in Articles of Incorporation).	
Nov. 5, 1996	Voters of **Perry, Brigham City, and Willard** approved a proposition to become part of UTA and adopted the optional 1/4 of 1% sales tax for its funding (Nov. 18, 1996 included in Articles of Incorporation).	
Nov. 7, 2000	Voters of **Salt Lake, Davis, and Weber Counties** approved the second 1/4 of 1% sales tax to fund additional light rail extensions, expanded bus service, and commuter rail.	Beginning April 1, 2001, the total sales tax rate is 1/2 of 1% in those counties and is distributed: • 0.50% for transit in Davis and Weber Counties; • 0.4375% for transit in Salt Lake County; and • 0.0625% for state highway including I-15 in Salt Lake County.
Mar. 5, 2003	**Legislature** allows a county that has not imposed a second 1/4 or 1% sales tax for transit expansion to impose a sales tax of 1/4 of 1% for allocation specified by the county for a fixed guideway system, a project or service for public transit, or a state highway involving new construction, renovation, improvement or an environmental study with approval of the voters within the county.	H.B. 136 "County Option Sales and Use Tax for Highways, Fixed Guideways, or Systems of Public Transit"; effective May 5, 2003.[84]
Mar. 3, 2004	• **Utah Legislature** adds language in 2004 allowing imposition of sales tax of "up to" 1/4 of 1%.	• H.B. 157 "Transportation Amendments" added "up to" language; effective date May 3, 2004.[85]

Source: Laws of Utah and the Utah Transit Authority, June 2004

UTA currently serves a population of over 1.7 million people, which is approximately 80 percent of Utah's total population, and serves an area of approximately fourteen hundred square miles.[86] The primary local financial support for UTA comes from a local option sales tax, which includes seven-sixteenths of 1 percent in Salt Lake County, 0.5 percent in Davis and Weber Counties, and 0.25 percent imposed in various cities in Utah, Box Elder, and Tooele Counties. In addition, UTA also charges a fare for its bus service that funds approximately 15 percent of the operating budget of the bus system and a fare for its light rail service which funds approximately 25 percent of the operating budget of the light rail system.[87]

UTA also receives a substantial portion of its funding from the federal government. Under the Federal Transit Act of 1998, Title III of the Transportation Equity Act for the Twenty-first Century (TEA-21), UTA received federal funds for 50 percent to 93 percent of the cost of substantially all property and equipment through contracts between UTA and the Federal Transit Administration. The Federal Transit Administration now allows capital grant funds to be used for preventative maintenance activities as well. In addition, UTA received a portion of its funding from federal preventative maintenance grants.[88]

UTA will need $4.4 billion in the next twenty-seven years to fund the construction of commuter rail, light rail extensions, bus rapid transit lines, and some expansion of existing systems.[89] An additional $1.7 billion will also be needed to fund bus and rail car replacements through the year 2030.[90] The Wasatch Front Regional Council has recently approved for public comment a plan which assumes that the equivalent of a 1/2-cent sales tax increase for transit will be allowed by the legislature and passed by the voters within UTA's jurisdiction by 2007.[91] The Plan includes forty miles of light rail additions, commuter rail from Brigham City to Payson, and Bus Rapid Transit serving areas in Weber, Davis, Salt Lake, Utah, and Tooele Counties. The additional sales tax revenue would generate approximately $130 million per year for construction and operation of transit improvements and allow much of the Plan to be completed before 2020.

The 2030 long range capital improvement needs reported for the other transit districts in the state are:
- $90 million for the Cache Valley Transit District and the Logan Transit District
- $90 million for the Park City Transit District
- $100 million for the Sun Tran Transit District (in St. George)[92]

LIGHT RAIL AND COMMUTER RAIL TRANSIT

Table 20-3 provides a history of the development of light rail and commuter rail transit for the last fifteen years. The Utah Transit Authority is the only transit district to date to provide rail service.

The cost of constructing and equipping a commuter rail system from Salt Lake City north to Weber County is estimated to be approximately $540 million, which includes a portion of the $185 million paid for the right-of-way. UTA has received grants from the Federal Transit Administration for much of the engineering and environmental work done to date and expects to receive federal funding for a significant portion of the construction. The annual operating cost is estimated to be $15 million. Construction began in 2005 with a projected completion date in 2008.[93]

Environmental impact statements were conducted on a Weber County to Salt Lake commuter rail line and on the West Valley and mid-Jordan light rail extensions. The draft environmental impact statement for the Mid-Jordan light rail extension was completed, and a final record of decision was issued by the Federal Transit Administration on the Weber County to Salt Lake commuter rail line in the Spring of 2005.

Table 20-3

Utah Transit Authority
Light Rail and Commuter Rail History

Date	Who and What	Notes
Mar. 12, 1990	**Utah Legislature** authorizes the imposition of a second 1/4 of 1% sales tax to fund a fixed guideway and expanded public transit system with approval of the voters within the county or municipality. In first class counties (Salt Lake County), 25% of the additional 1/4 of 1% sales tax must be used for improvements to I-15.	S.B. 108 "Public Choice on Transit Tax Amendments"; effective date January 1, 1991.[94]
Aug. 2, 1995	• **Federal Transit Administration** signed a "Full Funding Grant Agreement" with UTA indicating that the federal government will pay 80% of the $312 million cost to build the North/South light system from downtown Salt Lake City to Sandy.	
Mar. 3, 1999	• **Legislature** creates the Salt Lake Airport to University of Utah Light Rail Restricted Account and diverts a 1/64% sales tax generated in Salt Lake City and formerly used to fund Olympics for operation and maintenance of this line.	• H.B. 366 "Sales and Use Tax Diversions"; effective date May 3, 1999.[95]
	• **Legislature** in appropriations intent language, provides that if other funds are insufficient, additional operating funds would be provided from state revenues and state authorizations of local revenues for the Airport to University of Utah light rail line, not to exceed $5 million per year for a maximum 10 years.	• S.B. 3 "Appropriations Act II"; effective date March 22, 1999.[96]
Dec. 14, 1999	• Salt Lake Airport to University of Utah line is scaled back to a Main Street to Rice-Eccles Stadium extension at a cost of $105 million due to: • resistance in Congress for funding; and • time constraints of having the project done for the Olympics in February 2002.	• As a condition of obtaining federal funding for the Airport to University of Utah light rail line projected at a cost of $480 million UTA must demonstrate the ability to fund operating expenses.
Dec. 6, 1999	North/South light rail line from the Delta Center downtown Salt Lake City to 10,000 South in Sandy begins regular passenger service. The cost to construct the 15-mile line, 16 station line was $292 million.	
Feb. 29, 2000	**Legislature** directs UTA to develop a proposal for a commuter rail project, pursue federal funding, and begin negotiations for right-of-way acquisition. Capital cost for commuter rail are estimated at between $155 and $275 million and annual operating costs are estimated at between $10 and $15 million.	S.B. 1, "Appropriations Act"; effective July 1, 2000.[97]
June 26, 2000	Construction begins on a 2.5-mile light rail extension from downtown Main Street along 400 South to the Rice-Eccles Stadium at the University of Utah with 80% of the cost paid by the Federal Transit Administration.	
Dec. 15, 2001	Service began on the 2.3-mile light rail extension from downtown Main Street along 400 South to the Rice-Eccles football stadium at the University of Utah.	
May 20, 2002	Construction begins on a 1.5-mile light rail extension from Rice Eccles Stadium to the University Medical Center at a cost of extension is $89.4 million. The extension project cost includes adding seven TRAX cars, which will make a total of 40 TRAX cars in UTA's fleet.	

Date	Who and What	Notes
Sept. 20, 2002	Final agreement is signed between UTA and Union Pacific on the sale of 175 miles of rail right-of-way to UTA at a cost of $185 million. The right-of-way corridor runs 20 feet wide on the main line between Brigham City and Payson and includes the purchase of spur lines between (1) Sugar House and South Salt Lake; (2) Midvale, West Jordan, and South Jordan; (3) Woods Cross and South Ogden; and (4) the Utah County border and Lindon. Various ancillary parcels are also included.	
Nov. 7, 2000	Voters of **Salt Lake, Davis, and Weber Counties** approved the second 1/4 of 1% sales tax to fund additional light rail extensions, expanded bus service, and commuter rail.	Beginning April 1, 2001, the total sales tax rate is 1/2 of 1% in those counties and is distributed: • 0.50% for transit in Davis and Weber Counties; • 0.4375% for transit in Salt Lake County; and • 0.0625% for state highway including I-15 in Salt Lake County.
Mar. 5, 2003	**Legislature** allows a county that has not imposed a second 1/4 or 1% sales tax for transit expansion to impose a sales tax of 1/4 of 1% for allocation specified by the county for a fixed guideway system, a project or service for public transit, or a state highway involving new construction, renovation, improvement or an environmental study with approval of the voters within the county.	H.B. 136 "County Option Sales and Use Tax for Highways, Fixed Guideways, or Systems of Public Transit"; effective May 5, 2003.[98]
Sept. 29, 2003	Service begins on the 1.5-mile light rail extension from Rice Eccles Stadium to the University Medical Center which cost a total of $89.4 million.	

Source: Legislative Interim Reports, Laws of Utah, and the Utah Transit Authority, July 2004

AERONAUTICS

UDOT has general responsibility for regulating aeronautics in the state. It licenses all public-use airports in Utah and works closely with airport sponsors and managers to ensure that each functions as an integral part of the statewide system of airports. It also has a primary role in planning and programming federal and state aviation funds. It administers all federal and state funds for the construction, improvement, operation, and maintenance for publicly used airports within Utah.[99]

Utah currently has fifty-one public-use airports sponsored by local governments. Salt Lake City International Airport is Utah's largest airport and Delta Air Lines' third largest hub. In 2004, the facility served 18.3 million passengers and was ranked twenty-sixth busiest in the nation and fifty-first busiest in the world.[100] Utah also has many small airports that provide a critical, time-sensitive component of the rural transportation system.

An increasing demand for airport planning, development, and maintenance projects and a decline in federal dollars have resulted in a greater financial burden on state and local government to address airport infrastructure needs. Federal funding for thirty-five of these airports is available under the National Plan of Integrated Airport Systems for development projects only, selected by priority. The federal match on these projects is 90.94 percent, and UDOT typically provides half of the remaining 9.06 percent local share from the State Aviation Fund. The remaining sixteen airports are not eligible for federal funding under the National Plan of Integrated Airport Systems. All funding for these airports must come from state or local sources.[101]

State aviation funding comes from taxes on general and commercial aviation fuel. The state currently imposes a four cents per gallon aviation fuel tax for federally certificated (generally commercial) aircraft carriers and a nine cents per gallon aviation fuel tax for non-federally certificated aircraft carriers.[102] In addition, federally certificated aircraft carriers are eligible for a $0.015 cent per gallon refund for aviation fuel purchased at the Salt Lake City Airport.[103] Revenue from the aviation fuel tax not allocated to an airport is deposited in the Aeronautics Restricted Account to be used for construction, operation, and maintenance of publicly-used airports. Typically, the state aid to local airports is used for maintenance of runways, taxiways, and aprons in the form of crack sealing, slurry sealing, and overlays. Prior to 1999, the four cent per gallon tax rate for aviation fuel had not changed since it was enacted in 1931, when the motor fuel tax was the same rate. In 1999, the legislature approved an aviation fuel tax increase for non-federally certificated aircraft carriers. This increase provides an additional $500,000 annually for the statewide airport system.[104]

Table 20-4 shows how funds from the aviation fuel tax are currently distributed.

Table 20-4

Aviation Fuel Tax Funds Distribution			
Type of Air Carrier and Location Aviation Fuel Is Purchased	Tax Allocation per Gallon to Airport	Tax Allocation per Gallon to Aeronautical Operations	Total Tax Collected per Gallon
Federally certificated air carrier at Salt Lake City Airport (minus the amount for a refund or credit claimed under Section 59-13-404)	$0.015	$0.01	$0.025
Federally certificated air carrier at airport other than Salt Lake City Airport	$0.03	$0.01	$0.04
Non-federally certificated air carrier at Salt Lake City Airport	$0.00	$0.09	$0.09
Non-federally certificated air carrier at airport other than Salt Lake City Airport	$0.03	$0.06	$0.09

Source: Sections 59-13-402 and 59-13-404, Utah Code Annotated 1953, September 2004

Each airport in Utah has a long-range plan. In addition, the Wasatch Front Regional Council prepared the Metropolitan Airport System Plan in 1993, which is a master plan for all airports along the Wasatch Front, and UDOT updated the Utah Continuous Airport System Plan in 1993, which covers airports outside the Wasatch Front area. UDOT's priorities for the future are to expand the current five-year plan to include a ten- and twenty-year plan, to upgrade system airports by focusing on bringing airports up to Federal Aviation Administration safety standards, and to upgrade airport access by projects such as improving access roads to St. George Municipal Airport and to the Provo City Airport and building a TRAX extension from downtown Salt Lake City to the Salt Lake International Airport.[105]

Chapter 21

Relationship of State and Federal Governments

FEDERAL SUPREMACY

The Supremacy Clause in Article 6 of the United States Constitution provides that the U.S. Constitution, federal laws "made in pursuance thereof," and treaties made "under the authority of the United States," shall be "the supreme law of the land" notwithstanding any state law.[1] This clause is the basis of

> **In this chapter:**
>
> Federal Supremacy (p. 307)
> State Preemption Over Local Governments (p. 309)
> Federal Funds Received by State Agencies (p. 310)
> Influence of Federal Land Ownership in Utah (p. 310)

federal supremacy, the most important aspect of which is known as the doctrine of federal preemption. However, the Tenth Amendment attempts to limit this supremacy by reserving to the states and the people all powers not delegated to the federal government.[2]

Since the authority of the United States over the individual states is supreme on all subjects which the constitution has committed to it, an exercise of federal power generally prevails over state legislation or action. If the laws or public policy of the states come into conflict with the federal statutes,[3] or with administrative regulations properly adopted under federal law,[4] the state law must yield. State statutes or common-law rules may not set nor deny the benefits of a federal statute. The extent and nature of the legal consequences of an act which is made unlawful by federal law are determined by that law, notwithstanding conflicting state policy or law.[5] Also, when Congress, in the exercise of its constitutional powers, passes an act conferring power on a federal body, the states are deprived of authority to confer the same powers on a state body.[6]

Concurrent Power

Ordinarily state law is subordinate to federal law even where the field is one of concurrent power.[7] The supremacy of the exercise of congressional power regarding a given subject matter effectively negates the reserved power of the state.[8] State law, even if based on the acknowledged police power of the state, must always yield in case of conflict with the exercise by the federal government of any power it possesses under the law and the U.S. Constitution.[9]

In many matters, both the federal government and the states may exercise concurrent powers and enact legislation concerning the same subject matter. In these situations, the action of the state is valid unless preempted. When the subject is a local one, the states may legislate as long as their legislation is consistent with federal legislation.[10] Notwithstanding a matter being entrusted to Congress, it is competent for the state to supplement federal legislation and assist in its enforcement.[11]

State Laws

The enforcement of a state statute in the absence of federal legislation, or in the presence of consistent federal legislation, does not impair the constitutional supremacy of federal laws.[12] Where Congress has the power to regulate or control and fails to act, the states ordinarily may exercise that power.[13] If a federal statute does not occupy the whole field, it does not preclude states from enacting legislation to regulate situations not covered by the act.[14]

When Congress has purposely left untouched a part of a subject which is peculiarly adapted to local regulation, the state may legislate concerning the local matters unless the state or municipal statute conflicts with the federal law or infringes on its policy.[15] Thus, when the power given to Congress over a subject is not conclusive in its terms nor inconsistent with state action, the states may legislate on that subject until Congress evidences a purpose to totally exclude state action within the field.[16]

Exclusive Federal Authority

No state may be permitted without the consent of Congress to exercise those functions which the U.S. Constitution has delegated exclusively to Congress.[17] Among the major subjects thus removed from the sphere of state influence or activity are bankruptcy, foreign or international affairs, interstate and foreign commerce, copyrights and patents, national defense, naturalization, punishment of counterfeiting of securities and currency of the United States, and postal services.[18] There are also implied limitations upon the states in their attempts to tax the federal government and its agents.[19]

When the subject matter is national in character, so as to require uniformity of regulations affecting the states alike, the power of Congress is exclusive.[20] For example, by the National Labor Relations Act, as amended by the Labor Management Relations Act of 1947, safeguarding the right of employees to strike, Congress occupied this field and closed it to state regulation. Any concurrent state regulation of peaceful strikes for higher wages is invalid.[21]

National commerce is another area in which uniformity of regulations may be required. In *Maurer v. Hamilton,* the Court held that the Federal Motor Carrier Act did not invalidate state regulation of the size and weight of interstate trucks.[22] However, in *Castle v. Hayes Freight Lines, Inc.*, the Court held that an Illinois statute allowing for suspension of a carrier's of right to sue Illinois highways for the interstate transportation of goods was preempted by the Federal Motor Carrier Act.[23] In a number of situations the Court has invalidated statutes on the preemption ground when it appeared that the state laws sought to favor local economic interests at the expense of the interstate market.[24] On the other hand, when the Court has been satisfied that valid local interests, such as those in safety[25] or in the reputable operation of local business,[26] outweigh the restrictive effect on interstate commerce, the Court has rejected the preemption argument and allowed the state regulation to stand.

When Federal Law Is Not Exclusive

In determining whether Congress has occupied a particular field or whether state law is in conflict with federal law, the entire scheme of a federal statute and its content and purpose must be considered. The intent to occupy the field or the fact of conflict must be clearly shown.

It is often a perplexing question whether Congress has precluded state action or by the choice of selective regulatory measures has left the police power of the states undisturbed except as the state and federal regulations collide.[27]

Whether Congress and the agencies acting under it have excluded state action depends on the facts in the particular cases and the congressional intent, regardless of coincidence or terms in the state and federal statutes involved.[28] Thus, the nature of the power exerted by Congress, the object sought to be attained, and the character of the obligation imposed by the law are important in determining whether federal enactments preclude the enforcement of state laws on the same subject.[29]

Implied Preemption vs. Expressed Preemption

"Implied preemption" can be found in two situations. First, where Congress intends to "occupy the field."[30] Second, where the state law conflicts with the federal law.[31] Conflict occurs where either it is impossible to comply with both the state and federal laws or where the state law is inconsistent with the objectives or purposes of Congress.[32] "Express preemption" occurs when Congress expresses intent that federal law is to be dominant.[33] An unexpressed purpose of Congress to set aside statutes of states regulating their internal affairs is not lightly to be inferred, and ought not to be applied where the legislative command, read in the light of its history, remains ambiguous.[34] So the intention of Congress to exclude the states from exercising their reserved powers must be clearly manifested, and the courts will not lightly infer that Congress by mere passage of a federal act has impaired the traditional sovereignty of the states in that regard.[35]

While it has been held that state action may be excluded by clear implication or inconsistency as well as by express language, an intention wholly to exclude state action will not be implied unless, when fairly construed, the federal regulation on a subject is clearly in conflict with the state regulation on the same subject.[36] To justify the thwarting of state regulation, the conflict should be direct and positive so that the two acts cannot be reconciled or consistently stand together.[37]

The test of the validity of the state law is whether, under the circumstances of the particular case, such law stands as an obstacle to the accomplishment and execution of the full purposes and objectives of Congress.[38] A state law will not be considered in conflict with federal statutes if it does not impede the execution of the will and purpose of Congress.[39] If it does impede that purpose, only then must the state law yield. A state statute is in conflict with a federal statute when it is impossible to obey both the state and federal laws.[40]

Congressional Intent to Preempt

The U.S. Supreme Court outlined several principles courts can use in determining whether Congress intended to supersede the regulatory police power of the states by a federal act including:
- "The scheme of federal regulation may be so pervasive as to make reasonable the inference that Congress left no room for the States to supplement it. . ."[41]
- "[T]he act of Congress may touch a field in which the federal interest is so dominant that the federal system will be assumed to preclude enforcement of state laws on the same subject. . . "[42]
- "[T]he state policy may produce a result inconsistent with the objective of the federal statute."[43]

In a case involving warehouseman, the United States Supreme Court first looked at whether the matter in which the state was asserting "the right to act is in any way regulated by the Federal Act. If it is, the federal scheme prevails though it is a more modest, less pervasive regulatory plan than that of the state."[44]

STATE PREEMPTION OVER LOCAL GOVERNMENTS

Under the United States' system of federalism, the state is the level of general governmental power, elements of which are delegated upward to the federal government or downward to local levels of government. State preemptive capability over local governments is always assumed and is limited only by certain home rule provisions in state constitutions. Home rule provisions are usually granted by the state legislature to a local government giving the local government autonomy, based on certain conditions.[45] The view that municipal corporations have an inherent and autonomous right of local self-government has been generally denied.[46] It is established by a majority of decisions today that in the absence of constitutional limitations municipal corporations are subject to complete state regulation.[47] Any action by local governments in Utah directly in conflict with either the language or the plain meaning of the statutes is clearly preempted.

Prior to *Salt Lake City v. Allred*,[48] the Utah Supreme Court consistently held that if a municipality has enacting power, an ordinance promulgated pursuant to that power is void as having been preempted only if it directly conflicts with state statutes.[49] In *Salt Lake City v. Kusse*, the court declared that an ordinance is invalid if the "ordinance permits or licenses that which the statute forbids and prohibits, and vice versa."[50] However, in *Salt Lake City v. Allred*, the court adopted as its test, language which enunciated the direct conflict standard, but suggested that an ordinance could be preempted if the state legislature intended to preclude municipalities from legislating in the field or if the ordinance were inconsistent with state law.[51] Despite the indication that preemption can yield a result short of direct conflict with state statutes, the court apparently relied primarily on the direct conflict standard. Therefore, absent an express recognition of the preemption by occupation doctrine, only those ordinances directly in conflict with either the language or the plain meaning of the statutes are clearly preempted.

FEDERAL FUNDS RECEIVED BY STATE AGENCIES

In fiscal year 2006, Utah state agencies will receive more than $2.26 billion in federal funds (not including unemployment insurance; food stamps; taxpayer relief funds; or grants to schools, colleges, and universities). The largest portion ($1.357 billion or about 60%) of this has been appropriated for health and human services programs, primarily for Medicaid, child welfare, and grants for persons with disabilities. Figure 21-1 shows federal funds appropriated to state agencies in fiscal year 2006.

Figure 21-1[52]

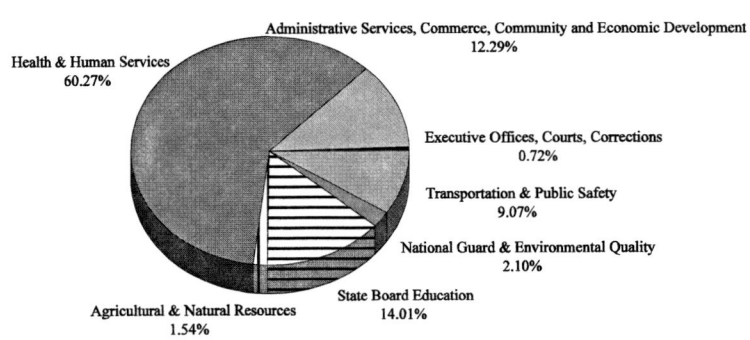

INFLUENCE OF FEDERAL LAND OWNERSHIP IN UTAH

In the mid to late 1800s, Congress passed legislation (e.g., the Homestead Act of 1862 and the Desert Lands Entry Act of 1877), which encouraged the settlement of the western United States through the sale of federally-owned land. Homestead entries peaked in 1910 and the majority of federal land transfers to private ownership took place prior to 1940.[53] Then in 1976, Congress enacted the Federal Land Policy Management Act which repealed homestead laws and established an express policy that public domain lands would generally remain federally-owned. The majority of federally-owned land is in twelve western states.

Land Managed by Federal Agencies in Utah

Of the 52.7 million acres in the state of Utah, the federal government owns about 35 million acres (66.5 percent).[54] Four federal agencies administer the majority of the federally-owned land. Table 21-1 shows the amount of land managed in Utah by those four federal agencies.

Table 21-1

Land Managed by Federal Agencies in Utah[55]

	Forest Service	National Park Service	Fish and Wildlife Service	Bureau of Land Management
Acres Managed	8,180,405	2,099,083	112,027	22,867,662
Percent of Total Utah Acres	15.5%	4%	0.2%	43.4%

Wilderness

In 1964, Congress passed the Wilderness Act which established the National Wilderness Preservation System. Areas designated as wilderness are generally undeveloped federal land greater than five thousand acres, relatively untouched by human activity, and without permanent improvements. Wilderness is managed to preserve the land's pristine character and is valued for solitude and primitive recreation. Timber harvesting, roads, buildings, or other activities that would alter the natural conditions of an area are generally prohibited in areas designated as wilderness. Some existing activities, such as mining and grazing, have been allowed under certain circumstances. The Forest Service, National Park Service, Fish and Wildlife Service, and the Bureau of Land Management (BLM) may make wilderness recommendations, but Congress holds the authority to designate wilderness. In Utah, 800,614 acres (about 1.5 percent of the state and 2.3 percent of all federal lands in Utah) have been designated as wilderness. Of this, 772,894 acres (about 9.5 percent of Forest Service lands in Utah) are Forest Service lands and 27,720 acres (about 0.1 percent of BLM lands in Utah) are Bureau of Land Management lands.[56]

In addition to areas already designated by Congress as wilderness, public lands that meet the basic criteria for wilderness designation can be identified as wilderness study areas (WSAs). The Federal Land Policy and Management Act of 1976 (FLPMA) required the BLM to review and identify possible wilderness study areas. In 1980, BLM completed an inventory of potential WSAs in the state. Currently there are about 3.3 million acres in 96 WSAs in Utah.[57] Under FLPMA, BLM is required to maintain the wilderness characteristics of all WSAs until Congress designates the WSA as wilderness or until it is released for other uses.

Payments in Lieu of Taxes

As noted in the federal preemption discussion, federal property is exempt from state and local taxation. In 1976 Congress enacted the Payments in Lieu of Taxes Act to provide some compensation to state and local governments for taxes that would have been collected if the federal land was privately owned. Payments in Lieu of Taxes require an annual appropriation from Congress. Since 1995, appropriations for PILT payments have been less than the amount authorized (but not required) under the Payments in Lieu of Taxes Act.[58] Figure 21-1 compares authorized with appropriated Payments in Lieu of Taxes paid to Utah from fiscal years 1999-2004.

Figure 21-2[59]

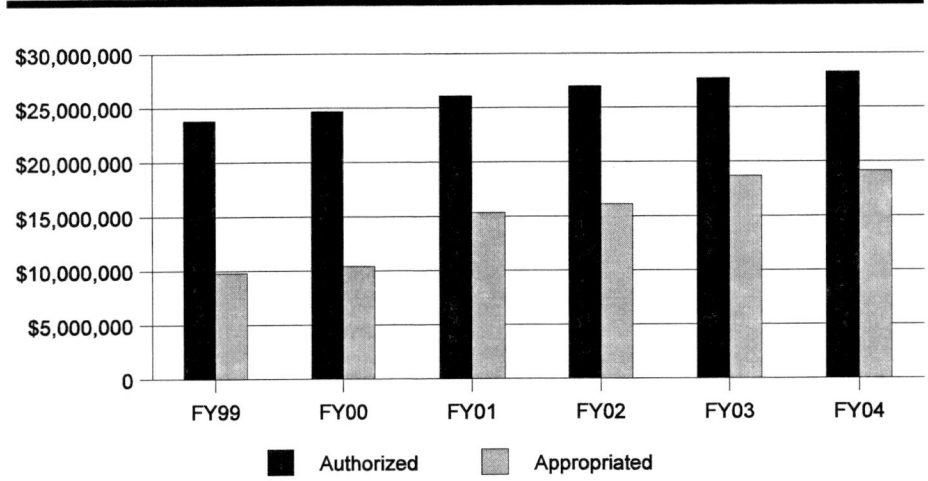

Impact of Federal Land Ownership

Federally-owned land is managed primarily for recreation, preservation, and natural resource development purposes. Controversy can result from federal land management when conflicting or competing interests and uses (e.g., land development, mineral extraction, environmental preservation, scenic beauty preservation, recreation, etc.) are at issue. In western states, where federal land ownership is significantly higher than in the other states, ownership and management of these lands has a direct affect on how people live. Rural communities in Utah are particularly impacted due to generally higher percentages of federal land ownership, a less diverse economic base, and greater impact of lost property tax revenue on local government budgets.

Chapter 22

Local Government

GENERAL BACKGROUND
Differences Between State & Local and Federal & State Relationships

In this chapter:

General Background (p. 313)
Counties (p. 314)
Municipalities (Cities and Towns) (p. 321)
Limited Purpose Local Governments (p. 332)

Local government entities are political subdivisions of the state. As political subdivisions, local government entities are not sovereign entities with inherent authority but are subject to the authority of the state. While the Utah Constitution imposes limitations on legislative authority with respect to local government, these entities still derive their authority from legislative enactments and are generally subject to legislative regulation and control.

While this state/local relationship is often compared to the relationship between the federal government and the states, there are some significant differences. Unlike local government entities, Utah, like all states, is a sovereign entity with certain inherent authority. Utah does not derive its authority from the federal government; rather, the federal government derives its authority from the states or from the people of the states.[1] It is only because of that derived authority and the supremacy clause of the U.S. Constitution that federal enactments take precedence over conflicting state laws, as discussed in Chapter 21, *Relationship of State and Federal Governments*. Unless there is a conflicting federal law, states are free to enact legislation and regulate behavior as they determine appropriate.

General Purpose Local Government vs. Limited Purpose Local Government

Counties, cities, and towns are units of local government that are general purpose governments. They are general purpose in nature because they are statutorily authorized to do whatever is reasonably necessary for the health, safety, morals, and welfare of their inhabitants, unless the legislature has specifically otherwise provided by statute.[2] They may provide services, criminalize certain behavior, and enforce the law through the exercise of the police power. Although counties, cities, and towns have been given broad general welfare powers, their authority with respect to fiscal matters is more narrow and is limited to those powers enumerated in statute.

In contrast to general purpose governments, limited purpose local government entities have not been given general welfare power. These limited purpose government entities may exercise only those powers and perform only those functions that are explicitly provided for in statute.[3] They are typically a provider of a specific service, such as water or sewer service, or perform a limited function, such as redevelopment. Limited purpose local governments include special districts, local districts, redevelopment agencies, and entities created under the Interlocal Cooperation Act.

COUNTIES

History

County government's lineage can be traced to the English shire of a thousand years ago. In England, two different county traditions developed: (1) the county as an administrative arm of the central government and (2) the county as a local government providing services directly to the people. Although the English county remained a leading unit of local government, smaller units, such as the parish and borough, became important providers of local services. These traditions later were transported to this country.[4]

In Utah, counties continue to act in many ways as an arm of state government, administering health and human services and fulfilling similar functions. Counties—particularly Salt Lake County—have also increasingly become providers of other local services that have traditionally been regarded as municipal-type services such as police, fire, water, sewer, and roads. In 1971, first and second class counties were statutorily authorized for the first time in Utah to provide a limited number of municipal services to the unincorporated area of the county.[5] Utah statute now authorizes all counties to provide many municipal-type services to areas outside municipalities.[6]

Current Status

Of the twenty-nine counties in Utah, the most populous county, Salt Lake, has a population of 935,295 whereas the least populous county, Daggett, has a population of 926.[7] San Juan County has the largest land area of 7,761 square miles whereas Davis County has the smallest land area of 275 square miles.[8] Figure 22-1 shows where each county and its county seat is located in Utah. Table 22-1 lists each county and its population.

Figure 22-1

Local Government • 315

Table 22-1

Classification of Counties and County Populations
Population as of July 1, 2004

Classification and County Name	Population	Population per Square Mile
First Class Counties (700,000 +)		
Salt Lake	935,295	1,237.2
Second Class Counties (125,000 - 700,000)		
Utah	403,352	198.3
Davis	261,208	949.8
Weber	208,633	385.6
Third Class Counties (31,000 - 125,000)		
Washington	109,924	44.6
Cache	97,467	83.7
Tooele	49,688	7.3
Box Elder	44,810	8.2
Iron	36,285	11.1
Summit	33,843	18.1
Fourth Class Counties (11,000 - 31,000)		
Uintah	26,671	6.2
Sanpete	23,649	14.6
Carbon	19,689	13.2
Sevier	19,455	9.8
Wasatch	18,139	15.5
Duchesne	15,004	4.6
San Juan	14,015	1.8
Millard	12,305	1.9
Fifth Class Counties (4,000 - 11,000)		
Emery	10,723	2.0
Juab	9,009	2.8
Grand	8,712	2.4
Morgan	7,614	12.2
Kane	6,178	1.5
Beaver	6,077	2.3
Garfield	4,427	0.8
Sixth Class Counties (Under 4,000)		
Wayne	2,494	1.0
Rich	2,054	1.3
Piute	1,393	1.8
Daggett	926	1.1

Source: Population from U.S. Census Bureau

Utah Constitutional Provisions

The Utah Constitution outlines some requirements and limitations relating to counties. These requirements and limitations are summarized below.

Counties Recognized as Legal Subdivisions

Article XI, Section 1 of the Utah Constitution recognizes counties as legal subdivisions of the state.[9] As legal subdivisions of the state, counties are dependent upon the legislature for any changes in their authority or responsibilities.

Moving a County Seat

The Utah Constitution provides that a county seat may be moved only when two-thirds of those voting on the proposition at a countywide general election vote in favor of moving the county seat. A proposition to move the county seat may not be submitted in the same county more than once in four years.[10]

Changing County Lines

The Utah Constitution provides that no territory may be stricken from any county unless a majority of the voters living in that county who vote on the proposition, as well as a majority of the voters living in the county to which it is to be annexed who vote on the proposition, vote in favor. An exception to the general rule is that counties sharing a common boundary may, through their county legislative bodies, make a minor adjustment, as defined by statute (currently one thousand feet),[11] to the common boundary. The legislature does not have the authority to change a county boundary.[12]

Optional Forms of County Government

Prior to 1972, the Utah Constitution required the legislature to "establish a system of county government that shall be uniform throughout the state."[13] In 1973, the Utah Constitution was amended to require the legislature to provide for optional forms of county government in statute.[14] The selection of an optional form is subject to voter approval as provided by statute.[15]

Public Debt Limits

Under the Utah Constitution, counties may not incur general obligation debt without voter approval.[16] General obligation debt is debt secured by property tax revenues. The total county indebtedness may not exceed 2 percent of the value of taxable property in the county.[17]

Changing County Boundaries

More than ninety county boundary changes have been made since the first six counties were designated in 1850 by the legislative assembly of the provincial State of Deseret.[18] The last county created is Daggett County, which was created in 1917 from territory taken from Uintah County. Although there have been several proposals for county boundary changes since then, the only major county boundary change occurred in 2003 when the Emery County and Grand County joint boundary was changed so that the portion of Green River City that had been in Grand County was moved to be within Emery County. In 2002, the Utah Constitution was changed to allow the county legislative bodies of two adjoining counties to make minor boundary adjustments. The major impetus for the constitutional amendment allowing a more streamlined process for a minor boundary change was the situation on the Utah County/Salt Lake County boundary on Traverse Ridge in Draper where lots were created that straddle the county boundary.

State statute provides four different ways to change county boundaries: (1) divide a county into two counties to create a new county, (2) consolidate two counties into one county, (3) make a major boundary adjustment between two counties, and (4) make a minor boundary adjustment between two counties. Each way to change county boundaries has its own statutory process as described below. State statute does not provide for a process to dissolve a county.

Dividing a County

The process to divide a county into two counties, thus creating a new county from an existing county, is citizen initiated. At least one-fourth of the registered voters from the area proposed to be a new county and also at least one-fourth of the registered voters from the remaining portion of the county must sign a petition requesting a new county be formed. The question is then voted upon by all voters. For the new county and also the remaining portion of the county, the election must pass by a majority vote in both the area proposed.[19]

Consolidating Counties

State statute provides a process whereby two counties may be consolidated into one county. A majority of voters in one county may petition that the consolidation question be placed before the voters. For the consolidation to occur, the ballot question must pass with a majority in both counties.[20]

Major Boundary Change

State statute provides a process whereby a portion of one county may be removed from that county and annexed to an adjoining county. A majority of voters in the territory proposed to be annexed may petition that the annexation question be placed before the voters of both full counties. For the annexation to occur, the ballot question must pass with a majority in each of the counties.[21]

Minor Boundary Adjustment

Counties sharing a common boundary may, in accordance with the Utah Constitution Article XI, Section 3, adjust all or part of the common boundary to move it up to one thousand feet from its location before the adjustment. The boundary adjustment is accomplished by the legislative bodies of both counties passing a joint resolution.[22]

Classification

Utah statute classifies counties according to population. Prior to 1987, counties were classified according to assessed valuation of property instead of population. Classification allows the legislature to grant different powers and apply different requirements to counties based on the characteristics of the classification.

Table 22-1 shows the population ranges for the six classifications outlined in statute and the population for each county obtained from the U.S. Census Bureau. For a county's classification to officially change, the lieutenant governor must issue a certificate of classification.[23] The classification shown in table 22-1 is based on the counties' population and may or may not reflect a county's official classification. The data in figures 22-2, 22-3, and 22-4 also are based on county population data obtained from the U.S. Census Bureau. Note that 75.7 percent of the state's population lives in just four counties: Salt Lake, Utah, Davis, and Weber.

Figure 22-2

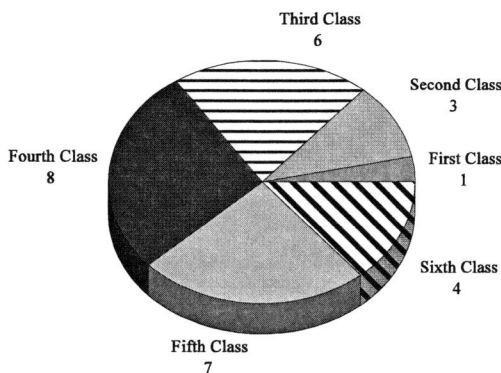

Number of Counties by Class

Figure 22-3

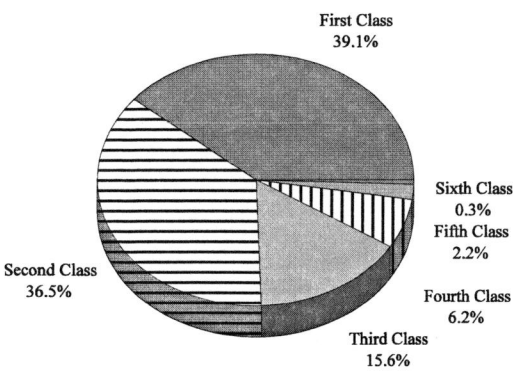

Percentage of State's Population by Class of County

Figure 22-4

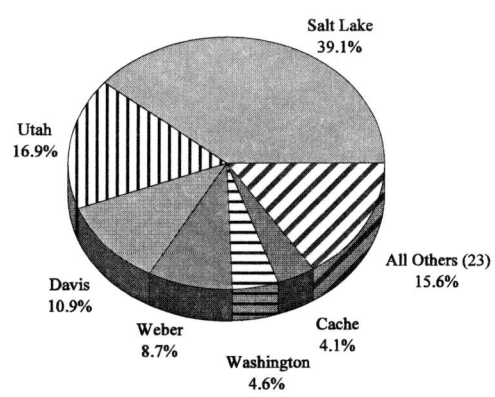

County Population as a Share of State Population

Local Government • 319

Forms of County Government[24]

Utah statute requires counties to operate under one of the following four forms of county government: (1) the county commission form, (2) the expanded county commission form, (3) the county executive-council form, or (4) the council-manager form. Unless a county adopts one of the other forms of government, the county is required to operate under the county commission form.

Grand County and Morgan County have adopted an optional form of county government similar to the expanded county commission form. Cache, Salt Lake, and Wasatch counties have adopted an optional form of county government similar to the county executive-council form. All other twenty-four counties operate under a three-member county commission form of government.

County Commission Form

Each county operating under a county commission form of government is governed by three county commissioners. These county commissioners act as both the county legislative body and the county executive and collectively exercise both legislative and executive powers, duties, and functions.[25]

Expanded County Commission Form

Each county operating under an expanded county commission form of government is governed by a county commission consisting of five or seven members. As with the county commission form, the county commission under the expanded county commission form of government exercises both legislative and executive powers, duties, and functions.[26]

County Executive-Council Form

A county operating under a county executive-council form of government is governed by an elected county council, an elected county executive, and such other officers and employees as are authorized by law. An optional plan, which is adopted by the county when the county changes its form of government, provides for the qualifications, time and manner of election, term of office, and compensation of the county executive. The county executive is the chief executive officer of the county. In the county executive-council form of county government, the county council is the county legislative body and exercises legislative powers, whereas the county executive exercises the executive powers.[27]

Council-Manager Form

A county operating under a council-manager form of government is governed by an elected county council, a county manager appointed by the council, and such other officers and employees as are authorized by law. The optional plan provides for the qualifications, time and manner of appointment, term of office, compensation, and removal of the county manager.

In the council-manager form of county government, the legislative powers of the county are vested in the county council, and the executive powers of the county are vested in the county manager. The county manager is the administrative head of the county government and has the powers, functions, and duties of a county executive, except as the county legislative body otherwise provides by ordinance. The county manager may not veto any ordinances enacted by the council.[28]

Uniform Fiscal Procedures[29]

State statute provides for uniform accounting, budgeting, and financial reporting procedures for counties. The statute requires counties to:
- Make financial plans for both current and capital expenditures

- Ensure that their executive staffs administer their respective functions in accordance with adopted budgets
- Provide the public and investors with information about the financial policies and administration of counties
- Provide for the optional use of performance budgeting and related accounting and reporting procedures
- Enable larger counties to evaluate and measure operating performance and provide data comparable with other cities

Counties are required to file with the state auditor both budgets and financial reports. Independent audits are required. The amount of fund balances are limited. Counties are limited from making any appropriations in excess of the estimated expendable revenue.

Land Use Regulation and Townships[30]

An important function of county government is the regulation of the use of land in the unincorporated areas of the county. State statute gives counties broad authority to enact ordinances regulating the use of land in the unincorporated parts of the counties.[31] Each county is required to adopt a general plan to address present and future needs of the county and the future development of land within the unincorporated area of the county.[32] Each county is also required to establish a planning commission to make recommendations to the county legislative body concerning the general plan, land use ordinances, and other land use decisions.[33]

A county may also divide some or all of the unincorporated area into one or more townships.[34] A township is a designation of a portion of a county's unincorporated area that provides protection from annexations by adjoining municipalities. State law prohibits an area within a township from being annexed to an adjoining municipality unless all of the area in the township is annexed or township voters or property owners approve of the annexation.[35] A township designation also allows more local input into land use issues. Each township may have a separate planning commission, thus giving township residents greater direct input into recommendations for land use regulations that affect the township area. Greater local control over planning and zoning issues is often a major factor leading an unincorporated area of a county to incorporate into a municipality.

MUNICIPALITIES (CITIES AND TOWNS)

History

Cities, towns, and villages have existed throughout the world for thousands of years. For the most part, these local units, which functioned as centers of commerce, were established to provide special local services to populations concentrated in relatively small geographical areas.

Current Status

In Utah, the term "municipality" refers to both cities and towns. There are no villages in Utah. As of September 2005, there are 241 municipalities in Utah.[36] Utah's biggest city, Salt Lake City, has a population of 178,605, whereas the smallest town, Ophir, has a population of twenty-five.[37] Table 22-2 lists each municipality and county and its population. Of Utah's total population of 2,389,039, about 85 percent or 2,041,928 live within municipalities.[38] Of Utah's 84,900 square miles, only about 2 percent of the land area is located within municipalities. Figure 22-5 shows where the municipalities are located in Utah.

Table 22-2

Population of Utah Municipalities and Counties
As of July 1, 2004

Beaver County	6,077	Balance of Cache County	6,468
Beaver	2,513		
Milford	1,414	**Carbon County**	19,689
Minersville	818	East Carbon	1,295
Balance of Beaver County	1,332	Helper	1,909
		Price	8,197
Box Elder County	44,810	Scofield	26
Bear River City	796	Sunnyside	382
Brigham City	17,149	Wellington	1,582
Corinne	645	Balance of Carbon County	6,298
Deweyville	311		
Elwood	717	**Daggett County**	926
Fielding	443	Manila	302
Garland	1,984	Balance of Daggett County	624
Honeyville	1,273		
Howell	233	**Davis County**	261,208
Mantua	786	Bountiful	41,173
Perry	2,916	Centerville	14,670
Plymouth	375	Clearfield	27,227
Portage	273	Clinton	16,447
Snowville	171	Farmington	13,882
Tremonton	6,205	Fruit Heights	4,743
Willard	1,650	Kaysville	21,749
Balance of Box Elder County	8,883	Layton	61,205
		North Salt Lake	9,555
Cache County	97,467	South Weber	5,486
Amalga	413	Sunset	5,000
Clarkston	661	Syracuse	16,158
Cornish	252	West Bountiful	4,755
Hyde Park	2,955	West Point	7,046
Hyrum	6,463	Woods Cross	7,859
Lewiston	1,781	Balance of Davis County	4,253
Logan	45,517		
Mendon	974	**Duchesne County**	15,004
Millville	1,487	Altamont	180
Newton	692	Duchesne	1,454
Nibley	2,657	Myton	550
North Logan	6,692	Roosevelt	4,437
Paradise	728	Tabiona	151
Providence	5,351	Balance of Duchesne County	8,232
Richmond	1,971		
River Heights	1,422	**Emery County**	10,723
Smithfield	7,801	Castle Dale	1,612
Trenton	437	Clawson	164
Wellsville	2,745	Cleveland	513

322 • *Local Government*

Elmo	369	Balance of Kane County	1,152
Emery	302		
Ferron	1,567	**Millard County**	12,305
Green River	954	Delta	3,126
Huntington	2,066	Fillmore	2,195
Orangeville	1,346	Hinckley	739
Balance of Emery County	1,830	Holden	393
		Kanosh	480
Garfield County	4,427	Leamington	211
Antimony	111	Lynndyl	127
Boulder	174	Meadow	250
Cannonville	135	Oak City	629
Escalante	743	Scipio	298
Hatch	115	Balance of Millard County	3,857
Henrieville	144		
Panguitch	1,476	**Morgan County**	7,614
Tropic	462	Morgan	2,748
Balance of Garfield County	1,067	Balance of Morgan County	4,866
Grand County	8,712	**Piute County**	1,393
Castle Valley	354	Circleville	487
Moab	4,825	Junction	171
Balance of Grand County	3,533	Kingston	137
		Marysvale	357
Iron County	36,285	Balance of Piute County	241
Brian Head	115		
Cedar City	22,224	**Rich County**	2,054
Enoch	3,955	Garden City	391
Kanarraville	304	Laketown	186
Paragonah	465	Randolph	477
Parowan	2,546	Woodruff	192
Balance of Iron County	6,676	Balance of Rich County	808
Juab County	9,009	**Salt Lake County**	935,295
Eureka	788	Alta	366
Levan	801	Bluffdale	6,087
Mona	1,079	Draper (part)**	32,219
Nephi	5,034	Herriman	7,826
Rocky Ridge	437	Holladay*	19,311
Santaquin (part)**	4	Midvale	27,019
Balance of Juab County	866	Murray	43,328
		Riverton	30,119
Kane County	6,178	Salt Lake City	178,605
Alton	138	Sandy	89,979
Big Water	417	South Jordan	36,791
Glendale	347	South Salt Lake	21,510
Kanab	3,528	Taylorsville	58,179
Orderville	596	West Jordan	89,011

	West Valley City	112,678
	Balance of Salt Lake County*	182,079
San Juan County		14,015
	Blanding	3,056
	Monticello	1,912
	Balance of San Juan County	9,047
Sanpete County		23,649
	Centerfield	1,044
	Ephraim	4,765
	Fairview	1,157
	Fayette	202
	Fountain Green	936
	Gunnison	2,661
	Manti	3,170
	Mayfield	416
	Moroni	1,269
	Mount Pleasant	2,688
	Spring City	997
	Sterling	250
	Wales	223
	Balance of Sanpete County	3,871
Sevier County		19,455
	Annabella	607
	Aurora	951
	Elsinore	743
	Glenwood	438
	Joseph	272
	Koosharem*	291
	Monroe	1,849
	Redmond	798
	Richfield	7,048
	Salina	2,406
	Sigurd	431
	Balance of Sevier County*	3,621
Summit County		33,843
	Coalville	1,423
	Francis	802
	Henefer	721
	Kamas	1,438
	Oakley	1,160
	Park City (part)**	7,881
	Balance of Summit County	20,418

Tooele County		49,688
	Grantsville	7,077
	Ophir	25
	Rush Valley	523
	Stockton	573
	Tooele	27,903
	Vernon	272
	Wendover	1,625
	Balance of Tooele County	11,690
Uintah County		26,671
	Ballard	598
	Naples	1,444
	Vernal	7,939
	Balance of Uintah County	16,690
Utah County		403,352
	Alpine	7,896
	American Fork	22,387
	Cedar Fort	317
	Cedar Hills	5,813
	Draper (part)**	823
	Eagle Mountain	8,190
	Elk Ridge	2,001
	Genola	1,159
	Goshen	817
	Highland	12,332
	Lehi	25,665
	Lindon	8,489
	Mapleton	6,129
	Orem	88,619
	Payson	14,542
	Pleasant Grove	27,116
	Provo	99,624
	Salem	4,838
	Santaquin (part)**	5,811
	Saratoga Springs	5,389
	Spanish Fork	22,839
	Springville	21,507
	Vineyard	135
	Woodland Hills	1,190
	Balance of Utah County*	9,724
Wasatch County		18,139
	Charleston	414
	Heber	8,800
	Midway	2,529
	Park City (part)**	1

Wallsburg	283
Balance of Wasatch County	6,112
Washington County	109,924
Enterprise	1,403
Hildale	1,980
Hurricane	9,748
Ivins	6,404
La Verkin	3,846
Leeds	622
New Harmony	195
Rockville	259
St. George	59,780
Santa Clara	5,661
Springdale	520
Toquerville	1,046
Virgin	472
Washington	11,521
Balance of Washington County*	6,467
Wayne County	2,494
Bicknell	342
Hanksville	200
Loa	510
Lyman	227
Torrey	168
Balance of Wayne County	1,047
Weber County	208,633
Farr West	4,256
Harrisville	4,780
Hooper	4,108
Huntsville	657
Marriott-Slaterville	1,418
North Ogden	16,328
Ogden	78,519
Plain City	4,159
Pleasant View	6,048
Riverdale	7,896
Roy	35,308
South Ogden	15,130
Uintah	1,223
Washington Terrace	8,395
West Haven	5,237
Balance of Weber County	15,171
All of Utah	2,389,039

Source: U.S. Census Bureau

* On August 10, 2005, the Utah Population Estimates Committee provided estimates for the following four incorporations and two annexations: Cottonwood Heights incorporation, 35,853; Central Valley incorporation, 471; Fairfield incorporation, 134; Apple Valley incorporation, 538; Holladay after annexation, 25,646; and Koosharem after annexation, 389.

** Part of Santaquin is located in Utah County and part is located in Juab County. Part of Park City is located in Summit County and part is located in Wasatch County. Part of Draper is located in Salt Lake County and part is located in Utah County.

Figure 22-5

Location of Municipalities in Utah

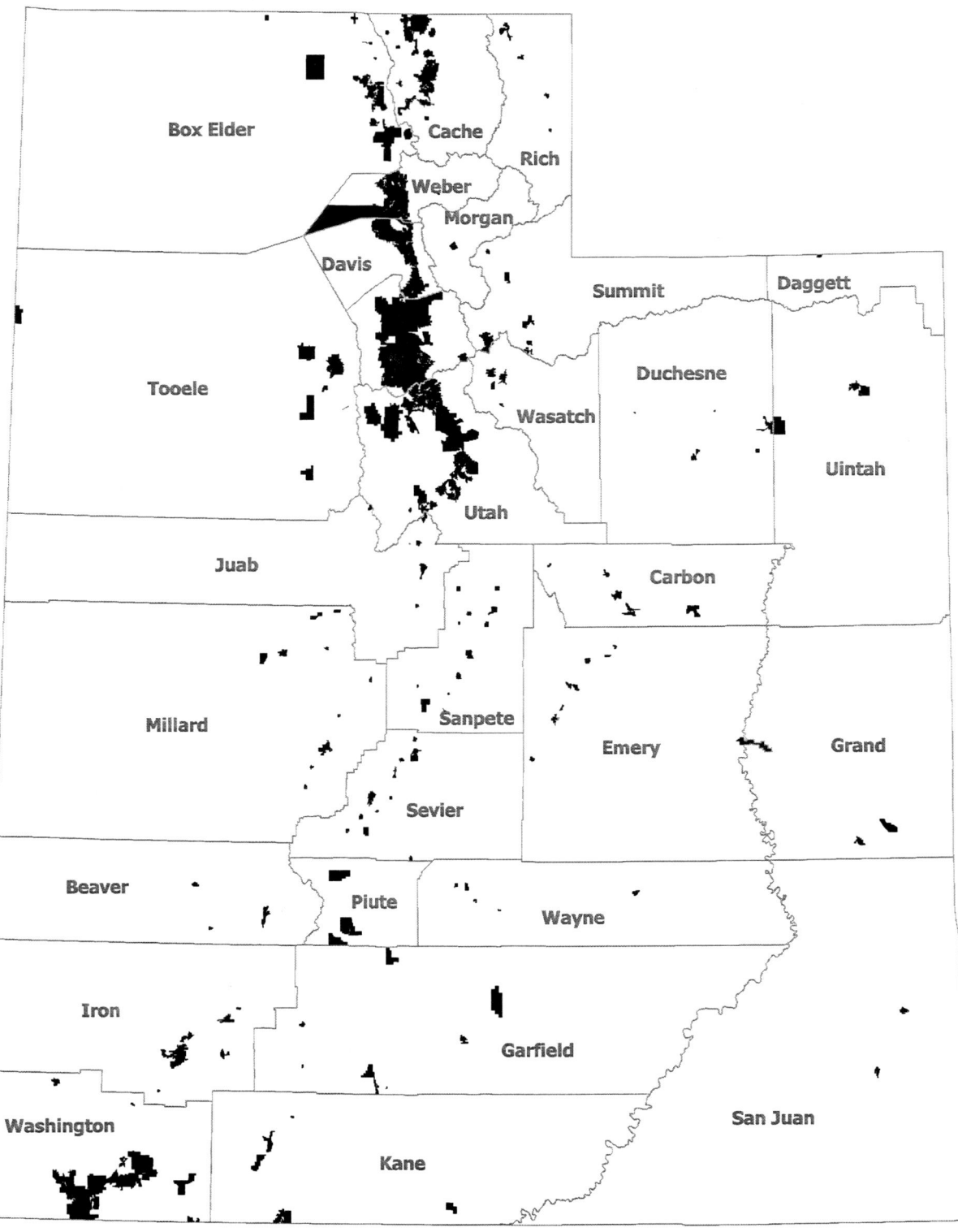

Utah Constitution Provisions

The Utah Constitution prohibits the legislature from creating any cities or towns by special laws. However, the constitution requires the legislature to provide by statute for the incorporation, organization, and dissolution of cities and towns and for their classification in proportion to population.[39]

Charter Cities

In 1933, the Utah Constitution was amended to allow cities and towns to adopt a charter through a process that requires voter approval first of a charter commission to draft a charter and then of the charter itself.[40] The charter provisions of the constitution set forth the powers given to charter cities.

The constitutional amendment came at a time when there was a trend among several states toward allowing more local autonomy. Enabling cities and towns to adopt a charter was seen as a way of allowing them greater local control. Only a few Utah municipalities ever adopted a charter, and the only remaining charter city is Tooele.

Municipalities Forbidden from Disposing of Water Rights

The Utah Constitution prohibits municipalities from leasing, selling, or disposing of any waterworks, water rights, or sources of water supply. All waterworks, water rights, and sources of water supply owned are to be preserved, maintained, and operated by the municipality for supplying its inhabitants with water at reasonable charges.[41]

Public Debt Limits

As with counties, the Utah Constitution prohibits municipalities from issuing general obligation debt without voter approval.[42] No part of the indebtedness may be incurred for other than strictly municipal purposes.[43] A municipality may not become indebted to an amount exceeding 4 percent of the value of the taxable property,[44] although a first or second class city may incur up to 4 percent additional debt and any other city or town may incur up to 8 percent additional debt for supplying the city or town with water, artificial lights, or sewers.[45]

Incorporation, Dissolution, and Boundary Changes

State statutes provide a process for municipal incorporation, dissolution, annexation, withdrawal, and boundary adjustments. Incorporation is the creation of a new city from the unincorporated part of a county. Municipalities may not overlap. Dissolution is the process of dissolving an existing city or town. Boundary changes can occur through annexation, withdrawal, or boundary adjustments with adjacent municipalities. For incorporation or any boundary changes, the statute requires the area to be contiguous and not create any peninsulas or leave any islands of unincorporated area. Each of the processes are briefly summarized below. The specifics of each process may be found in Title 10, Chapter 2, Incorporation, Classification, Boundaries, Consolidation, and Dissolution of Municipalities.

Incorporation

The municipal incorporation process is property owner initiated. An area proposed for incorporation must have at least one hundred residents. An area with one hundred to one thousand residents would incorporate as a town as described in the next paragraph. For areas with more than one thousand residents, the process to incorporate starts with a petition signed by property owners of at least 10 percent of the land area and 7 percent of the value of the private real property. This petition initiates a feasibility study which examines various issues including projected revenues and projected costs of the new municipality. State statute prohibits the incorporation if the feasibility study projects that the average annual revenue exceeds the average annual costs by more than 5 percent. If the results of the feasibility study allow incorporation, public hearings are held. The next step is an incorporation petition signed by property owners of at least one-third of the private land area and at least one-third of the value of all real property within the area proposed for incorporation. A successful incorporation petition places the question of incorporation on the ballot for all residents of the area to vote.[46]

The process to incorporate as a town (100 - 1,000 residents) starts with a petition signed by property owners of a majority of the land area and at least one-third of the value of private real property. The county may conduct a feasibility study, but is not required to do so. If a feasibility study is performed, the same 5 percent rule applies as with the incorporation of a city. Unlike the process for incorporating a city, the incorporation question for a town is not voted upon by the residents. Instead, the county legislative body is authorized to approve the incorporation if it determines that the incorporation is in the best interests of the citizens of the county and the proposed town.[47]

Annexation[48]

Municipal annexation for twenty-eight of Utah's twenty-nine counties requires the adoption of an annexation policy plan in addition to other requirements. The annexation policy plan contains a map of projected expansion with criteria that will guide the municipality's decision whether to grant future annexation requests. Municipalities within Salt Lake County (Utah's only first class county) are not required to adopt an annexation policy plan.

The municipal annexation process for most annexations is property owner initiated. The process to annex starts with an annexation petition signed by the owners of property representing a majority of the private land area and at least one-third of the value of the private real property in the area proposed for annexation. If property within an agriculture protection area is included in the area proposed for annexation, all of the owners of that property must sign the petition. If the area proposed for annexation is entirely government owned, each state or local government entity owning property in the area must sign the petition. The municipal legislative body may reject a petition for annexation. However, if the property tax rate for the area proposed for annexation is higher than the tax rate in the municipality, municipalities in first class counties (Salt Lake County) may not reject the annexation petition. A protest to the annexation may be filed by the county legislative body, special districts, neighboring municipalities, or private property owners within one-half-mile of the proposed annexation. If protested, the boundary commission examines whether projected revenues from the annexation area would exceed the projected costs by more than 5 percent. If the projected revenues exceed costs by more than 5 percent, state statute prohibits the annexation. Public hearings are held and the municipal legislative body makes the final decision limited by provisions in the statute.

For unincorporated islands within a municipality or for unincorporated peninsulas, the municipal legislative body may initiate the annexation process if the municipality has been providing municipal services to the area for more than a year. If the property owners of at least a majority of the land area and one-half of the private land value do not protest, the municipal legislative body may annex the island or peninsula. Additionally, a municipality may annex an area without a petition if the area is an unincorporated island with fewer than five hundred residents and the municipality has provided one or more municipal services to the area for at least a year. If a protest to the annexation is submitted by the owners of property representing 10 percent of the private land area and 10 percent of the value of private land in the area proposed for annexation, the municipality may not annex the area.

Boundary Adjustments[49]

Municipalities having common boundaries may adjust common boundaries unless property owners within that area protest. The protest must have signatures of property owners from at least 25 percent of the land area and 15 percent of the land value.

Withdrawal/Disconnection[50]

The municipal disconnection process is property owner initiated. The process to disconnect territory from a municipality is initiated by a petition signed by the property owners of at least a majority of the real property. The municipality holds a public hearing then makes its decision on whether or not to grant the disconnection request. The petitioners or the county may appeal the municipality's decision to district court. The district court hears evidence regarding the viability of the disconnection proposal and other criteria outlined in the statute. The court's order either ordering or rejecting disconnection outlines the findings and reasons.

Consolidation of Municipalities[51]

State statute also provides a process for consolidating municipalities. The process is initiated by either (1) resolutions passed by the municipalities wanting to consolidate or (2) petitions signed by at least 10 percent of the registered voters in each of the municipalities. A plan for consolidation is prepared setting forth the nature of obligations, assets, and liabilities of the municipalities. Public hearings and an election are held to determine the outcome of the proposal.

Dissolution of Municipalities[52]

A municipality may be dissolved by court order. The process is generally initiated by a voter petition. If the municipality has fewer than fifty residents, the process may also be initiated by an application submitted by the county legislative body. A voter petition requires a number of registered voter signatures equal to at least 25 percent of the votes cast in the last congressional election. A petition is not valid if it has been less than two years since incorporation or less than two years since an unsuccessful dissolution election. If the district court determines that a voter petition complies with statutory requirements, the court orders an election to determine the outcome of the dissolution request. If an election is held and a majority of those voting vote in favor of dissolution, the district court orders dissolution and winds down the affairs of the municipality, including making provisions for payments of debts, performance of contracts, and disposal of assets. If the dissolution process was initiated by an application of the county legislative body for a municipality with fewer than fifty residents, no election is required. Instead, the district court, upon making the necessary findings, simply orders dissolution and implements the same winding down provisions.

Classification[53]

Because the needs of large and small municipalities differ, the statute classifies municipalities according to population. The statute contains different powers and requirements based on classification.

The most recent population figures for municipalities from the U.S. Census Bureau and the Utah Populations Estimates Committee are for July 1, 2004. Based on these population figures and the classification ranges in the statute, table 22-3 shows the number of municipalities that fall into each of the classes and the total population for each of the classes. A municipality's official classification is determined by a declaration by the lieutenant governor and the official classification of some municipalities for various reasons does not conform to the population ranges outlined in the statute. Figures 22-6 and 22-7 show this information graphically.

Table 22-3

Classification of Municipalities

Classification	Population Range	Number of Municipalities	Total Population in Class
City of the first class	100,000 or more	2	291,283
City of the second class	65,000 through 99,999	5	445,752
City of the third class	30,000 through 64,999	11	480,295
City of the fourth class	10,000 through 29,999	22	440,951
City of the fifth class	1,000 through 9,999	97	382,473
Town	Under 1,000	104	44,603

Source: Population from U.S. Census Bureau; Classification from Utah Code Annotated Section 10-2-301.

Figure 22-6

Statewide Population Per Class of Municipality

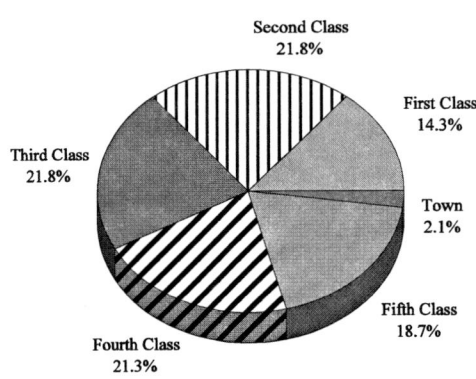

Source: Population from U.S. Census Bureau; Classification from Utah Code Annotated Section 10-2-301.

Figure 22-7

Municipalities Per Class

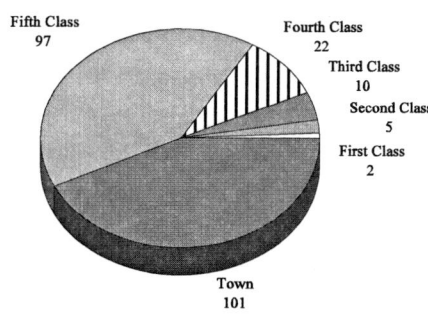

Source: Population from U.S. Census Bureau; Classification from Utah Code Annotated Section 10-2-301.

Forms of Municipal Government[54]

There are presently four basic forms of government under which a municipality may operate. They are (1) the five-member council form, (2) the six-member council form, (3) the council-mayor form, and (4) the council-manager form.[55]

In the five-member and six-member council forms and the council-manager form, the council is the governing body and exercises both legislative and executive powers. In both the five-member and six-member council forms, one of the council members is also the mayor. Under the five-member council form, the mayor is a voting member. Under the six-member council form, the mayor votes only in the event of a tie or in the appointment or dismissal of a city manager. In both the five-member and six-member council forms, the mayor exercises ceremonial and administrative functions.[56]

By contrast, the council-mayor form of government consists of a five- or seven-member council, which exercises legislative powers, and a mayor, who exercises executive powers. In the council-mayor form, the mayor has veto power over council enactments.[57] The mayor's veto may be overridden by a two-thirds vote of the council. City council members and mayors are elected to four-year terms except when needed to stagger the terms of a newly created municipality. Features of the different forms of government are summarized in table 22-4.

Table 22-4[58]

Optional Forms of Municipal Government				
Form of Government	Size of Council	Mayor	Separation of Powers	Mayor Has Veto Power
Five-Member Council	5 (including the mayor)	Yes	No	No
Six-Member Council	6 (including the mayor)	Yes	No	No
Council-Mayor	5 or 7	Yes	Yes	Yes
Council-Manager	5 or 7	No*	No	No mayor*

* Although a mayor is not specifically provided for in the code provisions related to the council-manager form of government, other provisions elsewhere in the code suggest that this form of government may include a mayor.

Another form of municipal government is mentioned in another part of the Utah Code, separate from the provisions relating to the previously mentioned four forms of municipal government. That form is referred to as a "manager form of government." It is established when a governing body adopts an ordinance establishing a manager form of government and appointing a person to act as city or town manager. Establishing this form of government does not require voter approval.[59]

A city's form of government is determined at the time of incorporation. Voters at the incorporation election select the form of government under which the new city will operate. A new town, by contrast, is initially required to operate under a five-member council form of government.[60]

A municipality retains the form of government under which it is currently operating until the municipality adopts another form of government. Changing the form of government under which a municipality operates may be initiated by either the governing body of the municipality or a citizen initiative. A change in the form of government requires voter approval. If the form of government is changed, it cannot be changed again for four years. If the ballot question fails, the same optional form of government may not be proposed for two years.[61]

A city retains its current form of government even after an increase in population results in a change of classification. However, a town operating under a five-member council form of government whose classification changes to fifth class city because of a population increase is required to change its form of government to a six-member council.[62]

Uniform Fiscal Procedures[63]

In state statute there are two similar but separate sets of provisions governing accounting, budgeting, and financial reporting procedures and requirements for municipalities. One set of provisions applies to cities, and the other set applies to towns. They include provisions that:
- Establish procedures for the adoption of a budget, including a requirement for notice and a public hearing on the budget
- Require cities and towns to make financial plans for both current fiscal period and capital expenditures
- Require cities and towns to file budgets and financial reports with the state auditor
- Establish property tax limits
- Require cities and towns to have a balanced budget
- Establish limits on the amount of money that may be accumulated in the general fund

Land Use Regulation

An important function of municipal government is the regulation of the use of land within the municipality. Like counties, municipalities are given broad statutory authority to enact ordinances regulating the use of land in the municipalities.[64] Each municipality is required to adopt a general plan to address present and future needs of the municipality and the future development of land within the municipality.[65] Each municipality is required to establish a planning commission to make recommendations to the municipal legislative body concerning the general plan, land use ordinances, and land use decisions.[66] Land use regulation is one of the most visible functions of municipal government and has one of the greatest impacts on residents.

LIMITED PURPOSE LOCAL GOVERNMENTS

Limited purpose local governments are generally created to provide a specific public service or a limited number of services. These governments are usually created to provide a service that a general purpose local government cannot or will not provide, or can provide but in a less efficient way. Limited purpose local governments include: special districts, local districts, special service districts, redevelopment agencies, and entities created under the Interlocal Cooperation Act.

Because limited purpose local governments are less known to the general public than are municipalities and counties, concerns about adequate accountability have been expressed. Very often, the general public is unaware that limited purpose local governments such as special districts even exist. Some independent special districts, for example, operate without significant oversight, and the public may have little, if any, input regarding the appointment of the districts' governing officials.

Special Districts[67]

A special district is a limited purpose local government created to meet service needs in a particular area. In Utah, special districts are created either by a county or a municipality which both are general-purpose governments. Approximately 95 percent of independent special districts have been created by counties. Some special districts have the power to levy taxes; others rely on user fees, grants, and other sources of revenue. Many special districts have authority to issue bonds to raise money to fund projects. Functions of special districts vary and include providing natural resource management, fire protection, housing and community development, mosquito abatement, and water and sewer service.

Special districts are typically created to address a problem or need that does not fit neatly into a single jurisdiction. Two examples may help explain the use of special districts.
1. A certain area of a county wants a swimming pool and recreation facility. The county cannot afford to build it for this area. The people of the area create a recreation district and build the facility themselves.
2. A river running through several counties may periodically overflow its banks. The best way to address this problem may be through a flood control district covering only the affected areas.

Also, counties and municipalities usually operate under debt and tax limitations. Special districts may circumvent debt and tax ceilings when demands for services exceed a jurisdiction's revenue-raising abilities. Special districts are also better suited to use service charges or user-fee financing to fund their operations.

Local Districts and Rewrite of Special District Statutes

The first special district was created shortly after statehood. Over the last hundred years various types of special districts have been created in the statutes to address different needs. Each of these different types of special districts had their own statutory provisions for how they are created, how they operate, and what their duties and powers are. Over the years, statutory provisions governing the creation and operation of about thirty different types of special districts had been enacted and were scattered throughout the code. In 1990, after a two-year legislative task force studied special districts, the legislature reorganized all the existing provisions related to the various types of special districts and gathered them into one place in the code (newly created Title 17A), organizing them into two general categories: independent and dependent.

At the conclusion of the 1990 task force work there were seventeen different types of independent special districts and thirteen types of dependent special districts. The 1990 work did not rewrite the various statutory provisions, rather it simply gathered the various provisions into one place in the code. In 1997, the Political Subdivisions Interim Committee started a multi-year rewrite of the special district statutes. One of the primary goals of this rewrite was to simplify and standardize, where possible, the statutory provisions for the various types of special districts. The rewritten statutory provisions are in a new Title 17B, and the special districts that have been categorized as independent districts are being given a new name of local districts. So far, provisions relating to the board of trustees and to the process for creation, dissolution, withdrawal, annexation, and other boundary changes have been standardized. The rewrite has not yet been completed, so a moratorium has been placed on the creation of a local district until the rewrite is complete, although the local district creation provisions may be used to create an independent special district.

Independent and Dependent Districts

As was mentioned earlier, in 1990 special districts were categorized into two categories: independent and dependent.

An independent special district operates independently of its creating entity. The independent special district is a separate legal entity. The creating entity does not control its budget or other aspects of the district. Currently, there are approximately 360 independent special districts in Utah that can be divided into twelve types. They are listed here with the number of each type in parentheses: cemetery maintenance districts (44); county improvement districts for water, sewerage, flood control, electric, and gas (53); county service areas (20); drainage districts (18); fire protection districts (8); irrigation districts (5); metropolitan water districts (6); mosquito abatement districts (15); public transit districts (2); special service districts (119); water conservancy districts (24); and regional service areas (1).[68]

By contrast, a dependent special district is not, in most cases, a separate legal entity. It is typically just a vehicle to provide funding for a particular service and is controlled by the county, city, or town that created the district. Currently the nine types of dependent special districts in the statute are county improvement districts, municipal improvement districts, parking and business improvement districts, soil conservation districts, municipal building authorities, pure sugar beet seed districts, special road districts, historical districts, and sprinkling districts.[69]

The following is an example of the need for dependent districts. An older part of a city does not have any sidewalks. Typically the cost of installing sidewalks is born by the developer when a new subdivision is developed. The city wants to install sidewalks in the older part of the city but does not want the entire city to bear the costs of these sidewalks in just one part of the city. The city creates a dependent municipal improvement special district for the area that will get the new sidewalks. Properties benefitting from the improvements are included within the district and are assessed an amount to pay for the cost of installing the sidewalks. The city performs the administrative aspects of operating the district. Because of the 'uniform and equal' taxation requirement in the Utah Constitution, a city cannot tax one portion of the city differently than the rest of the city.[70] Having the district is simply a way of imposing the cost of improvements on those receiving the benefit of the sidewalks rather than requiring the whole city to bear the costs. In this situation there is no need for the district to be a separate government body so the dependent type of district meets the need nicely.

Special Service Districts[71]

Because the term "special district" is so similar to the term "special *service* district," they are often confused and sometimes incorrectly used interchangeably, or one is used when the other is intended. As discussed in earlier sections, the term "special district" refers to all types of independent and dependent districts that are statutorily authorized to be created. "Special *service* district" refers only to the one type of independent special district that is discussed in this section.

A special *service* district is one of the twelve types of districts categorized in statute as independent special districts. Special service districts are unique among independent special districts because they are constitutionally based. Article XI, Section 7 of the Utah Constitution states that the legislature may by statute authorize counties, cities, and towns to establish a special service district to provide services that are specified in statute. The services listed in statute that a special service district may provide are water, sewerage, drainage, flood control, garbage, health care, transportation, recreation, fire protection and emergency medical or ambulance, jail facilities (in first class counties), street lighting, consolidated 911 and emergency dispatch, animal shelter and control, and economic development using federal mineral lease funds.[72]

The constitutional provision also states that each special service district is to be governed by the governing authority of the county, city, or town that creates the district. This is another feature of special service districts that distinguishes them from other independent special districts. Unlike other independent special districts, a special service district is constitutionally required to remain under the control of the county, city, or town that creates it, even though it is, like other independent special districts, a separate legal entity.[73]

The constitution also states that the legislature may authorize the creating county, city, or town to impose a property tax for district purposes and that the legislature may authorize the district to issue bonds. Both the imposition of a property tax and the issuance of bonds is conditioned on voter approval.[74]

Redevelopment Agencies[75]

Redevelopment agencies (RDAs) were first legislatively authorized in 1969.[76] They began as a tool to assist local government to revitalize declining areas. Since then, the legislature has expanded the types of projects that RDAs may undertake to include economic development and education housing development.

An RDA is a political subdivision of the state created to undertake or promote redevelopment, economic development, or education housing development. Both municipalities and counties are authorized in state statute to create an RDA.[77] An RDA is created by county or municipal ordinance. The geographic boundaries of an RDA created by a municipality are the same as the municipality's boundaries. The boundaries of an RDA created by a county are the boundaries of the unincorporated area of the creating county. An RDA is a separate legal entity from the municipality or county that created the RDA.

The driving force behind most if not all projects undertaken by an RDA is tax increment. Tax increment provides funding for redevelopment, economic development, or education housing development projects undertaken by the RDA. Tax increment is the amount of additional property tax revenue generated within a project area from an increase in the value of property located within the project area because of the development activities of the RDA. Tax increment is a major source of funding for agency projects and may also be used in other ways specified in statute.

In 1993, the legislature enacted legislation requiring that a taxing entity committee approve an agency's budget and the amount of tax increment to be used by the agency from a project area.[78] A taxing entity committee is comprised of representatives from each of the entities that impose a property tax on property located within the project area. Some uses of tax increment are not, however, subject to the approval of the taxing entity committee.

An RDA may undertake projects that have a defined territory that is a subset of the RDA's territory. As mentioned above, an RDA may create a project of three different types: redevelopment, economic development, and education housing development. Each of these types has a separate and distinct purpose and set of requirements.

The purpose of a redevelopment project is to redevelop an area, known as a project area, and to eliminate what is known as "blight." If the area is found to be a blighted area, retail sales of goods may be allowed as the primary objective of the project area. Acquiring property by eminent domain is prohibited.[79] In 2005, the legislature enacted a one-year moratorium on the adoption of new project area plans for redevelopment projects requiring a finding of blight.[80] The moratorium expires June 30, 2006.

The purpose of an economic development project is to create additional jobs or retain jobs within a project area.[81] Retail sales cannot be the primary objective of the project.[82] Incidental or subordinate development of retail sale of goods is allowed, and an economic benefit analysis and a finding of an economic benefit is required.[83]

The purpose of an education housing development project is to promote high density housing adjacent to a public or private institution of higher education.[84] These areas have many of the same restrictions as an economic development project area. Local school districts can exempt the school district portion of tax increment with written notice prior to the taxing agency's approval. In this event, school districts and the state school board have no vote in the budget approval process.[85] As of September 2005, there have not been any education housing development projects established in Utah.

All project area budgets adopted after May 2000 must allocate 20 percent of the tax increment for affordable income housing, unless the project area budget provides for the agency to receive no more than $100,000 in annual tax increment or the agency obtains a waiver of the 20 percent requirement from both the Olene Walker Housing Loan Fund Board and the taxing entity committee.[86]

Interlocal Cooperation Entities and Interlocal Cooperation Agreements[87]

Sometimes municipalities and counties are not equipped with finances or manpower to provide all of the services that their residents need. Also, it may be more economical to join efforts with another municipality or county to provide the service. To provide a way for local governments to make sure these needs are met, Utah law allows local governments to sign agreements and cooperate with other localities to provide services and facilities that will work best with the geography, economy, population, and other factors influencing the needs and development of their local communities. This allows local governments to make the most efficient use of their powers by enabling them to offer services on a basis of mutual advantage and thereby provide the benefit of economy of scale, economic development, and utilization of natural resources for the overall promotion of the general welfare of the state.

These agreements can create interlocal cooperation entities which are considered political subdivisions of the state. Depending upon how the agreement was written, the newly created entity may be separate legally from the public agencies that created them.

Public agencies may also enter into agreements to engage in joint or cooperative action, to exchange services that they are each authorized by statute to provide, or to provide law enforcement services to one or more other public agencies. For example, two or more Utah public agencies may create a Utah interlocal entity to provide sewage and wastewater treatment plants and facilities, provide electric and other energy services, or finance a facility to provide some other particular service. All of these services would be very costly for individual governments to provide, but when local governments work together, the costs drop and the services are better.

Interlocal cooperation entities may run either independently or by a joint board appointed by the public agencies entering into the agreement. The public agencies involved in an interlocal entity may appropriate funds to the administrative joint board or interlocal entity; sell, lease, give, or otherwise supply tangible and intangible property to the administrative joint board or interlocal entity; and provide personnel or services for the administrative joint board or interlocal entity as may be within its legal power to furnish.

Records from the state auditor's office show that thirty-four active entities have been created through the Interlocal Cooperation Act. As an example, the Intermountain Power Agency located in Millard County was created by a group of about thirteen municipalities. The Intermountain Power Agency generates electric power for the municipalities and sells the excess power. The municipalities wanted to create a stable source of power at a cheaper rate for their citizens. As another example, the Utah Local Government Trust was formed by interlocal agreement to provide municipalities, counties, school districts, and special districts with risk management and loss prevention programs.

Associations of Governments

Associations of governments implement the vision of multi-county or regional planning districts to coordinate planning and governmental activities within a specified geographic area of the state. These multi-county planning districts encompass and combine two or more counties to provide a framework to aid and encourage better coordination of and communication between plans and programs, facilitate more efficient and effective ways for the administration and delivery of services that will carry out the responsibilities of government, and provide and operate various types of services or to develop facilities that would be more efficient on a district basis.[88]

With these distinct advantages, regional planning districts appeared the obvious solution to the rising difficulties of government activities in the mid-1960s.

On the federal level, a presidential memorandum issued in 1966 recognized the problems with coordination of planning and requested federal agencies to coordinate and establish the multi-jurisdictional planning units with boundaries congruous with state planning and development districts. Subsequently, in 1967 and 1969, circulars were issued by the federal Bureau of the Budget encouraging the establishment of these state planning and development districts. In 1968, the federal Intergovernmental Cooperation Act, requested the creation of mechanisms to evaluate and review federal programs that heavily influence local planning and development.

In Utah, the basis for these planning districts was established in 1965 with the passage of the Interlocal Cooperation Act.[89] In 1966, in conjunction with federal developments, the State Advisory Planning Committee, under supervision of Governor Calvin L. Rampton issued a report recommending the creation of multi-county planning districts.[90] The governor released the official multi-county district boundaries in an executive order on May 17, 1970, to take effect two months later (July 1, 1970).[91] These districts were created to assist the state and local governments with multi-county planning, program integration, and optimization of economies of scale. As shown in figure 22.8, these associations are Bear River Association of Governments, Wasatch Front Regional Council, Mountainland Association of Governments, Uintah Basin Association of Governments, Southeast Association of Governments, Six County Association of Governments, and Five County Association of Governments.

In fact, Utah took to this concept almost out of necessity. Several factors pushed Utah to consider regional planning districts:
- Utah's rural county makeup—and its declining rural county population—enhanced the difficulty of providing effective state and federal programs
- These local government entities also found it difficult to resolve and develop support services for the rising social and economic problems of modern society
- Many state or federal programs encompassed boundaries broader than, and separate from, city and county lines, resulting in overlapping jurisdictions, duplication, and competition for resources (e.g., law enforcement and employment security)
- Various regional groups had been formed, but not in any organized fashion, increasing the difficulty of approving, funding, and administering government programs

Throughout the 1980s, associations of governments activity increased as the federal government pushed to give more service delivery control and responsibility to the states by using block grants.

Figure 22-8

Associations of Governments in Utah

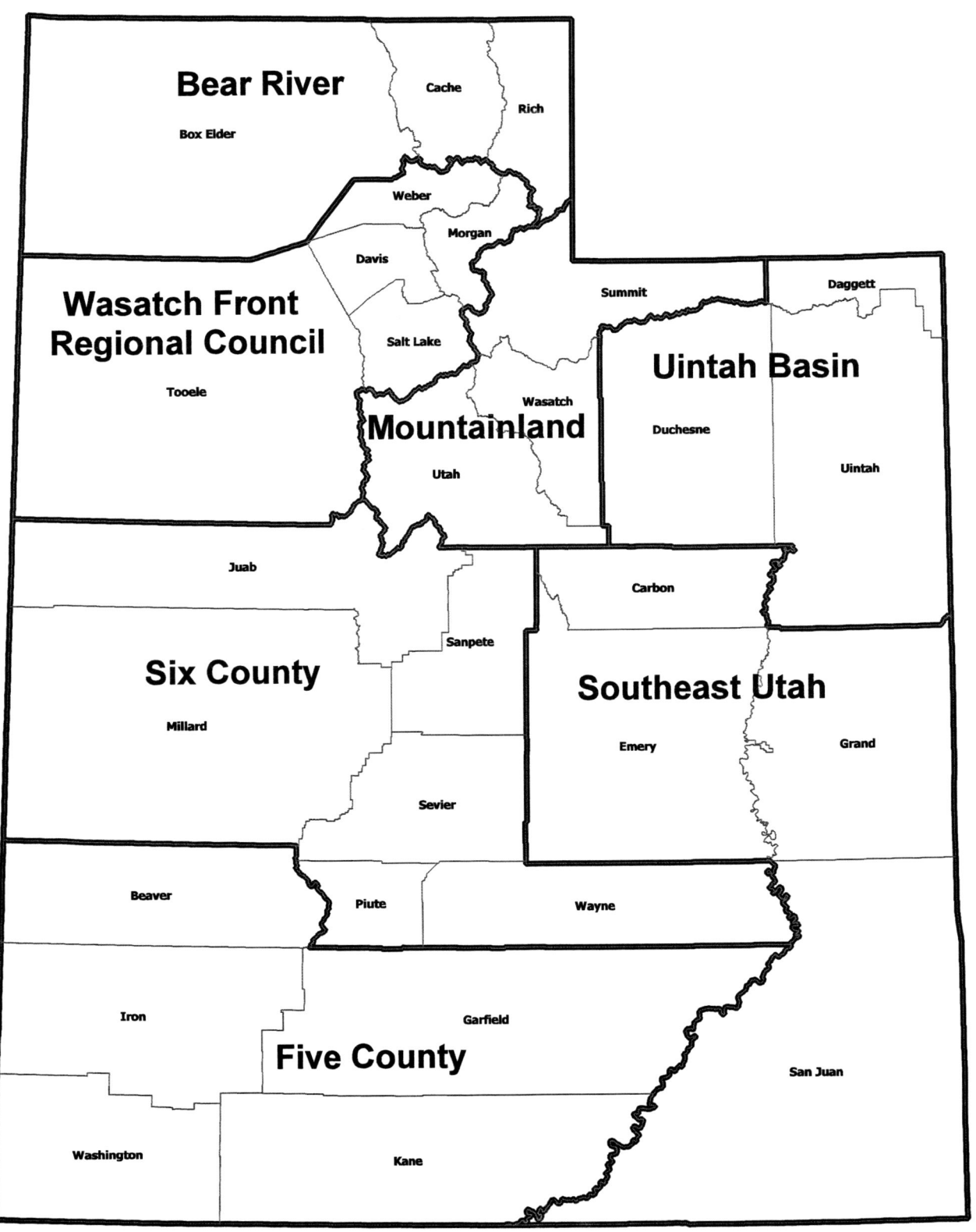

Utah's seven associations were formally established to:
- Provide a common forum to identify, discuss, study, and resolve area wide problems
- Achieve advantages of cooperative action that cannot be achieved individually and to make the most effective use of local leadership and staff resources
- Provide local input into state programs that are undergoing increasing decentralization to a regional level
- Serve as a multi-purpose "umbrella-type" organization to engage in and carry out planning and development programs with respect to existing and emerging problems of industry, commerce, transportation, population, housing, agriculture, public services, local governments, and any other matters which are relevant to an association's purposes
- Maintain liaison with members, governmental units and groups of organizations, and to serve as the regional voice for local governments
- Perform such other functions as may be deemed necessary under the direction of local elected officials

Some of the most important activities accomplished by associations of governments are those which the state's administration determine would be better addressed at a regional level by locally elected officials. The other alternative would be to increase state administrative oversight and staffing. The associations have allowed local officials to have a direct impact upon many programs such as Community Development Block Grants, Community Services Block Grants, Social Services Block Grants, and capital improvements planning and prioritization.

Services provided to the state by the associations of governments are as follows:
- Providing clearinghouse reviews and comment to the Governor's Office of Planning and Budget (GOPB)
- Providing federal register review and follow up
- Providing public lands research, comments, and follow up
- Participating in the Resource Conservation and Development Council
- Developing Economic Development Planning Strategies
- Serving as the GOPB State Data Center Affiliate
- Participating with GOPB Demographic and Economic Analysis
- Participating with GOPB and U.S. Bureau of the Census' State Data Center
- Disseminating feedback for local officials on state projects and proposals
- Participating in major state initiatives as identified by the Governor's Office, including:
  - Regional planning councils
  - Quality Growth Commission
  - Twenty-first Century Communities program
  - Utah Advisory Council on Intergovernmental Affairs
  - Local Government Comprehensive Planning Projects
- Providing comments as to the impact of state and federal actions on local government where appropriate through the Resource Development Coordinating Committee

Table 22-5 shows the varied activities of the seven associations of governments.[92]

Table 22-5

Activities of Utah's Seven Associations of Governments

HOUSING	Bear River	Wasatch Front	Mountain-lands	Uintah Basin	South-east	Six County	Five County
Planning	X	X	X	X	X	X	X
First Time Home Buyer Assistance	X			X	X	X	X
Major Home Repair or Replacement	X			X	X	X	X
Emergency Home Repair	X			X	X	X	X
Home Weatherization	X			X	X	X	X
Home Energy Assistance Target Program (HEAT)	X			X	X	X	X
Affordable Housing Planning	X	X	X	X	X	X	X
ECONOMIC DEVELOPMENT SERVICES	Bear River	Wasatch Front	Mountain-lands	Uintah Basin	South-east	Six County	Five County
Economic Development Planning	X	X	X	X	X	X	X
Revolving Loan Funds	X			X	X	X	X
Procurement Training Centers	X				X	X	
Business Assistance/Small Business Development (Resource) Centers					X		
Small Business Incubation			X		X		
Travel Region			X				
COMMUNITY DEVELOPMENT	Bear River	Wasatch Front	Mountain-lands	Uintah Basin	South-east	Six County	Five County
Community Development Block Grant Program	X	X	X	X	X	X	X
Geographic Information Systems	X	X	X	X		X	X
Planning Technical Assistance	X	X	X	X	X	X	X
Leadership Training	X		X	X		X	X
Environmental Reviews	X		X	X	X	X	X
Water Quality Planning		X	X			X	X
21st Century Planning Assistance	X		X	X	X	X	X

TRANSPORTATION PROGRAMS	Bear River	Wasatch Front	Mountain-lands	Uintah Basin	South-east	Six County	Five County
Regional Transportation Coordination	X	X	X	X			X
Transportation Assistance	X	X	X	X	X	X	X
Metropolitan Planning Organization		X	X				X
Air Quality		X	X				

EMERGENCY ASSISTANCE	Bear River	Wasatch Front	Mountain-lands	Uintah Basin	South-east	Six County	Five County
Emergency Food Assistance	X			X	X	X	X
FEMA Disaster Planning	X	X	X	X	X	X	X
Emergency Assistance	X			X	X	X	X

HUMAN SERVICES	Bear River	Wasatch Front	Mountain-lands	Uintah Basin	South-east	Six County	Five County
Aging Services	X		X	X	X	X	X
Congregate & Home Delivered Meals	X		X	X	X	X	X
In-Home Services/Alternatives to Nursing Home Care	X		X	X	X	X	X
Medicaid Waiver	X		X		X	X	X
Retired Senior Volunteer Programs (RSVP)			X	X		X	X
Community Services Block Grant	X			X	X	X	X
Social Services Block Grant	X		X	X	X	X	X

Chapter 23

Utah and the Future

LONG-TERM PROJECTIONS

Population

The Demographic and Economic Analysis section of the Governor's Office of Planning and Budget (GOPB) produces long-term population and demographic projections for the state. The latest long-term projections (completed in April 2005) show continued population growth at rates about twice as fast as the nation. In rounded numbers, the population projections for the state show a population of 2.8 million residents by 2010, an increase of 587,000 or about 26 percent over 2000. By 2020 Utah is projected to have 3.5 million residents, an increase of 653,000 or about 23 percent. By 2030 Utah's population is projected to be 4.1 million, an increase of 600,000 or 17 percent.[1] In short, the state is projected to continue to be one of the fastest growing states in the nation in terms of percent growth (see table 23-1).

Approximately 79 percent of this growth is projected to come from the state's natural increase and only 21 percent from net-migration. Natural increase is the difference between births and deaths over a given time. The reason natural increase is the dominant factor in Utah's population growth is the state's high birth rate as discussed in more detail in Chapter 1, *An Historical, Demographic, and Economic Overview of the State*. The number of births per year is projected to grow from an average of 50,900 in the 2000s to 69,000 in the 2020s. By comparison, deaths are expected to average 13,400 in the 2000s, to 19,700 in the 2020s. Net migration is projected to increase by an average of 20,000 per year in the 2000s and then only 11,000 per year in the 2020s.[2] Of the approximately 1.8 million increase in Utah's population between 2000 and 2030, about 386,000 will be in-migrants, the balance 1.4 million will be the result of natural increase.

Table 23-1

Utah Population Projections by County
2000-2030

County	2000 Population	2000 Percent of Total	2005 Population	2005 Percent of Total	2010 Population	2010 Percent of Total	2020 Population	2020 Percent of Total	2030 Population	2030 Percent of Total
Beaver	6,023	0.3%	6,335	0.3%	7,575	0.3%	11,549	0.3%	13,761	0.3%
Box Elder	42,860	1.9%	45,142	1.8%	49,254	1.7%	61,675	1.8%	73,833	1.8%
Cache	91,897	4.1%	102,477	4.1%	114,304	4.0%	147,776	4.3%	183,989	4.5%
Carbon	20,396	0.9%	19,205	0.8%	19,023	0.7%	20,982	0.6%	23,188	0.6%
Daggett	933	0.0%	967	0.0%	1,024	0.0%	1,141	0.0%	1,209	0.0%
Davis	240,204	10.7%	276,374	10.9%	304,502	10.8%	352,320	10.1%	382,219	9.4%
Duchesne	14,397	0.6%	15,043	0.6%	15,897	0.6%	19,021	0.5%	21,497	0.5%
Emery	10,782	0.5%	10,492	0.4%	10,346	0.4%	11,359	0.3%	12,536	0.3%
Garfield	4,763	0.2%	4,645	0.2%	4,955	0.2%	5,973	0.2%	6,747	0.2%
Grand	8,537	0.4%	8,691	0.3%	9,039	0.3%	9,751	0.3%	10,129	0.2%
Iron	34,079	1.5%	40,212	1.6%	48,772	1.7%	65,607	1.9%	77,493	1.9%
Juab	8,310	0.4%	8,917	0.4%	10,112	0.4%	12,798	0.4%	14,546	0.4%
Kane	6,037	0.3%	6,093	0.2%	6,618	0.2%	8,359	0.2%	9,783	0.2%
Millard	12,461	0.6%	13,305	0.5%	14,199	0.5%	18,386	0.5%	22,439	0.6%
Morgan	7,181	0.3%	8,525	0.3%	10,183	0.4%	16,200	0.5%	24,595	0.6%
Piute	1,436	0.1%	1,356	0.1%	1,503	0.1%	1,790	0.1%	1,797	0.0%
Rich	1,955	0.1%	2,086	0.1%	2,147	0.1%	2,447	0.1%	2,636	0.1%
Salt Lake	902,777	40.2%	970,748	38.4%	1,053,258	37.2%	1,230,817	35.4%	1,381,519	33.9%
San Juan	14,360	0.6%	14,444	0.6%	14,481	0.5%	15,419	0.4%	16,910	0.4%
Sanpete	22,846	1.0%	25,447	1.0%	27,904	1.0%	32,902	0.9%	35,181	0.9%
Sevier	18,938	0.8%	19,494	0.8%	21,038	0.7%	24,855	0.7%	26,892	0.7%
Summit	30,048	1.3%	36,417	1.4%	44,511	1.6%	65,001	1.9%	85,660	2.1%
Tooele	41,549	1.9%	51,835	2.1%	67,150	2.4%	95,696	2.8%	112,722	2.8%
Uintah	25,297	1.1%	26,317	1.0%	27,071	1.0%	29,289	0.8%	30,641	0.8%
Utah	371,894	16.6%	453,977	18.0%	527,502	18.6%	661,319	19.0%	804,112	19.8%
Wasatch	15,433	0.7%	20,138	0.8%	25,516	0.9%	37,082	1.1%	46,193	1.1%
Washington	91,104	4.1%	125,010	4.9%	162,544	5.7%	251,896	7.3%	353,922	8.7%
Wayne	2,515	0.1%	2,527	0.1%	2,764	0.1%	3,469	0.1%	3,943	0.1%
Weber	197,541	8.8%	212,707	8.4%	230,145	8.1%	271,339	7.8%	306,227	7.5%
TOTAL	2,246,553		2,528,926		2,833,337		3,486,218		4,086,319	

Source: Governor's Office of Planning and Budget, *State of Utah Long-Term Projections 2005-2050*

Demographics

Of all the demographic projections produced by GOPB the trend that has received the greatest attention is the large increase in Utah's school-age (ages 5-17) population as shown in figure 23-1. Between 2005 and 2015 the state is projecting an increase in this population from 538,492 to 694,359, an increase of 155,492.[3] During this ten-year period, Utah's school-age population will grow by about 2.9 percent per year. This is certainly a large increase and it will be a challenge to find the funds necessary to pay for the increased educational costs. However, it should be remembered that along with a growing school-age population will come a growing working-age population. During this same time period, Utah's working-age population (ages 18-64) is projected to increase from 1,184,212 to 1,503,562, an increase of 319,350. This is an average annual growth rate of 2.4 percent, just slightly less than the growth rate of the school-age population. During this ten-year period, the school-age dependancy ratio (the school-age dependancy ratio is defined as the number of school-age children ages 5 to 17 per 100 working-age adults ages 18-64) increases from thirty-five to thirty-eight. It might also be helpful to know that the state's school-age dependancy ratio has been much higher in the past than it is now or will be in 2015. In 1990, the state's school-age dependancy ratio stood at forty-eight.[4]

Figure 23-1

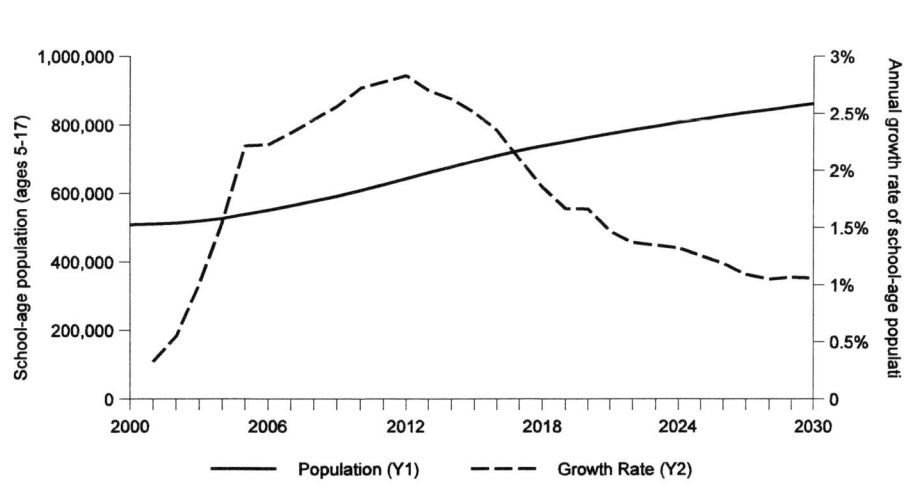

Source: 2005 Economic Report to the Governor

Furthermore, the increased dependancy ratio is a short-lived event. Between 2015 and 2030, the school-age population growth rate declines sharply from the 2.9 percent average annual growth rate previously mentioned for the ten years of 2005-15 to an annual average growth rate of only 0.08 percent for the next fifteen years. Equally important, the working-age population grows by 1.2 percent per year—a faster rate than the school-age population. The result is a decline in the school-age dependancy ratio from the thirty-eight to thirty-six. As a percent of total population, school-age children decline from 22.3 percent in 2015 to 20.7 percent in 2030.[5]

The growth in Utah's college-age population is also going to be strong. The state's eighteen to twenty-nine years of age population is projected to grow from its present population of 536,770 to 695,239 by 2030. This is an increase of 29.5 percent.[6]

In addition to the school-age population trends just discussed, Utah is expected to experience other important demographic changes as well over the next twenty-five years as shown in figure 23-2. For example, Utah's youngest children (ages 0-4) will decline from 9.7 percent of total population in 2005 to 8.8 percent in 2030. However, next in importance to the changes in school-age population is the increase in the number of elderly. The state's sixty-five and older population is projected to grow from 8.5 percent in 2000 to 10.7 percent in 2020 and to 13.0 percent in 2030 (see figure 23-3.[7] With the younger populations shrinking as a percent of Utah's population and the older age groups increasing, it should not be surprising that the state median age will increase. Between 2005 and 2020, the median age of the state is projected to increase from 28.5 to 31.9. By 2030 the median age will be 32.5. By comparison, the national median age will increase from 36.2 in 2005 to 39.0 in 2030.[8] As can be seen by these figures, though Utah will age, relative to the nation the state will continue to be very young.

Figure 23-2

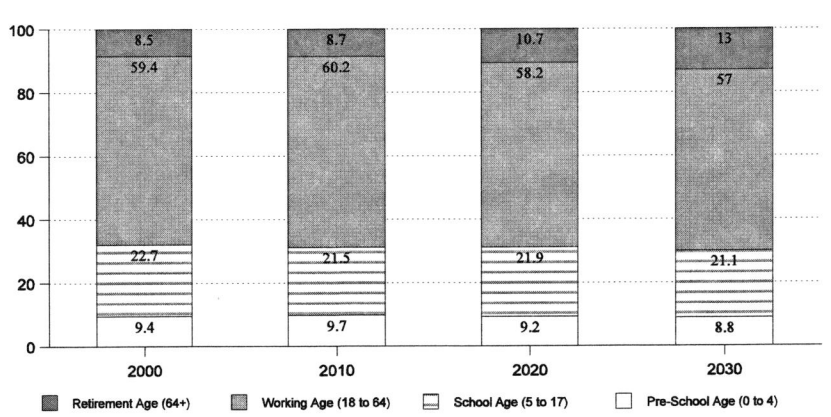

Figure 23-3

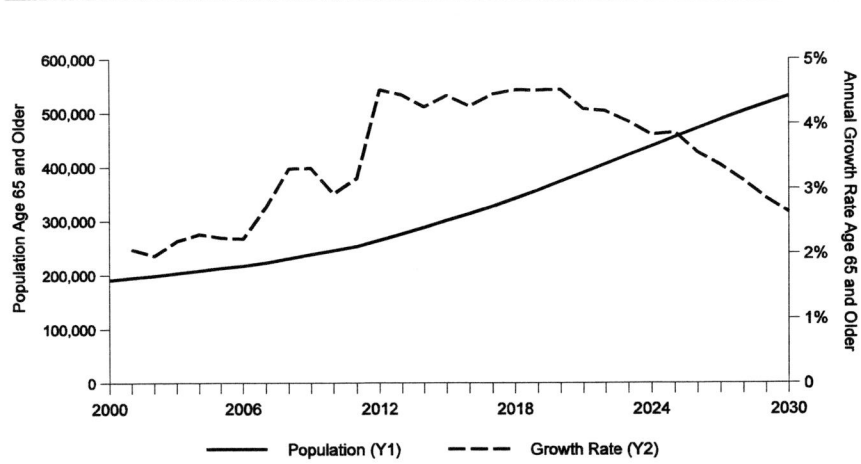

Another significant demographic change is the increase in the state's minority populations. Utah, which historically has had very small numbers of minorities, recently has seen some significant changes in this area. From 1900 to 1960, minorities represented less than 2 percent of Utah's population.[9] By 1970, minorities represented 5.5 percent of the state's population. By 1980 it had increased to 7.6 percent, by 1990 to 8.8 percent and by 2000 it had exploded to 14.7 percent.[10] By far the largest portion of Utah's minorities come from our southern neighbors. According to the 2000 Census, 55.4 percent of Utah's foreign born population is from Latin America, 80 percent of that coming from Mexico. Utah currently has over a quarter of a million people who identify themselves as Hispanic. This is by far the largest minority group in Utah composing 61 percent of all Utah minorities.[11] If such trends continue, by the 2010 Census, Utah's Hispanic population could account for 20 percent of the state's population. According to census counts, Whites accounted for 98 percent of the state's population from 1850 through 1960. By 2000, that percent had fallen to 85 percent and if the projections are correct it will fall further by 2010 and beyond. Thirty-five percent of the state's over half-million population increase in the 1990s consisted of minorities.[12]

Such trends are not unique to Utah. Many demographers call the large increase of immigrants in to the United States the Second Great Migration Wave. The First Great Migration Wave covered the years of 1880 to 1920, when most of the immigrants came from Western and Northern Europe.[13] This Second Great Migration Wave is having a profound impact on the United States. In 1900, the census reported that minorities accounted for 12.1 percent of the nation's population. By 1940 minorities had declined to 10.2 percent of the national population. Since then each census has shown a steady increase. By 1960, 11.4 percent of the nation's population consisted of minorities; by 1980 it had increased to 20.4 percent and by the 2000 census, 30.9 percent of nation were minorities.[14] As in Utah, the largest source of these immigrants is Latin America with Asian immigrants accounting for the second largest source.

Urbanization

Utah is currently the eighth most urban state in the nation with 88.2 percent of the population living in urban areas.[15] Nationally, 79.0 percent of the population lives in urban areas. Currently, three-fourths of the state's 2.4 million people live in just four of the state's twenty-nine counties Davis, Salt Lake, Utah and Weber. The concentration of the state's population is projected to continue. Between 2004 and 2030, the state is projected to increase in population from 2.4 million to 4.1 million an increase of 1.7 million. Two-thirds of this population growth is projected to occur in the four counties just mentioned. However, when four other counties adjacent to these four counties are added (Tooele, Summit, Wasatch and Morgan), 75 percent of the state's growth is accounted for. In other words, three out of every four new residents in Utah over the next quarter century are projected to reside within less than an hours drive of the state capitol. The only exception to this concentration of population in the state is Washington County in the southern part of the state. The population growth of this desert county is projected to outshine every other county. Its population is projected to grow from 116,209 to 351,196 and will go from 4.4 percent of the state's population in 2003 to an astounding 8.8 percent in 2030. It is expected to pass Weber County to become the fourth largest county in the state (see table 23-1).[16]

By comparison to these urbanization trends, between now and 2030, fifteen of Utah's twenty-nine counties are projected to have population increases of less than ten thousand and twelve counties are projected to have population increases of less than five thousand. In other words, in 2030 there will still be seven counties in the state with populations under ten thousand and thirteen counties (almost half) with populations under twenty thousand.

Employment

Utah's economy is projected to grow by an annual average rate of 2.1 percent between 2005 and 2030 as shown in table 2. This is more than twice the projected growth rate for the nation. From a total employment count of 1,482,410 in 2005 Utah's work force is projected to increase to 2,493,070 by 2030. The fastest growing industry sectors are both services. Professional/Business Services is projected to grow by an annual average rate of 2.6 percent and Education/Health Services is projected to grow by a remarkable 4.1 percent. Leisure/Hospitality services ranks third with a growth rate of 1.9 percent. Clearly the services industries continue to be the major growth industries of the past 25 years and for the next 25 years as well. Only one industry sector - Natural Resources/Mining is expected to show actual declines in employment. All other industries grow but at different rates.[17]

Figure 23-4

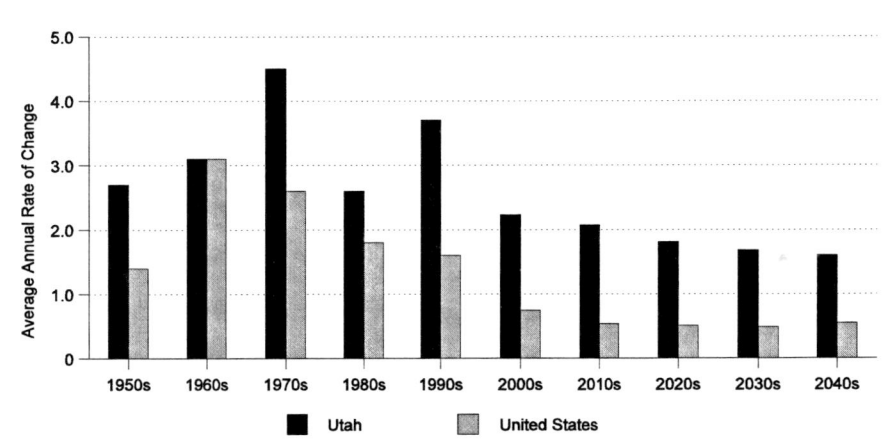

Table 23-2

Industry	2005		2010		2020		2030	
	\multicolumn{8}{c}{**Projected Industry Growth**}
Natural Resources/Mining	31,459	2.1%	29,895	1.7%	28,228	1.4%	27,576	1.1%
Construction	98,937	6.7%	114,959	6.6%	141,999	6.8%	161,705	6.5%
Manufacturing	123,039	8.3%	131,677	7.5%	150,920	7.2%	180,666	7.2%
Trade, Trans., Utilities	271,735	18.3%	305,185	17.4%	342,687	16.4%	378,185	15.2%
Information	33,770	2.3%	38,134	2.2%	41,166	2.0%	44,025	1.8%
Financial Activity	143,752	9.7%	163,555	9.3%	194,359	9.3%	221,565	8.9%
Professional/Business Services	199,315	13.4%	236,776	13.6%	301,647	14.5%	374,448	15.0%
Education/Health Services	156,429	10.6%	191,684	10.9%	294,044	14.1%	430,409	17.3%
Leisure/Hospitality	125,644	8.5%	146,355	8.3%	175,690	8.4%	201,267	8.1%
Other Services	81,394	5.5%	93,441	5.3%	113,366	5.4%	133,925	5.4%
Government	216,936	14.6%	246,064	17.1%	299,991	14.4%	339,299	13.6%

Source: 2005 Economic Report to the Governor

SUMMARY

That Utah's population and employment growth are projected to grow about twice as fast as the nation over the next twenty-five years bodes well for the state. However, this growth means that the state's biggest challenge will be meeting the demands spawned by this expected growth. Infrastructure needs are going to be significant. The demand for roads, drinking water, waste water, and schools to name just some are going to be enormous. For example, the Utah Department of

Transportation estimates that the transportation infrastructure needs through the year 2030 total $22.6 billion. That is an annual average of just under $1 billion a year—more than the state has ever spent in the past. The reconstruction of I-15 in Salt Lake County has made an enormous difference in the quality of transportation in the state's most populous county. Such improvements now must move on to the next two most populous counties, Utah County and Davis County and other parts of the state. Water development demands total $5.3 billion: $4.2 billion for drinking water and $1.1 billion for waste water projects. Part of this planning for water needs must include not only development of new sources but significant attention to conservation. Utah has one of the highest per capita water uses in the nation. Much of the reason for this is the large amount of water (82 percent) that is used for agricultural purposes.

The state must also meet the needs of an increasingly diverse population. As discussed, the state's minority population is increasing rapidly, especially the Hispanic population. Today 11 percent of the state's public school children are Hispanic—this number will continue to increase. Of all Utah's challenges, both today and in the near future, the most critical will be improving and funding the state's educational system. Next to providing order and safety for its citizens, education is the government's most important task—especially in the high-tech world facing Utah's citizens.

The strong employment growth projections for Utah are mainly the result of a very high birth rate. What is critical to the state's economic future is that all of these children have access to and indeed obtain a good education. If the state's fast growing workforce (relative to that of the nation's) is also a well-educated workforce, Utah's future has a great chance of being very bright.

Chapter 1 Endnotes

1. Allan Powell, *Utah History Encyclopedia* (Salt Lake City: University of Utah Press, 1994), 217; See also Richard Poll, *Utah's History* (Provo, UT: Brigham Young University Press, 1972), 13.

2. Powell, *Utah History Encyclopedia*, 217; Poll, *Utah's History*, 7-9.

3. Poll, *Utah's History*, 14-18.

4. Poll, *Utah's History*, 18.

5. Ibid., 19.

6. Thomas Alexander, *Utah: The Right Place* (Salt Lake City: Gibbs Smith Publisher, 1995), 23.

7. Alexander, *Utah: The Right Place*, 37.

8. Ibid., 28.

9. Ibid., 32.

10. Ibid., 34.

11. Ibid., 39.

12. Poll, *Utah's History*, 27.

13. Alexander, *Utah: The Right Place*, 40.

14. Ibid., 43.

15. Ibid.

16. Powell, *Utah History Encyclopedia*, 217; Poll, *Utah's History*, 177.

17. Powell, *Utah History Encyclopedia*, 217; Poll, *Utah's History*, 178.

18. Powell, *Utah History Encyclopedia*, 217; Poll, *Utah's History*, 180.

19. Poll, *Utah's History*, 113.

20. Ibid., 125-6.

21. Ibid., 133.

22. Ibid.

23. Alexander, *Utah: The Right Place*, see Chapter 11 for the Great Depression and World War II.

24. Ibid.

25. Powell, *Utah History Encyclopedia*, 491-493. The discussion of the Utah economy was written by Michael E. Christensen, Director of the Office of Legislative Research and General Counsel, for the *Utah History Encyclopedia* and is reprinted here by permission.

26. Office of the Governor, Utah Council of Economic Advisors, *2004 Economic Report to the Governor* (Salt Lake City: Governor's Office of Planning and Budget, January 2004), 68.

27. Office of the Governor, Utah Council of Economic Advisors, *2005 Economic Report to the Governor* (Salt Lake City: Governor's Office of Planning and Budget, January 2005), 33.

28. Governor's Office of Planning and Budget, State of Utah *Long Term Projections 2005-2050* (Salt Lake City: April 2005), 3.

29. Office of the Governor, *2005 Economic Report to the Governor*, 33.

30. Ibid., 39.

31. Office of the Governor, *2004 Economic Report to the Governor*, 102.

32. Utah Department of Workforce Services, *Trendlines: Perspectives on Utah's Economy* (Salt Lake City, May/June 2005), 27, http://jobs.utah.gov/wi/pubs/trendlines/current/tl.asp (accessed May 24, 2005).

33. Office of the Governor, *2004 Economic Report to the Governor*, 67-68.

34. Office of the Governor, *2005 Economic Report to the Governor*, 62, 98.

35. Ibid., 99.

36. American Chamber of Commerce Researchers Association, http://www.coli.org.

Chapter 2 Endnotes

1. Thomas E. Patterson, *The American Democracy* (New York: McGraw-Hill, 2003), 19.

2. *Black's Law Dictionary*, 8th ed. (Minnesota: Thompson West, 2004), 730.

3. Patterson, *American Democracy*, 48 (statement by Englishman James Bryce).

4. Gaillard Hunt, ed., *The Writings of James Madison* (New York: G.P. Putnam's Sons, 1904), 274.

5. *The Oxford Dictionary of Quotations*, 3rd ed. (Oxford: Oxford University Press, 1979), 1 (letter from Lord Acton to Bishop Mandell Creighton, April 3, 1887).

6. Virginia Gray and Russell L. Hanson, eds., *Politics in the American States* (CQ Press: Washington, D.C.), 49.

7. *Society of Separationists, Inc. v. Whitehead*, 870 P.2d 916, 921 (Utah 1993); Dale L. Morgan, *The State of Deseret* (Logan, Utah: Utah State University Press & Utah Historical Society, 1987), 7-27; see John J. Flynn, "Federalism and Viable State Government - The History of Utah's Constitution," *Utah Law Review* (September 1966): 311, 315.

8. *Society of Separationists*, 870 P.2d at 922-23; Flynn, "Federalism and Viable State Government," 315.

9. Morgan, *The State of Deseret*, 64-66; Jerome Bernstein, "A History of the Constitutional Convention of the Territory of Utah From 1849 to 1895" (master's thesis, Utah State University, 1961), 90; Martin B. Hickman, "Utah Constitutional Law" (unpublished Ph.D. dissertation, University of Utah, 1954), 41.

10. Hickman, "Utah Constitutional Law," 41, 43.

11. "Compromise of 1850," 31 Cong. Ch. 51, 9 Stat. 453 (1850).

12. *Society of Separationists*, 870 P.2d at 923; Morgan, *State of Deseret*, 93; Bernstein, "History of the Constitutional Convention," 91; Hickman, "Utah Constitutional Law," 45.

13. *Society of Separationists*, 870 P.2d at 923 (citing Hickman, "Utah Constitutional Law," 45); Andrew Love Neff, 1 *History of Utah 1847 to 1869,* ed. Leland H. Creer (Salt Lake City: Deseret News Press, 1940), 457-59.

14. Morgan, *State of Deseret*, 117 (citing *Deseret Evening News*, April 26, 1882); Bernstein, "History of the Constitutional Convention," 93.

15. *Society of Separationists*, 870 P.2d at 927; Church of Jesus Christ of Latter Day Saints, Scriptures, *Doctrine and Covenants*, "Official Declaration-1," http://scriptures.lds.org/od/1 (accessed May 23, 2005); Admission of Utah, H.R. Rep. No. 53-162, pt. 1, at 2-3 (1893).

16. *Society of Separationists*, 870 P.2d at 927-28; Flynn, *Federalism and Viable State Government*, 322; Hickman, "Utah Constitutional Law," 68.

17. Utah Enabling Act of July 16, 1894, 53 Cong. Ch. 138, 28 Stat. 107 (1894) (reprinted in *Utah Code Annotated* 1A (1991): 43).

18. *Society of Separationists*, 928 (citing Flynn, *Federalism and Viable State Government*, 323; Hickman, "Utah Constitutional Law," 72).

19. Utah Constitution, art. 1.

20. Jean Bickmore White, *The Utah State Constitution: A Reference Guide* (Westport, CT: Greenwood Press, 1998), 55.

21. Utah Constitution, art. 2.

22. Utah Constitution, art. 3.

23. Utah Constitution, art. 4, sec. 10; see also Utah Constitution, art. 4.

24. Utah Constitution, art. 5.

25. Utah Constitution, art. 7, sec. 6.

26. Utah Constitution, art. 6.

27. Utah Constitution, art. 7.

28. Utah Constitution, art. 8, secs. 4, 13.

29. Utah Constitution, art. 8.

30. Utah Constitution, art. 9.

31. Utah Constitution, art. 10.

32. Utah Constitution, art. 11.

33. Bickmore White, *Utah State Constitution*, 143.

34. David S. Monson, *Utah Voter Information Pamphlet: General Election, November 2, 1982* (Salt Lake City: State Elections Office, 1982), 21.

35. Utah Constitution, art. 12.

36. Utah Constitution, art. 13.

37. Utah Constitution, art. 14.

38. Utah Constitution, art. 15.

39. Utah Constitution, art. 16.

40. Utah Constitution, art. 17.

41. Utah Constitution, art. 18.

42. Utah Constitution, art. 19.

43. Utah Constitution, art. 20.

44. Utah Constitution, art. 21.

45. Utah Constitution, art. 22.

46. Utah Constitution, art. 23.

47. Utah Constitution, art. 24.

Chapter 3 Endnotes

1. Arthur Earl Bonfield, *State Administrative Rulemaking*, (Boston: Little, Brown & Co., 1986), 3.

2. *State v. Gallion*, 572 P.2d 683, 688 (Utah 1977).

3. Ibid., 689.

4. *Utah Code Annotated*, sec. 63-46a-4(4) (Supp. 2005).

5. *Utah Code Annotated*, sec. 63-46a-10(1)(e) (2004).

6. *Utah Code Annotated*, sec. 63-46a-5(2) and (3) (2004).

7. *Utah Code Annotated*, sec. 63-46a-12 (2004).

8. *Utah Code Annotated*, sec. 63-46a-11.5 (2004).

9. *Utah Code Annotated*, sec. 63-46a-11.5(3).

10. *Reauthorization of Administrative Rules*, 2002 Utah Laws ch. 325.

11. *Utah Administrative Rulemaking Act Amendments*, 2003 Utah Laws ch. 197; *Utah Code Annotated*, sec. 63-46a-3.5 (2004).

12. State of Utah, Governor's Executive Order, Governor Norman H. Bangerter, (March 22, 1988), http://www.rules.utah.gov/law/eo1988-03-22.htm (accessed August 17, 2005).

Chapter 4 Endnotes

1. Utah Constitution, art. 4, sec. 2; *Utah Code Annotated*, secs. 20A-2-102, 20A-3-101 (2003). Utah Constitution Article 4, Section 6 prohibits any person who is mentally incompetent, convicted of a felony, or convicted of treason or voting fraud from voting or holding a state office until the right to vote is restored as provided by the legislature. Section 20A-2-101.5 restores a convicted felon's voting rights when the felon is sentenced to probation, granted parole, or completed incarceration.

2. See *Utah Code Annotated*, sec. 20A-9-403(2)(a)(ii) (Supp. 2005) (regular primary elections); *Utah Code Annotated*, sec. 20A-9-802(3)(b) (2003) (Western States Presidential Primary).

3. See *Utah Code Annotated*, secs. 20A-2-104, -201 to -205 (2003 & Supp. 2005).

4. *Utah Code Annotated*, sec. 20A-3-302 (Supp. 2005).

5. *Utah Code Annotated*, secs. 20A-3-302, -303 (2003 & Supp. 2005).

6. *Utah Code Annotated*, sec. 20A-3-304 (Supp. 2005). Voters applying for an absentee ballot for the Western States Presidential Primary must file with the appropriate election officer no later than the Tuesday before election day.

7. *Utah Code Annotated*, secs. 20A-3-304(3)(b), -306(2) (2003 & Supp. 2005). The county clerk may establish a permanent absentee voter list that contains the name of any voter who requests permanent absentee voter status and who meets the absentee registration requirements. *Utah Code Annotated*, sec. 20A-3-304(4). An absentee ballot is not valid unless it is either received at the clerk's office before closing of polls on election day, or clearly postmarked before election day and received in the clerk's office before noon on the day of the official canvass following the election. *Utah Code Annotated*, sec. 20A-3-306(2). The dates of the official canvass vary depending upon the type of election. See *Utah Code Annotated*, secs. 20A-4-301 to -306 (2003 & Supp. 2005).

8. *Utah Code Annotated*, secs. 20A-3-401 to -413 (2003 & Supp. 2005).

9. *Utah Code Annotated*, sec. 20A-3-104 (2003).

10. *Utah Code Annotated*, secs. 20A-3-104, -105.5 (2003). A "provisional ballot" is defined as "a ballot voted provisionally by a person: a) whose name is not listed on the official register at the polling place; or b) whose legal right to vote is challenged as provided in [Title 20A]." *Utah Code Annotated*, sec. 20A-1-102(51) (Supp. 2005).

11. See *Help America Vote Act of 2002*, Pub. L. No. 107-252, 116 Stat. 1666-1730, codified at 42 U.S.C. secs. 15301-15545.

The Help America Vote Act was enacted to make federal elections more accessible and efficient, and to prevent fraud by a voter's use of multiple registrations under a single name. In 42 U.S.C. sec. 15482, voting information requirements are provided for voting by provisional ballot. If a person declares that he is a registered voter but his or her name does not appear on the official list of registered voters, that person will be allowed to cast a provisional ballot that will later be counted if a state or local election official can verify that the individual is registered.

The act requires states to create a uniform, centralized, and computerized statewide voter registration list that contains the name and registration information of every registered voter. This registration list will enable election officials to verify a valid registration when deciding whether or not to count a provisional ballot.

The act does not specify the conditions under which provisional ballots would be counted. However, the act does guarantee to a person voting by provisional ballot, access to a toll-free telephone number or an Internet website to discover whether the vote was counted, and if not counted, the reason why. Brain Kim, *Help America Vote*, Harvard Journal on Legislation 40 (2003): 579, 592.

12. *Utah Code Annotated*, sec. 20A-3-108 (2003).

13. The Utah Constitution designates that the term for senators shall be four years, but it also requires that nearly one half as practicable of the senate be elected every two years. The Utah State Constitution makes clear that this determination must be made by the legislature after each apportionment.

14. See *Utah Code Annotated*, sec. 17-27a-301(3)(c) (Supp. 2005).

15. See *Utah Code Annotated*, secs. 20A-8-101 to -404 (2003 & Supp. 2005).

16. See *California Democratic Party v. Jones*, 530 U.S. 567 (2000); *Tashjan v. Republican Party of Conn.* 479 U.S. 208 (1986).

17. *Utah Code Annotated*, secs. 20A-8-101 to -106 (2003).

18. *Utah Code Annotated*, secs. 20A-8-401 to -403 (2003 & Supp. 2005). Deadlines for political parties are scattered throughout *Utah Code Annotated*, Title 20A, Election Code; most can be found in *Utah Code Annotated*, Title 20A, Chapter 9, Candidate Qualifications and Nominating Procedures.

19. *Utah Code Annotated*, sec. 20A-9-202 (Supp. 2005).

20. Ibid., -202(4); *Utah Code Annotated*, sec. 20A-9-601 (2003).

21. *Utah Code Annotated*, sec. 20A-9-203 (Supp. 2005).

22. *Utah Code Annotated*, sec. 20A-9-502 (2003).

23. A person signing the signature sheet must be a registered voter and may not have signed another certificate of nomination petition for the same office.

24. *Utah Code Annotated*, sec. 20A-9-601 (2003).

25. *Utah Code Annotated*, sec. 20A-9-602 (2003).

26. *Utah Code Annotated*, sec. 20A-13-301 (2003).

27. *Utah Code Annotated*, sec. 20A-9-404 (2003).

28. Ibid., -404(3), (4).

29. *Utah Code Annotated*, sec. 20A-9-203(2).

30. The Utah Constitution specifically excepts from the referendum process a law that was passed by a two-thirds vote of each house of the Legislature.

31. *Gallivan v. Walker*, 54 P.3d 1069, 1080 (Utah 2002) (citing *Utah Power & Light Co. v. Provo City,* 74 P.2d 1191, 1205 (Utah 1937) (Larson, J., concurring)); *Public Employees' Ass'n v. State*, 610 P.2d 1272, 1273 (Utah 1980).

32. *Gallivan v. Walker*, 54 P.3d 1069, 1080 (Utah 2002) (citing *Utah Power & Light Co. v. Provo City,* 74 P.2d 1191, 1205 (Utah 1937) (Larson, J., concurring)); *Public Employees' Ass'n v. State*, 610 P.2d 1272, 1273 (Utah 1980).

33. National Conference of State Legislatures, LegisBrief, *Initiative, Referendum, and Recall: The Process,* by Jennifer Drage, Policy Associate (Denver: National Conference of State Legislatures, August-September 1999). In Utah, more signatures are required to place the proposed bill on the ballot than are required to send the proposed bill to the legislature. Compare "Direct Initiative Process" (notes 32-36 and accompanying text) with "Indirect Initiative Process" (notes 37-40 and accompanying text).

34. *Utah Code Annotated*, sec. 20A-7-202(1) (2003); Utah State Elections Office, "Application for an Initiative or Referendum," Online Application Form, http://elections.utah.gov/InitiativesandReferendums.htm (accessed April 29, 2005). The application must include a statement indicating whether or not persons will be paid for gathering the signatures for the petition. Section 20A-7-202(2)(e).

35. The lieutenant governor may reject an application if the proposed law: (1) is patently unconstitutional or nonsensical, (2) could not become law if passed, or (3) is identical or substantially similar to an initiative submitted for evaluation within two years prior to the date of the application. Section 20A-7-202(5).

36. *Utah Code Annotated*, secs. 20A-7-202.5, -502.5 (Supp. 2005). A summary of the initial fiscal impact estimate is printed on each petition signature sheet and the entire fiscal impact estimate is printed in the voter information pamphlet and ballot. *Utah Code Annotated*, secs. 20A-7-203(2), -209(2), -402(2), -503(2) (Supp. 2005).

37. Three days before each public hearing, the sponsor must notify the lieutenant governor, each state senator, state representative, and county commissioner or county council member in the county

in which the hearing will be held. Sponsors must also (1) publish a written notice of the hearing in at least one newspaper of general circulation in the region in which the hearing will be held; and (2) provide to the Lieutenant Governor's Office video or audio tapes or comprehensive minutes of the hearings. The Lieutenant Governor's Office will make any tapes or minutes available to the public. *Utah Code Annotated*, sec. 20A-7-204.1 (Supp. 2005).

38. A "legal signature" is the certified and verified signature of a "legal voter"—one who "is registered to vote or becomes registered to vote before the county clerk certifies the signatures on an initiative or referendum petition." *Utah Code Annotated*, sec. 20A-7-101(8), (9) (Supp. 2005).

Each signature sheet for an initiative or referendum petition must include a statutorily prescribed warning that it is a class A misdemeanor for an individual: (1) to sign his or her name more than once on the same measure; (2) sign another individual's name to the petition; or (3) sign the petition knowing he or she is not a registered voter and does not intend to become a registered voter before the county clerk certifies the signatures on the petition. *Utah Code Annotated*, sec. 20A-7-203(2)(f).

39. *Utah Code Annotated*, sec. 20A-7-202(4)(a).

40. *Utah Code Annotated*, sec. 20A-7-201(2)(a) (2003). The number of signatures required to equal 10 percent of all votes cast for governor in each state senate district can be found at Utah State Elections Office, "Other Elections Information," http://www.elections.utah.gov/signature_nos.htm (accessed May 10, 2005). The numbers are based on votes cast for governor in the 2004 general election. The Lieutenant Governor's Office suggests that petition sponsors gather more signatures than the required number because some people who sign the petition are not registered voters.

In addition, any voter who has signed a petition and desires to have his or her name removed from the petition, may do so by submitting a notarized statement—requesting removal of the signature—to the country clerk *before* the county clerk delivers the verified signatures to the Lieutenant Governor. *Utah Code Annotated*, sec. 20A-7-205(3) (2003).

41. The county clerk must (1) check by the June 15 before the general election that all persons who circulated and verified initiative petitions are at least eighteen years old and residents of Utah; (2) by July 1, certify that all signers are registered voters; and (3) deliver the petition packets to the lieutenant governor. *Utah Code Annotated*, sec. 20A-7-206(1) to (3) (Supp. 2005).

In both the initiative and referendum process, the county clerk submits the names of any individuals who have circulated and verified petitions but who are not at least eighteen years old or residents of Utah, to the county attorney and attorney general.

42. *Utah Code Annotated*, sec. 20A-7-201(2)(b).

43. *Utah Code Annotated*, sec. 20A-7-209 (Supp. 2005).

44. Sponsors who desire to challenge the wording of the impartial ballot title may petition for review by the Utah Supreme Court according to procedures outlined in *Utah Code Annotated*, sec. 20A-7-209(4).

45. *Utah Code Annotated*, sec. 20A-7-211 (2003).

46. *Utah Code Annotated*, sec. 20A-7-212 (2003).

47. *Utah Code Annotated*, sec. 20A-7-214 (Supp. 2005).

48. *Utah Code Annotated*, sec. 20A-7-201(1)(a).

49. The county clerk must (1) check by December 1 before the annual general session that all persons who circulated and verified initiative petitions are at least eighteen years old and residents of Utah; (2) by December 15, certify that all signers are registered voters; and (3) deliver the petition packets to the lieutenant governor. *Utah Code Annotated*, sec. 20A-7-206(4) to (6).

50. *Utah Code Annotated*, sec. 20A-7-201(1)(b).

51. *Utah Code Annotated*, sec. 20A-7-208(1) (2003).

52. A person seeking to have an initiative submitted to a county, city, or town where the local legislative body is elected from council districts must obtain the same signature percentages from each of a majority of council districts.

53. *Utah Code Annotated*, sec. 20A-7-506(1) (Supp. 2005). Any voter who has signed an initiative petition may have his or her signature removed from the petition by submitting a notarized statement indicating so to the local clerk *before* the local clerk delivers the petition to the county clerk to be certified. *Utah Code Annotated*, sec. 20A-7-505(3).

54. *Utah Code Annotated*, sec. 20A-7-506(2), (3).

55. The local legislative body may (1) adopt the proposed law and refer it to the people, (2) adopt the proposed law without referring it to the people, or (3) reject the proposed law. An adopted proposed law that is not referred to the people is subject to referendum as with other laws. *Utah Code Annotated*, sec. 20A-7-501(3) (2003).

56. Ibid., -501(3)(d).

57. Initiative petition sponsors may challenge the wording of the ballot title to the state supreme court, which shall examine the measure and hear arguments, and then certify to the local clerk a ballot title that fulfills the statutory requirements for a ballot title. A ballot title is required, to the best of the local attorney's ability, to give "a true and impartial statement of the purpose of the measure." In addition, it "may not intentionally be an argument, or likely to create prejudice, for or against the measure." *Utah Code Annotated*, sec. 20A-7-508(2) to (4).

58. *Utah Code Annotated*, sec. 20A-7-510 (2003). Within ten days of the local body's proclamation, any qualified voter who signed the initiative petition may challenge the local body's decision to the state supreme court, in accordance with procedures outlined in Subsections 20A-7-510(3), (4).

59. *Utah Code Annotated*, sec. 20A-7-511(1) (2003).

60. Ibid., -511(2).

61. *Utah Code Annotated*, sec. 20A-7-513 (Supp. 2005).

62. *Utah Code Annotated*, sec. 20A-7-302(1) (2003). Hereinafter, for purposes of referendum discussion, "the last legislative session" will mean the last legislative session at which the law was passed.

63. *Utah Code Annotated*, sec. 20A-7-301(1)(a) (2003).

64. *Utah Code Annotated*, sec. 20A-7-306(1) (2003).

65. Ibid., -306(2).

66. If the lieutenant governor refuses to accept and file any referendum petition, any voter may apply to the supreme court for an extraordinary writ to compel him to do so within ten days after the refusal.

67. *Utah Code Annotated*, sec. 20A-7-301(1)(b), (2).

68. *Utah Code Annotated*, sec. 20A-7-308 (2003). Sponsors have 15 days to challenge the wording of the ballot title, and the supreme court has five days to certify to the lieutenant governor an impartial ballot title which meets statutory requirements.

69. *Utah Code Annotated*, sec. 20A-7-310(1) to (3)(a) (2003).

70. *Utah Code Annotated*, sec. 20A-7-311 (2003).

71. *Utah Code Annotated*, sec. 20A-7-601(1) (Supp. 2005). The local law remains in effect until repealed by the voters by referendum.

72. A person seeking to have an initiative submitted to a county, city, or town where the local legislative body is elected from council districts must obtain the same signature percentages from each of a majority of council districts.

73. For "land use law," signatures must be equal to (1) in a first or second class county or city, 20 percent of all votes cast in the county or city for all candidates for governor at the last governor election; or (2) in a city of the third, fourth, or fifth class or a town, 35 percent of all the votes cast in the city or town for all candidates for governor at the last governor election. "Land use law" includes a land use development code, an annexation ordinance, and comprehensive zoning ordinances. *Utah Code Annotated*, sec. 20A-7-601(2).

74. *Utah Code Annotated*, sec. 20A-7-606(1) (2003). Any voter who has signed a referendum petition may have his signature removed from the petition by submitting a notarized statement indicating so to the local clerk *before* the local clerk delivers the petition to the county clerk to be certified.

75. Ibid., -606(2), (3).

76. *Utah Code Annotated*, sec. 20A-7-607 (2003).

77. *Utah Code Annotated*, sec. 20A-7-608 (2003).

78. Within ten days of the local body's proclamation, any qualified voter who signed the referendum petition proposing the law may challenge the local body's decision to the state supreme court, in accordance with procedures outlined in *Utah Code Annotated*, sec. 20A-7-610(3) to (5) (2003).

79. *Utah Code Annotated*, sec. 20A-7-601(3), (4).

80. *Utah Code Annotated*, sec. 20A-7-611 (2003).

81. Executive Branch www.utah.gov; Legislative Branch www.le.utah.gov; and Judicial Branch www.utcourts.gov.

82. *Utah Code Annotated*, sec. 20A-1-201.5 (2003).

83. *Utah Code Annotated*, sec. 20A-1-201 (2003).

84. Ibid.

85. *Utah Code Annotated*, sec. 20A-1-202 (2003).

86. Ibid.

87. *Utah Code Annotated*, sec. 20A-1-203 (Supp. 2005).

88. *Utah Code Annotated*, sec. 20A-2-300.6 (2003).

89. *Utah Code Annotated*, sec. 20A-2-301 (2003).

90. *Utah Code Annotated*, secs. 20A-7-701 to -706 (2003 & Supp. 2005).

91. *Utah Code Annotated*, sec. 20A-7-201 (2003).

92. *Utah Code Annotated*, sec. 52-4-1 to 52-4-10 (2002 & Supp. 2005).

93. *Utah Code Annotated*, sec. 52-4-1 (2002).

94. *Utah Code Annotated*, sec. 52-4-5 (Supp. 2005).

95. *Utah Code Annotated*, sec. 52-4-4 (2002).

96. Ibid.

97. Ibid.

98. *Utah Code Annotated*, sec. 52-4-5.

99. *Utah Code Annotated*, sec. 52-4-6 (2002).

100. *Utah Code Annotated*, Title 63, Chapter 2, Government Records Access and Management.

101. *Utah Code Annotated*, sec. 63-2-102 (2004).

102. *Utah Code Annotated*, sec. 63-2-201 (Supp. 2005). "A governmental entity shall provide a person with a certified copy of a record if the person requesting the record has a right to inspect it, the person identifies the record with reasonable specificity, and the person pays the lawful fees."

103. *Utah Code Annotated*, sec. 63-2-204(1) (Supp. 2005).

104. *Utah Code Annotated*, sec. 36-11-102(9) (2001).

105. *Utah Code Annotated*, sec. 36-11-401 (2001).

106. *Utah Code Annotated*, sec. 36-11-201 (Supp. 2005).

107. See *Rules of the Fifty-Sixth Legislature*, State of Utah, HR-38.01 to 38.07, SR-38.01 to 38.05 (2005).

108. Ibid., HR-38.02, SR-38.02.

109. Ibid.

110. Ibid., HR 38.04 to 38.07; SR 38.03 to 38.05.

111. Richard D. Poll, *Utah's History* (Provo, UT: Brigham Young University Press, 1978), 711-712; Journals of the House of Representatives and Senate (Salt Lake City: Utah Legislative Printing Office, 1979-2004).

112. Source: J. Brent Haymond et al., *The Utah State Legislature Centennial History 1896-1996* (Utah: The Office of the Third House, Utah State House of Representatives, 1996), 304-308.

Chapter 5 Endnotes

1. Utah Constitution, art. 7, sec. 2.

2. *Utah Code Annotated*, sec. 67-1-9 (2004).

3. Utah Constitution, art. 7, sec. 5.

4. Scott M. Matheson, *Out of Balance* (Salt Lake City: Gibbs M. Smith, Inc, 1986), 200.

5. *Utah Code Annotated*, sec. 67-1-1 (2004).

6. Utah Constitution, art. 7, sec. 10; *Utah Code Annotated*, sec. 67-1-1(3).

7. Utah Constitution, art. 7, sec. 10.

8. Utah Constitution, art. 7, sec. 6.

9. *Utah Code Annotated*, sec. 67-1-1.5 (2004).

10. Office of the state auditor, state treasurer, and attorney general.

11. *Utah Code Annotated*, sec. 67-1-3(1) (2004).

12. State of Utah, Office of the Governor, Boards and Commissions, *General Information*, http://www.governor.utah.gov/boards/newboardinformation.html (accessed May 31, 2005).

13. *Utah Code Annotated*, sec. 67-1a-2 (2004).

14. *Utah Code Annotated*, sec. 67-1-2.5 (2004).

15. http://www.governor.utah.gov/boards/home.html.

16. *Utah Code Annotated*, sec. 63-38-2 (2004).

17. *Utah Code Annotated*, Title 63, Chapter 5a, Disaster Response and Recovery Act.

18. *Utah Code Annotated*, sec. 63-53a-6 (Supp. 2005).

19. Utah Constitution, art. 7, sec. 5(3).

20. Sarah McCally Morehouse and Malcolm E. Jewell, *State Politics, Parties, and Policy* (Lanham, MD: Rowman and Littlefield Publishers, 2003), 168.

21. Utah Constitution, art. 7, sec. 8.

22. Ibid.

23. Ibid.

24. Thad Beyle, "The Governors," *Politics in the American States*, eds. Virginia Gray and Russell L. Hanson (Washington, D.C.: CQ Press, 2004), 215.

25. Utah Constitution, art. 7, sec. 6.

26. Utah Constitution, art. 8, sec. 8.

27. Ibid.

28. Ibid.

29. *Utah Code Annotated*, sec. 77-30-2 (2003).

30. 18 U.S.C. sec. 3182 (2000).

31. U.S. Constitution, art. 4, sec. 2, cl. 2.

32. *Utah Code Annotated*, sec. 78-30-4 (2002).

33. *Puerto Rico v. Branstad*, 483 U.S. 219 (1987).

34. Ibid. See also *Utah Code Annotated*, sec. 77-30-22 (2003).

35. Utah Constitution, art. 7, sec. 4.

36. *Utah Code Annotated*, sec. 39-1-3 (1998).

37. *Utah Code Annotated*, sec. 39-1-1 (1998).

38. Utah Constitution, art. 7, sec. 4.

39. *Utah Code Annotated*, sec. 39-1-3 (1998).

40. Beyle, "The Governors," 210.

41. Separately Elected Executive Branch Officials (SEP)—A score of 5 is given if the governor or a governor/lieutenant governor team is elected. A score of 4.5 is given if the governor or

governor/lieutenant governor team and one other official are elected. A score of 4 is given if the governor/lieutenant governor team and some process officials (e.g., attorney general, secretary of state, treasure, auditor) are elected. A score of 3 is given if the governor/lieutenant governor team, process officials, and some major and minor policy officials are elected. A score of 2.5 is given if the governor and six or fewer officials are elected but none are policy officials. A score of 2 is given if the governor and six or fewer officials are elected including one major policy official. A score of 1.5 is given if the governor and six or fewer officials are elected with two being major policy officials. A score of 1 is given if the governor and seven or more process and several major policy officials are elected.

Tenure Potential of Governors (TEP)—A score of 5 is given if the governor is elected for a four-year term with no restraint on reelection. A score of 4.5 is given if the governor is elected for a four-year term with only three terms permitted. A score of 4 is given if the governor is elected for a four-year term with only two terms permitted. A score of 3 is given if the governor is elected for a four-year term with no consecutive election permitted. A score of 2 is given if the governor is elected to a two-year term with no restraint on reelection. A score of 1 is given if the governor is elected to a two-year term with only two terms permitted.

Governor's Appointment Powers (AP)—Governor's appointment powers are measured in six major function areas (i.e., corrections, K-12 education, health, highways/transportation, public utilities regulation, and welfare) that are totaled and then averaged and rounded to the nearest .5 for the state score. A score of 5 is given if the governor makes an appointment and no other approval is needed. A score of 4 is given if the governor makes an appointment and a board, council, or legislature approves that appointment. A score of 3 is given if the governor and someone else jointly makes an appointment or if someone else makes the appointment and the governor approves it. A score of 2 is given if someone else makes an appointment and the governor and other body approves that appointment. A score of 1 is given if someone else makes an appointment and no other approval or confirmation is needed.

Governor's Budget Power (BP)—A score of 5 is given if the governor has full responsibility of its budget and the legislature may not increase the executive budget. A score of 4 is given if the governor has full responsibility and the legislature can increase the budget by special majority vote or subject to an item veto. A score of 3 is given if the governor has full responsibility and the legislature has unlimited power to change the executive budget. A score of 2 is given if the governor shares responsibility and the legislature has unlimited power to change the executive budget. A score of 1 is given if the governor shares responsibility with another elected official and the legislature has unlimited power to change the executive budget.

Governor's Veto Power (VP)—A score of 5 is given if the governor has item veto power and a special majority vote of the legislature is needed to override a veto (three-fifths of legislature elected or two-thirds of legislators present). A score of 4 is given if the governor has item veto power with a majority of the legislators elected needed to override a veto. A score of 3 is given if the governor has item veto power with only a majority of the legislators present needed to override a veto. A score of 2 is given if the governor has no item veto power with a special legislative majority needed to override a regular veto. A score of 1 is given if the governor has no item veto power and only a simple legislative majority needed to override a regular veto.

Gubernatorial Party Control (PC)—A score of 5 is given if the governor's party has a substantial majority (75 percent or more) in both houses of the legislature. A score of 4 is given if the governor's party has a simple majority in both houses (under 75 percent) or a substantial majority in one house and a simple majority in the other. A score of 3 is given if there is split party control in the legislature or a nonpartisan legislature. A score of 2 is given if the governor's party has a simple minority (25 percent or more) in both houses or simple minority in one and a substantial minority (under 25 percent) in the other. A score of 1 is given if the governor's party has a substantial minority in both houses.

42. Utah Constitution, art. 7, sec. 11.

43. Utah Constitution, art. 7, sec. 11.

44. Utah Office of Attorney General, *Opinion Request on Gubernatorial Succession*, Op. Att'y Gen. 03-001 (Utah 2003), http://attorneygeneral.utah.gov/Opinions_AttorneyGeneral/agop03001.htm (accessed November 2, 2005).

45. *Utah Code Annotated*, sec. 63-5b-201 (2004).

46. *Utah Code Annotated*, sec. 63-5b-201 (2004).

47. Utah Constitution, art. 6, sec. 19.

48. *Utah Code Annotated*, sec. 77-5-3 (2003).

49. *Utah Code Annotated*, sec. 67-1a-1 (2004).

50. See Lieutenant Governor Implementation, H.B. 2, 43rd Leg., 1st Special Sess. (Utah 1980); See also Revision of Executive Article, S.J.R. No. 7, 43rd Leg., General Sess. (Utah 1979).

51. Ibid.

52. *Utah Code Annotated*, sec 67-1a-6 (2004).

53. *Utah Code Annotated*, sec. 67-1a-7 (2004).

54. *Utah Code Annotated*, sec. 67-1a-2(2) (2004).

55. Lynne M. Ross, ed., *State Attorneys General* (Washington, D.C.: BNA Books, 1990), 3.

56. 43 Cong. Ch. 469; 18 Stat. 253 (1874).

57. Utah Constitution, art. 7, sec. 3(2).

58. Utah Constitution, art. 7, sec. 1.

59. Ross, *State Attorneys General*, vii, quote by Dave Frohnmayer.

60. Utah Constitution, art. 7, sec. 16; *Utah Code Annotated*, Title 67, Chapter 5, Attorney General.

61. Utah Constitution, art. 7, sec. 16. The scope of the attorney general's power under this section is unclear. The legislature has made clearer, more specific grants of power to the attorney general in statute. See *Utah Code Annotated*, Title 67, Chapter 5, Attorney General.

62. *Utah Code Annotated*, sec. 67-5-5 (2004).

63. Utah Constitution, art. 7, sec. 5.

64. See *Hansen v. Utah State Retirement Board*, 652 P.2d 1332 (Utah 1982).

65. Utah Constitution, art. 6, sec. 32; Utah Constitution, art. 8, sec. 12.

66. *Utah Code Annotated*, sec. 67-5-1 (2004).

67. State of Utah, Office of the Attorney General, *Opinions*, http://www.attygen.state.ut.us/ag opinions.html (accessed November 3, 2005).

68. Ross, *State Attorneys General*, 73; see also *Stenberg v. Carhart*, 530 U.S. 914, 940 (2000).

69. Ibid.

70. *Utah Code Annotated*, sec. 67-5-1(2) (2004); See also *Parker v. Rampton*, 497 p. 2d 848, 852 (Utah 1972) (Attorney General is "the chief legal officer of the state, and charged with the duty of representing its interests.")

71. *State v. Jiminez*, 588 P.2d 707 (Utah 1978).

72. Ross, *State Attorneys General*, 36.

73. Ross, *State Attorneys General*, 13.

74. *Hanson v. Barlow*, 456 P.2d 177 (Utah 1969).

75. Utah Constitution, art. 7, sec. 3.

76. Utah Constitution, art. 7, sec. 15; *Utah Code Annotated*, sec. 67-3-1(1)(a) (Supp. 2005).

77. *Utah Code Annotated*, sec. 67-3-1(3), (4)(a) (Supp. 2005).

78. State Auditor - Expansion of Duties, S.B. 200, 54the Leg. Gen. Sess. (Utah 2003).

79. *Utah Code Annotated*, sec. 67-3-1(1)(b) (Supp. 2005).

80. *Utah Code Annotated*, sec. 67-3-1(3)(a)(I) (Supp. 2005).

81. *Utah Code Annotated*, sec. 67-3-5 (2004).

82. *Utah Code Annotated*, sec. 67-3-1(7)(g) (Supp. 2005).

83. *Utah Code Annotated*, sec. 67-3-1(13) (Sup. 2005).

84. Utah Constitution, art. 7, sec. 15(2).

85. *Utah Code Annotated*, sec. 67-4-1(1) (2004).

86. *Utah Code Annotated*, sec. 67-4-1(1)(f) (2004) and sec. 67-4-11 (2004).

87. *Utah Code Annotated*, sec. 67-4-1(j) (2004).

88. *Utah Code Annotated*, sec. 67-4-11 (2004).

89. *Utah Code Annotated*, Title 51, Chapter 7, State Money Management Act.

90. *Utah Code Annotated*, sec. 51-7-2 (Supp. 2005).

91. State of Utah, Treasurer's Office, Public Treasurer's Investment Fund, *General Information,"* http://www.treasurer.state.ut.us/ptif.html (accessed November 3, 2005).

92. State of Utah, Utah Department of Administrative Services, http://www.das.utah.gov (accessed November 3, 2005).

93. *Utah Code Annotated*, sec. 63A-1-102(3) (2004).

94. Ibid., -102(7).

95. *Utah Code Annotated*, sec. 63A-1-105(2) (2004).

96. Utah Department of Administrative Services http://www.das.utah.gov/ (accessed May 31, 2005); *Utah Code Annotated*, Title 63, State Affairs in General.

97. State of Utah, Department of Administrative Services, Division of Archives, *About Us*, http://archives.utah.gov/abothar.htm (accessed November 3, 2005).

98. State of Utah, Department of Administrative Services, Office of State Debt Collection, *Organization*, http://debt.utah.gov/about.htm (accessed November 3, 2005).

99. State of Utah, Department of Administrative Services, Division of Facilities and Construction Management, Contact Info, *About DFCM*, http://dfcm.utah.gov/about/history.htm (accessed November 3, 2005).

100. Evan M. Berman et al., *Human Resource Management in Public Service* (Thousand Oaks, CA: Sage Publications, 2001), 18.

101. Ibid.

102. Expansion of Department of Administrative Services oversight to include Human Resource Management, H.B. 319, 56th Leg., Gen. Sess. (2005).

103. *Utah Code Annotated*, sec. 67-19-3.1 (2004).

104. *Utah Code Annotated*, sec. 67-19-7 (2004).

105. *Utah Code Annotated*, sec. 67-19-6.1 (Supp. 2005).

106. Under Section 67-19-6.1, which is effective July 1, 2006, DHRM and state agencies will enter into a field office agreement that will define the specific scope of services that will be performed by the agency and the DHRM field office.

107. *Utah Code Annotated*, sec. 63E-1-102 (2004).

108. *Utah Code Annotated*, Title 9, Chapter 3, Part 3, Heber Valley Historic Railroad Authority.

109. *Utah Code Annotated*, Title 53C, School and Institutional Trust Lands Management Act.

110. *Utah Code Annotated*, Title 63C, Chapter 7, Utah Communications Agency Network Act.

111. *Utah Code Annotated*, Title 4, Chapter 22, Dairy Promotion Act.

112. *Utah Code Annotated*, Title 9, Chapter 3, Part 4, Utah Science Center Authority.

113. *Utah Code Annotated*, Title 49, Utah State Retirement and Insurance Benefit Act.

114. *Utah Code Annotated*, Title 9, Chapter 4, Part 9, Utah Housing Corporation Act.

115. *Utah Code Annotated*, Title 9, Chapter 4, Part 11, Utah State Fair Corporation Act.

116. *Utah Code Annotated*, Title 63, Chapter 38f, Part 12, Utah Venture Capital Enhancement Act.

117. *Utah Code Annotated*, Title 31A, Chapter 33, Workers' Compensation Fund.

118. *Rules of the Fifty-Sixth Legislature*, State of Utah, SR-24.05, HR-24.05 (2005).

119. *Rules of the Fifty-Sixth Legislature*, State of Utah, JR-3.02 (2005).

120. *Consolidation of Data Processing and Telecommunications*, H.B. 274, 48th Leg., Gen. Sess. (Utah 1990).

121. *Digital State*, S.B. 188, 53rd Leg., Gen. Sess. (Utah 1999).

122. *Amendments Related to Information Technology*, S.B. 151, 55th Leg., Gen. Sess. (Utah 2003).

123. *Information Technology Governance Amendments*, H.B. 109, 56th Leg., Gen. Sess. (Utah 2005).

124. *Utah Code Annotated*, Title 63F, Chapter 1, Department of Technology Services.

125. Val Oveson (Chief Information Officer, State of Utah), Alan Sherwood (Deputy Chief Information Officer, State of Utah) in discussion with Richard C. North (Policy Analyst, Office of Legislative Research and General Counsel), 2004.

126. Glen Johnson (System Administrator, Office of Legislative Research and General Counsel) in discussion with Richard C. North (Policy Analyst, Office of Legislative Research and General Counsel), 2004.

127. Gordon Bissegger (Director, Court Administrative Services), Jerome E. Battle (Director, Court Information Technology Services) in discussion with Richard C. North (Policy Analyst, Office of Legislative Research and General Counsel), 2004.

Chapter 6 Endnotes

1. Utah Constitution, art. 9, sec. 2 and art. 5, sec. 12; *Utah Code Annotated*, secs. 36-1-101 and 36-1-201 (2001).

2. *Rules of the Fifty-Sixth Legislature*, State of Utah, HR-20.05, SR-20.05 (2005).

3. Utah Constitution, art. 6, sec. 2.

4. Utah Constitution, art. 6, sec. 16.

5. Utah Constitution, art. 6, sec. 15.

6. Utah Constitution, art. 7, sec. 8; Statutes relating to the initiative and referendum process do not permit the governor to veto laws adopted by the people.

7. Utah Constitution, art. 7, sec. 8.

8. Ibid.

9. Utah Constitution, art. 7, sec. 8; *Rules of the Fifty-Sixth Legislature*, State of Utah, JR-17.01 to 17.05 (2005).

10. The veto override bill retains its original passage and effective date, unless the bill had an early effective date. If the bill has an early effective date, the date of the veto override is the effective date of the bill. Utah Constitution, art. 7, sec. 8, ch. 4.

11. Utah Constitution, art. 7, sec. 6.

12. Utah Constitution, art. 7, sec. 6.

13. *Utah Code Annotated*, secs. 77-5-1 to -12 (2003); *Rules of the Fifty-Sixth Legislature*, State of Utah, SR-36.02 to 36.06, 37.24; HR-36.01 to 36.05, 37.10; JR-13.13 (2005).

14. Utah Constitution, art. 6, sec. 19.

15. The House Judiciary Standing Committee first investigates to see if there are sufficient grounds to exercise its impeachment power by weighing the evidence received from compelling witness testimony and document production. If impeachment is recommended, the speaker of the House appoints a Committee on Impeachment to prepare the Articles of Impeachment for submission to the House. The Resolution of Impeachment must pass the house by a constitutional two-thirds vote, after which it is presented to the president of the senate for prosecution in the senate.

16. Once the senate receives the Articles of Impeachment, and the president of the senate has served notice on the accused, the senate resolves itself into a Committee of the Whole by a constitutional majority vote. The Committee on Impeachment presents the Articles of Impeachment at the bar of the senate and to the defendant official. If the defendant official pleads not guilty, the senate will proceed to try the impeachment. (The "Committee of the Whole" is a procedure in which the entire membership of a single house constitutes a committee to consider legislative matters. It is used to permit an individual who is not a member of the house to address members on a bill before the Legislature, or when the senate hears impeachment proceedings.)

17. Utah Constitution, art. 7, sec. 6, cl. 2.

18. *Utah Code Annotated*, Title 36, Chapter 12, Legislative Organization, establishes the organization of interim legislative activities and outlines responsibilities of the professional staff offices.

19. "Leadership" in each house refers to the speaker of the house or president of the senate, the majority and minority leaders, whips, and assistant whips. Majority and minority leaders are elected by their respective caucuses and are responsible for: (1) conducting party caucuses; (2) managing the consideration of legislation on the floor of their houses; (3) informing members of agendas and

voting schedules; (4) mobilizing party strength to support or oppose legislation; and (5) communicating with the leadership of the other party particularly with respect to scheduling legislative business.

"Whip" and "assistant whips" are dependent upon the majority and minority leaders for their assignments but are usually responsible for reporting to the leadership any factors pertinent to the legislation being discussed and other business of concern to their respective parties. They also assist the leaders in encouraging support of party programs. The term "whip" is derived from foxhunting where the huntsman's assistant responsible for controlling the hounds is called the "whipper-in." Utah Legislature, Office of Legislative Research and General Counsel, Citizens' Guide, "Organization of the Utah Legislature," http://www.le.utah.gov (accessed May 31, 2005).

20. Utah Legislature, Office of the Legislative Fiscal Analyst, *Legislative Tool Box: Appropriation Process Budget Analysis*, ed. William J. Greer, Senior Fiscal Analyst (Salt Lake City, Oct. 12, 2004), 6-8, http://www.le.state.ut.us/lfa/reports/toolbox.pdf (accessed May 31, 2005).

21. *Rules of the Fifty-Sixth Legislature*, State of Utah, JR-3.02 (2005).

22. Utah Constitution, art. 13, sec. 5.

23. The legislative fiscal analyst reviews the subcommittee's portion of the budget and makes recommendations to the legislature on each item or program. The fiscal analyst also recommends specific funding levels (1) noting instances in which the executive branch may be failing to carry out the expressed intent of the legislature, (2) identifying proposed new services contained in the governor's budget, and (3) identifying appropriations requests that have previously been denied by the legislature. *Utah Code Annotated*, sec. 36-12-13 (2001).

24. *Utah Code Annotated*, sec. 36-12-1(1) (2001).

25. *Rules of the Fifty-Sixth Legislature*, State of Utah, SR-24.12 and HR-24.12 (2005).

26. Utah Constitution, art. 6, sec. 12.

27. Utah Constitution, art. 6, sec. 22.

28. Utah Constitution, art. 6, sec. 15.

29. Utah Constitution, art. 6, sec. 11.

30. Utah Constitution, art. 6, sec. 22.

31. Utah Constitution, art. 6, sec. 14.

32. Utah Constitution, art. 6, sec. 25.

33. Utah Constitution, art. 6, sec. 22.

34. Utah Constitution, art. 6, sec. 15.

35. *Utah Code Annotated*, secs. 52-4-1 to -10 (2002).

36. Utah Constitution, art. 6, sec. 11.

37. Utah Constitution, art. 6, sec. 22.

38. *Martineau v. Crabbe,* 150 P. 301, 304 (Utah 1915).

39. *Pass v. Kanell,* 100 P.2d 972, 974 (Utah 1940).

40. Utah Constitution, art. 6, sec. 14.

41. Utah Constitution Article 6, Section 25, provides that ". . . no act shall take effect until sixty days after the adjournment of the session at which it passed, unless the Legislature by a vote of two-thirds of all the members elected to each house, shall otherwise direct."

42. *Hargett v. Limbert,* 801 F.2d 368, 373 (10th Cir. 1986); *Mecham v. State Tax Commm'n,* 410 P.2d 1008, 1009 (Utah 1966). Legislative Joint Rule JR-4.20 provides that a delayed effective date may take effect with a majority vote of each house.

43. Legislative Joint Rule JR-4.19 requires the language: "This act takes effect upon approval by the governor, or the day following the constitutional time limit of art. 7, sec. 8 without the governor's signature, or in the case of a veto, the date of veto override."

44. The terms "retrospective" and "retroactive" as applied to laws are often used interchangeably and are deemed synonymous by some courts. *16B American Jurisprudence,* 2nd ed., (Minnesota: Thompson West, 1998) *Constitutional Law* sec. 690.

45. *Rules of the Fifty-Sixth Legislature,* State of Utah, JR-4.20.1 (2005).

46. *Utah Code Annotated,* sec. 68-3-3 (2004).

47. The rationale is that the bill takes effect on the 61st day after the legislative session, and then has retrospective operation to the specified date.

48. *Keegan v. State,* 896 P.2d 618 (Utah 1995); *State v. Higgs,* 656 P.2d 998, 1001 (Utah 1982).

49. *Evans,* 953 P2d at 437-38; *Roark v. Crabtree,* 893 P.2d 1058, 1062 (Utah 1995). *See Olsen,* 956 P.2d 257 (Utah 1998); *Keegan v. State,* 896 P.2d 618, 620 (Utah 1995); *State v. Abeyta,* 852 P.2d 993, 995 (Utah 1993); *State, Dep't of Social Servs. V. Higgs,* 656 P. 2d 998, 1001 (Utah 1982).

50. U.S. Constitution, art. 1, sec. 10; Utah Constitution, art. 1, sec. 18.

51. *Black's Law Dictionary,* 620.

52. Emily Shapiro, "Retroactivity of Statutes," *Minnesota House of Representatives Bill Drafting Manual* (1992), 12. A law is considered ex post facto if it has the "purpose or effect of creating a new crime, increasing the punishment for an existing crime, depriving a defendant of a defense available at the time the act was committed, or otherwise rendering an act punishable in a different, more disadvantageous manner than was true under the law at the time the act was committed." Ibid., 14.

53. *Rules of the Fifty-Sixth Legislature,* State of Utah, JR-4.21(2) (2005).

54. Norman J. Singer, *1A Sutherland Statutory Construction* (Minnesota: Thomson West, 2002), sec. 29:1.

55. Utah Constitution, art. 23, sec. 3.

56. *Rules of the Fifty-Sixth Legislature*, State of Utah, SR-25.01 and HR-25.01 (2005).

57. *Rules of the Fifty-Sixth Legislature*, State of Utah, SR-23.13 and HR-23.13 (2005).

58. *Rules of the Fifty-Sixth Legislature*, State of Utah, SR-25.03 and HR-25.03 (2005).

59. *Rules of the Fifty-Sixth Legislature*, State of Utah, SR-25.10 and HR-25.10 (2005).

60. *Rules of the Fifty-Sixth Legislature*, State of Utah, JR-7.01 to 7.08 (2005).

61. Adoption of the report implies approval of any amendments or bill substitutes provided by the standing committee.

62. *Rules of the Fifty-Sixth Legislature*, State of Utah, SR-25.14 and HR-25.14 (2005).

63. *Rules of the Fifty-Sixth Legislature*, State of Utah, HR-28.05 (2005).

64. *Rules of the Fifty-Sixth Legislature*, State of Utah, HR-30.06 (2005).

65. *Rules of the Fifty-Sixth Legislature*, State of Utah, SR-30.06 (2005).

66. *Rules of the Fifty-Sixth Legislature*, State of Utah, SR-30.01, SR-30.06 (2005).

67. *Rules of the Fifty-Sixth Legislature*, State of Utah, SR-25.14 (2005).

68. *Rules of the Fifty-Sixth Legislature*, State of Utah, JR-7.01 to 7.08 (2005).

69. Utah Constitution, art. 6, sec. 24.

70. If the presiding officer fails or refuses to sign a bill that the Legislature has passed, this failure will not invalidate the bill. A presiding officer's signature on a bill is simply a ministerial duty and not an exercise of legislative discretion. To hold otherwise would give the presiding officer, in effect, veto power over bills, which authority he does not have. The courts will examine the journals of each house to determine the proper enactment of the bill. *Dean v. Rampton*, 538 P.2d 169, 171 (Utah 1975); Singer, *1 Sutherland Statutory Construction*, sec. 14:8.

71. *Utah Code Annotated*, sec. 36-12-12 (2004).

72. Utah Constitution, art. 7, sec. 8.

73. Utah Constitution, art. 6, sec. 25.

74. Utah Constitution, art. 7, sec. 8.

75. Utah Constitution, art. 7, sec. 8.

76. Utah Constitution, art. 6, sec. 5.

77. Ibid.

78. *Utah Code Annotated*, sec. 20A-11-305 (2003).

79. Ballot access restrictions requiring candidates to disclose financial information are constitutional uses of legislative authority allowing states to regulate elections.

80. Utah Constitution Article 6, Section 6 provides that the following are not considered to be offices of profit or trust: "appointments in the State Militia, and offices of notary public, justice of the peace, United States commissioner, and postmaster of the fourth class."

81. Utah Constitution, art. 6, sec. 3.

82. Utah Constitution, art. 6, sec. 4.

83. Utah Constitution, art. 6, sec. 9; *Utah Code Annotated*, sec. 36-2-3 (2001).

84. *Utah Code Annotated*, secs. 36-2-2, -3 (2001); *Rules of the Fifty-Sixth Legislature*, State of Utah, JR-15.01 to 15.05 (2005).

85. Utah Constitution, art. 6, sec. 31.

86. Utah Constitution, art. 6, sec. 6.

87. *State v. Grover,* 125 P.2d 807, 813 (Utah 1942). See also *Shields v. Toronto*, 395 P.2d 829 (Utah 1964); *Romney v. Barlow*, 469 P.2d 497 (Utah 1970).

88. *Shields v. Toronto*, 395 P.2d 829 (Utah 1964).

89. Ibid., 835.

90. Utah Constitution, art. 6, sec. 10.

91. *State v. Evans,* 735 P.2d 29, 31 (Utah 1987).

92. Ibid., 32.

93. *Utah Code Annotated*, sec. 76-8-109 (2003); *Rules of the Fifty-Sixth Legislature*, State of Utah, JR-16.01 to 16.07 (2005).

94. The "Journal" is an official record maintained by each house on a daily basis indicating specific actions taken and the record of votes. Specific actions may include the introduction of bills, amendments, committee hearings, reports, floor action, and votes. The journal may refer to various speeches, but usually does not record their content.

95. *Rules of the Fifty-Sixth Legislature*, State of Utah, JR-16.05 (2005).

96. *Rules of the Fifty-Sixth Legislature*, State of Utah, JR-16.02 (2005).

97. Utah Constitution, art. 6, sec. 10.

98. Utah Constitution, art. 6, sec. 8.

99. This constitutional provision provides that "for words used in any speech or debate in either house, [members of the Legislature] shall not be questioned in any other place."

100. (1) *Gravel v. United States*, 408 U.S. 606, 616 (1972); (2) *Kilbourn v. Thompson*, 103 U.S. 168 (1881); (3) *Doe v. McMillan*, 412 U.S. 306 (1973); (4) *Gravel v. United States*, 408 U.S., at 616; (5) Ibid.; (6) *McSurely v. McClennan*, 553 F.2d 1277 (D.C. Cir. 1976); (7) *Consumers Union of United States v. Periodical Correspondents' Assoc.*, 515 F.2d 1341 (D.C. Cir. 1975); and (8) *National Ass'n of Social Workers v. Harwood*, 69 F.3d 622 (1st Cir. 1995).

101. *Walker v. Jones*, 733 F.2d 923 (D.D.C. Cir. 1984).

102. *Walker v. Jones*, 733 F.2d 923 (D.C. Cir. 1984); *United States v. Murphy*, 642 F.2d 699 (2nd Cir. 1980).

103. *United States v. Murphy*, 642 F.2d 699 (2d Cir. 1980).

104. See Greer, *Appropriation Process Budget Analysis*, 6-8.

105. *Utah Code Annotated*, sec. 63-38-2 (2004).

106. Ibid.

107. *Rules of the Fifty-Sixth Legislature*, State of Utah, JR-3.02 (2005).

108. Utah Constitution, art. 7, sec. 8.

109. Utah Constitution Article 6, Section 22, provides: "Except general appropriation bills and bills for the codification and general revisions of laws, no bill shall be passed containing more than one subject, which shall be clearly expressed in its title." Appropriations bills are not limited to the single subject rule with respect to the enumeration of approved fees in *Utah Code Annotated*, sec. 63-38-3 (2004).

110. *Utah Code Annotated*, sec. 63-38-3.

111. Utah Constitution, art. 13, sec. 5, cl. 2.

112. Ibid. Subsection (2)(b) makes an exception to the balanced budget requirement for "an appropriation or expenditure to suppress insurrection, defend the State, or assist in defending the United States in time of war."

113. Utah Legislature, Office of Legislative Research and General Counsel, Briefing Paper, *Tax Primer* (November, 2001), 35-38, http://www.le.state.ut.us/lrgc/briefingpapers/taxbrief.pdf (accessed May 9, 2005); Greer, *Appropriation Process Budget Analysis*, 22-24.

114. Utah Constitution, art. 10, sec. 5.

115. Utah Constitution, art. 13, sec. 5(6).

116. Utah Constitution, art. 6, sec. 1.

117. *Hansen v. State Retirement Bd.*, 652 P.2d 1332, 1341 (Utah 1982) (Crockett, J. concurring); *State v. Mason*, 78 P.2d 920, 925 (Utah 1938); *State ex rel. Nichols v. Cherry*, 60 P. 1103, 1103 (Utah 1900); *Kimball v. Grantsville City*, 57 P. 1, 4 (Utah 1899).

118. *Blue Cross and Blue Shield of Utah v. State,* 779 P.2d 634, 645 (Utah 1989). The Utah Supreme Court views the special laws ban as the flip side of the uniform operation of laws provision. "If a law satisfies the requirement of Article 1, Section 24 of the Utah Constitution, that all laws of a general nature have uniform operation, it will not violate Article 6, Section 26." Ibid. Utah's Supreme Court has defined special legislation as a law that "confers particular privileges or imposes peculiar disabilities, or burdensome conditions in the exercise of a common right; upon a class of persons arbitrarily selected from the general body of those who stand in precisely the same relation to the subject of the law." *Hulbert v. State*, 607 P.2d 1217, 1224 (Utah 1980).

119. *Saville v. Corless*, 151 P. 51 (Utah 1915).

120. Utah Constitution, art. 6, sec. 27.

121. *Albertson's Inc. v. Hansen*, 600 P.2d 982 (Utah 1979).

122. *Geis v. Continental Oil Co.*, 511 P.2d 725, 727 (Utah 1973).

123. *D'Orio v. Startup Candy Co.,* 266 P. 1037 (Utah 1928). The test is whether "skill" or "chance" is the dominating element that determines the game's result. Ibid., 1039.

124. Utah Constitution, art. 11, sec. 5.

125. A "special commission" is an entity separate and distinct from the municipal government, which intrudes into areas of purely municipal concern. *Tribe v. Salt Lake City Corp.*, 540 P.2d 499, 502-03 (Utah 1975).

126. Utah Constitution, Article 6, Section 28 provides: "The Legislature shall not delegate to any special commission, private corporation or association, any power to make, supervise or interfere with any municipal improvement, money, property or effects, whether held in trust or otherwise, to levy taxes, to select a capitol site, or to perform any municipal functions."

127. Utah Constitution, art. 6, sec. 29; *Utah Technology Finance Corporation v. Wilkinson*, 723 P.2d 406, 412 (Utah 1986).

128. Utah Constitution, art. 13, sec. 5(4).

129. *Mountain States Tel. & Tel. Co. v. Garfield County,* 811 P.2d 184, 187 (Utah 1991).

130. "Public purpose" is generally regarded as whatever is necessary for the preservation of the public health, safety, and welfare, and funds may be raised by taxation to embrace expenditures for the general welfare. *Carmichael v. Southern Coal & Coke Co.*, 301 U.S. 495, 514 (1937); *Daytona Beach v. King*, 181 So. 1 (Fla. 1938). "Public purpose" does not mean that the benefits from the funds to be raised are to spread equally over the whole community or a large portion of the community. A use may be "public" even though it primarily benefits the inhabitants of a small and restricted locality. *Milheim v. Moffat Tunnel Improv. Dist.*, 262 U.S. 710 (1923); *State ex rel. Charleston, C. & C.R. Co. v. Whitesides*, 9 S.E. 661 (S.C. 1889).

131. Utah Constitution, art. 5, sec. 1.

132. See Ibid., 687. The Utah Supreme Court clarified that Article 5, Section 1 of the Utah Constitution does limit the ability of the Legislature to delegate rulemaking authority to one of the Constitutional officers, in this case the Utah Attorney General.

133. *State v. Gallion*, 572 P.2d 683, 690 (Utah 1977) (Crockett, J., concurring).

134. U.S. Constitution, art. 1, sec. 2. In addition, census data is used to determine the boundaries of state and local political districts, and is useful to individuals overseeing "public and private sector issues involving health and education, transportation planning, community services, housing, consumer marketing, economic strategies, and social equity." Barry Edmonston, "Using U.S. Census Data to Study Population Composition," *North Dakota Law Review* 77 (2001): 711, 712.

135. The Bureau of the Census in the U.S. Department of Commerce conducts the census, which is required to be completed within nine months of the census date and reported by the Secretary to the President of the United States. 13 U.S.C. sec. 141(b) (2004).

136. U.S. Constitution, art. 1, sec. 2, cl. 3 ("representatives . . . shall be apportioned among the several States . . . according to their respective Numbers").

137. U.S. Constitution, art. 1, sec. 3; 2 U.S.C. sec. 2c (2004); Edmonston, "Using U.S. Census Data to Study Population Composition," 715.

138. Utah Constitution, art. 9, sec. 1 and 2.

139. J. Gerald Hebert et al., *The Realists' Guide to Redistricting – Avoiding the Legal Pitfalls*, (Illinois: American Bar Association Publishing, 2000), 5.

140. *Wesberry v. Sanders*, 376 U.S. 1, 7-8 (1964).

141. *Reynolds v. Sims*, 377 U.S. 533, 569, 579 (1964). Although *Reynolds v. Sims* is the foundation for the federal judiciary's development of variance standards for state legislative districting, the Court declined to delineate what population differences in equality would be permitted. The Court stated, "What is marginally permissible in one state may be unsatisfactory in another depending upon the particular circumstances of the case." Some population differences in equality in legislative plans might be justified if they were "based on legitimate considerations incident to the effectuation of a rational state policy. . . . " Ibid., 578-79.

142. The Voting Rights Act Amendments of 1975 extended protection to members of a language minority group. 42 U.S.C. sec. 1973(a) (1982).

143. Ibid. The Voting Rights Act of 1965 was enacted by Congress to enforce the Fifteenth Amendment of the United States Constitution, that no citizen's right to vote shall "be denied or abridged . . . on account of race, color, or previous condition of servitude." U.S. Constitution, amend. 15.

144. *Thornburg v. Gingles*, 478 U.S. 30 (1986).

145. *Shaw v. Reno (Shaw I)*, 509 U.S. 630 (1993); *Shaw v. Hunt (Shaw II)*, 517 U.S. 899 (1996).

146. The U.S. Supreme Court stated: "A reapportionment plan that includes in one district individuals who belong to the same race, but who are otherwise widely separated by geographical and political boundaries, and who may have little in common with one another but the color of their skin, bears an uncomfortable resemblance to political apartheid. It reinforces the perception that members of the same racial group – regardless of their age, education, economic status, or the community in which they live – think alike, share the same political interests, and will prefer the same candidates at the polls. We have rejected such perceptions elsewhere as impermissible racial stereotypes." *Shaw v. Reno*, 509 U.S. 630, 649 (1993).

147. "Gerrymandering" is defined as "[t]he practice of dividing a geographical area into electoral districts, often of highly irregular shape, to give one political party an unfair advantage by diluting the opposition's voting strength." *Black's Law Dictionary*, 8th ed. (Minnesota: Thompson West, 2004), 708.

148. *Davis v. Bandemer*, 478 U.S. 109 (1986).

149. Ibid., 127.

150. *Vieth v. Jubelirer*, 541 U.S. 267 (2004).

151. *Utah Code Annotated*, sec. 36-12-7 (2001).

152. *Utah Code Annotated*, sec. 36-12-12 (Supp. 2005).

153. Executive Article 7, Section 16 provides that the Attorney General is required to be the legal advisor to the "State officers, *except as otherwise provided by this Constitution*. . . ." The Utah Supreme Court, in *Hansen v. Utah State Retirement Board,* interpreted the term "state officers" as being limited to the "Governor, Lieutenant Governor, Auditor, Treasurer, and the Superintendent of Public Instruction, the departments over which they have direct supervisory control, and to the other state executive offices referred to in Article 7, insofar as the officers of those offices act within the scope of the duties of such office." *Hansen v. Utah State Retirement Board*, 652 P.2d 1332, 1336-37 (Utah 1982).

    The language, "except as otherwise provided by this Constitution," clarifies the constitutional authority the legislature has to appoint it own legal counsel. 1979 Utah Laws 1323 (Utah Constitution, art. 7, sec. 16 referring to Utah Constitution, art. 6, sec. 32).

154. The *Utah Code* is a complete codification and compilation of all effective and current laws of the state, classified according to subject matter.

155. Statutory responsibilities of the Office of Legislative Research and General Counsel are outlined in *Utah Code Annotated*, sec. 36-12-12 (Supp. 2005).

156. Statutory responsibilities of the Office of the Legislative Fiscal Analyst are outlined in *Utah Code Annotated*, sec. 36-12-13 (2001). See also *Rules of the Fifty-Sixth Legislature*, State of Utah, JR-3.02, 4.22, 4.22.1, 4.23, and 13.28.

157. Utah Code Annotated, sec. 36-12-13 (2001).

158. Utah Constitution Article 6, Section 33 provides that the legislative auditor "shall have authority to conduct audits of any funds, functions, and accounts in any branch, department, agency or political subdivision of this state and shall perform such other related duties as may be prescribed

by the Legislature. He shall report to and be answerable only to the Legislature." *Utah Code Annotated*, sec. 36-12-15 (Supp. 2005).

159. Statutory responsibilities of the Office of the Legislative Auditor General are outlined in *Utah Code Annotated*, sec. 36-12-15 (Supp. 2005).

160. *Utah Code Annotated*, sec. 36-13-1 (2001).

161. *Laws of Utah* (cited as "*Utah Laws*") are Utah's "session laws," or the chronological publication of laws enacted during a legislative session. The enrolled version of any legislation passed by the Legislature is compiled and published in the *Laws of Utah*. An enrolled bill that is either signed by the governor or allowed to become law without the governor's signature is listed in the *Laws of Utah* in accordance with chapter numbers assigned by the Office of Legislative Research and General Counsel, generally in order of the governor's action. Resolutions are included in the *Laws of Utah*, but not assigned a chapter number. Vetoed legislation is not assigned a chapter number and is included immediately following the governor's letters explaining the veto.

162. *Information Technology Commission*, 1994 Utah Laws ch. 241.

163. *Amendments to Information Technology*, 2003 Utah Laws ch. 209, codified at *Utah Code Annotated*, Title 63D, Chapter 1a, State Information Technology Act.

Chapter 7 Endnotes

1. Virginia Gray and Pete Eisinger, *American States and Cities*, Second Edition, Longman, 1997, 204.

2. Utah Constitution, art. 8, sec. 1.

3. Utah Constitution, art. 8, sec. 12; *Utah Code Annotated*, sec. 78-3-21 (Supp. 2005).

4. Utah Constitution, art. 7, sec. 4.

5. *Utah Code Annotated*, sec. 78-3-21 (Supp. 2005).

6. Utah Constitution, art. 8, sec. 4.

7. Utah Constitution, art. 8, sec. 4.

8. *Utah Code Annotated*, sec. 78-2a-1 (2002).

9. *Utah Code Annotated*, sec. 78-3a-102 (Supp. 2005).

10. *Utah Code Annotated*, sec. 78-5-101 (2002).

11. Utah Constitution, art. 8, sec. 3.

12. The Court of Appeals hears all appeals from state adjudicative proceedings except those of the Public Service Commission, State Tax Commission, School and Institutional Trust Lands Board of Trustees, Division of Forestry, Fire and State Lands actions reviewed by the Department of Natural Resources, Board of Oil, Gas, and Mining, and the State engineer. *Utah Code Annotated*, sec.

78-2a-3 (2002).

13. *Utah Code Annotated*, sec. 78-2a-2(4) (2002).

14. *Utah Code Annotated*, sec. 78-3-4 (Supp. 2005).

15. *Utah Code Annotated*, sec. 78-3-31 (2002).

16. *Utah Code Annotated*, sec. 78-3a-102(3).

17. *Utah Code Annotated*, sec. 78-3a-104(2) (Supp. 2005).

18. *Utah Code Annotated*, sec. 78-3-23 (2002).

19. Utah Constitution, art. 8, sec. 12.

20. *Utah Code Annotated*, sec. 78-3-21(1) (Supp. 2005).

21. *Utah Code Annotated*, sec. 78-3-22 (2002); Utah Code of Jud. Admin., R. 1-203 (2005).

22. *Utah Court Rules Annotated* (Charlottesville, VA: Matthew Bender & Co., Inc., 2005).

23. Utah Code of Jud. Admin., R. 1-203.

24. Utah Code of Jud. Admin., R. 2-203 (2005).

25. Utah Code of Jud. Admin., R. 1-204 (2005).

26. Ibid., -204(4).

27. Utah Code of Jud. Admin., R. 1-205 (2005).

28. Ibid.

29. *Utah Code of Jud. Admin.*, R. 2-103 (2005).

30. Utah Code of Jud. Admin., R. 2-103 (2005).

31. Utah Code of Jud. Admin., R. 2-212 (2005).

32. *Utah Code Annotated*, sec. 78-3-23.

33. *Utah Code Annotated*, sec. 78-3-24 (2002).

34. *Utah Code Annotated*, sec. 78-3-25 (2002).

35. Ibid., -25(3).

36. Utah Legislature, Office of the Legislative Auditor, *A Performance Audit of the Administrative Office of the Courts* (Salt Lake City: Legislative Printing Office, May 2004), 14.

37. *Utah Code Annotated*, sec. 78-3-24.

38. Utah Legislature, Senate Floor Debates, 45th Leg., 2nd Spec. Sess., Tuesday, March 27, 1984, Disc No. 6.

39. Justice Leonard H. Russon, "Views from the Bench: The Constitutional Guarantee of an Independent Judiciary," *Utah Bar Journal* 16, no. 4 (May 2003): 22.

40. *The Book of the States*, 2003 (Lexington, Ky.: Council of State Governments, 2003):247-250.

41. Utah Constitution, art. 8, sec. 8(1).

42. *Utah Code Annotated*, sec. 20A-12-102 (2003).

43. *Utah Code Annotated*, sec. 20A-12-103 (2003).

44. *Utah Court Rules Annotated*, "Manual of Procedures for Judicial Nominating Commissions," Appendix A (Charlottesville, VA: Matthew Bender & Co, Inc., 2005), 1454.

45. Utah Constitution, art. 8, sec. 8(1).

46. Ibid.

47. Utah Constitution, art. 8, sec. (3).

48. U.S. Department of Justice, Office of Justice Programs, Bureau of Statistics, *State Court Organization 1998*, by David B. Rottman et al. (Washington D.C., June 2000), Table 7, 34-48, http://www.ojp.usdoj.gov/bjs/abstract/sco98.htm (accessed May 24, 2005).

49. Utah Constitution, art. 8, sec. 9; *Utah Code Annotated*, sec. 20A-12-201 (2003).

50. Utah Constitution, art. 8, sec. 13.

51. Utah Constitution, art. 8, sec. 13.

52. Utah Constitution, art. 6, sec. 19.

53. Utah Constitution, art. 6, sec. 18.

54. Utah Constitution, art. 6, sec. 17.

55. Utah Constitution, art. 6, sec. 18.

56. Utah Constitution, art. 6, sec. 19.

57. *Resolution Initiating Impeachment Proceedings for Judge Ray M. Harding, Jr.*, H.R. 9, 55th Leg., Gen. Sess. (Utah 2003).

58. *Utah Code Annotated*, sec. 77-10a-2 (2003).

59. *Utah Code Annotated*, sec. 77-10a-13 (2003).

60. U.S. Constitution, amend. 6.

61. Utah Commission on Justice in the Twenty-First Century, "Doing Utah Justice: A Progress Report to the People of Utah" (Salt Lake City: Commission on Justice, 1991).

Chapter 8 Endnotes

1. *Compañia General de Tabacos de Filipinas v. Collector of Internal Revenue*, 275 U.S. 87 (1927).

2. Property tax is for calendar year 2003. Source: Utah State Tax Commission, Property Tax Division, *2003 Annual Statistical Report: Local, Personal, and Centrally Assessed Property* (September 1, 2004), 26; Utah State Tax Comm'n, Economic and Statistical Unit, *TC-23 Monthly Revenue Summary, Final Year-end, FY 2003-2004* (September 15, 2004).

3. Property tax is for calendar years 1982 to 2004. Source: Utah State Tax Comm'n, *Annual Reports, Fiscal Years 2000-2001 to 2003-2004*; Utah State Tax Comm'n, Property Tax Div., *Annual Statistical Reports: Local, Personal, and Centrally Assessed Property (1978-2003)*.

4. Jewell J. Rasmussen, *History of Utah's First Century of Taxation and Public Debt 1896 - 1995* (Utah: University of Utah, 1996), 11-12.

5. Utah Foundation, *Financing Government in Utah* (Utah: Utah Foundation, 2000), 11.

6. Ibid., 26.

7. Governor Olene S. Walker, *Recommendations on a Tax Structure for Utah's Future* (Salt Lake City, November 2004), 2; Utah Foundation, *Financing Government in Utah*, 26. Note that the state does not currently impose a general property tax for state purposes.

8. Rasmussen, *History of Utah's First Century of Taxation and Public Debt*, 4-7.

9. Utah Foundation, *Financing Government in Utah*, 28-32; Utah Constitutional Revision Commission, *Report of the Utah Constitutional Revision Commission 1994* (Utah: Legislative Printing, 1994).

10. Olene S. Walker, *Utah Voter Information Pamphlet: General Election November 5, 2002* (Utah: State Elections Office, 2002), 26-31. Note that except for a change in the membership of county boards of equalization, the constitutional amendment was not intended to change the substance of the Revenue and Taxation Article.

11. *See* Utah Foundation, *Financing Government in Utah*, 11-26.

12. Ibid.

13. Utah Constitution, art. 13, sec. 2.

14. Utah Constitution, art. 12, sec. 3.

15. Utah Constitution, art. 13, secs. 2 and 3.

16. Utah Constitution, art. 13, sec. 2.

17. Ibid.

18. Utah Constitution, art. 13, secs. 2 and 3.

19. *Utah Code Annotated*, sec. 59-4-101 (2004).

20. Ibid.

21. *Utah Code Annotated*, sec. 59-3-102 (2004).

22. See *Utah Code Annotated*, sec. 59-3-102.

23. Source: Utah State Tax Comm'n, *2003 Annual Statistical Report*, 26-30.

24. See Utah Constitution, art. 14, Public Debt. The debt limit for the state is established in Section 1 and the debt limit for local jurisdictions is established in Section 4.

25. See Utah Constitution, art. 14.

26. *Utah Code Annotated*, sec. 59-2-704 (2004).

27. Utah Constitution, art. 13, sec. 6; *Utah Code Annotated*, sec. 59-2-201 (2004).

28. Utah Constitution, art. 13, sec. 6; *Utah Code Annotated*, sec. 59-2-201, -203 (2004).

29. Source: Utah State Tax Comm'n, *Annual Statistical Reports: (1978-2003)*.

30. See Utah Constitution, art. 13, sec. 2; *Utah Code Annotated*, sec. 59-2-103 (2004).

31. *Utah Code Annotated*, sec. 59-2-303.1 (2004).

32. *Utah Code Annotated*, sec. 59-2-704.

33. *Utah Code Annotated*, sec. 59-2-1001 (2004).

34. *Utah Code Annotated*, secs. 59-2-1002, -1003, -1004 (2004).

35. *Utah Code Annotated*, sec. 59-2-103. Note that reductions in value, such as the residential exemption, or property tax relief, such as property tax relief for the poor, may be applied, resulting in a reduction in the value of property.

36. *Utah Code Annotated*, sec. 59-2-1331 (2004).

37. *Utah Code Annotated*, secs. 59-2-918, -919, -924 (2004 & Supp. 2005).

38. Utah Foundation, *Financing Government in Utah*, 25.

39. *Utah Code Annotated*, secs. 59-2-918, -919.

40. See *Utah Code Annotated*, sec. 59-2-924(2)(b).

41. *Utah Code Annotated*, sec. 59-2-919(4).

42. Ibid.

43. *Utah Code Annotated*, sec. 59-2-918, -919.

44. *Utah Code Annotated*, sec. 59-2-1004.

45. Ibid.

46. *Utah Code Annotated*, sec. 59-2-1007 (2004).

47. *Utah Code Annotated*, sec. 59-2-1006 (2004).

48. *Utah Code Annotated*, sec. 59-1-602 (2004).

49. Source: Utah State Tax Comm'n, *2003 Annual Statistical Report*, 33.

50. Source: Utah State Tax Comm'n, *Annual Statistical Reports: (1978-2003)*.

51. See Utah Constitution, art. 14.

52. Utah Foundation, *Financing Government in Utah*, 65-66.

53. Utah Foundation, *Financing Government in Utah*, 66-68.

54. *Utah Code Annotated*, sec. 59-12-107 (2004 & Supp. 2005).

55. *See* Utah Foundation, *Financing Government in Utah*, 85.

56. Ibid., 68-69.

57. Ibid., 71.

58. Ibid.

59. *Utah Code Annotated*, sec. 59-12-205 (2004 & Supp. 2005).

60. See *Utah Code Annotated*, Title 59, Chapter 12, Sales and Use Tax Act.

61. Ibid.

62. Ibid.

63. *See Quill Corp. v. North Dakota*, 504 U.S. 298 (1992).

64. 1999 Utah Laws ch. 191.

65. 2000 Utah Laws ch. 253; 2001 Utah Laws ch. 104; 2003 Utah Laws ch. 312; 2004 Utah Laws ch. 255; 2005 Utah Laws ch. 158; 2005 Utah Laws ch. 232.

66. *See* 2005 Utah Laws ch. 232.

67. See *Utah Code Annotated*, sec. 59-12-103 (2004 & Supp. 2005).

68. See *Utah Code Annotated*, sec. 59-12-103.

69. State and local sales and use tax exemptions are found in *Utah Code Annotated*, sec. 59-12-104 (2004 & Supp. 2005).

70. *Utah Code Annotated*, sec. 59-12-104(2), (8).

71. The Utah Tax Review Commission is created by *Utah Code Annotated*, sec. 59-1-901 (2004). *Utah Code Annotated*, sec. 59-1-903 (2004), provides that the duties of the Utah Tax Review Commission include reviewing state and local tax laws.

72. *Utah Code Annotated*, sec. 59-12-104.5 (2004).

73. Source: Utah State Tax Comm'n, Economic and Statistical Unit, *Fourth Quarter & Calendar Year 2004 Taxable Retail Sales, Services and Purchases in the State of Utah*, Research Publication 2005-07 (April 2005).

74. *Utah Code Annotated*, sec. 59-12-107.

75. Ibid.

76. Utah State Tax Comm'n, Utah Individual Income Tax Return, Form: 2004 TC-40 (2004).

77. A county imposing a transient room tax or a city or town imposing a municipality transient room tax or additional municipal transient room tax may collect the tax rather than contracting with the State Tax Commission to collect the tax. *Utah Code Annotated*, secs. 59-12-302, -354 (2004).

78. See *Utah Code Annotated*, Title 59, Chapter 12, Sales and Use Tax Act.

79. *Utah Code Annotated*, sec. 59-12-106 (2004 & Supp. 2005).

80. *Utah Code Annotated*, sec. 59-12-108 (2004).

81. Source: Utah State Tax Comm'n, *TC-23 Monthly Revenue Summary, FY 2003-2004*.

82. See *Utah Code Annotated*, sec. 59-12-103 for a description of the earmarking of state sales and use taxes.

83. Utah Foundation, *Financing Government in Utah*, 43.

84. Ibid.

85. Ibid.

86. Utah Foundation, *Financing Government in Utah*, 45-56.

87. Ibid., 48

88. Ibid., 47.

89. Ibid., 64.

90. Utah Foundation, *Financing Government in Utah*, 49-51, 61, 64.

91. Ibid., 50.

92. Ibid., 91.

93. Ibid., 93.

94. Utah Foundation, *Financing Government in Utah*, 93-95, 107-108.

95. Ibid., 94-95.

96. Other taxes, such as the taxes under the Radioactive Waste Facility Tax Act imposed by *Utah Code Annotated*, Title 59, Chapter 24, Radioactive Waste Facility Tax Act, are computed on the basis of gross receipts. However, for purposes of this chapter, these other taxes are addressed below under the discussion on "Other Taxes."

97. Utah Foundation, *Financing Government in Utah*, 154-56.

98. Ibid., 156-57.

99. See *Utah Code Annotated*, secs. 59-7-104, -201, and 59-10-104 (2004).

100. See *Utah Code Annotated*, secs. 59-10-103, -112 (2004 & Supp. 2005).

101. See *Utah Code Annotated*, sec. 59-10-111 (2004); 26 U.S.C. sec. 63 (2005).

102. *Utah Code Annotated*, sec. 59-10-114 (2004 & Supp. 2005). An example of a statute that governs the determination of state taxable income is *Utah Code Annotated*, sec. 59-10-112 (2004).

103. *Utah Code Annotated*, sec. 59-7-311 (Supp. 2005).

104. Ibid.

105. *Utah Code Annotated*, secs. 59-8-104, 59-8a-104 (2004).

106. Utah State Tax Comm'n, *Summary of 2002 State Income Tax Returns*, http://www.tax.utah.gov/esu/income/state02/state.htm (accessed July 21, 2005).

107. Ibid.

108. Utah State Tax Comm'n, *Utah Corporate Income Statistics Utah Apportioned Data for All Fields: Returns for 2002*, http://www.tax.utah.gov/esu/income/corp02/utiall.html (accessed July 21, 2005).

109. Ibid.

110. *Utah Code Annotated*, sec. 59-10-402 (2004).

111. *Utah Code Annotated*, sec. 59-10-404 (2004).

112. *Utah Code Annotated*, sec. 59-10-402, -403 (2004).

113. See *Utah Code Annotated*, sec. 59-10-402.

114. *Utah Code Annotated*, sec. 59-7-504 (2004). Although not expressly stated in statute, State Tax Commission Form TC-20, Corporation Franchise or Income Tax Return and Instructions, provides that a parent company filing a combined report with affiliated companies must make quarterly estimated payments if the aggregate state tax liability is $3,000 or more for all corporations included in the combined filings, including corporations paying only the minimum tax. Utah State Tax Comm'n, *Utah Corporation Franchise or Income Tax Return, Form: 2004 TC-20: Tax Return and Instructions* (Rev. Dec. 2004).

115. Utah State Tax Comm'n, *Utah Corporation Franchise or Income Tax Return, Form: 2004 TC-20: Tax Return and Instructions* (Rev. Dec. 2004).

116. Ibid.

117. *Utah Code Annotated*, secs. 59-7-505, -507 (2004). Exceptions to the return filing requirements are contained in sec. 59-7-505. These statutes do not expressly require that the tax due must be paid by the due date regardless of whether estimated payments are made, but penalties apply if there is an underpayment.

118. *Utah Code Annotated*, sec. 59-7-502 (2004). If a corporation's taxable year changes for federal income tax purposes, the corporation must file a short period return covering the period that is less than twelve months and is between the last day of the prior taxable year and the last day of the new taxable year. *Utah Code Annotated*, sec. 59-7-503 (2004).

119. *Utah Code Annotated*, secs. 59-8-105, 59-8a-105 (2004).

120. Ibid.

121. Utah Constitution, art. 13, sec. 5(5).

122. Office of the Governor, Governor's Office of Planning and Budget, *Budget Recommendations Fiscal Year 2006, Fiscal Year 2005 Supplements* (Salt Lake City, January 2005), 16-17.

123. Utah Constitution, art. 13, sec. 5(5).

124. Utah Foundation, *Financing Government in Utah*, 157; Rasmussen, *History of Utah's First Century of Taxation and Public Debt*, 15.

125. Utah Foundation, *Financing Government in Utah*, 152-154.

126. A mining occupation tax was effective for 1917 and 1918. In 1919, this tax was repealed and the property tax base increased to three times the net proceeds for metalliferous mines, the value of improvements, and ground at $5 per acre. Nonmetallic mines and minerals were subject to property tax assessment at their full value. In 1937, a mining occupation tax was enacted. Utah Foundation, *Financing Government in Utah*, 135; Rasmussen, *History of Utah's First Century of Taxation and Public Debt*, 20, 40-41.

127. Utah Foundation, *Financing Government in Utah*, 111.

128. *Licensing and Sale of Cigarettes*, 1923 Utah Laws ch. 52.

129. Utah Foundation, *Financing Government in Utah*, 148; Rasmussen, *History of Utah's First Century of Taxation and Public Debt*, 38.

130. Utah Foundation, *Financing Government in Utah*, 117.

131. Ibid., 148; Rasmussen, *History of Utah's First Century of Taxation and Public Debt*, 150.

132. Rasmussen, *History of Utah's First Century of Taxation and Public Debt*, 55-56.

133. Legislation imposing a severance tax on oil and gas production was passed by the Legislature in 1955 with an effective date of January 1, 1956. Utah Foundation, *Financing Government in Utah*, 136.

134. Rasmussen, *History of Utah's First Century of Taxation and Public Debt*, 63.

135. Ibid., 77.

136. *Municipal Energy Sales and Use Tax Act*, 1996 Utah Laws ch. 280.

137. *Brine Shrimp Royalty Act*, 1997 Utah Laws ch. 179.

138. *Radioactive Waste Tax Act*, 2001 Utah Laws ch. 314.

139. *State and Local Taxes, Fees, and Charges Related to Telecommunications*, 2003 Utah Laws ch. 253.

140. *Waste Tax and Fee Amendments*, 2003 Utah Laws ch. 295.

141. *Multi-Channel Video or Audio Service Tax Act*, 2004 Utah Laws ch. 300.

142. *Sexually Explicit Business and Escort Service Tax Act*, 2004 Utah Laws ch. 214.

143. Utah Constitutional Revision Commission, *Report of the Utah Constitutional Revision Commission 1994* (Utah: Legislative Printing, 1994).

144. Utah Constitution, art. 13, sec. 6.

145. Ibid.

146. *Utah Code Annotated*, sec. 59-1-206 (2004).

147. *Utah Code Annotated*, sec. 59-1-207 (2004); Utah State Tax Commission, *Tax Commissioners and Executive Director* (Salt Lake City, August 19, 2002), http://tax.utah.gov/commission.html (accessed June 9, 2005).

148. *Utah Code Annotated*, sec. 59-1-206.

149. Utah Constitution, art. 13, sec. 6.

150. Office of the Governor, Utah Council of Economic Advisors, *2005 Economic Report to the Governor* (Salt Lake City: Governor's Office of Planning and Budget, January 2005).

151. Ibid, 19.

152. U.S. Census Bureau, U.S. Bureau and Economic Analysis, http://www.census.gov/govs/www/estimate.html (accessed August 4, 2005).

153. U.S. Census Bureau, U.S. Bureau and Economic Analysis, http://www.census.gov/popest/states/ (accessed August 4, 2005).

154. U.S. Census Bureau, U.S. Bureau and Economic Analysis, http://www.bea.gov/bea/regional/spi/ (accessed August 4, 2005).

155. Utah State Tax Comm'n, Econ. and Statis. Unit, *Western States' Tax Burdens Fiscal Year 1999-2000*, Res. Pub. 2001-19 (Salt Lake City, June 2001).

156. Utah State Tax Comm'n, Econ. and Statis. Unit, *Western States' Tax Burdens, Fiscal Year 2002-2003, Initial State and Local Tax Burdens for Selected Western States*, Res. Pub. 2003-31 (Salt Lake City, December 2003).

157. The legislature reduced the state sales and use tax rate from 5 percent to 4.875 percent. (1994 Utah Laws ch. 290) during in the 1994 General Session. During the 1997 General Session, the Legislature further reduced the state sales and use tax rate from 4.875 percent to 4.75 percent. (1997 Utah Laws ch. 272). Income tax rates were reduced during the 1996 General Session. (1996 Utah Laws ch. 333). Property tax revenues were reduced through various legislative actions during the mid 1990s, including an increase in the residential property tax exemption to the maximum percentage of 45 percent allowed under the Utah Constitution and reductions in the minimum school program property tax levy. Between fiscal years 1995 and 2004, the net cumulative total of all tax reductions was $1,825,400,597. Office of the Governor, Utah Council of Economic Advisors, *2004 Economic Report to the Governor* (Salt Lake City: Governor's Office of Planning and Budget, January 2004), 83. Taxes on motor fuel and special fuel were raised during the 1997 General Session. (1997 Utah Laws ch. 272). Taxes on cigarettes were also raised during the 1997 and 2002 General Sessions. (1997 Utah Laws ch. 279; 2002 Utah Laws ch. 248).

158. Western States' Tax Burdens Fiscal Year 1999-2000. *Initial State and Local Tax Burdens for Selected Western States*, 4; Economic and Statistical Unit, Utah State Tax Commission, Research Publication 2001-19R, (Salt Lake City, October 2001).

159. *TC 23 Monthly Revenue Summary*. Final Year End. Fiscal year 2003-04. Economic and Statistical Unit. Utah State Tax Commission. September 14, 2004.

160. For households, the amount shown is a percentage of personal income. For businesses, the amount shown is a percentage of gross state product (GSP). Source: Utah State Tax Comm'n, Econ. and Statis. Unit, *Western States' Tax Burdens Fiscal Year 1999-2000*, Res. Pub. 2001-19 (Salt Lake City, June 2001), 33.

161. Utah State Tax Comm'n, *TC-23 Monthly Revenue Summary, FY 2003-2004*.

162. Utah Constitution, art. 10, sec. 4.

163. Utah State Tax Comm'n, *TC-23 Monthly Revenue Summary, FY 2003-2004*.

164. Ibid.

165. Utah Constitution, art. 13, sec. 5. Utah Constitution, art. 13, sec. 5 also provides that these proceeds may be used for "statutory refunds and adjustments and costs of collection and administration."

166. Utah State Tax Comm'n, *TC-23 Monthly Revenue Summary, FY 2003-2004*.

167. See *Utah Code Annotated*, secs. 17-36-1 to -54 (2001 & Supp. 2005).

168. University of Utah, Center for Public Policy and Administration, *2003 Survey of Local Government Finances* (Salt Lake City, March 2005).

169. Ibid.

170. Ibid.

171. Utah Legislature, Office of the Legislative Fiscal Analyst, *2004-2005 Appropriations Report* (Salt Lake City, April 2004).

172. Ibid.

173. Utah State Tax Comm'n, *Annual Report, Fiscal Years 2000-2001 to 2003-2004*.

174. Basic Data: Tax data: Utah State Tax Comm'n, *Annual Report, Fiscal Years 2000-2001 to 2003-2004*; Personal Income Data: Office of the Governor, *2005 Economic Report to the Governor*.

175. Basic Data: Tax Data: Utah State Tax Comm'n, *Annual Report, Fiscal Years 2000-2001 to 2003-2004*; Personal Income Data: Office of the Governor, *2005 Economic Report to the Governor*; Price Index: Executive Offices of the President and the Council of Economic Advisors, *Economic Report of the President, February 2005* (Washington, 2005).

Chapter 9 Endnotes

1. *Utah Code Annotated*, sec. 4-2-1 (Supp. 2005).

2. Utah Department of Agriculture and Food, News & Info, *2005 Utah Department of Agriculture and Food Annual Report*, 4, http://ag.utah.gov/AnnualReport.pdf (accessed Nov. 14, 2005).

3. *Utah Code Annotated*, sec. 4-7-2 (1995).

4. Utah Dep't of Agric. and Food, *2005 Annual Report*, 4.

5. *Utah Code Annotated*, sec. 4-2-7 (Supp. 2005).

6. Ibid.

7. *Utah Code Annotated*, sec. 4-2-4 (1995).

8. Utah Dep't of Agric. and Food, *2005 Annual Report*, 8-9.

9. Ibid., 8.

10. Ibid., 15.

11. *Utah Code Annotated*, secs. 4-18-5(e), 4-18-6, 4-19-2 (1995 & Supp. 2005).

12. Utah Dep't of Agric. and Food, *2005 Annual Report*, 15-17.

13. *Utah Code Annotated*, sec. 4-18-6.

14. *Utah Code Annotated*, sec. 4-19-2.

15. Utah Dep't of Agric. and Food, *2005 Annual Report*, 15.

16. Ibid.

17. Ibid.

18. Ibid.

19. Ibid.

20. Ibid.

21. Utah Dep't of Agric. and Food, *2005 Annual Report*, 15.

22. Ibid.

23. Ibid.

24. Ibid.

25. Utah Dep't of Agric. and Food, *2005 Annual Report*, 16.

26. Ibid.

27. Ibid., 16-17.

28. Ibid., 16.

29. Ibid., 17.

30. Ibid.

31. *Utah Code Annotated*, sec. 4-18-4 (Supp. 2005).

32. *Utah Code Annotated*, sec. 4-18-5 (1995).

33. Utah Dep't of Agric. and Food, *2005 Annual Report*, 18.

34. Ibid., 18-19.

35. Ibid., 18.

36. Ibid.

37. Ibid., 19.

38. Ibid.

39. Utah Dep't of Agric. and Food, *2005 Annual Report*, 19.

40. Utah Dep't of Agric. and Food, *Utah Department of Agriculture and Food Organizational Chart*, http://ag.utah.gov/AnnualReport.pdf (accessed Nov. 14, 2005).

41. Utah Dep't of Agric. and Food, *2005 Annual Report*, 11.

42. Ibid., 10.

43. *Utah Code Annotated*, sec. 4-31-16 (Supp. 2005).

44. Ibid.

45. *Utah Code Annotated*, sec. 4-31-2 (1995).

46. *Utah Code Annotated*, sec. 4-24-1 (1995).

47. *Utah Code Annotated*, sec. 4-24-4 (Supp. 2005).

48. *Utah Code Annotated*, secs. 4-24-1 to -30 (1995 & Supp. 2005).

49. *Utah Code Annotated*, sec. 4-24-4.

50. *Utah Code Annotated*, sec. 4-24-5.

51. *Utah Code Annotated*, sec. 4-24-7.

52. *Utah Code Annotated*, secs. 4-30-2(8) and 4-30-4 (Supp. 2005).

53. Ibid.

54. Utah Dep't of Agric. and Food, *2005 Annual Report*, 11.

55. *Utah Code Annotated*, Title 4, Chapter 39, Domesticated Elk Act.

56. *Utah Code Annotated*, sec. 4-39-104 (Supp. 2005).

57. *Utah Code Annotated*, sec. 4-32-4 (Supp. 2005).

58. *Utah Code Annotated*, sec. 4-32-2 (1995).

59. *Utah Code Annotated*, sec. 4-32-4.

60. *Utah Code Annotated*, sec. 4-32-7 (Supp. 2005).

61. *Utah Code Annotated*, sec. 4-37-102 (Supp. 2005).

62. Utah Dep't of Agric. and Food, *2005 Annual Report*, 12.

63. *Utah Code Annotated*, sec. 4-37-503 (Supp. 2005).

64. *Utah Code Annotated*, sec. 4-37-501 (Supp. 2005).

65. Utah Dep't of Agric. and Food, *2005 Annual Report*, 13.

66. Ibid.

67. Ibid.

68. Ibid.

69. Ibid.

70. Ibid.

71. Utah Dep't of Agric. and Food, *2005 Annual Report*, 13.

72. Utah Dep't of Agric. and Food, *Organizational Chart*.

73. *Utah Code Annotated*, Title 4, Chapter 14, Utah Pesticide Control Act.

74. *Utah Code Annotated*, sec. 4-14-3 (1995).

75. *Utah Code Annotated*, sec. 4-14-6(4) (1995).

76. *Utah Code Annotated*, sec. 4-14-4 (1995).

77. *Utah Code Annotated*, sec. 4-14-10 (Supp. 2005).

78. Ibid.

79. Utah Dep't of Agric. and Food, *2005 Annual Report*, 22.

80. Ibid.

81. *Utah Code Annotated*, Title 4, Chapter 13, Utah Fertilizer Act.

82. *Utah Code Annotated*, sec. 4-13-3 (Supp. 2005).

83. *Utah Code Annotated*, sec. 4-13-5 (1995).

84. *Utah Code Annotated*, Title 4, Chapter 14, Utah Pesticide Control Act.

85. *Utah Code Annotated*, sec. 4-14-3 (1995).

86. *Utah Code Annotated*, sec. 4-14-6(4) (1995).

87. *Utah Code Annotated*, Title 4, Chapter 15, The Utah Nursery Act.

88. *Utah Code Annotated*, sec. 4-15-4 (1995).

89. *Utah Code Annotated*, sec. 4-15-7 (1995).

90. Ibid.

91. *Utah Code Annotated*, Title 4, Chapter 16, Utah Seed Act.

92. *Utah Code Annotated*, sec. 4-16-6 (Supp. 2005).

93. Ibid.

94. Ibid.

95. *Utah Code Annotated*, sec. 4-16-9 (1995).

96. *Utah Code Annotated*, Title 4, Chapter 12, Utah Commercial Feed Act.

97. *Utah Code Annotated*, sec. 4-12-4 (1995).

98. *Utah Code Annotated*, sec. 4-12-5 (1995).

99. *Utah Code Annotated*, sec. 4-12-7 (1995).

100. Utah Dep't of Agric. and Food, *2005 Annual Report*, 23.

101. *Utah Code Annotated*, Title 4, Chapter 17, Utah Noxious Weed Act.

102. Utah Dep't of Agric. and Food, *2005 Annual Report*, 22.

103. *Utah Code Annotated*, sec. 4-17-3.5 (Supp. 2005).

104. *Utah Code Annotated*, sec. 4-17-4 (1995).

105. *Utah Code Annotated*, sec. 4-17-4.5 (1995).

106. Utah Dep't of Agric. and Food, *2005 Annual Report*, 20.

107. Ibid.

108. Ibid.

109. *Utah Code Annotated*, sec. 4-11-4 (Supp. 2005).

110. *Utah Code Annotated*, sec. 4-11-10 (1995).

111. Utah Dep't of Agric. and Food, *2005 Annual Report*, 20-21.

112. *Utah Code Annotated*, Title 4, Chapter 35, Insect Infestation Emergency Control Act.

113. *Utah Code Annotated*, sec. 4-35-4 (Supp. 2005).

114. Ibid.

115. Utah Dep't of Agric. and Food, *2005 Annual Report*, 20.

116. *Utah Code Annotated*, sec. 4-2-2 (Supp. 2005).

117. Utah Dep't of Agric. and Food, *2005 Annual Report*, 23.

118. Ibid., 24.

119. Utah Dep't of Agric. and Food, *Organizational Chart*.

120. *Utah Code Annotated*, secs. 4-5-3, -5 (1995 & Supp. 2005).

121. Ibid.

122. Ibid.

123. Ibid.

124. *Utah Code Annotated*, sec. 4-5-7 (Supp. 2005).

125. Utah Dep't of Agric. and Food, *2005 Annual Report*, 24-25.

126. Ibid., 26-27.

127. *Utah Code Annotated*, sec. 4-4-1 (1995).

128. Utah Dep't of Agric. and Food, *2005 Annual Report*, 25.

129. *Utah Code Annotated*, sec. 4-3-4 (1995).

130. *Utah Code Annotated*, sec. 4-3-5 (1995).

131. *Utah Code Annotated*, sec. 4-3-8 (Supp. 2005).

132. *Utah Code Annotated*, sec. 4-9-6 (Supp. 2005).

133. Ibid.

134. Ibid.

135. Utah Dep't of Agric. and Food, *2005 Annual Report*, 27.

136. Ibid.

137. *Utah Code Annotated*, sec. 4-10-5 (1995).

138. *Utah Code Annotated*, sec. 4-10-7 (1995).

139. Utah Dep't of Agric. and Food, *2005 Annual Report*, 27.

140. Ibid.

141. Utah Dep't of Agric. and Food, *2005 Annual Report*, 7.

142. Ibid.

143. Ibid.

144. *Utah Code Annotated*, sec. 4-23-2 (1995).

145. *Utah Code Annotated*, sec. 4-23-4 (Supp. 2005).

146. Utah Dep't of Agric. and Food, *2005 Annual Report*, 6.

147. Ibid.

148. *Utah Code Annotated*, sec. 4-38-4 (Supp. 2005).

149. Ibid.

150. *Utah Code Annotated*, sec. 4-38-16 (1995).

Chapter 10 Endnotes

1. *Utah Code Annotated*, secs. 7-1-102 (Supp. 2005), 13-1-1 (2001), 31A-1-102, -103, -104 (2003 & Supp. 2005).

2. U.S. Constitution, amend. 21.

3. Utah Department of Alcoholic Beverage Control, About UDABC, *About Liquor Control States*, http://www.alcbev.state.ut.us/Background/regulate.html (accessed May 31, 2005).

4. Two counties in Maryland are local jurisdictions that are also considered "control" jurisdictions. National Alcohol Beverage Control Association, *About NABC*, http://www.nabca.org/about/index.php (accessed May 31, 2005); see also Utah Dep't of Alcoholic Beverage Control, *69th Annual Report, Summary of Operations July 1, 2003 to June 30, 2004*, http://www.alcbev.state.ut.us/Background/2004annrpt.pdf (accessed May 31, 2005).

5. Utah Dep't of Alcoholic Beverage Control, *History of Utah Alcoholic Beverage Control: 1882-1995*, compiled by Earl F. Dorius (April 1995), 1-3.

6. *Utah Code Annotated*, sec. 32A-1-103 (2003).

7. Utah Dep't of Alcoholic Beverage Control, About UDABC, *Licenses and Permits General Information*, http://www.alcbev.state.ut.us/license_permit/gen_lic_perm.html (accessed May 31, 2005).

8. Ibid.

9. Ibid.

10. See, e.g., Utah Dep't of Alcoholic Beverage Control, *69th Annual Report*.

11. *Utah Code Annotated*, sec. 32A-1-102 (2003). Statutes also address the issuances of local licenses for certain businesses allowing consumption or possession of alcoholic beverages on their premises. *Utah Code Annotated*, Title 11, Chapter 10, Clubs Allowing Consumption of Liquor on Premises.

12. *Utah Code Annotated*, sec. 32A-1-106 (2003).

13. Ibid.

14. *Utah Code Annotated*, secs. 32A-1-106, -107 (2003 & Supp. 2005).

15. *Utah Code Annotated*, sec. 32A-1-104 (2003).

16. *Utah Code Annotated*, sec. 32A-1-107.

17. Ibid.

18. Ibid.

19. *Utah Code Annotated*, sec. 32A-1-104.

20. *Utah Code Annotated*, sec. 32A-1-108 (Supp. 2005).

21. Ibid.

22. *Utah Code Annotated*, sec. 32A-1-107.

23. *Utah Code Annotated*, sec. 32A-1-104.

24. Ibid.

25. *Utah Code Annotated*, sec. 13-1-1.

26. Utah Department of Commerce, *Fiscal Year 2004 Annual Report,* "Mission Statement" (Salt Lake City, October 1, 2004), 3, http://www.commerce.state.ut.us/report.pdf (accessed May 12, 2005).

27. 1941 Utah Laws ch. 5.

28. Ibid.

29. 1983 Utah Laws ch. 322.

30. Utah Dep't of Commerce, Administration, http://www.commerce.utah.gov (accessed May 13, 2005).

31. 1983 Utah Laws ch. 57.

32. 1937 Utah Laws ch. 19; 1941 Utah Laws ch. 7, 1st Spec. Sess.

33. *Utah Code Annotated*, sec. 13-2-2 (2001).

34. Thad LeVar (Commerce Manager, Division of Consumer Protection) in discussion with Mark Steinagel (Policy Analyst, Office of Legislative Research and General Counsel), August 12, 2004.

35. 1984 Utah Laws ch. 66.

36. Kathy Berg (Director, Division of Corporations and Commercial Code) in discussion with Mark Steinagel (Policy Analyst, Office of Legislative Research and General Counsel), September 2, 2004.

37. 1985 Utah Laws ch. 187.

38. Lauri Arensmeyer (Division of Occupational and Professional Licensing) in discussion with Mark Steinagel (Policy Analyst, Office of Legislative Research and General Counsel), September 17, 2004.

39. 1892 Utah Laws ch. 72.

40. *Utah Code Annotated*, sec. 58-1-106 (Supp. 2005).

41. *Appropriations Act*, S.B. 1, 55th Leg., Gen. Sess. (Utah 2004).

42. *Utah Code Annotated*, secs. 78-14-1 to -17 (2002 & Supp. 2005).

43. *Utah Code Annotated*, secs. 38-11-101 to -302 (2001 & 2005).

44. Bruce Scott Moio (Utility Analyst, Division of Public Utilities) E-mail message to Mark Steinagel (Policy Analyst, Office of Legislative Research and General Counsel), March 25, 2005.

45. *Utah Code Annotated*, sec. 54-4a-6 (2000).

46. 1983 Utah Laws ch. 246.

47. 1977 Utah Laws ch. 54.

48. *Utah Code Annotated*, sec. 54-10-2 (Supp. 2005).

49. *Utah Code Annotated*, sec. 54-10-4 (2000).

50. 1979 Utah Laws ch. 194.

51. Utah Dep't of Commerce, *Fiscal Year 2003 Annual Report* (Salt Lake City, October 1, 2003), 29.

52. *Utah Code Annotated*, sec. 61-2-5 (2000).

53. Utah Dep't of Commerce, *2003 Annual Report*, 29; Jennifer Eatchel (Division of Real Estate) in discussion with Mark Steinagel (Policy Analyst, Office of Legislative Research and General Counsel), September 7, 2004.

54. Utah Dep't of Commerce, *2003 Annual Report*, 29.

55. 2000 Utah Laws ch. 329.

56. Goodmortgage.com, *Mortgage Brokers vs. Your Bank*, http://www.goodmortgage.com/Mortgage_School/MSbrokervsbankerprocess.htm (accessed May 16, 2005); Bankrate, Inc., *Securing the Loan: Know Your Lenders* http://www.bankrate.com/brm/green/mtg/mort3c.asp (August 2004).

57. *Utah Code Annotated*, sec. 61-2-5.5 (Supp. 2005).

58. Ibid.

59. 1983 Utah Laws ch. 284.

60. *Utah Code Annotated*, sec. 61-1-18 (Supp. 2005).

61. *Utah Code Annotated*, sec. 61-1-18.5 (Supp. 2005).

62. Utah Division of Securities, *About the Division*, http://www.securities.state.ut.us/general_info.html (accessed May 16, 2005).

63. Utah Dep't of Commerce, *2003 Annual Report*, 33; Tony Taggart (Director, Division of Securities) in discussion with Mark Steinagel (Policy Analyst, Office of Legislative Research and General Counsel), September 22, 2004.

64. Utah Department of Financial Institutions, General Information, Department, *History*, http://www.dfi.utah.gov/history.htm (accessed May 16, 2005).

65. Ibid.

66. Orla Beth Peck (Supervisor of Credit Unions, Department of Financial Institutions) E-mail message to Patricia Owen (Associate General Counsel, Office of Legislative Research and General Counsel), March 31, 2005.

67. *Utah Code Annotated*, sec. 7-1-102 (Supp. 2005).

68. Ibid.

69. As of September 2005, the industrial banks industry is the largest industry regulated by the Department of Financial Institutions based on total assets of the banks. Also, as of June 30, 2005, the state had no state-chartered savings and loans or savings banks. Ed G. Leary (Commissioner, Department of Financial Institutions) e-mail message to Patricia Owen (Associate General Counsel, Office of Legislative Research and General Counsel), September 28, 2005.

70. 26 U.S.C. sec. 501(c)(14); *Utah Code Annotated*, sec. 7-9-34 (1995 & Supp. 2005).

71. See *Utah Code Annotated*, secs. 7-9-51, -53 (1995 & Supp. 2005).

72. See, e.g., *Utah Bankers Ass'n v. America First Credit Union, et. al.*, 912 P.2d 988 (Utah 1996).

73. See, e.g., *Utah Credit Union Act Amendments*, S.B. 237, 53rd Leg., Gen. Sess. (Utah 1999); *Amendments Related to Financial Institutions*, H.B. 162, 55th Leg., Gen. Sess. (Utah 2003). During the 2005 General Session, the Utah Legislature adopted H.J.R. 1, *Joint Resolution Related to Financial Institutions*, which affirmed certain actions taken by the legislature and urges congressional action related to financial institutions. The resolution, however, did not modify the

Utah Credit Union Act itself.

74. *Utah Code Annotated*, sec. 7-1-201 (Supp. 2005).

75. *Utah Code Annotated*, sec. 7-1-202 (Supp. 2005).

76. *Utah Code Annotated*, sec. 7-1-201.

77. *Utah Code Annotated*, sec. 7-1-301 (Supp. 2005).

78. Ibid.

79. Ibid.

80. Utah Dep't of Fin. Inst., *General Information*, http://www.dfi.utah.gov/GenInfo.htm (accessed May 31, 2005).

81. *Utah Code Annotated*, Title 7, Chapter 5, Trust Business.

82. See, e.g., *Utah Code Annotated*, sec. 7-8-16 (Supp. 2004).

83. *Utah Code Annotated*, sec. 7-1-501 (Supp. 2004); Utah Admin Code R331-14, Rule Governing Parties Who Engage in the Business of Issuing and Selling Money Orders, Traveler's Checks, and Other Instruments for the Purpose of Effecting Third-Party Payments, http://www.rules.utah.gov/publicat/code.htm (in effect March 1, 2005).

84. *Utah Code Annotated*, sec. 7-1-715 (Supp. 2004).

85. *Utah Code Annotated*, Title 7, Chapter 22, Regulation of Independent Escrow Agents.

86. *Utah Code Annotated*, Title 70D, Mortgage Financing Regulation.

87. *Utah Code Annotated*, Title 70C, Utah Consumer Credit Code.

88. *Utah Code Annotated*, Title 7, Chapter 23, Check Cashing Registration Act.

89. *Utah Code Annotated*, Title 7, Chapter 24, Title Lending Registration Act.

90. Utah Dep't of Fin. Inst., *Mortgage Lending*.

91. See 1909 Utah Laws ch. 121; 1907 Combined Laws of Utah ch. 7.

92. *Utah Code Annotated*, sec. 31A-1-102 (2003).

93. *Utah Code Annotated*, sec. 31A-2-102 (2003).

94. *Utah Code Annotated*, sec. 31A-2-103 (2003).

95. *Utah Code Annotated*, sec. 31A-2-104 (2003).

96. Utah Insurance Department, Industry Resources, Annual Report, *Organizational Chart*, (September 2003) http://www.insurance.utah.gov/FlowChart.pdf (accessed May 31, 2005).

97. Ibid.

98. *Utah Code Annotated*, sec. 31A-1-104 (2003).

99. Utah Ins. Dep't, Industry Resources, Annual Report, *Table A, Summary of Insurers Doing Business in Utah 2003*, http://www.insurance.utah.gov/TableA.htm (accessed May 31. 2005).

100. Utah Ins. Dep't, Industry Resources, Annual Report, *Insurance Company Rehabilitations/Liquidations*, http://www.insurance.utah.gov/liquidation.html (accessed May 31, 2005); *Utah Code Annotated*, Title 31A, Chapter 27, Insurers Rehabilitation and Liquidation.

101. Utah Ins. Dep't, *Insurance Company Rehabilitations*.

102. *Utah Code Annotated*, sec. 31A-23a-106 (2003).

103. Utah Ins. Dep't, "Forces for Change," Newsletter, August 2004, http://www.insurance.utah.gov/Newsletter.Ind.html (accessed September 3, 2004).

104. *Utah Code Annotated*, sec. 31A-19a-101 (2003).

105. See, e.g., *Utah Code Annotated*, secs. 31A-28-106, -210 (2003).

106. *Utah Code Annotated*, sec. 31A-2-216 (2003).

107. See *Utah Code Annotated*, Title 31A, Chapter 31, Insurance Fraud Act; Utah Insurance Department, Companies/Agents, Fraud, *FRAUD DIVISION TOLL FREE 1-877-372-8315*, http://www.insurance.utah.gov/FraudDiv.html (accessed May 31, 2005).

108. *Utah Code Annotated*, sec. 31A-29-104 (Supp. 2004).

109. *Utah Code Annotated*, sec. 31A-29-102 (2003).

110. National Right to Work Legal Defense Foundation, Inc., *Issue Paper: Employees in Right to Work States*, "Right to Work States" (Springfield, Virginia, 2003), http://www.nrtw.org/rtws.htm (accessed May 16, 2005).

111. *Utah Code Annotated*, sec. 34-34-4 (2001).

112. Utah Labor Commission, Labor Commission Home, http://laborcommission.utah.gov/index.html (accessed May 16, 2005).

113. Utah Foundation, *State and Local Government in Utah* (Salt Lake City: Utah Foundation, 1992), 201.

114. 1997 Utah Laws ch. 375.

115. *Utah Code Annotated*, sec. 34A-1-103 (2001).

116. *Utah Code Annotated*, sec. 34A-1-202 (2001).

117. Utah Constitution, art. 16, sec. 2.

Chapter 11 Endnotes

1. William Fulton, "The Job Hunt," *Governing, The Magazine of States and Localities* (Washington, D.C., Congressional Quarterly, Inc., June 2004), 62.

2. Utah Legislature, Office of Legislative Fiscal Analyst, *In Depth Budget Review for the Division of Business and Economic Development - A Report to the Executive Appropriations Committee*, by Andrea Wilko (Salt Lake City, September 13, 2004), 27.

3. Division of Business and Economic Development Board, Business Development Committee, *International Office Report*, submitted by Tina Lewis (Director, Department of Business and Economic Development International within the Utah Department of Community and Economic Development) (November 2004).

4. See *Utah Code Annotated*, secs. 9-2-205, 9-3-204, 9-4-201, 9-6-201, 9-7-201, 9-8-201, 9-9-102 (2003 & Supp. 2005).

5. See *Utah Code Annotated*, secs. 63-38f-202 to -204 (Supp. 2005).

6. *Utah Code Annotated*, sec. 63-38f-303 to -304 (Supp. 2005).

7. See *Utah Code Annotated*, secs. 63-38f-301 to -303, 63-38f-401 to -416, 63-38f-701 to -704, 63-38f-901 to -909 (Supp. 2005).

8. See *Utah Code Annotated*, secs. 63-38f-1406 to -1414 (Supp. 2005).

9. See *Utah Code Annotated*, sec. 9-1-202 (Supp. 2005).

10. See *Utah Code Annotated*, sec. 9-4-202 (2004).

11. See *Utah Code Annotated*, secs. 9-4-201 to -1408 (2003 & Supp. 2005).

12. See *Utah Code Annotated*, secs. 9-6-201 to -205 (2003 & Supp. 2005).

13. *Utah Code Annotated*, sec. 9-8-203 (2003).

14. *Utah Code Annotated*, sec. 9-8-204 (2003).

15. See *Utah Code Annotated*, secs. 9-7-201 to -205 (2003).

16. See *Utah Code Annotated*, secs. 9-9-102 to -104.5 (2003).

17. See *Utah Code Annotated*, secs. 63D-1a-201 to -204 (2004).

18. *Utah Code Annotated*, sec. 63-38f-1207 (Supp. 2005).

19. *Utah Code Annotated*, sec. 9-4-1103 (2003).

20. *Utah Code Annotated*, sec. 9-3-306 (2003).

21. *Utah Code Annotated*, secs. 9-3-402 to -407 (2003 & Supp. 2005).

22. See *Utah Code Annotated*, secs. 9-4-801, -802 (2003 & Supp. 2005).

23. See *Utah Code Annotated*, secs. 9-4-904 to -911 (2003 & Supp. 2005).

24. Utah Legislature, Office of the Legislative Auditor, *A Review of the Coordination of Utah's Employment And Training Programs*, Report 92-10 (Salt Lake City, 1992), 2, 5.

25. See Table 11-1, Comparison of Aid to Families with Dependent Children and Temporary Assistance to Needy Families.

26. Ibid.

27. See *Utah Code Annotated*, secs. 35A-1-206(7), 35A-3-201 to -207, 35A-4-501, 35A-4-508 (2001 & Supp. 2005).

28. *Utah Code Annotated*, sec. 35A-3-203 (Supp. 2005).

29. *Utah Code Annotated*, Title 35A, Chapter 4, Employment Security Act.

30. See *Utah Code Annotated*, sec. 35A-4-508.

31. Utah Department of Workforce Services, *2004 Annual Report* (Price, UT: Utah Department of Workforce Services, January 14, 2005), 4.

32. *Utah Code Annotated*, sec. 35A-1-207(1) (2001).

33. Ibid., -207(2).

1. Office of the Governor, Utah Council of Economic Advisors, *2005 Economic Report to the Governor* (Salt Lake City: Governor's Office of Planning and Budget, January 2005), 37.

2. Kathleen O'Leary Morgan and Scott Morgan, eds., *State Rankings 2005* (Lawrence, KS: Morgan Quitno, 2005), 115.

3. Office of the Governor, Utah Council of Economic Advisors, *2005 Economic Report to the Governor* (Salt Lake City: Governor's Office of Planning and Budget, January 2005), 32.

4. Kathleen O'Leary Morgan and Scott Morgan, eds., *State Rankings 2005* (Lawrence, KS: Morgan Quitno, 2005), 291.

5. Ibid., 140.

6. T. Ross Reeve and Pamela S. Perlich, "The Coming Boom in Utah's School Age and College Age Populations: State and County Scenarios," *Utah Economic and Business Review* 62, (September/October 2002): 2.

7. Office of the Governor, Utah Council of Economic Advisors, *2005 Economic Report to the Governor* (Salt Lake City: Governor's Office of Planning and Budget, January 2005), 24.

8. Utah Enabling Act, Pub. L. No. 53-138, 28 Stat. 107.

9. Utah Constitution, art. 10, sec. 1.

10. Utah Constitution, art. 10, sec. 2.

11. *Utah Code Annotated*, Title 20A, Chapter 14, Part 1, State School Board - Nomination and Election.

12. Utah Constitution, art. 10, sec. 3.

13. *Utah Code Annotated*, sec. 53A-1-401 (Supp. 2005).

14. *Utah Code Annotated*, sec. 53A-1-402 (Supp. 2005).

15. *Utah Code Annotated*, sec. 53A-1-401.

16. Utah Constitution, art. 10, sec. 3.

17. *Utah Code Annotated*, sec. 53A-1-303 (2000).

18. *Utah Code Annotated*, sec. 53A-1-301 (Supp. 2005).

19. *Utah Code Annotated*, sec. 53A-1-302 (2000).

20. *Utah Code Annotated*, sec. 53A-3-402 (Supp. 2005).

21. *Utah Code Annotated*, sec. 53A-3-301 (Supp. 2005).

22. *Utah Code Annotated*, sec. 53A-3-303 (2000).

23. *Utah Code Annotated*, sec. 53A-3-304 (2000).

24. *Utah Code Annotated*, Title 53A, Chapter 1a, Part 5, The Utah Charter Schools Act.

25. Utah State Office of Education, Programs, Finance and Statistics, Superintendent's Annual Report: Section II, Data Files 2003-04, *2004 Fall Enrollment by School* (November 22, 2004), http://www.k12.ut.us/data.

26. *Utah Code Annotated*, sec. 53A-1a-511 (Supp. 2005).

27. *Utah Code Annotated*, sec. 53A-25-301 (2000).

28. Utah Enabling Act, Pub. L. No. 53-138, 28 Stat. 107.

29. Utah Constitution, art. 10, secs. 1, 2.

30. Utah Constitution, art. 10, sec. 5.

31. Utah Constitution, art. 10, sec. 5.

32. Utah Constitution, art. 13, sec. 5.

33. *Utah Code Annotated*, sec. 53A-17a-102 (2000).

34. *Utah Code Annotated*, secs. 53A-17a-133, 53A-17a-134, 53A-17a-151 (Supp. 2005).

35. *Utah Code Annotated*, secs. 53A-16-101, 41-1a-1205, 59-16-101 (Supp. 2005).

36. 2004 Utah Laws ch. 257.

37. *Utah Code Annotated*, sec. 53A-1-409 (Supp. 2005).

38. Utah State Office of Educ., *Utah Statewide Scores on the Iowa Tests*, (Salt Lake City, January 11, 2005), http://www.usoe.org/EVAL/_IowaTestsNRT1/UtahNRTScoreReport%20Jan1104.pdf (accessed May 2, 2005).

39. U.S. Department of Education, National Center for Education Statistics, *National Assessment of Educational Progress, The Nation's Report Card* (last updated March 31, 2005), http://www.nces.ed.gov/nationsreportcard (accessed May 2, 2005).

40. Ibid.

41. ACT, Inc., *Average ACT Scores by State: 2004 ACT-Tested Graduates* (2004), http://www.act.org/news/data/04/states (accessed May 2, 2005).

42. College Entrance Examination Board, *School Report of AP Examinations 2003-2004 (By State)* (2004), http://www.collegeboard.com/student/testing/ap/exgrd_sum/2003 (accessed May 2, 2005).

Chapter 13 Endnotes

1. Utah Constitution, art. 10, sec. 2.

2. Utah Constitution, art. 10, secs. 2, 4.

3. *Utah Code Annotated*, sec. 53B-1-103 (Supp. 2005).

4. *Utah Code Annotated*, sec. 53B-1-104 (Supp. 2004).

5. Utah System of Higher Education, Finance and Figures, *Data Book 2004-2005*, "Enrollments" (Office of the Commission of Higher Education, February 2004).

6. Ibid., "Staffing."

7. National Center for Public Policy and Higher Education, *Policy Alert* "Community Colleges: Gateway or Blockade?," by Jane V. Wellman, May 2004.

8. The information and figures about Utah universities and colleges in the preceding three subsections is compiled from various sources including the Utah System of Higher Education, *Data Book*; the Utah System's Web site, *Utah Institutions*, http://www.utahsbr.edu/html/institutions.html; and the individual websites of Utah's colleges and universities, which are available on the Internet.

9. *Utah Code Annotated*, sec. 53B-2a-105 (Supp. 2005).

10. *Utah Code Annotated*, sec. 53B-2-104 (Supp. 2005).

11. *Utah Code Annotated*, sec. 53B-2-102 (2000).

12. Ibid.

13. *Utah Code Annotated*, sec. 53B-2a-102 (Supp. 2005).

14. *Utah Code Annotated*, sec. 53B-2a-108 (Supp. 2005).

15. *Utah Code Annotated*, sec. 53B-2a-107 (Supp. 2005).

16. Utah Constitution, art. 13, sec. 5.

17. *Utah Code Annotated*, sec. 53B-7-101 (2000).

18. *Utah Code Annotated*, sec. 53B-7-103 (2000).

19. The National Institute for Public Policy and Higher Education, *Measuring Up*, "State Reports: States at a Glance (Utah, 2002)," http://measuringup.highereducation.org (accessed May 12, 2005).

20. Ibid.

21. Utah System of Higher Education, *Data Book*, "Staffing," 2.

22. Utah System of Higher Education, *Data Book*, "Tuition and Fees," 4.

23. *Utah Code Annotated*, sec. 53B-7-101.5 (Supp. 2005).

24. The NCHEMS Information Center for State Higher Education Policymaking and Analysis, *Affordability: Percent of Family Income Needed to Pay for College - by Type of Institution* (2004), http://www.higheredinfo.org/dbrower/index.php?submeasure=75&year=2004&level=nation&mode=data&state=0 (accessed July 27, 2005).

25. National Center for Public Policy, *Policy Alert*.

26. Richard E. Kendall (Commissioner of Higher Education) memo to Utah Board of Regents, May 26, 2004, 1.

Chapter 14 Endnotes

1. *Utah Code Annotated*, sec. 19-1-104 (2002).

2. *Utah Code Annotated*, sec. 19-1-105 (1991).

3. *Utah Code Annotated*, sec. 19-1-106 (1991).

4. *Utah Code Annotated*, sec. 19-1-102 (2003).

5. Ibid.

6. *Utah Code Annotated*, sec. 19-1-201 (2003).

7. Ibid.

8. *Utah Code Annotated*, sec. 19-1-104 (2003).

9. *Utah Code Annotated*, sec. 19-1-202.

10. *Utah Code Annotated*, sec. 19-1-105 (2003).

11. Utah Department of Environmental Quality, Division of Air Quality, About DAQ, *Mission & Vision*, http://www.airquality.utah.gov/smlfltlogo.html (accessed May 20, 2005).

12. Utah Dep't Envtl. Quality, DEQ Documents, *DEQ At-A-Glance*, 6, http://www.eq.state.ut.us/references/deqataglance.pdf (accessed May 20, 2005).

13. Utah Dep't Envtl. Quality, Div. of Air Quality, About DAQ, *How the Department of Air Quality Is Structured*, http://www.airquality.utah.gov/structure.html (accessed May 20, 2005).

14. *Utah Code Annotated*, sec. 19-2-104 (2003).

15. Utah Dep't Envtl. Quality, Division of Drinking Water, *Drought Conditions/Water Conservation*, http://www.drinkingwater.utah.gov/ (accessed May 20, 2005).

16. Utah Dep't Envtl. Quality, *DEQ At-A-Glance*, 9.

17. *Utah Code Annotated*, sec. 19-4-103 (2003).

18. Utah Dep't Envtl. Quality, DEQ Documents, *DEQ 101*, "Drinking Water," Image 18, http://www.eq.state.ut.us/references/deq101.htm (accessed May 20, 2005).

19. Ibid.

20. Utah Dep't Envtl. Quality, Division of Environmental Response and Remediation, *Who We Are*, http://www.environmentalresponse.utah.gov/ (accessed May 20, 2005).

21. Utah Dep't Envtl. Quality, *DEQ At-A-Glance*, 11.

22. Utah Dep't Envtl. Quality, Div. of Envtl. Response & Remed., *What Is the Underground Storage Tank Program - Details*, "Utah's Underground Storage Tank Program Overview," http://www.undergroundtanks.utah.gov/ustcomp/utustsum.htm (accessed May 20, 2005).

23. Utah Dep't Envtl. Quality, Division of Solid and Hazardous Waste, *Mission Statement*, http://www.hazardouswaste.utah.gov/ (accessed May 20, 2005).

24. Utah Dep't Envtl. Quality, *DEQ At-A-Glance*, 12.

25. Utah Dep't Envtl. Quality, Div. of Solid and Hazardous Waste, Program Contacts, *Solid Waste Program*, http://www.hazardouswaste.utah.gov/sws.htm (accessed May 20, 2005).

26. Utah Dep't Envtl. Quality, *DEQ At-A-Glance*, 14.

27. Utah Dep't Envtl. Quality, Division of Radiation Control, *X-ray Section*, http://www.radiationcontrol.utah.gov/drc_xray.htm (accessed May 20, 2005).

28. Utah Dep't Envtl. Quality, Div. of Rad. Control, *Indoor Radon Program*, http://www.radiationcontrol.utah.gov/RADON.htm (accessed May 20, 2005).

29. Utah Dep't Envtl. Quality, Div. of Rad. Control, *Uranium Mills*, http://www.radiationcontrol.utah.gov/milllst.htm (accessed May 20, 2005).

30. Utah Dep't Envtl. Quality, Div. of Rad. Control, Transportation, *Radioactive Material Transportation*, http://www.radiationcontrol.utah.gov/RAM/RAMTrans_ciles/frame.htm (accessed May 20, 2005).

31. Utah Dep't Envtl. Quality, Div. of Rad. Control, *Low Level Waste*, http://www.radiationcontrol.utah.gov/drc_lows.htm (accessed May 20, 2005).

32. Utah Dep't Envtl. Quality, Div. of Rad. Control, *Radioactive Materials*, http://www.radiationcontrol.utah.gov/drc_ram.htm (accessed May 20, 2005).

33. Utah Dep't Envtl. Quality, Div. of Rad. Control, *Non-ionizing Radiation*, http://www.radiationcontrol.utah.gov/Drc_nion.htm (accessed May 20, 2005).

34. Utah Dep't Envtl. Quality, Div. of Rad. Control, *Generator Site Access*, http://www.radiationcontrol.utah.gov/DRC_prmt.htm (accessed May 20, 2005).

35. Utah Dep't Envtl. Quality, Division of Water Quality, *Our Mission*, http://www.waterquality.utah.gov/mission.htm (accessed May 23, 2005).

36. Utah Dep't Envtl. Quality, DEQ Documents, *DEQ 101*, "Water Quality," Image 4, http://www.eq.state.ut.us/references/DEQ101/4 (accessed May 23, 2005).

37. *Utah Code Annotated*, sec. 19-5-103 (2003).

Chapter 15 Endnotes

1. Utah Department of Health, Center for Health Data, Indicator-Based Information System for Public Health, Indicator Profile (hereinafter IBIS-PH), *Complete Indicator Profile of Life Expectancy at Birth*, http://ibis.health.utah.gov/view?xslt=indicator/complete_profile.xslt&xml=indicator/LifeExpect.xml (accessed March 22, 2005). A Utah female born in 2002 has a life expectancy of 79.92 years. Her U.S. counterpart has a life expectancy of 79.9 years. A Utah male born in 2002 has a life expectancy of 76.28 years. His U.S. counterpart has a life expectancy of 74.7 years.

2. Utah Dep't of Health, Office of the Executive Director, *2003 Utah Public Health Outcome Measures Report, Utah Department of Health* (Salt Lake City: Dep't of Health, 2003), 90-99, 114-121. See also, Utah Dep't of Health, Center for Health Data, Indicator-Based Information System for Public Health, http://www.ibis.health.utah.gov.

3. United Health Foundation, *America's Health: State Health Rankings - 2004 Edition* (Minnetonka, MN, 2004), http://www.unitedhealthfoundation.org/shr2004/components/index.html (accessed March 22, 2005).

4. United Health Foundation, *America's Health: State Health Rankings - 2004 Edition* (Minnetonka, MN, 2003), http://www.unitedhealthfoundation.org/shr2004/states/utah.html (accessed June 9, 2005).

5. Morgan Quitno Press, *2005 Healthiest State* (Lawrence, KN: Morgan Quitno Press, 2005), http://www.morganquitno.com/hc05fact.htm (accessed June 3, 2005).

6. Ibid.

7. Morgan Quitno Press, *1993 to 2005 Healthiest State Rankings* (Lawrence, KN: Morgan Quitno Press, 2005), http://www.morganquitno.com/hc93-05.htm (accessed June 3, 2005).

8. Utah Dep't of Health, IBIS-PH, *Complete Indicator Profile of Motor Vehicle Traffic Crash Deaths*, http://ibis.health.utah.gov/view (accessed June 3, 2005).

9. Utah Dep't of Health, IBIS-PH, *Complete Indicator Profile of Overweight or Obese*, http://ibis.health.utah.gov/view?xslt=indicator/complete_profile.xslt&xml=indicator/OvrwtObe.xml, citing A.H. Mokdad, et al., "The Spread of the Obesity Epidemic in the United States, 1991-1998," *Journal of the American Medical Association (JAMA)* 282, no. 16 (1999): 1519-1522, (accessed June 6, 2005).

10. Utah Dep't of Health, IBIS-PH, *Complete Indicator Profile of Cigarette Smoking Among Adults*, http://ibis.health.utah.gov/view?xslt=indicator/complete_profile.xslt&xml=indicator/CigSmokAdlt.xml (accessed June 6, 2005).

11. Utah Dep't of Health, *Complete Indicator Profile of Overweight or Obese*.

12. Utah Dep't of Health, IBIS-PH, *Complete Indicator Profile of Suicide Deaths*, http://ibis.health.utah.gov/view?xslt=indicator/complete_profile.xslt&xml=indicator/SuicDth.xml (accessed June 6, 2005). This figure is an average.

13. Utah Dep't of Health, Office of the Exec. Dir., *2003 Utah Public Health Outcome Measures Report* (Salt Lake City: Utah Dep't of Health, 2003), 105.

14. Institute of Medicine, National Academy of Sciences, *Care Without Coverage: Too Little, Too Late* (Washington D.C.: National Academies Press, 2002), 1-2, 7, http://books.nap.edu/html/care_without/reportbrief.pdf (accessed May 27, 2005). See also, Inst. of Med., Nat'l Acad. of Sci., *Hidden Costs, Value Lost: Uninsurance in America* (Washington D.C.: National Academies Press, 2003), 1-2, http://books.nap.edu/html/hidden_costs/reportbrief.pdf (accessed May 27, 2005).

15. Utah Dep't of Health, *Utah Health Status Update: Health Insurance in Utah* (Salt Lake City, July/August 2004), http://health.utah.gov/opha/publications/hsu/04JulAug_Insurance.pdf (accessed June 3, 2005). From 2003 to 2004, the number of Utahns without coverage at any given time increased from 9.1 percent (214,500 persons) to 10.2 percent (251,400 persons). Utah Dep't of Health, *Utah Health Status Update: Uninsured in Utah* (Salt Lake City, May 2005), http://health.utah.gov/opha/publications/hsu/05May-HealthIns.pdf (accessed June 22, 2005).

16. Utah Dep't of Health, IBIS-PH, *Health Insurance Coverage*, http://ibis.health.utah.gov/view?xslt=indicator/complete_profile.xslt&xml=indicator/HlthIns.xml (accessed June 6, 2005). This figure has been modified from that reported by the U.S. Current Population Survey. There may not be a statistical difference between the 2003 state and national rates.

17. Utah Dep't of Health, *Utah Health Status Update: Health Insurance in Utah*.

18. Utah Dep't of Health, Office of Public Health Assessment, Center for Health Data, *Health Insurance Coverage, 2003 Utah Health Status Survey Report* (Salt Lake City: Utah Dep't of Health, December 2004), xiii.

19. Ibid.

20. Utah Dep't of Health, *Utah Health Status Update: Health Insurance in Utah.*

21. Utah Insurance Department, *2004 Health Insurance Market Report* (Salt Lake City: October 5, 2004), 1-2.

22. Beginning January 1, 2006, Medicare will include a new Part D prescription drug benefit funded in part by state payments. These payments are commonly referred to as the "clawback" and are intended to approximate the savings states will realize in their Medicaid programs as Part D covers individuals formerly covered under Medicaid. This "phased-down State contribution" marks "the first time since the enactment of the Medicare and Medicaid programs in 1965 [that] a specific Medicare benefit will be financed in significant part by state payments." Schneider, Andy, *The "Clawback:" State Financing of Medicare Drug Coverage* (Washington, D.C.: The Kaiser Commission on Medicaid and the Uninsured, 2004), 1.

23. Utah Dep't of Health, Office of Health Care Statistics, *Health Outcome Evaluation of Utah's Primary Care Network (PCN): A New Medicaid Waiver*, by Wu Xu and Mike Martin (Salt Lake City), slide 16, http://health.utah.gov/hda/report/pcnPoster_files/frame.htm (accessed September 29, 2004).

Fiscal year 2003 contributions totaled $6.9 million. Utah Dep't of Health, *Utah Primary Care Network Annual Report, July 2002 - June 2003* (Salt Lake City: Utah Dep't of Health, 2003), 2, http://health.utah.gov/pcn/FY03AnnualReport.pdf (accessed June 9, 2005).

Fiscal year 2004 contributions by hospitals totaled $9.1 million. Vance Eggers (Actuarial Specialist, Division of Health Care Financing, Utah Dep't of Health) in discussion with Mark Andrews (Policy Analyst, Office of Legislative Research and General Counsel), March 23, 2005 and April 27, 2005.

24. Utah Ins. Dep't, *2004 Heath Insurance Market Report*, 2-3; U.S. Bureau of the Census, "Income Stable, Poverty Up, Numbers of Americans With and Without Health Insurance Rise, Census Bureau Reports," news release, August 26, 2004, http://www.census.gov/Press-Release/www/releases/archives/income_wealth/002484.html (accessed October 27, 2004); see Centers for Medicare and Medicaid Services, "Medicare Enrollment - All Beneficiaries as of July 2003" (September 17, 2004), http://www.cms.hhs.gov/statistics/enrollment/st03all.asp for Medicare enrollment data. U.S. Medicare enrollment as of July 1, 2003 was 40,172,605. This figure may not be comparable to the U.S. Census Bureau's national enrollment rate. The Medicaid percentage includes Primary Care Network enrollees.

25. Utah Ins. Dep't, *2004 Health Insurance Market Report*, 1-2.

26. Ibid.

27. Utah Ins. Dep't, *2004 Health Insurance Market Report*, 2-3. Figures are for 2003. See cautionary notes about membership estimates for employer sponsored self-funded plans. All figures are based on comprehensive (major medical) coverage only and do not include single disease or accident only coverage.

28. *Revised Statutes of Utah*, sec. 24-1-1098 (1898).

29. *Revised Statutes of Utah*, secs. 24-1-1107, -1108 (1898).

30. See *Utah Code Annotated*, Title 26, Health Code.

31. *Utah Code Annotated*, sec. 26A-1-106 (Supp. 2005). Where local resources are inadequate, the state may provide assistance and funding to local departments.

32. Title 26 of the Utah Code does not provide many specifics about how the Department of Health must be organized. In fact, the executive director retains broad discretion for organizing the department in whatever manner necessary to promote effectiveness and efficiency (sec. 26-1-13). The relatively few specifics governing the department's organization are found in the following statutes:

Utah Code Section	Function
26-1-7	Creates four committees within the department: Health Facility Committee, State Emergency Medical Services Committee, Health Data Committee, and Utah Health Care Workforce Financial Assistance Program Advisory Committee
26-1-26	Appoints a director of community health nursing
26-1-7.5	Creates the Utah Health Advisory Council (not part of the department)
26-1-20	Authorizes the creation of other advisory committees
26-18-2.1	Creates the Division of Health Care Financing (Medicaid)

33. See Utah Dep't of Health, Division of Community and Family Health Services, http://health.utah.gov/cfhs/index.html (accessed June 9, 2005).

34. Utah Legislature, Office of the Legislative Fiscal Analyst, *Fiscal Year 2005 Budget Recommendations to the Joint Appropriations Subcommittee for Health and Human Services: Utah Department of Health, Epidemiology and Laboratory Services* (Salt Lake City, 2004), 10. See Utah Dep't of Health, Utah Public Health Laboratory, Division of Epidemiology and Laboratory Services, "Bureau of Chemical And Environmental Services," http://health.utah.gov/els/chemistry/index.html (accessed June 6, 2005).

35. Utah Legislature, *2005 Budget Recommendations to the Subcommittee for Health and Human Services*, 10.

36. Ibid., 21.

37. Ibid., 21, 22.

38. Ibid., 16-19.

39. Ibid., 20.

40. Utah Dep't of Health, Utah Pub. Health Lab., Bureau of Laboratory Improvement, "Clinical Laboratory Certification," http://health.utah.gov/els/labimp/labcert/clialabcert.html (accessed June 8, 2005).

41. Utah Dep't of Health, Utah Pub. Health Lab., Bur. of Lab. Imprv., "Environmental Laboratory Certification," http://health.utah.gov/els/labimp/labcert/envlabcert.html (accessed June 8, 2005).

42. See Utah Dep't of Health, Utah Pub. Health Lab., Bureau of Microbiology, http://health.utah.gov/els/microbiology/index.html (accessed June 9, 2005).

43. See *Utah Code Annotated*, Title 26, Chapter 18, Utah Medical Assistance Act.

44. Smith, Vernon K., "Understanding Key Medicaid and Health Cost Drivers: What's Controllable and What's Not," presentation for the Health Chairs Meeting, National Conference of State Legislatures, Washington, D.C., June 16, 2005, slide 19, accessed September 7, 2005 at http://www.ncsl.org/programs/health/forum/chairs/healthchairsmtgb.htm. Figures are Health Management Associates estimates based on Congressional Budget Office Medicaid baseline March 2005. Expenditure distribution based on spending for services only and excludes disproportionate share hospital payments, supplemental provider payments, vaccines for children and administration.

45. Kent Roner (Director, Bureau of Financial Services, Division of Health Care Financing, Utah Department of Health) in discussion with Mark Andrews (Policy Analyst, Office of Legislative Research and General Counsel), October 19, 2004, updated by the bureau October 3, 2005. Figures include only service delivery costs, not the state's administrative overhead. Growth rates calculated by Mark Andrews.

46. Ibid. Fiscal year 2006 appropriations total $1.558 billion, an 11.9 percent increase over fiscal year 2005 expenditures.

47. Ibid.; Utah Legislature, Office of Legislative Fiscal Analyst, *2005-2006 Appropriations Report* (Salt Lake City, April 2005), 13, 15. General Fund expenditures exclude General Fund restricted accounts.

48. Utah Legislature, *2005-2006 Appropriations Report*, 13.

49. As used here, "enrollment" refers to "Medicaid eligibles," persons who have met Medicaid eligibility requirements. As in private health plans, not all who are eligible to use services do so.

50. Roner discussion with Andrews, October 2004. These figures are the 12-month moving averages of Medicaid eligibles calculated in June of each fiscal year. Due to people cycling in or out of the program, the twelve-month moving average is much lower than the unduplicated count of individuals who were eligible for the program at any time during the year. The unduplicated counts—the total number of unique persons eligible sometime during any given year—are as follows:

Fiscal year 1996: 225,684	Fiscal year 2001: 235,813
Fiscal year 1997: 225,493	Fiscal year 2002: 249,447
Fiscal year 1998: 217,775	Fiscal year 2003: 249,745
Fiscal year 1999: 222,114	Fiscal year 2004: 276,813
Fiscal year 2000: 222,360	Fiscal year 2005: 286,983

51. Roner discussion with Andrews, October 2004, with October 2005 update. Growth rates calculated by Mark Andrews.

52. See Utah Dep't of Health, "A Summary of Medical Assistance Programs in the State of Utah" (Salt Lake City, April 2005), http://health.utah.gov/eol/forms/pdffiles/medprosumapr05.pdf (accessed June 9, 2005). Federal statute defines at least forty-nine eligibility categories, twenty-one of which are optional. Schneider, Andy, *The Medicaid Resource Book* (Washington, D.C.: The Kaiser Commission on Medicaid and the Uninsured, 2002), 8.

53. John Strong (Acting Director, Bureau of Access, Division of Health Care Financing, Utah Dep't of Health) in discussion with Mark Andrews (Policy Analyst, Office of Legislative Research and General Counsel), May 27, 2005. As of May 21, 2005, 18,009 individuals were enrolled in the program.

54. Ibid. As of May 21, 2005, 73 individuals were enrolled in the program.

55. Ibid. As of April 30, 2005, 31,156 children were enrolled in the program.

56. Enrollment is expected to increase by 12,000 as a result of *Children's Health Care Coverage Amendments*, H.B. 114, 56th Leg., Gen. Sess. (Utah 2005) which appropriates an additional $16.3 million in state and federal funds to the program beginning in fiscal year 2006.

57. *Utah Code Annotated*, sec. 26-33a-104 (2000).

58. Utah Dep't of Health, Division of Health Systems Improvement, "The Division of Health Systems Improvement," http://www.health.state.ut.us/hsi/ (accessed June 9, 2004).

59. *Utah Code Annotated*, Title 26, Chapter 8a, Utah Emergency Medical Services System Act.

60. See Utah Dep't of Health, Division of Health Care Improvements, Office of Child Care Licensing, Child Care Licensing, http://health.utah.gov/licensing/ (accessed May 27, 2005).

61. Utah Legislature, Office of the Legislative Fiscal Analyst, *Fiscal Year 2005 Budget Recommendations to the Joint Appropriations Subcommittee for Health and Human Services: Utah Department of Health, Health Systems Improvement* (Salt Lake City, 2004), 11-12, 15-16. See Utah Dep't of Health, Bureau of Health Facility Licensing Certification and Resident Assessment, http://health.utah.gov/pcra (accessed June 9, 2005).

62. *Utah Code Annotated*, secs. 26-18-302, -304 (2000).

63. *Utah Code Annotated*, sec. 26-9-1 (2000). See Utah Dep't of Health, Division of Health Care Improvements, "Primary Care and Rural Health," http://health.utah.gov/primary_care.

64. *Utah Code Annotated*, sec. 26-4-7 (Supp. 2005) includes a complete list of the circumstances under which an OME investigation is required. Highway deaths are specifically excluded.

65. Utah Dep't of Health, Office of the Medical Examiner, "General Information," http://health.utah.gov/ome (accessed June 6, 2005).

66. A. Richard Melton (Deputy Director, Utah Department of Health) in discussion with Mark Andrews (Policy Analyst, Office of Legislative Research and General Counsel), November 15,

2005.

67. Utah Legislature, *2005-2006 Appropriations Report*, 13.

68. Ibid., 15. The fiscal year 2006 General Fund appropriation for the department is $323,978,900. Fiscal year 2006 General Fund appropriations for all programs total $1,990,562,800. Figures exclude appropriations from General Fund restricted accounts.

69. Ibid., 13.

70. *Utah Code Annotated*, sec. 26A-1-103 (Supp. 2005).

71. *Utah Code Annotated*, secs. 26A-1-106, -114 (Supp. 2005).

72. *Utah Code Annotated*, sec. 26A-1-108 (Supp. 2005). Local health departments "shall enforce state health laws, Department of Health, Department of Environmental Quality, and local health department rules, regulations, and standards. . . ."

73. *Utah Code Annotated*, sec. 26A-1-106. Where local resources are inadequate, the state may provide assistance and funding to local departments.

74. Utah Legislature, Office of the Legislative Fiscal Analyst, *Fiscal Year 2005 Budget Recommendations: Utah Department of Health–Local Health Departments*, prepared for the Joint Appropriations Subcommittee for Health and Human Services, 2004, 9.

Chapter 16 Endnotes

1. Utah Foundation, *State and Local Government in Utah* (Salt Lake City: Utah Foundation, 1992), 159.

2. Ibid.

3. See Utah Department of Social Services, *Unification of Social Services: The Utah Experience* (Salt Lake City: Utah Department of Social Services, January 1984), 1.

4. Ibid., 9.

5. *Utah Code Annotated*, sec. 62A-1-105 (Supp. 2005). In contrast to the Department of Health, the Legislature has been very specific about the organization of the Department of Human Services. Each of the divisions, offices, and boards discussed here are created and charged with specific duties by statute.

6. See *Utah Code Annotated*, secs. 62A-1-105, 62A-2-104 (2000 & Supp. 2005).

7. *Utah Code Annotated*, secs. 62A-1-109, 62A-14-104 (2000).

8. See *Utah Code Annotated*, Title 62A, Utah Human Services Code.

9. For an excellent overview of and answers to questions about services provided by the department, see Utah Department of Human Services, *Hot Tips Quick Reference Guide: Finding Your Way Around the Department of Human Services* (Salt Lake City, Revised July 2004),

http://hs.utah.gov/pdf/hot-tips.pdf (accessed May 27, 2005).

10. Utah Dep't of Human Servs., *Hot Tips Quick Reference Guide*, 24.

11. Ibid.

12. *Utah Code Annotated*, sec. 62A-3-302 (Supp. 2005).

13. *Utah Code Annotated*, secs. 62A-3-101, -104 (Supp. 2005).

14. *Utah Code Annotated*, Title 62A, Chapter 4a, Child and Family Services.

15. Utah Legislature, Office of the Legislative Auditor General, *A Performance Audit of Utah's Child Welfare System*, Report 93-06 (Salt Lake City, 1993).

16. *David C. v. Leavitt*, Case No. 93-C-206W, 1993WL 764518, at 1 (D. Utah May 5, 1993).

17. *David C. v. Leavitt*, Case No. 93-C-206W (D. Utah May 24, 1994) (Settlement Agreement).

18. Dep't of Human Servs., Office of Services Review, *A System Review of the Division of Child and Family Services: Fiscal Year 2004 Report* (Salt Lake City, September 2004).

19. *David C. v. Huntsman*, Case No. 2:93-CV-206C (D. Utah May 26, 2005) (Stipulation to Enter Order to Amend the Milestone Plan).

20. Richard Anderson (Director, Division of Child and Family Services) in discussion with Mark Andrews (Policy Analyst, Office of Legislative Research and General Counsel), December 15, 2004 (based on a draft report of a child welfare workforce survey by the American Public Human Services Association).

21. *Utah Code Annotated*, sec. 62A-5-103 (Supp. 2005).

22. Utah Dep't of Human Servs., *Hot Tips Quick Reference Guide*, 51.

23. *Utah Code Annotated*, sec. 62A-5-101 (Supp. 2005).

24. Utah Dep't of Human Servs., *Hot Tips Quick Reference Guide*, 55-56.

25. See *Utah Code Annotated*, Title 62A, Chapter 5, Part 2, Utah State Developmental Center.

26. *Utah Code Annotated*, sec. 62A-5-102 (Supp. 2005).

27. *Utah Code Annotated*, sec. 62A-15-103 (Supp. 2005).

28. *Utah Code Annotated*, sec. 17-43-301 (Supp. 2005).

29. See *Utah Code Annotated*, Title 62A, Chapter 15, Part 6, Utah State Hospital and Other Mental Health Facilities.

30. See Utah Dep't of Human Servs., *Hot Tips Quick Reference Guide*, 62-63 (substance abuse services priorities), 73 (mental health services priorities).

31. Ibid., 76.

32. Ibid.

33. Ibid., 76-84.

34. An incapacitated adult is an adult who "suffers from a mental or physical impairment that renders the person substantially incapable of: (i) caring for his personal safety; (ii) managing his financial affairs; or (iii) attending to and providing for such necessities as food, shelter, clothing, and medical care, to the extent that physical injury or illness may result." *Utah Code Annotated*, secs. 62A-14-102, -107 (2000).

35. *Utah Code Annotated*, sec. 62A-14-105 (2000).

36. Utah Dep't of Human Servs., *Hot Tips Quick Reference Guide*, 19.

37. *Utah Code Annotated*, sec. 62A-14-105.

38. *Utah Code Annotated*, sec. 62A-2-108 (Supp. 2005).

39. *Utah Code Annotated*, sec. 62A-2-101(17) (Supp. 2005).

40. Utah Dep't of Human Servs., *Hot Tips Quick Reference Guide*, 11.

41. *Utah Code Annotated*, sec. 62A-2-120 (Supp. 2005).

42. *Utah Code Annotated*, sec. 62A-2-106 (Supp. 2005).

43. *Utah Code Annotated*, sec. 62A-11-104 (Supp. 2005). The Office of Recovery Services does not collect child support in every case of court-ordered support. By law, some cases are automatically sent to the Office for enforcement. In other cases, one of the parties must request the Office's involvement. See Dep't of Human Servs., *Hot Tips Quick Reference Guide*, 85.

44. Dep't of Human Servs., *Hot Tips Quick Reference Guide*, 85.

45. Emma Chacon (Director, Office of Recovery Services, Department of Human Services) in discussion with Mark Andrews (Policy Analyst, Office of Legislative Research and General Counsel), November 8, 2004. Of the 74,025 cases on which support was collected, approximately 69,000 were child suport cases and 5,000 were support cases for children in custody of the state.

46. Ibid. Data for support cases is based on the federal fiscal year (October 1–September 30). Data for Medicaid cases is based on the state fiscal year (July 1–June 30).

47. Ibid. Collection rates are based on federal fiscal years. Utah's federal fiscal year 2004 collection rate increased to 59.8 percent. Another useful performance measure is the percentage of cases on which the office is able to collect current support due. This collection rate varies significantly by case type. In state fiscal year 2003, the office collected current support due on the 51 percent of cases involving public assistance and 79 percent of cases not involving public assistance. Utah Dep't of Human Servs., *Outcome Report*, by Brad McGarry et al. (Salt Lake City, November 2003) 19, 34, http://www.dhs.utah.gov/reports.htm (accessed May 26, 2005). The rate for all cases in state fiscal year 2004 was 60.6 percent. Chacon, 2004.

48. Don Thompson (Supervisor, Self-Assessment Unit, Office of Recovery Services) in discussion with Mark Andrews (Policy Analyst, Office of Legislative Research and General Counsel), November 2004.

49. Chacon, 2004. Outstanding child support, including support for children in custody of the state, totaled $313.3 million in federal fiscal year 2004. Outstanding payments for Medicaid reimbursement totaled $24.3 million in state fiscal year 2004. Combined arrears totaled $337.7 million. Realistically, not all of the arrears are collectable.

50. Utah Legislature, Office of the Legislative Fiscal Analyst, *2005-2006 Appropriations Report* (Salt Lake City, April 2005): 13, 41, 118. "General Fund" excludes restricted accounts.

Chapter 17 Endnotes

1. *Utah Code Annotated*, sec. 63-34-3 (2004).

2. *Utah Code Annotated*, sec. 65A-1-4 (2004).

3. *Utah Code Annotated*, sec. 65A-1-3 (2004).

4. *Utah Code Annotated*, sec. 65A-1-2 (2004).

5. *Utah Code Annotated*, sec. 65A-8-6(3) (2004).

6. *Utah Code Annotated*, sec. 65A-8a-103 (2004).

7. State of Utah, Department of Natural Resources, Division of Forestry, Fire and State Lands, *Forest Stewardship*, http://www.ffsl.utah.gov/stewardship.htm (accessed on Nov. 29, 2005).

8. State of Utah, Department of Natural Resources, Division of Forestry, Fire and State Lands, *Forestry Assistance*, http://www.ffsl.utah.gov/mmforestryassist.htm (accessed on Nov. 29, 2005).

9. *Utah Code Annotated*, secs. 65A-4-3, 65A-5-1 (2004).

10. *Utah Code Annotated*, sec. 65A-9-1 (2004).

11. *Utah Code Annotated*, sec. 40-6-15 (1998).

12. *Utah Code Annotated*, sec. 40-6-4 (1998).

13. State of Utah, Department of Natural Resources, Division of Oil, Gas, and Mining, *Utah Minerals Program*, http://www.ogm.utah.gov/minerals/default.htm (accessed Nov. 29, 2005).

14. State of Utah, Department of Natural Resources, Division of Oil, Gas, and Mining, *Utah Coal Program*, http://www.ogm.utah.gov/coal/Default.htm (accessed Nov. 29, 2005).

15. State of Utah, Department of Natural Resources, Division of Oil, Gas, and Mining, *Utah oil and Gas*, http://www.ogm.utah.gov/oilgas/default.HTM (accessed Nov. 29, 2005).

16. *Utah Code Annotated*, sec. 40-6-14 (Supp. 2005).

17. State of Utah, Department of Natural Resources, *FY 2004-2005 Annual Report & Directory of Services*, (Salt Lake City: Department of Natural Resources, September 2005), 27.

18. Ibid., 25.

19. *Utah Code Annotated*, sec. 63-11-17.1 (2004).

20. *Utah Code Annotated*, secs. 63-11-12, -14 (2004).

21. *Utah Code Annotated*, sec. 63-11-17 (2004).

22. State of Utah, Department of Natural Resources, Division of State Parks & Recreation, http://www.stateparks.utah.gov/ (accessed Nov. 29, 2005).

23. Ibid.

24. *Utah Code Annotated*, sec. 73-18-1 (Supp. 2005).

25. State of Utah, Department of Natural Resources, Division of State Parks & Recreation, *OHV Safety and Education*, http://www.stateparks.utah.gov/ohv/default.htm (accessed Nov. 29, 2005).

26. *Utah Code Annotated*, sec. 63-11-17.8 (2004).

27. *Utah Code Annotated*, sec. 63-11a-503 (2004).

28. State of Utah, Department of Natural Resources, Division of Water Resources, *50 Year History*, http://www.water.utah.gov/mission/history.pdf (accessed Nov. 29, 2005).

29. Ibid.

30. Ibid.

31. Ibid.

32. Ibid.

33. *Utah Code Annotated*, secs. 73-10-1.5, -18 (1989).

34. *Utah Code Annotated*, sec. 73-10-1 (Supp. 2005).

35. State of Utah, Department of Natural Resources, Division of Water Resource, *Water Conservation*, http://www.conservewater.utah.gov/ (accessed Nov. 29, 2005).

36. *Utah Code Annotated*, Title 73, Chapter 10, Board of Water Resources- Division of Water Resources.

37. State of Utah, Department of Natural Resources, Division of Water Rights, *Water Right Information*, http://www.waterrights.utah.gov/wrinfo/default.asp (accessed on Nov. 29, 2005).

38. Ibid.

39. *Utah Code Annotated*, sec. 73-2-1.1 (1989).

40. *Utah Code Annotated*, sec. 73-2-14 (Supp. 2005).

41. *Utah Code Annotated*, sec. 73-3-25 (Supp. 2005).

42. State of Utah, Department of Natural Resources, Division of Water Rights, *Dam Safety*, http://www.waterrights.utah.gov/daminfo/default.asp (accessed Nov. 29, 2005).

43. *Utah Code Annotated*, sec. 73-3-29 (Supp. 2005); State of Utah, Department of Natural Resources, Division of Water Rights, *Stream Alteration Information Page*, http://www.waterrights.utah.gov/strmalt/default.asp (accessed Nov. 29, 2005).

44. *Utah Code Annotated*, sec. 23-14-1 (2003).

45. State of Utah, Department of Natural Resources, Division of Wildlife Resources, *A brief history of the Utah Fish & Game by Edwin and LeeAnn Rawley*, http://www.wildlife.utah.gov/about/history.html (accessed Nov. 29, 2005).

46. *Utah Code Annotated*, sec. 23-14-2 (2003).

47. *Utah Code Annotated*, sec. 23-14-2.6 (2003).

48. U.S. Fish & Wildlife Service, *2001 National and State Economic Impacts of Wildlife Watching*, 10, http://library.fws.gov/nat_survey2001_economics.pdf (accessed Nov. 29, 2005).

49. State of Utah, Department of Natural Resources, Division of Wildlife Resources, *Ecology & Habitat*, http://www.wildlife.utah.gov/habitat/ (accessed Nov. 29, 2005).

50. State of Utah, Department of Natural Resources, Division of Wildlife Resources, http://wildlife.utah.gov/index.php (accessed Nov. 29, 2005).

51. State of Utah, Department of Natural Resources, Division of Wildlife Resources, *Law Enforcement*, http://wildlife.utah.gov/law/ (accessed Nov. 29, 2005).

52. State of Utah, Department of Natural Resources, Division of Wildlife Resources, *Hunter Education*, http://wildlife.utah.gov/huntereducation/ (accessed Nov. 29, 2005).

53. State of Utah, Department of Natural Resources, Division of Wildlife Resources, *Conservation Outreach*, http://wildlife.utah.gov/outreach/ (accessed Nov. 29, 2005).

54. State of Utah, Department of Natural Resources, Division of Wildlife Resources, *Dedicated Hunter Program*, http://wildlife.utah.gov/dh/ (accessed Nov. 29, 2005).

55. State of Utah, Department of Natural Resources, Division of Wildlife Resources, *Habitat Program*, http://www.wildlife.utah.gov/habitat/habitat_program.html (accessed Nov. 29, 2005).

56. *Utah Code Annotated*, secs. 63-73-5, -6 (2004).

57. *Utah Code Annotated*, sec. 63-73-2 (2004).

58. State of Utah, Department of Natural Resources, Utah Geological Survey, *Energy & Minerals Program*, http://geology.utah.gov/emp/index.htm (accessed Nov. 29, 2005).

59. State of Utah, Department of Natural Resources, Utah Geological Survey, *Geological Hazards Program*, http://geology.utah.gov/ghp/index.htm (accessed Nov. 29, 2005).

60. State of Utah, Department of Natural Resources, Utah Geological Survey, *Geologic Mapping Program*, http://geology.utah.gov/gmp/index.htm (accessed Nov. 29, 2005).

61. State of Utah, Department of Natural Resources, Utah Geological Survey, *Groundwater & Paleontology Program*, http://geology.utah.gov/esp/index.htm (accessed Nov. 29, 2005).

62. State of Utah, Department of Natural Resources, Utah Geological Survey, *Geologic Information & Outreach Program*, http://geology.utah.gov/giop/index.htm (accessed Nov. 29, 2005).

63. *Utah Code Annotated*, sec. 63-34-14 (Supp. 2005).

64. *Utah Code Annotated*, sec. 63-34-13 (2004).

Chapter 18 Endnotes

1. Morgan Quitno Press, Crime State Rankings 2005, Crime in the 50 United States, (Lawrence, KS, 2005) Kathleen O'Leary Morgan and Scott Morgan, Editors.

2. Ibid.

3. Utah Comm'n on Crim. & Juv. Justice, Crime Statistics: Utah versus the United States (Salt Lake City, Utah 2004) http://justice.utah.gov/Research/CrimeStats/UtahCompareUS.htm (accessed June 24, 2005).

4. Ibid.

5. Ibid.

6. Morgan Quitno Press, Crime State Rankings 2005, Crime in the 50 United States, (Lawrence, KS, 2005) Kathleen O'Leary Morgan and Scott Morgan, Editors.

7. Utah Comm'n on Crim. & Juv. Justice, Crime Statistics: Utah versus the United States (Salt Lake City, Utah 2004) http://justice.utah.gov/Research/CrimeStats/UtahCompareUS.htm (accessed June 24, 2005).

8. Morgan Quitno Press, Crime State Rankings 2005, Crime in the 50 United States, (Lawrence, KS, 2005) Kathleen O'Leary Morgan and Scott Morgan, Editors.

9. Utah Comm'n on Crim. & Juv. Justice, *Crime Statistics: Utah versus the United States* (Salt Lake City, Utah 2004) http://justice.utah.gov/Research/CrimeStats/UtahCompareUS.htm (accessed June 24, 2005).

10. Ibid.

11. Ibid. The Mountain States include Arizona, Colorado, Idaho, Montana, Nevada, New Mexico, Utah, and Wyoming.

12. U.S. Department of Justice, Federal Bureau of Investigation, *Uniform Crime Reports* (Washington D.C., 2003), http://www.fbi.gov (accessed September 21, 2004).These states included: Arkansas, Iowa, Kansas, Mississippi, Nebraska, Nevada, New Mexico, Utah, and West Virginia.

13. Ibid.

14. Utah Department of Corrections, 1982 Through 2004 (midyear) Utah Department of Corrections (Cliff Butter, Research Consultant, Utah Department of Corrections), August 24, 2005.

15. U.S. Department of Justice, Prison and Jail Inmates at Midyear 2004, Bureau of Justice Statistics Bulletin (Paige M. Harrison and Allen J. Beck, Ph.D.), April 2005. The Western States are Alaska, Arizona, California, Colorado, Hawaii, Idaho, Montana, Nevada, New Mexico, Oregon, Utah, Washington, and Wyoming.

16. U.S. Department of Justice, Prison and Jail Inmates at Midyear 2004, Bureau of Justice Statistics Bulletin Paige M. Harrison and Allen J. Beck, Ph.D.), April 2005.

17. Felony and Misdemeanor Fines and Imprisonment Statutory References: Felony and misdemeanor fines, see Utah Code Annotated, sec. 76-3-301; Corporate fines, see *Utah Code Annotated*, sec. 76-3-302; Felony imprisonment, see *Utah Code Annotated*, sec. 76-3-203; Capital felony penalties, see *Utah Code Annotated*, sec. 76-3-206; Misdemeanor imprisonment, see *Utah Code Annotated*, sec. 76-3-204; Infraction penalty, see *Utah Code Annotated*, sec. 76-3-205.

18. *Utah Code Annotated*, sec. 76-3-302 (2003).

19. *Utah Code Annotated*, sec. 77-15a-101 (2003).

20. *Utah Code Annotated*, sec. 76-3-203 (2003).

21. *Utah Code Annotated*, sec. 76-3-406 (2003).

22. *Utah Code Annotated*, Title 63, Chapter 25a, Part 3, Sentencing Commission.

23. Utah Constitution, art. 7, sec. 12.

24. *Utah Code Annotated*, sec. 77-27-2 (2003).

25. *Utah Code Annotated*, sec. 77-27-5 (Supp. 2005).

26. *Utah Code Annotated*, sec. 77-27-2 (2002).

27. *Utah Code Annotated*, sec. 76-3-203.

28. *Utah Code Annotated*, sec. 77-27-5.

29. *Utah Code Annotated*, sec. 77-27-7(1) (2003).

30. *Utah Code Annotated*, sec. 77-27-7(2).

31. *Utah Code Annotated*, sec. 77-27-13(5)(a) (2003).

32. *Utah Code Annotated*, sec. 77-27-5(3).

33. *Utah Code Annotated*, sec. 77-27-11 (2003).

34. *Utah Code Annotated*, sec. 64-13-3 (2002).

35. Arturo Perez (Senior Policy Specialist, National Conference of State Legislatures) E-mail message to Jami Momberger (Policy Analyst, Office of Legislative Research and General Counsel), October 15, 2004.

36. William J. Greer (Senior Fiscal Analyst, Office of the Legislative Fiscal Analyst) telephone discussion with Stewart E. Smith (Policy Analyst, Office of Legislative Research and General Counsel), July 27, 2005.

37. William J. Greer (Senior Fiscal Analyst, Office of Legislative Fiscal Analyst) E-mail message to Jami Momberger (Policy Analyst, Office of Legislative Research and General Counsel), September 28, 2004.

38. Office of the Legislative Fiscal Analyst, *2005-2006 Appropriations Report, Utah Legislature 2005 General Session, April 2005 Special Session* (Salt Lake City, April 2005), 39.

39. Arturo Perez (Senior Policy Specialist, National Conference of State Legislatures) E-mail message to Jami Momberger (Policy Analyst, Office of Legislative Research and General Counsel), October 15, 2004.

40. Utah Department of Corrections, *FY 2006 Budget Recommendation – Department of Corrections*, presentation by William J. Greer (Senior Fiscal Analyst, Office of Legislative Fiscal Analyst) to Executive Offices and Criminal Justice Appropriations Subcommittee, 56th Leg., January 26, 2005.

41. Ibid.

42. Ibid.

43. Utah Dep't of Corrs., *Utah Department of Corrections Jail Program Report* (Salt Lake City: Utah Dep't of Corrs., September 2, 2003).

44. Ibid.

45. *Utah Code Annotated*, sec. 64-13c-303 (2002).

46. Ibid.

47. Ibid.

48. *Utah Code Annotated*, sec. 62A-7-102 (Supp. 2005).

49. *Utah Code Annotated*, sec. 62A-7-104 (Supp. 2005).

50. Ibid.

51. Ibid.

52. *Utah Code Annotated*, sec. 62A-7-109 (Supp. 2005).

53. *Utah Code Annotated*, sec. 62A-7-108 (2000).

54. *Utah Code Annotated*, sec. 62A-7-112 (2000).

55. *Utah Code Annotated*, sec. 62A-7-114 (2000).

56. *Utah Code Annotated*, sec. 53-1-107 (2002).

57. *Utah Code Annotated*, sec. 53-1-108 (2002).

58. *Utah Code Annotated*, Title 53, Chapter 8, Utah Highway Patrol.

59. *Utah Code Annotated*, sec. 53-10-401 (1998).

60. *Utah Code Annotated*, secs. 53-10-301 to -303 (2002).

61. *Utah Code Annotated*, Title 53, Chapter 2, Emergency Management.

62. *Utah Code Annotated*, Title 53, Chapter 3, Uniform Driver License Act.

63. *Utah Code Annotated*, Title 53, Chapter 10, Part 2, Bureau of Criminal Identification.

64. *Utah Code Annotated*, Title 53, Chapter 6, Peace Officer Standards and Training.

Chapter 19 Endnotes

1. 1917 Utah Laws ch. 47; *Utah Code Annotated*, sec. 54-4-1 (1975).

2. *Utah Code Annotated*, sec. 54-4-1(1); Utah Foundation, *State and Local Government in Utah* (Salt Lake City: Utah Foundation, 1992), 198.

3. Steve Mecham (Chair, Public Service Commission) in discussion with Richard C. North (Policy Analyst, Office of Legislative Research and General Counsel), 2004.

4. Utah Legislature, Office of Legislative Research and General Counsel, *Energy Policy Issues and Legislative Options* (Salt Lake City: Legislative Printing Office, November 2001), 6.

5. 1975 Utah Laws ch. 9, 1st Spec. Sess.

6. 1995 Utah Laws ch. 9. That act provided a PSC regulated process by which competitors and the existing local exchange carrier would cooperate to de-regulate the provision and pricing of telephone services. Upon completion of the requirement, that a competitive telecommunications market had developed in Utah, the existing local exchange carrier could pricing flexibility. Qwest Communication was granted pricing flexibility in 2005 per Utah Code, 54-8b-2.3.

7. 1983 Utah Laws ch. 246.

8. *Utah Code Annotated*, sec. 54-4a-3 (Supp. 2005).

9. 1983 Utah Laws ch. 246; *Utah Code Annotated*, sec. 54-4a-4 (2000).

10. 1977 Utah Laws ch. 54.

11. 1989 Utah Laws ch. 225.

12. *Utah Code Annotated*, sec. 54-10-2 (Supp. 2005).

13. 1977 Utah Laws ch. 54; *Utah Code Annotated*, secs. 54-10-5, -7 (2000).

14. 1977 Utah Laws ch. 54; *Utah Code Annotated*, secs. 54-10-4, -5, -7 (2000).

15. Utah Legislature, Office of Legislative Research and General Counsel, *Report of the Electrical Deregulation and Customer Choice Task Force* (Salt Lake City: Legislative Printing Office, November 1998), 1.

16. Ibid., 15.

17. "British Thermal Unit" is the quantity of heat necessary to raise the temperature of one pound of water one degree Fahrenheit. *Webster's Ninth New Collegiate Dictionary* (Springfield, MA: Merriam-Webster, 1985).

18. Data complied using information obtained from the U.S. Department of Energy, Energy Information Administration, *State Energy Price and Expenditure Report, 2001*, "Table 1 - Energy Price and Expenditure Estimates by Source, Selected Years, 1970-2001, United States;" "Table 1 - Energy Price and Expenditure Estimates by Source, Selected Years, 1970-2001, Utah," http://tonto.eia.doe.gov/FTPROOT/state/pr_all.pdf (accessed May 25, 2005).

19. Ibid.

20. Data compiled using information obtained from the U.S. Department of Energy, Energy Information Administration, Natural Gas Residential Price table grouped by area. http://tonto.eia.doe.gov/dnav/ng/ng_pri_sum_a_EPG0_PRS_DMcf_a.htm (accessed August 9, 2005).

21. Data compiled using information obtained from the U.S. Department of Energy, Energy Information Administration, Natural Gas Residential Price table grouped by area. http://tonto.eia.doe.gov/dnav/ng/ng_pri_sum_a_EPG0_PRS_DMcf_a.htm (accessed August 9, 2005).

Chapter 20 Endnotes

1. 1975 Laws of Utah ch. 204, sec. 4.

2. Utah Department of Transportation, Inside UDOT, *The Final Four Strategic Goals*, by Bethany Eller (August 15, 2003), http://www.udot.utah.gov/index.php/m=c/tid=39 (accessed May 17, 2005).

3. *Utah Code Annotated*, sec. 72-1-202 (Supp. 2005).

4. *Utah Code Annotated*, secs. 72-1-202, -203 (2001 & Supp. 2005).

5. *Utah Code Annotated*, secs. 72-1-301, -303 (Supp. 2005).

6. *Utah Code Annotated*, sec. 72-1-204 (2001).

7. Utah Dep't of Transp., Inside UDOT, *Statewide Transportation Improvement Program*, by Bret Anderson (September 19, 2004), http://www.udot.utah.gov/index.php/m=c/tid=33 (accessed May 17, 2005).

8. 23 C.F.R. Part 450, Planning Assistance and Standards.

9. Utah Dep't of Transp., *Utah Transportation 2030: State of Utah Long Range Transportation Plan - Draft Final* (Salt Lake City, October 2003).

10. Utah Dep't of Transp., Inside UDOT, *Transportation 2030 FAQs*, by Joni DeMille (August 15, 2003), http://www.udot.utah.gov/index.php/m=c/tid=33 (accessed May 17, 2005).

11. 23 U.S.C. sec. 134.

12. Utah Legislature, Transportation Planning Task Force, *Transportation Planning Task Force Report to the Transportation Interim Committee*, Appendix E, 55th Leg. (November 19, 2003).

13. *Transportation Amendments and Highway Jurisdictional Transfer Task Force*, S.B. 25, 56th Leg., Gen. Sess. (Utah 2005).

14. Utah Dep't of Transp., Systems Planning and Programming, *Annual Statistical Summary*, Appendix A (Salt Lake City, 2004).

15. *Utah Code Annotated*, Title 72, Chapter 4, Designation of State Highways Act.

16. Utah Dep't of Transp., *Annual Statistical Summary*, Appendix A.

17. Ibid.

18. Ibid.

19. Utah Constitution, art. 13. sec. 5.

20. *Utah Code Annotated*, sec. 72-2-103 (Supp. 2005).

21. *Utah Code Annotated*, secs. 72-2-107, -108 (2001).

22. 1923 Utah Laws ch. 39.

23. 1941 Utah Laws ch. 53.

24. See *Utah Code Annotated*, secs. 53-12-103(6), 72-2-118 (Supp. 2005).

25. *Utah Code Annotated*, sec. 72-2-118.

26. Mark Bleazard, Office of Legislative Fiscal Analyst, *Centennial Highway Program FY 1997-2017 dated 2/15/05* (February 15, 2005).

27. Ibid.

28. Ibid.

29. Ibid.

30. *Transportation Investment Act*, H.B. 1008, 56th Leg., 1st Spec. Sess. (Utah 2005).

31. Ibid.

32. *Transportation Corridor Preservation*, H.B. 53, 51st Leg., Gen. Sess. (Utah 1996).

33. *Utah Code Annotated*, secs. 59-12-103(5), -1201 (2004 & Supp. 2005).

34. *Utah Code Annotated*, sec. 72-5-403 (Supp. 2005).

35. *Local Corridor Preservation Funding*, S.B. 8, 56th Leg., Gen. Sess. (Utah 2005).

36. 1937 Utah Laws ch 40.

37. 1947 Utah Laws ch. 47.

38. 1951 Utah Laws ch. 47.

39. 1961 Utah Laws ch. 57.

40. 1977 Utah Laws ch. 117.

41. 1981 Utah Laws ch. 135.

42. 1982 Utah Laws ch. 30.

43. *Utah Code Annotated*, sec. 59-12-103(5) (Supp. 2005).

44. *Utah Code Annotated*, sec. 72-2-108 (2001).

45. 26 U.S.C. sec. 4081.

46. 26 U.S.C. sec. 9503.

47. Utah Dep't of Transp., *Annual Statistical Summary*, 15.

48. Transportation Equity Act for the 21st Century, Pub. L. No. 105-178, as amended by Title IX of Pub. L. No. 105-206.

49. Safe, Accountable, Flexible, Efficient Transportation Equity Act: A Legacy for Users, Pub. L. No. 109-59.

50. 23 C.F.R. Part 450, Planning Assitance and Standards.

51. Utah Legislature, *Transportation Planning Task Force Report*, 8-9 & Appendix A.

52. Utah Dep't of Transp., Inside UDOT, *Statewide Transportation Improvement Program*, by Bret Anderson (September 19, 2004), http://www.udot.utah.gov/index.php/m=c/tid=33 (accessed

May 17, 2005).

53. *Utah Code Annotated*, sec. 72-1-201 (2001).

54. Utah Dep't of Transp., *Utah Transportation 2030: State of Utah Long Range Transportation Plan - Draft Final* (Salt Lake City, October 2003).

55. Utah Dep't of Transp., *Report to the Transportation Planning Task Force* (September 8, 2004), 22-26.

56. Utah Dep't of Transp., *Utah Transportation 2030*, 57.

57. See Utah Dep't of Transp., *Utah Transportation 2030*, 53-55; *Utah Code Annotated*, Title 72, Chapter 12, Travel Reduction Act.

58. *Access Management Incentives in Transportation*, H.B. 66, 53rd Leg., Gen. Sess. (Utah 1999).

59. *State Highway Access Management*, H.B. 218, 54th Leg., Gen. Sess. (Utah 2001).

60. Utah Dep't of Transp., Inside UDOT, Project Development, Right of Way, *UDOT Access Management Program*, by Tim Boschert (August 20, 2003), http://www.udot.utah.gov/index.php/m=c/tid=314 (accessed May 17, 2005).

61. Utah Dep't of Transp., *Utah Transportation 2030*, 65.

62. *Utah Code Annotated*, Title 72, Chapter 9, Motor Carrier Safety Act.

63. *Utah Code Annotated*, sec. 72-9-301 (2001).

64. 1978 Utah Laws ch. 8, 1981 Utah Laws ch. 135, 1984 Utah Laws ch. 55, 1987 Utah Laws ch. 139.

65. 1997 Utah Laws ch. 272.

66. Utah State Tax Commission, Economic Information and Statistical Unit, *Annual Report Fiscal Year 2002-2003*, by Jodi Monaco et al. (2003), 8, 10, 12; Utah State Tax Comm'n, *Annual Report of the Utah State Tax Commission, Fiscal Year July 1, 1986 to June 30, 1987*, ed. W. Lee Shaw (1987), 33, 61, 75.

67. Office of the Governor, Utah Council of Economic Advisors, *2004 Economic Report to the Governor* (Salt Lake City: Governor's Office of Planning and Budget, January 2004), 64; Utah State Tax Comm'n, *Annual Report Fiscal Year 2002-2003*, 8, 10, 12.

68. *Utahns For Better Transportation v. United States DOT*, 305 F.3d 1152 (10th Cir. 2002).

69. H.C.R. 201, 2005 Second Special Session, *Resolution Approving Legacy Parkway Settlement Agreement*.

70. 1969 Utah Laws ch. 12, 1st Spec. Sess.

71. *Utah Code Annotated*, sec. 17A-2-1038 (2004).

72. *Utah Code Annotated*, sec. 17A-2-1042 (2004).

73. *Utah Code Annotated*, secs. 59-12-501, -502, -1001, and -1501.

74. *Utah Code Annotated*, sec. 17A-2-1044 (2004).

75. *Utah Code Annotated*, sec. 59-12-501 (2004).

76. 1969 Utah Laws ch. 12, 1st Spec. Sess.

77. 1973 Utah Laws ch. 15.

78. 1974 Utah Laws ch. 59.

79. 1974 Utah Laws ch. 12.

80. 1974 Utah Laws ch. 2.

81. 1974 Utah Laws ch. 1, 2nd Spec. Sess.

82. 1977 Utah Laws ch. 50.

83. 1990 Utah Laws ch. 191.

84. 2003 Utah Laws ch. 282.

85. 2004 Utah Laws ch. 336.

86. Utah Transit Authority, Finance Department, *Comprehensive Annual Financial Report: For Fiscal Year Ended December 31, 2003* (Salt Lake City, June 1, 2004), 43.

87. Wasatch Front Regional Council et al., *Report to the Transportation Planning Task Force of the Utah Legislature* (Salt Lake City, July 2004), 9.

88. Utah Transit Authority, *Comprehensive Annual Financial Report*, 27.

89. Wasatch Front Regional Council et al., *Report to the Transportation Planning Task Force of the Utah Legislature* (Salt Lake City, July 2004), Appendix 3.

90. Wasatch Front Regional Council, *Long Range Plan Communique* (Salt Lake City, April 2004), 1.

91. Ibid.

92. Utah Legislature, *Transportation Planning Task Force Report*, 9.

93. U.S. Department of Transportation, Federal Transit Administration, *Record of Decision: Weber County to Salt Lake City Commuter Rail Project*, (April 29, 2005), http://www.rideuta.com/calendarAndNews/commuterRail/files/recordDecision.pdf (accessed November 18, 2005).

94. 1990 Utah Laws ch. 191.

95. 1999 Utah Laws ch. 133.

96. 1999 Utah Laws ch. 310.

97. 2000 Utah Laws ch. 344.

98. 2003 Utah Laws ch. 282.

99. *Utah Code Annotated*, secs. 59-13-402, 72-10-303 (2001 & 2004).

100. Salt Lake City International Airport, Fast Facts, *A Snapshot of Salt Lake City International Airport*, http://www.slcairport.com/73.asp (accessed May 17, 2005).

101. Utah Dep't of Transp., *Utah Transportation 2030*, 41-44.

102. *Utah Code Annotated*, sec. 59-13-402 (2004).

103. *Utah Code Annotated*, sec. 59-13-404 (2004).

104. Utah Dep't of Transp., *Utah Transportation 2030*, 44.

105. Ibid., 41-44.

Chapter 21 Endnotes

1. U.S. Constitution, art. 6, cl. 2.

2. U.S. Constitution, amend. 10.

3. *Swift & Co. v. Wickham*, 382 U.S. 111 (1965).

4. *Fry v. United States*, 421 U.S. 542 (1975).

5. *Sola Elec. Co. v. Jefferson Elec. Co.*, 317 U.S. 173 (1942).

6. *In re Kings County Lighting Co.*, 72 F. Supp. 767 (D.C.N.Y. 1947).

7. *Sperry v. Florida*, 373 U.S. 379 (1963) *on remand*, 159 So. 2d 229 (Fla. 1963).

8. Ibid.

9. *Free v. Bland*, 369 U.S. 663 (1962).

10. *Florida Lime & Avocado Growers, Inc. v. Paul*, 373 U.S. 132 (1963), *reh'g denied*, 374 U.S. 858 (1963).

11. *Molnar v. Curtin*, 77 N.Y.S.2d 553 (N.Y. App. Div. 1948), *aff'd*, 80 N.E.2d 356 (N.Y. Ct. App. 1948).

12. *Davega City Radio v. State Labor Relations Bd.*, 22 N.E.2d 145 (N.Y. Ct. App. 1939).

13. *Amalgamated Meat Cutters & Butcher Workmen, v. Johnson*, 286 P.2d 182 (Kan. 1955).

14. *Innes v. Tobin*, 240 U.S. 127 (1916).

15. *S. Pac. Co. v. Arizona*, 325 U.S. 761 (1945).

16. *Hines v. Davidowitz*, 312 U.S. 52 (1941).

17. *Crosby v. Nat'l Foreign Trade Council*, 530 U.S. 363 (2000).

18. U.S. Constitution, art. 1, sec. 8.

19. Ibid.

20. *Minnesota Rate Cases*, 230 U.S. 352 (1913).

21. *Amalgamated Ass'n of St., Elec. Ry. & Motor Coach Employees v. Wisconsin Employment Relations Bd.*, 340 U.S. 383 (1951).

22. *Maurer v. Hamilton*, 309 U.S. 598 (1940).

23. *Castle v. Hayes Freight Lines, Inc.*, 348 U.S. 61 (1954).

24. *See Chicago v. Atchison, T. & S.F. Ry.*, 357 U.S. 77 (1958), which invalidated a city ordinance regulating interterminal transportation despite the fact that the ICC had not exercised its regulatory authority.

25. *See Lloyd A. Fry Roofing Co. v. Wood*, 344 U.S. 157 (1952); *Terminal R.R. Ass'n v. Brotherhood of R.R. Trainmen*, 318 U.S. 1 (1943).

26. *See Union Brokerage Co. v. Jensen*, 322 U.S. 202 (1944); *Townsend v. Yeomans*, 301 U.S. 441 (1937).

27. *Rice v. Santa Fe Elevator Corp.*, 331 U.S. 218 (1947).

28. *California v. Zook*, 336 U.S. 725 (1949), *reh'g denied*, 337 U.S. 921 (1949).

29. *Hines v. Davidowitz*, 312 U.S. 52 (1941).

30. *Crosby v. Nat'l Foreign Trade Council*, 530 U.S. 363 (2000).

31. Ibid.

32. Ibid.

33. Foyle v. Lederle Lab., 674 F. Supp. 530, 532 (E.D.N.C. 1987).

34. *Penn Dairies v. Milk Control Comm'n of Pennsylvania*, 318 U.S. 261 (1943).

35. *City of Burbank v. Lockheed Air Terminal, Inc.*, 411 U.S. 624 (1973).

36. *Kelly v. Washington*, 302 U.S. 1 (1937).

37. Ibid.

38. *Florida Lime & Avocado Growers, Inc. v. Paul*, 373 U.S. 132 (1963).

39. *In re Morgan*, 194 P.2d 800 (Cal. Ct. App. 1948).

40. *Crosby v. Nat'l Foreign Trade Council*, 530 U.S. 363 (2000).

41. *Rice v. Santa Fe Elevator Corp.*, 331 U.S. 218 (1947).

42. Ibid.

43. Ibid.

44. Ibid, 236.

45. *Black's Law Dictionary*, 16th ed. p. 738, (Minnesota: West Publishing Co, 1990).

46. Norman J. Singer, *1 Sutherland Statutory Construction*, 6th ed. (Minnesota: Thomson West, 2002), sec. 4:07.

47. *Lentini v. Kenner*, 211 So. 2d 311 (La. 1968); *Larke v. Morrissey*, 230 A.2d 562 (Conn. 1967); *Nordine v. Illinois Power Co.*, 199 N.E.2d 34 (Ill. Ct. App. 1964).

48. *Salt Lake City v. Allred*, 430 P.2d 371 (Utah 1967), *rev'd on reh'g*, 437 P.2d 434 (Utah 1968).

49. See, e.g., *Salt Lake City v. Kusse*, 93 P.2d 671 (Utah 1939); *American Fork City v. Charlier*, 134 P. 739 (Utah 1913); *Tooele City v. Hoffman*, 134 P. 558 (Utah 1913).

50. *Salt Lake City v. Kusse*, 93 P.2d 671, 673 (Utah 1939).

51. *Salt Lake City v. Allred*, 430 P.2d 371 (Utah 1967), *rev'd on reh'g*, 437 P.2d 434 (Utah 1968).

52. Chart created from e-mail data sent from John E. Massey (Legislative Fiscal Analyst, Office of the Legislative Fiscal Analyst) to Michael E. Christensen (Director, Office of Legislative Research and General Counsel), March 17, 2005 on file with Office of Legislative Research and General Counsel.

53. U.S. Department of State, Congressional Research Service, *Federal Land Management Agencies: Background on Land and Resources Management*, RL32393, coordinated by Carol Hardy Vincent (Washington, D.C.: Cong. Research Serv., August 2, 2004), 6, http://www.ncseonline.org/nle/crsreports/04Aug/RL32393.pdf (accessed June 7, 2005).

54. See U.S. General Services Administration, Office of Governmentwide Policy, *Overview of the United States Government's Owned and Leased Real Property: Federal Real Property Profile as of September 30, 2003*, "Table 16" (Washington, D.C.: U.S. Gen. Serv. Admin., September 30, 2003), 16, http://www.gsa.gov/gsa/cm_attachments/GSA_DOCUMENT/Annual%20Report%20%20FY2003-R4_R2M-n11_0Z5RDZ-i34K-pR.pdf (accessed June 7, 2005).

55. U.S.D.A. Forest Service, Land Areas of the National Forest System, *Land Areas Report as of September 30, 2003*, "Table 4: Areas by State" (Washington, D.C., September 30, 2003), http://www.fs.fed.us/land/staff/lar/ (accessed June 7, 2005).

For the National Park Service and U.S. Fish and Wildlife Service, see Cong. Research Serv., *Federal Land Management Agencies,* http://www.ncseonline.org/nle/crsreports/ 04Aug/RL32393.pdf. For the U.S. Bureau of Land Management, see U.S. Department of the Interior, Bur. of Land Mgmt., *Public Land Statistics,*
2003 (Washington, D.C.: Bur. of Land Mgmt., 2003), http://www.blm.gov/natacq/pls03/ (accessed June 8, 2005).

56. Cong. Research Serv., *Federal Land Management Agencies*, Table 5.

57. U.S. Dep't of Int., Bur. of Land Mgmt., Office & Centers: Utah, *Questions and Answers Regarding Wilderness Study Areas*, http://www.ut.blm.gov/utahwilderness/qandas.htm (accessed September 21, 2005) and telephone conversation between J Brian Allred, Office of Legislative Research and General Counsel and Margaret Kelsey, Bureau of Land Management, Utah Office (September 21, 2005).

58. Cong. Research Serv., *Federal Land Management Agencies*, Figure 3.

59. U.S. Dep't of Int., Bur. of Land Mgmt., *Payments in Lieu of Taxes – Total State Payment Results* (Washington, D.C.: Bur. of Land Mgmt.), http://www.blm.gov/pilt/state.php (accessed June 8, 2005); U.S. Dep't of Int., Bur. of Land Mgmt., *Charts - U.S. Department of the Interior, Bureau of Land Management Payment In Lieu of Taxes For Fiscal Years 1999-2004, Total Payments by County (Utah)*, by Bill Howell, Dep't of Int. Budget Office, (Washington, D.C.: Bur. of Land Mgmt., March 7, 2005).

Chapter 22 Endnotes

1. See United States Constitution, Preamble and Tenth Amendment

2. See *Utah Code Annotated*, sec. 17-50-302 (Supp. 2005)(counties); sec. 10-8-84 (2003)(cities); sec. 10-8-94 (2003)(towns).

3. See Utah Constitution, art. 11, sec. 8.

4. Utah Foundation, *State and Local Government in Utah* (Salt Lake City: Utah Foundation, December 1992), 221.

5. 1971 Utah Laws ch. 1, 1st Spec. Sess.

6. See *Utah Code Annotated*, sec.17-34-1 (Supp. 2005).

7. U.S. Census Bureau, population estimates as of July 1, 2004.

8. Utah Association of Counties.

9. See Utah Constitution, art. 11, sec. 1.

10. See Utah Constitution, art. 11, sec. 2.

11. *Utah Code Annotated*, sec. 17-2-13 (Supp. 2005).

12. See Utah Constitution, art. 11, sec. 3.

13. Utah Constitution, 1896.

14. *Amending Article Eleven Section Four Constitution*, 39th Leg., Gen. Sess. (Utah 1971). This amendment was passed by the legislature on March 11, 1971; passed by voters in November 1972; became effective on January 1, 1973.

15. See Utah Constitution, art. 11, sec. 4.

16. Utah Constitution, art. 14, sec. 3(1).

17. Utah Constitution, art. 14, sec. 4(1).

18. Utah Foundation, *State and Local Government*, 222.

19. See *Utah Code Annotated*, sec. 17-3-3 (Supp. 2005).

20. See *Utah Code Annotated*, sec. 17-2-4 (Supp. 2005).

21. See *Utah Code Annotated*, sec. 17-2-9 (Supp. 2005).

22. See *Utah Code Annotated*, sec. 17-2-13 (Supp. 2005).

23. See *Utah Code Annotated*, Title 17, Chapter 50, Part 5, Classification.

24. See *Utah Code Annotated*, Title 17, Chapter 52, Forms of County Government.

25. See *Utah Code Annotated*, sec. 17-52-501 (2001).

26. See *Utah Code Annotated*, sec. 17-52-502 (2001).

27. See *Utah Code Annotated*, sec. 17-52-504 (2001).

28. See *Utah Code Annotated*, sec. 17-52-505 (2001).

29. See *Utah Code Annotated*, Title 17, Chapter 36, Uniform Fiscal Procedures.

30. See *Utah Code Annotated*, Title 17, Chapter 27a, County Land Use, Development, and Management Act.

31. See *Utah Code Annotated*, sec. 17-27a-102 (Supp. 2005).

32. See *Utah Code Annotated*, sec. 17-27a-401 (Supp. 2005).

33. See *Utah Code Annotated*, sec. 17-27a-301 (Supp. 2005).

34. See *Utah Code Annotated*, sec. 17-27a-306 (Supp. 2005).

35. See *Utah Code Annotated*, sec. 10-2-427 (2001).

36. Utah Dep't of Info. Tech. Serv., Automated Geo. Ref. Cntr., State Geographic Information Database, Layer: SGID.U024.Municipalities2005, (State Tax Commission Boundary Data as of January 1, 2005) http://agrc.utah.gov/agrc_sgid/sgidintro.html (accessed November 28, 2005); Utah

Gov. Office of Planning and Budget, Utah Population Estimates Committee, ??Title of Memo, by Robert Spendlove, August 10, 2005.

37. U.S. Census Bureau, population estimates as of July 1, 2004.

38. Ibid.

39. Utah Constitution, art. 11, sec. 5.

40. Ibid.

41. Utah Constitution, art. 11, sec. 6.

42. Utah Constitution, art. 14, sec. 3(1).

43. Ibid., sec. 3(2).

44. Utah Constitution, art. 14, sec. 4(1).

45. Ibid., sec. 4(3).

46. *Utah Code Annotated*, Title 10, Chapter 2, Part 1, Incorporation.

47. *Utah Code Annotated*, sec. 10-2-125 (2003).

48. *Utah Code Annotated*, Title 10, Chapter 2, Part 4, Annexation.

49. *Utah Code Annotated*, sec. 10-2-419 (2003).

50. *Utah Code Annotated*, Title 10, Chapter 2, Part 5, Restriction of Municipal Limits.

51. *Utah Code Annotated*, Title 10, Chapter 2, Part 6, Consolidation of Municipalities.

52. *Utah Code Annotated*, Title 10, Chapter 2, Part 7, Dissolution of Municipalities.

53. *Utah Code Annotated*, Title 10, Chapter 2, Part 3, Classification of Municipalities.

54. *Utah Code Annotated*, Title 10, Chapter 3, Part 12, Optional Forms of Municipal Government.

55. *Utah Code Annotated*, sec. 10-3-101(1) (Supp. 2005).

56. Ibid.

57. Ibid., -101(2).

58. *Utah Code Annotated*, Title 10, Chapter 3, Part 12, Optional Forms of Municipal Government.

59. *Utah Code Annotated*, sec. 10-3-830 (2003).

60. *Utah Code Annotated*, sec. 10-3-106 (2003).

61. *Utah Code Annotated*, sec. 10-3-1207 (2003).

62. *Utah Code Annotated*, sec. 10-2-303(1)(b) (Supp. 2005).

63. *Utah Code Annotated*, Title 10, Chapter 5, Uniform Fiscal Procedures Act for Utah Towns; Title 10, Chapter 6, Uniform Fiscal Procedures Act for Utah Cities.

64. See *Utah Code Annotated*, sec. 10-9a-102 (Supp. 2005).

65. See *Utah Code Annotated*, sec. 10-9a-401 (Supp. 2005).

66. See *Utah Code Annotated*, sec. 10-9a-301 (Supp. 2005).

67. *Utah Code Annotated*, Title 17A and Title 17B, Chapter 2, Local Districts.

68. *Utah Code Annotated*, Title 17A, Chapter 2, Independent Special Districts.

69. *Utah Code Annotated*, Title 17A, Chapter 3, Dependent Special Districts.

70. Utah Constitution, art. 13, sec. 2.

71. *Utah Code Annotated*, Title 17A, Chapter 2, Part 13, Special Service Districts.

72. *Utah Code Annotated*, sec. 17A-2-1304 (Supp. 2005).

73. Utah Constitution, art. 11, sec. 7.

74. Ibid.

75. *Utah Code Annotated*, Title 17B, Chapter 4, Redevelopment Agencies Act.

76. *Neighborhood Development Program*, 1969 Utah Laws ch. 5.

77. *Utah Code Annotated*, sec. 17B-4-201 (Supp. 2005).

78. *Redevelopment Amendments*, 1993 Utah Laws ch. 50.

79. See *Utah Code Annotated*, sec. 17B-4-1101 (2004).

80. See *Utah Code Annotated*, sec. 17B-4-402 (2004).

81. *Utah Code Annotated*, sec. 17B-4-102(11) (Supp. 2005).

82. *Utah Code Annotated*, sec. 17B-4-1005 (Supp. 2005).

83. *Utah Code Annotated*, sec. 17B-4-403 (Supp. 2005).

84. *Utah Code Annotated*, sec. 17B-4-102(12) (Supp. 2005).

85. *Utah Code Annotated*, sec. 17B-4-1004(5) (Supp. 2005).

86. *Utah Code Annotated*, sec. 17B-4-504 (2004).

87. *Utah Code Annotated*, Title 11, Chapter 13, Interlocal Cooperation Act.

88. AOG Study, Utah Advisory Council on Intergovernmental Relations, October 1993.

89. *Cooperative Agreements*, 1965 Utah Laws ch. 14.

90. Information about AOGs on GOPB Web site http://www.governor.state.ut.us/planning/aog/creation.htm (accessed November 28, 2005).

91. Ibid.

92. John S. Williams (Executive Director, Five County Association of Governments, Elected Spokesperson for Seven Associations of Governments), *Activities of Utah's Seven Associations of Governments*, Table distributed to Political Subdivisions Interim Committee, 55th Leg. (May 19, 2004).

Chapter 23 Endnotes

1. Governor's Office of Planning and Budget, *State of Utah Long Term Projections 2005-2050* (Salt Lake City: Governor's Office of Planning and Budget, April 2005), 3.

2. Ibid., 4.

3. Calculated from data in the Office of the Governor, Utah Council of Economic Advisors, *2003 Economic Report to the Governor* (Salt Lake City: Governor's Office of Planning and Budget, January 2003), 25.

4. Office of the Governor, Utah Council of Economic Advisers, *2005 Economic Report to the Governor* (Salt Lake City: Governor's Office of Planning and Budget, January 2005), 19.

5. Ibid.

6. Ibid, 22.

7. Ibid.

8. Governor's Office of Planning and Budget, *State of Utah Long Term Projections 2005-2050*, 6.

9. Office of the Governor, Utah Council of Economic Advisers, *2004 Economic Report to the Governor* (Salt Lake City: Governor's Office of Planning and Budget, January 2004), 170.

10. Ibid.

11. Ibid, 167.

12. Office of the Governor, Utah Council of Economic Advisors, *2004 Economic Report to the Governor* (Salt Lake City: Governor's Office of Planning and Budget, January 2004), 167-168.

13. Ibid.

14. Ibid, 170.

15. U.S. Bureau of the Census, *Census 2000*, Summary File 1, Final National File (Washington D.C.: Bureau of the Census, 2002).

16. Governor's Office of Planning and Budget, *State of Utah Long Term Projections 2005-2050* (Salt Lake City: Governor's Office of Planning and Budget, April 2005), 3.

17. Office of the Governor, Utah Council of Economic Advisers, *2005 Economic Report to the Governor* (Salt Lake City: Governor's Office of Planning and Budget, January 2005), 25.

INDEX

absentee ballot (43, 44)
administrative rules (37-41, 81, 82, 118)
Administrative Rules Review Committee (37-41, 82)
administrative services (63, 81, 82, 84, 89, 90, 124, 163, 164, 188, 208, 273, 278, 286)
aeronautics (285, 304, 305)
aging (247-249, 341)
Agricultural Advisory Board (163)
agriculture (2, 3, 5, 9, 10, 12, 65, 163-169, 171, 176, 230, 261, 328, 339)
AIDS (242)
air quality (165, 229, 231, 341)
Air Quality Board (229, 231)
airports (304, 305)
alcoholic beverage (173-175)
amendment (23, 27, 32, 34, 51, 70, 75, 77, 100, 101, 103, 109, 110, 112, 130, 133, 168, 173, 224, 307, 313, 317, 327)
annexation (53, 318, 321, 325, 327, 328, 333)
apportionment (23, 31, 45, 111, 260, 293)
Asian affairs (198)
assessment (33, 110, 134, 136, 137, 147, 148, 165, 203, 215, 216, 236, 244, 245, 250, 251, 285)
assessor (46, 138)
Association of Counties (314)
attorney (29, 45, 46, 48, 50, 52, 53, 55, 63, 66, 70, 71, 73, 76-78, 83, 110, 113, 118, 129, 130, 178, 282)
attorney general (29, 45, 50, 55, 63, 66, 70, 71, 73, 76-78, 110, 113, 129, 178, 282)
audit (79, 80, 114, 124, 148, 199, 200, 249, 286)
auditor (29, 45, 46, 55, 63, 66, 71, 73, 79, 80, 112-114, 124, 138, 199, 200, 249, 321, 332)
authorities (25, 71, 78, 110, 129, 174, 200, 239, 250, 287, 295, 334)
aviation fuel (147, 305)
aviation fuel tax (147, 305)
ballot (27, 43, 44, 49, 50, 52-56, 64, 75, 76, 105, 208, 318, 328, 332)

Bear River (202, 259, 322, 337)
Bear River Commission (259)
beer tax (147, 159)
Big Game Control (261)
bills (28, 29, 58, 96, 98-106, 108, 113, 114)
birth rate (16, 19, 205, 343, 349)
Black affairs (198)
blind (44, 212)
block grants (196, 200, 337, 339)
Board of Education (29, 31, 201, 207-209, 211, 212, 215-217, 220, 223, 276)
Board of Pardons (29, 30, 70, 267, 270, 271)
Board of Regents (220, 222-224, 227)
bonds (32, 81, 135, 199, 292, 299, 333, 335)
Brigham Young (1, 7-9, 59)
Brigham Young University (1, 59)
budget officer (49, 52)
building board (82, 223)
burden of proof (138)
business administrator (211)
business and labor (173)
charter school (211, 212)
child abuse (78)
child care (199-201, 239, 244, 245)
Church of Jesus Christ of Latter-day Saints (7)
circuit court (125, 298)
cities (6, 10, 13, 14, 24, 32, 46, 48, 109, 110, 117, 135, 156, 196, 257, 258, 282, 299, 302, 313, 321, 327, 332, 334)
city attorney (129)
city commission (46)
city council (32, 46, 331)
city manager (331)
city recorder (48)
classification of counties (316)
classification of municipalities (329, 330)
clerks (47, 50, 52, 53, 55, 56, 76)
climate (1-5, 9, 14, 178)
codified (44, 104, 115, 127, 272)
College of Applied Technology (220-223)
College of Eastern Utah (221, 222)
Colorado Plateau (1-3, 263, 264)

Colorado River Basin (165, 259)
commissioner of higher education (220, 227)
commissioner of public safety (276)
communication (10, 54, 64, 68, 103, 114, 115, 123, 212, 222, 282, 337)
community affairs (192)
community and economic development (191-195, 198, 274)
community development (192, 196, 198, 200, 333, 339, 340)
commutation (271)
Congress (8, 9, 25, 27, 34, 47, 55, 63, 76, 88, 112, 140, 200, 237, 244, 259, 293, 303, 307-311)
constable (46)
constitution (1-35, 39, 43, 45-49, 52, 53, 55, 63-66, 69-71, 73, 74, 76, 77, 79, 80, 93-96, 99-101, 103-114, 117-119, 122, 124, 126-128, 130, 133-137, 139, 140, 147, 148, 152, 154, 155, 173, 189, 207-209, 212, 213, 219, 223, 224, 271, 289, 307, 308, 313, 317, 318, 327, 334, 335)
constitutional amendment (70, 75, 77, 101, 110, 133, 224, 317, 327)
constitutional convention (25, 34, 35)
Constitutional Revision Commission (133, 148)
consumer protection (78, 176-178)
convention (25, 34, 35, 48, 195)
cooperation (71, 165, 168, 200, 232, 246, 277, 287, 313, 332, 336, 337)
corporate franchise tax (143)
corporations (23, 32, 79, 80, 88, 89, 143-146, 176, 178, 270, 309, 310)
correctional industries (273)
council of state governments (126)
council-manager (320, 331)
council-manager form (320, 331)
council-mayor form (331)
counties (5, 13-15, 24, 32, 52, 55, 56, 85, 119, 121, 133, 135, 137-139, 148, 156, 173, 196, 202, 212, 246, 254, 264, 274, 286-289, 293, 298-304, 313, 314, 316-318, 320-322, 327, 328, 332-337, 347-349)

county assessor (46, 138)
county attorney (46, 48, 50, 77)
County Boards of Equalization (133)
county clerk (38, 43, 44, 46, 49-53)
county commission (46, 121, 320)
county jail (273)
county service areas (334)
court administrator (107, 117, 121, 123, 124, 130)
court of appeals (30, 44, 45, 118, 119, 122, 125-127, 201, 277, 298)
crime (14, 26, 27, 31, 37, 78, 101, 128, 129, 235, 267, 269, 271, 273, 275, 277-279)
criminal cases (178)
deaf (212)
debt (24, 27, 33, 80-82, 133, 135, 139, 147, 148, 214, 291, 317, 327, 333)
debt limits (135, 317, 327)
decentralization (85, 339)
declaration of rights (23, 26)
democrat (9, 59, 61)
Democratic Party (46, 47)
Department of Administrative Services (63, 81, 82, 84, 89)
Department of Agriculture and Food (163, 166-168, 171)
Department of Commerce (65, 111, 173, 176, 178, 180, 181, 281, 282)
Department of Corrections (267, 269, 271, 272, 274)
Department of Financial Institutions (173, 182-185, 199)
Department of Health (168, 199-201, 230, 235, 239-247)
Department of Human Services (244, 247, 248, 251, 275)
Department of Natural Resources (119, 167, 193, 241, 253, 255-264)
Department of Public Safety (267, 276)
Department of Transportation (234, 281, 285, 293, 294, 302, 349)
Department of Workforce Services (17, 191, 199, 200, 202, 247)
dependent children (200)
Deseret (8, 25, 27, 219, 317)
development center (278)

disabilities (85, 109, 201, 216, 237, 242, 247, 249, 310)
disconnection (329)
district court (30, 38, 44, 45, 117, 119, 121, 122, 124, 125, 129, 170, 261, 281, 329)
district superintendent of schools (211)
districts (30-32, 45, 46, 48, 50, 51, 53, 54, 81, 111, 112, 114, 119, 121, 125, 132, 135, 136, 138, 139, 142, 156, 157, 161, 163, 165, 207, 208, 210, 211, 213-215, 257, 258, 261, 298-300, 302, 313, 328, 332-337)
drinking water (229, 231, 232, 234, 239, 246, 349)
drinking water board (229, 231)
driver license (278)
earmarking (142)
economic development (6, 140, 165, 191-196, 198, 202, 230, 274, 335, 336, 339, 340)
education (10, 11, 17, 23, 29, 31-33, 40, 67, 68, 71, 80, 87, 88, 108-112, 115, 123, 133, 139, 142, 147, 153, 154, 158, 181, 197, 199, 201, 202, 205-217, 219-227, 236, 243, 245, 250, 254, 257-259, 262, 263, 273, 275, 276, 278, 289, 335, 336, 347-349)
election judges (44)
elections (27, 32, 43-50, 52, 54-56, 75, 76, 105, 125, 127, 133, 225)
electoral college (48)
emergency management (277)
Emergency Medical Services Committee (240)
eminent domain (69, 265, 335)
employment security (201, 337)
employment service (200)
enabling act (25, 27, 88, 207, 212)
energy (12, 69, 109, 148, 193, 196, 233, 256, 263, 281, 283, 284, 336, 340)
enrollment (100, 102, 103, 210, 211, 215, 222, 225, 237, 238, 243, 244)
environmental quality (165, 168, 229-231, 241, 242, 246)
environmental response and remediation (231, 232)
ethnic minorities (216)

executive branch (29, 37, 39-41, 54, 58, 63, 67, 68, 71, 81, 90, 96, 108, 110, 114, 185, 198, 271)
expositions (88, 199)
extradition (70)
family health services (240, 241)
family services (247, 249, 251)
federal (7, 9, 11, 12, 23-26, 31, 32, 34, 37, 39, 44, 48, 55, 63, 65, 67-71, 75, 76, 79, 80, 84, 85, 88, 101, 108, 109, 111, 112, 117, 121, 124, 125, 128-130, 134, 140, 143, 146, 155, 158, 165, 167, 168, 171, 174, 183, 184, 192, 194, 196, 197, 200, 202, 208, 212-215, 221, 230-234, 237, 238, 241-247, 249, 251, 254-256, 258-262, 264, 269, 271, 273, 276-278, 281-283, 287-289, 291-295, 298, 299, 302-305, 307-313, 335, 337, 339)
federal aid (9, 293)
federal system (309)
fees (31, 33, 57, 82, 86, 108, 109, 134, 148, 151, 152, 155-158, 169, 171, 180, 181, 212-214, 224, 225, 289, 291, 292, 333)
finance (10, 12, 19, 80, 81, 83, 96, 105, 110, 114, 147, 165, 211, 221, 273, 278, 301, 336)
finances (156, 299, 336)
financial institution (181, 183, 184)
financing (83, 88, 133, 138-140, 142, 143, 147, 164, 165, 184, 185, 205, 212, 219, 224, 237, 240, 242-244, 258, 333)
fine arts (192, 196)
fire marshal (278)
fire protection (254, 333, 334)
flood control (165, 257, 333, 334)
food stamps (199, 201, 310)
form of municipal government (332)
gas (1, 11, 119, 147, 180, 253, 255, 256, 263, 278, 281-284, 290, 293, 334)
General Election (30-32, 34, 44-51, 53-55, 66, 76, 101, 110, 127, 133, 208, 317)
general obligation bonds (135, 292)
General Session (28, 40, 50, 57, 68, 70, 81, 89, 90, 93-95, 98, 107, 111, 115, 152, 184, 193, 211, 270, 273)
geographic boundaries (111, 125, 335)

Index • 439

government (1, 6, 7, 10-12, 17, 23-26, 28, 29, 31, 32, 34, 37, 39, 41, 43-46, 54, 56, 57, 63-65, 67, 68, 70, 71, 74-76, 78-85, 87, 90, 106-110, 113, 115, 124, 127, 129-131, 133, 138-143, 147, 153, 156, 158, 171, 173, 176, 178, 182, 187, 188, 194, 198, 199, 213, 223, 229, 231, 233, 236-238, 242, 245, 247, 249-251, 258, 263-265, 270, 277, 281, 286, 287, 302-304, 307-309, 311-314, 317, 320, 321, 328, 331-337, 339, 348)

government operations (65, 68, 75, 108)

governmental services (135)

governor (8, 12, 13, 15, 16, 19, 20, 25, 28-31, 40, 41, 45, 47, 49-53, 55, 58, 63-71, 73-77, 80, 81, 84, 90, 93-96, 101, 102, 104, 105, 107, 108, 111, 113, 114, 126-128, 133, 147-149, 152, 160, 161, 166, 169, 175, 176, 178, 180, 181, 184, 185, 188, 193-199, 205-209, 220, 222, 223, 229, 259, 260, 263, 271, 272, 276, 277, 281, 282, 285, 286, 296, 318, 329, 337, 345, 347, 348)

grand jury (117, 129, 130)

gross receipts tax (143)

Grover Cleveland (26)

gubernatorial appointments (93)

habeas corpus (24, 26)

hazardous waste (148, 229, 231-233, 241)

health (11, 12, 17, 21, 24, 34, 56, 69, 71, 110, 111, 123, 142, 158, 163, 166-168, 176, 177, 179, 180, 185-187, 189, 199-202, 212, 229-247, 249, 250, 255, 256, 261, 271-273, 310, 313, 314, 334, 348)

health advisory council (240)

health and human services (142, 158, 200, 202, 241, 245, 246, 310, 314)

health care financing (237, 240, 242-244)

Health Data Committee (240, 244)

Health Facility Committee (240)

hearing impaired (212)

Heber Valley Historic Railroad (88, 198, 199)

high birth rate (16, 19, 205, 343, 349)

higher education (31, 33, 40, 68, 80, 87, 115, 142, 147, 153, 158, 197, 199, 202, 213, 219-227, 278, 336, 347)

highway patrol (63, 276, 277)

highway safety (276, 277, 295)

highway system (288, 293, 294)

highway user (289, 293)

highways (71, 141, 155, 276, 285, 286, 288-296, 298, 301, 304, 308)

Hispanic affairs (198)

history (1, 2, 5-9, 12, 13, 25, 30, 43, 59, 61, 76, 82, 84, 100, 133, 142, 147, 148, 174, 182, 192, 197, 229, 247, 257-259, 261, 271, 299, 302, 303, 309, 314, 321)

homestead exemption (34)

hospitals (237, 241, 245)

house of representatives (28, 29, 44, 50, 59, 61, 69, 73, 74, 93-97, 100-103, 105, 106, 109, 111, 115, 128)

human services (142, 158, 200, 202, 241, 244-251, 275, 310, 314, 341)

impeachment (29, 30, 70, 74, 76, 80, 93, 94, 124, 128)

income tax (33, 68, 108, 131, 132, 141-147, 152, 154, 155, 158, 159, 161, 184, 213, 224)

incorporation (32, 299-301, 325, 327-329, 332)

indebtedness (317, 327)

Indian affairs (192, 193, 198)

Industrial Commission (188)

industrial promotion (194)

information technology (81, 89, 90, 93, 114, 115, 117, 130, 164, 177, 188, 198, 199, 242, 273, 278)

inheritance tax (147)

initiative (28, 43, 49-53, 55, 69, 94, 97, 109, 185, 261, 263, 332)

institute of fine arts (196)

institutional boards (223)

insurance premium tax (86, 147, 159)

interim committees (89, 95-97, 102, 105, 113)

interlocal cooperation (313, 332, 336, 337)

Interlocal Cooperation Act (313, 332, 336, 337)

internal audit (148, 286)

interstate (24, 67, 125, 143, 184, 259, 293, 308)

introduction of bills (106)

John C. Fremont (6)
judicial branch (54, 90, 117, 123, 128, 199)
Judicial Conduct Commission (31, 119, 128)
judicial council (30, 56, 117, 118, 120-124, 127, 128, 271)
judicial districts (257)
judicial powers (30)
judiciary (30, 71, 94, 117, 119, 122-126)
justice court (30, 44, 46, 121-123)
juvenile court (44, 45, 121, 122, 124, 126, 249)
labor (4, 10, 23, 34, 85, 173, 187-189, 202, 274, 308)
laboratory services (240, 241)
law enforcement (24, 33, 142, 241, 257, 261, 262, 271, 277-279, 289, 336, 337)
law library (197)
legal counsel (77, 113)
Legislative Auditor General (112, 114, 199, 249)
legislative branch (37, 54, 58, 81, 90, 93, 107, 110, 115)
legislative committees (95, 97, 113, 114)
Legislative Fiscal Analyst (50, 68, 96, 107, 108, 112-114, 158, 191, 241, 243, 245, 246, 251, 273, 274, 291, 310)
legislative general counsel (113)
Legislative Management Committee (89, 95, 97, 113, 114)
legislative powers (109, 320, 331)
legislative process (70, 99, 102, 107, 111)
legislative research (50, 53, 55, 90, 95, 97, 100, 102-104, 108, 111-114, 123, 178, 180-182, 184, 197, 237, 243-245, 249, 251, 273, 281, 282, 310, 311)
Legislative Research and General Counsel (50, 53, 55, 90, 95, 97, 100, 102-104, 108, 111-114, 123, 178, 180-182, 184, 197, 237, 243-245, 249, 251, 273, 281, 282, 310, 311)
legislative rules (58, 59, 94, 96, 102, 103, 106)
legislature (25, 27-35, 37, 38, 40, 43, 45, 49-52, 55-59, 61, 63, 64, 66-71, 74-77, 79-81, 88-90, 93-115, 117-119, 124-127, 130, 132-134, 138, 140, 143, 147, 148, 152, 153, 158, 161, 165, 169, 171, 174, 177, 178, 184, 189, 191-193, 196, 200, 201, 207, 209, 211, 212, 216, 219, 222-227, 229, 230, 237, 239, 241, 243, 245-247, 249-251, 253, 255, 257, 258, 260-264, 271, 273, 277, 281, 282, 285, 288, 290-295, 298-305, 309, 310, 313, 317, 318, 327, 333-335)
library division (193, 197)
licenses (39, 170, 171, 174-176, 186, 234, 245, 251, 262, 278, 304, 310)
licensing (58, 67, 83, 90, 109, 147, 164, 166, 167, 173, 176-178, 180, 181, 185, 244, 245, 248, 250, 251, 278)
lieutenant governor (29, 30, 45, 47, 49, 50, 52, 53, 55, 58, 63, 64, 67, 71, 73, 75, 76, 113, 318, 329)
lobbying (43, 58, 107)
local governments (14, 23, 32, 33, 40, 81, 82, 110, 117, 129-133, 135, 140-142, 149, 156, 192, 196, 199, 247, 249, 277, 304, 307, 309-311, 313, 332, 333, 336, 337, 339)
local health (230, 235, 239, 241, 242, 246)
local health department (246)
local school board (55, 210, 211, 214)
local school districts (45, 336)
mandamus (70)
manufacturing (10, 12, 16, 17, 19, 144, 152, 176, 273, 348)
marshal (278)
mayor (32, 46, 331)
medicaid (78, 237, 240, 242-245, 248, 251, 310, 341)
medical assistance (242, 243)
medical examiner (240, 241, 245)
medicare (237, 238, 245)
mental health (56, 123, 247, 249, 250, 271-273)
militia (23, 28, 33, 71, 105)
Millard Fillmore (8)
mining (9, 10, 12, 15, 19, 119, 135, 136, 147, 253, 255-257, 263, 311, 348)
mining severance tax (147)
money management (80)
money management council (80)

Index • 441

Mormon pioneers (9)
Mormon settlement (1, 7-9)
motor fuel tax (147, 158, 290, 291, 305)
motor pool (83)
municipal improvement districts (334)
municipal-type services (156, 314)
national conference of state legislatures (49, 242, 273)
natural resources (7, 12, 17, 119, 151, 164, 167, 192, 193, 241, 253-264, 336, 348)
office of education (197, 209-211, 215)
oil and gas severance tax (147)
oil, gas, and mining (119, 256)
open meetings (57)
pardon (70)
parks (1, 166, 167, 253, 257, 258, 287)
parole (30, 43, 250, 267, 270-275)
peace officer (279)
per pupil expenditures (207)
performance (31, 56, 79, 84, 85, 114, 123, 124, 128, 171, 192, 195, 202, 203, 205, 215-217, 244, 249-251, 321, 329)
performance audit (124, 249)
personal income (19, 149-153, 159-161, 206, 225, 296)
personnel management (84, 278)
Planning Commission (46, 321, 332)
planning coordinator (68, 199)
police (279, 307-309, 313, 314)
police officers (279)
political parties (43, 46-48, 54, 56)
political subdivisions (32, 39, 56, 85, 87, 109, 110, 112, 139, 140, 196, 260, 313, 333, 336, 339)
pollution (14, 165, 231, 295)
polygamy (9, 25)
population (1, 5, 8-10, 13-16, 32, 109, 111, 112, 140, 159, 160, 192, 206, 207, 211, 225, 236-238, 269, 273, 274, 287, 293, 301, 314, 316, 318, 321, 322, 325, 327, 329, 330, 332, 336, 339, 343-349)
powers (23-25, 28-30, 32, 37, 64, 65, 70-73, 77, 79, 93, 95, 106, 109, 110, 117, 124, 148, 173, 184, 185, 187, 188, 196, 208, 211, 230, 239, 258, 276, 281, 307, 309, 313, 318, 320, 327, 329, 331, 333, 336)

presidential electors (48)
primary election (43, 46-48)
prison facilities (273)
privilege tax (134, 148)
probation (43, 179, 270-273)
Procurement Policy Board (83)
prohibition (24, 64, 109, 174, 188)
property tax (33, 131-140, 142, 143, 147, 152, 213, 214, 299, 300, 312, 317, 328, 332,
prosecution (33, 131-140, 142, 143, 147, 152, 213, 214, 299, 300, 312, 317, 328, 332, 335)
public assistance (77, 78, 94, 101, 128, 129, 182)
public education (43, 200, 201, 247, 251)
public health (31, 87, 108, 115, 133, 139, 142, 147, 154, 199, 205-208, 210-215, 226, 243, 245)
public health service (24, 69, 110, 163, 230, 232, 234-236, 239, 241, 242, 244-247, 256, 261)
public lands (247)
public safety (23, 27, 34, 169, 258, 311, 339)
public schools (68, 85, 87, 88, 142, 250, 257, 267, 276, 277)
Public Service Commission (34, 149, 207-209, 211-213, 233, 259)
public utilities (115, 119, 176, 180, 181, 281, 282)
public utilities and technology (11, 71, 135, 144, 148, 176, 180, 181, 281-283)
purchasing (283)
radiation (83, 164, 170, 174, 225, 296)
Radiation Control Board (229, 231, 233, 234)
railroad (229, 233)
real estate (6, 9, 11, 32, 88, 198, 199)
reapportionment (10, 12, 19, 78, 93, 123, 176, 181, 199, 233)
recorder (93, 111, 112)
recovery services (46, 48, 51)
recreation (248, 251, 264)
redevelopment (1, 2, 157, 253, 255, 257, 258, 311, 312, 333, 334)
redistricting (232, 313, 332, 335)
referendum (93, 111, 112, 207)
regional councils (28, 43, 49-55, 94, 109)

registration (202, 203)
rehabilitation (24, 43, 44, 56, 58, 76, 83, 109, 151, 152, 155, 164, 168, 169, 176, 181, 185, 214, 289, 291-293)
reprieve (88, 164, 165, 186, 202, 250, 262, 271, 275)
republican (70)
Republican Party (46-48, 59, 61)
resolution (46, 47)
respite (50, 52, 56, 58, 94, 97, 101, 104, 105, 120, 124, 128, 179, 184, 200, 298, 318)
retention election (70, 249)
retirement (31, 45, 46, 56, 121, 126-128)
Retirement and Independent Entities Committee (31, 63, 77, 80, 85-89, 109, 113, 128, 237)
Retirement Board (89)
retirement office (77, 80, 86, 88, 113)
retirement system (88)
revenue (86)
revenue and taxation (23, 32, 33, 107-109, 114, 131-133, 135, 138-143, 147, 149-161, 171, 174, 199, 212-214, 224, 226, 255, 281, 288, 289, 291-294, 296, 298, 302, 305, 312, 321, 327, 333, 335)
revenue bonds (23, 33, 133)
revenue sharing (199)
right to work (140)
right-of-way (187, 188)
risk manager (298, 302-304)
Rules Committee (83)
salaries (98, 102, 103)
sales and use tax (23, 31, 34, 67, 105, 124, 223, 263)
sales tax (131, 140-142, 148, 152, 153, 155, 159, 161, 291-293, 299, 301, 303, 304)
Salt Lake City (108, 140, 151, 152, 294, 296, 298-304)
Salt Lake Community College (1, 3, 9, 12-14, 17, 21, 25, 32, 34, 59, 64, 96, 110, 124, 130, 133, 147-149, 151-153, 156, 158, 176, 181, 188, 191, 200, 205-207, 216, 221, 235-237, 241, 243, 245, 247-249, 251, 256, 262, 267, 273, 274, 277, 281, 282, 287, 288, 294, 296, 299, 301-305, 310, 314, 321, 323, 343, 345, 347, 348)

school-age children (221, 222)
securities (149, 205, 345)
senate (80, 81, 176, 181, 182, 308)
separation (28-31, 44, 45, 50, 57, 59, 65, 66, 69, 70, 73-75, 81, 89, 93-107, 109, 111, 114, 115, 124-128, 148, 175, 176, 180, 181, 184, 185, 188, 195-197, 208, 220, 222, 229, 271, 272, 276, 281, 282, 285, 286)
separation of powers (95, 110, 249, 331)
service areas (95, 110, 331)
sheriff (245, 334)
Snow College (46)
social services (221, 222)
solid and hazardous waste (229, 247, 339, 341)
Southern Utah University (229, 231-233)
special (221)
special district (27-29, 32, 43, 44, 46, 49, 53-55, 64, 66, 68, 70, 71, 75, 76, 79, 80, 87, 93, 94, 96, 97, 109, 110, 114, 133-135, 138, 139, 147, 152, 155-157, 161, 174, 197, 232, 233, 237, 239-241, 264, 273, 289-291, 293, 296, 298-300, 313, 321, 327, 328, 332-335, 337)
special fuel tax (43, 46, 49, 55, 298, 333, 334)
special service district (147, 290, 291, 293)
standing committees (32, 334, 335)
state aid (95, 98, 123)
state auditor (208, 305)
State Board of Education (45, 55, 63, 66, 73, 79, 80, 321, 332)
State Board of Regents (29, 31, 201, 207-209, 211, 212, 215-217, 220, 223, 276)
state boundaries (220, 222-224)
state budget (23, 27)
state budget office (41, 67, 68, 131, 158, 159, 274, 291)
state constitution (68)
state engineer (24, 27, 32, 45, 71, 76)
state fair (119, 260, 261)
state fire marshal (88, 198, 199)
state highway system (278)
state history (288, 293)
state hospital (192, 197)
state lands (250, 251)

state library (34, 119, 212, 253-255)
state militia (97, 193, 197)
State of Deseret (71, 105)
state roads (8, 25, 27, 317)
state senate (288)
state supreme court (28, 50, 59, 66, 69, 73, 93-97, 100, 101, 104, 106, 109, 115, 127, 128)
state tax commission (45, 52, 54, 125)
state treasurer (33, 119, 131, 132, 135, 137, 138, 140, 141, 146, 148, 151, 152, 256, 296, 321)
statehood (45, 55, 63, 66, 73, 77, 79-81, 199)
street lighting (1, 8-10, 25, 27, 31, 32, 34, 35, 61, 63, 76, 133, 178, 239, 333)
substance abuse (335)
superintendent of public instruction (179, 247, 249, 250)
surplus property (29, 31, 63, 113, 199, 209)
surveyor (83)
systems (46)
Tax Review Commission (2, 31, 32, 56, 69, 81, 83, 85-88, 114, 117, 130, 147, 164, 165, 207, 213, 226, 227, 231, 232, 237, 240, 241, 244, 245, 258, 260, 261, 278, 285-288, 294, 295, 301, 302, 304, 340)
tax system (141)
taxes (131, 143)
termination (32, 33, 79, 108-110, 112, 125, 131-138, 140-156, 158-161, 184, 195, 206, 214, 289, 296, 298, 305, 311, 312, 333)
Territory of Utah (82, 271)
tourism (25, 27, 63)
tourist (10, 16, 88, 151, 192, 193, 195, 199, 230)
town council (15)
towns (46)
transient room tax (8, 24, 32, 46, 48, 135, 156, 196, 257, 299, 313, 321, 327, 332, 334)
transportation (10-12, 17, 21, 24, 68, 71, 109, 111, 136, 144, 153, 155, 194, 195, 234, 281, 285-289, 291-296, 298, 299, 301, 302, 304, 305, 308, 334, 339, 341,
Transportation Commission (141)

travel (10-12, 17, 21, 24, 68, 71, 109, 111, 136, 144, 153, 155, 194, 195, 234, 281, 285-289, 291-296, 298, 299, 301, 302, 304, 305, 308, 334, 339, 341, 349)
travel development (285-288, 299)
treasurer (58, 83, 96, 193, 195, 258, 287, 295, 340)
trial by jury (193, 195)
truth in taxation (29, 45, 46, 55, 63, 66, 73, 77, 79-81, 113, 199, 299)
tuition (26)
U.S. Congress (132, 138)
U.S. Constitution (212-214, 222, 224-226)
U.S. Forest Service (55, 76)
U.S. House of Representatives (26, 70, 101, 109, 111, 112, 124, 130, 173, 307, 308, 313)
U.S. Senate (258, 288)
U.S. Supreme Court (44, 111)
unemployment benefits (44)
unemployment insurance (46, 112, 124, 130, 140, 309)
union pacific (201)
University of Deseret (20, 151, 201, 310)
University of Utah (6, 304)
University of Utah Medical Center (219)
Upper Colorado River Commission (1, 12, 25, 31, 133, 156, 221, 224, 263, 303)
urban sprawl (12)
Utah Arts Council (259)
Utah College of Applied Technology (14)
Utah Constitution (196)
Utah Highway Patrol (221-223)
Utah State Bar (23, 25-35, 39, 43, 45, 49, 55, 63-66, 69-71, 73, 74, 76, 77, 79, 80, 93-96, 99-101, 103-111, 113, 114, 117-119, 122, 126-128, 133-137, 139, 140, 147, 148, 152, 154, 155, 189, 207-209, 212, 213, 219, 224, 271, 289, 313, 317, 318, 327, 334, 335)
Utah State Legislature (276)
Utah State University (29, 76, 118, 119, 122, 127)
Utah Supreme Court (61)
Utah Technology Finance Corporation (25, 31, 167-169, 221)

Utah Transit Authority (30, 31, 37, 40, 44, 45, 49, 50, 56, 76, 101, 104-106, 109, 110, 113, 117-119, 121-124, 127-129, 277, 281, 310)
vehicle registration (110)
veto (142, 288, 298, 299, 301-304)
veto override (83, 151, 152, 155, 214, 289, 291, 293)
visually impaired (29, 49, 50, 52, 53, 63, 69-71, 93, 94, 101-104, 108, 114, 320, 331)
vocational rehabilitation (93, 94, 101, 104)
voter assistance (212)
voters (202)
voting machines (56)
Wasatch Front (26, 28, 32-35, 43, 44, 47-56, 69, 101, 109, 110, 133, 214, 299-304, 317, 318, 321, 329, 332)
water (27)
Water and Power Board (195, 236, 245, 262, 282, 287, 288, 294, 298, 299, 302, 305, 337)
Water Quality Board (1-4, 7, 23, 32-34, 133, 134, 141, 157, 164, 165, 167, 170, 180, 229, 231, 232, 234, 239, 241, 246, 253, 255-261, 264, 283, 313, 314, 323, 327, 333, 334, 340, 349)
water resources (258)
water rights (229, 234)
Weber State University (4, 165, 253, 255, 258-261)
welfare (23, 32-34, 133, 164, 253, 260, 261, 327)
Wildlife Board (221)
wildlife resources (11, 71, 78, 82, 88, 107, 110, 176, 194, 199, 200, 209, 247, 249, 251, 310, 313, 336)
wine and liquor tax (261, 262)
Workers' Compensation Fund (167, 168, 171, 253, 261-263)
workforce services (147)
write-in candidate (80, 89)
Youth Parole Authority (17, 191, 199, 200, 202, 203, 247)
zoning (53, 264, 321)